Statistical Decision Theory and Related Topics III

Volume 1

Jack C. Kiefer
1924—1981

Statistical Decision Theory and Related Topics III

Volume 1

Edited by

Shanti S. Gupta and James O. Berger

Department of Statistics
Purdue University
West Lafayette, Indiana

1982

ACADEMIC PRESS
A Subsidiary of Harcourt Brace Jovanovich, Publishers
New York London
Paris San Diego San Francisco São Paulo Sydney Tokyo Toronto

Proceedings of the Third Purdue Symposium
June 1-5, 1981

ACADEMIC PRESS, INC.
111 Fifth Avenue, New York, New York 10003

United Kingdom Edition published by
ACADEMIC PRESS, INC. (LONDON) LTD.
24/28 Oval Road, London NW1 7DX

Library of Congress Cataloging in Publication Data
Main entry under title:

Statistical decision theory and related topics III.

Proceedings of the Third Purdue Symposium on Statistical Decision Theory and Related Topics, held at Purdue University on June 1-5, 1981.
Includes index.
1. Statistical decision--Congresses. I. Gupta, Shanti Swarup Date. II. Berger, James O. III. Purdue Symposium on Statistical Decision Theory and Related Topics (3rd : 1981 : Purdue University) IV. Purdue University.
QA279.4.S743 1982 519.5'42 82-11528
ISBN 0-12-307501-7 (v. 1)

PRINTED IN THE UNITED STATES OF AMERICA

82 83 84 85 9 8 7 6 5 4 3 2 1

CONTENTS

Numbers in parentheses refer to AMS 1980 subject classifications

CONTRIBUTORS

Numbers in parentheses indicate the pages on which the authors' contributions begin.

M. C. Agrawal (37), Institute of Mathematical Statistics, University of Umeå, 90187 Umeå, Sweden

Robert E. Bechhofer (61), School of Operations Research and Industrial Engineering, Cornell University, Ithaca, New York 14853

James Berger (109), Department of Statistics, Purdue University, West Lafayette, Indiana 47907

Roger L. Berger (143), Department of Statistics, The Florida State University, Tallahassee, Florida 32306

L. Mark Berliner (157), Department of Statistics, Ohio State University, Columbus, Ohio 43210

M. E. Bock (169), Department of Statistics, Purdue University, West Lafayette, Indiana 47907

Robert Bohrer (195), Department of Mathematics, University of Illinois, Urbana, Illinois 61801

Lawrence D. Brown (205), Department of Mathematics, Cornell University, Ithaca, New York 14853

Raymond J. Carroll (231), Department of Statistics, The University of North Carolina, Chapel Hill, North Carolina 27514

Arthur Cohen (243), Department of Statistics, Rutgers University, New Brunswick, New Jersey 08903

William W. Davis (271), Lockheed Research Laboratories, Palo Alto, California 94304

Morris H. DeGroot (271, 291), Department of Statistics, Carnegie-Mellon University, Pittsburgh, Pennsylvania 15213

Persi Diaconis (315), Department of Statistics, Stanford University, Stanford, California 94305

Morris L. Eaton (329), Department of Theoretical Statistics, University of Minnesota, Minneapolis, Minnesota 55455

F. Eicker (353), Abteilung Statistik, Dortmund University, 46 Dortmund-Hombruch, West Germany

Thomas S. Ferguson (385), Department of Mathematics, University of California at Los Angeles, Los Angeles, California 90024

Stephen E. Fienberg (291), Department of Statistics, Carnegie-Mellon University, Pittsburgh, Pennsylvania 15213

David Freedman (315), Department of Statistics, University of California, Berkeley, California 94720

Zvi Galil (1), Department of Mathematics, Tel Aviv University, Tel Aviv, Israel

J. K. Ghosh (403), Indian Statistical Institute, Calcutta 700 035, India

Shanti S. Gupta (457, 473), Department of Statistics, Purdue University, West Lafayette, Indiana 47907

R. Helmers (497), Mathematisch Centrum, 1009 AB Amsterdam, The Netherlands

Robert N. Holt, Jr. (231), School of Accounting, University of Georgia, Athens, Georgia 30602

Ping Hsiao (513), Department of Mathematics, Wayne State University, Detroit, Michigan 48202

Deng-Yuan Huang (457), Institute of Mathematics, Academia Sinica, Taipei, Taiwan

Jiunn Tzon Hwang (205), Department of Mathematics, Cornell University, Ithaca, New York 14853

S. N. Joshi (403), Indian Statistical Institute, Calcutta 700 035, India

J. Kiefer (1), Department of Statistics, University of California at Berkeley, Berkeley, California 94720

Radhika V. Kulkarni (61), School of Operations Research and Industrial Engineering, Cornell University, Ithaca, New York 14853

Gunnar Kulldorff (37), Institute of Mathematical Statistics, University of Umeå, 90187 Umeå, Sweden

Klaus-J. Miescke (473), Department of Mathematics, Mainz University, 6500 Mainz, West Germany

David Ruppert (231), Department of Statistics, The University of North Carolina, Chapel Hill, North Carolina 27514

H. B. Sackrowitz (243), Department of Statistics, Rutgers University, New Brunswick, New Jersey 08903

B. K. Sinha (403), Department of Mathematics and Statistics, University of Pittsburgh, Pittsburgh, Pennsylvania 15260

W. R. Van Zwet (497), Department of Mathematics, University of Leiden, 2300 RA Leiden, The Netherlands

PREFACE

The Third Purdue Symposium on Statistical Decision Theory and Related Topics was held at Purdue University during the period June 1 – 5, 1981. The symposium brought together many prominent leaders and a number of younger researchers in statistical decision theory and related areas. This volume contains, in two parts, the invited papers presented at the symposium and includes works on general decision theory, multiple decision theory, optimum experimental design, sequential and adaptive inference, Bayesian analysis, robustness, and large sample theory. These research areas have seen rapid developments since the preceding Purdue Symposium in 1976, developments reflected by the variety and depth of the works in this volume.

We are extremely grateful to Dr. Felix Haas, Executive Vice President and Provost, and to Dr. Allan H. Clark, Dean of the School of Science, for the encouragement and financial support provided by Purdue University. The symposium was also supported by the National Science Foundation under grant MCS8024665, by the Office of Naval Research under grant N00014-81-G-0047, and by the U. S. Army Research Office under grant DAG29MO81. We sincerely thank these agencies for their assistance, and in particular wish to thank Dr. E. J. Wegman of the Office of Naval Research, Dr. Alvin Thaler of the National Science Foundation, and Dr. Robert L. Launer of the U. S. Army Research Office. Thanks also are due to the organizations supporting the research efforts of the editors: the Office of Naval Research grant N00014-75-C-0455, for S. S. Gupta, and the National Science Foundation grant MCS8101670A1, and the Alfred P. Sloan Foundation, for J. O. Berger.

Many individuals contributed to the success of the symposium. The program for the symposium was developed under the guidance of an advisory committee composed of S. S. Gupta (Chairman), Purdue University; R. E. Bechhofer, Cornell University; J. O. Berger, Purdue University; J. C. Kiefer, University of California at Berkeley; G. Kulldorff, University of Umeå; C. R. Rao, University of Pittsburgh; and H. E. Robbins, Columbia University. The excellence of the program was due in large part to the efforts of these colleagues.

In presiding over the sessions at the symposium, valuable contributions were also made by J. Blum, University of California at Davis; E. Csaki, Institute of Mathematics of the Hungarian Academy of Sciences; R. Farrell, Cornell University; L. Gleser, Purdue University; P. K. Goel, Purdue University; S. Ikeda, Soka University; R. L. Launer, U. S. Army Research Office; G. McCabe,

Purdue University; G. C. McDonald, General Motors Research Laboratories; G. Meeden, Iowa State University; D. S. Moore, Purdue University; I. Olkin, Stanford University; P. S. Puri, Purdue University; J. Rustagi, Ohio State University; E. Samuel-Cahn, Hebrew University; E. Wegman, Office of Naval Research; and S. Zacks, State University of New York at Binghamton. We are thankful to all these colleagues. Finally, faculty and students in Purdue's Department of Statistics were instrumental in seeing that local arrangements and activities went smoothly.

Numerous colleagues at Purdue and elsewhere served as referees for the papers appearing in this volume. We thank them for their efforts, which in many cases resulted in a strengthening of the papers. The assistance of Academic Press in preparing this volume for publication is also happily acknowledged. Finally, for her skill and patience throughout all stages of the preparation for the symposium and of this volume, and for her very accurate and attractive typing of the contents of this volume, we are deeply grateful to Norma Lucas.

Approximately two months after the end of the symposium, Jack C. Kiefer died. He was instrumental in the planning and promotion of this symposium, and of the two earlier Purdue symposia held in 1970 and 1976. Jack's greatness as a statistician is undeniable and will no doubt be well documented elsewhere. Upon learning of his death, however, our reaction (and that of many others at Purdue and elsewhere) was simply that we had just lost a wonderful friend. To our friend we dedicate this volume.

CONTENTS OF VOLUME 2

Numbers in parentheses refer to AMS 1980 subject classifications

ON THE CHARACTERIZATION OF D-OPTIMUM WEIGHING DESIGNS FOR $n \equiv 3 \pmod 4$

Z. Galil[1]

Department of Mathematics
Tel Aviv University
Tel Aviv, Israel

J. Kiefer[1]

Department of Statistics
University of California at Berkeley
Berkeley, California, U.S.A.

I. INTRODUCTION

Let k and n be positive integers with $k \leq n$, and let $\mathcal{X} = \mathcal{X}(k,n)$ be the set of all n x k matrices $X = \{x_{ij}\}$ consisting entirely of entries ±1. We seek a D-optimum X*, i.e., one that maximizes det(X'X) over $\mathcal{X}$. The weighing, fractional factorial, and first order regression settings where this problem arises, a partial history, and a list of known results, are given in Galil and Kiefer [2] (hereafter denoted GK). As described there, the most interesting unsolved cases are those for which $n \equiv 3 \pmod 4$, and the present article is devoted entirely to improving knowledge on the structure of a D-optimum X* in those cases.

WE HEREAFTER ASSUME $n \equiv 3 \pmod 4$.

Ehlich [1] developed the pioneering approach to this subject for the saturated case k = n, and its main aspects are easily

[1]This research was supported by the National Science Foundation under grant no. MCS 78-25301. The first author was also supported by the Israel Commission for Basic Research.

ISBN 0-12-307501-7

extended to the general case $k \leq n$. In the remaining paragraphs of this section, except for the last one in which we summarize this paper's contents, we list, from GK, the main results of that development which we shall use herein. Let $\mathcal{C} = \mathcal{C}(k,n)$ be the class of all symmetric k x k matrices with diagonal elements n and off-diagonal entries -1 or 3. (The conclusions that follow are valid if in addition $\mathcal{C}$ is restricted to positive-definite matrices.) Let

$$(1.1) \qquad \Psi(k,n) = \max_{C \in \mathcal{C}(k,n)} \det C.$$

It can be shown that letting symmetric C have off-diagonal entries $\equiv 3 \pmod 4$ other than -1 or 3 can only reduce det C. Every X in $\mathcal{X}$ can be transformed, by multiplying certain columns by -1, into an $\tilde{X}$ for which the entries of $\tilde{X}'\tilde{X}$ are all $\equiv 3 \pmod 4$, and hence

$$\max_{X \in \mathcal{X}} \det(X'X) \leq \Psi(k,n).$$

Even if we find a C with det C = $\Psi(k,n)$, we must still either find an X that satisfies X'X = C or show that no such X exists and pursue a further development - see Section 7. Nevertheless, a first step is to determine $\Psi(k,n)$ and the C's achieving it.

A *block* of size r is an r x r matrix with diagonal entries n and off-diagonal entries 3. A *block matrix* in $\mathcal{C}(k,n)$ with s blocks, of sizes $r_1, r_2, \ldots, r_s$ satisfying $\Sigma_1^s r_i = k$, has diagonal blocks of those sizes and all other elements -1. Such a block matrix C has

$$(1.2) \qquad \det C = (n-3)^{k-s}\{1 - G\}\Pi_1^s(n - 3 + 4r_i),$$

$$G = \Sigma_1^s r_i/(n - 3 + 4r_i).$$

The Ehlich development shows that $\Psi(k,n)$ is achieved only by a block matrix. Let $\mathcal{B} = \mathcal{B}(k,n)$ be the subset of $\mathcal{C}(k,n)$ consisting of block matrices with *blocks of only one size or blocks of only two contiguous sizes*. The Ehlich theory shows that if $C \in \mathcal{C}$ and $\det C = \Psi(k,n)$, then $C \in \mathcal{B}$. (The original method of proof in Ehlich ([1], p. 443) only shows that *some* maximizing C is in $\mathcal{B}$, but this is easily strengthened by showing (i) if there are 3 or more different r_i's we can alter some pair of them so as to improve det C *strictly* and (ii) with $s \geq 3$ and only two block sizes with $r_2 - r_1 \geq 2$, we can either *strictly* improve det C, or can obtain the same value of det C with blocks of at least 3 sizes, except for some possibilities with $r_1 = 1$, $r_2 = 3$ that are handled separately.)

For any C_s in $\mathcal{B}$ having s blocks, u of size r and v of size r + 1, we have

$$u + v = s, \quad ur + v(r + 1) = sr + v = k. \tag{1.3}$$

From (1.2) and (1.3),

$$\begin{aligned} D_{k,n}(s) &\stackrel{\text{def}}{=} \det C_s \\ &= (n-3)^{k-s}(n - 3 + 4r)^{u}(n + 1 + 4r)^{v}\{1 - G\} \\ &= (n-3)^{k-s}(n - 3 + 4r)^{(r+1)s-k}(n + 1 + 4r)^{k-sr}\{1 - G\}, \end{aligned}$$

(1.4)

$$\begin{aligned} 1-G &= 1 - ur/(n - 3 + 4r) - v(r + 1)/(n + 1 + 4r) \\ &= [k(n - 3) + 4sr(r + 1)]/(n + 4r + 1)(n + 4r - 3). \end{aligned}$$

Thus,

$$\Psi(k,n) = \max_s D_{k,n}(s). \tag{1.5}$$

We use the notation of ceiling and floor functions, $\lfloor x \rfloor$ and $\lceil x \rceil$, for the greatest integer $\leq x$ and least integer $\geq x$. For C_s in $\mathcal{B}$ having blocks of sizes r and r + 1 as in (1.3), we define the maximum block size to be R. Thus, we have R = r + 1 unless v = 0, when R = r. Furthermore

$$r = \begin{cases} \lfloor k/s \rfloor & \text{if } u > 0, \\ (k/s) - 1 & \text{if } u = 0, \end{cases}$$

(1.6)

$$R = \lceil k/s \rceil .$$

An ambiguity occurs in the definition of r, u, and v only if $s|k$. We may remove the ambiguity either by assuming always that

(1.7)

(a) $u > 0$ (hence $r = k/s$ and $v = 0$ if k/s = integer)

(b) $v > 0$ (hence $r + 1 = k/s$ and $u = 0$ if k/s = integer).

For computational simplicity we use (1.7)(a) in Section 2 and (1.7)(b) in Section 4, as we shall repeat there. Thus, s determines R and, once the convention (1.7)(a) or (b) is chosen, s determines r; but not conversely.

We denote by s_{OPT}, r_{OPT}, R_{OPT}, any set of values that maximizes $D_{k,n}(s)$. Sometimes there is more than one maximizing set. In GK we showed that a solution was

(1.8) $$\{s_{OPT} = k,\ r_{OPT} = R_{OPT} = 1\} \Leftrightarrow n \geq 2k - 5$$

and that k is the unique value of s_{OPT} if $n > 2k - 5$. When $n = 2k - 5$ the single other solution is

(1.9) $$s_{OPT} = k - 1,\ r_{OPT} = 1,\ R_{OPT} = 2.$$

IN THE REMAINDER OF THIS PAPER WE MAY HENCE ASSUME $n \geq 2k - 5$.

In Section 2 we follow Ehlich to derive simple inequalities on s_{OPT}, r_{OPT}, R_{OPT}. (The value of R_{OPT} is crucial for our construction methods.) Exact determination of these quantitites is not simple, as one sees from the extensive computer study of $D_{n,n}(s)$ needed by Ehlich (described in Comment 6 of Section 2) to show $s_{OPT} = 7$ for $n \geq 63$ when $k = n$. In the comments of Section 2 we show how better inequalities can be obtained by studying in detail the various cases of congruence, and how s_{OPT} can sometimes be determined exactly in this way. (As an illustration, we show by this method that $s_{OPT} = 7$ if $n - k = 3$ and $n \equiv 7$ or 11(mod 12), or if $n - k = 4$ or 5 and $n \equiv 3$(mod 8), there being four cases (k,n) of "ties" where also $s_{OPT} = 8$.) However, Ehlich's and our approach, of first obtaining simple inequalities and then supplementing these by a finer calculation comparing $D_{k,n}(s)$ among s-values not eliminated by the inequalities, is useful because the number of such s-values is often small. The number of such s-values to be compared is roughly $n/(2k - n)$, and the calculations following (2.15) imply that, as $n \to \infty$ with $k/n \to 1 - \lambda > 1/2$, the numbers of such s-values is within 1 of $(1 - 2\lambda)^{-1}$ as $n \to \infty$. Thus, in all "practical" cases except when k/n is near 1/2, the number of such s-values is reasonably small. In Section 3 we treat the simpler asymptotic determination of s_{OPT} as $k,n \to \infty$. In Section 4 we determine exactly those pairs of (k,n) for which there is a "tie" for neighboring s-values in the sense that $D_{k,n}(s) = D_{k,n}(s + 1)$ for some s. This must be the case when two neighboring values of s_{OPT} exist, as they did in the special case (1.8) - (1.9), and it turns out that neighboring s_{OPT}-values are the only cases of neighboring ties, i.e., $D_{k,n}$ can have no other "flat" places on the domain of integral s. The pairs (k,n) of this type turn out to be certain ones satisfying $2k - n = d$ for a fixed small d. For these and other small values of d, we determine s_{OPT} for the "series" $\{(k,n): 2k - n = d\}$, in Section 5. (Although, as we just mentioned, k/n near 1/2 means more s-values to be compared, small values of d allow this comparison to be carried out easily analytically.) In Section 6 we develop an approximate formula for s_{OPT}, for general k,n. In Section 7 we discuss briefly the problem of construction of an optimum X, described earlier.

II. SIMPLE INEQUALITIES

Throughout this section we adopt the convention (1.7)(a). The basic inequalities are on values of r or R that *cannot* be optimum, and we use whichever of these gives the better inequality on s_{OPT}, and also obtain inequalities on r_{OPT} and R_{OPT} from them.

We shall only detail an extension of the argument in Ehlich's Lemmas 3.1 and 3.2, and then comment briefly on finer arguments that yield slight improvements.

An upper bound on s_{OPT}, *lower bound on* r_{OPT} *or* R_{OPT}. Suppose $\bar{s}$ is a proposed value of s_{OPT} and $C_{\bar{s}}$ is the corresponding block matrix with blocks of two adjacent sizes (or one if $\bar{s}|k$). Of course, $\bar{s} \leq k$. Let $\rho = 2r$ if $v = 0$ and $\rho = 2r + 1$ if $v > 0$, and consider the family $\{C(x), 0 \leq x \leq r\}$ of block matrices of the following form: Of the $\bar{s}$ blocks in $C_{\bar{s}}$ keep $\bar{s} - 2$ intact, say blocks number $3, 4, \ldots, \bar{s}$. The first two blocks, of size r, r (respectively, $r, r + 1$) if $\rho = 2r$ (respectively, $2r + 1$) are eliminated and blocks of size $x, \rho - x$ are introduced. As x varies, it is easily seen from (1.2) that det $C(x)$ is proportional to

$$f(x) = (n-3+4x)(n-3+4\rho-4x)\left(1-\beta-\frac{x}{n-3+4x}-\frac{\rho-x}{n-3+4\rho-4x}\right),$$

(2.1)

$$\beta = \Sigma_3^{\bar{s}} r_i/(n-3+4r_i).$$

Since f is quadratic and $f(0) = f(\rho)$, if $f'' \equiv -16(1-2\beta) > 0$, decreasing x to 0 from the value r it has in $C_{\bar{s}}$ will increase det $C(x)$ so $s_{OPT} \neq \bar{s}$. Changing s need not mean changing r. However, if $(1-2\beta) < 0$ whenever $r = \bar{r}$ (regardless of the value of $\bar{s}$), we conclude that $r_{OPT} \neq \bar{r}$.

If $v=0$ $(R = r)$, we have

$$(n-3+4r)(1-2\beta) = n-3+4r - 2(\bar{s}-2)r$$

$$= n-3+8r - 2k.$$

If $v > 0$ $(R = r + 1)$, we have

$$(n+1+4r)\beta = (u-1)r(n+1+4r)/(n-3+4r)+(v-1)(r+1)$$
$$\geq (u-1)r+(v-1)(r+1)$$

and thus

$$(n+1+4r)(1-2\beta) \leq (n+1+4r) - 2(u-1)r - 2(v-1)(r+1)$$
$$= n+3+8r-2k.$$

From the previous paragraph, we conclude that s can be reduced in both cases while increasing the determinant, if $\bar{s}$ corresponds to r for which

(2.2) $r < (2k-n-3)/8$

or, alternatively (the first case being more restrictive in terms of R than the second), if $\bar{s}$ corresponds to R for which

(2.3) $R < (2k-n+3)/8.$

Thus, since (2.2) and (2.3) are conditions that hold for all $\bar{s}$ with such r or R, we have

(2.4)
$$r_{OPT} \geq (2k-n-3)/8,$$
$$R_{OPT} \geq (2k-n+3)/8.$$

Since $r \leq k/\bar{s}$, (2.2) is satisfied if $\bar{s} > 8k/(2k-n-3)$, so that

(2.5) $s_{OPT} \leq 8k/(2k-n-3).$

(The inequality on s obtained from (2.3) is less good.) Of course, we can actually write $r_{OPT} \geq \lceil (2k-n-3)/8 \rceil$ and similarly for R_{OPT}, and thus $s_{OPT} \leq \lfloor k/\lceil (2k-n-3)/8 \rceil \rfloor$.

Comments and refinements. 1. We know (Section 4) exactly when two *successive* values of s can both be optimum, and we know s_{OPT}, r_{OPT}, and R_{OPT} in all those cases. In all other cases, (2.5) holds with strict inequality; and the strict inequality holds for the smallest s_{OPT} in any event. The question of strict inequality in (2.4) requires further consideration: if the unimodality conjecture described in (6.1) is false (which we doubt), it is conceivable that two separated values of s_{OPT} could exist, and these might yield the same or different r_{OPT} and R_{OPT} values (since r is not strictly decreasing in s); but the strict inequality in (2.4) holds for the largest r_{OPT} or R_{OPT} even if there are such ties.

2. The inequalities can be sharpened by considering dependence on v in the second case, $v > 0$. If $1 \leq v \leq \bar{s} - 2$, (2.2) is improved slightly by taking $\rho = 2r$; but for $v = \bar{s} - 1$, $u = 1$, the treatment above gives the best one can do with this argument, so (2.2) is binding if the inequality is not to depend on v. We shall not use this minor improvement in the sequel, but considerations of this kind are important if one wants to determine better bounds. We now give an example of this treatment.

When $k = n$ the proof of Ehlich (Lemma 3.1) that $s_{OPT} \leq 7$ requires detailed calculation of $1 - 2\beta$ when $\bar{s} = 8$ and $n \equiv 3 (\text{mod } 8) (u = 5)$ or $n \equiv 7 (\text{mod } 8) (u = 1)$. The analogue for showing, *sometimes*, that $s_{OPT} = 7$ for the nonsaturated case $k < n$, is more complicated because k can have any congruence q (mod 8). (We can at best hope to obtain $s_{OPT} \leq 8$ from (2.5).) Suppose, then, that $\bar{s} = 8$ (hence $k \geq 8$) and $k = n-B = 8r + v$, r and v integers, $r \geq 1$, $0 \leq v \leq 7$. Then the largest possible β, attained when min(v,6) of the 6 blocks have size $r + 1$, is

$$(2.6) \qquad \beta = \frac{(6-v)r}{12r+B-3+v} + \frac{v(r+1)}{12r+B+1+v}, \quad 0 \leq v \leq 6,$$

$$\beta = \frac{6(r+1)}{12r+B+8}, \qquad v = 7.$$

This is $\geq 1/2$ iff

$$(2.7) \qquad 4r(v+9-3B) \geq (B-3+V)(B+1-v), \quad 0 \leq v \leq 6,$$

$$B \leq 4, \qquad v = 7.$$

An examination of the various possible cases shows that this is satisfied $\forall r \geq 1$ if $0 \leq B \leq 3$ (for both $n \equiv 3$ and $7 (\text{mod } 8)$); and, for $B = 4$ or 5, if $v = 11 - B (n \equiv 3 (\text{mod } 8))$. Among these cases, we find $\beta = 1/2$ in (2.6) only when B = 4 or 5 or when B = 3 and $v = 0$, so we might have a "tie" ($s_{OPT} = 8$ as well as 7) in those cases. However, a check of the cases of ties (Section 4) shows that in the above domain s_{OPT} can be 8 as well as 7 only when $(n,k) = (19,15)$, $(19,14)$, $(27,22)$, or $(11,8)$. In all the cases where (2.7) is satisfied, improvement if $\bar{s} \geq 9$ is easily checked. Thus, we have obtained $s_{OPT} \leq 7$ for $0 \leq n - k \leq 3$ and for "half-the cases" $n-k = 4$ or 5 (namely, those with $n \equiv 3 \pmod 8$), with s_{OPT} also 8 for the four values (n,k) noted above. In comment 5 on the lower bound, below, the two bounds obtained by this finer argument will be combined. This extends Ehlich's inequality for the saturated case to "near-saturated" cases, and it is seen how finer calculations were required than those that yielded (2.5). Of course, even this refinement does not yield *necessary* conditions for $s_{OPT} \leq 7$, since it was based on the single mode of improvement of det C through altering only two block sizes. (Illustrations of how more block sizes must be altered in finer arguments will be encountered in the verification of the cases $d = 13, 15, 17$ of (5.1), and in Section 6.) When k/n is near 9/10 and (2.5) yields only $s_{OPT} \leq 9$, an analogous argument can be used to delimit some cases in which $s_{OPT} \leq 8$, etc.; the argument is now longer because there are many more combinations (B,v) that are possible for $\bar{s} = 9$. We omit details.

Lower bound on s_{OPT}, *upper bound on* r_{OPT} *or* R_{OPT}. We now consider $\tilde{C}(x)$, obtained from $C_{\bar{s}}$ by replacing one block of size R in $\tilde{C}_{\bar{s}}$ by two blocks, of size x and R-x. From (1.2), the determinant of C(x) is proportional to

$$g(x) = (n-3+4x)(n-3+4R-4x)\ \{1-\gamma-\frac{x}{n-3+4x}-\frac{R-x}{n-3+4R-4x}\},$$

$$\gamma = \frac{ur}{n-3+4r}+\frac{(v-1)R}{n-3+4R}.$$

(Note that $\gamma = (\bar{s}-1)r/(n-3+4r)$ if $v = 0$, $R = r$.)

We suppose $R \geq 2$, which means $\tilde{C}(1) \neq C_{\bar{s}}$. (The case $R = 1$ is covered by (1.8).) Since g is quadratic and $g(0) = g(R)$, $\det \tilde{C}(1) > \det C_{\bar{s}}$ if $0 < g'(0) = 8R(1-2\gamma)$. If $v = 0$ $(R=r, r\bar{s}=k)$, we have

$$(n-3+4r)(1-2\gamma) = n-3+4r-2(\bar{s}-1)r$$
$$= n-3-2k+6r.$$

If $v > 0$, we have

$$(n-3+4r)(1-2\gamma) \geq n-3+4r-2ur-2(v-1)(r+1)$$
$$= n-1-2k+6r.$$

We conclude, as with the earlier bounds, that we can improve on $C_{\bar{s}}$ if

(2.9) $\quad r > (2k-n+3)/6$

or, alternatively, if

(2.10) $\quad R > (2k-n+7)/6.$

In particular,

(2.11) $\quad r_{OPT} \leq (2k-n+3)/6,$

$\quad\quad\quad R_{OPT} \leq (2k-n+7)/6.$

As before, we obtain from $\bar{R} \geq k/\bar{s}$ and (2.10) (which yields a better inequality than (2.9))

(2.12) $\quad s_{OPT} \geq 6k/(2k-n+7).$

Again, (2.9), (2.10), and (2.11) can be written in a stronger form, corresponding to that described below (2.5).

Comments and refinements. 3. We cannot replace the inequality in (2.12) by strict inequality even in the case that s_{OPT} is known to be unique, because the existence of the new matrix $\tilde{C}(1)$ with $\det \tilde{C}(1) = \det C'_{\bar{s}}$ does not guarantee existence of a *block matrix in* with $s > \bar{s}$ unless $R = 2$. (The upper bound argument for $\bar{s}$ gave a smaller number of blocks, and a further argument gives a block matrix with at most $\bar{s}$ - 1 blocks.)

4. In place of differentiating g, one can obtain the results from evaluation of $C(1) - C_{\bar{s}}$ by modifying appropriately the calculations (3.2) - (3.3) of GK.

5. Within the case $v > 0$, the value $v = 1$ shows that this kind of argument can't yield a better bound that does not depend on v. The analogue of (2.6) is now, from (2.8) with $\bar{s} = 6$, $k = 6r + v = n-B$ $(r \geq 1,\ 0 \leq v \leq 5)$,

$$(2.13)\qquad \begin{aligned} \gamma &= \frac{(6-v)r}{10r+B-3+v} + \frac{(v-1)(r+1)}{10r+B+1+v}, && 1 \leq v \leq 5, \\ \gamma &= \frac{5r}{10r+B-3}, && v = 0. \end{aligned}$$

This is < 1/2 iff

$$(2.14)\qquad \begin{aligned} &r(10B-18-2v) > (v-3)^2-B^2, && 1 \leq v \leq 5, \\ &B > 3, \qquad v = 0. \end{aligned}$$

Thus, for $r \geq 1$ we obtain $\gamma < 1/2$ for all $B > 3$ and all possible cases of congruence $n \equiv 3 \pmod 4$; and for $B = 3$ we have $\gamma < 1/2$ if $v > 0$, which means $n \equiv 7$ or $11 \pmod{12}$. (In addition, we have $\gamma = 1/2$ if $B = 3$ and $v = 0$, or if $B = 2$ and $v = 1$; but note Comment 3 above on the inapplicability of the argument in this case.)

Thus, in the saturated case $B = 0$ (or cases of small B) we cannot obtain $s_{OPT} \geq 7$ by this argument, and indeed Ehlich resorted to another argument to obtain this conclusion (Comment 6, below). However, for $B \geq 4$ we always have $s_{OPT} \geq 7$ for at least some of the possible congruences. Combining this with the results of Comment 2 on the upper bound, we have shown $s_{OPT} = 7$ for all (k,n) satisfying some of the possible congruences, when $3 \leq n - k \leq 5$; namely, for $n-k = 3$ if $n \equiv 7$ or $11 \pmod{12}$ and for $n-k = 4,5$ if $n \equiv 3 \pmod 8$; and the value $s_{OPT} = 7$ is unique in this domain except for a tie with $s_{OPT} = 8$ when $(n,k) =$ (19,15), (19, 14), (27,22), and (11,8).

On reading Ehlich's proof that $s_{OPT} = 7$ for $k = n \geq 63$ (see Comment 6, below), it is perhaps surprising that one can obtain s_{OPT} exactly in the cases noted above (each an infinite family of n, k) by these simple refined versions of Ehlich's method. (As we have mentioned, he also used division into cases by congruence, but when $k = n$ this did not determine s_{OPT} from the β- and γ- inequalities.) However, since s_{OPT} can not always be determined exactly in this way, we now discuss other tools. (For larger s_{OPT}-values, the method can again be used, as for the upper bound. But obtaining agreement of the two bounds becomes less possible as s_{OPT} increases. We omit details.)

6. Having used inequalities of the previous type and a few small n calculations of $1 - 2\beta$ to show $s_{OPT} = 6$ or 7 for $k = n > 39$, Ehlich completes his proof that $s_{OPT} = 7$ for $n \geq 63$ by the following two steps: (A) He shows analytically that $D_{n,n}(7) > D_{n,n}(6)$ if $n \geq 10^4$; (B) he verifies $D_{n,n}(7) > D_{n,n}(6)$ by computer for $63 \leq n < 10^4$.

This suggests trying to improve the argument of (A) to reduce the values 10^4 and, thus, the computing needed in (B); and then to carry out analogous computations in nonsaturated cases, sometimes for other values of s_{OPT}. An improvement of (A) is in fact possible if one takes account of congruences of n (mod 7 and mod 6) in computing a lower bound on $D_{n,n}(7)$ and upper bound on $D_{n,n}(6)$: it turns out that the effect of the congruence on the value of $D_{k,n}(s)$ is very slight. Specifically, if one writes $\log D_{k,n}(s)$ from (1.4) in terms of n, k, v, s with the substitution $r = (k-v)/s$, and expands in usual fashion as $n \to \infty$, one finds that the coefficient of terms in v is $O(n^{-2})$, the $O(n^{-1})$ coefficient vanishing. Of course, k and s determine v, but for the sake of obtaining the bounds now under discussion this calculation shows that the actual fine structure dependence on congruence is slight. However the dependence enters when one tries to bound $D_{k,n}(s)$ by considering (1-G) and the remaining factor separately (as Ehlich did), because the former is decreasing in v and the latter is increasing, whereas these effects largely cancel in the product. With care in estimating $D_{n,n}(s)$ by not bounding the two factors separately, one can thus obtain a sequence c_n that approaches 0 more rapidly than in Ehlich's estimate and such that

$$(1+c_n)D_{n,n}(7)/D_{n,n}(6) > 2\cdot 3^6\cdot 11^6\cdot 5^{-5}\cdot 7^{-7} = 1.0036$$
$$= \lim_n D_{n,n}(7)/D_{n,n}(6).$$

A corresponding computation can be carried out for $k < n$ and other values of s_{OPT}, but it seems an overwhelming task to try to determine s_{OPT} for every n, k in this way. We shall determine s_{OPT} exactly for certain cases near the "very regular" border $n = 2k - 5$ (see (1.8)-(1.9)), in Section 5, and asymptotically as $n \to \infty$ and $k/n \to 1-\lambda > 1/2$, in Section 3. For other "practical" values, the bounds can be combined with a small computer search, to obtain s_{OPT} for a given n,k: compute $\log D_{k,n}(s)$ from (1.4) for s between the values given by (2.5) and (2.12). A list of the values of s_{OPT} for $k \le n \le 100$, obtained by this procedure, is found in Table 1. An indication of the number of values s that must be compared can be seen upon writing $k/n = 1 - \lambda$ in (2.5) and (2.12), yielding

$$\text{(2.15)} \qquad \frac{6(1-\lambda)}{1-2\lambda+7/n} \le s_{OPT} \le \frac{8(1-\lambda)}{1-2\lambda-3/n}\ .$$

For n large, as λ increases from 0 toward 1/2, the lower and upper bound in (2.15) increase by unity each time $w = (1-\lambda)/(1-2\lambda)$ passes through a value near an integer multiple of 1/6 or 1/8, respectively. Thus, the set of s values to be searched oscillates slightly as λ increases, but has size roughly $2w = 1 + (1-2\lambda)^{-1}$, which increases with λ. The first 10 of the limiting intervals $\lceil 6w \rceil$ to $\lfloor 8w \rfloor$ of s-values that must be

Table 1

Optimum Number of Blocks for $k \leq n \equiv 3 \pmod 4$.

Ties occur when 2k-n = 5;7 (every other case); 9, 11; 17 (every third case).

Key: $\overline{j}$ means a tie, $s_{OPT} = j$ or $j + 1$.

k \ n	7	11	15	19	23	27	31	35	39	43	47	51	55	59	63
6	$\overline{5}$														
7	7														
8		$\overline{7}$													
9		$\overline{6}$													
10		$\overline{5}$	$\overline{9}$												
11		$\overline{5}$	8												
12			$\overline{6}$	$\overline{11}$											
13			$\overline{6}$	$\overline{9}$											
14			6	$\overline{7}$	$\overline{13}$										
15			6	$\overline{7}$	11										
16				7	$\overline{8}$	$\overline{15}$									
17				6	$\overline{8}$	$\overline{12}$									
18				6	8	$\overline{9}$	$\overline{17}$								
19				6	7	$\overline{9}$	14								
20					7	9	$\overline{10}$	$\overline{19}$							
21					7	8	$\overline{10}$	$\overline{15}$							
22					6	$\overline{7}$	10	$\overline{11}$	$\overline{21}$						
23					6	7	9	$\overline{11}$	17						
24						7	8	11	$\overline{12}$	$\overline{23}$					
25						7	8	9	$\overline{12}$	$\overline{18}$					
26						6	7	9	11	$\overline{13}$	$\overline{25}$				
27						6	7	9	10	$\overline{13}$	20				
28							7	8	$\overline{9}$	12	$\overline{14}$	$\overline{27}$			
29							7	8	9	11	$\overline{14}$	$\overline{21}$			
30							6	7	8	10	13	$\overline{15}$	$\overline{29}$		
31							6	7	8	10	11	$\overline{15}$	23		
32								7	9	9	11	14	$\overline{16}$	$\overline{31}$	
33								7	8	9	10	12	$\overline{16}$	$\overline{24}$	
34								6	7	8	10	$\overline{11}$	15	$\overline{17}$	$\overline{33}$
35								6	7	8	9	11	13	$\overline{17}$	26

Table 1 (continued).

Optimum Number of Blocks for $k \leq n \equiv 3 (\mathrm{mod}\ 4)$.

Ties occur when $2k-n = 5;7$ (every other case); 9, 11; 17 (every third case).

Key: $\overline{j}$ means a tie, $s_{OPT} = j$ or $j + 1$.

k \ n	39	43	47	51	55	59	63	67	71	75	79	83	87	91	95	99
36	7	8	9	10	12	16	$\overline{18}$	$\overline{35}$								
37	7	7	8	10	12	14	$\overline{18}$	$\overline{27}$								
38	6	7	8	9	11	13	17	$\overline{19}$	$\overline{37}$							
39	6	7	8	9	10	12	14	$\overline{19}$	29							
40		7	8	8	10	11	$\overline{13}$	18	$\overline{20}$	$\overline{39}$						
41		7	7	8	9	11	13	15	$\overline{20}$	$\overline{30}$						
42		6	7	8	9	10	12	14	19	$\overline{21}$	$\overline{41}$					
43		6	7	8	9	10	11	14	16	$\overline{21}$	32					
44			7	7	8	9	11	12	15	19	$\overline{22}$	$\overline{43}$				
45			7	7	8	9	10	12	14	16	$\overline{22}$	$\overline{33}$				
46			7	7	8	9	10	11	13	$\overline{15}$	20	$\overline{23}$	$\overline{45}$			
47			6	7	8	8	9	11	12	15	17	$\overline{23}$	35			
48				7	7	8	9	10	12	13	16	21	$\overline{24}$	$\overline{47}$		
49				7	7	8	9	10	11	13	16	18	$\overline{24}$	$\overline{36}$		
50				7	7	8	8	10	10	12	14	17	22	$\overline{25}$	$\overline{49}$	
51				6	7	8	8	9	10	12	13	16	19	$\overline{25}$	38	
52					7	7	8	9	10	11	13	15	$\overline{17}$	23	$\overline{26}$	$\overline{51}$
53					7	7	8	9	9	11	12	14	17	19	$\overline{26}$	$\overline{39}$
54					7	7	8	8	9	10	11	13	15	18	24	$\overline{27}$
55					6	7	7	8	9	10	11	12	14	18	20	$\overline{27}$
56						7	7	8	9	9	11	12	14	16	19	25
57						7	7	8	8	9	10	11	13	15	18	21
58						7	7	8	8	9	10	11	12	14	16	$\overline{19}$
59						6	7	7	8	9	10	10	12	13	15	19
60							7	7	8	8	9	10	11	12	15	17
61							7	7	8	8	9	10	11	12	14	16
62							7	7	8	8	9	9	10	12	13	15
63							7	7	7	8	9	9	10	11	13	14
64								7	7	8	8	9	10	11	12	13
65								7	7	8	8	9	10	11	11	13
66								7	7	7	8	9	9	10	11	13
67								7	7	7	8	8	9	10	11	12

Table 1 (continued).

Optimum Number of Blocks for $k \leq n \equiv 3 \pmod 4$.

Ties occur when 2k-n = 5;7 (every other case); 9, 11; 17 (every third case).

Key: $\bar{j}$ means a tie, $s_{OPT} = j$ or $j + 1$.

k \ n	71	75	79	83	87	91	95	99
68	7	7	8	8	9	10	10	11
69	7	7	8	8	9	9	10	11
70	7	7	7	8	8	9	10	11
71	7	7	7	8	8	9	10	10
72		7	7	8	8	9	9	10
73		7	7	8	8	9	9	10
74		7	7	7	8	8	9	10
75		7	7	7	8	8	9	9
76			7	7	8	8	9	9
77			7	7	7	8	8	9
78			7	7	7	8	8	9
79			7	7	7	8	8	9
80				7	7	8	8	8
81				7	7	7	8	8
82				7	7	7	8	8
83				7	7	7	8	8
84					7	7	7	8
85					7	7	7	8
86					7	7	7	8
87					7	7	7	8
88						7	7	7
89						7	7	7
90						7	7	7
91						7	7	7
92							7	7
93							7	7
94							7	7
95							7	7
96								7
97								7
98								7
99								7

searched for large n are given in Table 2.

Table 2.

Interval of s-values to which (2.15) limits search for s_{OPT}, for n large.

Interval of λ-values	$\lceil 6w \rceil$ to $\lfloor 8w \rfloor$
(0, 1/10)	[7, 8]
(1/10, 1/8)	[7, 9]
(1/8, 1/6)	[8, 9]
(1/6, 1/5)	[8, 10]
(1/5, 3/14)	[9, 10]
(3/14, 1/4)	[9, 11]
(1/4, 5/18)	[10, 12]
(5/18, 2/7)	[10, 13]
(2/7, 3/10)	[11, 13]
(3/10, 5/16)	[11, 14]

Thus, for example, if $\lambda = 1/9$, s_{OPT} is 7, 8, or 9 for n sufficiently large; examining (2.15) more closely, we see that [7, 9] is in fact the interval if $n > 63$. We next turn to the exact determination of s_{OPT} for fixed λ as $n \to \infty$.

III. ASYMPTOTICS

We think of $k,n \to \infty$ while s is fixed or bounded; when this last is not the case, as in the verification of (3.3), further care is needed. Write $k/n = b > \frac{1}{2}$, and substitute into (1.4). We obtain

$$D_{k,n}(x) = (n-3)^k s^{-s}(s+4b)^{s-1}(s+4b-bs)[1+0(n^{-1})]. \tag{3.1}$$

Thus, asymptotically we need only maximize $(1+4b/s)^{s-1}(1-b+4b/s)$ with respect to s for each b, and Table 2 gives the values of s to which we can limit our search. One obtains $s_{OPT} = 7$ for λ near 0, then $s_{OPT} = 8$, etc.; the first few intervals of λ-values (the "near-saturated" cases) that yield a given s_{OPT}-value are, as $n \to \infty$, with $k/n \to 1-\lambda$,

$$\text{(3.2)} \qquad \lim s_{OPT} = \begin{cases} 7 & \text{for} \quad 0 \leq \lambda < .08837, \\ 8 & \text{for} \quad .08837 < \lambda < .17027, \\ 9 & \text{for} \quad .17027 < \lambda < .22494, \end{cases}$$

and one can continue in this manner. In particular, for $k/n \to 1$ in any way as $n \to \infty$, it is easy to see that s_{OPT} is eventually 7.

For comparison, when n is 99 we have $s_{OPT} = 7$ for $0 \leq \lambda \leq .111$, $s_{OPT} = 8$ for $.121 \leq \lambda \leq .192$, $s_{OPT} = 9$ for $.202 \leq \lambda \leq .242$; for fixed λ, (3.2) may overestimate s_{OPT} slightly.

When λ is near 1/2, we approach the domain (1.8) where $s_{OPT} = k$, $R_{OPT} = 1$. Writing $b = 1/2 + \varepsilon$ with $\varepsilon > 0$, and noting that $s \to \infty$ as $\varepsilon \to 0$ by (2.12), we find that the logarithm of $(1 + 4b/s)^{s-1}(1-b+4b/s)$ (see just under (3.1)) is

$$2-\log 2 + 2\varepsilon - 2\varepsilon^2 - 10/3s^2 + 4\varepsilon/s + O((\varepsilon+s^{-1})^3)$$

as $\varepsilon \to 0$ and $s \to \infty$. From this one can show that the maximum is given at

$$\text{(3.3)} \qquad s_{OPT} \approx 5/3\varepsilon$$

as $\varepsilon \to 0$. This is meaningful if, having first let $n \to \infty$, we then let $\varepsilon \to 0$. A closer examination of the $O(n^{-1})$ term in (3.1) shows that its behavior as $n \to \infty$ and $s \to \infty$ is $3/n + O(1/ns+s^2/n^2)$, and one can then verify that (3.3) is valid for $\varepsilon = o(n^{-1/2})$.

The approximation (3.3) is reasonably accurate for moderate n and even fairly large ε. For example, when $\varepsilon = 1/5$, (3.3) gives 11.7; from Table 1, for $n = 31$ and $k = 22$, we have $s_{OPT} = 10$, and for $n = 59$, $k = 41$, we have $s_{OPT} = 11$. Even for $2k-n = d$, an integer ≥ 5, so that $\varepsilon \approx d/2n$, the approximation gives approximately the right ratio of k/s_{OPT} and thus of R_{OPT}, although the absolute error from s_{OPT} is unbounded: for d = 5, 7, 9, 11, 17, the approximation gives for $k/s_{OPT} \approx 3k/5 \approx 3d/20$ the values .75, 1.05, 1.35, 1.65, 1.95, 2.25, 2.55, compared with the actual values 1, 1.33, 2.00, 2.00, 2.25, 2.77, 3.00, recorded in Section 5.

Improvement of the estimate (3.1) means inclusion of terms of order n^{-2} in the expansion of $\log D_{k,n}(s)$, which includes dependence on v and, thus, greater complexity.

IV. NEIGHBORING TIES

In this section we determine the pairs (k,n) for which there is an s with

$$D_{k,n}(s) = D_{k,n}(s+1). \tag{4.1}$$

In Section 5 it is then shown that $s_{OPT} = s$ or $s + 1$ (only) for the values satisfying (4.1). The five "tied series", as we will call them, turn out to be pairs (k, n) and corresponding s in (4.1) for which

$$\begin{aligned}(2k-n,s) = (5,k-1);\ (7,3(k-1)/4) \text{ when } n \equiv 3 (\text{mod } 8);\\ (9,k/2);\ (11,(k-1)/2);\ (17,(k-1)/3) \text{ when } n \equiv 3 (\text{mod } 12).\end{aligned} \tag{4.2}$$

The proof that the pairs (k,n) satisfying (4.2), and only those, satisfy (4.1), is divided into two cases, of which (A) below is simplest. Of the two possible conventions of u, v we choose (1.7)(b), with $v > 0$, throughout this section.

(A) *Cases where* (4.1) *holds with the same value of* R *for* s *as for* s + 1. We let u refer to the design with s blocks, which thus has u blocks of size r and s-u of size r+1; the design with s+1 blocks has u+r+1 blocks of size r and s-u-r of size r+1. We write $n-3 = 4m$. Then, from (1.4), (4.1) says

$$4^{k-2}m^{k-s}(m+r)^{u-1}(m+r+1)^{s-u-1}A' = 4^{k-2}m^{k-s-1}(m+r)^{u+r} \times (m+r+1)^{s-u-r-1}B', \tag{4.3}$$

where

$$A' = 4A = 4\{4(m+r)(m+r+1)-mk-(k+u)r\},$$

(4.4)

$$B' = 4B = 4\{4(m+r)(m+r+1)-mk-(k+u+r+1)r\}.$$

Simplifying, we obtain from (4.3),

$$(4.5) \qquad m(m+r+1)^r A = (m+r)^{r+1} B.$$

Since m+r and m+r+1 are relatively prime, (4.5) implies $(m+r)^{r+1} \mid mA$ and hence $mA \geq (m+r)^{r+1}$, which from (4.4) implies

$$(4.6) \qquad 4m(m+r+1) > (m+r)^r.$$

It is easily seen that (4.6) is false for $r = 3\ \forall m$; and, since $(m+r)^r/(m+r+1)$ is increasing (has positive logarithmic derivative) for $r \geq 1$, it follows that (4.6) and hence (4.3) is false for all $r \geq 3$, $\forall m$.

The remainder of the solution in case (A) is found by checking that u is an integer such that $u \geq 0$, $s-u > 0$, $u+r+1 \geq 0$, and $s-u-r > 0$. For $r = 1$ this implies $0 \leq u < k-2$ (the last from $s-u-1 > 0$ and $s \leq k-1$), and the formula for u, from (4.5), is $u = (m+1)(2m+6-k)$. Thus, the condition $0 \leq u < k-2$ becomes $2m+4 < k \leq 2m+6$, or $(n+5)/2 < k \leq (n+9)/2$. The only solutions are $k = (n+9)/2$ and $k = (n+7)/2$, and in the latter case the integrality of $s = (u+k)/2$ shows we must have $n \equiv 3 \pmod 8$. These are of course the series $2k-n = 9$ and 7 of (4.2).

There remains the possibility $r = 2$ in (A). (This can be disposed of in a number of ways.) We now have, from (4.5),

$$(4.7) \qquad u = \frac{(4m+12-k)(m+2)}{2} - \frac{3(m+2)^3}{3m+8},$$

so that $3(m+2)^3/(3m+8)$ must be an integral multiple of 1/2. This is possible only if $m = 0$, $n = 3$, for which (4.7) gives $u = 9-k$, impossible for $k \leq n$.

(B) *Cases in which, if* R *is the maximum block size for* s *blocks, then* R-1 *is the maximum for* s+1 *blocks.* We now suppose the s blocks consist of v of size r+1 and u = s-v of size r; and that the s+1 blocks consist of s+v-r+1 of size r and r-v = u+r-s of size r-1. Thus, $v \leq r$. (It is easily checked that these are the right values.) Again, u and v always refer to the s blocks. In order for (4.1) to hold we have, in place of (4.5),

$$m(m+r)^{r-2v-1}(m+r+1)^{v-1}A = (m+r-1)^{r-v-1}B^* \tag{4.8}$$

where A (rewritten from (4.4) in terms of v) and B* (after some simplification) are given by

$$\begin{aligned} A &= 4(m+r)(m+r+1)-k(m+r+1)+v(r+1), \\ B^* &= 4(m+r)(m+r-1)-k(m+r-1) - (r-v)(r-1). \end{aligned} \tag{4.9}$$

If $r-2v-1 < 0$, the power of m+r in (4.8) can be transferred to the other side to make it a positive power, and similarly for $(m+r-1)^{-1}$ if r = v. In any event, m+r is relatively prime to m+r+1 and m+r-1, and the last two have at most a factor 2 in common, so that, writing $[x]^+ = \max(x,0)$, we see that $(m+r+1)^{v-1}$ and $(m+r-1)^{r-v-1}$ (when $r-v-1 \geq 0$) have at most a factor $2^{[r-3]^+}$ in common. (This maximum factor occurs when v = 2 and $2^{[r-3]^+} | (m+r+1)$, or when v = r-2 and $2^{[r-3]^+} | (m+r-1)$; in fact, the common factor is 1 if m+r is even or if v = 1 or r or r-1, and is at most $2^{\max([v-1]^+,[r-v-1]^+)}$ otherwise.) Thus, we have, from (4.8) upon transferring terms if necessary to have positive powers on both sides,

$$(m+r)^{|r-2v-1|}(m+r+1)^{v-1}(m+r-1)^{|r-v-1|} \,\Big|\, 2^{[r-3]^+}mAB^*, \tag{4.10}$$

and hence it is necessary that the left side of (4.10) is

$$\leq 2^{[r-3]^+}16(m+r)^2(m+r-1)(m+r+1)m \tag{4.11}$$

in order that (4.8) be satisfied.

The total of exponents on the left side of (4.10) is at least r-2 (attained when v = (r-1)/2, r odd). Also, for $r \geq 10$, we have $(m+r)^2(m+r-1)(m+r+1)m < (m+r-1)^5$. Consequently, from (4.10) and (4.11), (4.8) can be satisfied for $r \geq 10$ only if $(m+r-1)^{r-7} < 2^{r+1}$. This is impossible for $r \geq 10$ if $m \geq 2$, and in the trivial cases m = 0, 1 we have $7 \geq n \geq r$. Thus, (4.10) is impossible for $r \geq 10$. For $r \leq 9$, certain other values can be eliminated by the same method with the use of the improved factor noted above (4.10); for example, for r = 8, 9 values $v \leq r-5$ can be eliminated, as can the values v = 1, r-1, r for $r \geq 6, 5, 4$, respectively.

For $r \leq 9$, the various possibilities can be listed; for each r, there are some values of v that can be eliminated by using (4.10)-(4.11), perhaps with the possible improvement on the factor $2^{[r-3]^+}$ noted just above (4.10). The remaining values of v can then be checked in each case by solving (4.8) for k seeing whether the resulting expression can be an integer. The calculations are tedious but straightforward, and, rather than to take the space to give them all, we treat in some detail here, for illustration, only the value r = 6. When r = 6, the values v = 1, 5, 6 are eliminated by the remark at the end of the previous paragraph, and the value v = 4 can be handled similarly. There remain the values v = 2 and 3, which can not be eliminated by using (4.10). Instead, we solve (4.8) for k. The general form of this (valid for all r and m), from (4.9) with (4.8) being abbreviated $\alpha A = \beta B^*$, is

$$(4.12) \qquad k = 4(m+r) - \frac{\alpha v(r+1) + \beta(r-v)(r-1)}{\beta(m+r-1) - \alpha(m+r+1)}$$

$$= 4(m+r) - F \text{ (say)}.$$

Thus, a necessary condition for (4.8) to hold is that F be an integer. For our case r = 6, v = 2, we obtain

$$F = \frac{14m(m+6)(m+7)+20(m+5)^3}{(m+5)^4-m(m+6)(m+7)^2} = \frac{34m^3+482m^2+2088m+2500}{17m^2 + 206m + 625}$$

$$= 2m + 4 + \frac{2m^2 + 14m}{17m^2 + 206m + 625},$$

which is obviously never an integer for $m \geq 1$. A similar development holds for $v = 3$, and also for the other cases that must be studied in this manner for $4 \leq r \leq 9$.

For each of the values $r = 1$, 2, and 3, respectively, the analogous development yields a single series of solutions and no others, namely, the series of (4.2) for $2k-n = 5$, 11, and 17 (the last with $n \equiv 3 \pmod{12}$).

V. CHARACTERIZATION OF s_{OPT} FOR THE "SERIES" $k = (n+d)/2$, $d \leq 17$

We fix d at any odd integral value ≥ 5 and consider the series of settings $(k,n) = ((n+d)/2, n)$ with $n \geq d$. (For $d < 5$, see (1.8).)

The basic idea is that, in order to show $s_{OPT} = g(n,d)$ uniquely, we show that altering C_s (the block matrix with blocks of at most two sizes) to some C^* increases the determinant from the value $D_{k,n}(s)$, if either (a) $s > g(n,d)$ or (b) $s < g(n,d)$; in the case of the five series of (4.2) in which two values $s = g(n,d)$ and $g(n,d)-1$ yield the same value $D_{k,n}(s)$, we show both values (and no others) are s_{OPT} by the same demonstration with (b) replaced by (b') $s < g(n,d)-1$.

The demonstration becomes more complicated as d increases. In GK, part (b') for $d = 5$ was handled by letting C^* be obtained from C_s by replacing a block of size R in the latter by one each of sizes $R-1$ and 1. This no longer always suffices, as one can check when $d = 13$ and $s < g(n,13)$ (given in (5.1)) with $r = 2$. What does work is to replace 2 blocks of size 3 by 3 blocks of size 2. Unfortunately, the corresponding calculation when s_{OPT}/n is smaller and r_{OPT} is larger (which occurs as d grows) is more tedious to carry out exactly, and having characterized s_{OPT} exactly for $d \le 17$, we shall then outline an argument for general d but will only take the space here to give $\lim_{n\to\infty} g(n,d)/n$ for general d. Our exact result is

THEOREM. *For* $5 \le d \le 17$ (d *odd*), $(k,n) = ((n+d)/2,n)$, $d \le n \equiv 3 \pmod 4$, *the only values of* s_{OPT} (*with accompanying* r_{OPT} *and* R_{OPT}) *are:*

(5.1)

$$\underline{d=5}: \quad s_{OPT} = \begin{cases} k=(n+5)/2, & r_{OPT} = 1^*, \quad R_{OPT} = 1, \\ k-1=(n+3)/2, & r_{OPT} = 1, \quad R_{OPT} = 2. \end{cases}$$

$\underline{d=7}$: *If* $n \equiv 3 \pmod 8$,

$$s_{OPT} = \begin{cases} (3k+1)/4 = (3n+23)/8, & r_{OPT} = 1, \; R_{OPT} = 2, \\ (3k-3)/4 = (3n+15)/8, & r_{OPT} = 1, \; R_{OPT} = 2, \end{cases}$$

if $n \equiv 7 \pmod 8$,

$$s_{OPT} = (3k-1)/4 = (3n+19)/8, \quad r_{OPT} = 1, \; R_{OPT} = 2.$$

$$\underline{d=9}: \quad s_{OPT} = \begin{cases} (k+2)/2 = (n+13)/4, & r_{OPT} = 1, \; R_{OPT} = 2, \\ k/2 = (n+9)/4, & r_{OPT} = 2^*, \; R_{OPT} = 2. \end{cases}$$

$$\underline{d=11}: \quad s_{OPT} = \begin{cases} (k+1)/2 = (n+13)/4, & r_{OPT} = 1, \; R_{OPT} = 2, \\ (k-1)/2 = (n+9)/4, & r_{OPT} = 2, \; R_{OPT} = 3. \end{cases}$$

$$\underline{d=13}: \quad s_{OPT} = \lfloor (4k+3)/9 \rfloor = \lfloor (2n+29)/9 \rfloor, \; r_{OPT}=2, \; R_{OPT}=3.$$

$$\underline{d=15}: \quad s_{OPT} = \lfloor (13k+25)/36 \rfloor = \lfloor (13n+245)/72 \rfloor, r_{OPT}=2, R_{OPT}=3.$$

(5.1) (continued)

<u>d=17</u>: *if* $n \equiv 3 \pmod{12}$,

$$s_{OPT} = \begin{cases} (k+2)/3 = (n+21)/6, & r_{OPT} = 2,\ R_{OPT} = 3, \\ (k-1)/3 = (n+15)/6, & r_{OPT} = 3,\ R_{OPT} = 4; \end{cases}$$

if $n \equiv 7 \pmod{12}$,

$$s_{OPT} = k/3 = (n+17)/6, \qquad r_{OPT} = 3^*,\ R_{OPT} = 3;$$

if $n \equiv 11 \pmod{12}$,

$$s_{OPT} = (k+1)/3 = (n+19)/6,\ r_{OPT} = 2, \quad R_{OPT} = 3.$$

(*In the three values marked* *, *the value is given for* r_{OPT} *under the convention* $u > 0$ *of* (1.7)(a), *and must be reduced by* 1 *for the value under the convention* $v > 0$ *of* (1.7)(b).)

The value $d = 5$ was covered in (1.8)-(1.9), but we include it here for unity of exposition.

Proof. We divide the demonstration into several parts.

1. *Series with ties*. We treat the values $d = 5, 7, 9, 11, 17$ first because these are simplest; we remarked, just above the statement of the theorem, on the difficulty of proof in other cases, but in these five cases the proof mentioned there can be used to improve C_s to C^* if s is too small.

(a) *Lower bound on* s_{OPT}. We first show s_{OPT} is $\geq$ the value given in (5.1). It is convenient in this proof to adopt the convention of (1.7)(b), so that always $R = r+1$ and $v > 0$ and thus

(5.2) $\quad k-sr-1 \geq 0.$

Using (1.7)(b) means reducing by 1 the values r with * as described at the end of the theorem. We compare $D_{k,n}(s)$ with $D^* = \det C^*$ where C^* is obtained from C_s by replacing a block of size $R = r+1$ by blocks of size 1 and r. From (1.2) we obtain, after some simple arithmetic, and with G of (1.4) referring to

$D_{k,n}(s)$ and $L = n + 4r + 1$,

$$L^{2-v}(L-4)^{1-u}(L-4r-4)^{s+1-k}[D^*-D_{k,n}(s)]$$

$$= L(L-4)^2(L-4r)\{1-G+ \frac{r+1}{L} - \frac{1}{L-4r} - \frac{r}{L-4}\}$$

$$(5.3)\quad - L^2(L-4)(L-4r-4)\{1-G\}$$

$$= 8rL(L-4)\{1-2G+2(r+1)L^{-1}\}$$

$$= 8r[L(L-2-2k+2r) + 8(k-1-sr)(r+1)]$$

$$= 8r[(2k-d+4r+1)(6r-d-1)+8(k-1-sr)(r+1)].$$

If $d = 5, 7, 9, 11$ and $r \geq 2$, we have $6r - d - 1 \geq 0$ and thus (noting (5.2)) that (5.3) is > 0 when $d \leq 9$ or when $d = 11$, $r = 2$, and $s < (k-1)/2$. The latter shows $s_{OPT} \geq (k-1)/2$ when $d = 11$. For $d = 5, 7, 9$, it remains still to consider only $r = 1$, for which (5.3) is > 0 iff

$$(5.4)\qquad s < k(1- \frac{d-5}{8}) + \frac{(d-5)^2}{16} - 1.$$

This becomes $s < k-1$ for $d = 5$; $s < \frac{3}{4}(k-1)$ for $d = 7$, $s < k/2$ for $d = 9$. Thus, $s_{OPT} \geq k-1, \frac{3}{4}(k-1), k/2$ in the respective cases; for $d = 7$ and $n \equiv 7 \pmod 8$ this implies $s_{OPT} \geq (3k-1)/4$.

When $d = 17$ and $r \geq 3$, we have $6r-d-1 \geq 0$ and thus (5.3) is > 0 if $r > 3$ or $r = 3$ and $s < (k-1)/3$. Hence, $s_{OPT} \geq (k-1)/3$. This implies $s_{OPT} \geq k/3$ if $n \equiv 7 \pmod{12}$ and $s_{OPT} \geq (k+1)/3$ if $n \equiv 11 \pmod{12}$.

This completes the proof that s_{OPT} is at least the smaller of the two values of s in each of the cases $d = 5, 7, 9, 11, 17$, or is at least the single value given in the subcases of $d = 7, 17$ when there is a unique s_{OPT}.

(b) *Upper bound on* s_{OPT}. When $d = 5$, $s_{OPT} \leq k$ is trivial. We next show that if $d > 5$ and s is too large we can increase the determinant from the value $D_{k,n}(s)$ as follows: Firstly, by (1.8) we know $s_{OPT} \leq k-1$ if $d > 5$, so (with the $v > 0$ convention) $r_{OPT} \geq 1$ then. In the cases $d = 7, 9, 11$, for $k > s >$ the value(s) of s_{OPT} in the theorem's statement, we have $r = 1$ and $s \geq \frac{1}{2}(k+1)+1$, from which $u = 2s-k \geq 3$. We shall now shown that if $d = 7, 9, 11$ and if s is such that $r = 1$ and $u \geq 2$, so that there are at least 2 blocks of size 1, then combining 2 blocks of size 1 into a block of size 2 yields a C^{**} with determinant $D^{**} > D_{k,n}(s)$, if $s > s_{OPT}$ of the theorem's statement. In fact, if we put $r = 1$ and $s-1$ for s in (5.3), $[D^*-D_{k,n}(s)]$ there is $[D_{k,n}(s)-D^*]$ here, which is thus proportional to

$$(2k-d+5)(5-d) + 16(k-s), \tag{5.5}$$

which is negative (D^* larger) if

$$s > k(1- \frac{d-5}{8}) + \frac{(d-5)^2}{16} . \tag{5.6}$$

Hence, for $d = 7, 9, 11$, we have $s_{OPT} \leq (3k+1)/4$, $(k+2)/2$, $(k+1)/2$, and $s_{OPT} \leq (3k-1)/4$ if $d = 7$ and $n \equiv 7 \pmod 8$. This yields the desired result except for $d = 17$.

For $d = 17$, (5.6) always holds, so $r_{OPT} > 1$ and $s_{OPT} \leq k/2$. For $k/2 \geq s > (k+2)/3$ there are at least 3 blocks of size 2 in C_s, and C_{s-1} is obtained by replacing the 3 blocks of size 2 by 2 blocks of size 3. This yields (with $r = 2$ and G referring to C_s, and with the substitution $k = (n+d)/2$ for use in the other cases of d below)

$$\begin{aligned}
&(n-3)^{s-k}(n+5)^{4-u}(n+9)^{1-v}[D_{k,n}(s)-D_{k,n}(s-1)] \\
&= (n+5)^4(n+9)\{1-G\} - (n-3)(n+5)(n+9)^3\times \{1-G+ \frac{6}{n+5} - \frac{6}{n+9}\} \\
&= (48n+368)(n+5)(n+9)\{1-G\} - 24(n-3)(n+9)^2 \\
&= [24n+184][2(n+5)(n+9)-(n-3)(n+d)- \frac{3(n-3)(n+9)^2}{3n + 23} - 48s].
\end{aligned} \tag{5.7}$$

This is negative (C_{s-1} better than C_s) iff

(5.8) $$s > \left[\frac{71n}{3} + \frac{1073}{9} + \frac{512}{9(3n + 23)} - d(n-3)\right]/48.$$

For d = 17 the right side of (5.8) is easily seen to be $< (n+21)/6$ if $n \geq 17$ (the smallest possible value); thus, C_{s-1} is better than C_s if $s > (n+21)/6$, so $s_{OPT} \leq (n+21)/6$. This (and the implications $s_{OPT} \leq (n+17)/6$ or $\leq (n+19)/6$ when $n \equiv 7$ or 11 (mod 12)) complete the proof for d = 17.

2. *The cases* d = 13, 15. We consider the expression (5.7) when s is such that this formula applies: $k/2 \geq s > s-1 \geq k/3$. From $u = 3s-k$ we see that there are always at least 3 blocks of size 2 among the s blocks in this range, and for the case of s-1 blocks $v = k-2(s-1)$ shows that there are at least 2 blocks of size 3 among the s-1 blocks. Thus, the exchange of (5.7) is always possible.

For d = 13, (5.7) is negative (C_{s-1} better than C_s) iff

(5.9) $$s > [2n + 89/3 + 32/3(3n + 23)]/9,$$

and is positive if the opposite inequality holds. Since $32/3(3n + 23) < 1/3$ for $n \geq 13$, we conclude that (5.7) is $\{^<_>\}$ 0 iff $s\{^>_<\} \lfloor (2n + 29)/9 \rfloor$. For d = 15, the analogue of (5.9) is

(5.10) $$s > [13n + 739/3 + 256/3(3n + 23)]/72.$$

For $n \geq 15$, we have $256/3(3n + 23) < 5/3$ and thus the right side of (5.10) is $y = [13n + 245 + x]/72$ where $4/3 < x < 3$. Hence, if $n = 4m+3$, we have $y = [13m + 62 + x/4]/18$ and thus $\lfloor y \rfloor = \lfloor (13m + 62)/18 \rfloor$. We conclude that (5.7) is $\{^<_>\}$ 0 iff $s\{^>_<\} \lfloor (13n + 245)/72 \rfloor$.

The above calculation shows that the s_{OPT} stated in (5.1) gives the unique maximum of $D_{k,n}(s)$ over the crucial interval $k/3 + 1 \leq s \leq k/2$. Values of $s > k/2$ or $\leq k/3$ are excluded by the fact that $r_{OPT} \geq 2$ implies $s_{OPT} \leq k/2$ and that $R_{OPT} \leq 3$, $r_{OPT} \leq 2$ implies $s_{OPT} > k/3$.

It is interesting that successive values of g(4m+3,d) - g(4m-1,d) (where again $g(n,d) = s_{OPT}$) go through a cycle of length 9 when d = 13 and of length 18 when d = 15.

VI. GENERAL APPROXIMATION TO s_{OPT}

Some ideas for the determination of s_{OPT} in general arise from the calculations of the previous section on the series $k = (n+d)/2$, $d \leq 17$. The simple inequalities of Section 2 did not suffice, and we had to study $D_{k,n}(s)$ in detail, either in a crucial interval of s values with constant R and with s_{OPT} in its interior, or else in two neighboring intervals with different R values and s_{OPT} on their boundary. At the same time, we had to rule out s-values outside the crucial interval. For general (k,n) the analogue to this last is intuitively plausible but we do not have a general proof. A sufficient condition for our program of characterizing s_{OPT} to work is the

(6.1) *Unimodality conjecture:* $D_{k,n}(s)$ *is unimodal in* s.

Indeed, this was seen to be valid in all our numerical investigations. But a complete proof, even of unimodality in the interval of s-values not excluded by the simple inequalities of Section 2, would entail an analysis of $D_{k,n}(s) - D_{k,n}(s+1)$ involving calculations like those of Sections 4 and 5. In particular, the case where R differs for s and s+1 (part (B) of Section 4) seems the messiest to analyze.

Assuming this unimodality, we want a formula, or at least an accurate estimate, for s_{OPT}. The expression (5.7) suggests an approach for finding a general expression for s_{OPT} that holds for larger values of d than those of the previous section, but the details are more difficult to carry out because, as r increases, the analogue of (5.7) in the crucial interval $k/(r+1)+1 \leq s \leq k/r$ becomes more complicated. We cannot guarantee, as we did in each of (5.8), (5.9), (5.10), that the influence of a vanishing remainder term (of the form $c/(3n + 23)$ in the above) is also absent for all small n. Thus, although one can carry out a detailed analysis for each pair (k,n), we still do not have a simple presentation that covers all cases. We now indicate the idea of the development, an approximation to s_{OPT}, and an asymptotic formula.

Suppose, for fixed k, n, r, that s is an integer satisfying

$$k/(r+1) \leq s-1 < s \leq k/r. \tag{6.2}$$

Write

$$f(n,r) = (n+4r-3)^{r+1} - (n-3)(n+4r+1)^{r}. \tag{6.3}$$

Then from (1.4), with G, u, and v again referring to the value s, and by a calculation like that used earlier, where now we replace r+1 of the blocks of size r by r of size r+1 or vice versa, we have

$$\begin{aligned}[(n-3)^{s-k}(n+4r-3)^{r-u+2}(n+4r+1)^{1-v}/f(n,r)]\\ [D_{k,n}(s)-D_{k,n}(s-1)]\\ = (n+4r+1)(n+4r-3)\{1-G\}-4r(r+1)(n-3)\\ \times (n+4r+1)^{r}/f(n,r).\end{aligned} \tag{6.4}$$

This expression is $\{\substack{<\\=\\>}\}$ 0, respectively, iff

$$\begin{aligned} s\{\substack{>\\=\\<}\} &\frac{(n+4r+1)(n+4r-3)-k(n-3)}{4r(r+1)} - \frac{(n-3)(n+4r+1)^{r}}{f(n,r)}\\ &= \frac{2(n+4r+1)(n+4r-3)-(n+d)(n-3)}{8r(r+1)} - \frac{(n-3)(n+4r+1)^{r}}{f(n,r)} \qquad (6.5)\\ &= p(k,n,r) \quad \text{(say)},\end{aligned}$$

where we have again written $d = 2k-n$.

Write

$$h(k,n,r) = \lfloor p(k,n,r) \rfloor. \tag{6.6}$$

In the next two paragraphs (A) and (B), we make some brief

remarks about (6.5). We mostly ignore "ties" in what follows, having covered these in Section 4.

(A) If $s_0 = h(k,n,r)$ satisfies $k/(r+1)+1 \leq s_0 \leq k/r-1$, it follows from (6.5) that, on the interval $k/(r+1) \leq s \leq k/r$, $D_{k,n}(s)$ is nondecreasing up to s_0 and (from (6.5) with s replaced by s+1) nonincreasing thereafter, so that it has an *internal* maximum on this interval at s_0 (unique except for a possible "tie").

(B) On the other hand, if $p(k,n,r) \geq k/r$, $D_{k,n}(s)$ is nondecreasing for $k/(r+1) \leq s \leq k/r$; and if $p(k,n,r-1) - 1 \leq k/r$, $D_{k,n}(s)$ is nonincreasing for $k/r \leq s \leq k/(r-1)$. Hence, if $p(k,n,r-1) - 1 \leq k/r \leq p(k,n,r)$, and if $k/(r+1) + 1 \leq \lfloor k/r \rfloor \leq k/(r-1)-1$, then $D_{k,n}(s)$ has an internal maximum on the interval $k/(r+1) \leq s \leq k/(r-1)$ at $s = \lfloor k/r \rfloor$ (unique except for a possible "tie").

In both of the preceding paragraphs, the maximizing value of s is indeed s_{OPT} if the unimodality conjecture (6.1) is valid.

Expanding f(n,r) in powers of n for fixed r, we have

$$f(n,r)/8r(r+1) = \Sigma_{j\geq 0} n^{r+1-j} \binom{r+1}{j} [(4r-3)^j - (4r-4j+1) \times (4r+1)^{j-1}]/8r(r+1)$$

$$= n^{r-1} + \frac{(r-1)(12r-1)}{3} n^{r-2}$$

$$+ \frac{(r-1)(r-2)(48r^2-8r+3)}{6} n^{r-3}$$

$$+ \frac{(r-1)(r-2)(r-3)(320r^3-80r^2+60r-7)}{30} n^{r-4}$$

$$+ O(n^{r-5}),$$

and hence, by a straightforward but tedious computation, that

$$\frac{8r(r+1)(n-3)(n+4r+1)^r}{f(n,r)} = n^2 + \frac{16r-10}{3}n + \frac{4r^2-140r+1}{9} \tag{6.7}$$
$$- \frac{128(r-1)(2r^2+5r+2)}{135}n^{-1} + O(n^{-2}).$$

Thus, for fixed r,

$$p(k,n,r) = \frac{1}{8r(r+1)}\left\{\frac{(32r+7-3d)n}{3} + 3d + \frac{284r^2-4r-55}{9}\right. \tag{6.8}$$
$$\left. + \frac{128(r-1)(2r^2+5r+2)}{135n} + O(n^{-2})\right\}.$$

Suppose $n \to \infty$, $k \to \infty$, with $d = 2k-n$ fixed. Then, under the unimodality conjecture (6.1), we obtain from (6.8) and from (A), (B) respectively for the two lines of (6.9) below,

Asymptotic formula for s_{OPT}: For fixed d, let r be the unique integer satisfying one of the two inequalities of (6.9). Then

$$\lim_n \frac{s_{OPT}}{n} = \begin{cases} \dfrac{32r+7-3d}{24r(r+1)} & \text{if } \dfrac{20r-5}{3} \le d < \dfrac{20r+7}{3}, \\[2ex] 1/2r & \text{if } \dfrac{20r-13}{3} \le d \le \dfrac{20r-5}{3}. \end{cases} \tag{6.9}$$

For successive values of r the two lines of (6.9) mesh to include all odd values of $d \ge 5$.

One can check the agreement of this formula with the results of the theorem of Section 5, the asymptotic ratios obtained from (5.1) for $d = 5,\ldots,17$ being precisely those for (r, line of (6.9)) = (1,2), (1,1), (2,2), (2,2), (2,1), (2,1), (3,2). In fact, for these small values of d, in the three "line 1 of (6.9)" cases the integer part of the approximation of (6.8), with or without the n^{-1} term, is always the correct value of s_{OPT}. (The asymptotic condition $20r-5 < 3d < 20r+7$ of (6.9) of course does not generally correspond to (A) when we look at nonasymptotic behavior.) An approximation to s_{OPT} that is fairly accurate for both the situations (A) and (B) is suggested by those paragraphs:

Let $\hat{p}$ be the approximation to p through terms of order n^0 (or n^{-1}) in (6.8). Put $\bar{r} = \min\{r: k^{-1}(1+r)\hat{p}(k,n,r) \geq 1\}$. Then $s^* = \lfloor \hat{p}(k,n,\bar{r}) \rfloor$ approximates s_{OPT}. (Obvious slight modifications are possible.) A numerical investigation for values $n \leq 199$, with $(n+5)/2 \leq k \leq n$, shows that this approximation is quite good, usually yielding s_{OPT} exactly and rarely being off by more than 1. Replacing $\hat{p}$ by $\hat{p}-1$ in the definition of $\bar{r}$, and increasing s* where necessary to make it monotone in k, improve somewhat; inclusion of $O(n^{-1})$ terms matters less. Although the above calculations leading to an approximation for s_{OPT} are based on an expansion in powers of n for fixed r, the approximation turns out to be quite good even for values of (k,n) near saturation, for which cases r (corresponding to s_{OPT}) is of order n and the successive terms in the expansion (6.8) are all of the same order in n. This is evidently because the terms after the first three decrease rapidly; for example, for k = n = d = 7r (about what occurs near saturation), the term in n^{-1} is only about .001 times the sum of the first three terms.

VII. CONSTRUCTION OR NONCONSTRUCTIBILITY

When k = n, the Ehlich theory leading to (1.5) is rarely implementable in the sense of there existing an X with $\det(X'X) = \Psi(n,n)$. Specifically, $\Psi(n,n)$ is infrequently a square, which is necessary for such an X to exist; the only two values of n < 200 for which $\Psi(n,n)$ is square, other than the trivial value n = 3, are 91 and 147 (misprinted 47 in GK). It is not known whether an X with $\det(X'X) = \Psi(n,n)$ is constructible for any n > 3.

When k < n we do not of course have squareness of $D_{k,n}(s_{OPT})$ as a condition for constructibility of an X with $\det(X'X) = \Psi(k,n)$. Nonconstructibility in the cases (k,n) = (13,15) (both s_{OPT} = 6 and 7 in (5.1), d = 11), (14,15), and (9,11) with

$s_{OPT} = 7$, was demonstrated by a computer search of the tree of possibilities, somewhat reduced by observing certain symmetries, as described in Galil and Kiefer [3].

The pairs (k,n) for which X attaining $\Psi(k,n)$ had been obtained by 1979 are listed in Galil and Kiefer [2], [3]. These were sometimes obtained by computer search (see also Mitchell [6]) and sometimes by combinatorics; the construction of an X in the case (1.8) as a submatrix of a Hadamarad matrix (or of a union of such matrices - see GK) is well known, and that of an X satisfying (1.9) is described in Galil and Kiefer [3].

Recently we obtained new combinatorial methods that yield X's attaining $\Psi(k,n)$ for infinitely many (k,n), including many of those listed in (5.1). This is described in Galil and Kiefer [4].

When $\Psi(k,n)$ is not attainable by an X, one must both find a likely optimality candidate X* and must also methodically show no X exists which is better. Williamson [7] carried this out for $k = n = 7$, although a simpler proof of optimality is possible then - see GK, p. 1300. For $k = n = 11$ Ehlich, in unpublished work described in outline by GK, found and proved optimality of X's yielding three nonisomorphic X'X forms.

In cases of "ties" among the determinants of nonisomorphic X'X's, such as that just described or those of (5.1) where X's yielding both values of s_{OPT} exist, these X's are compared further in terms of other optimality criteria in Galil and Kiefer [3], [5]. For example, if $\det C_s = \det C_{s+1}$ with s and s+1 both optimum, it can be shown that C_s is better than C_{s+1} in terms of the Φ_p-optimality criterion $\Phi_p(C) = (k^{-1}\mathrm{tr}\, C^{-p})^{1/p}$, $0 < p < \infty$, and $\Phi_\infty(C)$ = maximum eigenvalue of C^{-1}.

REFERENCES

[1] Ehlich, H. (1964). Determinantenabschätzungen für binäre Matrizen mit n ≡ 3 mod 4. *Math. Z.* *84*, 438-447.

[2] Galil, Z. and Kiefer, J. (1980a). D-optimum weighing designs. *Ann. Statist.* *8*, 1293-1306.

[3] Galil, Z. and Kiefer, J. (1980b). Optimum weighing designs. In *Recent Developments in Statistical Inference and Data Analysis* (K. Matusita, ed.). North Holland, Amsterdam.

[4] Galil, Z. and Kiefer, J. (1981a). Construction of optimum block matrices for weighing designs with n ≡ 3(mod 4). To appear in *Ann. Statist.*

[5] Galil, Z. and Kiefer, J. (1981b). Comparison among D-optimum designs. To appear.

[6] Mitchell, T. J. (1974). Computer construction of "D-optimal" first-order designs. *Technometrics* *16*, 211-220.

[7] Williamson, J. (1946). Determinants whose elements are 0 and 1. *Amer. Math. Monthly* *53*, 527-534.

ECONOMICS OF SOME TWO-PHASE SAMPLING STRATEGIES FOR REGRESSION ESTIMATION

M. C. Agrawal and Gunnar Kulldorff

Institute of Mathematical Statistics
University of Umeå
Umeå, Sweden

I. INTRODUCTION

The regression estimator of the population mean $\bar{Y}$, say, for a characteristic y presumes that the population mean $\bar{X}$, say, for an auxiliary characteristic x is known. If the knowledge about $\bar{X}$ is lacking, we can take recourse to two-phase sampling for regression estimation. This consists in drawing a (usually large) sample in the first phase to estimate $\bar{X}$, followed by selection of a (usually small) sample in the second phase to estimate $\bar{Y}$. As regards the selection of the second-phase sample there exist two approaches:

(i) The second-phase sample is drawn as a sub-sample from the first-phase sample,

(ii) the second-phase sample is drawn independently from the whole population.

In the second approach we shall distinguish two alternatives depending on whether or not we identify which units are common to the two samples.

The two-phase sampling procedure employing (i) will be denoted by P_1. Approach (ii) employed without identification of units common to the two samples will be denoted by P_2, while the same approach combined with identification of common units will be denoted by P_3. Based on these three procedures, we consider three estimators for the purpose of comparison under a fixed cost.

ISBN 0-12-307501-7

Consider a population of size N. Let n_i' and n_i $(i = 1,2,3)$ denote the sample sizes in the first and second phases, respectively, for the procedure P_i. Further, let $\bar{x}_i'$ and $\bar{x}_i$ $(i = 1,2,3)$ be the sample means of the characteristic x based on n_i' and n_i units, respectively, and $\bar{y}_i$ be the sample mean of the characteristic y based on n_i units. Furthermore, let S_x^2 and S_y^2 denote the population variances for x and y, and let ρ be the correlation coefficient between x and y in the population.

Under the procedure P_1, the difference estimator of $\bar{Y}$ is defined as $\bar{y}_1 + k_1(\bar{x}_1' - \bar{x}_1)$, where k_1 is constant. This estimator has its minimum variance when $k_1 = \beta$, where $\beta = \rho\, S_y/S_x$ is the regression coefficient of y on x, and

$$t_1 = \bar{y}_1 + \beta(\bar{x}_1' - \bar{x}_1)$$

is called the two-phase regression estimator.

If we employ the procedure P_2, we can express the difference estimator of $\bar{Y}$ as $\bar{y}_2 + k_2(\bar{x}_2' - \bar{x}_2)$, where k_2 is constant. This estimator has its minimum variance when $k_2 = \beta\gamma$, where

$$\gamma = (\frac{1}{n_2} - \frac{1}{N})/(\frac{1}{n_2'} + \frac{1}{n_2} - \frac{2}{N}).$$

The estimator

$$t_2 = \bar{y}_2 + \beta\gamma(\bar{x}_2' - \bar{x}_2)$$

was considered by Rao [3].

For the procedure P_3, Rao [3] proposed the estimator

$$t_3 = \bar{y}_3 + \beta(\bar{x}_3'' - \bar{x}_3),$$

where $\bar{x}_3''$ is the mean based on distinct units in the two samples.

Our objective in this paper is to undertake an investigation about the performance of the three strategies, viz., strategy 1 (P_1,t_1), strategy 2 (P_2,t_2) and strategy 3 (P_3,t_3), when the total expected cost is fixed. A cost-based comparison of these strategies is called for as the procedures P_2 and P_3 entail an additional cost in observing the characteristic x on the units drawn in the second-phase sample.

Throughout this paper, samples are taken to be drawn according to simple random sampling without replacement, and it is assumed that $\rho \neq 0$.

II. COST FUNCTIONS

Let c_1 and c_3 be the costs per unit for measuring x in the first and second phases, respectively, and c_2 be the cost per unit for measuring y in the second phase. It will be assumed that $c_1 < c_2$; otherwise there is no reason for using two-phase sampling. We allow c_1 and c_3 to assume different values without any specific order. Then, for strategy 1 (P_1,t_1), the cost of the survey is assumed to be

$$C_1 = c_1 n_1' + c_2 n_1.$$

For strategy 2 (P_2,t_2) (based on independent samples, and identification of common units missing), the total cost can be given by

$$C_2 = c_1 n_2' + (c_2 + c_3) n_2. \tag{2.1}$$

For strategy 3 (P_3,t_3), the total cost is assumed to be $c_1 n_3' + c_2 n_3 + c_3(\nu - n_3')$, where ν is the number of distinct units in the two samples. The expected cost will then be

$$C_3 = c_1 n_3' + c_2 n_3 + c_3 n_3 \left(1 - \frac{n_3'}{N}\right). \tag{2.2}$$

We shall compare strategies 1 and 2 when $C_1 = C_2$, and strategies 1 and 3 when $C_1 = C_3$. However, we shall not compare strategies 2 and 3 directly, as they normally apply to different practical circumstances and do not compete. If a comparison were to be made, we should allow for different values of c_3, since strategy 3 involves an operation of identifying common units which is not needed for strategy 2.

III. A COMPARISON OF STRATEGIES 1 AND 2

The variances of t_1 and t_2 are

$$(3.1)\qquad V(t_1) = \left(\frac{\rho^2}{n_1'} + \frac{1-\rho^2}{n_1} - \frac{1}{N}\right) S_y^2$$

and (see Rao [3])

$$(3.2)\qquad V(t_2) = \left(\frac{1}{n_2} - \frac{1}{N}\right)\left(1 - \frac{\frac{1}{n_2} - \frac{1}{N}}{\frac{1}{n_2'} + \frac{1}{n_2} - \frac{2}{N}}\rho^2\right) S_y^2.$$

In order to compare strategy 1 with strategy 2 for the same total cost, we shall consider n_2' and n_2 as fixed and choose

$$n_1' = n_2' + \frac{c_3}{c_1} n_2$$

and

$$n_1 = n_2,$$

so that $C_1 = C_2$. Under strategy 1, we have the inherent restriction $n_1 \leq n_1'$ (but we need not assume that $n_2 \leq n_2'$), which will be satisfied if and only if

$$\frac{n_2'}{n_2} + \frac{c_3}{c_1} \geq 1.$$

We also have the restriction $n_1' \leq N$, which is satisfied if and only if

$$\frac{c_3}{c_1} \leq \frac{N-n_2'}{n_2}.$$

If the sample sizes n_2' and n_2 satisfy these conditions, we have

$$[V(t_2)-V(t_1)]S_y^{-2}\rho^{-2} = \frac{1-n_2'n_2/N^2}{n_2'+n_2-2n_2'n_2/N} - \frac{1}{n_2'+(c_3/c_1)n_2},$$

which yields

$$V(t_1) \lesseqgtr V(t_2) \text{ according as } \frac{c_3}{c_1} \gtreqless \frac{(N-n_2')^2}{N^2-n_2'n_2}.$$

We notice that this comparison is independent of ρ. The right hand side of the latest relation is less than unity and less than $(N-n_2')/n_2$ but larger than $1-n_2'/n_2$. Thus, the inequality

$$\frac{c_3}{c_1} > \frac{(N-n_2')^2}{N^2-n_2'n_2} \tag{3.3}$$

implies that $n_1 \le n_1'$. If (3.3) holds and if $c_3/c_1 \le (N-n_2')/n_2$, then the choice made above for n_1' and n_1 makes stategy 1 more efficient than strategy 2.

If $c_3/c_1 > (N-n_2')/n_2$, we can choose

$$n_1' = N$$

and

$$n_1 = (1 + \frac{c_3}{c_2})\, n_2 - \frac{c_1}{c_2}\,(N-n_2'),$$

so that $C_1 = C_2$. We then have

$$[V(t_2)-V(t_1)]S_y^{-2} = \rho^2\, \frac{(N-n_2')(N-n_2)}{N(Nn_2'+Nn_2-2n_2'n_2)} + (1-\rho^2)(\frac{1}{n_2} - \frac{1}{n_1}),$$

which is positive for all ρ since $n_1 > n_2$.

We can therefore conclude that, if (3.3) holds (e.g. when $c_1 \leq c_3$), we can choose sample sizes n_1' and n_1 independent of ρ so that $V(t_1) < V(t_2)$ for all ρ. If $c_1 \leq c_3$, then strategy 1 is better than strategy 2 in the sense that, whatever be the sample sizes for strategy 2, we can obtain a smaller variance for the same cost by using strategy 1 with appropriate sample sizes.

It is natural to ask if the superiority of strategy 1 to strategy 2 can be extended beyond the condition (3.3) by some other choice of n_1' and n_1. Quite generally, we can set

$$(3.4) \qquad n_1' = n_2' + \lambda \frac{c_3}{c_1} n_2$$

and

$$(3.5) \qquad n_1 = n_2[1+(1-\lambda) \frac{c_3}{c_2}],$$

so that $C_1 = C_2$ for any value of λ. The case $\lambda = 1$ will mean a sole increase in the first-phase sample size under P_1, while $\lambda = 0$ implies an exclusive raise in the second-phase sample size.

We can thus express

$$[V(t_2)-V(t_1)]S_y^{-2} = \rho^2 \left\{ \frac{\frac{1}{n_2 n_2'} - \frac{1}{N^2}}{\frac{1}{n_2'} + \frac{1}{n_2} - \frac{2}{N}} - \frac{1}{n_2' + \lambda \frac{c_3}{c_1} n_2} \right\}$$

$$+ (1-\rho^2) \frac{1}{n_2} \left\{ 1 - \frac{1}{1+(1-\lambda) \frac{c_3}{c_2}} \right\},$$

which implies that strategy 1 is better than strategy 2 for all $\rho \neq 0$ if and only if

$$(3.6) \qquad \lambda > \frac{c_1}{c_3} \frac{(N-n_2')^2}{N^2-n_2 n_2'} \quad \text{and} \quad \lambda \leq 1.$$

From this we conclude that, if (3.3) does not hold, we can not choose a value of λ independent of ρ such that strategy 1 is superior to strategy 2 for any value of ρ.

IV. A COMPARISON OF STRATEGIES 1 AND 3

The variance of t_3, as obtained by Rao [3], is

$$(4.1) \qquad V(t_3) = \{\rho^2 E(\frac{1}{\nu}) + \frac{1-\rho^2}{n_3} - \frac{1}{N}\} S_y^2,$$

where

$$(4.2) \qquad E(\frac{1}{\nu}) = \sum_{j=0}^{n_3''} W_j,$$

$$W_o = \frac{1}{n_3'+n_3},$$

$$W_{j+1} = \frac{W_j(n_3'-j)(n_3-j)}{(N-j)(n_3'+n_3-1-j)} \qquad (j = 0,1,\ldots,n_3''-1),$$

$$n_3'' = \min(n_3', n_3).$$

To compare strategy 1 with strategy 3 for the same total expected cost, we consider n_3' and n_3 as the basis and choose

$$n_1' = n_3' + \frac{c_3}{c_1} n_3 \, (1 - \frac{n_3'}{N})$$

and

$$n_1 = n_3,$$

so that $C_1 = C_3$. The restriction $n_1 \leq n_1'$ is satisfied if and only if

$$\frac{1-n_3'/n_3}{1-n_3'/N} \leq \frac{c_3}{c_1},$$

e.g., if $n_3 \leq n_3'$ or $c_1 \leq c_3$. The restriction $n_1' \leq N$ is satisfied if and only if $n_3 \leq Nc_1/c_3$, e.g., if $c_3 \leq c_1$. The sample sizes n_3' and n_3 will normally satisfy these conditions. From (3.1) and (4.1), we then get

$$V(t_1) \lesseqgtr V(t_3) \text{ according as } \frac{c_3}{c_1} \gtreqless \left(\frac{1}{E(1/\nu)} - n_3'\right) \frac{N}{n_3(N-n_3')} .$$

We notice that this comparison is independent of ρ. The right hand side of the latest relation is less than 1, since $E(1/\nu) > 1/E(\nu)$ and $E(\nu) = n_3' + n_3 - n_3'n_3/N$. It is larger than $(1-n_3'/n_3)/(1-n_3'/N)$, since $E(1/\nu) < 1/n_3$. Thus, the inequality

$$\text{(4.3)} \qquad \frac{c_3}{c_1} > \left(\frac{1}{E(1/\nu)} - n_3'\right) \frac{N}{n_3(N-n_3')}$$

implies that $n_1 \leq n_1'$. If (4.3) holds and if $c_3/c_1 \leq N/n_3$, the choice made for n_1' and n_1 above makes strategy 1 more efficient than strategy 3.

If $c_3/c_1 > N/n_3$, we can choose

$$n_1' = N$$

and

$$n_1 = n_3 + \frac{1}{c_2}(c_3n_3 - c_1N)\left(1 - \frac{n_3'}{N}\right),$$

so that $C_1 = C_3$. We then have

$$[V(t_3) - V(t_1)]S_y^{-2} = \rho^2\left[E\left(\frac{1}{\nu}\right) - \frac{1}{N}\right] + (1-\rho^2)\left(\frac{1}{n_3} - \frac{1}{n_1}\right),$$

which is positive for all ρ since $E(1/\nu) > 1/N$ and $n_1 > n_3$.

We therefore conclude that, if (4.3) holds (e.g. when $c_1 \leq c_3$), we can choose sample sizes n_1' and n_1 independent of ρ so that $V(t_1) < V(t_3)$ for all ρ. If $c_1 \leq c_3$, then strategy 1 is better than strategy 3 in the sense that, whatever be the sample sizes for strategy 3, we can obtain a smaller variance for the same total expected cost by using strategy 1 with appropriate sample sizes.

More generally, we can set

$$(4.4)\qquad n_1' = n_3' + \lambda \frac{c_3}{c_1} n_3(1 - \frac{n_3'}{N})$$

and

$$(4.5)\qquad n_1 = n_3[1+(1-\lambda) \frac{c_3}{c_2} (1 - \frac{n_3'}{N})],$$

so that $C_1 = C_3$ for any value of λ. The special case $\lambda = 1$ was considered above. The difference of the variances of t_1 and t_3 is thus expressible as

$$[V(t_3)-V(t_1)]S_y^{-2} = \rho^2 \left[E(\frac{1}{\nu}) - \frac{1}{n_3' + \lambda \frac{c_3}{c_1} n_3(1 - \frac{n_3'}{N})} \right]$$

$$+ (1-\rho^2) \frac{1}{n_3} \left[1- \frac{1}{1+(1-\lambda) \frac{c_3}{c_2} (1 - \frac{n_3'}{N})} \right],$$

which implies that strategy 1 is better than strategy 3 for all $\rho \neq 0$ if and only if

$$(4.6)\qquad \lambda > \frac{c_1}{c_3} (\frac{1}{E(1/\nu)} - n_3') \frac{N}{n_3(N-n_3')} \quad \text{and } \lambda \leq 1.$$

We, therefore, conclude that, if (4.3) does not hold, we can not choose a value of λ independent of ρ such that the corresponding strategy 1 is better than strategy 3 for any value of ρ.

V. OPTIMUM ALLOCATION FOR THE THREE STRATEGIES

In order to make a quantitative comparison between different strategies discussed in the preceding sections, it will be fair to consider sample sizes chosen for each strategy according to optimum allocation in the sense of minimizing the variance for a specified cost C (or expected cost for strategy 3). We assume that $C < Nc_2$, i.e., that the available resources are less than the cost of a complete enumeration of the y-values.

5.1 *Optimum Allocation for Strategy* 1

We know (see, e.g., Cochran ([2], p. 341)) that, for a fixed total cost C, the minimum variance for the estimator t_1 is given by

$$\min V(t_1) = [\frac{1}{C}\{\sqrt{c_1\rho^2} + \sqrt{c_2(1-\rho^2)}\}^2 - \frac{1}{N}]\, S_y^2$$

for

$$n_1' = \frac{C}{c_1 + \sqrt{c_1 c_2 (1-\rho^2)/\rho^2}}$$

and

$$n_1 = \frac{C}{c_2 + \sqrt{c_1 c_2 \rho^2/(1-\rho^2)}}.$$

The restriction $n_1 \le n_1'$ is, however, violated by this solution, if and only if $\rho^2 < c_1/(c_1 + c_2)$. The restriction $n_1' \le N$ is violated if and only if

$$C > Nc_1 \text{ and } \rho^2 > [1 + \frac{c_1}{c_2}(\frac{C}{Nc_1} - 1)^2]^{-1}.$$

We should also bear in mind that two-phase sampling is not always better than one-phase sampling. In practice we should, therefore, replace strategy 1 by one-phase sampling with C/c_2 units for observing the characteristic y only (so that the total cost is C) and the sample mean $\bar{y}$ as estimator, whenever this modification renders

$$(5.1) \qquad V(\bar{y}) = (\frac{c_2}{C} - \frac{1}{N}) S_y^2$$

smaller than $V(t_1)$.

This modification and the two restrictions mentioned previously lead to three separate cases which are spelt out in Chart 1 in terms of ρ^2, C/N, c_1 and c_2. These cases are illustrated in Figure 1 as

(I) zone of preference for two-phase sampling in the form of strategy 1,

(II) zone of preference for complete enumeration in the first phase (leading to the usual regression estimation without recourse to two-phase sampling)

(III) zone of preference for one-phase sampling and the estimator $\bar{y}$.

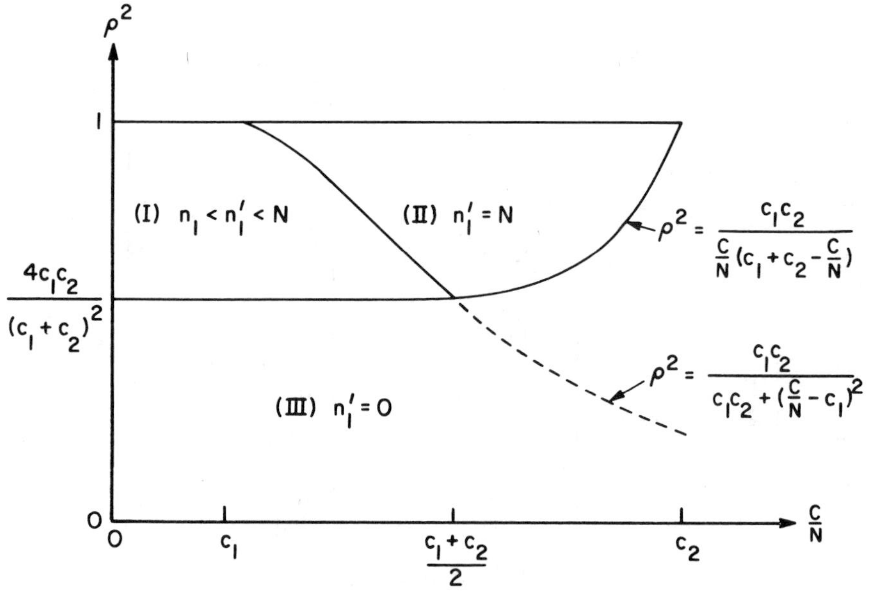

Figure 1. Schematic illustration of how the three cases in Chart 1 depend on ρ^2, C/N, c_1 and c_2.

Chart I. Optimum allocation for the modified strategy 1.

Case	Condition	Optimum n'_1	Optimum n_1	$\min V(t_1)S_y^{-2} + \frac{1}{N}$
I	$\rho^2 \geq \frac{4c_1c_2}{(c_1+c_2)^2}$ and $\frac{C}{N} \leq c_1 + \sqrt{c_1c_2 \frac{1-\rho^2}{\rho^2}}$	$\frac{C}{c_1 + \sqrt{c_1c_2 \frac{1-\rho^2}{\rho^2}}}$	$\frac{C}{c_2 + \sqrt{c_1c_2 \frac{\rho^2}{1-\rho^2}}}$	$\frac{1}{C}\left(\sqrt{c_1\rho^2} + \sqrt{c_2(1-\rho^2)}\right)^2$
II	$\rho^2 \geq \frac{c_1c_2}{\frac{C}{N}(c_1+c_2-\frac{C}{N})}$ and $\rho^2 \geq \frac{c_1c_2}{c_1c_2+(\frac{C}{N}-c_1)^2}$	N	$\frac{C-Nc_1}{c_2}$	$\frac{\rho^2}{N} + \frac{c_2(1-\rho^2)}{C-Nc_1}$
III	$\rho^2 \leq \frac{4c_1c_2}{(c_1+c_2)^2}$ or $\frac{C}{N} \geq \frac{c_1+c_2}{2} + \sqrt{\frac{(c_1+c_2)^2}{4} - \frac{c_1c_2}{\rho^2}}$	0	$\frac{C}{c_2}$	$\frac{c_2}{C}$

5.2 *Optimum Allocation for Strategy 2*

With a view to minimizing the variance of t_2 for specified cost C, we insert

$$n_2' = \frac{C-(c_2+c_3)n_2}{c_1}$$

in (3.2) and obtain $V(t_2) = v(z;a,b,\rho)S_y^2/N$, where

$$v(z;a,b,\rho) = z-1- \frac{(z-1)^2\rho^2}{\frac{az}{z-b}+z-2},$$

$z = N/n_2$, $a = Nc_1/C$ and $b = N(c_2+c_3)/C$. The function v(z) can be minimized numerically under the restrictions $b \leq z \leq N$ if $a \geq 1$, $b \leq z \leq \min\{N,b/(1-a)\}$ if $a < 1$, for different values of ρ^2, a and b. The minimum value of $V(t_2)$ thus obtained should then be compared with $V(\bar{y})$ in (5.1) for one-phase sampling with C/c_2 units. By 'modified strategy 2' we mean that strategy 2 is replaced by one-phase sampling and the estimator $\bar{y}$, whenever the latter is more efficient.

The optimum allocation for strategy 2 is considerably simplified when the population size $N \to \infty$. From (3.2) we then obtain

$$\lim_{N\to\infty} V(t_2) = \left(\frac{\rho^2}{n_2'+n_2} + \frac{1-\rho^2}{n_2}\right) S_y^2.$$

Writing the cost function (2.1) as $C_2 = c_1(n_2'+n_2) + (c_2+c_3-c_1)n_2$ and assuming a fixed total cost C, we can employ Cauchy's inequality and obtain

$$\min \lim_{N\to\infty} V(t_2) = \left[\sqrt{c_1\rho^2} + \sqrt{(c_2+c_3-c_1)(1-\rho^2)}\right]^2 S_y^2/C \tag{5.2}$$

for

$$n_2 = \frac{C}{c_2+c_3-c_1+\sqrt{c_1(c_2+c_3-c_1)\rho^2/(1-\rho^2)}}$$

and

$$n_2' = n_2\left(\sqrt{\frac{(c_2+c_3-c_1)\rho^2}{c_1(1-\rho^2)}} - 1\right).$$

If $c_1 = c_3$, we have

$$\min \lim_{N\to\infty} V(t_2) = \min \lim_{N\to\infty} V(t_1).$$

In general, the difference between the left and right hand sides has the same sign as c_3-c_1.

Comparison with one-phase sampling (with C/c_2 units), when $N \to \infty$, leads us to conclude that strategy 2 is more efficient if and only if

$$|\rho| > \frac{\sqrt{c_1c_2} + \sqrt{c_3(c_2+c_3-c_1)}}{c_2+c_3}.$$

In Section 6, we shall undertake a numerical investigation to examine the performance of strategy 2 vis-a-vis strategy 1 under optimum allocation.

5.3 *Optimum Allocation for Strategy* 3

From the cost function (2.2) for strategy 3 we can determine either n_3 or n_3' as a function of the other, and then insert it in $V(t_3)$ given by (4.1). We thus obtain a function of only one sample size, and can find the minimum by comparing its values for all possible integer values of the sample size. The restriction to an integer value will be somewhat unfair in comparison with strategy 1, for which the optimum allocation has been determined without such a restriction. In order to reduce this handicap as much as possible we minimize $V(t_3)$ with respect to n_3', which should normally be larger than n_3, after making the insertion

$$n_3 = \frac{C-c_1 n_3'}{c_2+c_3(1-n_3'/N)} .$$

Since this quantity will generally not be an integer, we can not use formula (4.2) for $E(1/\nu)$ if $n_3 < n_3'$. We will then use another expression for $E(1/\nu)$ (vide Rao [4], Agrawal [1]) given by

$$E(\frac{1}{\nu}) = \sum_{j=0}^{N-n_3'} U_j \quad \text{if} \quad n_3 \leq n_3',$$

where

$$U_o = 1/N$$

and

$$U_{j+1} = U_j \frac{(N-n_3'-j)(N-n_3-j)}{(N-j)(N-j-1)} \qquad (j = 0,1,\ldots,N-n_3'-1).$$

The minimum value of $V(t_3)$ thus obtained should be compared with $V(\bar{y})$ in (5.1). If $\bar{y}$ is more efficient than t_3 we should modify strategy 3 accordingly.

When the population size $N \to \infty$, we have

$$\lim_{N\to\infty} E(\frac{1}{\nu}) = \frac{1}{n_3' + n_3} ,$$

$$\lim_{N\to\infty} V(t_3) = (\frac{\rho^2}{n_3'+n_3} + \frac{1-\rho^2}{n_3}) S_y^2$$

and

$$\lim_{N\to\infty} C_3 = c_1 n_3' + (c_2+c_3)n_3,$$

which is the same limiting situation as for strategy 2. Hence,

$$\min \lim_{N\to\infty} V(t_3) = \min \lim_{N\to\infty} V(t_2)$$

as given in (5.2).

In Section 6, we shall carry out a numerical computation to examine the relative efficiency of strategy 3 compared to strategy 1 under optimum allocation.

VI. NUMERICAL COMPARISONS UNDER OPTIMUM ALLOCATION

In Tables 1 and 2, we have computed the relative efficiencies of t_2 and t_3 with respect to t_1. We have employed the minimum variances for each estimator to compute these relative efficiencies. Besides, we have indicated in the tables such places where, if any of these estimators is less efficient than the simple arithmetic mean $\bar{y}$, we have replaced the variance of the less efficient estimator by the variance of $\bar{y}$. We have also indicated when any of the optimum values of n_1', n_2' and n_3' is, for some combination of the parameters, equal to the population size. Let V_1, V_2 and V_3 denote the minimum variances for the modified strategies 1, 2 and 3, respectively.

We present below some salient features noted from these tables.

(i) Both V_1/V_2 and V_1/V_3 decrease with c_3/c_1. As long as two-phase sampling remains superior to one-phase sampling and none of the optimum sample sizes hits N, the decrease with c_3/c_1 is roughly linear.

(ii) When $c_1 \leq c_3$, V_1/V_2 and V_1/V_3 are below 1, as we know from Sections 3 and 4. If Nc_1/C is not large, t_1 may be more efficient than t_2 even for $c_3 < c_1$. But, the relative order between V_1 and V_3 depends effectively on c_3/c_1. When $c_1 = c_3$, we have $.999 \lesssim V_1/V_3 < 1$.

(iii) The relative efficiency of t_2 with respect to t_1 increases with Nc_1/C, provided the other parameters are held fixed. Under the same circumstances as stated in (i), the difference $(V_1/V_2)_{N=\infty}-V_1/V_2$ seems to be roughly proportional to C/Nc_1.

Table 1. Relative efficiency of (modified) strategy 2 with respect to (modified) strategy 1 under optimum allocation (V_1/V_2).

$\frac{Nc_1}{C}$	ρ^2	c_3/c_1	0.5			1.0			2.0		
		c_2/c_1	5	10	20	5	10	20	5	10	20
.5	.60		.9326	.9783	.9946	.9303°	.9347	.9724	.9303°	.8589	.9310
	.80		.8962	.9597	.9853	.8130	.9175	.9640	.6886	.8443	.9242
	.90		.8889*	.9490	.9793	.8000*	.9035	.9577	.6667*	.8255	.9175
	.95		.8889*	.9474*	.9748	.8000*	.9000*	.9509	.6667*	.8182*	.9069
1	.60		1.0097	1.0087	1.0072	.9477°	.9686	.9861	.9477°	.8980	.9468
	.80		.9784	.9944	1.0004	.9153	.9591	.9813	.8131	.8962	.9454
	.90		.9639	.9858	.9956	.9077	.9538	.9781	.8158	.8964	.9450
	.95		.9566	.9805	.9922	.9050	.9510	.9759	.8199	.8978	.9452
2	.60		1.0418	1.0234	1.0136	.9690	.9847	.9931	.9535°	.9161	.9546
	.80		1.0186	1.0130	1.0089	.9595	.9797	.9906	.8625	.9201	.9561
	.90		1.0056	1.0060	1.0052	.9564	.9773	.9889	.8741	.9253	.9582
	.95		.9981	1.0013	1.0024	.9572	.9766	.9881	.8874	.9317	.9609
4	.60		1.0562	1.0305	1.0168	.9850	.9924	.9965	.9560°	.9241	.9585
	.80		1.0379	1.0224	1.0132	.9802	.9899	.9953	.8850	.9316	.9614
	.90		1.0257	1.0162	1.0102	.9787	.9887	.9945	.8995	.9388	.9647
	.95		1.0172	1.0115	1.0076	.9793	.9885	.9941	.9142	.9464	.9683
∞	.60		1.0698	1.0375	1.0200	1	1	1	.9582°	.9332	.9623
	.80		1.0565	1.0318	1.0176	1	1	1	.9064	.9428	.9667
	.90		1.0453	1.0265	1.0152	1	1	1	.9232	.9517	.9711
	.95		1.0357	1.0216	1.0129	1	1	1	.9383	.9602	.9754

* indicates that n_1' and n_2' hit N.

o indicates that t_2 is replaced by $\bar{y}$ in one-phase sampling.

Table 2 (continued). Relative efficiency of (modified) strategy 3 with respect to (modified) strategy 1 under optimum allocation (V_1/V_3).

N	$\frac{C}{c_1}$	ρ^2	c_3/c_1	0.5			1.0			2.0		
			c_2/c_1	5	10	20	5	10	20	5	10	20
100	50	.60		1.0674	1.0350	1.0186	.9991	.9994	.9997	$.9535^{o}$	.9354	.9639
		.80		1.0514	1.0285	1.0158	.9990	.9995	.9997	.9104	.9465	.9691
		.90		1.0399	1.0228	1.0133	.9990	.9994	.9997	.9281	.9559	.9737
		.95		1.0311	1.0183	1.0109	.9993	.9993	.9997	.9426	.9641	.9779
100	100	.60		1.0644	1.0328	1.0174	.9992	.9995	.9996	$.9477^{o}$	.9394	.9661
		.80		1.0446	1.0248	1.0139	.9993	.9996	.9996	.9209	.9529	.9724
		.90		1.0320	1.0189	1.0111	.9994	.9997	.9997	.9409	.9635	.9778
		.95		1.0228	1.0142	1.0088	.9995	.9997	.9998	.9562	.9720	.9825
100	200	.60		1.0481	1.0257	1.0143	.9994	.9996	.9998	$.9303^{o}$	.9532	.9721
		.80		1.0106	1.0128	1.0093	.9999	.9998	.9998	.9930	.9767	.9817
		.90		1*	1.0019	1.0049	1*	1.0000	.9999	1*	.9985	.9905
		.95		1*	1*	1.0004	1*	1*	1.0000	1*	1*	.9997

* indicates that n_1' and n_3' hit N, and consequently the ratio of the variances V_1/V_3 is unity.

o indicates that t_3 is replaced by $\bar{y}$ in one-phase sampling.

Table 2 (continued). Relative efficiency of (modified) strategy 3 with respect to (modified) strategy 1 under optimum allocation (V_1/V_3).

N	$\frac{C}{c_1}$	ρ^2	c_3/c_1 →	0.5			1.0			2.0		
			c_2/c_1 →	5	10	20	5	10	20	5	10	20
400	50	.60		1.0691	1.0366	1.0197	.9996	.9995	.9999	.9571[o]	.9335	.9625
		.80		1.0554	1.0308	1.0171	.9996	.9996	.9998	.9070	.9435	.9670
		.90		1.0442	1.0257	1.0147	.9997	.9999	.9997	.9240	.9523	.9714
		.95		1.0347	1.0209	1.0122	.9998	.9999	.9996	.9389	.9608	.9759
400	100	.60		1.0690	1.0365	1.0194	.9998	.9999	.9999	.9560[o]	.9343	.9631
		.80		1.0545	1.0303	1.0168	.9998	.9998	.9999	.9081	.9446	.9679
		.90		1.0432	1.0250	1.0143	.9998	.9999	.9999	.9253	.9536	.9724
		.95		1.0339	1.0203	1.0120	.9998	.9999	.9999	.9401	.9619	.9767
400	200	.60		1.0682	1.0356	1.0189	.9998	.9999	.9999	.9535[o]	.9358	.9641
		.80		1.0523	1.0289	1.0160	.9998	.9999	.9999	.9110	.9469	.9693
		.90		1.0407	1.0234	1.0135	.9998	.9999	.9999	.9286	.9563	.9740
		.95		1.0316	1.0188	1.0112	.9999	.9999	.9999	.9432	.9644	.9783
∞	All finite values	.60		1.0698	1.0375	1.0200	1	1	1	.9582[o]	.9332	.9623
		.80		1.0565	1.0318	1.0176	1	1	1	.9064	.9428	.9667
		.90		1.0453	1.0265	1.0152	1	1	1	.9232	.9517	.9711
		.95		1.0357	1.0216	1.0129	1	1	1	.9383	.9602	.9754

* indicates that n_1' and n_3' hit N, and consequently the ratio of the variances V_1/V_3 is unity.

o indiates that t_3 is replaced by $\bar{y}$ in one-phase sampling.

(iv) An increase in c_2/c_1, for fixed values of the other parameters, tends to bolster up the efficiency of the relatively lagging estimator.

(v) An increase in C has a small boosting effect on the efficiency of t_1 or t_3 according as $V_1/V_3 > 1$ or $V_1/V_3 < 1$.

VII. COMPARISON OF THE STRATEGIES WHEN β IS UNKNOWN

If β is estimated by the sample regression coefficient b, then the three estimators can be expressed as

$$t_1 = \bar{y}_1 + b(\bar{x}_1' - \bar{x}_1)$$

$$t_2 = \bar{y}_2 + b\gamma(\bar{x}_2' - \bar{x}_2)$$

$$t_3 = \bar{y}_3 + b(\bar{x}_3'' - \bar{x}_3).$$

We shall carry out a comparison of the above estimators under a superpopulation model that has often been considered in the context of regression estimation. Let the regression model in the superpopulation be

$$y_i = \alpha + \beta x_i + e_i \qquad (i = 1,2,\ldots,N), \tag{7.1}$$

where, for given x_i's, the e_i's are independent random variables with mean zero and variance $\sigma_y^2(1-\rho^2)$, where σ_y and ρ are now parameters of the superpopulation. Further, it is assumed that x_i's $(i = 1,2,\ldots,N)$ are drawn from a normal population with mean μ_x and variance σ_x^2.

Using the model (7.1), we can write after some algebra

$$t_1 - \bar{Y} = \bar{e}_n - \bar{e}_N + \beta(\bar{x}_1' - \bar{X}) + \frac{(\bar{x}_1'-\bar{x}_1)\sum_{i=1}^{n_1} e_i(x_i-\bar{x}_1)}{\sum_{i=1}^{n_1}(\bar{x}_i-\bar{x}_1)^2}, \tag{7.2}$$

where

$$\bar{e}_n = \sum_{i=1}^{n_1} e_i/n_1$$

and

$$\bar{e}_N = \sum_{i=1}^{N} e_i/N.$$

From (7.2), we obtain

$$E\{(t_1-\bar{Y})^2 \mid x\} = (\frac{1}{n_1} - \frac{1}{N})\sigma_y^2(1-\rho^2) + \beta^2(\bar{x}_1'-\bar{X})^2 + \sigma_y^2(1-\rho^2)\frac{(\bar{x}_1' - \bar{x}_1)^2}{\sum_{i=1}^{n_1}(x_i-\bar{x}_1)^2}. \tag{7.3}$$

In order to average over the distribution of x_i's, we need to evaluate the expected value of the last term on the right hand side of (7.3). For this purpose, we express

$$\bar{x}_1' - \bar{x}_1 = \frac{(n_1'-n_1)(\bar{x}_1^* - \bar{x}_1)}{n_1'},$$

where

$$\bar{x}_1^* = \frac{\sum_{i=1}^{n_1'-n_1} x_i}{n_1' - n_1},$$

and thus,

$$E\left\{\frac{(\bar{x}_1'-\bar{x}_1)^2}{\sum_{i=1}^{n_1}(x_i-\bar{x}_1)^2}\right\} = \left(\frac{n_1'-n_1}{n_1'}\right)^2 E\left[\frac{\{(\bar{x}_1^*-\mu_x)-(\bar{x}_1-\mu_x)\}^2}{\sum_{i=1}^{n_1}(x_i-\bar{x}_1)^2}\right]$$

$$= (\frac{1}{n_1} - \frac{1}{n_1'})\frac{1}{n_1-3}.$$

Hence, the expected mean square error (EMSE) of t_1 is

$$(7.4)\quad E\,M(t_1) = (\frac{1}{n_1} - \frac{1}{N})\sigma_y^2(1-\rho^2)+(\frac{1}{n_1'} - \frac{1}{N})\rho^2\sigma_y^2 + (\frac{1}{n_1} - \frac{1}{n_1'})\,\frac{\sigma_y^2(1-\rho^2)}{n_1-3}$$

$$= (\frac{1}{n_1'} - \frac{1}{N})\sigma_y^2+(\frac{1}{n_1} - \frac{1}{n_1'})\,\frac{n_1-2}{n_1-3}\,\sigma_y^2(1-\rho^2).$$

The EMSE of t_2 under the superpopulation model (7.1) is similarly obtained as

$$(7.5)\quad E\,M(t_2) = (\frac{1}{n_2} - \frac{1}{N})\sigma_y^2(1-\rho^2)+(\frac{1}{n_2'} - \frac{1}{N})\gamma\,\rho^2\sigma_y^2 + (\frac{1}{n_2'} + \frac{1}{n_2})\,\frac{\gamma^2\sigma_y^2(1-\rho^2)}{n_2-3}$$

$$= \gamma(\frac{1}{n_2'} - \frac{1}{N})\sigma_y^2+ \gamma^2\{\frac{n_2-2}{n_2-3}\,(\frac{1}{n_2'} + \frac{1}{n_2})- \frac{2}{N}\}\,(1-\rho^2)\sigma_y^2.$$

The EMSE of t_3, as obtained by Rao [3], under the superpopulation model (7.1) is

$$(7.6)\quad E\,M(t_3) = [E(\frac{1}{\nu}) - \frac{1}{N}]\sigma_y^2+[\frac{1}{n_3} - E(\frac{1}{\nu})]\,\frac{n_3-2}{n_3-3}\,\sigma_y^2(1-\rho^2).$$

It is interesting to note that, if we approximate $(n_i-2)/(n_i-3)$ $(i = 1,2,3)$ by unity in the EMSE expressions (7.4-6), these are transformed into the same form as the variance expressions (when β is known) in Sections 3 and 4, except that ρ and σ_y now refer to the superpopulation, and hence, in a cost-based comparison, all the earlier conditions (obtained in Sections 3 and 4) for the superiority of t_1 over t_2 and t_3 hold approximately when β is not known. However, if the approximation is not tenable, then a comparison of (7.4) and (7.5) via (3.4) and (3.5) reveals that, under the superpopulation model (7.1), t_1 is better than t_2 if, besides the earlier condition (3.6), the inequality

$$\rho^2 \geq \frac{1}{n_2-2} \tag{7.7}$$

holds, which is normally a weak condition in practice. Similarly, comparing (7.4) and (7.6) via (4.4) and (4.5), we find that, if the superpopulation model (7.1) is assumed, t_1 would fare better than t_3 under the condition (4.6) provided

$$\rho^2 \geq \frac{1}{n_3-2} .$$

ACKNOWLEDGMENT

We thank Magnus Jansson for his help in the computer work.

REFERENCES

[1] Agrawal, M. C. (1981). On averaging over distinct units in replicated samples. To appear in *Math. Operationsforsch. Statist. Ser. Statist.*

[2] Cochran, W. G. (1977). *Sampling Techniques*, Third edition. John Wiley & Sons, New York.

[3] Rao, P.S.R.S. (1972). On two-phase regression estimator. *Sankhyā Ser. A 34*, 473-476.

[4] Rao, P.S.R.S. (1975). On the two-phase ratio estimator in finite populations. *J. Amer. Statist. Assoc. 70*, 839-845.

CLOSED ADAPTIVE SEQUENTIAL PROCEDURES FOR SELECTING THE BEST OF $k \geqq 2$ BERNOULLI POPULATIONS[1]

Robert E. Bechhofer and Radhika V. Kulkarni

School of Operations Research and Industrial Engineering
Cornell University
Ithaca, New York, U.S.A.

I. INTRODUCTION AND SUMMARY

1.1 *Summary*

The goal of selecting that one of $k \geqq 2$ Bernoulli populations which has the largest single-trial "success" probability $p_{[k]} = \max\{p_1,\ldots,p_k\}$ is treated. Consideration is restricted to procedures which take no more than n observations from any one of the k populations. One such procedure is the single-stage procedure of Sobel and Huyett [54] which takes exactly n observations from each of the k populations. We propose a one-at-a-time adaptive sampling rule (R^*) which when used in conjunction with a particular stopping rule (S^*) and terminal decision rule (T^*) achieves the same probability of a correct selection as does the single-stage procedure uniformly in $\underset{\sim}{p} = (p_1,\ldots,p_k)$. Letting N denote the random total number of observations to terminate sampling using the procedure (R^*,S^*,T^*) we show that $n \leqq N \leqq kn-1$; for $p_{[k]} \to 0$ we have $P\{N = kn-1|\underset{\sim}{p}\} \to 1$ while for $p_{[1]} \to 1$ we have $P\{N = n|\underset{\sim}{p}\} \to 1$. For $k = 2$ the sampling rule R^* (the conjugate sampling rule $\bar{R}^*$) which is *stationary* is *optimal* in the sense that it minimizes $E\{N|(p_1,p_2)\}$ uniformly in (p_1,p_2) for $p_1 + p_2 > 1$ ($p_1 + p_2 < 1$) among all sampling rules which use (S^*,T^*) and which take no more than n observations from either

[1]Research supported by U. S. Army Research Office - Durham Contract DAAG-29-80-C-0036, and Office of Naval Research Contract N00014-75-C-0586.

ISBN 0-12-307501-7

population; R^* has additional optimal properties for $k = 2$. The procedure (R^*,S^*,T^*) is generalized for $k > 2$ to accommodate such goals as "Selecting the s $(1 \leqq s \leqq k-1)$ "best" Bernoulli populations with regard to order," and is shown to have desirable properties for these goals as well. Some conjectures are made concerning the optimality of (R^*,S^*,T^*) for $k > 2$. The performance of (R^*,S^*,T^*) is compared for $k \geqq 2$ with that of other sequential selection procedures that have been proposed in the literature.

1.2 *Introduction*

Let Π_i $(1 \leqq i \leqq k)$ denote $k \geqq 2$ Bernoulli populations with corresponding single-trial "success" probabilities p_i. Denote the ordered values of the p_i by $p_{[1]} \leqq \cdots \leqq p_{[k]}$; the values of the p_i and the pairing of the Π_i with the $p_{[j]}$ $(1 \leqq i, j \leqq k)$ are assumed to be completely unknown.

Statistical procedures for the problem of selecting the "best" population, i.e., the one associated with $p_{[k]}$, have received considerable attention in recent years. In a fundamental paper, Sobel and Huyett [54] proposed a *single-stage* procedure employing the indifference-zone approach of Bechhofer [4] with the "distance measure" $\Delta_{i,j} = p_i - p_j$; their procedure was shown by Hall [26] to have the optimum property of being "most economical" among single-stage procedures. Paulson [40], [41], using the distance measures $\Delta_{i,j}$ and p_i/p_j, proposed the first *sequential* procedure for this problem. His *open* procedure permitted the elimination of "non-contending" populations; it employed a fixed number of stages with a random number of observations per stage, the total number of observations (N) required for termination being an *unbounded* random variable. Bechhofer, Kiefer and Sobel [6], Section 12.6.1.4, using the distance measure $p_i(1-p_j)/p_j(1-p_i)$ (and $\Delta_{i,j}$) also proposed an *open* sequential procedure employing a vector-at-a-time (VT) sampling rule.

Spurred on by the potential of application of such methods in clinical trials and related areas, there followed a period of considerable research activity focusing on sequential procedures for this problem; these studies were spearheaded intially by Milton Sobel, George Weiss, David Hoel and their collaborators: Sobel and Weiss [55] - [59]; Kiefer and Weiss [34], [35]; Hoel [27]; Hoel and Sobel [28]; Hoel, Sobel, Weiss [29]; Nebenzahl and Sobel [37]. During the period of 1973-1980 a large number of additional papers appeared; all employed the measure of distance $\Delta_{i,j}$ (except Taheri and Young [60] who used p_i/p_j). These papers are listed among our references. An excellent review of many of these proposed procedures (and others), with particular reference to adaptive sampling for clinical trials, is contained in Hoel, Sobel and Weiss [31]. A recent text by Büringer, Martin and Schriever [14] gives an in depth comprehensive survey of these procedures (and many additional ones); it treats their derivation, performance characteristics, and uses, and provides extensive tables for their implementation.

Concurrently, the Bernoulli selection problem was studied employing the subset approach of Gupta [22]. The early key papers using this approach are Gupta, Huyett and Sobel [23] and Gupta and Sobel [24]; an up-to-date summary of more recent results using the subset approach is contained in Gupta and Panchapakesan [25], Section 13.2.

The problem of allocating observations among treatments when the total available number of observations is fixed (fixed patient horizon), with the objective of assigning a higher proportion of the total number of available observations to the population with the larger success probability has been studied in the medical context by Armitage [3], Anscombe [2], Colton [16], Cornfield, Halperin and Greenhouse [17], Zelen [65], and Canner [15], among others. For comments concerning this formulation of the problem see Sobel and Weiss [59].

A somewhat related class of procedures directed toward solutions of the so-called 2-armed (or multi-armed) bandit problem was investigated by many research workers: Robbins [46], [47]; Bradt, Johnson and Karlin [13], Isbell [33], Feldman [19], Smith and Pyke [53], Fabius and van Zwet [18], Berry [8], [9], and Rodman [48], among others. These papers are *not* concerned with the Bernoulli *selection* problem, but rather focus on minimizing or maximizing appropriate objective functions, the principal tool used being dynamic programming.

II. THE k-POPULATION BERNOULLI SELECTION PROBLEM

2.1 *Earlier Approaches*

Before we describe our objectives and approach, it will be helpful to sketch the chronological development of certain statistical aspects of the Bernoulli selection problem. It perhaps is of historical interest to note that the Sobel-Huyett [54] and Gupta-Huyett-Sobel [23] papers made no reference to the potential applicability of their procedures to the drug selection problem or to clinical trials. Such a reference appears first in Paulson [40] (although Armitage [3], Anscombe [2] and Colton [16] had earlier considered such applications). Sobel and Weiss [55] treated the special case $k = 2$, and emphasized the desirability of minimizing the number of patients on the poorer treatment. With this objective in mind they studied the performance of the *play-the-winner* (PW) sampling rule (introduced earlier by Robbins [46], [47], and proposed specifically for clinical trials by Zelen [65]). The two procedures studied by Sobel-Weiss [55] employed PW and VT sampling rules, the latter having been proposed earlier by Bechhofer, Kiefer and Sobel [6] (B-K-S); both procedures suffered from the fact that the expected total number of observations ($E\{N\}$) required to terminate experimentation approached infinity both for PW and VT as either $p_{[1]} \to 1$ or $p_{[2]} \to 0$. To overcome this problem for VT for $k = 2$, Kiefer and Weiss [34] suggested a *truncated* version of the B-K-S VT - procedure, and permitted the possibility of a third terminal decision, i.e., "The two populations are essentially the same." (Later, Kiefer and Weiss [35] proposed an analogous *truncated* version of the Sobel-Weiss PW sampling rule.) The procedures of Sobel and Weiss [57] for $k = 2$ and [58] for $k \geq 3$ which employed PW sampling and a *stopping rule based on inverse sampling* also were vulnerable to $p_{[k]} \to 0$ since then $E\{N\} \to \infty$.

The Sobel-Weiss [58] procedure was the first (after Paulson [40], [41]) to consider the case $k \geq 3$ for the distance measure $\Delta_{i,j}$. Although most investigators studied only the $k = 2$ case, Hoel and Sobel [28], Sobel and Weiss [59], Hoel, Sobel and Weiss [30], and Schriever [49] considered the $k \geq 3$ case. All restricted consideration to the goal of selecting the "best" population.

Further work on *closed* procedures for $k = 2$ was carried out by Hoel [27], Nebenzahl and Sobel [37], Berry and Sobel [10], Fushimi [20], Kiefer and Weiss [35], Simon, Weiss and Hoel [52], Schriever [50] and Tamhane [62]. Bofinger [12] and Schriever [49] appear to be the only authors to have considered *closed* procedures for $k \geq 3$. Most of these procedures employed some variant of PW sampling rules designed to minimize $E\{N\}$ and/or $E\{N_{(1)}\}$, the expected number of observations taken from the population associated with $p_{[1]}$.

2.2 *Our Approach*

In this paper we have limited consideration to *closed* procedures, i.e., procedures for which the total number of observations taken from any of the $k \geq 2$ populations is a *bounded* random variable. We are disenchanted with open procedures because we believe that they are of little practical use. (This, of course, is a criticism of all of the ranking and identification procedures described in Bechhofer, Kiefer and Sobel [6], and in a hypothesis testing or acceptance sampling context of the Wald sequential probability ratio test.) Even if E{N} is "small" relative to the kn required by the best competing single-stage procedure, the distribution of N is usually highly skewed to the right, and hence "large" values of N occur with positive (albeit small) probabilities. This fact discourages the use of such procedures.

Our reference point is the single-stage procedure of Sobel and Huyett [54] which takes exactly n observations from each of the $k \geq 2$ populations. We were able to characterize a class of closed sequential procedures which achieve the same probability of a correct selection as does the Sobel-Huyett (S-H) procedure, uniformly in $\tilde{p}$. Within this class we have found adaptive procedures which are uniformly in $\tilde{p}$ superior in terms of E{N} to the S-H procedure. For k = 2 our procedure is *optimal* within a certain class.

Our closed sequential procedures for $k \geq 2$ are applicable to a broad class of general ranking and selection goals such as the one described in equation (6) of Bechhofer [4], namely, "To select the k_t "best" populations, the k_{t-1} "second best" populations, etc., and finally the k_1 "worst" populations." Here $k_1, k_2, \ldots, k_t$ $(t \leq k)$ are positive integers such that $\sum_{i=1}^{t} k_i = k$. To illustrate our procedure we consider in Section 3 the case $t = 2$, $k_1 = k - s$, $k_2 = s$ $(1 \leq s \leq k-1)$ which we call Goal I, and in Section 4 the case $t = s+1$, $k_1 = k - s$, $k_2 = k_3 = \ldots = k_{s+1} = 1$ $(1 \leq s \leq k-1)$ which we call Goal II. Other goals not given by (6) in Bechhofer [4] can be handled similarly.

The main difference between our present formulation of the problem and that adopted in all of the previous papers in this category is that the so-called "least-favorable configuration" of the p-values (which plays a central role when *designing* an experiment using the indifference-zone approach) is of no concern to us. Our interest is focused on the probability of achieving a correct selection for a given n for the particular goal considered, and in accomplishing this objective with minimum cost (e.g., minimum E{N} needed to achieve a correct selection). A special virtue of all of our procedures for $k \geq 2$ is that no special tables of constants are necessary to carry out the procedures, and the procedures are very easy to implement.

We assume throughout that the response (success or failure) of an experiment is known sufficiently soon that it can influence the choice of population for the next experiment. This condition is not met in most clinical trials (although it often can be realized in testing in the physical sciences). Even if this condition is not met the procedures can sometimes be used to advantage. (See Remark 5.3.) Also, modifications of the procedure can be made to good effect if the responses are delayed.

III. SINGLE-STAGE PROCEDURES

In this section we consider single-stage procedures for the Goal I and Goal II Bernoulli selection problems. Let $S_i(F_i)$ denote a "success" ("failure") from Π_i $(1 \leq i \leq k)$. If n observations are taken from Π_i, let $y_{i,n}$ denote the number of successes yielded by Π_i $(1 \leq i \leq k)$.

3.1 *Single-Stage Procedure for Goal I*

PROCEDURE FOR GOAL I. (selecting the s $(1 \leq s \leq k-1)$ "best" of k populations *without* regard to order):

Sampling rule (R_{SS}): Take n observations from each of the k populations.

(3.1a)

Terminal decision rule (T_{SS}): Compute $y_{i,n}$ $(1 \leq i \leq k)$.

Let A_1, $A_2 \subset A = \{1,2,\ldots,k\}$ denote two disjoint sets of order s and k-s, respectively, such that

(3.1b) $$y_{i_1,n} \geqq y_{i_2,n}$$

for all $i_1 \in A_1$ and for all $i_2 \in A_2$. If there are r sets $A^{(i)} = \{A_1,A_2\}$ $(1 \leqq i \leqq r)$ satisfying (3.1b), then select one of them at random and announce for the selected set that A_1, A_2 are associated with $\{p_{[k]},p_{[k-1]},\ldots,p_{[k-s+1]}\}$ and $\{p_{[k-s]},\ldots,p_{[1]}\}$, respectively.

3.2 *Single-Stage Procedure for Goal II*

PROCEDURE FOR GOAL II (Selecting the s $(1 \leqq s \leqq k-1)$ "best" of k populations *with* regard to order):

Sampling rule (R_{SS}): Take n observations from each of the k

(3.2a) populations.

Terminal decision rule (T_{SS}): Compute $y_{i,n}$ $(1 \leqq i \leqq k)$.

Let $A_1,A_2,\ldots,A_{s+1} \subset A = \{1,2,\ldots,k\}$ denote s+1 disjoint sets, $A_1,\ldots,A_s$ of order one, A_{s+1} of order k-s, such that

(3.2b) $$y_{i_j,n} \geqq y_{i_{j+1},n} \quad (1 \leqq j \leqq s)$$

for $i_j \in A_j$ $(1 \leqq j \leqq s)$ and for all $i_{s+1} \in A_{s+1}$. If there are r sets $A^{(i)} = \{A_1,A_2,\ldots,A_{s+1}\}$ $(1 \leqq i \leqq r)$ satisfying (3.2b), then select one of them at random and announce for the selected set that $A_1,A_2,\ldots,A_s$ and A_{s+1} are associated with $p_{[k]},p_{[k-1]},\ldots,p_{[k-s+1]}$ and $\{p_{[k-s]},\ldots,p_{[1]}\}$, respectively.

Example 3.1. $(k = 5,\ s = 3,\ n = 3)$

Π_1	Π_2	Π_3	Π_4	Π_5
S_1	S_2	S_3	S_4	F_5
S_1	S_2	S_3	S_4	F_5
S_1	S_2	F_3	F_4	F_5

Then $A^{(1)} = \{\{1\}, \{2\}, \{3\}, \{4,5\}\}$

$A^{(2)} = \{\{1\}, \{2\}, \{4\}, \{3,5\}\}$

$A^{(3)} = \{\{2\}, \{1\}\ \{3\}\ \{4,5\}\}$

$A^{(4)} = \{\{2\}, \{1\}, \{4\}, \{3,5\}\}.$

Hence select one of $A^{(i)}$ $(1 \leqq i \leqq 4)$ at random.

Remark 3.1. The single-stage procedures given in this section for Goals I and II coincide for s = 1. The case s = 1 was studied in detail by Sobel and Huyett [54]. In that paper the common sample size n was chosen to guarantee certain indifference-zone probability requirements (as in Bechhofer [4]) given by their equations (5) and (13).

IV. A CLASS OF SEQUENTIAL PROCEDURES

We now propose a class of sequential procedures for the Goal I and Goal II Bernoulli selection problems. Let S_i^m (F_i^m) denote a success (failure) from Π_i at stage m $(1 \leqq i \leqq k,$ $1 \leqq m \leqq kn)$. Let $n_{i,m}$ denote the total number of observations taken from Π_i through stage m, and let $z_{i,m}$ denote the total number of successes yielded by Π_i through stage m $(1 \leqq i \leqq k,\ 1 \leqq m \leqq kn)$.

Theorem 5.1 (in Section 5.1) relates to a class of sequential selection procedures which employs a very general class of sampling rules, and a particular stopping and terminal decision rule specific to the goal (Goal I or Goal II) under consideration.

Throughout the remainder of this paper we shall let R denote an arbitrary sampling rule which takes no more than n observations from any of the k populations. The basis for specifying n (e.g., to guarantee an indifference-zone probability requirement as in Sobel and Huyett or because of availability of observations or because of other economic considerations) is of no concern to us here.

4.1 *A Class of Sequential Procedures for Goal* I

PROCEDURE FOR GOAL I (Selecting the s ($1 \leq s \leq k-1$) "best" of k populations *without* regard to order):

Sampling rule (R): Arbitrary, the only restriction being

(4.1a) that at most n observations can be taken from any of the k populations. Thus, e.g., one-at-a-time sampling, vector-at-a-time sampling, or multistage sampling can be used.

Stopping rule (S^*): Stop sampling at the *first* stage m at which there exist two disjoint sets $A_1, A_2 \subset A = \{1,2,\ldots,k\}$ with A_1 of order s and A_2 of order k-s, such that

(4.1b) $$z_{i_1,m} \geq z_{i_2,m} + n - n_{i_2,m}$$

for all $i_1 \in A_1$ and for all $i_2 \in A_2$.

Terminal decision rule (T^*): If r sets $A^{(i)} = \{A_1, A_2\}$

(4.1c) ($1 \leq i \leq r$) satisfy (4.1b), then select one of them at random and announce for the selected set that A_1 and A_2 are associated with $\{p_{[k]}, p_{[k-1]}, \ldots, p_{[k-s+1]}\}$ and $\{p_{[k-s]}, \ldots, p_{[1]}\}$, respectively.

Examples 4.1. For (k = 3, s = 1, n = 1), stop if

Π_1	Π_2	Π_3		Π_1	Π_2	Π_3
		S_3^1		F_1^1	F_2^2	

Then $A^{(1)} = \{\{3\}, \{1,2\}\}$. Hence, select $A^{(1)}$.

Examples 4.2. For ($k = 3$, $s = 2$, $n = 1$), stop if

Π_1	Π_2	Π_3
		F_3^1

Π_1	Π_2	Π_3
S_1^1		F_3^2

Then $A^{(1)} = \{\{1,2\}, \{3\}\}$. Hence, select $A^{(1)}$.

Example 4.3. For ($k = 5$, $s = 2$, $n = 3$), stop if

Π_1	Π_2	Π_3	Π_4	Π_5
S_1^{10}	S_2^7	S_3^4	F_4^3	S_5^1
S_1^{11}	S_2^8	S_3^5		F_5^2
	F_2^9	F_3^6		

Then $A^{(1)} = \{\{1,2\}, \{3,4,5\}\}$ and $A^{(2)} = \{\{1,3\}, \{2,4,5\}\}$.

Hence, select one of $A^{(i)}$ ($i = 1,2$) at random.

4.2 *A Class of Sequential Procedures for Goal II*

PROCEDURE FOR GOAL II (Selecting the s ($1 \leqq s \leqq k-1$) "best" of k populations *with* regard to order):

Sampling rule (R): Arbitrary, the only restriction being that

(4.2a) at most n observations can be taken from any of the k populations.

Stopping rule (S^*): Stop sampling at the *first* stage m at which there exist $s+1$ disjoint sets $A_1, A_2, \ldots, A_s, A_{s+1} \subset A = \{1,2,\ldots,k\}$ with $A_1, \ldots, A_s$ of order one, A_{s+1} of order $k-s$, such that

(4.2b) $$z_{i_j,m} \geqq z_{i_{j+1},m} + n - n_{i_{j+1},m} \quad (1 \leqq j \leqq s)$$

for $i_j \in A_j$ ($1 \leqq j \leqq s$) and for all $i_{s+1} \in A_{s+1}$.

Terminal decision rule (T^*): If r sets $A^{(i)} = \{A_1, A_2, \ldots, A_{s+1}\}$
(4.2c) $(1 \leq i \leq r)$ satisfy (4.2b) then select one of them at random and announce for the selected set that $A_1, A_2, \ldots, A_s$ and A_{s+1} are associated with $p_{[k]}, p_{[k-1]}, \ldots, p_{[k-s+1]}$ and $\{p_{[k-s]}, \ldots, p_{[1]}\}$, respectively.

Example 4.4. For (k = 5, s = 3, n = 3), stop if

Π_1	Π_2	Π_3	Π_4	Π_5
S_1^6	S_2^4	F_3^3	F_4^2	F_5^1
S_1^7	F_2^5	S_3^{13}	S_4^{11}	F_5^{10}
S_1^8	F_2^9		F_4^{12}	

Then $A^{(1)} = \{\{1\}, \{3\}, \{2\}, \{4,5\}\}$ and $A^{(2)} = \{\{1\}, \{3\}, \{4\}, \{2,5\}\}$. Hence, select one of $A^{(i)}$ (i = 1,2) at random.

V. COMPARISON OF SOME PERFORMANCE CHARACTERISTICS OF THE SINGLE-STAGE AND SEQUENTIAL PROCEDURES

In this section we compare the probability of a correct selection achieved by our class of sequential procedures with that of the corresponding single-stage procedures. We do the same for the total number of observations required to terminate experimentation for the sequential procedures and the total sample size required by the corresponding single-stage procedures.

5.1 *Probability of a Correct Selection*

If two or more populations have a common p-value, assume that the populations are tagged in such a way that the ordering of the k populations is unique. Then a correct selection (CS) for Goal I is achieved if the selected sets A_1, A_2 are associated with $\{p_{[k]}, p_{[k-1]}, \ldots, p_{[k-s+1]}\}$, $\{p_{[k-s]}, \ldots, p_{[1]}\}$, respectively;

analogously, a correct selection for Goal II is achieved if the selected sets $A_1, A_2, \ldots, A_{s+1}$ are associated with $\{p_{[k]}\}$, $\{p_{[k-1]}\}, \ldots, \{p_{[k-s+1]}\}$, $\{p_{[k-s]}, \ldots, p_{[1]}\}$, respectively.

We now state our first key theorem relating the P{CS} achieved by our sequential procedures and the P{CS} achieved by the corresponding single-stage procedures.

THEOREM 5.1.

$P_I\{CS|(R_{SS}, T_{SS})\} \equiv P_I\{CS|(R, S^*, T^*)\}$ *uniformly in* $\underset{\sim}{p} = (p_1, \ldots, p_k)$ *for Goal* I, *and analogously for Goal* II.

Proof. See Appendix .

Remark 5.1. Note that if the weak inequality in (4.1b) and (4.2b) were replaced by a strict inequality, the associated stopping rules would involve *curtailment* of the sampling process. Then the conclusion of Theorem 5.1 would be obvious since the resulting sequential procedure and the single-stage procedure *always* lead to the *same* terminal decision. However, such is not the case when the weak inequality is used. For example, for $k \geqq 2$, $s = 1$, $n \geqq 1$, we see that (4.1b) calls for stopping if (say) the sequence S_i^j $(1 \leqq j \leqq n)$ were obtained for *any* i $(1 \leqq i \leqq k)$ in which situation (4.1c) would select Π_i. However, for that same initial sequence curtailed sampling would require that at least one more observation be taken from *all* populations Π_j $(j \neq i, 1 \leqq j \leqq k)$; if these additional observations were such that a total of r-1 additional populations also yielded n S's, then the curtailment terminal decision rule would select one of these r n-success populations at random (which is what the single-stage procedure would do). Thus (4.1b) and (4.1c) permit earlier stopping than under curtailment, but sometimes may lead to a different terminal decision than under curtailment.

Remark 5.2. If sampling continues beyond the stage called for by (4.1b) for Goal I or (4.2b) for Goal II then the P{CS} is not increased (provided that the total number of observations taken from any population is at most n). VT sampling for the Bernoulli selection problem *always* requires at least as large a total number of observations as would be required by a one-at-a-time sampling rule (and, in fact, often a very much larger total) to achieve the same P{CS} for a given data set. Thus, unless VT sampling is used for (say) "blocking" purposes for the Bernoulli, it should ordinarily be avoided. For an example of the latter situation see Tamhane [61].

Remark 5.3. In some areas of application, e.g., in certain types of clinical trials and in reliability-life studies, the experiments may be started at different times, and the outcomes (successes or failures) from the k populations may be staggered or spaced over time. This might be the case in experiments which are designed in single-stages as with Sobel-Huyett and for which n observations are to be taken from each of the k populations. In such situations for (say) Goal I, the stopping rule (4.1b) and the terminal decision rule (4.1c) can be applied as each success or failure is recorded. Then (4.1b) permits the possibility of an *early terminal decision* although successes and failures will continue to be recorded as they occur after that point. These later observations make it possible to estimate the p_i $(1 \leqq i \leqq k)$ more precisely. They may lead to a different terminal decision, but they will not increase the probability of a correct selection.

Remark 5.4. If the common sample size n of the Sobel-Huyett single-stage procedure was chosen to guarantee the indifference-zone probability requirements given by their equations (5) or (13), then a fortiori our class of sequential procedures for $s = 1$ guarantees these same probability requirements. Although Sobel-Huyett did not consider Goal I or Goal II for $s > 1$, an analogous result would hold for those goals as well.

Remark 5.5 For large n the normal approximation to the binomial distribution can be used (as in Sobel-Huyett) to obtain an excellent approximation to the P{CS} achieved by the single-stage procedure for Goal I or Goal II for specified s and given $\underset{\sim}{p}$. This computed P{CS} thus holds for our general class of sequential procedures for the same specified s and given $\underset{\sim}{p}$.

Remark 5.6. A single-stage procedure for selecting the *multinomial* event which has the largest probability is described in Bechhofer, Elmaghraby and Morse [5]; only the case s = 1 was considered. Alam and Thompson [1] proposed a single-stage procedure for the case s = k-1. The sequential procedures employing *vector-at-a-time* (VT) sampling and (S^*,T^*) for the Bernoulli selection problem given for Goal I ($1 \leqq s \leqq k-1$) and Goal II ($1 \leqq s \leqq k-1$) in Section 4 of the present paper are directly applicable to the multinomial selection problem (with obvious interpretations of notation).

A sequential procedure employing multinomial VT sampling *with curtailment* was proposed for the multinomial selection problem (s = 1) by Gibbons, Olkin and Sobel [21], pp. 178-183. Our procedure improves on the G-O-S procedure in that it achieves the same P{CS} uniformly in $\underset{\sim}{p}$ as does theirs (and the single-stage procedure), but our procedure requires at most as many (and usually less) vector-stages to terminate sampling. These results with accompanying computations are contained in Bechhofer and Kulkarni [7].

5.2 *Total Number of Observations to Terminate Sampling*

In Sections 4.1 and 4.2 we described a class of sequential procedures for Goals I and II, respectively. For each the sampling rule is arbitrary, the only restrictions being that the rule adopted take no more than n observations from any of the k populations, and that it be used in conjunction with (4.1b) and (4.1c) for Goal I or (4.2b) and (4.2c) for Goal II. If we denote by N the random total number of observations that have been taken from the k populations when sampling stops, then it can be shown that using (4.1b) and (4.1c) for Goal I we have

(5.1) $$\min\{sn, (k-s)n\} \leqq N \leqq kn,$$

or using (4.2b) and (4.2c) for Goal II we have

(5.2) $$sn \leqq N \leqq kn;$$

if an arbitrary one-at-a-time sampling rule is used, then

(5.3) $$N \leqq kn-1$$

for both Goal I and Goal II. Examples 4.1 and 4.2 show that the lower bound in (5.1) and the upper bound in (5.3) can be achieved for appropriate sampling rules and outcomes. That the procedures are closed is of particular practical importance.

For either Goal I or Goal II with given (k, s, n), the distribution of N and hence $E\{N|\underset{\sim}{p}\}$ (and other related performance characteristics of the sequential procedure) depend on $\underset{\sim}{p}$ and the specific sampling rule that is used. In Sections 6 and 7 we propose a particular sampling rule which has highly desirable properties when used in conjunction with $(\mathcal{S}^*,\mathcal{T}^*)$.

VI. AN OPTIMAL SEQUENTIAL PROCEDURE FOR k = 2

In this section and the next we continue to restrict attention to arbitrary sampling rules $\mathcal{R}$ which take no more than n observations from any of the k populations, and which are used in conjunction with (4.1b) and (4.1c) for Goal I or (4.2b) and (4.2c) for Goal II. We seek sampling rules within this class which have desirable properties. Indeed we have been successful in constructing an *optimal* rule for k = 2 for several definitions of optimality which are of considerable practical importance. Our results are summarized in Theorems 6.1, 6.2 and 6.3, below.

In the sequel we let $N_{(i)}$ $(N^S_{(i)}, N^F_{(i)})$ denote the random number of observations (successes, failures) that have been taken from the population with parameter $p_{[i]}$ $(1 \leq i \leq k)$ when sampling stops. Also let $N^S = \sum_{i=1}^{k} N^S_{(i)}$ and $N^F = \sum_{i=1}^{k} N^F_{(i)}$. Then $N = \sum_{i=1}^{k} N_{(i)} = N^S + N^F$. We are particularly interested in $E\{N\}$. However, also of concern is $E\{\sum_{i=1}^{k-1} N_{(i)}\}$, the expected total number of observations taken from the "inferior" populations, i.e., those having the smaller p-values; this quantity is especially important in clinical trials where ethical considerations play an important role, and p_i is the probability of a "success" using treatment i $(1 \leq i \leq k)$. (See Hoel, Sobel and Weiss [31].) For the same reason $E\{N^F\}$ is important. In each case we seek to make $E\{N\}$, $E\{\sum_{i=1}^{k-1} N_{(i)}\}$ and $E\{N^F\}$ as *small* as possible. It is obvious that for these objectives it is sufficient to restrict attention to one-at-a-time sampling rules.

6.1 *Minimization of* $E\{N\}$

We use the following notation for k = 2. For a state $(z_{1,m}, n_{1,m}; z_{2,m}, n_{2,m})$ which does not satisfy (4.1b), let $D_m = D_m(z_{1,m}, n_{1,m}; z_{2,m}, n_{2,m})$ denote the sampling decision at stage m $(m = 0, 1, \ldots, 2n-1)$. $D_m = i$ means that at stage m the next observation is to be taken from Π_i $(i = 1,2)$; $D_m = (1,2)$ means that at stage m the next observation is to be taken at random from Π_1 or Π_2.

Sampling rule (R^*):

$$(6.1) \quad D_m = \begin{cases} 1 & \text{if } n_{1,m} - z_{1,m} < n_{2,m} - z_{2,m} \\ & \text{or} \\ & n_{1,m} - z_{1,m} = n_{2,m} - z_{2,m} \text{ and } z_{1,m} > z_{2,m}, \\ 2 & \text{if } n_{1,m} - z_{1,m} > n_{2,m} - z_{2,m} \\ & \text{or} \\ & n_{1,m} - z_{1,m} = n_{2,m} - z_{2,m} \text{ and } z_{1,m} < z_{2,m}, \\ (1,2) & \text{if } n_{1,m} - z_{1,m} = n_{2,m} - z_{2,m} \text{ and } z_{1,m} = z_{2,m}. \end{cases}$$

THEOREM 6.1. *Among all sampling rules R used in conjunction with* (S^*,T^*) *for* $k = 2$, R^* *minimizes* $E\{N|(p_1,p_2)\}$ *for* $p_1 + p_2 > 1$. *The conjugate sampling rule* $\bar{R}^*$ *(in which* $n_{i,m} - z_{i,m}$ *and* $z_{i,m}$ *in* R^* *are replaced by* $z_{i,m}$ *and* $n_{i,m} - z_{i,m}$, *respectively, for* $i=1,2$) *minimizes* $E\{N|(p_1,p_2)\}$ *for* $p_1 + p_2 < 1$. *Both* R^* *and* $\bar{R}^*$ *minimize* $E\{N|(p_1,p_2)\}$ *for* $p_1 + p_2 = 1$, *and (for symmetry) one can choose between them with probability* (1/2, 1/2).

Proof. The proof of Theorem 6.1 is quite long, and therefore is not given here. It is given in detail in Kulkarni [36] along with the proofs of Theorems 6.2 and 6.3 which are stated below. These proofs will be published elsewhere.

Remark 6.1. Note that R^* and $\bar{R}^*$ are *stationary*, i.e., the rules are *independent* of n. (Contrast this result with the one described in Remark 6.5.)

Example 6.1. To illustrate the sequential procedure which employs (R^*,S^*,T^*) for $k = 2$, $s = 1$ and $n = 7$ we give the following stopping sequence:

	Π_1	Π_2
Cycle 1	F_1^1	S_2^2
		F_2^3
Cycle 2	S_1^7	S_2^4
	F_1^8	S_2^5
		F_2^6
Cycle 3 is		S_2^9
truncated by S^*		S_2^{10}

Π_2 is selected after S_2^{10}. Note that we regard the sampling as proceeding in *cycles*; within each cycle (except perhaps the last one) the outcomes from each population are a sequence of successes followed by a single failure. Here the last cycle is *truncated* by S^*.

Remark 6.2. Note from S_2^4 of Example 6.1 that R^* is *not* a PW sampling rule. (See Robbins [47], Zelen [65], Sobel and Weiss [55].) R^* is PW within a cycle, but may not be PW as sampling progresses from one cycle to the next. *Play-the-loser* for $\bar{R}^*$ corresponds to PW for R^*. Most of the sequential procedures proposed in the literature for the Bernoulli selection problem employ a PW sampling rule.

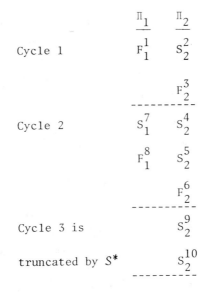

Remark 6.3. If the experimenter knows that $p_1 + p_2 > 1$ $(p_1 + p_2 < 1)$ then he presumably would use R^* $(\bar{R}^*)$. However, lacking such knowledge he may be prepared to assume that (p_1, p_2) represent the outcome of a random sample of size two taken from a Beta distribution $B(a,b)$: $[\Gamma(a+b)/\Gamma(a)\Gamma(b)]x^{a-1}(1-x)^{b-1}$, $0 \leqq x \leqq 1$, $a,b > 0$. Since $P\{p > 1/2 | (a,b)\} > 1/2$ for $a > b$, he may wish to replace the assumption $p_1 + p_2 > 1$ ($p_1 + p_2 < 1$) by the assumption $a > b$ ($a < b$), and chose (a,b) accordingly to model his assessment of the particular situation under study. Then he can use the following empirical sampling rule R^*_E in conjunction with (S^*,T^*).

Empirical sampling rule (R^*_E).

At stage m estimate p_i $(i = 1,2)$ by $\hat{p}_{i,m}=(z_{i,m}+a)/(n_{i,m}+a+b)$.

(6.2) If $\hat{p}_{1,m} + \hat{p}_{2,m} > 1$ use R^*,

$\hat{p}_{1,m} + \hat{p}_{2,m} < 1$ use $\bar{R}^*$,

$\hat{p}_{1,m} + \hat{p}_{2,m} = 1$ use either R^* or $\bar{R}^*$.

Remark 6.4. Based on limited calculation for selected (a,b) and $n \leqq 10$ it appears that the $E\{N\}$ - values obtained for R^*_E and the optimal Bayes sampling rule are very close. Here the expectation is taken w.r.t. the prior Beta density.

Note. Since $\hat{p}_{i,m} \to p_i$ $(i = 1,2)$ for $m \to \infty$, an error in the choice of the particular (a,b) will have little effect on the performance of (R^*_E,S^*,T^*) when n is large.

6.2 *Minimization of* $E\{N_{(1)}\}$.

We had mentioned that in clinical trials it would be desirable to minimize the expected total number of observations taken from the populations with small p-values. Our next theorem addresses that issue for $k = 2$.

THEOREM 6.2. *Among all sampling rules R used in conjunction with* (S^*,T^*) *for* $k = 2$, R^* *minimizes* $E\{N_{(1)}|(p_1,p_2)\}$ *for* $p_{[2]} > 1/2$.

Remark 6.5. If $p_{[2]} < 1/2$ it is not possible to find a *stationary* sampling rule which when used in conjunction with

(S^*,T^*) for k = 2 will minimize $E\{N_{(1)}|(p_1,p_2)\}$ for all (p_1,p_2) as is illustrated by the following example.

Example 6.2. Let k = 2 and suppose that $p_{[1]} = 0.085$, $p_{[2]} = 0.250$. Suppose that $z_{1,1} = 1$, $n_{1,1} = 1$, $z_{2,1} = 0$, $n_{2,1} = 0$. Using dynamic programming (DP) it can be shown that at stage 1 the sampling rule that minimizes $E\{N_{(1)}\}$ for this particular pair $(p_{[1]},p_{[2]})$ with $p_{[2]} < 1/2$ and outcome (1,1; 0,0) is "Select the next observation from Π_2 if n = 2; select the next observation from Π_1 if n = 3." Thus the optimal sampling rule depends on n, and hence is *not* stationary.

6.3 *Minimization of* $E\{N^F\}$.

In clinical trials it is undesirable to obtain failures with *any* of the treatments employed in the trial. Our next theorems relate to that problem for k = 2.

THEOREM 6.3A. *Among all sampling rules R used in conjunction with (S^*,T^*) for k = 2, R^* minimizes* $E\{N^F|(p_1,p_2)\}$ *for* $p_1+p_2 > 1$.

THEOREM 6.3B. *Among all sampling rules R used in conjunction with (S^*,T^*) for k = 2, $\bar{R}^*$ minimizes* $E\{N^F|(p_1,p_2)\}$ *for* $p_{[2]} < 1/2$.

Remark 6.7. If $p_1 + p_2 < 1$ and $p_{[2]} > 1/2$ there exist points (p_1,p_2) such that neither R^* nor $\bar{R}^*$ when used in conjunction with (S^*,T^*) for k = 2 will minimize $E\{N^F|(p_1,p_2)\}$, as is illustrated by the following example.

Example 6.3. Let k = 2 and suppose that n = 2 and $p_{[1]} = 0.10$, $p_{[2]} = 0.55$. Suppose that $z_{1,1} = 1$, $n_{1,1} = 1$, $z_{2,1} = 0$, $n_{2,1} = 0$; using DP it can be shown that at stage 1 the R that minimizes $E\{N^F\}$ for this particular pair $(p_{[1]},p_{[2]})$ and outcome is R^*. Suppose now that $z_{1,1} = 0$, $n_{1,1} = 1$, $z_{2,1} = 0$, $n_{2,1} = 0$; using DP it can be shown that at stage 1 the R that minimizes $E\{N^F\}$ for the same particular pair $(p_{[1]},p_{[2]})$, but different outcome is $\bar{R}^*$.

Theorems 5.1, 6.1, 6.2 and 6.3 summarize four highly desirable properties of R^* when used in conjunction with (S^*,T^*) for the two-population Bernoulli selection problem. In Section 7 we consider sampling rules for the k-population ($k \geqq 3$) problem.

VII. A PROPOSED SAMPLING RULE FOR GOALS I AND II FOR k > 2

In this section we propose a natural generalization to $k > 2$ of the sampling rule R^*. This *generalized* R^* (which we still will refer to as R^* since it reduces to R^* when $k = 2$) when used in conjunction with (S^*,T^*) is thus a member of the class of sequential procedures described in Section 4; hence Theorem 5.1 applies. We describe some of its desirable properties in Section 7.1, and conjecture an optimal property in Section 7.2.

Generalized sampling rule (R^*):

At stage m ($0 \leqq m < kn-1$), if sampling has not stopped, take the next observation from the population which has the smallest number of failures among all Π_i for which $n_{i,m} < n$ ($1 \leqq i \leqq k$). If there is a tie among such equal-number-of-failure populations, take the next observation from that one of them which has the largest number of successes. If there is a further tie among such equal-number-of success populations, select one of them at random and take the next observation from it.

Remark 7.1. We can think of the sampling rule R^* as proceeding in cycles. Before the start of sampling the populations are arranged in random order, say, $\Pi_1',\Pi_2',\ldots,\Pi_k'$. The first cycle is started by taking one observation at a time from Π_1' until a failure is obtained. Then observations are taken one at a time from Π_2' until a failure is obtained. This process is continued until every population has produced a sequence of successes followed by a single failure. Then the first cycle is complete, and every population has produced exactly one failure (unless *truncation* has occurred during the cycle). Cycle i is started by taking observations from the population which has the largest *cumulative* number of successes through cycle i - 1 ($1 \leqq i \leqq c$) where c is the random total number of cycles until the termination of sampling. That population is sampled until a failure is obtained. The cycle is continued by sampling from the population which has the second largest *cumulative* number of successes through cycle i - 1, and sampling from that population is continued until a failure is obtained. This process is continued until in cycle i every population has produced a sequence of successes followed by a single failure. Then the ith cycle is complete, and every population has produced a cumulative number of exactly i failures (unless *truncation* has occurred during the ith cycle). If within a cycle two or more populations which have not yet been sampled in that cycle have the same *cumulative* number of successes through cycle i - 1, then they are sampled in random order.

Remark 7.2. Sampling rule R^* had been proposed earlier for $k \geqq 2$ by a referee of Sobel and Weiss [58]; see the sampling rule $\hat{R}_I$ referred to on pp. 1809 and 1824 of their paper. This sampling rule was to be used in conjunction with a stopping rule based on *inverse sampling*. However, as noted above, our motivation for proposing R^* is that it is a natural generalization to $k > 2$ of the sampling rule of (6.1).

Example 7.1. To illustrate the sequential procedure which employs (R^*,S^*,T^*) for k = 3, s = 1, n = 8 we give the following stopping sequence:

	Π_1	Π_2	Π_3
	S_1^5	S_2^1	F_3^4
Cycle 1	F_1^6	S_2^2	
		F_2^3	
	S_1^9	S_2^7	S_3^{13}
Cycle 2	S_1^{10}	F_2^8	F_3^{14}
	S_1^{11}		
	F_1^{12}		
Cycle 3 is truncated by S^*	S_1^{15}		
	S_1^{16}		

Π_1 is selected after S_1^{16}.

Remark 7.3. The stopping sequences given in Examples 4.1 - 4.4 could have been obtained using (R^*, S^*, T^*).

Example 7.2. We illustrate Theorem 5.1 by calculating in Table 7.1 the *exact* P{CS} when (R_{SS}, T_{SS}) and (R^*, S^*, T^*) are used for k = 3, s = 1, n = 1 (as in Examples 4.1).

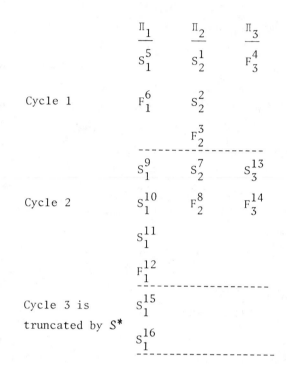

Table 7.1.

Exact P{CS} for k = 3, s = 1, and n = 1.

Outcomes leading to CS[1/] for (R_{SS}, T_{SS})	Probability of outcome and then CS[1/]	Stopping sequences leading to CS[1/] for (R^*, S^*, T^*)	Probability of stopping sequence and then CS[1/]
(S_1, S_2, S_3)	$p_1 p_2 p_3 \frac{1}{3}$	S_3^1	$\frac{1}{3} p_3$
(F_1, S_2, S_3)	$(1-p_1) p_2 p_3 \frac{1}{2}$	$F_1^1 \; S_3^2$	$\frac{1}{3}(1-p_1)\frac{1}{2} p_3$
(S_1, F_2, S_3)	$p_1 (1-p_2) p_3 \frac{1}{2}$	$F_2^1 \; S_3^2$	$\frac{1}{3}(1-p_2)\frac{1}{2} p_3$
(F_1, F_2, S_3)	$(1-p_1)(1-p_2) p_3$	$F_1^1 \; F_2^2$	$\frac{1}{3}(1-p_1)\frac{1}{2}(1-p_2)$
(F_1, F_2, F_3)	$(1-p_1)(1-p_2)(1-p_3) \frac{1}{3}$	$F_2^1 \; F_1^2$	$\frac{1}{3}(1-p_2)\frac{1}{2}(1-p_1)$

$$P\{CS\} = \frac{1}{3} - \frac{1}{3}(p_1+p_2-2\,p_3) + \frac{1}{6}[2\,p_1 p_2 - (p_1+p_2)p_3]$$

[1/] For simplicity of notation in this example we have assumed that $\max(p_1, p_2) < p_3$.

7.1 *Some Properties of the Procedure* (R^*, S^*, T^*)

The sequential procedure employing (R^*, S^*, T^*) has the following properties for $k \geqq 2$:

a) $P\{CS \mid (R^*, S^*, T^*), \underset{\sim}{p}\} = P\{CS \mid (R_{SS}, T_{SS}), \underset{\sim}{p}\}$ uniformly in $\underset{\sim}{p}$ for both Goal I and Goal II.

b) For Goal I

$$\min\{sn, (k-s)n\} \leqq N \leqq kn - 1,$$

and for Goal II

$$sn \leqq N \leqq kn - 1$$

for all $\underset{\sim}{p}$. These bounds on N can be achieved.

c) $\frac{1}{kn}(100) \leqq \frac{kn - E\{N\}}{kn}(100) \leqq \frac{k-s}{k}(100)$

for Goal II and analogously for Goal I for all $\underset{\sim}{p}$.

Here (kn - E{N})100/kn is the percent saving in expected total number of observations if (R^*,S^*,T^*) is used in place of the corresponding single-stage procedure. This saving is *always* positive and can be very large for $p_{[1]} \to 1$.

d) $P\{N = sn|\underset{\sim}{p}\} \to 1$ for $p_{[1]} \to 1$ for Goals I and II,

$P\{N = kn-s|\underset{\sim}{p}\} \to 1$ for $p_{[k]} \to 0$ for Goal I,

$P\{N = kn-1|\underset{\sim}{p}\} \to 1$ for $p_{[k]} \to 0$ for Goal II.

e) Populations with small p-values tend to be sampled less frequently.

f) No special tables of constants are necessary to carry out (R^*,S^*,T^*) for $k \geqq 2$, and it is very easy to implement.

We note from b) that using R^* instead of an arbitrary R With (S^*,T^*) yields a smaller upper bound (kn-1 instead of kn) for N. The fact that the sequential procedure employing (R^*,S^*,T^*) is *closed* increases its potential for use in real-life applications.

7.2 *Some Conjectures Concerning the Procedure* (R^*,S^*,T^*)

For $k > 2$ we make a conjecture for (R^*,S^*,T^*) that is a generalization of Theorem 6.1. The conjecture is made only for the case $s = 1$; when $s > 1$ the situation is much more complicated, and it is very difficult to conjecture an optimal sampling rule even for a limited region of the parameter space. (See Remark 7.7.)

Conjecture 7.1. Among all sampling rules R used in conjunction with (S^*,T^*) for $k > 2$, $s = 1$, R^* minimizes $E\{N|\underset{\sim}{p}\}$ for $p_{[1]} + p_{[2]} > 1$.

Note: If this conjecture is true then for $s = k-1$ generalized $\bar{R}^*$ (defined in the obvious way) minimizes $E\{N|\underset{\sim}{p}\}$ for $p_{[k]} + p_{[k-1]} < 1$.

Remark 7.4. Conjecture 7.1 was checked numerically for k = 3, s = 1, n = 1(1)6 over a fairly fine grid in the region $p_{[1]} + p_{[2]} > 1$, and was found to be true.

Remark 7.5. For k = 3, s = 1, n = 1(1)6 the condition $p_{[1]} + p_{[2]} > 1$ of Conjecture 7.1 is not necessary. For example, it was found by solving the dynamic programming equations on the computer that R^* minimizes $E\{N|\underset{\sim}{p}\}$ for $(p_{[1]}, p_{[2]}, p_{[3]}) =$ (0.35, 0.5, 0.7).

Remark 7.6. For k = 3, s = 1 it is not possible to find a stationary sampling rule that minimizes $E\{N|\underset{\sim}{p}\}$ for all $\underset{\sim}{p}$ such that $p_{[1]} + p_{[2]} < 1$ as is illustrated by the following example:

Example 7.1. (k = 3, s = 1, n $\geqq$ 3). Let $(p_{[1]}, p_{[2]}, p_{[3]}) =$ (0.4, 0.5, 0.6).

Consider the outcomes

Π_1	Π_2	Π_3
	S_2^4	S_3^1
	S_2^5	S_3^2
		F_3^3 .

For n = 3 the optimal sampling rule takes the next observation from Π_1 while R^* takes the next observation from Π_2. However, for n = 4 the optimal sampling rule takes the next observation from Π_2. Thus the optimal sampling rule is not stationary.

Remark 7.7. For (k = 3, s = 2, n = 3), Goal I, the following example shows that R^* used with (S^*, T^*) does not minimize $E\{N|\underset{\sim}{p}\}$ for any $\underset{\sim}{p}$ such that $0 < p_{[1]} \leqq p_{[3]} < 1$:

Example 7.2.

Π_1	Π_2	Π_3
S_1^3	F_2^2	F_3^1
S_1^4		

R^* takes the next observation from Π_1. However, the optimal sampling rule takes no more observations from Π_1, but chooses at random between Π_2 and Π_3 for the next observation. (A similar example can be constructed for $k > 3$, $k > s > 1$.)

In Theorems 6.1 - 6.3 and Conjecture 7.1 we have limited consideration to a class of sampling rules which take at most n observations from each of the k populations, and which are used in conjunction with (S^*,T^*). We believe that the conclusions given in these theorems and conjecture hold for a broader class of stopping and terminal decision rules. Our belief is summarized in the following conjecture.

Conjecture 7.2. Among all sampling rules R used in conjunction with a stopping rule (S) and terminal decision rule (T) which achieve the same P{CS} as (R_{SS},T_{SS}) uniformly in $\underset{\sim}{p}$, (R^*,S^*,T^*) has the optimal properties described in Theorems 6.1 - 6.3 and Conjecture 7.1.

VIII. PERFORMANCE OF (R^*,S^*,T^*) RELATIVE TO THAT OF OTHER BERNOULLI SELECTION PROCEDURES

For the purpose of comparing the performance characteristics of (R^*,S^*,T^*) with those of some competing Bernoulli selection procedures, we have categorized the latter into two groups: those that achieve the same P{CS} as (R^*,S^*,T^*) uniformly in $\underset{\sim}{p}$, and those that do not.

8.1 *Procedures Having the Same* P{CS} *as* (R^*, S^*, T^*)

a) Hoel [27] proposed a closed sequential procedure for k = 2 employing a PW sampling rule (R_{PW}). It can be shown that Hoel's procedure employs the stopping rule (S^*) and terminal decision rule (T^*). His stopping rule depends on a constant r which is actually the same for specified $\{\Delta^*, P^*\}$ as the n-value necessary to implement the Sobel-Huyett single-stage procedure (R_{SS}, T_{SS}) for the same specification. Thus (R_{PW}, S^*, T^*) achieves the same P{CS} uniformly in $\underset{\sim}{p}$ as do (R^*, S^*, T^*) and (R_{SS}, T_{SS}). Hoel gives tables of r-values for $\Delta^* = 0.1, 0.2, 0.3$ and $P^* = 0.90, 0.95, 0.99$. Using these (r = n)-values for (R^*, S^*, T^*) and (R_{PW}, S^*, T^*) we have found by exact calculations (for configurations with $p_{[1]} = p_{[2]}$ and $p_{[2]} = p_{[1]} + \Delta^*$) that $E\{N|\underset{\sim}{p}; (R^*, S^*, T^*)\} < (>) E\{N|\underset{\sim}{p}; (R_{PW}, S^*, T^*)\}$ if $p_1 + p_2 > 1$ (< 1); however, $E\{N|\underset{\sim}{p}; (\bar{R}^*, S^*, T^*)\} < < E\{N|\underset{\sim}{p}; (R_{PW}, S^*, T^*)\}$ if $p_1 + p_2 < 1$. The $E\{N|R^*\}$ and $E\{N|\bar{R}^*\}$ inequalities for $p_1 + p_2 > 1$ and $p_1 + p_2 < 1$, respectively, follow, of course, from Theorem 6.1. Moreover, it follows from Theorem 6.2 that $E\{N_{(1)}|\underset{\sim}{p}; (R^*, S^*, T^*)\} < E\{N_{(1)}|\underset{\sim}{p}; (R_{PW}, S^*, T^*)\}$ if $p_{[2]} > 1/2$; in fact, it appears from our computations that the inequality holds for all $p_{[2]} > p_{[1]}$. See also Pradhan and Sathe [43].

b) Nebenzahl and Sobel [37] proposed two sequential procedures, the first employing a vector-at-a-time sampling rule (R_{VT}) and the second employing a PW sampling rule (R_{PW}), both stopping when a fixed *total* number of observations n_T had been taken. They (N-S) chose n_T to guarantee the $\{\Delta^*, P^*\}$ indifference-zone probability requirement. N-S showed that for the same n_T both procedures achieved the same P{CS} uniformly in $\underset{\sim}{p}$, and that the total number of observations taken from the population with $p_{[1]}$ was never more for R_{PW} than for R_{VT}. If n_T is even (odd) it can be shown that the P{CS} using (R^*, S^*, T^*) with $n = n_T/2$ $((n_T+1)/2)$ is equal to that achieved by the N-S procedures with n_T, uniformly in $\underset{\sim}{p}$. Also, if n_T is even (odd) then E{N} using (R^*, S^*, T^*) with

$n = n_T/2$ ($n = (n_T+1)/2$) is smaller (smaller except when $p_1 = p_2 = 0$) than that obtained using the N-S procedures with n_T, uniformly in $\underset{\sim}{p}$. See Büringer, Martin and Schriever [14], p. 262, for further comments. Also see Pradhan and Sathe [42], [44].

c) Bofinger [12] proposed a variant of a PW sampling rule with *curtailment* which is applicable to the Bernoulli selection problem for $k \geqq 2$. She considered our Goal I, her "best" populations being the ones associated with $\{p_{[1]}, p_{[2]}, \ldots, p_{[k-s]}\}$. (Her PW corresponds to our play-the-loser.) Bofinger's procedure achieves the same P{CS} uniformly in $\underset{\sim}{p}$ as does (R_{SS}, T_{SS}) which uses the same n-value, and hence also as does (R, S^*, T^*). It would appear that *generalized* $(\bar{R}^*, S^*, T^*)$ would have smaller E{N} than that of Bofinger's procedure, at least for $s = k-1$ when $p_{[k]} + p_{[k-1]} < 1$. (See our Conjecture 7.1.) However, we have made no computations to verify this assertion.

8.2 *Procedures Having Different* P{CS} *from* (R^*, S^*, T^*)

a) Sobel and Weiss [58] proposed open sequential procedures for $k \geqq 2$ employing VT and several PW sampling rules all of which employed a stopping rule based on inverse sampling. All of the Sobel-Weiss (S-W) procedures stopped sampling as soon as any population produced r successes. The constant r was chosen to guarantee the $\{\Delta^*, P^*\}$ probability requirement, and was shown to have the same value for all of their procedures. (Berry and Young [11] proved that these procedures using the same r achieved the same P{CS} uniformly in $\underset{\sim}{p}$.) However, if r of the S-W procedures and n of the Sobel-Huyett (S-H) procedure were chosen to guarantee the *same* $\{\Delta^*, P^*\}$ requirement, then the P{CS} achieved by these procedures is *not* the same uniformly in $\underset{\sim}{p}$. If (R^*, S^*, T^*) is used with the S-H n, then from Theorem 5.1 we have that the P{CS} achieved by (R^*, S^*, T^*) and (R_{SS}, T_{SS}) is the same uniformly in $\underset{\sim}{p}$, but this P{CS} differs from that of the S-W procedures which use the corresponding r. This fact makes it difficult to compare the E{N} - values for (R^*, S^*, T^*) with those of the S-W procedures.

If $p_{[1]} \to 1$ then the S-W procedures which use one-at-a-time sampling have smaller E{N} than does the corresponding (R^*, S^*, T^*). However, if $p_{[k]} \to 0$ then $E\{N\} \to \infty$ for the S-W procedures while $N \leq kn-1$ for (R^*, S^*, T^*).

b) Berry and Sobel [10] proposed a closed sequential procedure for k = 2 employing a PW sampling rule. Sampling stops when either population produces r successes or both produce at least c failures. The constants (r,c) were chosen to guarantee the $\{\Delta^*, P^*\}$ requirement; Berry and Sobel (B-S) recommend the choice r = c as optimal. As with the S-W procedure, the B-S procedure has a P{CS} - function which differs from that of (R_{SS}, T_{SS}) if r = c and n are chosen to guarantee the same $\{\Delta^*, P^*\}$ requirement. A fortiori the B-S procedure has a different P{CS} - function than does (R^*, S^*, T^*) which uses the n of (R_{SS}, T_{SS}).

The B-S procedure has very desirable E{N} behavior relative to that of (R^*, S^*, T^*), but less desirable P{CS} behavior. When we determined n and r corresponding to the nine (Δ^*, P^*) combinations for $\Delta^* = 0.1, 0.2, 0.3$ and $P^* = 0.90, 0.95, 0.99$ and set $p_{[2]} - p_{[1]} = \Delta^*$ with $p_{[2]}$ varying we found that $E\{N|(B\text{-}S)\} < E\{N|(R^*, S^*, T^*)\}$ except in a small neighborhood of $(p_{[1]}, p_{[2]}) = (1/2-\Delta^*/2, 1/2+\Delta^*/2)$ where $P\{CS|(R^*, S^*, T^*)\}$ achieves its minimum in the preference zone. (*Note:* $P\{CS|(B\text{-}S)\}$ achieves its minimum in the preference zone at $(p_{[1]}, p_{[2]}) = (1/3-\Delta^*/2, 1/3 + \Delta^*/2)$ and at $(2/3 - \Delta^*/2, 2/3 + \Delta^*/2)$; this result is an asymptotic ($P^* \to 1$) one.) However, $P\{CS|(B\text{-}S)\} < P\{CS|(R^*, S^*, T^*)\}$ except in approximately this same small neighborhood. Thus it appears that the decrease in E{N} for B-S is purchased at the cost of a decrease in P{CS}. (Small changes in P{CS} result in large changes in E{N} when the P{CS} is close to unity.) We also found that $\max\{N|(B\text{-}S)\} > \max\{N|(R^*, S^*, T^*)\}$ for most $\{\Delta^*, P^*\}$ of interest.

c) Schriever [49] generalized the B-S procedure to k > 2. His procedure which employs a PW sampling rule stops sampling when any population produces r successes or every population produces at least c failures. The constants (r,c) are chosen to guarantee the $\{\Delta^*, P^*\}$ requirement; Schriever too recommended the choice $r = c$ as optimal. At this time we do not have sufficient exact calculations to compare the performance of Schriever's procedure with that of (R^*, S^*, T^*) for $k > 2$.

ACKNOWLEDGMENT

The writers are pleased to acknowledge the constructive suggestions of Professors V. G. Kulkarni, T. J. Santner and A. C. Tamhane.

NOTE ADDED IN PROOF

Additional references, [66]-[71], came to our attention after the writing of the paper. We are indebted to Professors Levin and Robbins for making a preliminary copy of their paper [67] available to us, and to a referee for suggesting Robbins [68]. Professor Sugimura kindly sent us copies of references [66], [69], [70] and [71]. Additional references published in Japanese journals are cited in Büringer, H., Martin, H. and Schriever, K-H [14].

APPENDIX: *Proof of Theorem* 5.1

We shall prove Theorem 5.1 for the case $s = 1$; the proof for $s > 1$ proceeds in a similar manner. In this Appendix we denote $p_{[i]}$ by p_i, i.e., $p_1 \leqq p_2 \leqq \cdots \leqq p_k$ are the ordered p's. For $0 \leqq m \leqq kn$ define

$$\Omega_m^n = \{x_m = (y_{1,m}, n_{1,m}; \ldots; y_{k,m}, n_{k,m}):\ 0 \leqq y_{i,m} \leqq n_{i,m},$$

$$\sum_{i=1}^{k} n_{i,m} = m\}$$

where $y_{i,m}$ and $n_{i,m}$ are the number of successes and number of observations, respectively, from π_i through stage m ($1 \leq i \leq k$). (Here π_i has probability of success p_i.) To emphasize the dependence of $y_{i,m}$ and $n_{i,m}$ on x_m we shall use the notation:

$$y_i(x_m) = y_{i,m}, \; n_i(x_m) = n_{i,m} \quad (1 \leq i \leq k).$$

For $0 \leq m \leq kn$ define the set of stopping states at stage m by

$$S_m^n = \{x_m \in \Omega_m^n: \exists \, i \text{ s.t. } y_i(x_m) \geq y_j(x_m)+n-n_j(x_m) \;\; \forall j \neq i\}$$

and the set of continuation states at stage m by $C_m^n = \Omega_m^n \setminus S_m^n$. Let

$$S^n = \bigcup_{m=0}^{kn} S_m^n \text{ and } C^n = \bigcup_{m=0}^{kn} C_m^n.$$

Define the probability of reaching state x_m along any feasible path using sampling rule R by

$$P_R(x_m) = a_R(x_m)P(x_m)$$

where

$$P(x_m) = \prod_{i=1}^{k} p_i^{y_i(x_m)} (1-p_i)^{n_i(x_m)-y_i(x_m)}$$

and $a_R(x_m)$ is the randomization coefficient employed by R. If it is not possible to reach state x_m using R, then it is clear that $P_R(x_m) = 0$. In this situation define $a_R(x_m) = 0$. Note that $a_R(x_m)$ depends only on the rule R and in particular is independent of the p_i's; $a_R(x_m)$ can and usually does depend on the data.

Example A.1. Suppose that R is PW for k = 2 with the following modification: if at any stage the number of successes and failures is the same for both populations, then take the next observation from one of them at random.

Let $n = 4$, $x_5 = (2,3;\ 1,2)$. It is possible to reach state x_5 along different sampling paths; two such paths are:
$s_1 = S_2^1\ F_2^2\ S_1^3\ S_1^4\ F_1^5$ and $s_2 = S_1^1\ F_1^2\ S_2^3\ F_2^4\ S_1^5$.
Now,

(A.1) $$P\{\text{reaching state } x_5 \text{ along } s_1\}$$

$$= \frac{1}{2}\, p_2(1-p_2)p_1^2(1-p_1) = \frac{1}{2}\, P(x_5)$$

and

(A.2) $$P\{\text{reaching state } x_5 \text{ along } s_2\}$$

$$= \frac{1}{2}\, p_1(1-p_1)p_2(1-p_2)\frac{1}{2}\, p_1 = \frac{1}{4}\, P(x_5).$$

Thus we see that for the particular paths of our example the coefficients in (A.1) and (A.2), above, depend on the sampling rule R and the path followed. For any particular R, $a_R(x_m)$ is the sum of *all* such coefficients. To illustrate this latter point consider the following example.

Example A.2. Let $R = R_{SS}$. Here

$$P_R(x_{kn}) = a_R(x_{kn})P(x_{kn})$$

where

$$P(x_{kn}) = \prod_{i=1}^{k} p_i^{y_i(x_{kn})}(1-p_i)^{n-y_i(x_{kn})}$$

and

$$a_R(x_{kn}) = \prod_{i=1}^{k} \binom{n}{y_i(x_{kn})}\ .$$

Let $K = \{1,2,\ldots,k\}$ and $A \subseteq K$, $A \neq \emptyset$. Let W_A denote the set of all stopping states, x_{kn}, which would lead to selection at random from the populations in A, using (R_{SS}, T_{SS}), i.e.,

$$W_A = \{x_{kn} \in \Omega_{kn}^n : y_i(x_{kn}) = \max_{1 \leqq j \leqq k} y_j(x_{kn}) \ \forall\, i \in A$$

$$y_i(x_{kn}) < \max_{1 \leqq j \leqq k} y_j(x_{kn}) \ \forall\, i \notin A\}.$$

Next let V_A denote the set of all stopping states, x_m, which for some m lead to selection at random from the populations in A, using (R,S^*,T^*), i.e.,

$$V_A = \{x_m \in S_m^n (1 \leqq m \leqq kn): y_i(x_m) \geqq y_j(x_m) + n - n_j(x_m)$$

$$\forall\, j \neq i \quad \text{iff} \quad i \in A\}.$$

Let $x_m \in \Omega_m^n$ $(0 \leqq m \leqq kn)$ and $x_{kn} \in \Omega_{kn}^n$. We will say that $x_m \subset x_{kn}$ if it is possible to augment x_m by the remaining observations which have not yet been taken to obtain x_{kn}, i.e., if

$$0 \leqq y_j(x_{kn}) - y_j(x_m) \leqq n - n_j(x_m) \quad (1 \leqq j \leqq k).$$

Example A.3. Let k = 2, n = 2 and suppose that $x_2 = (0,1;\ 1,1) \in \Omega_2^2$, and $x_4 = (1,2;\ 1,2) \in \Omega_4^2$. Then $x_2 \subset x_4$ since

$$0 \leqq y_j(x_4) - y_j(x_2) \leqq 2 - n_j(x_2) \quad (j = 1,2).$$

Let $x_m \subset x_{kn}$. Define the 'difference' between the original state and the augmented state by

$$d(x_m,x_{kn}) = \{y_1(d(x_m,x_{kn})),n_1(d(x_m,x_{kn}));\ldots;$$

$$\ldots;y_k(d(x_m,x_{kn})),n_k(d(x_m,x_{kn}))\}$$

where

$$\begin{cases} y_j(d(x_m,x_{kn})) = y_j(x_{kn}) - y_j(x_m) \\ \\ n_j(d(x_m,x_{kn})) = n - n_j(x_m) \end{cases} \qquad (1 \leqq j \leqq k).$$

Thus,

$$P(d(x_m,x_{kn}))=\prod_{i=1}^{k} p_i^{y_i(x_{kn})-y_i(x_m)}(1-p_i)^{n-n_i(x_m)-y_i(x_{kn})+y_i(x_m)}$$

and

$$\text{(A.3)}\qquad P(x_m)P(d(x_m,x_{kn})) = \prod_{i=1}^{k} p_i^{y_i(x_{kn})}(1-p_i)^{n-y_i(x_{kn})} = P(x_{kn}).$$

Since p_k is the largest of the p's and $k \in A$ implies correct selection with probability $1/|A|$, we can write

$$\text{(A.4)}\qquad P\{CS|(R_{SS},T_{SS})\} = \sum_{A:\ A\subseteq K,\ k\in A}\ \sum_{x_{kn}\in W_A} \frac{1}{|A|} P_{R_{SS}}(x_{kn})$$

and

$$\text{(A.5)}\qquad P\{CS|(R,S^*,T^*)\} = \sum_{A:\ A\subseteq K,\ k\in A}\ \sum_{x_m\in V_A} \frac{1}{|A|} P_R(x_m).$$

For $x_m \in S_m^n$ let $E^n(x_m)$ denote the set of all possible augmentations x_{kn} of x_m, i.e.,

$$E^n(x_m) = \{x_{kn} \in \Omega_{kn}^n:\ x_m \subset x_{kn}\}.$$

To prove Theorem 5.1 we shall use the following lemmas.

LEMMA A.1. *Let* $x_m \in S_m^n$. *Then,*

$$\sum_{x_{kn}\in E^n(x_m)} \prod_{i=1}^{k} \binom{n-n_i(x_m)}{y_i(x_{kn})-y_i(x_m)} P(d(x_m,x_{kn})) = 1.$$

Proof. When we consider all possible augmentations of x_m we have k independent binomial distributions with parameters $(n-n_i(x_m),p_i)$ $(1 \leq i \leq k)$. Hence, l.h.s.

$$= \sum_{y_1=0}^{n-n_1(x_m)} \cdots \sum_{y_k=0}^{n-n_k(x_m)} \prod_{i=1}^{k} \binom{n-n_i(x_m)}{y_i} p_i^{y_i}(1-p_i)^{n-n_i(x_m)-y_i}$$

$$= \prod_{i=1}^{k} \sum_{y_i=0}^{n-n_i(x_m)} \binom{n-n_i(x_m)}{y_i} p_i^{y_i}(1-p_i)^{n-n_i(x_m)-y_i}$$

$$= 1.$$

LEMMA A.2. *Let* $x_m \in V_A$ *and suppose that* $x_m \subset x_{kn}$. *Then* $x_{kn} \in \bigcup_{B \supseteq A} W_B$. *In other words, if* x_m *is a stopping state using R which leads to selection among the populations in* A, *then if* x_m *is augmented to obtain* x_{kn}, *we will at most randomize among the elements of a superset of* A.

Proof. $x_m \in V_A$

$$\Rightarrow y_i(x_m) \geqq y_j(x_m) + (n-n_j(x_m)) \ \forall\, j \neq i, \ \forall\, i \in A.$$

Hence, $x_m \subset x_{kn}$

$$\begin{aligned} \Rightarrow y_i(x_{kn}) &\geqq y_i(x_m) \\ &\geqq y_j(x_m) + (n-n_j(x_m)) \ \forall\, j \neq i \\ &\geqq y_j(x_m) + (y_j(x_{kn}) - y_j(x_m)) \\ &= y_j(x_{kn}), \end{aligned}$$

i.e., $y_i(x_{kn}) \geqq y_j(x_{kn}) \quad \forall\, j \neq i, \ \forall\, i \in A$

and possibly for some $i \notin A$. Thus it follows that $y_i(x_{kn}) = \max_{1 \leqq j \leqq k} y_j(x_{kn})$, at least for all $i \in A$. Hence, $x_{kn} \in W_B$ for some $B \supseteq A$. Therefore,

$$x_m \subset x_{kn} \Rightarrow x_{kn} \in \bigcup_{B \supseteq A} W_B. \qquad \square$$

Note. If $x_{kn} \in W_A$ and if $x_m \in S^n$ is s.t. $x_m \subset x_{kn}$ for some m, then $x_m \in \bigcup_{B \subseteq A} V_B$.

LEMMA A.3. *Let* $x_{kn} \in \Omega^n_{kn}$ *and suppose* R *is any sampling rule which takes no more than* n *observations per population. Then,*

$$\sum_{x_m \subset x_{kn},\ x_m \in S^n} a_R(x_m) \prod_{i=1}^{k} \binom{n-n_i(x_m)}{y_i(x_{kn})-y_i(x_m)} = \prod_{i=1}^{k} \binom{n}{y_i(x_{kn})}.$$

Proof. Consider an arbitrary state x_{kn} of outcomes (successes and failures) to which (R_{SS}, T_{SS}) is applied. Also consider the possible stopping states $x_m \subset x_{kn}$. If (R, S^*, T^*) is used instead of (R_{SS}, T_{SS}) for the same x_{kn}, we will stop at some stopping state $x_m \subset x_{kn}$. Clearly,

$$P\{\text{termination using } (R,S^*,T^*) \mid x_{kn} \text{ using } R_{SS}\} = 1$$

$$\Rightarrow \sum_{x_m \subset x_{kn}} \frac{P\{\text{terminate at state } x_m;\ \text{complete } x_m \text{ to } x_{kn}\}}{P_{R_{SS}}(x_{kn})} = 1,$$

i.e.,

$$\sum_{x_m \subset x_{kn}} \frac{P\{\text{terminate at state } x_m\}P\{\text{complete } x_m \text{ to } x_{kn} \mid x_m\}}{P_{R_{SS}}(x_{kn})} = 1,$$

i.e.,

$$\sum_{x_m \subset x_{kn}} \frac{P_R(x_m)\left[\prod_{i=1}^{k} \binom{n-n_i(x_m)}{y_i(x_{kn})-y_i(x_m)} P(d(x_m,x_{kn}))\right]}{P_{R_{SS}}(x_{kn})} = 1,$$

i.e.,

$$\sum_{x_m \subset x_{kn}} \frac{a_R(x_m)P(x_m)\left[\prod_{i=1}^{k} \binom{n-n_i(x_m)}{y_i(x_{kn})-y_i(x_m)} P(d(x_m,x_{kn}))\right]}{\prod_{i=1}^{k} \binom{n}{y_i(x_{kn})} P(x_{kn})} = 1,$$

i.e.,

$$\sum_{x_m \subset x_{kn}} \frac{a_R(x_m) \prod_{i=1}^{k} \binom{n-n_i(x_m)}{y_i(x_{kn})-y_i(x_m)} P(x_m)P(d(x_m,x_{kn}))}{\prod_{i=1}^{k} \binom{n}{y_i(x_{kn})} P(x_{kn})} = 1.$$

Using equation (A.3) we obtain

$$\sum_{x_m \subset x_{kn}} \frac{a_R(x_m) \prod_{i=1}^{k} \binom{n-n_i(x_m)}{y_i(x_{kn})-y_i(x_m)} P(x_{kn})}{\prod_{i=1}^{k} \binom{n}{y_i(x_{kn})} P(x_{kn})} = 1.$$

Thus

$$\sum_{x_m \subset x_{kn}} a_R(x_m) \prod_{i=1}^{k} \binom{n-n_i(x_m)}{y_i(x_{kn})-y_i(x_m)} = \prod_{i=1}^{k} \binom{n}{y_i(x_{kn})}. \qquad \square$$

LEMMA A.4. *Let* $x_{kn} \in W_B$, $k \in B$. *Then,*

$$\text{(A.6)} \qquad \sum_{\substack{A:\ A \subseteq B, \\ k \in A}} \frac{1}{|A|} \sum_{\substack{x_m:\ x_m \subset x_{kn}, \\ x_m \in V_A}} a_R(x_m) \prod_{i=1}^{k} \binom{n-n_i(x_m)}{y_i(x_{kn})-y_i(x_m)}$$

$$= \frac{1}{|B|} \prod_{i=1}^{k} \binom{n}{y_i(x_{kn})}.$$

Proof. If $|B| = 1$, then the lemma is true by Lemma A.3, since $A \subseteq B$, $k \in A \Rightarrow A = B$ and $x_m \subset x_{kn} \Rightarrow x_m \in V_A = V_B$.

Suppose $|B| > 1$.

Let $r \in B$, $r \neq k$. Now, $r,k \in B$ and $x_{kn} \in W_B$

$$\Rightarrow y_r(x_{kn}) = y_k(x_{kn}) = \max_{1 \leq j \leq k} y_j(x_{kn}).$$

Since $y_r(x_{kn}) = y_k(x_{kn})$, and recalling that the pairing of the $p_{[i]}$ with the Π_j $(1 \leq i,j \leq k)$ is completely unknown (and that the populations are tagged in such a way that their ordering is unique), it can be seen that interchanging the labels r and k would lead to the same stopping states contained in x_{kn} with the same randomization coefficients. Thus

$$\text{(A.7)}\qquad \sum_{\substack{A:\ A\subseteq B,\\ k\in\bar{A}}} \frac{1}{|A|} \sum_{\substack{x_m\subset x_{kn},\\ x_m\in V_A}} a_{\mathcal{R}}(x_m) \prod_{i=1}^{k} \binom{n-n_i(x_m)}{y_i(x_{kn})-y_i(x_m)}$$

$$= \sum_{\substack{A:\ A\subseteq B,\\ r\in\bar{A}}} \frac{1}{|A|} \sum_{\substack{x_m\subset x_{kn},\\ x_m\in V_A}} a_{\mathcal{R}}(x_m) \prod_{i=1}^{k} \binom{n-n_i(x_m)}{y_i(x_{kn})-y_i(x_m)} .$$

Hence, the l.h.s. of (A.6)

$$= \frac{1}{|B|} \sum_{r\in B} \sum_{\substack{A:\ A\subseteq B,\\ k\in\bar{A}}} \frac{1}{|A|} \sum_{\substack{x_m\subset x_{kn},\\ x_m\in V_A}} a_{\mathcal{R}}(x_m) \prod_{i=1}^{k} \binom{n-n_i(x_m)}{y_i(x_{kn})-y_i(x_m)}$$

which using (A.7)

$$= \frac{1}{|B|} \sum_{r\in B} \sum_{\substack{A:\ A\subseteq B,\\ r\in\bar{A}}} \frac{1}{|A|} \sum_{\substack{x_m\subset x_{kn},\\ x_m\in V_A}} a_{\mathcal{R}}(x_m) \prod_{i=1}^{k} \binom{n-n_i(x_m)}{y_i(x_{kn})-y_i(x_m)}.$$

The above equals

$$\frac{1}{|B|} \sum_{A:\ A\subseteq B} \sum_{r\in A} \frac{1}{|A|} \sum_{\substack{x_m\subset x_{kn},\\ x_m\in V_A}} a_{\mathcal{R}}(x_m) \prod_{i=1}^{k} \binom{n-n_i(x_m)}{y_i(x_{kn})-y_i(x_m)}$$

$$= \frac{1}{|B|} \sum_{A:\ A\subseteq B} \sum_{\substack{x_m\subset x_{kn},\\ x_m\in V_A}} a_{\mathcal{R}}(x_m) \prod_{i=1}^{k} \binom{n-n_i(x_m)}{y_i(x_{kn})-y_i(x_m)}$$

$$= \frac{1}{|B|} \sum_{x_m\subset x_{kn}} a_{\mathcal{R}}(x_m) \prod_{i=1}^{k} \binom{n-n_i(x_m)}{y_i(x_{kn})-y_i(x_m)}$$

by the note following Lemma A.2,

$$= \frac{1}{|B|} \prod_{i=1}^{k} \binom{n}{y_i(x_{kn})}$$

by Lemma A.3.

We now proceed with our proof of Theorem 5.1.

Proof. From equation (A.5) we have

$$P\{CS|(\mathcal{R},\mathcal{S}^*,\mathcal{T}^*)\} = \sum_{\substack{A:\ A\subseteq K,\\ k\in \bar{A}}} \frac{1}{|A|} \sum_{x_m\in V_A} P_{\mathcal{R}}(x_m)$$

$$= \sum_{\substack{A:\ A\subseteq K,\\ k\in \bar{A}}} \frac{1}{|A|} \sum_{x_m\in V_A} a_{\mathcal{R}}(x_m)P(x_m).$$

Using Lemma A.1 we can write

$$P\{CS|(\mathcal{R},\mathcal{S}^*,\mathcal{T}^*)\} = \sum_{\substack{A:\ A\subseteq K,\\ k\in \bar{A}}} \frac{1}{|A|} \sum_{x_m\in V_A} a_{\mathcal{R}}(x_m)P(x_m) \sum_{x_{kn}\in E^n(x_m)}$$

$$\times \left\{ \prod_{i=1}^{k} \binom{n-n_i(x_m)}{y_i(x_{kn})-y_i(x_m)} P(d(x_m,x_{kn})) \right\}$$

$$= \sum_{\substack{A:\ A\subseteq K,\\ k\in \bar{A}}} \frac{1}{|A|} \sum_{x_m\in V_A} a_{\mathcal{R}}(x_m) \sum_{B:\ B\subseteq K} \sum_{\substack{x_{kn}\in W_B,\\ x_{kn}\supset x_m}}$$

$$\times \left\{ \prod_{i=1}^{k} \binom{n-n_i(x_m)}{y_i(x_{kn})-y_i(x_m)} P(x_m)P(d(x_m,x_{kn})) \right\}.$$

As a consequence of Lemma A.2 the l.h.s. equals

$$\sum_{\substack{A:\ A\subseteq K,\\ k\in \bar{A}}} \frac{1}{|A|} \sum_{x_m\in V_A} a_{\mathcal{R}}(x_m) \sum_{B:\ A\subseteq B} \sum_{\substack{x_{kn}\in W_B\\ x_{kn}\supset x_m}}$$

$$\times \left\{ \prod_{i=1}^{k} \binom{n-n_i(x_m)}{y_i(x_{kn})-y_i(x_m)} P(x_m)P(d(x_m,x_{kn})) \right\}$$

which using equation (A.3) can be written as

$$= \sum_{\substack{A:\ A \subseteq K,\\ k \in \bar{A}}} \frac{1}{|A|} \sum_{x_m \in V_A} a_{\mathcal{R}}(x_m) \sum_{B:\ A \subseteq B} \sum_{\substack{x_{kn} \in W_B,\\ x_{kn} \supset x_m}}$$

$$\times \left\{ \prod_{i=1}^{k} \binom{n-n_i(x_m)}{y_i(x_{kn})-y_i(x_m)} P(x_{kn}) \right\}$$

$$= \sum_{\substack{B:\ B \subseteq K\\ k \in \bar{B}}} \sum_{x_{kn} \in W_B} \sum_{\substack{A:\ A \subseteq B,\\ k \in \bar{A}}} \sum_{\substack{x_m:\ x_m \subset x_{kn},\\ x_m \in V_A}} \frac{1}{|A|} a_{\mathcal{R}}(x_m)$$

$$\times \left\{ \prod_{i=1}^{k} \binom{n-n_i(x_m)}{y_i(x_{kn})-y_i(x_m)} P(x_{kn}) \right\}$$

$$= \sum_{\substack{B:\ B \subseteq K\\ k \in \bar{B}}} \sum_{x_{kn} \in W_B} P(x_{kn}) \sum_{\substack{A:\ A \subseteq B\\ k \in \bar{A}}} \frac{1}{|A|} \sum_{\substack{x_m:\ x_m \subset x_{kn},\\ x_m \in V_A}} a_{\mathcal{R}}(x_m)$$

$$\times \prod_{i=1}^{k} \binom{n-n_i(x_m)}{y_i(x_{kn})-y_i(x_m)}.$$

Finally, using Lemma A.4, this reduces to

$$\sum_{\substack{B:\ B \subseteq K,\\ k \in \bar{B}}} \sum_{x_{kn} \in W_B} P(x_{kn}) \frac{1}{|B|} \prod_{i=1}^{k} \binom{n}{y_i(x_{kn})}$$

$$= \sum_{\substack{B:\ B \subseteq K,\\ k \in \bar{B}}} \frac{1}{|B|} \sum_{x_{kn} \in W_B} P_{\mathcal{R}_{SS}}(x_{kn}) = P\{CS \mid (\mathcal{R}_{SS}, \mathcal{T}_{SS})\}. \qquad \square$$

REFERENCES

[1] Alam, K. and Thompson, J. R. (1972). On selecting the least probable multinomial event. *Ann. Math. Statist. 43*, 1981-1990.

[2] Anscombe, F. J. (1963). Sequential medical trials. *J. Amer. Statist. Assoc. 58*, 365-383.

[3] Armitage, P. (1960,1975). *Sequential Medical Trials.* Wiley, New York.

[4] Bechhofer, R. E. (1954). A single-sample multiple decision procedure for ranking means of normal populations with known variances. *Ann. Math. Statist. 25*, 16-39.

[5] Bechhofer, R. E., Elmaghraby, S. and Morse, N. (1959). A single-sample multiple decision procedure for selecting the multinomial event which has the highest probability. *Ann. Math. Statist. 30*, 102-119.

[6] Bechhofer, R. E., Kiefer, J. and Sobel, M. (1968). *Sequential Identification and Ranking Procedures.* The University of Chicago Press, Chicago.

[7] Bechhofer, R. E. and Kulkarni, R. V. (1981). Closed sequential procedures for selecting the multinomial events which have the largest probabilities. In preparation.

[8] Berry, D. A. (1972). A Bernoulli two-armed bandit. *Ann. Math. Statist. 43*, 871-897.

[9] Berry, D. A. (1978). Modified two-armed bandit strategies for certain clinical trials. *J. Amer. Statist. Assoc. 73*, 339-345.

[10] Berry, D. A. and Sobel, M. (1973). An improved procedure for selecting the better of two binomial populations. *J. Amer. Statist. Assoc. 68*, 979-984.

[11] Berry, D. A. and Young, D. H. (1977). A note on inverse sampling procedures for selecting the best binomial population. *Ann. Statist. 5*, 235-236.

[12] Bofinger, E. (1978). Selection using "Play-the-winner" sampling for non-negative observations. *Comm. Statist. A-Theory Methods A7(15)*, 1489-1499.

[13] Bradt, R. N., Johnson, S. M. and Karlin, S. (1956). On sequential designs for maximizing the sum of n observations. *Ann. Math. Statist.* *27*, 1060-1074.

[14] Büringer, H., Martin, H. and Schriever, K-H. (1980). *Nonparametric Sequential Selection Procedures.* Birkhauser, Basel, Boston, Stuttgart.

[15] Canner, P. L. (1970). Selecting one of two treatments when the responses are dichotomous. *J. Amer. Statist. Assoc.* *65*, 293-306.

[16] Colton, T. (1963). A model for selecting one of two medical treatments. *J. Amer. Statist. Assoc.* *58*, 388-400.

[17] Cornfield, J., Halperin, M. and Greenhouse, S. W. (1969). An adaptive procedure for sequential clinical trials. *J. Amer. Statist. Assoc.* *64*, 759-770.

[18] Fabius, J. and van Zwet, W. R. (1970). Some remarks on the two-armed bandit. *Ann. Math. Statist.* *41*, 1906-1916.

[19] Feldman, D. (1962). Contributions to the two-armed bandit problem. *Ann. Math. Statist.* *33*, 847-856.

[20] Fushimi, M. (1973). An improved version of a Sobel-Weiss play-the-winner procedure for selecting the better of two binomial populations. *Biometrika* *60*, 517-523.

[21] Gibbons, J. D., Olkin, I. and Sobel, M. (1977). *Selecting and Ordering Populations.* Wiley, New York.

[22] Gupta, S. S. (1956). On a decision rule for a problem in ranking means. Ph.D. Thesis (Mimeo Ser. No. 150), Institute of Statist., Univ. of North Carolina, Chapel Hill.

[23] Gupta, S. S., Huyett, M. J. and Sobel, M. (1957). Selection and ranking problems with binomial populations. *Transactions of the American Society for Quality Control*, 635-643.

[24] Gupta, S. S. and Sobel, M. (1960). Selecting a subset containing the best of several populations. *Contributions to Probability and Statistics*, I. Olkin et al (eds.). Stanford University Press, Stanford, California, 224-248.

[25] Gupta, S. S. and Panchapakesan, S. (1979). *Multiple Decision Procedures: Theory and Methodology of Selecting and Ranking Populations.* Wiley, New York.

[26] Hall, W. J. (1959). The most economical character of Bechhofer and Sobel decision rules. *Ann. Math. Statist.* *30*, 964-969.

[27] Hoel, D. G. (1972). An inverse stopping rule for play-the-winner sampling. *J. Amer. Statist. Assoc.* *67*, 148-151.

[28] Hoel, D. G. and Sobel, M. (1972). Comparison of sequential procedures for selecting the best binomial population. *Proceedings of the Sixth Berkeley Symposium on Mathematical Statistics and Probability*, L. LeCam, J. Neyman and E. L. Scott (eds.). University of California Press, Berkeley, 53-69.

[29] Hoel, D. G., Sobel, M. and Weiss, G. H. (1972). A two-stage procedure for choosing the better of two binomial populations. *Biometrika* *59*, 317-322.

[30] Hoel, D. G., Sobel, M. and Weiss, G. H. (1975). Comparison of sampling methods for choosing the best binomial population with delayed observations. *J. Statist. Comput. Simulation* *3*, 299-313.

[31] Hoel, D. G., Sobel, M. and Weiss, G. H. (1975). A survey of adaptive sampling for clinical trials. *Perspectives in Biometry*, R. M. Elashoff (ed.). Academic Press, New York, 29-61.

[32] Hoel, D. G. and Weiss, G. H. (1975). A clinical trial design with a fixed maximum number of failures. *Comm. Statist.* *4(5)*, 429-436.

[33] Isbell, J. (1959). On a problem of Robbins. *Ann. Math. Statist.* *30*, 606-610.

[34] Kiefer, J. E. and Weiss, G. H. (1971). A truncated test for choosing the better of two binomial populations. *J. Amer. Statist. Assoc.* *66*, 867-871.

[35] Kiefer, J. E. and Weiss, G. H. (1974). Truncated version of a play-the-winner rule for choosing the better of two binomial populations. *J. Amer. Statist. Assoc.* *69*, 807-809.

[36] Kulkarni, R. V. (1981). Closed adaptive sequential procedures for selecting the best of $k \geq 2$ Bernoulli populations. Unpublished Ph.D. dissertation, Cornell University, Ithaca, New York.

[37] Nebenzahl, E. and Sobel, M. (1972). Play-the-winner sampling for a fixed sample size binomial selection problem. *Biometrika* *59*, 1-8.

[38] Nordbrook, E. (1976). An improved play-the-winner sampling procedure for selecting the better of two binomial populations. *J. Amer. Statist. Assoc. 71*, 137-139.

[39] Nordbrook, E. (1976). A sequential design for binomial clinical trails. *Comm. Statist. A-Theory Methods* A5(*15*), 1469-1478.

[40] Paulson, E. (1967). Sequential procedures for selecting the best one of several binomial populations. *Ann. Math. Statist. 38*, 117-123.

[41] Paulson, E. (1969). A new sequential procedure for selecting the best one of k binomial populations (Abstract), *Ann. Math. Statist. 40*, 1865-1866.

[42] Pradhan, M. and Sathe, Y. S. (1973). Play-the-winner sampling for a fixed sample size with curtailment. *Biometrika 60*, 424-427.

[43] Pradhan, M. and Sathe, Y. S. (1974). Equivalence between fixed sample size rule and Hoel's inverse sampling rule for play-the-winner. *J. Amer. Statist. Assoc. 69*, 475-476.

[44] Pradhan, M. and Sathe, Y. S. (1976). Modification of fixed even sample-size procedure for play-the-winner. *Comm. Statist. A-Theory Methods* A5(*4*), 365-371.

[45] Rabie, M. (1978). Selecting the better of two binomial populations. Unpublished M.S. thesis, Cornell University, Ithaca, New York.

[46] Robbins, H. (1952). Some aspects of the sequential design of experiments. *Bull. Amer. Math. Soc. 58*, 527-535.

[47] Robbins, H. (1956). A sequential design problem with a finite memory. *Proc. Nat. Acad. Sci. U.S.A. 42*, 920-923.

[48] Rodman, L. (1978). On the many-armed bandit problem. *Ann. Prob. 6*, 491-498.

[49] Schriever, K-H. (1978/79). A truncated play-the-winner procedure for selecting the best of $k \geq 3$ binomial populations. *Bull. Math. Statist.* (*Fukuoka*) *18*, No. 1-2, 21-23.

[50] Schriever, K-H. (1979). A truncated vector-at-a-time procedure with a symmetrical stopping-rule for selecting the better of two binomial populations. *Rep. Statist. Appl. Res. Un. Japan. Sci. Engrs.* 26, 6-10.

[51] Simon, R. and Weiss, G. H. (1975). A class of adaptive sampling schemes for selecting the better of two binomial populations. *J. Statist. Comput. Simulation* 4, 37-47.

[52] Simon, R., Weiss, G. H. and Hoel, D. G. (1975). Sequential analysis of binomial clinical trials. *Biometrika* 62, 195-200.

[53] Smith, C. V. and Pyke, R. (1965). The Robbins-Isbell two-armed bandit problem with finite memory. *Ann. Math. Statist.* 36, 1375-1386.

[54] Sobel, M. and Huyett, M. J. (1957). Selecting the best one of several binomial populations. *Bell System Tech. J.* 36, 537-576.

[55] Sobel, M. and Weiss, G. H. (1970). Play-the-winner sampling for selecting the better of two binomial populations. *Biometrika* 57, 357-365.

[56] Sobel, M. and Weiss, G. H. (1971). A comparison of play-the-winner and vector-at-a-time sampling for selecting the better of two binomial populations with restricted parameter values. *Trabajos Estadist. Investigacion Oper.* 22, 195-206.

[57] Sobel, M. and Weiss, G. H. (1971). Play-the-Winner rule and inverse sampling in selecting the better of two binomial populations. *J. Amer. Statist. Assoc.* 66, 545-551.

[58] Sobel, M. and Weiss, G. H. (1972). Play-the-winner rule and inverse sampling for selecting the best of $k \geqq 3$ binomial populations. *Ann. Math. Statist.* 43, 1808-1826.

[59] Sobel, M. and Weiss, G. H. (1972). Recent results on using the play-the-winner sampling rule with binomial selection problems. *Proceedings of the Sixth Berkeley Symposium on Mathematical Statistics and Probability*, L. LeCam, J. Neyman and E. L. Scott (eds.). University of California Press, Berkeley, 717-736.

[60] Taheri, H. and Young, D. H. (1974). A comparison of sequential sampling procedures for selecting the better of two binomial populations. *Biometrika* 61, 585-592.

[61] Tamhane, A. C. (1980). Selecting the better Bernoulli treatment using a matched samples design. *J. Roy. Statist. Soc. Ser. B.* 42, 26-30.

[62] Tamhane, A. C. (1981). A curtailed sampling procedure and a sequential procedure for selecting the better Bernoulli treatment using a matched samples design. Submitted for publication.

[63] Thionet, P. (1975). Contribution to the study of "play-the-winner" sequential selection procedure. *Proceedings of the 40th Session of the International Statistical Institute 4*, 392-395.

[64] Wei, L. J. and Durham, S. (1978). The randomized play-the-winner rule in medical trials. *J. Amer. Statist. Assoc. 73*, 840-843.

[65] Zelen, M. (1969). Play the winner rule and the controlled clinical trial. *J. Amer. Statist. Assoc. 64*, 131-146.

[66] Asano, C., Jojima, K. and Sugimura, M. (1977). Extended versions of sequential optimum selection plan with play-the-winner sampling and the stopping rules in a finite population. *Res. Inst. Fund. Inform. Sci. Res. Rep. 69*, 1-17.

[67] Levin, B. and Robbins, H. (1981). Selecting the highest probability in binomial or multinomial trials. Submitted for publication in *Proc. Nat. Acad. Sci. U.S.A.*

[68] Robbins, H. (1974). A sequential test for two binomial populations. *Proc. Nat. Acad. Sci. U.S.A. 71*, 4435-4436.

[69] Sugimura, M. and Asano, C. (1978). Selecting the best one of several treatments. *Rep. Fac. Engrg. Oita Univ. 4*, 59-68.

[70] Sugimura, M., Suesada, S. and Asano, C. (1975). A certain truncated sequential design based on Markov chains for selecting one of two medical treatments. *Rep. Fac. Engrg. Oita Univ. 1*, 43-53.

[71] Sugimura, M., Suesada, S. and Asano, C. (1976). Truncated and untruncated sequential designs based on Markov chains for selecting one of two treatments. *Rep. Fac. Engrg. Oita Univ. 2*, 37-56.

ESTIMATION IN CONTINUOUS EXPONENTIAL FAMILIES: BAYESIAN ESTIMATION SUBJECT TO RISK RESTRICTIONS AND INADMISSIBILITY RESULTS[1]

James Berger

Department of Statistics
Purdue University
West Lafayette, Indiana, U.S.A.

I. INTRODUCTION

Suppose we observe $\underset{\sim}{X} = (X_1,\ldots,X_p)$, where the X_i are independent and have positive densities

$$f_i(x_i|\theta_i) = \beta_i(\theta_i)t_i(x_i)e^{\theta_i x_i}$$

with respect to Lebesgue measure on $\mathcal{X}_i \subset R^1$. It is desired to estimate $\underset{\sim}{\theta} = (\theta_1,\ldots,\theta_p)$ where the loss in estimating $\underset{\sim}{\theta}$ by an estimate

$$\underset{\sim}{\delta}(\underset{\sim}{x}) = (\delta_1(\underset{\sim}{x}),\ldots,\delta_p(\underset{\sim}{x}))$$

is sum of squares error loss

$$L(\underset{\sim}{\theta},\underset{\sim}{\delta}) = \sum_{i=1}^{p}(\theta_i-\delta_i(\underset{\sim}{x}))^2.$$

The parameter space will be taken to be the natural parameter space, i.e.

$$\Theta = \{\underset{\sim}{\theta} = (\theta_1,\ldots,\theta_p): \int_{\mathcal{X}_i} t_i(x_i)e^{\theta_i x_i}dx_i < \infty \text{ for } i=1,\ldots,p\}.$$

[1]Research supported by the Alfred P. Sloan Foundation and by the National Science Foundation under Grants MCS78-02300A3 and MCS81-01670.

ISBN 0-12-307501-7

An important feature of an estimator $\underset{\sim}{\delta}$ is its risk function (or expected loss)

$$R(\underset{\sim}{\theta},\underset{\sim}{\delta}) = E_{\underset{\sim}{\theta}} L(\underset{\sim}{\theta},\underset{\sim}{\delta}(\underset{\sim}{X})).$$

Two problems of major importance in this simultaneous estimation framework are as follows. Problem I involves classification of inadmissible and admissible estimators, and development of estimators offering significant improvement upon standard estimators that happen to be inadmissible. The most studied example of this is estimation of a multivariate normal mean $\underset{\sim}{\theta}$ in which the usual estimator $\underset{\sim}{\delta}^{o}(\underset{\sim}{x}) = \underset{\sim}{x}$ is inadmissible if $p \geq 3$ (Stein [18]).

Problem II is the problem of robust Bayesian estimation. In Bayesian estimation, a prior distribution (possibly improper) $\pi(d\underset{\sim}{\theta})$ on Θ is determined, and nominally one would want to use the Bayes estimator $\underset{\sim}{\delta}^{\pi}$, defined as that estimator minimizing the Bayes risk

$$r(\pi,\underset{\sim}{\delta}) = E^{\pi} R(\underset{\sim}{\theta},\underset{\sim}{\delta}) = \int R(\underset{\sim}{\theta},\underset{\sim}{\delta})\pi(d\underset{\sim}{\theta})$$

(or more generally minimizing the posterior expected loss). The determination of π is often very inexact, however, and hence it is important to consider the robustness (with respect to the specification of π) of the estimator selected. A general discussion of Bayesian robustness is given in Berger [3], in which it is argued that good measures of robustness can be obtained from $R(\underset{\sim}{\theta},\underset{\sim}{\delta})$. If, for example, a minimax estimator $\underset{\sim}{\delta}^{o}$ is the classical estimator for a problem, then if one restricts consideration to estimators satisfying

$$R(\underset{\sim}{\theta},\underset{\sim}{\delta}) \leq R(\underset{\sim}{\theta},\underset{\sim}{\delta}^{o}) + C, \tag{1.1}$$

it will be ensured that $r(\pi,\underset{\sim}{\delta}) \leq r(\pi,\underset{\sim}{\delta}^{o}) + C$ no matter how badly the prior distribution is misspecified. One can thus formally state as a Bayesian robustness problem

Problem II*: Select the estimator $\underset{\sim}{\delta}$ which minimizes $r(\pi,\underset{\sim}{\delta})$ subject to (1.1).

At first sight it may seem that the robustness requirement (1.1) is excessively harsh, but it will be seen that (1.1) can often be attained with surprisingly little sacrifice in Bayes risk (compared to the nominally optimal but often nonrobust Bayes estimator $\underset{\sim}{\delta}^{\pi}$). Constraints other than (1.1) may sometimes be more natural. For example, in some problems it may be more reasonable to require that $R(\underset{\sim}{\theta},\underset{\sim}{\delta}) \leq R(\underset{\sim}{\theta},\underset{\sim}{\delta}^{o})(1+C)$.

Problem II* is also frequently crucial in successful resolution of Problem I. This is because, if $\underset{\sim}{\delta}^{o}$ is a "standard" estimator which happens to be inadmissible, then the class of estimators better than $\underset{\sim}{\delta}^{o}$ is precisely the class of estimators satisfying (1.1) with $C = 0$. In selecting among these improved estimators it seems inescapable that prior information must be employed (see Berger [2] and [5]). Hence a reasonable solution would be determine a prior distribution π and solve Problem II* when $C = 0$ in (1.1).

Problem II* has been considered for various situations in Hodges and Lehmann [13], Efron and Morris [11], Shapiro [15] and [16], Bickel [7] and [8], and Berger [4]. Exact mathematical solution is unfortunately very messy. For example, if $\underset{\sim}{X}$ has a normal distribution with identity covariance matrix, so that $\underset{\sim}{\delta}^{o}(\underset{\sim}{X}) = \underset{\sim}{X}$ is the usual estimator, the solution to Problem II* can be typically shown to be a (generalized) Bayes estimator with respect to a prior measure concentrated on a countably infinite number of shells. It is an extremely difficult numerical problem to determine the appropriate shells and their masses, and the resulting estimator is an abdominable mess. For this reason we will consider a slightly modified version of Problem II*, one which is tractable mathematically and yields reasonably simple estimators.

The starting point for the investigation will be Stein's

unbiased estimator of risk, discussed for this setting in Hudson [14] and Berger [1], which leads to the representation

$$(1.2) \qquad R(\underset{\sim}{\theta},\underset{\sim}{\delta}) - R(\underset{\sim}{\theta},\underset{\sim}{\delta}^{o}) = E_{\underset{\sim}{\theta}}[\mathcal{D}\, \underset{\sim}{\delta}(\underset{\sim}{X})],$$

where $\mathcal{D}$ is usually a nonlinear differential operator. The condition (1.1) will clearly be satisfied if

$$(1.3) \qquad \mathcal{D}\, \underset{\sim}{\delta}(\underset{\sim}{x}) \leq C,$$

and so we can formulate

Problem II**: Select the estimator which minimizes $r(\pi,\underset{\sim}{\delta})$ subject to (1.3).

The solutions to Problem II** seem to be very close to the solutions to Problem II*, and their comparative simplicity makes them considerably more attractive from a practical viewpoint.

Analysis in generality of any of the problems mentioned here is extremely difficult, and hence we will consider only various special cases. Section 2 will develop the needed form of the representation (1.2). Section 3 will present some results concerning Problem I, namely classification of inadmissible estimators. Section 4 will give an explicit solution to Problem II** when $\underset{\sim}{X}$ has a spherically symmetric normal distribution. The most important example of the theory in Section 4, namely the analysis when π is a conjugate prior, is presented in Section 5. The resulting estimators will be seen to have the rather startling property (for $p > 1$) of having nearly optimal Bayes risk even when C is very small (i.e., even when the estimators are constrained to have risks which never exceed the risk of the minimax estimator $\underset{\sim}{\delta}^{o}(\underset{\sim}{x}) = \underset{\sim}{x}$ by more than a very small amount.) Section 5 can be understood (for the most part) without having read the previous sections.

II. THE UNBIASED ESTIMATOR OF RISK

We begin by stating some conditions on the densities $f_i(x_i|\theta_i)$ and the estimators that will be considered. These are chosen for convenience of application, and can undoubtedly be generalized. The following notations will be used thoughout the paper:

$$\mathcal{X} = \mathcal{X}_1 \times \mathcal{X}_2 \times \ldots \times \mathcal{X}_p, \quad t(\underset{\sim}{x}) = \prod_{i=1}^{p} t_i(x_i), \tag{2.1}$$

$$\beta(\underset{\sim}{\theta}) = \prod_{i=1}^{p} \beta_i(\theta_i), \quad f(\underset{\sim}{x}|\underset{\sim}{\theta}) = \prod_{i=1}^{p} f_i(x_i|\theta_i) = \beta(\underset{\sim}{\theta})t(\underset{\sim}{x})e^{\underset{\sim}{\theta}\underset{\sim}{x}^t},$$

$$h'(y) = \frac{d}{dy}h(y), \quad h^{(i)}(\underset{\sim}{x}) = \frac{\partial}{\partial x_i}h(\underset{\sim}{x}), \quad h^{(i,j)}(\underset{\sim}{x}) = \frac{\partial^2}{\partial x_i \partial x_j}h(\underset{\sim}{x}),$$

$$\nabla h(\underset{\sim}{x}) = (h^{(1)}(\underset{\sim}{x}),\ldots,h^{(p)}(\underset{\sim}{x})), \quad \nabla^2 h(\underset{\sim}{x}) = \sum_{i=1}^{p} h^{(i,i)}(x),$$

$$\underset{\sim}{\gamma}(\underset{\sim}{x}) = \underset{\sim}{\delta}(\underset{\sim}{x}) - \underset{\sim}{\delta}^o(\underset{\sim}{x}).$$

The estimator $\underset{\sim}{\delta}^o$ is to be thought of as the "standard" estimator or estimator under investigation, and $\underset{\sim}{\delta}$ as a competing estimator.

Condition 1.

(i) The $\mathcal{X}_i$ are (possibly infinite) intervals (a_i,b_i);

(ii) the functions t_i are differentiable and

$E_{\underset{\sim}{\theta}}|\nabla \log t\ (\underset{\sim}{X})|^2 < \infty$;

(iii) $E_\theta|\underset{\sim}{\delta}^o(\underset{\sim}{X})|^2 < \infty$.

Condition 2. For $i = 1,\ldots,p$ and all $\underset{\sim}{\theta} \in \Theta$, γ_i satisfies

(i) except possibly for $(x_1,\ldots,x_{i-1},x_{i+1},\ldots,x_p)$ in a set of probability zero, $\gamma_i(\underset{\sim}{x})$ is a continuous piecewise differentiable function of x_i and

$$\lim_{x_i \to a_i} \{\gamma_i(\underset{\sim}{x}) t_i(x_i) e^{\theta_i x_i}\} = \lim_{x_i \to b_i} \{\gamma_i(\underset{\sim}{x}) t_i(x_i) e^{\theta_i x_i}\} = 0;$$

(ii) $E_\theta[\gamma_i^2(\underset{\sim}{X})] < \infty$ and $E_{\underset{\sim}{\theta}}|\gamma_i^{(i)}(\underset{\sim}{X})| < \infty$.

Condition 3. For some positive differentiable functions m_o and g,

(i) $\underset{\sim}{\delta}^o(\underset{\sim}{x}) = \nabla \log m_o(\underset{\sim}{x}) - \nabla \log t(\underset{\sim}{x})$;

(ii) $\underset{\sim}{\gamma}(\underset{\sim}{x}) = 2\nabla \log g(\underset{\sim}{x})$.

Comment. If $\pi(d\underset{\sim}{\theta})$ is a (generalized) prior distribution on $\bar{\Theta}$ (the closure of Θ) and the marginal density of $\underset{\sim}{X}$, given by

$$m(\underset{\sim}{x}) = t(\underset{\sim}{x}) \int_{\bar{\Theta}} e^{\underset{\sim}{\theta}\underset{\sim}{x}^t} \beta(\underset{\sim}{\theta})\pi(d\underset{\sim}{\theta}), \tag{2.2}$$

is finite, then it is well known that the Bayes estimator of $\underset{\sim}{\theta}$ is

$$\underset{\sim}{\delta}^\pi(\underset{\sim}{x}) = \nabla \log m(\underset{\sim}{x}) - \Delta \log t(\underset{\sim}{x}). \tag{2.3}$$

Furthermore, Berger and Srinivasan [6] show that any admissible estimator must be of this form. Hence the restrictions in Condition 3 are natural.

THEOREM 1. *If Conditions* 1, 2, *and* 3(i) *hold, then*

$$R(\underset{\sim}{\theta},\underset{\sim}{\delta}) - R(\underset{\sim}{\theta},\underset{\sim}{\delta}^o) = E_\theta[2\sum_{i=1}^p \gamma_i^{(i)}(\underset{\sim}{X}) + 2\sum_{i=1}^p \gamma_i(\underset{\sim}{X}) \frac{\partial}{\partial X_i} \log m_o(\underset{\sim}{X}) + \sum_{i=1}^p \gamma_i^2(\underset{\sim}{X})]. \tag{2.4}$$

If, furthermore, Condition 3(ii) *holds, then*

$$R(\underset{\sim}{\theta},\underset{\sim}{\delta}) - R(\underset{\sim}{\theta},\underset{\sim}{\delta}^o) = E_\theta[\frac{4}{g(X)} \mathcal{D}\, g(\underset{\sim}{X})], \tag{2.5}$$

where

$$\mathcal{D}\, g(\underset{\sim}{X}) = \nabla^2 g(\underset{\sim}{X}) + \nabla g(\underset{\sim}{X}) \cdot \nabla \log m_o(\underset{\sim}{X}). \tag{2.6}$$

Proof. Although versions of this theorem are given in Hudson [14] and Berger [1], we sketch the proof under this set of assumptions. Clearly

$$(2.7)\qquad R(\underset{\sim}{\theta},\underset{\sim}{\delta})-R(\underset{\sim}{\theta},\underset{\sim}{\delta}^{o}) = \sum_{i=1}^{p} E_{\theta}[2\gamma_i(\underset{\sim}{X})(\delta_i^{o}(\underset{\sim}{X})-\theta_i)+\gamma_i^2(\underset{\sim}{X})].$$

Now

$$(2.8)\qquad E_{\underset{\sim}{\theta}}[\gamma_i(\underset{\sim}{X})\theta_i] = \int_{\prod_{j\neq i}\mathcal{X}_j} \beta(\underset{\sim}{\theta}) \prod_{j\neq i} [t_j(x_j)e^{\theta_j x_j}]$$

$$\times \int_{a_i}^{b_i} \gamma_i(\underset{\sim}{x})t_i(x_i)\theta_i e^{\theta_i x_i} dx_i \prod_{j\neq i} dx_j.$$

Observe, using Conditions 1 and 2 and the Cauchy-Schwartz inequality, that

$$(2.9)\qquad E_{\underset{\sim}{\theta}}[\frac{1}{t_i(X_i)}|\frac{\partial}{\partial X_i}\{\gamma_i(\underset{\sim}{X})t_i(X_i)\}|]$$

$$= E_{\underset{\sim}{\theta}}|\gamma_i^{(i)}(\underset{\sim}{X})+\gamma_i(\underset{\sim}{X})\frac{d}{dX_i}\log t_i(X_i)|$$

$$\leq E_{\underset{\sim}{\theta}}|\gamma_i^{(i)}(\underset{\sim}{X})| + \{[E_{\underset{\sim}{\theta}}\gamma_i^2(\underset{\sim}{X})][E_{\underset{\sim}{\theta}}(\frac{d}{dX_i}\log t_i(X_i))^2]\}^{1/2}$$

$$< \infty.$$

It further follows from Condition 2 that, with probability one, $\gamma_i(\underset{\sim}{x})t_i(x_i)$ is absolutely continuous on $[c,d]$ for $a_i < c < d < b_i$, which together with (2.9) establishes the validity (with probability one) of the integration by parts

$$\int_c^d \gamma_i(\underset{\sim}{x})t_i(x_i)\theta_i e^{\theta_i x_i} dx_i = \gamma_i(\underset{\sim}{x})t_i(x_i)e^{\theta_i x_i}\Big|_{x_i=c}^{x_i=d}$$

$$- \int_c^d [\gamma_i^{(i)}(\underset{\sim}{x})t_i(x_i)+\gamma_i(\underset{\sim}{x})t_i'(x_i)]e^{\theta_i x_i} dx_i.$$

Letting $c \to a_i$, $d \to b_i$, applying Condition 2(i) and using the resulting expression in (2.8) gives the equality

$$E_{\underset{\sim}{\theta}}[\gamma_i(\underset{\sim}{X})\theta_i] = -E_{\underset{\sim}{\theta}}[\gamma_i^{(i)}(\underset{\sim}{X})] - E_{\underset{\sim}{\theta}}[\gamma_i(\underset{\sim}{X}) \frac{d}{dX_i} \log t_i(X_i)].$$

Applying this in (2.7) and using Condition 3(i) yields (2.4). Equation (2.5) follows by a direct calculation.

III. INADMISSIBILITY

Proofs of inadmissibility of various estimators $\underset{\sim}{\delta}^o$ using theorems analogous to Theorem 1 have been carried out in Hudson [14] and Berger [1] in a rather haphazard manner. A systematic approach to the problem would be to attempt to solve

$$\mathcal{D}\, g(\underset{\sim}{x}) = 0 \tag{3.1}$$

(see (2.6)) for g, and observe that if a solution $g > 0$ is found then

$$\mathcal{D}[g(\underset{\sim}{x})]^\alpha = \alpha[g(\underset{\sim}{x})]^{\alpha-1}\mathcal{D}\, g(\underset{\sim}{x}) + \alpha(\alpha-1)[g(\underset{\sim}{x})]^{\alpha-2}\sum_{i=1}^{p}[g^{(i)}(\underset{\sim}{x})]^2$$

$$= \alpha(\alpha-1)[g(\underset{\sim}{x})]^{\alpha-2}\sum_{i=1}^{p}[g^{(i)}(\underset{\sim}{x})]^2 < 0$$

for $0 < \alpha < 1$. From (2.5) it would follow that the estimator

$$\underset{\sim}{\delta}(\underset{\sim}{x}) = \underset{\sim}{\delta}^o(\underset{\sim}{x}) + \underset{\sim}{\gamma}(\underset{\sim}{x}) = \underset{\sim}{\delta}^o(\underset{\sim}{x}) + 2\alpha\nabla \log g(\underset{\sim}{x})$$

has smaller risk than $\underset{\sim}{\delta}^o$ for all $\underset{\sim}{\theta}$.

Unfortunately, closed form solution of (3.1) is possible only in certain special cases, such as when $p = 1$, when $\underset{\sim}{X}$ has a spherically symmetric normal distribution and $\underset{\sim}{\delta}^o$ is a spherically symmetric estimator, and when the X_i are from Gamma distributions with equal degrees of freedom and

$$\nabla \log m_o(\underset{\sim}{x}) = (x_1^{-1},\ldots,x_p^{-1}) + \nabla \log \phi(\sum_{i=1}^{p} x_i^2).$$

We will consider the situation when p = 1 as an example.

THEOREM 2. *Let* p = 1 *and suppose that Condition* 1 *holds and that* δ^o *is as in Condition* 3(i). *Define*

$$\psi_1(x) = \int_a^x \frac{1}{m_o(y)}\, dy \text{ and } \psi_2(x) = \int_x^b \frac{1}{m_o(y)}\, dy,$$

and suppose for all $x \in \mathcal{X} = (a,b)$ *that either* $\psi_1(x) < \infty$ *or* $\psi_2(x) < \infty$. *Letting* ψ_i (i = 1 *or* 2) *be the finite function chosen, assume further that*

(i) $E_\theta | \frac{d}{dX} \log \psi_i(X)|^2 < \infty$, *and*

(ii) $\lim_{x\to a}\{t(x)e^{\theta x} \frac{d}{dx} \log \psi_i(x)\} = \lim_{x\to b}\{t(x)e^{\theta x} \frac{d}{dx} \log \psi_i(x)\}=0.$

Then δ^o *is inadmissible and a better estimator is given by*

$$\delta(x) = \delta^o(x) + \gamma(x), \tag{3.2}$$

where

$$\gamma(x) = 2\alpha \frac{d}{dx} \log \psi_i(x)$$

and $0 < \alpha < 1$.

Proof. We begin by verifying Condition 2 of Section 2. Only the condition $E_\theta|\gamma'(X)| < \infty$ is not immediately obvious. But

$$\gamma'(x) = -\frac{1}{2\alpha}\gamma^2(x) - \gamma(x) \frac{d}{dx} \log m_o(x),$$

so

$$E_\theta|\gamma'(X)| \le \frac{1}{2\alpha} E_\theta[\gamma^2(X)]+\{[E_\theta\gamma^2(X)][E_\theta(\frac{d}{dX} \log m_o(X))^2]\}^{1/2}.$$

All terms are finite by assumption (the finiteness of

$E_\theta(\frac{d}{dX}\log m_o(X))^2$ following from Condition 1 (ii) and (iii)).

Theorem 1 thus applies, and it is easy to check that $\mathcal{D}\psi_i(x)=0$. The discussion preceding this theorem completes the proof.

Comment. Because m_o is continuous and positive, ψ_i will be finite for all $a < x < b$ if it is finite for any x. Hence only the behavior of $m_o(x)$ at the boundaries of $\mathcal{X}$ is relevant to the admissibility problem.

Example. Suppose X has a Gamma distribution, i.e. has density on $\mathcal{X} = (0,\infty)$

$$f(x|\theta) = (-\theta)^\alpha x^{\alpha-1}e^{\theta x}/\Gamma(\alpha).$$

(The natural parameter space here is $\Theta = (-\infty,0)$. It is easy to transpose the results below to the more common parametrization in which $\Theta = (0,\infty)$, however.) Clearly $t(x) = x^{\alpha-1}$, so that $E_\theta|\frac{d}{dX}\log t(X)|^2 < \infty$ if and only if $\alpha = 1$ or $\alpha > 2$. Henceforth assume that $\alpha > 2$.

Suppose, now, that

$$(3.3)\qquad m_o(y) = \begin{cases} k_1y^r(1+o(1)) & \text{as } y \to 0 \\ k_2y^s(1+o(1)) & \text{as } y \to \infty. \end{cases}$$

If $r < 1$ then ψ_1 is finite, while if $s > 1$ then ψ_2 is finite. In either case it is easy to verify the remaining conditions needed to apply Theorem 2, and hence (3.2) gives a better estimator.

Observe that the possible inadmissibility of δ^o due to the behavior of $m_o(y)$ at ∞ is of little practical concern since for reasonable (generalized) priors (see 2.2) m(y) will not be blowing up at ∞. Inadmissibility due to the behavior of $m_o(y)$ near zero is of concern, however, as can be seen by considering the prior distribution

$$\pi(d\theta) = \frac{2}{\pi(1+\theta^2)}\, d\theta.$$

A simple calculation gives

$$m(y) = \frac{2y^{\alpha-1}}{\pi\Gamma(\alpha)} \int_{-\infty}^{0} (-\theta)^{\alpha} e^{y\theta} \frac{d\theta}{(1+\theta^2)}$$

$$= \frac{2}{\pi\Gamma(\alpha)} \int_0^{\infty} \frac{\eta^{\alpha} e^{-\eta}}{y^2+\eta^2}\, d\eta.$$

Clearly

$$\lim_{y\to 0} m(y) = \frac{2\Gamma(\alpha-1)}{\pi\Gamma(\alpha)} = \frac{2}{(\alpha-1)\pi},$$

and

$$m(y) = \frac{2\alpha}{\pi y^2}(1+o(1)) \quad \text{as } y \to \infty.$$

Hence (3.3) is satisfied with $r = 0 < 1$, so the Bayes estimator with respect to π, given by $\delta^{\pi}(x) = \nabla \log m(x) - \nabla \log t(x)$, is inadmissible. (Although π is proper, it can be checked that the Bayes risk for the problem is infinite. Hence δ^{π} is being defined as the estimator minimizing the posterior expected loss.)

It can be shown that if π has α moments, then $m(y) = O(y^{\alpha-1})$ as $y \to 0$, which (since $\alpha > 2$) means that r will be greater than 1 and the inadmissibility theorem will not apply.

Comment. Once δ^{o} has been determined to be inadmissible, the problem of selecting a good improvement still remains. As mentioned in the introduction, one possible method of tackling this problem is to solve Problem II** with $C = 0$. A second method which might have some potential is to exploit the relationship between (2.6) and diffusion processes (first observed by Brown [9]). The operator $\mathcal{D}$ happens to be the infinitesimal generator of the diffusion process on $\mathcal{X}$ which has local mean $\underset{\sim}{\mu}(\underset{\sim}{x}) = \nabla \log m_o(\underset{\sim}{x})$ and local covariance matrix $2I$. It will typically be the case that the diffusion is transient if and only if $\mathcal{D}\, g(\underset{\sim}{x}) = 0$ has a suitable positive solution, i.e., if and only if the estimator $\underset{\sim}{\delta}^{o}$ is inadmissible. Furthermore, if X_t denotes a (random) sample path of the (transient) diffusion and $E_{\underset{\sim}{x}}$ stands for expectation when the process starts at $\underset{\sim}{x}$ at time $t = 0$, then for appropriate positive functions h the function

$$g_h(\underset{\sim}{x}) = E_{\underset{\sim}{x}} \int_0^{\infty} h(X_t)dt$$

will be finite and satisfy $\mathcal{D}\, g_h(\underset{\sim}{x}) < 0$. Thus a large class of improved estimators

$$\underset{\sim}{\delta}(\underset{\sim}{x}) = \underset{\sim}{\delta}^{o}(\underset{\sim}{x}) + 2\nabla \log g_h(\underset{\sim}{x})$$

could be produced, and perhaps h could be chosen to accomodate the available prior information. Formidable difficulties are unfortunately also encountered in this approach to the problem.

IV. RESTRICTED RISK BAYES RULES

Using (2.4), (2.5) and (2.6), and providing Conditions 1 and 3(i) hold, we can formally state Problem II** as that of minimizing $r(\pi,\underset{\sim}{\delta})$ among all estimators satisfying Conditions 2 and 3(ii) and also satisfying

$$\mathcal{D}_C g(\underset{\sim}{x}) \equiv \nabla^2 g(\underset{\sim}{x}) + \nabla g(\underset{\sim}{x})\cdot\nabla \log m_o(\underset{\sim}{x}) - \frac{C}{4}\, g(\underset{\sim}{x}) \leq 0 \tag{4.1}$$

or, equivalently,

$$\mathcal{D}^{*}_{C}\underset{\sim}{\gamma}(\underset{\sim}{x}) \equiv 2\sum_{i=1}^{p} \gamma_i^{(i)}(\underset{\sim}{x}) + 2\sum_{i=1}^{p} \gamma_i(\underset{\sim}{x}) \frac{\partial}{\partial x_i} \log m_o(\underset{\sim}{x}) + \sum_{i=1}^{p} \gamma_i^2(\underset{\sim}{x}) - C \leq 0. \tag{4.2}$$

This is basically a calculus of variations minimization problem with side constraints, and the answer will typically be that the solution, δ^C, must be a smooth blending of the unconstrained minimizing estimator δ^π and estimators arising from solutions to $\mathcal{D}_C g(x) = 0$ (or $\mathcal{D}^*_C \gamma(x) = 0$).

The major problem in determining δ^C is that of solving the elliptic partial differential equation $\mathcal{D}_C g(x) = 0$. Indeed, as discussed at the beginning of Section 3, this can only be solved in closed form for certain special cases. In this section we will analyze the spherically symmetric normal situation.

If X has a p-variate normal distribution with identity covariance matrix, its distribution is as in (2.1) with

$$t(x) = e^{-|x|^2/2} \text{ and } \beta(\theta) = (2\pi)^{-p/2}e^{-|\theta|^2/2}.$$

Suppose now that the prior distribution $\pi(d\theta)$ is symmetric about a point $\mu = (\mu_1,\ldots,\mu_p)$, so that the marginal density of X will be of the form

$$m(x) = h(|x-\mu|^2). \tag{4.3}$$

The Bayes estimator for this problem can be written (see (2.3))

$$\delta^\pi(x) = x + \frac{2h'(|x-\mu|^2)}{h(|x-\mu|^2)}(x-\mu). \tag{4.4}$$

In trying to solve Problem II**, it is natural to restrict attention to estimators which are spherically symmetric about μ, i.e., to estimators of the form

$$\delta(x) = x-\rho(|x-\mu|^2)(x-\mu). \tag{4.5}$$

To put this in the general framework of section 2, we can define

$$\delta^o(x) = x, \quad g(x) = \phi(|x-\mu|^2), \tag{4.6}$$

$$\rho(|x-\mu|^2) = -\frac{4\phi'(|x-\mu|^2)}{\phi(|x-\mu|^2)}, \quad \gamma(x) = -\rho(|x-\mu|^2)(x-\mu),$$

so that an estimator of the form (4.5) can be written

$$\text{(4.7)} \qquad \underset{\sim}{\delta}(\underset{\sim}{x}) = \underset{\sim}{\delta}^{o}(\underset{\sim}{x}) + \underset{\sim}{\gamma}(\underset{\sim}{x}) = \underset{\sim}{\delta}^{o}(\underset{\sim}{x}) + 2\nabla \log g(\underset{\sim}{x}),$$

which is the form assumed in (2.1) and Condition 3(ii). For convenience, we will denote the corresponding quantities for $\underset{\sim}{\delta}^{\pi}$ by $g^{\pi}(\underset{\sim}{x})$, $\rho^{\pi}(\underset{\sim}{x})$, and $\underset{\sim}{\gamma}^{\pi}(\underset{\sim}{x})$, and note that

$$\text{(4.8)} \qquad \rho^{\pi}(\underset{\sim}{x}) = -\frac{2h'(|\underset{\sim}{x}-\underset{\sim}{\mu}|)^2}{h(|\underset{\sim}{x}-\underset{\sim}{\mu}|^2)} .$$

A simple calculation using (4.6) shows that $\mathcal{D}_C g(\underset{\sim}{x})$ in (4.1) can be written (letting $r = |\underset{\sim}{x}-\underset{\sim}{\mu}|^2$)

$$\text{(4.9)} \qquad \bar{\mathcal{D}}_C \phi(r) \equiv \mathcal{D}_C g(\underset{\sim}{x}) = 2p\phi'(r) + 4r\,\phi''(r) - \frac{C}{4}\phi(r)$$

$$= \frac{1}{4}\phi(r)[-2p\,\rho(r)+r\rho^2(r)-4r\rho'(r)-C].$$

The following lemmas present the solutions to the differential equation

$$\text{(4.10)} \qquad \bar{\mathcal{D}}_C \phi(r) = 0.$$

LEMMA 1.

(i) *If* $C = 0$, *positive solutions to* (4.10) *exist for all* $r > 0$ *only if* $p > 2$, *and are given (up to a multiplicative constant) by*

$$\text{(4.11)} \qquad \phi_{C,\lambda}(r) = \begin{cases} \lambda + r^{(2-p)/2} & \textit{for } \lambda \geq 0 \\ 1 & \textit{for } \lambda = \infty. \end{cases}$$

(We will use λ *to index the solutions.)*

(ii) If $C > 0$, *the positive solutions to* (4.10) *are given (up to a multiplicative constant) by*

$$\phi_{C,\lambda}(r) = \begin{cases} r^{(2-p)/4}[\lambda I_\nu(\frac{1}{2}\sqrt{Cr})+K_\nu(\frac{1}{2}\sqrt{Cr})] & \text{for } \lambda \geq 0 \\ r^{(2-p)/4} I_\nu(\frac{1}{2}\sqrt{Cr}) & \text{for } \lambda = \infty, \end{cases} \tag{4.12}$$

where $\nu = |p-2|/2$ *and* I_ν *and* K_ν *are the modified Bessel functions determined by*

$$I_\nu(r) = e^{-i\pi\nu/2} J_\nu(re^{i\pi/2}),$$

$$K_\nu(r) = \frac{\pi}{2} e^{i\pi\nu/2}[e^{i\pi(\nu+1)/2} I_\nu(r) - Y_\nu(re^{i\pi/2})],$$

where J_ν *and* Y_ν *are the Bessel functions of the first and second kind respectively and of order* ν.

Proof. When $C = 0$, (4.10) can be solved explicitly, yielding (4.11) as solutions. For $C > 0$, making the transformation $w(r) = r^{p/4}\phi(r)$ in (4.10) results in the equivalent differential equation

$$w''(r) + [\frac{-C}{16r} - \frac{p}{4}(\frac{p}{4}-1)\frac{1}{r^2}]w(r) = 0.$$

The positive solutions to this equation are known to be of the form $w_\lambda(r) = \sqrt{r}\,[\lambda I_\nu(\frac{1}{2}\sqrt{Cr})+K_\nu(\frac{1}{2}\sqrt{Cr})]$ for $\lambda \geq 0$ and $w_\infty(r) = \sqrt{r}\, I_\nu(\frac{1}{2}\sqrt{Cr})$. Transforming back gives the desired result.

LEMMA 2. *The functions* ρ *(as defined in (4.6)) corresponding to the* $\phi_{C,\lambda}$ *are*

(i) *when* $C = 0$ *and* $p \geq 2$, *given by*

$$\rho_{C,\lambda}(r) = \begin{cases} \dfrac{2(p-2)}{\lambda r^{p/2}+r} & \text{for } \lambda \geq 0 \\ 0 & \text{for } \lambda = \infty; \end{cases} \tag{4.13}$$

(ii) *when* $C > 0$ *and* $p > 1$, *given by*

$$(4.14)\qquad \rho_{C,\lambda}(r) = \begin{cases} -\dfrac{\sqrt{C}}{\sqrt{r}}\dfrac{[\lambda I_{\nu+1}(\frac{1}{2}\sqrt{Cr}) - K_{\nu+1}(\frac{1}{2}\sqrt{Cr})]}{[\lambda I_{\nu}(\frac{1}{2}\sqrt{Cr}) + K_{\nu}(\frac{1}{2}\sqrt{Cr})]} & \text{for } \lambda \geq 0 \\[2ex] -\dfrac{\sqrt{C}}{\sqrt{r}}\dfrac{I_{\nu+1}(\frac{1}{2}\sqrt{Cr})}{I_{\nu}(\frac{1}{2}\sqrt{Cr})} & \text{for } \lambda = \infty; \end{cases}$$

(iii) *when* $C > 0$ *and* $p = 1$, *given by the expressions in* (4.14) *minus* $2/r$.

Proof. The results follow from straightforward calculation and the fact that $\lambda I'_{\nu}(y) + K'_{\nu}(y) = \lambda I_{\nu+1}(y) - K_{\nu+1}(y) + \frac{\nu}{y}[\lambda I_{\nu}(y) + K_{\nu}(y)]$.

Some knowledge of the behavior of the functions $\rho_{C,\lambda}$ will be needed and is given in the following lemma.

LEMMA 3.

(i) $\rho_{C,\lambda}(r)$ *is decreasing and continuous in* λ *and hence*

$$\rho_{C,\infty}(r) \leq \rho_{C,\lambda}(r) \leq \rho_{C,0}(r).$$

Furthermore

$$\rho_{C,0}(r) = \begin{cases} 0 & \text{if } C = 0 \text{ and } p \leq 2 \\ 2(p-2)/r & \text{if } C = 0 \text{ and } p > 2 \\ \sqrt{C}\,/\,\sqrt{r} & \text{if } C > 0 \text{ and } p = 1 \\ \dfrac{\sqrt{C}}{\sqrt{r}}\dfrac{K_{\nu+1}(\frac{1}{2}\sqrt{Cr})}{K_{\nu}(\frac{1}{2}\sqrt{Cr})} & \text{if } C > 0 \text{ and } p > 1, \end{cases}$$

$$\rho_{C,\infty}(r) = \begin{cases} 0 & \textit{if } C = 0 \\ -\dfrac{\sqrt{C}}{\sqrt{r}} \coth(\frac{1}{2}\sqrt{Cr}) & \textit{if } C > 0,\ p = 1 \\ -\dfrac{\sqrt{C}}{\sqrt{r}} \dfrac{I_{\nu+1}(\frac{1}{2}\sqrt{Cr})}{I_\nu(\frac{1}{2}\sqrt{Cr})} & \textit{if } C > 0,\ p > 1. \end{cases}$$

(ii) *As a function of* r, $\rho_{C,\lambda}(r)$ *has bounded derivatives on compact sets in* $(0,\infty)$.

(iii) *As* $r \to 0$,

(a) *when* $p = 1$

$$\rho_{C,\lambda}(r) = \begin{cases} (1-\frac{4\lambda}{\pi})\dfrac{\sqrt{C}}{\sqrt{r}}(1+o(1)) & \textit{if } \lambda \neq \frac{\pi}{4} \textit{ and } \lambda < \infty \\ -\frac{C}{6}(1+o(1)) & \textit{if } \lambda = \frac{\pi}{4} \\ -\frac{2}{r}(1+o(1)) & \textit{if } \lambda = \infty; \end{cases}$$

(b) *when* $p = 2$

$$\rho_{C,\lambda}(r) = \begin{cases} \dfrac{-4}{r \log r}(1+o(1)) & \textit{if } \lambda < \infty \\ -\frac{C}{4}(1+o(1)) & \textit{if } \lambda = \infty; \end{cases}$$

(c) *when* $p \geq 3$

$$\rho_{C,\lambda}(r) = \begin{cases} \dfrac{2(p-2)}{r}(1+o(1)) & \textit{if } \lambda < \infty \\ -\dfrac{C}{2p}(1+o(1)) & \textit{if } \lambda = \infty. \end{cases}$$

Proof. The fact that $\rho_{C,\lambda}(r)$ is decreasing in λ follows from simply differentiating with respect to λ in (4.13) and (4.14) and observing that the derivative is negative. The remainder of the lemma follows from well known properties and asymptotic expansions of the modified Bessel functions.

In general, I_ν and K_ν are expressible in closed form for half integer ν (corresponding to odd dimensions p). In all cases, tables of I_ν and K_ν exist for small and moderate integer and half integer values of ν (i.e. all p of moderate size), so one need not resort to numerical work to evaluate the $\rho_{C,\lambda}$.

The function $\rho_{C,0}(r)$, being the largest solution to (4.10), will be of particular interest. The following lemma gives some indication of its behavior for $C > 0$ and $p > 1$. (The $C = 0$ and $p = 1$ cases were dealt with in Lemma 3(i).)

LEMMA 4. *If* $C > 0$

(i) *and* $p = 3$, *then*

$$\rho_{C,0}(r) = \frac{\sqrt{C}}{\sqrt{r}} + \frac{2}{r} \; ;$$

(ii) *and* $p = 5$, *then*

$$\rho_{C,0}(r) = \frac{\sqrt{C}}{\sqrt{r}} + \frac{4}{r} + \frac{4}{r(2+\sqrt{Cr})} \; ;$$

(iii) *and* $p = 2$, *then*

$$\rho_{C,0}(r) = \frac{2}{r}\,\frac{\displaystyle\int_0^\infty \frac{\cos(t\sqrt{Cr}/2)}{(t^2+1)^{3/2}}\,dt}{\displaystyle\int_0^\infty \frac{\cos(t\sqrt{Cr}/2)}{(t^2+1)^{1/2}}\,dt} \; ;$$

(iv) *then as* $r \to \infty$,

$$\rho_{C,0}(r) = \frac{\sqrt{C}}{\sqrt{r}} + \frac{(p-1)}{r} + \frac{(p-3)(p-1)}{2r\sqrt{Cr}} + O(r^{-2}).$$

Proof. Simple calculation from known formulas and expansions for the modified Bessel functions.

At this point, the estimators (for which Conditions 2 and 3 hold) which satisfy (4.1) (or $\bar{\mathscr{D}}_C\phi(r) \leq 0$) can be described. They are the estimators corresponding to functions $\rho(r)$ which

(i) are continuous and piecewise differentiable;

(ii) satisfy $\rho_{C,\infty}(r) \leq \rho(r) \leq \rho_{C,0}(r)$;

(iii) satisfy $\sqrt{r}\,\rho(r) \to 0$ as $r \to 0$ when $p = 1$, and satisfy

$$\int_0^{\varepsilon} r\rho'(r)dr < \infty \quad \text{when } p = 2;$$

(iv) have the property that for any given point r_o, corresponding to which is the λ_o such that $\rho_{C,\lambda_o}(r_o) = \rho(r_o)$, $\rho(r)$ much be greater than or equal to $\rho_{C,\lambda_o}(r)$ for all $r \geq r_o$. The graph of $\rho(r)$ can thus follow any curve $\rho_{C,\lambda}(r)$, but if it departs from such a curve it must go up and to the right.

The properties (i), (ii), and (iii) above are conditions which ensure that the estimator (4.5) satisfies Conditions 2 and 3(ii) of Section 2. (Property (ii) above is also, of course, needed to ensure that $\bar{\mathscr{D}}_C\phi(r) \leq 0$.) When $p = 1$, the estimator will violate Condition 2(i) unless $\sqrt{r}\,\rho(r) \to 0$ (ensuring continuity of the estimator as $r = |x-\mu|^2 \to 0$). For $p > 1$, discontinuity at $r = 0$ is allowed by Condition 2(i). The moment requirements in Condition 2 can be shown (using Lemma 3(iii)) to be satisfied for the estimators corresponding to $\rho_{C,\infty}(r)$ and $\rho_{C,0}(r)$ when $p \geq 3$, and hence by $\rho(r)$ satisfying properties (i), (ii), and (iv) above. Property (iii) above ensures satisfaction of the moment requirements in Condition 2 for $p = 1$ and $p = 2$. (It is possible to show using Lemma 3(iii) that, when $p = 1$, only $\rho_{C,\pi/4}$ satisfies Condition 2, while when $p = 2$ only $\rho_{C,\infty}$ satisfies Condition 2.)

We now proceed with the theorem formalizing the nature of the solution to Problem II**. Let $\tilde{\delta}^C$ denote the "optimal" estimator, i.e., the estimator which minimizes $r(\pi,\underset{\sim}{\delta})$ among all spherically symmetric (about $\underset{\sim}{\mu}$) estimators satisfying Conditions 2 and 3 of Section 2 and for which $\bar{\mathcal{D}}_C(r) \le 0$ (which implies that $R(\underset{\sim}{\theta},\underset{\sim}{\delta}) \le R(\underset{\sim}{\theta},\underset{\sim}{\delta}^o) + C = p + C$). Also, let ρ_C and ϕ_C be defined, as usual, by

$$(4.15)\qquad \rho_C(r) = -4\phi_C'(r)/\phi_C(r),$$

$$\underset{\sim}{\delta}^o(\underset{\sim}{x}) = \underset{\sim}{x} - \rho_C(|\underset{\sim}{x}-\underset{\sim}{\mu}|^2)(\underset{\sim}{x}-\underset{\sim}{\mu}).$$

THEOREM 2. *If, for all* $r \in [a,b]$ $(a > 0,\ b < \infty)$, $\rho_C(r) \ne \rho^\pi(r)$, *then it must be true that* $\rho_C(r) = \rho_{C,\lambda}(r)$ *for some* λ *and all* $a \le r \le b$.

Proof. We will consider the case $\rho_C(r) < \rho^\pi(r)$ for $a \le r \le b$. The other cases are dealt with by similar arguments. To argue by contradiction, suppose there does not exist a λ such that $\rho_C(r) = \rho_{C,\lambda}(r)$ for all $a \le r \le b$.

Let λ^* be such that $\rho_{C,\lambda^*}(b) = \rho_C(b)$. (Such a λ^* must exist by Lemma 3(i), since it can be shown that $\rho_C(r)$ must be between $\rho_{C,\infty}(r)$ and $\rho_{C,0}(r)$ to satisfy $\bar{\mathcal{D}}_C\phi_C(r) \le 0$.) Define

$$d = \sup_{a \le r \le b} \{r: \rho_{C,\lambda^*}(r) \ne \rho_C(r)\}.$$

By continuity, $a < d \le b$. Next, choose $\varepsilon > 0$ so that $d - \varepsilon > a$ and $\rho_C(r) < \rho_{C,\lambda^*}(r) < \rho^\pi(r)$ for $d - \varepsilon < r < d$. (It can be shown that if $\rho_C(r_1) \ge \rho_{C,\lambda^*}(r_1)$ for some $d - \varepsilon < r_1 < d$, then it cannot be true that $\bar{\mathcal{D}}_C\phi_C(r) \le 0$ for all $r_1 < r < d$.) Without loss of generality, it can be assumed that b and ε were chosen so that $|\rho_C'(r)| < k_1 < \infty$ for $d - \varepsilon < r \le d$. Also, let

$$k_2 = |\sup_{a \le r \le b} \rho_{C,\lambda^*}'(r)|$$

(which is finite by Lemma 3(ii)). Observe that, for any $k \ge 2(k_1+k_o)$ and any point $r_o \in (d-\frac{\varepsilon}{2},d)$, the function

$\psi(r) = \rho_{C,\lambda^*}(r_o) + k(r-r_o)$ must intersect $\rho_C(r)$ at some point $d - \varepsilon < r_1 < r_o$. (Choose r_1 to be the first point of intersection if several exist.) Finally, define

$$\tilde{\rho}(r) = \begin{cases} \rho_C(r) & \text{for} \quad r \leq r_1 \text{ or } r \geq d \\ \psi(r) & \text{for} \quad r_1 \leq r \leq r_o \\ \rho_{C,\lambda^*}(r) & \text{for} \quad r_o \leq r \leq d. \end{cases}$$

Now it is clear that the estimator

$$\tilde{\delta}(\underset{\sim}{x}) = \underset{\sim}{x} - \tilde{\rho}(|\underset{\sim}{x}-\underset{\sim}{\mu}|^2)(\underset{\sim}{x}-\underset{\sim}{\mu})$$

will satisfy Conditions 2 and 3 of Section 2 if $\underset{\sim}{\delta}^C$ does. To verify that $\mathcal{D}_C\tilde{\phi}(r) \leq 0$ (where $\tilde{\rho}(r) = -4\tilde{\phi}'(r)/\tilde{\phi}(r)$), it is only necessary to check (see (4.9)) that

$$\xi(r) = -2p\psi(r) + r\psi^2(r) - 4r\psi'(r) - C \leq 0$$

for $r_1 \leq r \leq r_o$. (By assumption on ρ_C and definition of ρ_{C,λ^*}, $\mathcal{D}_C\tilde{\phi}(r) \leq 0$ for $r \leq r_1$ and $r \geq r_o$.) From the definition of $\psi(r)$ it is clear that

$$\xi(r) = -2p[\rho_{C,\lambda^*}(r_o)+k(r-r_o)]$$
$$+ r[\rho^2_{C,\lambda^*}(r_o)+2k\rho_{C,\lambda^*}(r_o)(r-r_o)+k^2(r-r_o)^2] - 4rk - C.$$

Observe, however, from (4.9) and the fact that $\mathcal{D}_C\phi_{C,\lambda^*}(r) = 0$, that

$$-2p\rho_{C,\lambda^*}(r_o) = -r_o\rho^2_{C,\lambda^*}(r_o) + 4r_o\rho'_{C,\lambda^*}(r_o),$$

and hence

$$\xi(r) = -2pk(r-r_o) + (r-r_o)\rho^2_{C,\lambda^*}(r_o) + 2k(r-r_o)\rho_{C,\lambda^*}(r_o)$$
$$+ rk^2(r-r_o)^2 + 4r_o\rho'_{C,\lambda^*}(r_o) - 4rk.$$

A moments reflection reveals that the k_1 and k_2 which work for a given ε also work for all smaller ε. By choosing ε small enough we can ensure that $r \geq \frac{1}{2} r_o$ for $r_1 \leq r \leq r_o$, and hence that

$$\begin{aligned} 4r_o\rho'_{C,\lambda^*}(r_o) - 4rk &\leq 4r_o\rho'_{C,\lambda^*}(r_o) - 2r_ok \\ &\leq 4r_ok_2 - 4r_o(k_1+k_2) \\ &= -4r_ok_1. \end{aligned}$$

Thus

$$\xi(r) \leq (r-r_o)[-2pk+\rho^2_{C,\lambda^*}(r_o)+2k\rho_{C,\lambda^*}(r_o)+rk^2(r-r_o)]-4r_ok_1.$$

As $\varepsilon \to 0$, the expression in square brackets above stays bounded, but $(r-r_o) \to 0$ when $r_1 \leq r \leq r_o$. Hence $\xi(r) \leq 0$ for $r_1 \leq r \leq r_o$ and small enough ε, completing the argument that $\tilde{\rho}(r)$ indeed satisfies $\bar{\mathcal{D}}_C\tilde{\phi}(r) \leq 0$.

To complete the proof, we must show that $r(\pi,\tilde{\delta}) < r(\pi,\delta^C)$, contradicting the supposed optimality of δ^C. But it is well known that, for any estimator δ,

$$\begin{aligned} r(\pi,\delta) - r(\pi,\delta^\pi) &= E^m|\gamma(X)-\gamma^\pi(X)|^2 \\ &= E^m\{[\rho(|X-\mu|^2)-\rho^\pi(|X-\mu|^2)]^2|X-\mu|^2\}, \end{aligned}$$

where m indicates that the expectation is with respect to the marginal distribution of X. From this and the fact that, by construction, $\tilde{\rho}(r)$ is closer to $\rho^\pi(r)$ than $\rho_C(r)$ is to $\rho^\pi(r)$ for $r_1 < r < d$, the desired conclusion follows.

It will typically be the case that

$$\rho^\pi(r) = k_1 + k_2r + o(r) \qquad (4.16)$$

as $r \to 0$, where $k_1 > 0$ and $k_2 \neq 0$. (This can be seen by considering (4.8) and expanding $h(r)$ in a Taylors series, for typical π.)

When this is true, it can be seen from Lemma 3(iii) that if $\rho_{C,\lambda}(r)$ is positive as $r \to 0$, it blows up at such a rate that $\rho_C(r)$ (the optimal solution) cannot equal $\rho_{C,\lambda}(r)$ for sufficiently small r. Hence, by Theorem 2, $\rho_C(r)$ must equal $\rho^\pi(r)$ on some interval $(0,b_1)$. (When this is the case and (4.16) holds, it is easy to verify that ρ_C will satisfy Conditions 2 and 3 - see the discussion after Lemma 4 - so no technical difficulties will be encountered.) Intervals in which $\rho_C(r)$ equals some $\rho_{C,\lambda}(r)$ and equals $\rho^\pi(r)$ will then alternate. The structure of $\rho_C(r)$ will thus usually be of the following form: for some numbers $0 = a_0 < b_1 \le a_1 \le b_2 \le \ldots$,

$$(4.17) \qquad \rho_C(r) = \begin{cases} \rho^\pi(r) & \text{for } a_i \le r \le b_{i+1} \\ \rho_{C,\lambda_i}(r) & \text{for } b_i \le r \le a_i, \end{cases}$$

where the λ_i are determined by the continuity constraints $\rho^\pi(b_i) = \rho_{C,\lambda_i}(b_i)$. The at first sight formidable task of finding the optimal sequences $\{a_i\}$ and $\{b_i\}$ is greatly simplified by the observation that, after b_i (and hence λ_i) have been selected, the subsequent a_i can only be a point for which $\rho_{C,\lambda_i}(a_i)=\rho^\pi(a_i)$. There will almost never be more than one or two points at which $\rho_{C,\lambda_i}(r)$ and $\rho^\pi(r)$ are equal for $r > b_i$, so the possibilities for the a_i are very limited. Furthermore, it will often happen that $\rho^\pi(r) > \rho_{C,0}(r)$ for $r \ge k$, in which case $\rho_C(r)$ must equal $\rho_{C,0}(r)$ for $r > k$. (This follows from Theorem 2 and Lemma 3(i).) Hence there will typically be very few b_i (and a_i) (i.e., very few switches between ρ^π and the $\rho_{C,\lambda}$), so that numerical minimization of the Bayes risk of estimators satisfying (4.17) over the b_i (and a_i) is quite feasible. This is particularly true because of the following relatively simple formula that can be used for the Bayes risk of δ^C.

LEMMA 5. *If*

$$\delta^C(x) = x - \rho_C(|x-\mu|^2)(x-\mu),$$

and ρ_C *is as in* (4.17), *then*

$$(4.18) \qquad r(\pi,\delta^C) = p + \frac{S_p}{2}\sum_{i\geq 1}\{4[2b_i^{p/2}h'(b_i)-2a_{i-1}^{p/2}h'(a_{i-1}) - \int_{a_{i-1}}^{b_i}\frac{(h'(r))^2}{h(r)}r^{p/2}dr] + \int_{b_i}^{a_i} Ch(r)r^{(p-2)/2}dr\},$$

where $h(|x-\mu|^2)$ *is the marginal density of* X *and* S_p *is the surface area of the unit* p*-sphere given by* $S_p = 2\pi^{p/2}/\Gamma(p/2)$.

Proof. From (2.5) and the observation that $R(\theta,\delta^0) = p$, it follows that

$$r(\pi,\delta^C) = p + E^{\pi}E_{\theta}[\frac{4}{g_C(X)}\mathcal{D}\, g_C(X)]$$

$$= p + E^h[\frac{4}{g_C(X)}\mathcal{D}\, g_C(X)].$$

Making the transformation $r = |x-\mu|^2$, noting that $\mathcal{D}\, g(x) = \mathcal{D}_C g(x) + \frac{C}{4}g(x)$, and using (4.9) gives

$$r(\pi,\delta^C) = p + \int_0^\infty \frac{4}{\phi_C(r)}[\bar{\mathcal{D}}_C\phi_C(r) + \frac{C}{4}\phi_C(r)]h(r)(\frac{1}{2}S_p r^{(p-2)/2}dr).$$

Now, from (4.17) and (4.8) it follows that

$$\phi_C(r) = \begin{cases} \phi_\pi(r) \equiv \sqrt{h(r)} & \text{for } a_i \le r \le b_{i+1} \\ \phi_{C,\lambda_i}(r) & \text{for } b_i \le r \le a_i. \end{cases}$$

Furthermore,

$$\bar{\mathcal{D}}_C\phi_\pi(r) + \frac{C}{4}\phi_\pi(r) = 2p\phi_\pi'(r) + 4r\phi_\pi''(r)$$

$$= \frac{ph'(r)}{\sqrt{h(r)}} + \frac{2rh''(r)}{\sqrt{h(r)}} - \frac{r[h'(r)]^2}{[h(r)]^{3/2}},$$

while, by definition, $\bar{\mathcal{D}}_C\phi_{C,\lambda_i}(r) = 0$. Hence

$$r(\pi,\underset{\sim}{\delta}^C) = p + \frac{S_p}{2}\sum_{i\ge 1}\{4\int_{a_{i-1}}^{b_i}\left[\frac{ph'(r)}{h(r)} + \frac{2rh''(r)}{h(r)} - \frac{r(h'(r))^2}{(h(r))^2}\right]$$

$$\times h(r)r^{(p-2)/2}dr + \int_{b_i}^{a_i} Ch(r)r^{(p-2)/2}dr\}.$$

Integrating by parts gives

$$\int_{a_{i-1}}^{b_i} h''(r)r^{p/2}dr = h'(r)r^{p/2}\Big|_{a_{i-1}}^{b_i} - \int_{a_{i-1}}^{b_i} h'(r)\frac{p}{2}r^{(p-2)/2}dr,$$

which when used above gives the desired result.

V. AN EXAMPLE

In this section we present perhaps the most important example of the theory of the preceding section, namely the analysis for conjugate priors. (Although conjugate priors are usually not robust, that is of no concern here because of the risk restrictions employed.) Thus we assume $\pi(d\underset{\sim}{\theta})$ is a $\mathcal{N}_p(\underset{\sim}{\mu},\tau^2 I)$ distribution. Since $\underset{\sim}{X}$ is $\mathcal{N}_p(\underset{\sim}{\theta},I)$, it follows that the marginal distribution of $\underset{\sim}{X}$ is $\mathcal{N}_p(\underset{\sim}{\mu},(1+\tau^2)I)$, i.e., the marginal density is

$$h(r) = [2\pi(1+\tau^2)]^{-p/2} e^{-r/[2(1+\tau^2)]},$$

where $r = |\underset{\sim}{x}-\underset{\sim}{\mu}|^2$. Hence (see (4.8))

$$\rho^{\pi}(r) = \frac{-2h'(r)}{h(r)} = \frac{1}{1+\tau^2}.$$

It is easy to see in this case (as indicated in the discussion after Theorem 2) that the optimal estimator is

$$\underset{\sim}{\delta}^C(\underset{\sim}{x}) = \underset{\sim}{x} - \rho_C(|\underset{\sim}{x}-\underset{\sim}{\mu}|^2)(\underset{\sim}{x}-\underset{\sim}{\mu}), \tag{5.1}$$

where

$$\rho_C(r) = \begin{cases} \rho^{\pi}(r) = 1/(1+\tau^2) & \text{for} \quad 0 < r \leq b \\ \rho_{C,0}(r) & \text{for} \quad b \leq r \end{cases} \tag{5.2}$$

and b is defined by

$$\rho^{\pi}(b) = (1+\tau^2)^{-1} = \rho_{C,0}(b). \tag{5.3}$$

(Lemma 3(i) and Lemma 4 describe $\rho_{C,0}(r)$.) Furthermore, using Lemma 5, a calculation (again using integration by parts) yields for the Bayes risk of $\underset{\sim}{\delta}^C$ the formula

$$r(\pi,\underset{\sim}{\delta}^C) = p - \frac{p}{(1+\tau^2)}\psi_p\left(\frac{b}{1+\tau^2}\right) + C\left(1-\psi_p\left(\frac{b}{1+\tau^2}\right)\right) - \frac{2}{(1+\tau^2)\Gamma(p/2)}\left[\frac{b}{2(1+\tau^2)}\right]^{p/2} e^{-b/[2(1+\tau^2)]}, \tag{5.4}$$

where $\psi_\nu(z)$ is the cumulative distribution function of the chi-square distribution with ν degrees of freedom.

To obtain some idea as to the effectiveness of the estimators $\underset{\sim}{\delta}^C$, we will present some tables of their risks. It is convenient to consider, instead of $r(\pi,\underset{\sim}{\delta}^C)$, the normalized relative savings risk of Efron and Morris [11] given by

$$\text{(5.5)} \qquad \mathrm{RSR}(\pi,\underset{\sim}{\delta}) = \frac{r(\pi,\underset{\sim}{\delta})-r(\pi,\underset{\sim}{\delta}^{\pi})}{r(\pi,\underset{\sim}{\delta}^{o})-r(\pi,\underset{\sim}{\delta}^{\pi})}.$$

This measures the proportion of the potential Bayesian improvement over $\underset{\sim}{\delta}^o(\underset{\sim}{x}) = \underset{\sim}{x}$ which is lost by the estimator $\underset{\sim}{\delta}$. The other side of the coin is the "robustness" of the estimator, which in this case is indicated by C, the amount by which the estimator could be worse than $\underset{\sim}{\delta}^o$. To put this on the same scale as RSR, we will formally consider the "relative robustness risk"

$$\mathrm{RRR}(\pi,\underset{\sim}{\delta}) = \frac{\sup_{\underset{\sim}{\theta}}[R(\underset{\sim}{\theta},\underset{\sim}{\delta})-R(\underset{\sim}{\theta},\underset{\sim}{\delta}^{o})]}{r(\pi,\underset{\sim}{\delta}^{o})-r(\pi,\underset{\sim}{\delta}^{\pi})}.$$

(This measure is also realistic in the sense that one would be concerned about the possible harm in using $\underset{\sim}{\delta}$ instead of $\underset{\sim}{\delta}^o$ relative to the maximum potential gain available.) Thus small RSR indicates near optimality from a Bayesian viewpoint, while small RRR indicates near optimality from a classical or minimax or Bayesian robustness viewpoint.

For the remainder of the section, we will state results for the situation where $\underset{\sim}{X}$ is $\mathcal{N}_p(\underset{\sim}{\theta},\sigma^2 I)$, since this is the practical situation.

THEOREM 3. *If* $\underset{\sim}{X}$ *is* $\mathcal{N}_p(\underset{\sim}{\theta},\sigma^2 I)$ *and* $\underset{\sim}{\theta}$ *is* $\mathcal{N}_p(\underset{\sim}{\mu},\tau^2 I)$, *then*

$$\text{(5.6)} \qquad \underset{\sim}{\delta}^C(\underset{\sim}{x}) = \underset{\sim}{x} - \rho_C^*(|\underset{\sim}{x}-\underset{\sim}{\mu}|^2/\sigma^2)(\underset{\sim}{x}-\underset{\sim}{\mu}),$$

where (letting $r = |\underset{\sim}{x}-\underset{\sim}{\mu}|^2/\sigma^2$)

$$\text{(5.7)} \qquad \rho_C^*(r) = \begin{cases} \sigma^2/(\sigma^2+\tau^2) & \text{for } 0 < r \le b \\ \rho_{C/\sigma^2,0}(r) & \text{for } b \le r \end{cases}$$

and b *is defined by*

(5.8) $$\sigma^2/(\sigma^2+\tau^2) = \rho_{C/\sigma^2,0}(b).$$

Furthermore,

(5.9) $$RRR(\pi,\underset{\sim}{\delta}^C) = \frac{C(\sigma^2+\tau^2)}{p\sigma^4},$$

and

(5.10) $$RSR(\pi,\underset{\sim}{\delta}^C) = [1-\psi_p(y)][1+RRR(\pi,\underset{\sim}{\delta}^C)] - \frac{(y/2)^{p/2}e^{-y/2}}{\Gamma(1+p/2)},$$

where $y = b\sigma^2/(\sigma^2+\tau^2)$ *depends only on* p *and* $RRR(\pi,\underset{\sim}{\delta}^C)$.

Proof. Formulas (5.6) through (5.10) follow from the preceding analysis after dividing $\underset{\sim}{X}$, $\underset{\sim}{\theta}$ and $\sqrt{C}$ by σ, and observing that

$$R(\underset{\sim}{\theta},\underset{\sim}{\delta}^o) = r(\pi,\underset{\sim}{\delta}^o) = p\sigma^2 \text{ and } r(\pi,\underset{\sim}{\delta}^\pi) = \frac{p\sigma^2\tau^2}{\sigma^2+\tau^2}.$$

The last statement of the theorem follows trivially from (5.8) and Lemma 3(i) when C = 0 or p = 1, while for C > 0 and p > 1 (5.8) can be written

$$\frac{\sigma^2}{\sigma^2+\tau^2} = \frac{[C/\sigma^2]^{1/2}}{[y(\sigma^2+\tau^2)/\sigma^2]^{1/2}} \frac{K_{\nu+1}\left(\frac{1}{2}\left[\frac{C}{\sigma^2}\frac{y(\sigma^2+\tau^2)}{\sigma^2}\right]^{1/2}\right)}{K_\nu\left(\frac{1}{2}\left[\frac{C}{\sigma^2}\frac{y(\sigma^2+\tau^2)}{\sigma^2}\right]^{1/2}\right)}$$

or

$$1 = \left[\frac{p\ RRR}{y}\right]^{1/2} \frac{K_{\nu+1}(\frac{1}{2}[py\ RRR]^{1/2})}{K_\nu(\frac{1}{2}[py\ RRR]^{1/2})}.$$

The pleasant feature of using RRR and RSR, as indicated in Theorem 3, is that, for a given p, $RSR(\pi,\underset{\sim}{\delta}^C)$ depends on C, σ^2, and τ^2 only through $RRR(\pi,\underset{\sim}{\delta}^C)$. The following corollaries and tables present interesting special cases. The proofs are immediate from Theorem 3, Lemma 3(i), and Lemma 4.

COROLLARY 1. *If* C > 0 *and* p = 1, *then*

$$\delta^C(x) = \begin{cases} x - \dfrac{\sigma^2}{\sigma^2+\tau^2}(x-\mu) & \text{if} \quad |x-\mu|^2 \le C(\sigma^2+\tau^2)^2/\sigma^4 \\ x - \dfrac{\sqrt{C}}{|x-\mu|}(x-\mu) & \text{if} \quad |x-\mu|^2 \ge C(\sigma^2+\tau^2)^2/\sigma^4, \end{cases}$$

$$RRR(\pi,\delta^C) = C(\sigma^2+\tau^2)/\sigma^4 \qquad (\equiv RRR \textit{ for short}),$$

and

$$RSR(\pi,\delta^C) = [1-\psi_1(RRR)][1+RRR] - [2RRR/\pi]^{1/2}e^{-RRR/2}.$$

Table 1. $RRR(\pi,\delta^C)$ vs. $RSR(\pi,\delta^C)$ for p = 1, C > 0.

RRR	0	.002	.02	.10	.2	.4	.6	.8	1.0	1.4	4	5	∞
RSR	1	.93	.80	.58	.45	.32	.24	.18	.16	.10	.0120	.006	0

COROLLARY 2. *If* C > 0 *and* p = 2, *then*

$$\underset{\sim}{\delta}^C(\underset{\sim}{x}) = \begin{cases} \underset{\sim}{x} - \dfrac{\sigma^2}{\sigma^2+\tau^2}(\underset{\sim}{x}-\underset{\sim}{\mu}) & \textit{if} \quad |\underset{\sim}{x}-\underset{\sim}{\mu}|^2 \le b\sigma^2 \\ \underset{\sim}{x} - \dfrac{\sqrt{C}}{|\underset{\sim}{x}-\underset{\sim}{\mu}|}\dfrac{K_1(\frac{1}{2}|\underset{\sim}{x}-\underset{\sim}{\mu}|\sqrt{C}/\sigma^2)}{K_0(\frac{1}{2}|\underset{\sim}{x}-\underset{\sim}{\mu}|\sqrt{C}/\sigma^2)}(\underset{\sim}{x}-\underset{\sim}{\mu}) & \textit{if} \quad |\underset{\sim}{x}-\underset{\sim}{\mu}|^2 \ge b\sigma^2, \end{cases}$$

$$RRR(\pi,\underset{\sim}{\delta}^C) = C(\sigma^2+\tau^2)/[2\sigma^4],$$

and

$$RSR(\pi,\underset{\sim}{\delta}^C) = e^{-y/2}[1 - \frac{y}{2} + RRR(\pi,\underset{\sim}{\delta}^C)].$$

(See Theorem 3 for the definitions of b and y. Note that an integral representation for K_1/K_0 is given in Lemma 4.)

Table 2. $RRR(\pi,\underset{\sim}{\delta}^C)$ vs. $RSR(\pi,\underset{\sim}{\delta}^C)$ for p = 2, C > 0.

RRR	0	.024	.073	.135	.20	.28	.36	.44	.52
RSR	1	.41	.31	.24	.19	.16	.13	.11	.089

COROLLARY 3. *If* $C \geq 0$ *and* $p = 3$, *then*

$$\underset{\sim}{\delta}^C(\underset{\sim}{x}) = \begin{cases} \underset{\sim}{x} - \dfrac{\sigma^2}{\sigma^2+\tau^2}(\underset{\sim}{x}-\underset{\sim}{\mu}) & \text{if } |\underset{\sim}{x}-\underset{\sim}{\mu}|^2 \leq (\sigma^2+\tau^2)y \\ \underset{\sim}{x} - \left[\dfrac{\sqrt{C}}{|\underset{\sim}{x}-\underset{\sim}{\mu}|} + \dfrac{2\sigma^2}{|\underset{\sim}{x}-\underset{\sim}{\mu}|^2}\right](\underset{\sim}{x}-\underset{\sim}{\mu}) & \text{if } |\underset{\sim}{x}-\underset{\sim}{\mu}|^2 \geq (\sigma^2+\tau^2)y, \end{cases}$$

$$RRR(\pi,\underset{\sim}{\delta}^C) = C(\sigma^2+\tau^2)/[3\sigma^4],$$

$$RSR(\pi,\underset{\sim}{\delta}^C) = [1-\psi_3(y)[1+RRR] - \frac{(y/2)^{3/2}e^{-y/2}}{3\sqrt{\pi}/4},$$

and

$$y = \{\frac{3}{2}RRR + \frac{4}{3} + RRR[1+8/(3RRR)]^{1/2}\}.$$

Table 3. $RRR(\pi,\underset{\sim}{\delta}^C)$ vs. $RSR(\pi,\underset{\sim}{\delta}^C)$ for p = 3, $C \geq 0$.

RRR	0	.025	.075	.1	.135	.2	.4	.7	1.0	1.5
RSR	.296	.203	.151	.133	.116	.091	.052	.027	.014	.008

COROLLARY 4. *If* $C = 0$ *and* $p \geq 3$, *then*

$$\underset{\sim}{\delta}^C(\underset{\sim}{x}) = \begin{cases} \underset{\sim}{x} - \dfrac{\sigma^2}{\sigma^2+\tau^2}(\underset{\sim}{x}-\underset{\sim}{\mu}) & \text{if } |\underset{\sim}{x}-\underset{\sim}{\mu}|^2 \leq 2(p-2)(\sigma^2+\tau^2) \\ \underset{\sim}{x} - \dfrac{2(p-2)\sigma^2}{|x-\mu|^2}(\underset{\sim}{x}-\underset{\sim}{\mu}) & \text{if } |\underset{\sim}{x}-\underset{\sim}{\mu}|^2 \geq 2(p-2)(\sigma^2+\tau^2), \end{cases}$$

$$RRR(\pi,\underset{\sim}{\delta}^C) = 0,$$

and

$$\mathrm{RSR}(\pi,\underset{\sim}{\delta}^{C}) = [1-\psi_p(2(p-2))] - \frac{(p-2)^{p/2}e^{-(p-2)}}{\Gamma(1+p/2)}.$$

Table 4. $\mathrm{RSR}(\pi,\underset{\sim}{\delta}^{C})$ for $p \geq 3$, $C = 0$.

p	3	4	5	6	7	8	9	10	15
RSR	.296	.135	.0727	.0427	.0267	.0174	.0117	.008	.0016

Tables 1 through 4 exhibit the almost startlingly impressive performance of the estimators $\underset{\sim}{\delta}^{C}$, especially for $p > 1$. When $p = 1$, a substantial sacrifice in Bayes risk improvement must be made if small RRR is desired. For $p = 2$ and $p = 3$, however, the situation is more promising. When $p = 3$, for example, one can guarantee that $\underset{\sim}{\delta}^{C}$ is no more than 10% worse than $\underset{\sim}{\delta}^{o}$ at a cost of only 13.3% of the potential Bayes risk improvement. (Note, in contrast, that the conjugate prior Bayes estimator $\underset{\sim}{\delta}^{\pi}$ has $\mathrm{RRR}(\pi,\underset{\sim}{\delta}^{\pi}) = \infty$.) Table 4 is particularly startling since $C = 0$, i.e., $\mathrm{RRR}(\pi,\underset{\sim}{\delta}^{C}) = 0$ so $\underset{\sim}{\delta}^{C}$ is minimax. When $p \geq 5$ one attains virtually all of the possible Bayesian gains at no cost (in terms of possible worsened performance compared to $\underset{\sim}{\delta}^{o}$). Of course, as discussed in Berger [4], this exceptional behavior is due to the Stein effect in simultaneous estimation. It is interesting that, even when $p = 2$, there is apparently considerable benefit derived from this effect.

ACKNOWLEDGMENTS

The author would like to thank Burgess Davis and Herman Rubin for several valuable discussions of these problems.

REFERENCES

[1] Berger, J. (1980). Improving on inadmissible estimators in continuous exponential families with applications to simultaneous estimation of gamma scale parameters. *Ann. Statist.* *8*, 545-571.

[2] Berger, J. (1980). A robust generalized Bayes estimator and confidence region of a multivariate normal mean. *Ann. Statist. 8*, 716-761.

[3] Berger, J. (1980). *Statistical Decision Theory: Foundations, Concepts, and Methods*. Springer-Verlag, New York.

[4] Berger, J. (1981). Bayesian robustness and the Stein effect. To appear in *J. Amer. Statist. Assoc.*

[5] Berger, J. (1982). Selecting a minimax estimator of a multivariate normal mean. *Ann. Statist. 10*.

[6] Berger, J. and Srinivasan, C. (1978). Generalized Bayes estimators in multivariate problems. *Ann. Statist. 6*, 783-801.

[7] Bickel, P. J. (1980). Minimax estimation of the mean of a normal distribution when the parameter space is restricted. Technical Report, University of California at Berkeley.

[8] Bickel, P. J. (1980). Minimax estimation of the mean of a normal distribution subject to doing well at a point. Technical Report. University of California at Berkeley.

[9] Brown, L. (1971). Admissible estimators, recurrent diffusions, and insoluble boundary value problems. *Ann. Math. Statist. 42*, 855-904.

[10] Brown, L. (1981). The differential inequality of a statistical estimation problem. Technical Report, Cornell University, Ithaca.

[11] Efron, B. and Morris, C. (1971). Limiting the risk of Bayes and empirical Bayes estimators - Part I: the Bayes case. *J. Amer. Statist. Assoc. 66*, 807-815.

[12] Ghosh, M. and Parsian, A. (1980). Admissible and minimax multiparameter estimation in exponential families. Technical Report, Iowa State University, Ames.

[13] Hodges, J. L., Jr. and Lehmann, E. L. (1952). The use of previous experience in reaching statistical decisions. *Ann. Math. Statist. 23*, 392-407.

[14] Hudson, M. (1978). A natural identity for exponential families with applications in multiparameter estimation. *Ann. Statist. 6*, 473-484.

[15] Shapiro, S. H. (1972). A compromise between Bayes and minimax approaches to estimation. Technical Report No. 31, Department of Statistics, Stanford University, Stanford.

[16] Shapiro, S. H. (1975). Estimation of location and scale parameters - a compromise. *Comm. Statist.* *4(12)*, 1093-1108.

[17] Srinivasan, C. (1980). Admissible generalized Bayes estimators and exterior boundary value problem. *Sankhyā*.

[18] Stein, C. (1955). Inadmissibility of the usual estimator for the mean of a multivariate normal distribution. *Proc. Third Berkeley Symp. Math. Statist. Prob.* *1*, 197-206. University of California Press, Berkeley.

[19] Stein, C. (1973). Estimation of the mean of a multivariate distribution. *Proc. Prague Symp. Asymptotic Statist.*, 345-381.

[20] Strawderman, W. E. and Cohen, A. (1971). Admissibility of estimators of the mean vector of a multivariate normal distribution with quadratic loss. *Ann. Math. Statist.* *42*, 270-296.

A MINIMAX AND ADMISSIBLE SUBSET SELECTION RULE FOR THE LEAST PROBABLE MULTINOMIAL CELL[1]

Roger L. Berger

Department of Statistics
The Florida State University
Tallahassee, Florida, U.S.A.

I. INTRODUCTION

In this paper, subset selection problems for the multinomial distribution are considered. In these problems, the aim is to select a non-empty subset of the cells which contains the cell with the lowest cell probability. Having restricted attention to rules which have a high probability of including the least probable cell, the goal is to find a rule which effectively excludes the cells associated with the larger cell probabilities. This leads to the use of the number of non-best cells selected as a measure of the loss to the experimenter. In this paper, a subset selection rule is presented which is minimax and admissible for this problem. The rule is simple and easy to implement and in some cases is similar to a rule proposed and studied by Nagel [10].

Alam and Thompson [1] considered the problem of selecting the single least probable cell. The subset selection problem for the multinomial distribution has been previously considered by Gupta and Nagel [8], Nagel [10], Panchapakesan [12], and Gupta and Huang [7]. Berger [3] described a class of minimax multinomial selection rules. Minimax selection rules for multinomial and other distributions have been considered by Berger [2] and

[1]This research was supported by the U.S. Army Research Office Grant No. DAAG29-79-C-0158.

ISBN 0-12-307501-7

Bjørnstad [5]. Berger and Gupta [4] found minimax and admissible subset selection rules for location parameters but the class of selection rules considered was restricted. To this author's knowledge, this is the first time minimax and admissible subset selection rules have been derived for the multinomial problem.

Section 2 contains the necessary notation for a formulation of the problem. The selection rule is defined in Section 3. The minimaxity and admissibility of the rule is proven in Section 4.

II. NOTATION AND FORMULATION

Let $\underset{\sim}{X} = (X_1,\ldots,X_k)$ be a multinomial random vector with $\sum_{i=1}^{k} X_i = n$. $\underset{\sim}{x}$ and $\underset{\sim}{y}$ will denote vectors in the sample space of $\underset{\sim}{X}$. Let $\underset{\sim}{p} = (p_1,\ldots,p_k)$ be the unknown cell probabilities with $\sum_{i=1}^{k} p_i = 1$. The ordered cell probabilities will be denoted by $p_{[1]} \leq \cdots \leq p_{[k]}$. The goal of the experimenter is to select a subset of the cells including the *best* cell, the cell associated with $p_{[1]}$. A *correct selection*, CS, is the selection of any subset which contains the best cell.

The action space A for a subset selection problem is the $2^k - 1$ non-empty subsets of $\{1,2,\ldots,k\}$. In general a selection rule is, for each $\underset{\sim}{x}$, a probability distribution on A. But as described in Berger [2], for our purposes a selection rule can be defined by the *individual selection probabilities*, $\psi(\underset{\sim}{x}) = (\psi_1(\underset{\sim}{x}),\ldots,\psi_k(\underset{\sim}{x}))$, where $\psi_i(\underset{\sim}{x})$ is the probability of including the ith cell having observed $\underset{\sim}{X} = \underset{\sim}{x}$. A necessary and sufficient condition on ψ to insure the existence of selection rule which always selects a non-empty subset is $\sum_{i=1}^{k} \psi_i(\underset{\sim}{x}) \geq 1$ for all $\underset{\sim}{x}$.

Let P^* be a preassigned fixed number such that $1/k < P^* < 1$. As is traditional, the only selection rules to be considered are those which satisfy the <u>*P*-condition*</u>, viz., $\inf_{\underset{\sim}{p}} P_{\underset{\sim}{p}}(CS|\psi) \geq P^*$. The set of all selection rules which satisfy the P*-condition will be denoted by $\mathcal{D}_{P^*}$.

The loss to be used herein is the number of non-best cells selected, S'. A *non-best cell* is any cell for which $p_i > p_{[1]}$. Thus the risk for a selection rule ψ at a parameter point $\underset{\sim}{p}$, i.e., the expected number of non-best cells selected, can be calculated from the individual selection probabilities by

$E_{\underset{\sim}{p}}(S'|\psi) = \sum_{i \in a(\underset{\sim}{p})} E_{\underset{\sim}{p}}\psi_i(\underset{\sim}{X})$ where $a(\underset{\sim}{p}) = \{i \in \{1,2,\ldots,k\}: p_i > p_{[1]}\}$.

This definition of the loss and risk differs from the definition used elsewhere (see e.g. Berger [2]) if $p_{[1]} = p_{[2]}$ but it agrees with the usual definition if $p_{[1]} < p_{[2]}$ and has the advantage of being permutationally invariant. It is easily checked that the minimax and admissible selection rule to be derived herein is also minimax and admissible for the definition of S' used in Berger [2].

The subset selection problem as defined above is invariant under the group of permutations on the sample space. See Ferguson [6] for the general definitions of invariance. If a selection rule is invariant under the group of permutations then these two relationships are true about the individual selection probabilities: (1) For every $i \in \{2,\ldots,k\}$ and every $\underset{\sim}{x}$, $\psi_i(\underset{\sim}{x}) = \psi_1(\underset{\sim}{y})$ where $y_1 = x_i$, $y_i = x_1$ and $y_j = x_j$ for j not equal to 1 or i; and (2) For every $i \in \{1,\ldots,k\}$, $\psi_i(\underset{\sim}{x}) = \psi_i(\underset{\sim}{y})$ where $x_i = y_i$ and $(y_1,\ldots,y_{i-1}, y_{i+1},\ldots,y_k)$ is a permutation of $(x_1,\ldots,x_{i-1}, x_{i+1},\ldots,x_k)$. Permutationally invariant selection rules will be of interest since, by Theorem 2, page 156 of Ferguson [6], a selection rule is admissible in the class of all selection rules if it is admissible in the class of invariant selection rules.

Finally, some results involving Schur functions and stochastic majorization will be used in the subsequent sections. All the notations, definitions and conventions will be as presented in Proschan and Sethuraman [13] and Nevius, Proschan and

Sethuraman [11] and will not be repeated herein.

III. A CLASS OF SELECTION RULES

In this section a class of selection rules is defined. The form of these rules is examined and the fact that these rules satisfy the P*-condition for certain values of P* is proven.

Selection rules of the following form will be examined. Let $0 < c \leq 1$ be a fixed constant. Define the individual selection probabilities by

$$\text{(3.1)} \qquad \psi_i^*(\underset{\sim}{x}) = \begin{cases} 1 & \displaystyle\sum_{\substack{j=1 \\ j \neq i}}^{k} c^{x_j} < M \\ \alpha & \qquad = \\ 0 & \qquad > \end{cases}$$

where the numbers $0 \leq \alpha < 1$ and $0 < M \leq k-1$ are chosen so that $E_{\underset{\sim}{p}_0} \psi_i^*(\underset{\sim}{X}) = P^*$ where $\underset{\sim}{p}_0 = (1/k, \ldots, 1/k)$. The ψ_i^* defined by (3.1) satisfy the invariance property (1) of Section 2 so in the future all the discussion will be in terms of ψ_1^*. Now further constraints will be placed on c which will further limit the form of ψ_1^*. For each $\underset{\sim}{y}$, define $A(\underset{\sim}{y}) = \{\underset{\sim}{x}\colon\ x_1 = y_1$ and $(x_2, \ldots, x_k)$ is a permutation of $(y_2, \ldots, y_k)\}$.

LEMMA 3.1. *There exists* $\varepsilon > 0$ *such that, if* $1 - \varepsilon < c < 1$, *then*

$$\text{(3.2)} \qquad \psi_1^*(\underset{\sim}{x}) = \begin{cases} 1 & x_1 < t \text{ or } x_1 = t \textit{ and } \displaystyle\sum_{j=2}^{k} c^{x_j} < M \\ \alpha & \underset{\sim}{x} \in A(\underset{\sim}{y}) \\ 0 & \textit{otherwise} \end{cases}$$

for some $t \in \{0, \ldots, n\}$ *and some* $\underset{\sim}{y}$.

Proof. Let $f(c, \underset{\sim}{x}) = \sum_{j=2}^{k} c^{x_j}$. Clearly $f(c,\underset{\sim}{x}) = f(c,\underset{\sim}{y})$ for every c if $\underset{\sim}{x} \in A(\underset{\sim}{y})$. The lemma will be true if the following two facts are true for every $1 - \varepsilon < c < 1$: (i) $f(c,\underset{\sim}{x}) \neq f(c,\underset{\sim}{y})$ if $\underset{\sim}{x} \notin A(\underset{\sim}{y})$ and (ii) $f(c,\underset{\sim}{x}) > f(c,\underset{\sim}{y})$ if $x_1 > y_1$. To see (i), fix $\underset{\sim}{x}$ and $\underset{\sim}{y}$ with $\underset{\sim}{x} \notin A(\underset{\sim}{y})$. Then $f(c,\underset{\sim}{x})$ and $f(c,\underset{\sim}{y})$ are two different polynomials in c. Hence $f(c,\underset{\sim}{x}) = f(c,\underset{\sim}{y})$ for only a finite number of values for c. But $f(1,\underset{\sim}{x}) = k-1 = f(1,\underset{\sim}{y})$. So there exists $\varepsilon > 0$ such that if $1 - \varepsilon < c < 1$ then $f(c,\underset{\sim}{x}) \neq f(c,\underset{\sim}{y})$. By considering all such pairs $\underset{\sim}{x}$ and $\underset{\sim}{y}$ (there are only a finite number of such pairs in the sample space) and taking the minimum ε obtained, an $\varepsilon > 0$ which works for any pair $\underset{\sim}{x}$ and $\underset{\sim}{y}$ is obtained. To see (ii), note that

$$\frac{d}{dc} f(c,\underset{\sim}{x})\Big|_{c=1} = \sum_{j=2}^{k} x_j = n-x_1 < n-y_1 = \sum_{j=2}^{k} y_j$$

$$= \frac{d}{dc} f(c,\underset{\sim}{y})\Big|_{c=1}.$$

Since $f(c,\underset{\sim}{x})$ and $f(c,\underset{\sim}{y})$ are continuous functions of c, condition (i) implies either $f(c,\underset{\sim}{x}) > f(c,\underset{\sim}{y})$ for every $1 - \varepsilon < c < 1$ or $f(c,\underset{\sim}{x}) < f(c,\underset{\sim}{y})$ for every $1 - \varepsilon < c < 1$. The inequality of the derivatives implies $f(c,\underset{\sim}{x}) > f(c,\underset{\sim}{y})$.

Note that every value of c satisfying $1 - \varepsilon < c < 1$ gives rise to the same ordering of the $\underset{\sim}{x}$'s. That is if the $\underset{\sim}{x}$'s in the sample space were to be ordered according to the value of the function $\sum_{j=2}^{k} c^{x_j}$, the same ordering would result from every c satisfying $1 - \varepsilon < c < 1$. Thus (3.2) defines only one selection rule, not different selection rules for different values of c.

Henceforth it will be assumed that c has been chosen so that ψ_1^* has the form given in (3.2).

To insure that the selection rule ψ^* will always select at least one cell, the individual selection probabilities must satisfy $\sum_{i=1}^{k} \psi_i^*(\underset{\sim}{x}) \geq 1$ for all $\underset{\sim}{x}$. This will be true if $P^* \geq P_{\underset{\sim}{p}_0}(X_1 < n/k) + P_{\underset{\sim}{p}_0}(\underset{\sim}{X} = (n/k,\ldots,n/k))/k$. This lower bound converges to 1/2 as $n \to \infty$. On the other hand, if $P^* \leq P_{\underset{\sim}{p}_0}(X_1 \leq n/k - 2)$, then $\sum_{i=1}^{k} \psi_i^*(\underset{\sim}{X})$ will equal to zero for $\underset{\sim}{x}$ in $\{\underset{\sim}{x}\colon\ x_i \geq n/k - 1,\ i = 1,\ldots,k\}$ and there are sample points in this set. This upper bound also converges to 1/2 as $n \to \infty$. Thus, roughly speaking, the rule ψ^* can be used only for $P^* \geq 1/2$. In practice P^* is usually chosen to be near one so this is not a serious restriction. In the following theorem the range of possible P^* values is restricted even further in order to ensure that ψ^* satisfies the P^*-condition.

THEOREM 3.1. *Let* $P^* \geq P_{\underset{\sim}{p}_0}(X_1 < n(k-1)/k)$. *Then*

$$\inf_{\underset{\sim}{p}} P_{\underset{\sim}{p}}(CS|\psi^*) = \inf_{\underset{\sim}{p}\in P_1} E_{\underset{\sim}{p}}\, \psi_1^*(\underset{\sim}{X}) = E_{\underset{\sim}{p}_0}\, \psi_1^*(\underset{\sim}{X}) = P^*$$

where $P_1 = \{\underset{\sim}{p}\colon\ p_1 = p_{[1]}\}$.

Proof. The first equality is true by the invariance of ψ^*. The last equality is true by the definition of ψ^*. Only the middle equality remains to be proven.

Let $\underset{\sim}{p} \in P_1$. Define $\underset{\sim}{p}'$ by $p_1' = \ldots = p_{k-1}' = p_1$ and $p_k' = 1-(k-1)p_1$. First it will be shown that $E_{\underset{\sim}{p}}\psi_1^*(\underset{\sim}{X}) \geq E_{\underset{\sim}{p}'}\psi_1^*(\underset{\sim}{X})$. Since $c > 0$, c^x is a convex function of x. Thus $\sum_{i=2}^{k} c^{x_i}$ is a Schur convex function of $(x_2,\ldots,x_k)$. Thus $\psi_1^*(t, x_2,\ldots,x_k)$ is a Schur concave function of $(x_2,\ldots,x_k)$ on the set $\{(x_2,\ldots,x_k)\colon \sum_{i=2}^{k} x_k = n-t\}$. The conditional distribution of $(X_2,\ldots,X_k)$ given $X_1 = t$ is a multinomial distribution. So, by Application 4.2a of Nevius, Proschan and Sethuraman [11], $E_{\underset{\sim}{p}}(\psi_1^*(X)|X_1 = t)$ is a Schur concave function of $(p_2,\ldots,p_k)$ for fixed p_1. Thus

$E_{\underset{\sim}{p}}(\psi_1^*(\underset{\sim}{X})|X_1=t) \geq E_{\underset{\sim}{p}'}(\psi_1^*(\underset{\sim}{X})|X_1=t)$ since $(p_2',\ldots,p_k')$ majorizes $(p_2,\ldots,p_k)$. On the other hand, $P_{\underset{\sim}{p}}(X_1 < t) = P_{\underset{\sim}{p}'}(X_1 < t)$ and $P_{\underset{\sim}{p}}(X_1=t) = P_{\underset{\sim}{p}'}(X_1=t)$ since these probabilities depend only on p_1 and $p_1 = p_1'$. Hence

$$\begin{aligned} E_{\underset{\sim}{p}}\psi_1^*(\underset{\sim}{X}) &= P_{\underset{\sim}{p}}(X_1 < t) + E_{\underset{\sim}{p}}(\psi_1^*(\underset{\sim}{X})|X_1=t)P_{\underset{\sim}{p}}(X_1=t) \\ &\geq P_{\underset{\sim}{p}'}(X_1 < t) + E_{\underset{\sim}{p}'}(\psi_1^*(\underset{\sim}{X})|X_1=t)P_{\underset{\sim}{p}'}(X_1=t) \\ &= E_{\underset{\sim}{p}'}\psi_1^*(\underset{\sim}{X}). \end{aligned}$$

It remains to show that, for any $\underset{\sim}{p}$ of the form $(p,\ldots,p,q)$ where $q = 1-(k-1)p$ and $p \leq 1/k$, $E_{\underset{\sim}{p}}\psi_1^*(\underset{\sim}{X}) \geq E_{\underset{\sim}{p}_0}\psi_1^*(\underset{\sim}{X})$. By examining the derivative of $p^{n-x_k}(1-(k-1)p)^{x_k}$ with respect to p, it is easily verified that this expression is a non-decreasing function of p on $0 \leq p \leq 1/k$ if $x_k \leq n/k$. If $P^* \geq P_{\underset{\sim}{p}_0}(X_1 < n(k-1)/k)$ then $t \geq n-n/k$. Thus $\psi_1^*(\underset{\sim}{x}) < 1$ implies $x_k \leq n/k$. This further implies that if $\psi_1^*(\underset{\sim}{x}) < 1$ then $P_{\underset{\sim}{p}}(\underset{\sim}{X}=\underset{\sim}{x}) = n!p^{n-x_k}(1-(k-1)p)^{x_k}/(x_1!\ldots x_k!) \leq n!\,(1/k)^{n-x_k}(1-(k-1)(1/k))^{x_k}/(x_1!\ldots x_k!) = P_{\underset{\sim}{p}_0}(\underset{\sim}{X}=\underset{\sim}{x})$. Let $T = \{\underset{\sim}{x}: \psi_1^*(\underset{\sim}{x}) = 0$. Then

$$\begin{aligned} E_{\underset{\sim}{p}}\psi_1^*(\underset{\sim}{X}) &= 1-\sum_{\underset{\sim}{x}\varepsilon T} P_{\underset{\sim}{p}}(\underset{\sim}{X}=\underset{\sim}{x}) - (1-\alpha)\sum_{\underset{\sim}{x}\varepsilon A(\underset{\sim}{y})} P_{\underset{\sim}{p}}(\underset{\sim}{X}=\underset{\sim}{x}) \\ &\geq 1-\sum_{\underset{\sim}{x}\varepsilon T} P_{\underset{\sim}{p}_0}(\underset{\sim}{X}=\underset{\sim}{x}) - (1-\alpha)\sum_{\underset{\sim}{x}\varepsilon A(\underset{\sim}{y})} P_{\underset{\sim}{p}_0}(\underset{\sim}{X}=\underset{\sim}{x}) \\ &= E_{\underset{\sim}{p}_0}\psi_1^*(\underset{\sim}{X}). \end{aligned}$$

This verifies the middle equality.

The result of Nevius, Proschan and Sethuraman used in the above proof was also proved by Rinott [14].

A CS is sometimes defined slightly differently. If more than one cell probability is tied with $p_{[1]}$, then the selection of any subset which contains any one of these "best" cells might be termed a CS. The result of Theorem 3.1 is unchanged if this definition is used. Let $P_2 = \{\underset{\sim}{p}: \; p_1 = p_{[1]} < p_{[2]}\}$. P_1 is the closure of P_2. Since $E_{\underset{\sim}{p}}\psi_1^*(\underset{\sim}{X})$ is a continuous function of $\underset{\sim}{p}$, the infimum over P_2 is the same as the infimum over P_1.

Further values of P* for which ψ^* will satisfy the P* condition are given by Theorem 3.2.

THEOREM 3.2. *Let* $P^* = P_{\underset{\sim}{p}_0}(X_1 < t)$ *for some* t. *Then*

$$\inf_{\underset{\sim}{p}} P(CS|\psi^*) = P^*.$$

Proof. If $P^* = P_{\underset{\sim}{p}_0}(X_1 < t)$, then $\psi_1^*(\underset{\sim}{x}) = 1$ if $x_1 < t$ and $\psi_1^*(\underset{\sim}{x}) = 0$ if $x_1 \geq t$. The equality follows from the MLR property of the binomial distribution.

The values of P* specified by Theorem 3.2 correspond to certain simple rules, investigated by Nagel [10], for selecting the most probable cell.

Henceforth it will be assumed that P* was chosen so that the condition of either Theorem 3.1 or 3.2 is satisfied. The restriction used in the proof of Theorem 3.1 that $P_{\underset{\sim}{p}}(\underset{\sim}{X}=\underset{\sim}{x}) \leq P_{\underset{\sim}{p}_0}(\underset{\sim}{X}=\underset{\sim}{x})$ for all $\underset{\sim}{x}$ with $\psi_1^*(\underset{\sim}{x}) < 1$ is rather strong. The fact that ψ^* satisfies the P*-condition for some smaller values of P*, as given by Theorem 3.2, leads the author to believe that ψ^* satisfies the P*-condition for a wider range of values. But this has not been proven.

IV. MINIMAXITY AND ADMISSIBILITY OF THE SELECTION RULE ψ^*

In this section the minimaxity and admissibility of the selection rule ψ^*, defined by (3.1) and (3.2), in the class of rules $\mathcal{D}_{P^*}$ with respect to the loss S' is proven. First the minimaxity of ψ^* will be investigated.

THEOREM 4.1. *If* $P^* \geq P_{\underset{\sim}{p}_0}(X_1 \leq n/2) - (k-1)P_{\underset{\sim}{p}_0}(\underset{\sim}{X} = (n/2, n/2, 0, \ldots 0))/2$ *then* ψ^* *is minimax with respect to* S'.

Remark 4.1. If n is an odd number, the second term in this lower bound for P* is zero. The only case in which this lower bound is larger (more restrictive) than the bound given in Theorem 3.1 is if k = 2 and n is even. In this case, this bound is the same as that given in Section 3 to ensure

$$\sum_{i=1}^{k} \psi_i^*(\underset{\sim}{x}) \geq 1.$$

The following two lemmas will be used in the proof of Theorems 4.1 and 4.2.

LEMMA 4.1. (a) *If* $\psi \in \mathcal{D}_{P^*}$ *then* $E_{\underset{\sim}{p}_0}\psi_i(\underset{\sim}{X}) \geq P^*$ *for* $1 \leq i \leq k$.

(b) *The minimax value for* S' *is* $(k-1)P^*$.

(c) *If* ψ *is minimax then* $\sum_{i=2}^{k} E_{\underset{\sim}{p}_0}\psi_i(\underset{\sim}{X}) = (k-1)P^*$.

Proof. These facts follow from the observation that $E_{\underset{\sim}{p}}\psi_1(\underset{\sim}{X})$ is a continuous function of $\underset{\sim}{p}$ for any selection rule and $\underset{\sim}{p}_0$ can be considered as the limit of a sequence of parameter points for which $p_i = p_{[1]} < p_{[2]}$. See Theorem 3.1 of Berger [2] for a similar proof with more details.

LEMMA 4.2. *If* $P^* \geq P_{\underset{\sim}{p}_0}(X_1 \leq n/2) - (k-1)P_{\underset{\sim}{p}_0}(\underset{\sim}{X} = (n/2, n/2, 0, \ldots, 0))/2$ *then* $S(\underset{\sim}{x}) = \sum_{i=1}^{k} \psi_i^*(\underset{\sim}{x})$ *is a Schur concave function of* $\underset{\sim}{x}$ *on the sample space.*

Proof. The inequality assumed for P* and the definition (3.2) of ψ^* implies either $t > n/2$ or $t = n/2$, $\underset{\sim}{y} = (n/2, n/2, 0, \ldots, 0)$ and $\alpha \geq \frac{1}{2}$. (Recall t is defined to be an integer). Suppose $\underset{\sim}{x}$ majorizes $\underset{\sim}{y}$. Without loss of generality it will be

assumed that $x_1 \geq x_2 \ldots \geq x_k$ and $y_1 \geq y_2 \geq \ldots \geq y_k$. Let
$$f(c,\underset{\sim}{x}) = \sum_{i=2}^{k} c^{x_i}.$$

Case 1. $y_1 < t$ or $y_1 = t$ and $f(c,\underset{\sim}{y}) < M$. Then $S(\underset{\sim}{y}) = k \geq S(\underset{\sim}{x})$.

Case 2. $y_1 = t = n/2$, $f(c,\underset{\sim}{y}) = M$. Then $\underset{\sim}{y} \varepsilon A(n/2,n/2,0,\ldots,0)$. Since $\underset{\sim}{x}$ majorizes $\underset{\sim}{y}$, either $\underset{\sim}{x} \varepsilon A(n/2, n/2,0,\ldots,0)$ or $x_1 > t$. In the first case $S(\underset{\sim}{y}) = S(\underset{\sim}{x})$ and in the second case $S(\underset{\sim}{y}) = (k-2) + 2\alpha \geq (k-1) = S(\underset{\sim}{x})$ since $\alpha \geq \frac{1}{2}$.

Case 3. $y_1 = t > n/2$. Since $\sum_{i=1}^{k} x_i = n = \sum_{i=1}^{k} y_i$, $x_1 \geq y_1 > n/2$ implies $x_i < n/2 < t$ and $y_i < n/2 < t$ for $2 \leq i \leq k$. So $\sum_{i=2}^{k} \psi_i^*(\underset{\sim}{x}) = k-1 = \sum_{i=2}^{k} \psi_i^*(\underset{\sim}{x})$. If $x_1 > y_1$, $\psi_1^*(\underset{\sim}{y}) \geq 0 = \psi_1^*(\underset{\sim}{x})$. If $x_1 = y_1$, then $(x_2,\ldots,x_k)$ majorizes $(y_2,\ldots,y_k)$. ψ_1^* is a Schur concave function of $(x_2,\ldots,x_k)$ for fixed x_1 (as in the proof of Theorem 3.1) so $\psi_1^*(\underset{\sim}{y}) \geq \psi_1^*(\underset{\sim}{x})$. In either case, $S(\underset{\sim}{y}) \geq S(\underset{\sim}{x})$.

Case 4. $y_1 > t$. As in Case 3, $x_i < n/2 \leq t$ and $y_i < n/2 \leq t$ for $2 \leq i \leq k$ so $S(\underset{\sim}{y}) = k-1 = S(\underset{\sim}{x})$.

Proof of Theorem 4.1. $S(\underset{\sim}{x})$ is a Schur concave function of $\underset{\sim}{x}$ by Lemma 4.2. By Application 4.2a of Nevius, Proschan and Sethuraman [11], $E_{\underset{\sim}{p}} S(\underset{\sim}{X}) = \sum_{i=1}^{k} E_{\underset{\sim}{p}} \psi_i(\underset{\sim}{X})$ is a Schur concave function of $\underset{\sim}{p}$ and thus is maximized at $\underset{\sim}{p}_0$. By the definition of ψ^*, $E_{\underset{\sim}{p}_0} S(\underset{\sim}{X}) = kP^*$. Fix $\underset{\sim}{p}$. Assume $p_j = p_{[1]}$.

$$
\begin{aligned}
(k-1)P^* &= kP^* - P^* \\
&\geq E_{\underset{\sim}{p}} S(\underset{\sim}{X}) - P^* \\
&\geq E_{\underset{\sim}{p}} S(\underset{\sim}{X}) - P_{\underset{\sim}{p}}(CS|\psi^*) \\
&= E_{\underset{\sim}{p}} S(\underset{\sim}{X}) - E_{\underset{\sim}{p}} \psi_j^*(\underset{\sim}{X}) \\
&= \sum_{\substack{i=1 \\ i\neq j}}^{k} E_{\underset{\sim}{p}} \psi_i^*(\underset{\sim}{X}) \geq \sum_{i\varepsilon a(\underset{\sim}{p})} E_{\underset{\sim}{p}} \psi_i^*(\underset{\sim}{X}) = E_{\underset{\sim}{p}}(S'|\psi^*).
\end{aligned}
$$

By Lemma 4.1b, ψ^* is minimax with respect to S'.

Remark 4.2. The proof of Theorem 4.1 also shows that ψ^* is minimax with respect to the loss S, the number of populations selected, which was investigated by Berger [2], Bjørnstad [5] and many others. See these two papers for further references. But no admissibility claims can be made for ψ^* for the loss S.

Now the admissibility of ψ^* will be proved.

Theorem 4.2. *ψ^* is admissible with respect to* S'.

Proof. By Theorem 2, page 156 of Ferguson [6], it suffices to prove that ψ^* is admissible in the class of permutation invariant rules in $\mathcal{D}_{P^*}$. Let $\underset{\sim}{p} = (p,q,\ldots,q)$ where $(k-1)q+p = 1$ and $1-\varepsilon < p/q < 1$ for the ε specified by Lemma 3.1. For any invariant rule ψ

$$
\begin{aligned}
E_{\underset{\sim}{p}}(S'|\psi) &= \sum_{i=2}^{k} \sum_{\underset{\sim}{x}} \psi_i(\underset{\sim}{x}) n! \prod_{j=1}^{k} (p_j^{x_j}/x_j!) \\
&= \sum_{\underset{\sim}{x}} \psi_1(\underset{\sim}{x}) \sum_{i=2}^{k} [n!(p_1^{x_i}/x_i!)(p_i^{x_1}/x_1!) \prod_{\substack{j=2 \\ j\neq i}}^{k} (p_j^{x_j}/x_j!)] \\
&= \sum_{\underset{\sim}{x}} \psi_1(\underset{\sim}{x}) \sum_{i=2}^{k} n! q^n (p/q)^{x_i} / (x_1! \ldots x_k!).
\end{aligned}
$$

By Lemma 4.1a, every permutation invariant rule in $\mathcal{D}_{P^*}$ satisfies

$E_{\underset{\sim}{p}_0}\psi_1(\underset{\sim}{X}) \geq P^*$. By the Neymann-Pearson Lemma (see Lehmann [9]) any such individual selection probability, ψ_1, which minimizes $E_{\underset{\sim}{p}}(S'|\psi)$ must satisfy

$$\psi_1(\underset{\sim}{x}) = \begin{cases} 1 & q^n \sum_{i=2}^{k} (p/q)^{x_i} < C/k^n \\ 0 & \qquad\qquad\qquad > \end{cases}$$

where C is a constant and the factorials have cancelled from both sides of the inequalities. This is equivalent to

$$(4.1) \qquad \psi_1(\underset{\sim}{x}) \begin{cases} 1 & \sum_{i=2}^{k} c^{x_i} < M \\ 0 & \qquad\quad > \end{cases}$$

where $c = p/q$ and $M = C/(qk)^n$. (4.1) is the form given by (3.1) and, since $1-\varepsilon < p/q < 1$, (4.1) is of the form (3.2) by Lemma 3.1. Furthermore, by Lemma 3.1 the set of $\underset{\sim}{x}$ in the sample space for which $\sum_{i=2}^{k} c^{x_i} = M$ is $A(\underset{\sim}{y})$ for some $\underset{\sim}{y}$. Since $\psi_1(\underset{\sim}{x})$ is invariant, $\psi_1(\underset{\sim}{x})$ is constant on $A(\underset{\sim}{y})$. So $\psi_1(\underset{\sim}{x})$ must be exactly of the form (3.2). (The Neyman-Pearson Lemma would have allowed different values of α for different $\underset{\sim}{x}$'s in $A(\underset{\sim}{y})$). Thus ψ_1^* corresponds to the unique permutation invariant rule in $\mathcal{D}_{P^*}$ which minimizes $E_p(S'|\psi)$. Thus ψ^* is admissible among the permutation invariant rules in $\mathcal{D}_{P^*}$.

The results of Sections 3 and 4 show that for fixed values of k and n, if P* is sufficiently large, ψ^* is minimax and admissible with respect to S'. This result could be extended if ψ^* could be shown to satisfy the P*-condition for smaller values of P* since the bound on P* in Theorem 3.1 is usually the largest. More work is needed to find minimax and admissible selection rules for smaller values of P*.

The problem of selecting a subset containing the most probable cell also leads to rules of the form (3.1) where now $c \geq 1$. But the author has been unable to verify the P*-condition except in certain special cases corresponding to Theorem 3.2. This problem too requires further investigation.

REFERENCES

[1] Alam, K. and Thompson, J. R. (1972). On selecting the least probable multinomial event. *Ann. Math. Statist. 43*, 1981-1990.

[2] Berger, R. L. (1979). Minimax subset selection for loss measured by subset size. *Ann. Statist. 7*, 1333-1338.

[3] Berger, R. L. (1980). Minimax subset selection for the multinomial distribution. *J. Statist. Plann. Inference 4*, 391-402.

[4] Berger, R. L. and Gupta, S. S. (1979). Minimax subset selection rules with applications to unequal variance (unequal sample size) problems. *Scand. J. Statist. 7*, 21-26.

[5] Bjørnstad, J. F. (1978). The subset selection problem. II. On the optimality of some subset selection procedures. Mimeo. Series 78-27, Dept. of Statist., Purdue Univ.

[6] Ferguson, T. S. (1967). *Mathematical Statistics: A Decision Theoretic Approach.* Academic Press, New York.

[7] Gupta, S. S. and Huang, D. Y. (1975). On subset selection procedures for Poisson populations and some applications to the multinomial selection problems. *Applied Statistics,* R. P. Gupta (ed.). North Holland, Amsterdam.

[8] Gupta, S. S. and Nagel, K. (1967). On selection and ranking procedures and order statistics from the multinomial distribution. *Sankhyā Ser. B 29*, 1-34.

[9] Lehmann, E. L. (1959). *Testing Statistical Hypotheses.* John Wiley, New York.

[10] Nagel, K. (1970). On subset selection rules with certain optimality properties. Ph.D. Thesis, Purdue University.

[11] Nevius, S. E., Proschan, F. and Sethuraman, J. (1977). Schur functions in statistics II. Stochastic majorization. *Ann. Statist.* 5, 263-274.

[12] Panchapakesan, S. (1971). On subset selection procedures for the most probable event in a multinomial distribution. *Statistical Decision Theory and Related Topics*, S. S. Gupta and J. Yackel (eds.). Academic Press, New York.

[13] Proschan, F. and Sethuraman, J. (1977). Schur functions in statistics I. The preservation theorem. *Ann. Statist.* 5, 256-262.

[14] Rinott, Y. (1973). Multivariate majorization and rearrangement inequalities with some applications to probability and statistics. *Israel J. Math.* 15, 60-77.

UNIFORM IMPROVEMENTS ON THE CERTAINTY EQUIVALENT RULE IN A STATISTICAL CONTROL PROBLEM[1]

L. Mark Berliner

Department of Statistics
Ohio State University
Columbus, Ohio, U.S.A.

I. THE CONTROL PROBLEM

The problem considered here arises when it is desired to choose values for design variables in a linear model so that the resulting dependent random variable will be close to a prescribed constant. For discussions and applications of this problem, see Aoki [1], Dunsmore [6]), Lindley [7], and Zellner [12].

The analysis here concerns the following transformed version of the problem as given in Basu [2] and Zaman [11. Consider the linear model

$$y = z^t\beta + \varepsilon,$$

where β is an unknown p-vector, z is an arbitrary p-vector, and $\varepsilon \sim N(0,\sigma^2)$; σ^2, possibly unknown. Furthermore, an estimate (independent of ε) of β, say $\hat{\beta}$, is available. Assume that $\hat{\beta} \sim N_p(\beta,\Lambda)$, where Λ is a known, positive definite matrix. The goal is to choose a controller $z_c(\hat{\beta})$ which performs well with respect to a control risk function R_c given by

$$(1.1) \qquad R_c(z_c,\beta) = E(y-y^*)^2 = E([z_c(\hat{\beta})]^t\beta + \varepsilon - y^*)^2,$$

where y^* is a non-zero constant, and the expectation is taken

[1]Research supported in part by the National Science Foundation under Grant MSC-7802300 and by the Office of Naval Research under Contract N00014-78-C-0543 (NR042-403).

ISBN 0-12-307501-7

over both $\hat{\beta}$ and ε. Computation in (1.1) yields

$$R_c(z_c,\beta) = \sigma^2 + (y^*)^2 E[(y^*)^{-1}[z_c(\hat{\beta})]^t\beta - 1]^2. \tag{1.2}$$

Now, consider the following transformation:

$$X = \Lambda^{-1/2}\hat{\beta}$$

$$\theta = \Lambda^{-1/2}\beta$$

$$\delta = (y^*)^{-1}\Lambda^{-1/2}z_c(\hat{\beta}).$$

Application of this transformation in (1.2) yields the equivalent problem of choosing a decision rule $\delta(x) = (\delta_1(x),\ldots,\delta_p(x))^t$, based on an observation $X \sim N_p(\theta, I)$, θ unknown, subject to incurring a loss,

$$L(\delta,\theta) = (\theta^t\delta - 1)^2. \tag{1.3}$$

This version of the control problem will be considered below.

The approach here is decision theoretic; control rules are evaluated in terms of their risk (expected loss) functions, $R(\delta,\theta) = E_\theta L(\delta(X),\theta)$. Our interest is the proposition of rules which dominate, in risk, the rule $\delta_m(x) = |x|^{-2}x$. ($|x|^2 = \sum_{i=1}^{p} x_i^2$.) This rule is the *certainty equivalent* controller. For brevity, discussion of the "certainty equivalent principle" (also known as the "separation principle") is omitted. The reader is referred to Aoki [1], Basu [2], and Zellner [12] for such discussions. However, in the spirit of this principle, note that the loss function implies that δ should be an estimator, in some sense, of the quantity $|\theta|^{-2}\theta$. Clearly, δ_m is the maximum likelihood estimator of this quantity.

As will be seen, a theorem of Zaman [11] implies that δ_m is inadmissible in all dimensions. (In fact, note that δ_m has infinite risk when p is 1 or 2.)

II. PREVIOUS RESULTS

Most previous results are concerned with spherically symmetric (s.s.) rules, i.e., rules of the form $\delta(x) = \Psi(|x|)x$. Many inadmissibility results are based on the asymptotic behavior of s.s. rules as $|x| \to \infty$. In particular, suppose that for some constant c,

$$\delta(x) \approx (|x|^2+c)^{-1}x \tag{2.1}$$

for $|x|$ sufficiently large. The essence of the available results is that if $c > 5-p$, then δ is inadmissible. (See Zaman [10] and Berger, Berliner, and Zaman [4] for precise theorems.) Related work of Zaman [10] and Takeuchi [9] also concerns rules of the form (2.1). In particular, Zaman [10] showed that the value $c = 5-p$ is *asymptotically optimal* (i.e., for all $|\theta|$ sufficiently large, $\delta(x) \approx (|x|^2+5-p)^{-1}x$ has the smallest risk of all rules of the form (2.1)). Berger, Berliner, and Zaman [5] studied the admissibility of s.s. generalized Bayes controllers. Of special interest in this paper, it was shown that, under suitable regularity conditions on generalized prior measures, the corresponding generalized Bayes rules, that are given by $\delta(x) \approx (|x|^2+5-p)^{-1}x$ for $|x|$ large, are admissible.

Three other results are directly applied in the discussion below. These results are paraphrased here. The reader is referred to the indicated references for precise statements.

RESULT 1. (Zaman [11]). *If* $\delta(x) = \Psi(|x|)x$ *is admissible, then*

i) $0 \leq \Psi(r) \leq 1$.

ii) $\lim_{r\to 0} \Psi(r) = 1$.

iii) $\Psi(r)$ *is a* $C^{(\infty)}$ - *function.*

Note that Result 1; i), ii), imply that δ_m is inadmissible. In

Result 2, and the rest of the paper, the following notation is used:

Definition. For any function Ψ, let

$$T_1(\Psi(r)) = \min\{1; \Psi(r)\}.$$

Result 1 can be viewed as a partial motivation of Result 2.

RESULT 2. (Zaman [11].) *Let* $\delta_0(x) = \Psi_0(|x|)x$. *If* $P_\theta(\Psi_0(|X|) > 1) > 0$, *then* δ *given by* $\delta(x) = T_1(\Psi_0(|x|))x$ *dominates* δ_0.

The next domination result was given by Berliner [5]. The derivation of this result is based on an integration by parts technique for risk analysis first introduced by Stein [8]. See Berliner [5] for a discussion and recent references.

For any differentiable function $\psi(r)$ let

$$\psi'(r) = \frac{d\psi(r)}{dr}.$$

Also, for all real η define the quantities $\xi(\Psi)$ and $\zeta(\Psi)$ by

$$\xi(\Psi) = \int_0^\infty \frac{d}{dr}\,[r^{(p+1)}\Psi^2(r)\exp(-\tfrac{1}{2}r^2)]\,\exp(r\eta)dr$$

and

$$\zeta(\Psi) = [r^{(p+1)}\Psi^2(r)\exp(-\tfrac{1}{2}r^2)\exp(r\eta)]\Big|_0^\infty.$$

RESULT 3. (Berliner [5]). *Let* $\delta(x) = \Psi(|x|)x$ *and* $\delta_0(x) = \Psi_0(|x|)x$. *Suppose that both* Ψ *and* Ψ_0 *are continuous, piece-wise differentiable functions on* $(0,\infty)$ *such that, for all real* η, *the following conditions hold:* (i) $\xi(\Psi) < \infty$, (ii) $\xi(\Psi_0) < \infty$, (iii) $|\zeta(\Psi)| < \infty$, *and* (iv) $|\zeta(\Psi_0)| < \infty$. *If*

$$\Psi(r)\{2r\Psi'(r)+(p+1-r^2)\Psi(r)+2\} \qquad (2.2)$$

$$\geq \Psi_0(r)\{2r\Psi_0'(r)+(p+1-r^2)\Psi_0(r)+2\}$$

for all $r > 0$, *and with strict inequality on a set of positive Lebesgue measure, then* δ *dominates* δ_0.

III. MAIN RESULTS

Theorems 1 and 2 below present classes of procedures which dominate δ_m. These theorems are direct applications of Result 3.

THEOREM 1. *Assume* $p \geq 6$. *Let* $\delta(x) = \Psi(|x|)x$ *where* $\Psi(r) = (r^2-g(r))^{-1}$. *Suppose that*

i) $g(r)$ *is continuous, piece-wise differentiable, and non-decreasing,*

ii) $g(r)$ *is not identically zero,*

and iii) $0 \leq g(r) \leq \min\{2(p-5);\ h(r^2,p)\}$, *where* $h(r^2,p)$ *is given by*

$$h(r^2,p) = \frac{r^2[r^2+3(p-3)-((r^2+11-p)^2+32(p-5))^{1/2}]}{2(r^2+p-3)}.$$

Then δ *dominates* δ_m.

Proof. First, note that δ_m clearly satisfies the requirements of Result 3 (when $p \geq 3$). It is also easy to verify that δ satisfies these requirements.

Step 1. To apply Result 3, let $\Psi_0(r) = r^{-2}$ and $\Psi(r) = (r^2-g(r))^{-1}$. Computing (2.2) in this case yields

$$(3.1)\qquad (r^2-g(r))^{-1}\{-2r(2r-g'(r))(r^2-g(r))^{-2} + (p+1-r^2)(r^2-g(r))^{-1}+2\}$$
$$\geq r^{-2}\{2r(-2r^{-3}) + (p+1-r^2)r^{-2}+2\}.$$

Simplification of (3.1) yields

$$(3.2) \qquad (r^2-g(r))^{-3}\{2r(g'(r)-2r) + [(p+1-r^2)+2(r^2-g(r))](r^2-g(r))\} \geq r^{-2}[(p-3)r^{-2}+1].$$

It is easy to check that $g(r) \leq h(r^2,p)$ implies that $g(r) < r^2$ for all $r^2 > 0$. Using this fact, an algebraic manipulation of (3.2) implies the equivalent inequality

$$(3.3) \qquad 2rg'(r)+r^{-4}g(r)\{[2(p-5)-g(r)]r^4 + [g(r)-3(p-3)]g(r)r^2+(p-3)g^2(r)\} \geq 0.$$

Since $g'(r) \geq 0$ it is sufficient to verify that

$$(3.4) \qquad [2(p-5)-g(r)]r^4+[g(r)-3(p-3)]g(r)r^2+(p-3)g^2(r) \geq 0.$$

Step 2. Let $Q(g)$ denote the L.H.S. of (3.4). Note that $Q(g)$ can be written as (suppressing the dependence of g on r)

$$(3.5) \qquad Q(g) = (r^2+p-3)g^2-r^2(r^2+3(p-3))g+2(p-5)r^4.$$

Clearly $Q(g)$ is an upward opening quadratic function of g. Consider the smallest root, say $\tilde{g}$, of $Q(g)$. The quadratic formula implies that $\tilde{g} = h(r^2,p)$. Next, inspection of $h(r^2,p)$ implies that $h(r^2,p) > 0$ when $r^2 > 0$ (and, of course, $p \geq 6$). Hence, $Q(g) \geq 0$ for all $g \leq \tilde{g}$. Finally, the dominance assertion then follows directly.

The remainder of this section is devoted to the development of a readily applicable version of Theorem 1. The motivation of this discussion is twofold. First, the function $h(r^2,p)$ in Condition iii) of Theorem 1 is rather cumbersome. Second, the specific g functions to be discussed in Section 4 are easily bounded by linear functions of r^2.

THEOREM 2. *Assume* $p \geq 6$. *Let* δ *be defined as in Theorem* 1. *Suppose that the corresponding* g *function satisfies Conditions* i) *and* ii) *of Theorem* 1. *If*

$$0 \leq g(r) \leq (p-5)\min\{1; r^2/y^*\}$$

where $y^* > 0$ *satisfies* $h(y^*,p) = p-5$, *then* δ *dominates* δ_m.

The proof is based on the following lemma.

LEMMA 1. *For* $p \geq 6$ *and* $y \geq 0$, $h(y,p)$ *is an increasing, concave function of* y.

The proof of Lemma 1 is a straightforward differentiation argument and is omitted.

Proof of Theorem 2. By Theorem 1 it is sufficient to verify that $g(r) \leq \min\{(p-5); h(r^2,p)\}$.

First, by Lemma 1, $h(r^2,p) \leq p-5$ iff $r^2 \leq y^*$. Now consider a graph of $h(r^2,p)$ as a function of r^2. The formula for the line connecting the origin and the point at which $h(r^2,p) = p-5$ is $[(p-5)/y^*]r^2$. Therefore, by concavity, $[(p-5)/y^*]r^2 \leq h(r^2,p)$ for all $r^2 \leq y^*$.

We close this section with a few remarks. First, the limit as $r^2 \to \infty$ of $h(r^2,p)$ is $3(p-3)/2$. Lemma 1 implies that if $p > 11$, Condition iii) of Theorem 1 simply reduces to $0 \leq g(r) \leq h(r^2,p)$. (Since $3(p-3)/2 < 2(p-5)$ when $p > 11$.)

Second, Theorem 2 can be generalized in the following sense. Theorem 2 is an application of Theorem 1 where the implicit upper bound on g is lowered from $2(p-5)$ to $p-5$. The same analysis could be performed for other upper bounds (moderated by the remark immediately above) if desired. However, Theorem 2 does include the important asymptotically optimal case.

Finally, the computation of y^* is required. For convenience, a partial list of the values of y^* (computed numerically) is given in Table 1.

Table 1. Selected Values of y*

p	y*	p	y*
6	7.605551	15	20.000000
7	9.123106	16	21.280110
8	10.582576	17	22.549834
9	12.000000	18	23.810250
10	13.385165	19	25.062258
11	14.744563	20	26.306624
12	16.082763	25	32.433981
13	17.403124	30	38.440307
14	18.708204	40	50.206556

IV. PROPOSED CONTROL RULES

First, the following limitation in the application of Result 3 is noted. Substitution of $\Psi_0 = \Psi_m$ in (2.2) forces the R.H.S. of the inequality to be (positive) unbounded as $r \to 0$ (see (3.2)). Meanwhile, the L.H.S. of (2.2) remains bounded as $r \to 0$ for any admissible (or nearly admissible, in the sense of Result 1; i), ii)) rule. Hence, the differential inequality (2.2) cannot yield admissible alternatives to δ_m. In the case of Theorems 1 and 2, this fact is reflected in the implicit restriction that the Ψ functions satisfying the conditions of these theorems are bounded from below by $K|x|^{-2}$, for some constant K, as $|x| \to 0$. However, the combination of Result 2 and these theorems leads to reasonable alternatives to δ_m for $p \geq 6$.

PROPOSITION 1. *Assume* $p \geq 6$. *Let* $\delta(x) = \Psi(|x|)x$. *Suppose* δ *satisfies the assumptions of Theorem* 1 (*or* 2). *Then* δ_T *given by*

$$\delta_T(x) = T_1(\Psi(|x|))x$$

dominates δ_m.

Proof. Obvious.

Remark. Unfortunately, the rules δ_T are also inadmissible since they violate the smoothness requirement of Result 1.

The final point of this discussion is the suggestion of functions $g(|x|)$ for actual use in the application of Theorem 2 and Proposition 1. The functions described below arise naturally as parts of a certain class of generalized Bayes rules. The reader is referred to Berger [3] and Berliner [5] discussions. Only the required facts are given here.

Let $n \geq 1/2$. For $v > 0$ define the function $r_n(v)$ by

$$r_n(v) = \frac{v\int_0^1 \lambda^n \exp(-\frac{1}{2} v\lambda)d\lambda}{\int_0^1 \lambda^{(n-1)} \exp(-\frac{1}{2} v\lambda)d\lambda}.$$

The following facts concerning r_n are needed here:

LEMMA 2. *(Berger* [3].) *If* $n \geq 1/2$, *then*

i) $0 < r_n(v) < 2n$.

ii) $r_n'(v) \geq 0$.

iii) $\lim_{v\to\infty} r_n(v) = 2n$.

iv) $\lim_{v\to\infty} r_n(v)/v = n/(n+1)$.

v) $r_n(v)/v \leq n/(n+1)$.

Now, let $v = a|x|^2$ for some constant $a > 0$. Next, for $p \geq 6$, define $r^*(v)$ by $r^*(v) = r_n(v)$ for $n = (p-5)/2$. Then, clearly, by Lemma 2, $r^*(a|x|^2) \to p-5$ as $|x|^2 \to \infty$. Hence, the rule $\delta(x) = (|x|^2 - r^*(a|x|^2))^{-1}x$ is asymptotically optimal.

Also, by Lemma 2, note that

$$r^*(a|x|^2) \leq [(p-5)/(p-3)]a|x|^2.$$

Then, to apply Theorem 2, we require that

$a \leq (p-3)/y^*$.

PROPOSITION 2. *Assume* $p \geq 6$. *Let* δ^* *be given by*

$$\delta^*(x) = T_1([|x|^2 - r^*(a|x|^2)]^{-1})x.$$

Then for any constant a *such that* $0 < a \leq (p-3)/y^*$, δ^* *dominates* δ_m.

Proof. The proof is a direct application of the above arguments, Lemma 2, and Proposition 1.

V. COMMENTS

i) The rules δ^* proposed above display desirable properties:

a) They are relatively easy to compute.

b) Their behavior for $|x|$ large is similar to that of the generalized Bayes, admissible rules discussed in Berliner [5].

c) They are asymptotically optimal.

However, they are not admissible since the smoothness requirement of Result 1 is violated.

ii) A common criterion for choosing among decision rules is minimaxity. We simply note here that δ_m is minimax when $p \geq 3$. Hence, δ^* is also minimax. See Berliner [5] for proofs and discussion.

iii) Another natural control procedure often considered is the uniform measure, generalized Bayes rule $\delta_u(x) = (1+|x|^2)^{-1}x$. This rule is admissible for $p \leq 4$, but inadmissible for $p \geq 5$. Several authors have shown that δ_u is dominated by δ_m when $p \geq 5$. Hence, the rules δ^* proposed above also dominate δ_u when $p \geq 6$. For further discussion, references for the above results, and another class of rules which dominate δ_u, see Berliner [5].

ACKNOWLEDGMENTS

I wish to express my appreciation to Jim Berger for his help and comments. My thanks also go to Jayne Sage for programming the computations for Table 1.

REFERENCES

[1] Aoki, M. (1967). *Optimization of Stochastic Systems.* Academic Press, New York.

[2] Basu, A. (1974). Control level determination in regression models. Technical Report 139, Economic Series, Institute for Mathematical Studies in the Social Sciences, Stanford University.

[3] Berger, J. (1980). A robust generalized Bayes estimator and confidence region for a multivariate normal mean. *Ann. Statist. 8*, 716-761.

[4] Berger, J., Berliner, L. M., and Zaman, A. (1981). General admissibility and inadmissibility results for estimation in a control problem. Mimeograph Series #79-34, Statistics Department, Purdue University.

[5] Berliner, L. M. (1981). Improving on inadmissible estimators in the control problem. Technical Report 229, Department of Statistics, The Ohio State University.

[6] Dunsmore, I. R. (1969). Regulation and optimization. *J. Roy. Statist. Soc. Ser. B 31*, 160-170.

[7] Lindley, D. V. (1968). The choice of variables in multiple regression. *J. Roy. Statist. Soc. Ser. B 30*, 31-66.

[8] Stein, C. (1973). Estimation of a mean of a multivariate distribution. *Proc. Prague Symp. Asymptotic Statist.*, 345-381.

[9] Takeuchi, K. (1968). On the problem of fixing the level of independent variables in a linear regression function. IMM 367, Courant Institute of Math. Sciences, New York University.

[10] Zaman, A. (1977). An application of Stein's method to the problem of single periold control of regression models. Technical Report 231, Economic Series, Institute for mathematical studies in the Social Sciences, Stanford University.

[11] Zaman, A. (1981). A complete class of theorem for the control problem, and further results on admissibility and inadmissibility. *Ann. Statist.* 9, 812-821.

[12] Zellner, A. (197). *An Introduction to Bayesian Inference in Econometrics*. John Wiley, New York.

EMPLOYING VAGUE INEQUALITY INFORMATION IN THE ESTIMATION OF NORMAL MEAN VECTORS[1]

(Estimators that shrink to closed convex polyhedra)

M. E. Bock

Department of Statistics
Purdue University
West Lafayette, Indiana, U.S.A.

I. INTRODUCTION

Consider the problem of estimating the mean vector θ of a p dimensional normal random vector X with covariance I_p where p is three or more. Let the possible values of θ be all of $\mathbb{R}^p$ and define the loss function for an estimator $\hat{\theta}$ of θ to be

$$L(\theta,\hat{\theta}) = ||\hat{\theta}-\theta||^2,$$

the square of the Euclidean norm.

James and Stein [1] exhibited estimators which shrink to a fixed vector (say zero) in the parameter space yet have the property that they are minimax and dominate the maximum likelihood estimator. Sclove, Morris and Radhakrishnan [3] noted that estimators with this property exist which shrink to linear manifolds when p is greater than or equal to the dimension of the linear manifold plus three. One of the estimators they considered has the form

$$(\hat{\theta}(X))_i = \bar{X} + (X_i-\bar{X})(1-c/s)^+$$

where c is in (0, 2(p-3)) and

[1]This research was supported by National Science Foundation Grants MCS-78-02300 and MCS-81-01670.

ISBN 0-12-307501-7

$$\bar{X} = \sum_{j=1}^{p} X_j/p \text{ and } s = \sum_{j=1}^{p} (X_j-\bar{X})^2.$$

This estimator shrinks to the linear manifold which consists of vectors whose components are all equal in $\mathbb{R}^p$. The dimension of this manifold is one and the estimator is minimax if p is greater than or equal to four, which is three plus the dimension of the manifold.

A fixed vector or a linear manifold are special cases of a closed convex polyhedron, which is the solution set for a finite system of linear inequality constraints. Suppose that vague inequality information about θ is present in the following form: One suspects that the mean vector θ satisfies the following finite system of linear inequality constraints:

$$A_i^t\theta \leq b_i,$$

where A_i is a known p-dimensional vector and b_i is a known scalar, $i = 1,\ldots,n$. Let Q be the closed convex polyhedron which satisfies these constraints. (We will assume that the system is solveable and that Q is not empty.) A class of estimators is exhibited in Section 2 such that the estimators shrink X to Q in the direction of P(X) the closest point of Q to X. Some of the estimators dominate $\hat{\theta}_0$ the maximum likelihood estimator and are of course minimax. A dominating estimator is exhibited for any estimator $\hat{\theta}$ which assumes the value X when X is not in Q.

The shrinkage estimator is robust in the following sense: If θ is actually in Q, then any estimator which shrinks X to Q by the choice of a value in the interval (X,P(X)] has a smaller loss than the estimator whose value is X when X is not in Q, no matter what the distribution of X. For θ not in Q, the estimators considered improve most in expected loss for values of θ close to Q. Thus one is rewarded most in using these estimators when the vague inequality information that θ is in Q is correct or "nearly correct". The shrinkage is done under the following condition:

Shrink X to Q only if P(X) lies on a face of Q with dimension d_0 such that

$$p \geq d_0 + 3,$$

i.e. the codimension of the face $(p-d_0)$ is three or more.

Section 2 of the paper provides the exact statement of these results in a theorem as well as the proof of the theorem. An appendix follows with proofs of lemmas used in the proof of the theorem.

II. A CLASS OF ESTIMATORS

In the theorem of this section dominating estimators $\hat{\theta}_g$ are given for any estimator $\hat{\theta}_1(X)$ which assumes the value X when X is not inside the convex closed polyhedron Q. If one completely specifies the values of $\hat{\theta}_1$ by defining $\hat{\theta}_1(X)$ to be X for X in Q, then $\hat{\theta}_1$ is the maximum likelihood estimator $\hat{\theta}_0$. The estimators that dominate $\hat{\theta}_0$ are also minimax estimators since $\hat{\theta}_0$ is minimax with constant risk for all values of θ.

THEOREM. *Assume that the* p-*dimensional random vector* X *is normally distributed with mean vector* θ *in* $\mathbb{R}^p$ *and identity covariance matrix. Let* Q *be the closed convex polyhedron which is the solution to a finite system of linear inequalities, i.e.*

$$Q = \{Y \text{ in } \mathbb{R}^p:\ A_i^t Y \leq b_i,\ i = 1,\ldots,n\}$$

where A_i *are known* p-*dimensional vectors and* b_i *are known scalars. Define* $\hat{\theta}_1(X)$ *to be any estimator of* θ *satisfying*

$$\hat{\theta}_1(X) = X \text{ for } X \text{ not in } Q.$$

Define P(X) *to be the orthogonal projection of* X *to* Q *and let* d *be the codimension of the face of* Q *in whose relative interior* P(X) *lies. Define*

$$\hat{\theta}_g(X) = \begin{cases} \hat{\theta}_1(X), & \textit{for } X \textit{ in } Q \textit{ and for } X \textit{ not in } Q \textit{ but } d \leq 2; \\ P(X)+g(||X-P(X)||^2)(X-P(X)), & \textit{for } X \textit{ not in } Q \textit{ and } d \geq 3, \end{cases}$$

where g *is a real-valued differentiable function defined on non-negative real values* t, *satisfying*

a) $g(t) \leq 1$;

b) $(1-g(t))\ (2d-t(1-g(t))) \geq 4tg'(t)$ *with strict inequality for a set of* t *values with positive Lebesgue measure;*

c) $\lim_{t\to\infty} t^{\frac{1}{2}}(1-g(t))\exp(-t/2) = 0$ *and*

$\lim_{t\to 0} t^{\frac{1}{2}}(1-g(t+c))\exp(-t/2) = 0$ *for any* $c > 0$.

Then $\hat{\theta}_g$ *dominates* $\hat{\theta}_1$ *under squared error loss* $||\hat{\theta}-\theta||^2$. *It is assumed that* Q *is not empty.*

Remark. The conditions given in c) assure that the usual "integration by parts" analysis of the risk is legitimate.

Example. If we define a constant c in $(0,\ 2(d-2))$ and set

$g(t) = 1-c/t$,

then g satisfies the conditions of the theorem. It is a function used by James and Stein (1).

III. OUTLINE OF THE PROOF BY PARTS

A. Because every vector's projection to Q lies in the relative interior of some face of Q and there are a finite number of faces of Q, it suffices to show the following: For each face $\mathcal{J}$ of Q with codimension greater than or equal to three, the expected value of

$$\nabla(X) = ||\hat{\theta}_g(X)-\theta||^2 - ||\hat{\theta}_1(X)-\theta||^2$$

is negative where the expectation is taken over all values of X whose projection to Q lies in the relative interior of that face $\mathcal{J}$ of Q. To exhibit this result, both the relative interior of the face of Q and the projection of X to the face are carefully described. (The description is actually valid for faces with co-dimension less than three.)

B. It is shown that the values of X over which the expected value of $\nabla(X)$ is taken are those whose projections to a certain pointed polyhedron S lie in the relative interior of a certain face F of S. (The convex polyhedron Q is shown to be the sum of a linear subspace L and a pointed polyhedron S (i.e., one with vertices) where S lies in $L^{\perp}$ the orthogonal complement space of L. A face $\mathcal{J}$ in Q may be written as the sum of L and a face F of S. The codimension of $\mathcal{J}$ is equal to the codimension d_F of F in $L^{\perp}$. The vectors exterior to Q whose projections to Q lie in the relative interior of $\mathcal{J}$ are those whose projections to S lie in the relative interior of F.)

C. Assume that one of the vertices in the face F is the zero vector and define N to be the linear subspace N generated by F and define $N^{\perp}$ to be its orthogonal complement space in $L^{\perp}$. (If the assumption is not true, make a translation of the whole problem, replacing S by S_F and F by F_0 which does have the zero vector for a vertex.)

D. A lemma shows that $P_S(X)$ is in F^I if and only if $P_N(X)$ is in F^I and $P_{N^{\perp}}(X)$ is in a certain face C of S^p, the polar cone of S. See Figure 1. Because $P_S(X)$ in F^I implies $P_S(X)$ equals $P_N(X)$, we may replace $P_S(X)$ in $\nabla(X)$ by $P_N(X)$ to obtain $\nabla^*(X)$ which is a function of X only through $P_{N^{\perp}}(X)$. Also, the lemma implies that the expectation of $\nabla(X)$ over S such that $P_S(X)$ is in F^I is equivalent to the expectation of $\nabla^*(X)$ over X such that

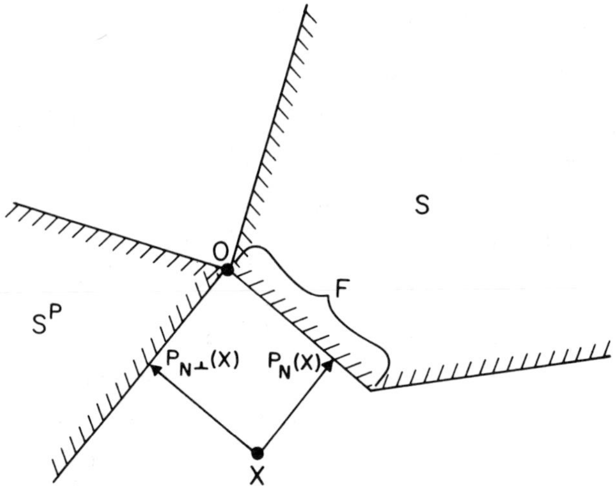

Figure 1.

$P_N(X)$ is in F^I and $P_{N^\perp}(X)$ in C. This is clearly the product of the probability that $P_N(X)$ is in F^I and the expectation of $\nabla^*(X)$ taken over X such that $P_{N^\perp}(X)$ is in C.

E. The face C may be written as the sum of a linear subspace M in $N^\perp$ and a pointed cone C_0 in $M^\perp$, the orthogonal complement of M in $N^\perp$. Thus we can evaluate ∇^* over X such that $P_{M^\perp}(P_{N^\perp}(X))$ is in C_0^I.

F. It is possible to describe C_0 as the union of simplicial cones whose relative interiors are disjoint. (See Definition 7 in the appendix.) So the expectation of $\nabla^*(X)$ is a sum of expectations of $\nabla^*(X)$ over X values in the relative interior of each of these simplicial cones. The original conditions of the theorem on the estimator may then be used to show that each expectation in the summand is negative.

IV. PROOF OF THE THEOREM

A. By Lemma 4 of the appendix, P(X) lies in the relative interior of some face of Q. Let H be the finite collection of faces of Q with codimension three or more. Define

$$h(t) = 1-g(t)$$

and note that if P(X) is in $\mathcal{T}^I$, the relative interior of a face $\mathcal{T}$ in H, then

$$\hat{\theta}_g(X) = X-h(||X-P(X)||^2)(X-P(X)).$$

Write the risk difference as

$$R(\theta,\hat{\theta}_g)-R(\theta,\hat{\theta}_1) = E[||\hat{\theta}_g(X)-||\ ^2] - E[||\hat{\theta}_1-\theta||^2]$$

$$= \sum_{\mathcal{T} \text{ in } H} E[I_{\mathcal{T}^I}(P(X))[2(\theta-X)^t(X-P(X))h(||X-P(X)||^2)$$

$$+ h^2(||X-P(X)||^2)||X-P(X)||^2]].$$

It suffices to show that each expectation in the sum is nonnegative. Let $\mathcal{T}$ be a fixed face in H and consider its corresponding expectation in the sum that forms the risk difference.

B. Stoer and Witzgall [4] noted a thoerem of Motzkin [2] shows that a closed convex polyhedron Q can be decomposed into the sum of a linear subspace L and a pointed polyhedron S in $L^\perp$, the orthogonal complement space of L. (See Lemma 6 in the appendix.) The projection of X to Q may be written as

$$P(X) = P_L(X) + P_S(P_{L^\perp}(X))$$

where P_L and $P_{L^\perp}$ and P_S are the projections to L, $L^\perp$ and S respectively. Setting

$$Y = P_{L^\perp}(X), \text{ and } \eta = P_{L^\perp}(\theta),$$

we have that

$$X-P(X) = Y-P_S(Y)$$

and

$$(X-\theta)^t(X-P(X)) = (Y-\eta)^t(Y-P_S(Y)).$$

By Lemma 6 of the appendix, P(X) lies in $\mathcal{J}^I$ if and only if $P_S(Y)$ lies in the relative interior of some face F of S with codimension d_F in $L^\perp$ equal to the codimension of $\mathcal{J}$.

The expectation corresponding to $\mathcal{J}$ in the sum for the risk difference is

$$(*)\quad E[(2(\eta-Y)^T(Y-P_S(Y))h(||Y-P_S(Y)||^2)$$
$$+ h^2(||Y-P_S(Y)||^2)||Y-P_S(Y)||^2)I_{F^I}(P_S(Y))]$$

To prove the theorem it suffices to show that each of these expectations (*) is negative.

C. Let $V_1,\ldots,V_m$ be the vertices of S. Since one or more of them belong to F, define V_F to be the vertex with lowest subscript in F. Define a new polyhedron S_F by subtracting V_F from each vector in S. The set F_0 formed by subtracting V_F from each vector in F is a face in the pointed polyhedron S_F and the codimension of F_0 is equal to that of F. Observe that one of the vertices of F_0 is the zero vector. (Note that now and in the future comments the vectors are all restricted to lie in $L^\perp$ and we speak of the codimension with respect to that space.) Note that $P_S(Y)$ lies in the relative interior of F if and only if $(P_S(Y)-V_F)$ lies in the relative interior of F_0. See, too, that $(P_S(Y)-V_F)$ is $P_{S_F}(Y-V_F)$. Define

$$Z = Y-V_F \text{ and } \rho = \eta-V_F.$$

Thus we can rewrite (*) as

$$(**)\quad E[(2((Z-P_{S_F}(Z))^t(\rho-P_{S_F}(Z))$$

$$-\ ||Z-P_{S_F}(Z)||^2)h(||Z-P_{S_F}(Z)||^2)$$

$$+\ h^2(||Z-P_{S_F}(Z)||^2)||Z-P_{S_F}(Z)||^2)I_{F_0^I}(P_{S_F}(Z))].$$

D. Let N be the linear subspace in $L^\perp$ generated by F_0 and let $N^\perp$ be its orthogonal complement space in $L^\perp$. Then according to Lemma 9, $P_{S_F}(Z)$ is in F_0^I if and only if $P_N(Z)$ is in F_0^I and $P_{N^\perp}(Z)$ is in C where

$$C = N^\perp \cap S_F^p$$

and S_F^p is the polar cone of S_F. The Remark accompanying Lemma 9 implies that C has dimension d_F equal to the codimension of F_0 and C is a face of S_F^p. According to Lemma 8, $P_{S_F}(Z)$ is $P_N(Z)$ if $P_{S_F}(Z)$ is in F_0^I. Noting that $P_{N^\perp}(Z)$ is $(Z-P_{S_F}(Z))$, we may re-write (**) as

$$-E[(2((||P_{N^\perp}(Z)||^2-(P_{N^\perp}(\rho))^tP_{N^\perp}(Z))h(||P_{N^\perp}(Z)||^2)$$

$$-\ h^2(||P_{N^\perp}(Z)||^2)||P_{N^\perp}(Z)||^2)I_C(P_{N^\perp}(Z))I_{F_0^I}(P_N(Z))].$$

(We have used the fact that $P_N(Z)$ and $P_{N^\perp}(Z)$ are orthogonal as well as the fact that $P_N(\rho)$ and $P_{N^\perp}(Z)$ are orthogonal.) Let $P_L, P_{L^\perp}, P_{N^\perp}$ and P_N be the symmetric idempotent projection matrices to the linear subspaces $L, L^\perp, N^\perp$, and N respectively. Then $P_N(Z)$ is normally distributed with mean $P_N(P_{L^\perp}\theta-V_F)$ and covariance $P_NP_{L^\perp}P_N$. Also $P_N(Z)$ is independent of $P_{N^\perp}(Z)$ which is normally distributed with mean $P_{N^\perp}(P_{L^\perp}\theta-V_F)$ and covariance $P_{N^\perp}P_{L^\perp}P_{N^\perp}$. Because $P_N(Z)$ is independent of $P_{N^\perp}(Z)$, the last expectation is equal to the product of the probability that $P_N(Z)$ is in F_0^I and the expectation

$$E[(2(P_{N^\perp}(\rho)-P_{N^\perp}(Z))^t P_{N^\perp}(Z)h(||P_{N^\perp}(Z)||^2)$$

$$+ h^2(||P_{N^\perp}(Z)||^2)||P_{N^\perp}(Z)||^2)I_C(P_{N^\perp}(Z))].$$

Because d_F is positive the probability is positive and to show that (**) is negative it suffices to show that the last expectation is negative.

E. Because C is a face of S_F^p, it is also a polyhedral cone. By Lemma 4, $P_{N^\perp}(Z)$ in C implies that $P_{N^\perp}(Z)$ is in the relative interior of some face of C. But $P_{N^\perp}(Z)$ is in the relative interior of those faces with dimension less than d_F only for a set of Lebesgue measure zero in the d_F-dimensional space $N^\perp$. So assume that $P_{N^\perp}(Z)$ is in C^I, the only face of C with dimension d_F. Define M to be the lineality space of C in $N^\perp$ with dimension (d_F-r) and let $M^\perp$ be its orthogonal complement space in $N^\perp$. Then the pointed cone

$$C_0 = M^\perp \cap C$$

has dimension r. By Lemma 6, $P_{N^\perp}(Z)$ is in C^I if and only if $P_{M^\perp}(P_{N^\perp}(Z))$ is in C_0^I.

Define U to be $P_M(P_{N^\perp}(Z))$ and ρ_U to be $P_M(P_{N^\perp}(\rho))$ and W to be $P_{M^\perp}(P_{N^\perp}(Z))$ and ρ_W to be $P_{M^\perp}(P_{N^\perp}(\rho))$. Applying the orthogonality of P_M and $P_{M^\perp}$, the last expectation is

$$(***)\ E[(2((\rho_W-W)^t W + (\rho_U-U)^t U)h(||U||^2+||W||^2)$$

$$+ h^2(||U||^2 + ||W||^2)(||U||^2 + ||W||^2))I_{C_0^I}(W)].$$

Let P_M and $P_{M^\perp}$ be the symmetric idempotent projection matrices to the linear subspaces M and $M^\perp$ respectively. Then U is normally distributed and its mean is ρ_U and its covariance Σ_U is $P_M P_{N^\perp} P_{L^\perp} P_{N^\perp} P_M$. Note that U is independent of W which is normally distributed with mean ρ_W and covariance Σ_W equal to $P_{M^\perp} P_{N^\perp} P_{L^\perp} P_{N^\perp} P_{M^\perp}$. Using the independence of U and W, a standard integration by parts argument implies that

$$(****)\quad E[2(U-\rho_U)^t Uh(||U||^2 + ||W||^2) I_{C_0^I}(W)]$$

$$= E[2I_{C_0^I}(W)((d_F-r)h(||U||^2+||W||^2)$$

$$+ 2h'(||U||^2+||W||^2)||U||^2)].$$

Next we will evaluate

$$(*****)\quad E[2(W-\rho_W)^t Wh(||U||^2+||W||^2) I_{C_0^I}(W)].$$

F. Let $C_1,\ldots,C_{n_0}$ be a simplicial decomposition of C_0, i.e. the C_i are simplicial cones of dimension r whose union is C_0 and whose relative interiors are disjoint. (See Definition 7 and remark in the appendix.) Note that except for a set of Lebesgue measure zero in $M^\perp$, any vector in C_0^I is in C_i^I the relative interior of C_i for some i. Thus $I_{C_0^I}(W)$ may be replaced by

$$\sum_{i=1}^{n_0} I_{C_i^I}(W)$$

in the last expectation since the C_i^I are disjoint. Then the last expectation is the sum of the expectations

$$E[2(W-\rho_W)^t W\, h(||U||^2+||W||^2) I_{C_i^I}(W)],\quad i = 1,\ldots,n_0.$$

Let $A_1^i,\ldots,A_r^i$ be the r linearly independent vectors which generate C_i and which form the columns of the matrix A^i. By Lemma 5, W is in C_i^I if and only if W is $A^i\alpha^i$ where α^i is a vector of positive components. Because A_j^i, $j = 1,\ldots,r$, are independent vectors in the r dimensional space $M^\perp$, it is always true that W has a representation in the form $A^i\alpha^i$, for $i = 1,\ldots,n_0$. Thus W is in C_i^I if and only if

$$T = [(A^i)^t A^i]^{-1}(A^i)^t W$$

is a vector of positive components. Now T is normally distributed with mean τ equal to $[(A^i)^t A^i]^{-1}(A^i)^t \rho_W$ and covariance

$$\Sigma = [(A^i)^t A^i]^{-1}(A^i)^t P_{M^\perp}P_{N^\perp}P_{L^\perp}P_{N^\perp}P_{M^\perp}A^i[(A^i)^t A^i]^{-1}.$$

Because the columns of A^i are contained in $M^\perp$ which is contained in $N^\perp$ which is contained in $L^\perp$, we have that A^i is $P_{L^\perp}P_{N^\perp}P_{M^\perp}A^i$. Thus Σ is $[(A^i)^t A^i]^{-1}$ since $P_{L^\perp}$ is idempotent. Thus the last expectation is

$$E[2(\prod_{j=1}^{r} I_{(0,\infty)}(T_j))\{(T-\tau)^t\Sigma^{-1}T\ h(T^t\Sigma^{-1}T+||U||^2)\}].$$

By Lemma 10, this equals

$$E[2(\prod_{j=1}^{r} I_{(0,\infty)}(T_j))\{r\ h(T^t\Sigma^{-1}T+||U||^2)+2h'(T^t\Sigma^{-1}T+||U||^2)\ T^t\Sigma^{-1}T\}].$$

Using the definition of T, this may be written as

$$E[2I_{C_i^I}(W)(rh(||U||^2+||W||^2)+2h'(||U||^2+||W||^2)||W||^2)].$$

Summing the last expectation over $i = 1,\ldots,n_0$, we may represent (*****) as

$$E[2I_{C_0^I}(W)(rh(||U||^2+||W||^2)+2h'(||U||^2+||W||^2)||W||^2)].$$

Incorporating the final representations for (****) and (*****), we may write (***) as

$$E[(-2d_F h(||U||^2+||W||^2)-4h'(||U||^2+||W||^2)(||U||^2+||W||^2)$$
$$+ h^2(||U||^2+||W||^2)(||U||^2+||W||^2))I_{C_0^I}(W)].$$

Recalling that h(t) is (1-g(t)) and assumptions a) and b) of the theorem, the integrand is negative for a set of values with positive Lebesgue measure. Thus the expectation (***) is negative as was to be shown.

V. APPENDIX

Definitions. Every closed convex polyhedron Q in $\mathbb{R}^p$ is described by a finite system of linear inequalities

$$Q = \{Y \text{ in } \mathbb{R}^p: \ A_i^t Y \leq b_i, \ i = 1,\ldots,n\}$$

where A_i is a vector and b_i is a scalar, i = 1,...,n. A linear inequality in the description is defined to be a *nonsingular inequality* if at least one vector in the polyhedron satisfies it strictly, i.e. if there is a vector Y_0 in Q such that

$$A_i^t Y_0 < b_i,$$

then

$$\{A_i^t Y \leq b_i\}$$

is a nonsingular inequality for Q.

A *relative interior point* of the polyhedron Q is a point of the polyhedron Q which strictly satisfies every nonsingular inequaltiy.

LEMMA 1. *Suppose there is a vector* P(X) *in the convex set* K *which is the orthogonal projection of the vector* X *to* K. *Then for all* Y *in* K,

$$(X-P(X))^t(Y-P(X)) \leq 0.$$

Proof. Suppose that $(X-P(X))^t(Y-P(X))$ is positive for some Y in K and define

$$M = \max\{||X-P(X)||^2, ||Y-P(X)||^2\}.$$

Then, by the Cauchy-Schwartz inequality and the definition of M,

$$0 < \rho \leq 1$$

where

$$\rho = (X-P(X)))^t(Y-P(X))/M.$$

Thus Y* is a member of K where

$$Y^* = \rho Y+(1-\rho)P(X).$$

Note that

$$\begin{aligned} ||X-Y^*||^2 &= ||(X-P(X))-\rho(Y-P(X))||^2 \\ &= ||X-P(X)||^2 + \rho^2||Y-P(X)||^2-2\rho(X-P(X))^t(Y-P(X)) \\ &= ||X-P(X)||^2 + \rho^2\{||Y-P(X)||^2-2M\}. \end{aligned}$$

The term multiplying ρ^2 is negative by the definition of M. This implies that Y* is closer to X than P(X), a contradiction to the definition of P(X). Thus, the original supposition leads to a contradiction.

LEMMA 2. *Let zero be contained in the convex set* K *which is contained in the convex set* Q. *Assume that* P(X) *the projection of the vector* X *to* Q *lies in the relative interior of* K. *Then*

$$(X-P(X))^t P(X) = 0.$$

Proof. We assume that P(X) is not zero. The following lemma (3.2.9, page 90) is given in Stoer and Witzgall [4]:

LEMMA. [*Let* K *be a convex set. If* X *is a vector in the relative interior of* K, *then for each vector* Y *in the linear manifold generated by* K *there exists a positive scalar* ε *such that the vectors* $(X+\varepsilon(Y-X))$ *and* $(X-\varepsilon(Y-X))$ *are in* K.]

Because P(X) is a relative interior point of K and because zero is in K, the LEMMA cited above implies that the line segment $[0,(1+\varepsilon)P(X)]$ is in K where ε is a positive constant.

Let Y be the projection of X to the linear subspace spanned by the vector P(X):

$$Y = \beta\, P(X)$$

where

$$\beta = (P(X))^t X/||P(X)||^2.$$

We know that β is greater than or equal to one since zero in Q implies

$$(X-P(X))^t(0-P(X)) \leq 0,$$

by Lemma 1. Because $\beta\, P(X)$ and $(X-\beta P(X))$ are orthogonal, so are $(\beta-1)P(X)$ and $(X-\beta\, P(X))$; thus

$$||X-P(X)||^2 = ||X-\beta P(X)||^2 + (\beta-1)^2||P(X)||^2.$$

If β is not one, then $\beta\, P(X)$ is closer to X than P(X). If $\beta\, P(X)$ is in Q, then this is a contradiction to the definition of P(X). Assume that $\beta\, P(X)$ is not in Q. Then

$$||X-P(X)||^2 = ||(X-(1+\varepsilon)P(X))+\varepsilon\, P(X)||^2$$

$$= ||X-(1+\varepsilon)P(X)||^2 + \varepsilon^2||P(X)||^2 + 2(X-(1+\varepsilon)P(X))^t P(X)\varepsilon.$$

The last term in the above equality may be written as

$$2(X-\beta P(X)+(\beta-1-\varepsilon)P(X))^t P(X)\varepsilon$$

$$= 2(\beta-1-\varepsilon)\varepsilon||P(X)||^2$$

since the orthogonality of $\beta\, P(X)$ and $(X-\beta\, P(X))$ implies the orthogonality of $\varepsilon\, P(X)$ and $(X-\beta\, P(X))$. Thus

$$||X-P(X)||^2 = ||X-(1+\varepsilon)P(X)||^2+[(\beta-1)^2-(\beta-1-\varepsilon)^2]||P(X)||^2.$$

Since β is greater than or equal to one and $\beta\, P(X)$ is not in Q we have

$$\beta > 1+\varepsilon.$$

This implies along with the last equality that $(1+\varepsilon)P(X)$ is closer to X than P(X), which is a contradiction to the definition of P(X). So β equals one. The definition of β implies the conclusion of the lemma.

LEMMA 3. *Let* F *be a convex set containing zero. Assume that* F *is contained in the convex set* Q *and that* P(X) *the projection of the vector* X *to* Q *lies in the relative interior of* F. *Then* (X-P(X)) *is the projection of* X *to the polar cone* Q^p *of* Q. *Furthermore,* P(X) *is also the projection of* X *to* Q^{pp} *the polar cone of the polar cone of* Q.

Proof. We make use of a lemma (2.7.5, page 51) of Stoer and Witzgall [4]:

LEMMA: [*Let* C *in* $\mathbb{R}^n$ *be a cone. If* X *in* $\mathbb{R}^n$ *admits an orthogonal decomposition* X = Y+Z *with* Y *in* C, Z *in* C^p *and* $Y^tZ = 0$, *then* Y *and* Z *are the projections of* X *into* C *and* C^p.]

Since P(X) is in Q, we have P(X) in Q^{pp} which contains Q. By Lemma 2, P(X) and (X-P(X)) are orthogonal. Using the LEMMA cited above it only remains to show that (X-P(X)) is in Q^p.

Because Lemma 1 implies that for any Y in Q,

$$(X-P(X))^t(Y-P(X)) \leq 0,$$

we have that for any Y in Q,

$$(X-P(X))^t Y \leq 0$$

since P(X) and (X-P(X)) are orthogonal. Thus (X-P(X)) is in Q^p.

LEMMA 4. *Any point in a closed convex polyhedron is a relative interior point of some face of the polyhedron.*

Proof. Suppose that the point X is in the closed convex polyhedron Q. Suppose X is not a relative interior point of Q. (Since Q is a face of itself, then X would be a relative interior point of a face if X were a relative interior point of Q.) Then the set I_Q is nonempty where

$$Q = \{Z: \ A_i^t Z \leq b_i, \ i = 1,\ldots,n\} \text{ and}$$

$$I_Q = \{i: \ A_i^t X = b_i \text{ and } \{A_i^t Z \leq b_i\} \text{ is a nonsingular inequality for } Q\}.$$

Note I_Q is contained in {1,...,n}. Then X is in the face F of Q where F is the intersection of Q and the hyperplanes of the form

$$\{Y: \ A_i^t Y = b_i\}$$

and i is in I_Q. Because the inequalities are nonsingular for Q, F is a proper face of Q. If X is a relative interior point of F, we are done. Suppose X is not a relative interior point of F (which is also a closed convex polyhedron). Then the set I_F is nonempty where

$$F = \{Z: \ D_i^t Z \leq c_i, \ i = 1,\ldots,m\} \text{ and}$$

$$I_F = [i: \ D_i^t X = c_i \text{ and } \{D_i^t Z \leq c_i\} \text{ is a nonsingular inequality for } F].$$

We can conclude X is also in a proper face G of F which is a proper face of Q distinct from F. If X is not a relative interior point of G, we can continue in the same fashion to find another proper face of Q which contains X. Because Q has a finite number of faces, the process must end.

LEMMA 5. *Let C be a polyhedral cone generated by d independent vectors A_i which form the columns of a matrix A. The vector X lies in the relative interior C^I of C if and only if the components of the vector*

$$\alpha = (A^tA)^{-1}A^tX$$

are positive and X is $A\alpha$.

Proof. Note that X is in C^I if and only if X has the form $A\beta$ where the components of the vector β are positive. Suppose X is in C^I, i.e. X is $A\beta$ where the components of β are positive. Then $A(A^tA)^{-1}A^tX$ is $A(A^tA)^{-1}A^tA\beta$ which equals $A\beta$ which is X. So X equals $A\alpha$. Now $(A^tA)^{-1}A^tX$ equals $(A^tA)^{-1}A^tA\beta$ which equals β, a vector with positive components. Suppose the components of α are positive and X is $A\alpha$. Then X is in C^I.

LEMMA 6. *For p-dimensional vectors A_i and scalars b_i, define Q to be a closed convex polyhedron given by*

$$Q = \{X \text{ in } \mathbb{R}^p: \ A_i^tX \le b_i, \ i = 1,\ldots,n\}.$$

Define the linear subspace (called the lineality space of Q)

$$L = \{X \text{ in } \mathbb{R}^p: \ A_i^tX=0, \ i = 1,\ldots,n\}$$

and let $L^\perp$ be its orthogonal complement space. Define the pointed polyhedron S by

$$S = Q \cap L^\perp.$$

Then the codimension of a face F_I of Q is equal to the codimension in $L^\perp$ of the face

$$F_I^* = F_I \cap S$$

of S. Furthermore the vector X lies in the relative interior of F_I if and only if $P_{L^\perp}(X)$ lies in the relative interior of F_I^*, where $P_{L^\perp}$ is the projection to $L^\perp$.

Remark. F_I is $L \oplus F_I^*$, the direct sum of L and F_I^*.

Proof. A theorem of Motzkin [2] cited in Stoer and Witzgall [4] shows that Q is $L \oplus S$. For I a subset of $\{1,\ldots,n\}$, define the face F_I to be

$$F_I = Q \cap \{X: A_i^t X = b_i, \text{ for } i \text{ in } I\}.$$

The definition of F_I^* implies that

$$F_I^* = \{X \text{ in } S: \ A_i^t X = b_i, \text{ for } i \text{ in } I\}.$$

It is clear that F_I^* is a face of S when we write

$$S = \{X \text{ in } L^\perp: \ A_i^t X \le b_i, \ i = 1,\ldots,n\}.$$

(Proof of Remark: Clearly F_I is contained in $(P_L(F_I) \oplus P_{L^\perp}(F_I))$. It suffices to show that $P_L(F_I)$ is L and $(L \oplus P_{L^\perp}(F_I))$ is contained in F_I and $P_{L^\perp}(F_I)$ is F_I^*. Assume that F_I is nonempty. Let X_0 be in F_I. Then for any X in L, and each i in I,

$$A_i^t(X+P_{L^\perp}(X_0)) \le b_i$$

since $A_i^t X$ is zero and $A_i^t P_{L^\perp}(X_0)$ is $A_i^t X_0$. The same sort of reasoning shows that for each i not in I,

$$A_i^t(X+P_{L^\perp}(X_0)) \le b_i.$$

Thus $(X+P_{L^\perp}(X_0))$ is in F_I for any X in L and any X_0 in F_I. This implies $P_L(F_I)$ is L and $(L \oplus P_{L^\perp}(F_I))$ is contained in F_I.

Now we show that $P_{L^{\perp}}(F_I)$ is $(F_I \cap S)$: Let Z be in F_I. Then for each i in I,

$$b_i = A_i^t Z$$

$$= A_i^t (P_L(Z) + P_{L^{\perp}}(Z))$$

$$= 0 + A_i^t P_{L^{\perp}}(Z).$$

Also, for each i not in I,

$$b_i \leq A_i^t Z = 0 + A_i^t P_{L^{\perp}}(Z).$$

Thus $P_{L^{\perp}}(Z)$ is in $(F_I \cap S)$ which implies that $P_{L^{\perp}}(F_I)$ is in $(F_I \cap S)$. Since $(F_I \cap S)$ is contained in F_I and is also contained in $L^{\perp}$, we have that $(F_I \cap S)$ is contained in $P_{L^{\perp}}(F_I)$. Thus $P_{L^{\perp}}(F_I)$ is $(F_I \cap S)$. q.e.d. Remark.)

Returning to the proof of the lemma, we note that by definition the dimension of F_I is the dimension of the linear manifold generated by F_I. Since F_I is $(L \oplus F_I^*)$ by the Remark, the dimension of F_I is the dimension of L plus the dimension of F_I^*. The codimension of F_I is defined to be p minus the dimension of F_I. This must be the dimension of $L^{\perp}$ minus the dimension of F_I^*, i.e. the codimension of F_I^* in $L^{\perp}$.

The inequalities which describe F_I are

$$\{X: \; A_i^t X \leq b_i, \text{ for } i = 1,\ldots,n; \; -A_j^t X \leq -b_j \text{ for } j \text{ in } I\}.$$

The possible nonsingular inequalities of F_I are of the form

$$A_i^t X \leq b_i$$

where i is not in I.

The inequalities which describe F_I are the same inequalities which describe F_I^* plus the restriction that the vectors of F_I^* lie in $L^{\perp}$. So the possible nonsingular inequalities for F_I^* are also those of F_I where the vectors are constrained to lie in $L^{\perp}$. But for i not in I

$$\begin{aligned} b_i &> A_i^t X \\ &= A_i^t (P_L(X) + P_{L^{\perp}}(X)) \\ &= A_i^t P_{L^{\perp}}(X). \end{aligned}$$

Thus an inequality is nonsingular for F_I if and only if it is a nonsingular inequality for F_I^*. Thus a vector X is in the relative interior of F_I if and only if $P_{L^{\perp}}(X)$ is in the relative interior of F_I^*.

Definition 7. (Simplicial decomposition of a pointed cone). Define a simplicial cone of dimension d to be the pointed cone generated by d linearly independent vectors. A simplicial decomposition of a pointed cone of dimension d is the description of the pointed cone as the union of a finite number of simplicial cones of dimension d whose relative interiors are pairwise disjoint.

Remark. A simplicial decomposition exists for any pointed cone. (To see this, note that a pointed cone is generated by a finite number of vectors. Consider a hyperplane which passes through the interior of the cone and bisects it in such a fashion that the intersection of the cone and hyperplane is a pointed polyhedron whose vertices are among the generators of the cone. The pointed polyhedron would be a face of the polytope with vertex at zero created by the bisection. A simplicial decomposition of the polyhedron exists and generates a simplicial decomposition for the cone.)

LEMMA 8. *Let* F *be a convex set containing zero and suppose that* F *is contained in the convex set* K. *Let* N *be the linear subspace generated by* F. *If* $P_K(X)$ *is the projection of the vector* X *to* K *and* $P_K(X)$ *lies in the relative interior* F^I *of* F, *then* $P_K(X)$ *equals* $P_N(X)$, *the projection of* X *to* N.

Proof. Because F is contained in K and $P_K(X)$ lies in F, we have that $P_K(X)$ equals $P_F(X)$ the projection of X to F. Because zero is in F, the linear manifold generated by F is also the linear subspace generated by F. Clearly $P_N(X)$ lies in N. By the LEMMA of Stoer and Witzgall stated in the proof of Lemma 2 of this appendix, there is a positive scalar ε such that $(P_F(X)+\varepsilon(P_N(X)-P_F(X)))$ is in F. Then F contains

$$Z = P_F(X)+\varepsilon/(1+\varepsilon)(P_N(X)-P_F(X))$$

$$= 1/(1+\varepsilon)(P_F(X)+\varepsilon(P_N(X)-P_F(X)) + \varepsilon/(1+\varepsilon)P_F(X)$$

since F is convex.

Since F is contained in N, we have $P_F(X)$ equal to $P_F(P_N(X))$. But

$$||P_N(X)-Z||^2 = (1-\varepsilon/(1+\varepsilon))^2||P_N(X)-P_F(X)||^2,$$

which is less than $||P_N(X)-P_F(X)||^2$ unless $P_N(X)$ equals $P_F(X)$. This would be a contradiction to the definition of $P_F(X)$ (equal to $P_F(P_N(X))$) since it would imply that Z is closer to $P_N(X)$ than $P_F(X)$. Thus we must have $P_F(X)$ equal to $P_N(X)$.

LEMMA 9. *Let zero be contained in the convex set* K *which is contained in the convex set* Q. *Define* N *to be the linear subspace generated by* K *and let* $N^\perp$ *be its orthogonal complement space. Define*

$$C_K = N^\perp \cap Q^P$$

where Q^P *is the polar cone of* Q *and let* P_Q, P_N, *and* $P_{N^\perp}$ *be the projections to* Q, N, *and* $N^\perp$ *respectively. Then* $P_Q(X)$ *is in the relative interior* K^I *of* K *if and only if* $P_N(X)$ *is in* K^I *and* $P_{N^\perp}(X)$ *is in* C_K.

Remark. In the case that Q is a pointed convex polyhedron with a vertex at zero, then Q^p and Q^{pp} are convex polyhedral cones. As noted by H. P. Wynn [5], C_K is a face of Q^p whose dimension is equal to the codimension of K.

Proof. Assume that $P_N(X)$ is in K^I and $P_{N^\perp}(X)$ is in C_K. Then $P_N(X)$ is in Q^{pp} since K^I is in Q which is in Q^{pp}. Also $P_{N^\perp}(X)$ is in Q^p by the definition of C_K. Furthermore $P_N(X)$ and $P_{N^\perp}(X)$ are orthogonal since N is a linear subspace. By the LEMMA cited in the proof of Lemma 2, $P_N(X)$ equals $P_{Q^{pp}}(X)$ the projection of X to Q^{pp}. Because $P_N(X)$ is in Q, then $P_{Q^{pp}}(X)$ is in Q. Because Q is contained in Q^{pp} we have that $P_Q(X)$ equals $P_{Q^{pp}}(X)$. Thus $P_Q(X)$ equals $P_N(X)$ and is in K^I.

Assume that $P_Q(X)$ is in K^I. Then by Lemma 8, $P_Q(X)$ is $P_N(X)$. Thus $P_N(X)$ is in K^I. By Lemma 3, $(X-P_Q(X))$ is $P_{Q^p}(X)$. But $P_{N^\perp}(X)$ is $(X-P_N(X))$ which is $(X-P_Q(X))$. Thus $P_{N^\perp}(X)$ is in both N and Q^p, which implies that $P_{N^\perp}(X)$ is in C_K.

LEMMA 10. *Let* T *be an* r *dimensional normal random vector with mean* τ *and covariance* Σ. *Assume that* h *is a real-valued differentiable function defined on* $(0,\infty)$ *satisfying*

$$(*)\quad \lim_{t\to\infty} t^{\frac{1}{2}}h(t)\exp(-t/2) = 0$$

$$(**)\quad \lim_{t\to 0} t^{\frac{1}{2}}h(t+c)\exp(-t/2) = 0 \text{ for any } c > 0.$$

Then

$$E[(\prod_{j=1}^{r} I_{(0,\infty)}(T_j))T^t\Sigma^{-1}(T-\tau)h(T^t\Sigma^{-1}T)]$$

$$= E[(\prod_{j=1}^{r} I_{(0,\infty)}(T_j))(rh(T^t\Sigma^{-1}T)+2h'(T^t\Sigma^{-1}T)T^t\Sigma^{-1}T)].$$

Proof. Let u be $(T-\tau)^t\Sigma^{-1}(T-\tau)$, and let v be $T^t\Sigma^{-1}T$. Note that

$$\frac{d}{dT_j}\{\exp(-\tfrac{1}{2}u)T_j h(v)\} = (\Sigma^{-1}(T-\tau))_j \exp(-\tfrac{1}{2}u)T_j h(v)$$

$$+ \exp(-\tfrac{1}{2}u)h(v)+2(\Sigma^{-1}T)_j T_j \exp(-\tfrac{1}{2}u)h'(v).$$

Thus

$$\left[\exp(-\tfrac{1}{2}u)T_j h(v)\right]_{T_j=0}^{T_j=\infty} = \int_0^\infty [-(\Sigma^{-1}(T-\tau))_j T_j h(v)+h(v)$$

$$+ 2(\Sigma^{-1}T)_j T_j h'(v)]\exp(-\tfrac{1}{2}u)dT_j.$$

Using (*) and (**) we have

$$\int_0^\infty (\Sigma^{-1}(T-\tau))_j T_j h(v)\exp(-\tfrac{1}{2}u)dT_j$$

$$= \int_0^\infty h(v)\exp(-\tfrac{1}{2}u)dT_j + \int_0^\infty 2(\Sigma^{-1}T)_j T_j h'(v)dT_j.$$

Now multiply both sides of the equation by $\prod_{i\neq j} I_{(0,\infty)}(T_i)$ and integrate both sides of the equation with respect to the other T_i's. Then summing over j yields the appropriate result.

REFERENCES

[1] James, W. and Stein, C. (1961). Estimation with quadratic loss. *Proc. Fourth Berkeley Symp. Math. Statist. Prob.* 1. Univ. of California Press, Berkeley, 361-379.

[2] Motzkin, T. (1936). *Beitrage zur Theorie der linearen Ungleichungen.* Azriel, Jerusalem.

[3] Sclove, S. L., Morris, C., and Radhakrishnan, R. (1972). Non-optimality of preliminary-test estimators for the mean of a multivariate normal distribution. *Ann. Math. Statist.* 43, 1481-1490.

[4] Stoer, J. and Witzgall, (1970). *Convexity and Optimizationn in Finite Dimensions I* Springer-Verlag, Berlin.

[5] Wynn, H. P. (1975). Integrals for one-sided confidence bounds: A general result. *Biometrika* 62, 393-396.

MULTIPLE THREE-DECISION RULES FOR PARAMETRIC SIGNS: A REVIEW[1]

Robert Bohrer

Department of Mathematics
University of Illinois
Urbana, Illinois, U.S.A.

I. INTRODUCTION

In his Keynote Address to the preceding (1976) Purdue Decision Theory Conference, Neyman [10] posed open problems in multiple decision theory. These are motivated by his work in comparing several combinations of treatments, as with mixtures of agricultural treatments arising in his 1930's work ([9] and [11]) or in combination drug treatments for cancer arising in his continued work for the National Institutes of Health.

The problem is to determine a best, or at least good, rule for using data to determine which among several parameters are positive and which are negative. As a "type I error" criterion, it is required that

(1) $P\{\text{no incorrect decisions}\} > 1-\alpha$

regardless of what the true values of the parameters might be. Although several results can be obtained regarding best decision rules for rather general data structures, the practical frame of reference in work to date has been that of the general linear model, as in Section 2.1 of [12]. In these cases, one desires to decide the signs of the parameters $\{\underset{\sim}{x}'\underset{\sim}{\beta}: \ x \text{ in } X^*\}$, which are linear functions of a p-dimensional parameter, $\underset{\sim}{\beta}$. Estimators, $\hat{\underset{\sim}{\beta}}$, for $\underset{\sim}{\beta}$ are available, which have the normal $N(\underset{\sim}{\beta}, B\ \sigma^2)$ distribution, i.e.,

[1]Research supported by the National Science Foundation under Grants MCS 75-07978, MCS 78-04017, and MSC 02581.

ISBN 0-12-307501-7

are unbiased estimators for $\underset{\sim}{\beta}$ with covariance matrix $B\sigma^2$, where B is known. Also at hand is an independent estimator S^2 for σ^2 having the $\sigma^2\chi^2(v)/v$ distribution.

It is seen that the best two-decision (+ or -) rule for deciding about one parameter is to decide that its sign is the same as that of its estimator.

Since the protection of (1) must be guaranteed for parameter values which are arbitrarily close to 0, it is seen that this best rule makes an incorrect decision half of the time about any single parameter. For p parameters, the chance (1) is worse, e.g., it is 2^{-p} if the parameters are estimated independently. Thus, to achieve (1) with reasonable α values requires a third decision, viz., "inconclusive data", for each parameter. With such three-decision rules, one seeks to maximize the expected number of correct decisions, subject to (1).

Note that an interesting dual problem arises in the ranking and selection literature when one seeks to group parameters into those better or worse than some standard but is indifferent about which decision to make for parameters sufficiently close to the standard. A solution to this problem, not considered here, are developed by Tong [14].

II. RULES BASED ON t-TESTS

In [2], rules are defined in terms of the t-statistics, $t_{\underset{\sim}{x}} = \underset{\sim}{x}'\hat{\underset{\sim}{\beta}}/(S\sqrt{\underset{\sim}{x}'B\underset{\sim}{x}})$. Namely, one decides that $\underset{\sim}{x}'\underset{\sim}{\beta}$ is positive if $t_{\underset{\sim}{x}} > c$ or negative if $t_{\underset{\sim}{x}} < -c$, and decides the data are inconclusive about $\underset{\sim}{x}'\underset{\sim}{\beta}$ otherwise, where c is determined to satisfy (1).

Are these rules any good? Are they best in any sense? Simple calculation shows that the chance of correct decision about a parameter of any non-zero magnitude is a non-central t-probability which increases to 1 as the number of experimental replications increases or, for a fixed design, as the magnitude of the parameter increases. For a single parameter, Bahadur [1] shows a sense in which this rule is optimal. For a finite number, $p > 1$, of parameters, Section 5 in [2] shows how Spjøtvoll's work applies to prove how these rules maximize the minimum expected number of correct decisions, subject to a bound α^* on the expected number of incorrect decisions. Note that this maximin optimality is closely related to the proposed goal, but that the expected number of incorrect decisions always exceeds P(> 0 incorrect decisions) (cf. (1)) by an amount decreasing to 0 as α approaches 0. Optimal rules in the problem as originally posed are considered in Section 4, below.

An important practical question remains, however. Namely, for what c-value is (1) attained? The general answer is by geometric probability; and this answer depends delicately on the set X^* defining the set of parameters.

In [2], it is shown that c-values for two limiting cases of interest are obtained from existing tables. For a finite number of independently estimated parameters, the c-values are the α-points of the Studentized maximum distribution. For the case of deciding about all linear functions of $\underset{\sim}{\beta}$, i.e., when $X^* = R^p$, the c-values are those tabled by Hochberg and Quade [8] for another problem. These latter c-values, of course, provide conservative values for any subset X^* of R^p.

For other conservative c-evaluations, the string of relations in Section 2.1 of [4] can be used to derive some such from existing methods of Bonferroni, Tukey, and Scheffé, and from the Studentized maximum modulus distribution.

These methods are exemplified in [2] by application in some 2-by-2 factorial designs. Critical values are determined from existing tables, and "powers" of exact and conservative methods are compared by evaluating the relative "P-effect sizes", i.e., the size of the true parameter value necessary in order to be correctly classified with chance P.

III. DECIDING THE SIGNS OF SIMPLE EFFECTS

In a 2^k factorial experiment, the simple effect of a factor in the presence of m specified other factors is the difference between expected observations with all m+1 factors present and that with only the m specified factors present. Simple interactions are differences of simple effects. The usual main effects and interactions in factorial experiments are all just sums and differences of simple effects and simple interactions, so that the latter give a more detailed, but more complex, summary of factor effects.

Example 1. In screening of two drugs in a 2-by-2 factorial design, where the levels for each drug are 0 (= absent) or 1 (= present), with cell expectations M_{ij} (i,j = 0,1), the four simple effects and one simple interaction are $M_{10}-M_{00}$, $M_{01}-M_{00}$, $M_{11}-M_{10}$, $M_{11}-M_{01}$, and $M_{11}-M_{10}-M_{01}+M_{00}$.

Example 2. In similar screening of k drugs, particularly interesting simple effects are the k comparisons of single drugs withe the control, viz., $M_{\tilde{v}}-M_{\tilde{0}}$, where $\tilde{v}$ is one of the rows of the k-by-k identity matrix. For example, with k = 2 and $\tilde{v}$ = 10, we have the simple effects $M_{10}-M_{00}$, as in Example 1.

3.1 *How Not to Decide the Signs of Simple Effects* $M_{\tilde{v}}-M_{\tilde{0}}$

Suppose one wants to decide the sign of a comparison of a factor with the control, e.g., of the simple effect, $M_{10\cdots0}-M_{\tilde{0}}$, of factor 1 with the control. In some classrooms and laboratories of my acquaintence, the common wisdom uses Yates algorithm to calculate the main effect of factor 1 and the interactions of factor 1 with all other factor combinations. If the main effect is greater-than the 1%-point of its null distribution while all the interactions test to be 0 at the 5% level, then the simple effect of factor 1 is judged positive. The author hastens to note that Fisherian classes and labs are not such places, as attested by

Yates in [11] and in a vigorous letter to the author.

For the case of a 2^3 experiment, with no 3-factor interaction in the model, a Monte Carlo study by Neyman [9] found values for the 8 cell means such that $M_{100}-M_{000}$ is negative, but such that the rule above decided that it was positive 9 times in 30, i.e., 30% of the time. Subsequently, Traxler [15] used numerical integration to find the exact probability of this incorrect decision to be .29 (although this misclassification probability goes rapidly to 0 as experimental replications increases. Thus, in drug screening, a worse-than-nothing drug would be retained for use by itself 30% of the time, far more often than the test sizes would suggest.

The cause of this seeming paradox is the fact that simple effects can combine algebraically to yield zero interactions and positive main effect, even though $M_{100}-M_{000}$ is negative. In [6] this algebra is worked out, along with the probability calculus which reduces the search for worst-case parameters to a single dimension. It is then demonstrated, in examples close in spirit to Neyman's, that: (i) if no 3-factor interaction is included in the model, the chance of misclassification can be over 90%, (ii) if included in the model but not its analysis, the chance of misconduct is above 3/8, while (iii) if included in both model and analysis, the chance of misconduct is about 1/4. Moreover, all of (i) - (iii) obtain independent of the number of replications of the experiment.

3.2 *How to Decide above Simple Effects*

To decide about simple effects and interactions, [6] suggests that the decision about each parameter should not involve estimates for other parameters. In fact, [2] shows how to make such decisions in an optimal way, based on estimators for the parameters in question only. The only problem with implementing these rules is determination of the critical points to achieve (1).

In [4], some entertaining but intricate geometric probability and numerical analysis is used to determine exact critical points for Examples 1 and 2, above. In addition, Section 2 in [4] cites several methods for obtaining conservative critical points. For these examples, the Bonferroni method always gives the sharpest (often nearly sharp) conservative method, while a Tukey-type method can often be used for a poor-second or -third best evaluation. Other competitors for second-best in various situations are based on the Studentized maximum modulus distribution and a sharpened-Scheffé method, while an unsharpened Scheffé method does uniformly worst. For problems wherein the number of parameters for decision is not >>p (the dimension of $\underset{\sim}{\beta}$), the Bonferroni method would appear to be the only serious competitor to the hard-to-evaluate exact critical points.

In discussion of Neyman's 1976 Keynote [10], Professor Scheffé's crypto-analysis was, "Dunnett's done it!" In fact, Appendix B in [4] shows that Dunnett's [7] work gives too-liberal rules in the present case, wherein to decide positive-is-negative is as bad as deciding negative-is-positive.

IV. ON OPTIMAL RULES SUBJECT TO (1)

As noted in Section 2, rules based on t-statistics are optimal among those which satisfy, not (1) but, a type I error criterion closely related to (1). Is the optimal rule subject to (1) any different? The answer is, "Yes," as shown in [5] and [3] for the case of deciding about only two parameters. The key to the work is to picture how a decision rule subdivides the $(\hat{\beta}_1, \hat{\beta}_2)$-plane into the 9 decision sets, (++),(+0),(+-),(+),(00),(0-),(-+),(-0),(--). For the rules, above, based on t-tests, all these regions are rectanges, defined as the intersection of the "inconclusive data" regions, $\{\hat{\beta}: \hat{\beta}_i < cS\}$, for the two parameters. For cases when one parameter is large, while the other is close to zero, it might seem possible to reduce the no-decision region to be centered on the axis with half-width as small as the α-point of the $\hat{\beta}_i$

distribution. In fact, when the $\hat{\beta}_i$ are independent and the (00) (no decision) region is expanded rectangularly to achieve (1), the resulting "Celtic cross" subdivision is shown in [5] to improve the minimum chance of correct decision, relative to the t-test rule.

Even more positively, subject to mild and reasonable symmetry and convexity properties, a maximin correct-decision rule, which satisfies (1) when both parameters approach zero, is shown in [5] to be the solution to a linear programming problem. In fact, there are two solutions to this problem, i.e., two maximin rules, as detailed in [5] and [3], respectively. These two rules coincide only in cases of independent parameter estimators.

The first optimal rule, studied in [5], has the double-cross shape. That is, the two-decision regions ((++),(+-),(-+),(--)) are infinite rectangles, the region of indecision about at least one parameter is the intersection of two strips, and the no-decision region, (00), is a cross of the same width embedded therein. Critical points and probabilities of correct decision are tabled for a large number of parameter pairs and for cases of both independent and dependent estimators. When parameter estimators are dependent, it is shown that the Double Cross violates (1), but only minutely, when one parameter approaches zero and the other is of opposite sign and increases without limit. Even when the Double Cross is exactly maximin under (1), there exist parameter pairs for which the Celtic cross improves on its expected number of correct decisions, showing the non-existence of a globally optimal rule.

In [3], the second linear programming solution to the maximin problem is investigated. In this case, all four two-decision regions have the same probability when parameters are zero. This requires larger values for pairs of estimators to be classed as having the same sign, relative to the Double Cross. Consequently, this optimal rule, which is shown to satisfy (1) for all parameter values, has quite smaller expected number of correct decisions when both parameters have rather large values, both with the same sign. On the other hand, because of the increase of the no-decision region required by (1) and its decreased two-decision regions, this rule has relatively very good expectation of correct classification when only one of the two parameters is rather large. Thus, one's choice of decision rule, among those which do comparably if not identically when parameters are both nearly zero, might well depend on the alternatives envisaged in practice. To protect against cases wherein at most one parameter is large, the second maximin rule is preferred. If both parameters are thought to be large, then the Double Cross, or the sub-optimal Spjøtvoll or Celtic Crosses, would be preferred.

For the case of deciding the signs of three parameters, solution to a corresponding linear programming problem can be shown to give maximin rules which have hideous global properties. In this case, the corresponding triple-cross rule does well globally. And the search goes on for a definition of optimality for which the optimal rules are good globally...and for those optimal rules.

ACKNOWLEDGMENT

I am grateful to Professor Neyman for his initiation of and interaction in this work.

REFERENCES

[1] Bahadur, R. R. (1952-3). A property of the t-statistic. *Sankhyā 12*, 79-88.

[2] Bohrer, R. (1979). Multiple three-decision rules for parametric signs. *J. Amer. Statist. Assoc. 74*, 432-437.

[3] Bohrer, R. (1981). Optimal multiple decision problems: principles and procedures. *Proceedings of the 1981 Berkeley Interdisciplinary Cancer Study Conference.* L. LeCam and J. Neyman, Editors. North-Holland, Amsterdam.

[4] Bohrer, R., Chow, W., Faith, R., Joshi, V. M., and Wu, C.-F. (1981). Multiple three-decision rules for factorial simple effects: Bonferroni wins again.! *J. Amer. Statist. Assoc.* *76*, 119-124.

[5] Bohrer, R. and Schervish, M. (1980). An optimal multiple decision rule for signs of parameters. *Proc. Nat. Acad. Sci.* *77*, 52-56.

[6] Bohrer, R. and Sheft, J. (1979). Misclassification probabilities in 2^p factorial experiments. *J. Statist. Plan. and Inference* *3*, 79-84.

[7] Dunnett, C. W. (1955). A multiple comparison procedure for comparing several treatments with a control. *J. Amer. Statist. Assoc.* *50*, 1096-1121.

[8] Hochberg, Y. and Quade, D. (1975). One-sided simultaneous confidence bounds on regression surfaces with intercepts. *J. Amer. Statist. Assoc.* *70*, 889-891.

[9] Neyman, J. (1935). Complex experiments. Contribution to the Discussions of the Paper by F. Yates. *J. Roy. Statist. Soc. Suppl.* *2*, 235-242.

[10] Neyman, J. (1976). Synergistic effects and the corresponding optimal version of the multiple comparison problem. *Statistical Decision Theory and Related Topics, II*, S. S. Gupta and D. S. Moore (eds.). Academic Press, New York.

[11] Neyman, J. and Yates, F. (1936). Correspondence. Complex experiments. *J. Roy. Statist. Soc. Suppl.* 3, 83-85.

[12] Scheffé, Henry (1959). *The Analysis of Variance.* Wiley & Sons, New York.

[13] Spjøtvoll, E. (1972). On the optimality of some multiple comparison procedures. *Ann. Math. Statist.* *43*, 398-411.

[14] Tong, Y. L. (1969). On partitioning a set of normal populations by their locations with respect to a control. *Ann. Math. Statist.* *40*, 1300-1324.

[15] Traxler, R. (1976). A snag in the history of factorial experiments. *On the History of Statistics and Probability*, D. B. Owen (ed.). Marcel Dekker, New York.

A UNIFIED ADMISSIBILITY PROOF

Lawrence D. Brown[1] and Jiunn Tzon Hwang[2]

Department of Mathematics
Cornell University
Ithaca, New York, U.S.A.

I. INTRODUCTION

This paper contains an admissibility proof for a variety of generalized Bayes estimators. The context is the problem of estimating the natural mean vector of an exponential family under a quadratic-form loss.

The ambition of the paper is two-fold. One is to establish the admissibility of certain natural procedures whose admissibility was previously in question, and to enable the proposal of new admissible procedures in certain situations. The second is to provide a simpler, more transparent proof even in previously established cases - a proof which also displays the similarity of all problems within the context of the theorem.

The theorem here includes Karlin's theorem on the admissibility of linear estimators in one-parameter exponential families. See Karlin [19]; also Cheng [10], Zidek [25] and Ghosh and Meeden [12].

But, the result here is not limited to one parameter exponential families; and covers a wide variety of generalized Bayes estimators, not merely linear estimators. In this same sense the

[1]Research supported in part by National Science Foundation grant MCS 7824175.

[2]Research supported in part by National Science Foundation grant MCS 8003568.

ISBN 0-12-307501-7

proof here may be thought of as a double extension of Cheng's [10] proof of Karlin's theorem.

There is another proof in the literature with considerable superficial similarity to the proof here. Zidek [25] gives a proof of admissibility in a very general one parameter context. See also Portnoy [21]. Zidek's theorem also contains Karlin's theorem. It may even be that Zidek's theorem includes much of ours in the one parameter situation, however Zidek's main regularity condition is relatively obscure in the general case. The precise connection is therefore not easy to establish.

The principal elements of our proof are Blyth's lemma, Green's Theorem (integration by parts), and the Cauchy-Schwartz inequality. Zidek's proof involves exactly these same elements, but they are applied differently and hence lead to a different result.

II. SETTING

Introduce the standard elements of an estimation problem: the sample space, $\mathcal{X}$, the parameter space, Θ, and decision space, $\mathcal{A}$, each contained in $\mathbb{R}^p$. Assume the unknown distribution on $\mathcal{X}$ is from an exponential family with densities

$$f_\theta(x) = e^{\theta \cdot x - \psi(\theta)}$$

relative to a σ-finite Borel measure, ν, on $\mathcal{X}$. Take Θ to be the natural parameter space,

$$\Theta = \{\boldsymbol{\theta}: \int e^{\theta \cdot x} \nu(dx) < \infty\}.$$

Assume Θ is open in $\mathbb{R}^p$. Then

$$E_\theta(X) = \nabla\psi(\theta).$$

See, for example, Barndorff-Nielson [1]. Assume for now that the loss function is

$$(2.1) \qquad L(\theta,a) = ||a - \nabla\psi(\theta)||^2 = ||a - E_\theta(X)||^2.$$

Other quadratic type losses will be considered later. The risk of a non-randomized estimator δ: $\mathcal{X} \to \mathcal{A}$ is

$$R(\theta,\delta) = E_\theta(L(\theta,\delta(X)).$$

For convenience, introduce the notation

$$I_x h = \int h(\theta)e^{\theta\cdot x-\psi(\theta)}d\theta.$$

Let G be a non-negative measure on Θ with differentiable density g. Assume $G(K) < \infty$ for every compact $K \subset \Theta$. Suppose

$$(2.2) \qquad I_x(||\nabla g||) < \infty \quad \text{for all } x \in \mathcal{X}.$$

Then, *define*

$$\delta_g(x) = x + \frac{I_x(\nabla g)}{I_x g}$$

with the obvious convention that $\frac{I_x(\nabla g)}{\infty} = 0$. As motivation for this definition, note that if $\Theta = \mathbb{R}^p$ and if $I_x g < \infty$ then

$$(2.3) \qquad \delta_g(x) = x + \frac{I_x(\nabla g)}{I_x g} = \frac{I_x(g\ \nabla\psi)}{I_x g}$$

$$= \frac{\int_\Theta \nabla\psi(\theta)f_\theta(x)g(\theta)d\theta}{\int_\Theta f_\theta(x)g(\theta)d\theta}$$

by Green's theorem and (2.2). Thus in this case δ_g is the generalized Bayes estimator corresponding to g. The expression (2.3) is frequently valid also when $\Theta \neq \mathbb{R}^p$, and in these cases δ_g is again the appropriate generalized Bayes estimator. See the remark following (5.1).

III. BASIC RESULT FOR $\Theta = \mathbb{R}^p$

Impose two conditions on the generalized density, g, in addition to the mild conditions implicit in Section 2:

The *growth condition*,

$$\int_{\mathbb{R}^p - S} \frac{g(\theta)}{||\theta||^2 \ell n^2(||\theta|| \vee 2)} d\theta < \infty \tag{3.1}$$

where $S = \{\theta: ||\theta|| \leqq 1\}$ and $a \vee b = \max\{a,b\}$.

And, the *asymptotic flatness condition*,

$$\int I_x\{g||\frac{\nabla g}{g} - \frac{I_x \nabla g}{I_x g}||^2\}\nu(dx) < \infty. \tag{3.2}$$

This form of the condition is not easy to verify. A more transparent but slightly less general condition is

$$\int_{\mathbb{R}^p} \frac{||\nabla g(\theta)||^2}{g(\theta)} d\theta < \infty. \tag{3.3}$$

LEMMA 3.1. *Equation* (3.3) *implies Equation* (3.2).

Proof. $I_x(g||\frac{\nabla g}{g} - \frac{I_x \nabla g}{I_x g}||^2)$

$$= I_x(\frac{||\nabla g||^2}{g}) - \frac{||I_x \nabla g||^2}{I_x g}$$

$$\leqq I_x(\frac{||\nabla g||^2}{g})$$

and

$$\int_{\mathcal{X}} I_x(\frac{||\nabla g||^2}{g})\nu(dx) = \int \frac{||\nabla g(\theta)||^2}{g(\theta)} d\theta.$$

One final minor technical assumption is

$$\sup\{R(\theta,\delta_g): \theta \varepsilon K\} < \infty \text{ for all compact sets } K \subset \Theta. \tag{3.4}$$

Here is the basic theorem for $\Theta = \mathbb{R}^p$ and ordinary quadratic loss (2.1).

THEOREM 3.1. *Assume* (3.1), (3.2) *and* (3.4). *Then* δ_g *is admissible.*

Before proving Theorem 3.1, we first introduce some notations. Let

$$B(g,\delta) = \int R(\theta,\delta)g(\theta)d\theta.$$

The sequence $h_n\colon \Theta \to [0,1]$ of absolutely continuous functions will be explicitly defined later so that, for every n, $h_n(\theta) = 1$ if $\theta \in S$ for some set S with $\int_S g(\theta)d\theta > 0$, and

$h_n(\theta) = 0$ for $||\theta|| > n$. Let $g_n(\theta) = h_n^2(\theta)g(\theta)$ and let

$$\Delta_n = B(g_n,\delta_g) - B(g_n,\delta_{g_n}).$$

In common with many admissibility proofs, the proof of Theorem 3.1 is based on Blyth's method. See Blyth [6], Stein [22] as well as page 386 of Berger's book [4]. The proof is easily supplied below.

Blyth's method: δ_g *is admissible if* $\exists\{h_n\} \ni \Delta_n \to 0$.

Proof. Suppose δ_g not admissible and let $R(\theta,\delta') \leqq R(\theta,\delta_g)$ with $\delta' \neq \delta_g$(a.e.(ν)). Let $\delta'' = (\delta' + \delta_g)/2$. Then $R(\theta,\delta'') < R(\theta,\delta_g)$ $\forall\theta$ by Jensen's inequality. Then

$$\begin{aligned}\Delta_n &= \sup\{B(g_n,\delta_g) - B(g_n,\delta)\colon \delta\}\\ &\geqq B(g_n,\delta_g) - B(g_n,\delta'')\\ &= \int (R(\theta,\delta_g) - R(\theta,\delta''))g_n(\theta)d\theta\\ &\geqq \int_S (R(\theta,\delta_g) - R(\theta,\delta''))g(\theta)d\theta.\end{aligned}$$

This implies

$$\Delta_n \not\to 0,$$

which is a contradiction.

Proof of Theorem 3.1. A familiar algebraic manipulation yields

$$(3.5)\quad \Delta_n = \int \|\delta_g(x) - \delta_{g_n}(x)\|^2 (I_x g_n)\nu(dx)$$

because

$$\Delta_n = \iint (\|\delta_g(x) - \nabla\psi(\theta)\|^2 - \|\delta_{g_n}(x) - \nabla\psi(\theta)\|^2) f_\theta(x)\nu(dx) g_n(\theta)d\theta$$

$$= \int \{(\delta_g(x) - \delta_{g_n}(x)) \cdot (\delta_g(x) + \delta_{g_n}(x) - 2\frac{I_x(g_n\nabla\psi)}{I_x g_n})(I_x g_n)\nu(dx)$$

$$= \int \|\delta_g(x) - \delta_{g_n}(x)\|^2 (I_x g_n)\nu(dx).$$

Hence, by the differentiability of g and h_n,

$$\Delta_n = \int \left\| \frac{I_x(\nabla g)}{I_x g} - \frac{I_x(\nabla g_n)}{I_x g_n} \right\|^2 (I_x g_n)\nu(dx)$$

$$= \int \left\| \frac{I_x(\nabla g)}{I_x g} - \frac{I_x(h_n^2 \nabla g)}{I_x g_n} - \frac{I_x(g\nabla h_n^2)}{I_x g_n} \right\|^2 (I_x g_n)\nu(dx).$$

Continuing from the above,

$$\Delta_n \leq 2\int \left\| \frac{I_x(\nabla g)}{I_x g} - \frac{I_x(h_n^2 \nabla g)}{I_x g_n} \right\|^2 (I_x g_n)\nu(dx)$$

$$+ 2\int \left\| \frac{I_x(g\nabla h_n^2)}{I_x g_n} \right\|^2 (I_x g_n)\nu(dx)$$

$$= 2(B_n + A_n). \quad \text{(say)}$$

Showing $A_n \to 0$:

$$A_n = 4\int \left|\left| \frac{I_x(gh_n \nabla h_n)}{I_x(gh_n^2)} \right|\right|^2 (I_x g_n)\nu(dx)$$

$$\leqq 4\int I_x(g||\nabla h_n||^2)\nu(dx) \quad \text{(by Cauchy-Schwarz inequality)}$$

$$= 4\int ||\nabla h_n(\theta)||^2 g(\theta)d\theta.$$

Let

$$\text{(3.6)} \qquad h_n(\theta) = \begin{cases} 1 & ||\theta|| \leqq 1 \\ 1 - \dfrac{\ell n(||\theta||)}{\ell n(n)} & 1 \leq ||\theta|| \leq n \\ 0 & ||\theta|| \geqq n, \end{cases}$$

$$n = 2,3,\ldots .$$

Clearly

$$\text{(3.7)} \qquad ||\nabla h_n(\theta)||^2 = \frac{1}{||\theta||^2 \ell n^2(n)} \chi_{1\leqq||\theta||\leqq n}(\theta)$$

$$\leqq \frac{1}{||\theta||^2 \ell n^2 \; (||\theta|| \vee 2)} \chi_{||\theta||\geq 1}(\theta).$$

Note that $||\nabla h_n(\theta)||^2 \to 0$ for each $\theta \in \Theta$. Condition (3.1) (the growth condition) and the bound in (3.7) yield that

$$\int \sup_n ||\nabla h_n(\theta)||^2 g(\theta)d\theta < \infty.$$

Hence $A_n \to 0$ by the dominated converence theorem.

Showing $B_n \to 0$:

The integrand of B_n is

$$||I_x(g_n \frac{I_x(\nabla g)}{I_x g} - h_n^2 \nabla g)||^2 / I_x g_n$$

$$= ||I_x(g_n(\frac{I_x \nabla g}{I_x g} - \frac{\nabla g}{g}))||^2 / I_x g_n$$

$$\leqq I_x(g_n||\frac{I_x(\nabla g)}{I_x g} - \frac{\nabla g}{g}||^2) \qquad \text{(Cauchy-Schwarz)}$$

$$\leqq I_x(g||\frac{I_x(\nabla g)}{I_x g} - \frac{\nabla g}{g}||^2) \quad \text{since} \quad g_n = h_n^2 g \leqq g.$$

Note the integrand of B_n approaches zero for each x. Apply the flatness condition (3.2) with the above bound to get $B_n \to 0$ by the dominated convergence theorem.

Hence

$$\Delta_n \leqq A_n + B_n \to 0.$$

So δ_g is admissible by Blyth's method.

IV. APPLICATIONS OF THEOREM 3.1

The following is an interesting general Corollary to Theorem 3.1.

COROLLARY 4.1. *If* $\Theta = \mathbb{R}^p$ *and* $p = 1$ *or* $p = 2$ *then the estimator* $\delta(x) = x$ *is admissible.*

Proof. Let $g = 1$. Then $\delta_g(x) = x$ since $\nabla g \equiv 0$. In this case, the regularity conditions of Theorem 3.1 are trivial to verify.

When $p = 1$ then this corollary is a special case of Karlin's theorem. The result for $p = 2$ is new, although special cases have been previously established as noted in Examples 4.1 and 4.2, below.

Example 4.1; *Normal distributions.* Suppose $X \sim N(\theta, I)$. By Corollary 4.1, *if* $p = 1$ *or* $p = 2$ *then* $\delta(x) = x$ *is admissible.* (For $p = 1$ there are proofs of this result which predate Karlin's paper. See Blyth [6], and Hodges and Lehmann [13]. For $p = 2$, the first proof of this result is in Stein [23]).

In general:

(i) If $g(\theta) \leqq ||\theta||^{2-p-\varepsilon}$ for some $\varepsilon > 0$ and

$$||\frac{\nabla g(\theta)}{g(\theta)}|| = O(\frac{1}{||\theta||})$$

then (3.1) and (3.3) are easy to check. Hence δ_g is admissible.

(ii) If $g(\theta) \leqq ||\theta||^{2-p}$ and

$$||\frac{\nabla g(\theta)}{g(\theta)}|| = O(\frac{1}{||\theta||}) \text{ and } \left|\frac{\partial^2 g(\theta)}{\partial\theta_i \partial\theta_j}\right| = O(\frac{1}{||\theta||^2})$$

then (3.2) can be verified with some difficulty. (Extend Lemma 3.4.1 of Brown (1971).) Condition (3.1) is still easy to check. Hence δ_g is admissible. Note that if $g(\theta) = ||\theta||^{+r}$ is smooth, as above, then $\delta_g(x) - x \sim rx/||x||^2$ as $||x|| \to \infty$. See Brown [7] and [8] or Berger and Srinivasan [5].

The generalized Bayes estimators arising out of the prior $g(\theta)$ satisfying (i) or (ii) are the commonly proposed admissible estimators. See, for example, Strawderman [24] and Berger [3]. The above results are also valid for the case $X \sim N(\theta, \Sigma)$ with Σ a known, non-singular covariance matrix. (Only the asymptotic formula for $\delta_g(x)$ need be modified.)

Example 4.2; *Poisson distributions.* Suppose X_i are independent Poisson variables with mean λ_i, $i = 1,\ldots,p$. Then the natural parameter is $\theta = (\theta_1,\ldots,\theta_p)$ with $\theta_i = \ell n\ \lambda_i$; and $\Theta = \mathbb{R}^p$. Again by Corollary 4.1, if $p = 1$ or $p = 2$ then $\delta(x) = x$ is admissible. This result for $p = 2$ was conjectured in Brown [8] and proved in Peng [20].

In general if g satisfies (i) of Example 4.1 then δ_g is admissible. If g satisfies (ii) of Example 4.1 then δ_g is *probably* also admissible, but we have not yet checked (3.2).

If $g(\theta) = ||\theta||^{-r}$ then

$$(\delta_g(x)-x)_i = \frac{r \ln x_i}{\sum_{j=1}^{p} \ln^2(x_j+1)}$$

as $x_i \to \infty$. These admissible estimators are thus similar to the (probably inadmissible) estimators in Peng [20] and in Hwang [15] improving on $\delta(x) = x$. Problems involving the weighted quadratic loss function first used by Clevenson and Zidek [11] may be treated using Theorem 2, to follow.

V. EXTENSIONS OF THE BASIC THEOREM

The basic theorem can be extended in several significant directions with only minor modifications of the proof. This section outlines three such directions and concludes with a unified statement of the resultant extended theorem. One combined effect of these extensions is to drop the previous assumption that $\Theta = \mathbb{R}^p$.

Other choices of $\{h_n\}$: In order for Blyth's method to be valid, one needs only to choose h_n so that $h_n(\theta) \geq 1$ (or even any positive number not necessary 1, as in Corollary 5.1) for all θ in a set S with $\int_S g(\theta) > 0$ and

$$(5.0) \qquad \int h_n^2(\theta) g(\theta) d\theta < \infty.$$

This latter condition will automatically be satisfied if for every n

(5.1) Closure $\{\theta: h_n(\theta) > 0\}$ is a compact subset of Θ.

The condition (5.1) is also convenient for establishing the validity of (2.3) for the prior density $h_n^2(\theta)g(\theta)$, as exploited in the algebraic manipulations in the proof of Theorems 3.1 or 5.1.

In order to show that $A_n \to 0$ as in the proof of Theorem 3.1 it is desired to choose $\{h_n\}$ so that

$$\int ||\nabla h_n(\theta)||^2 g(\theta)d\theta \to 0. \tag{5.2}$$

As in that proof this is usually accomplished by choosing $\{h_n\}$ so that $\nabla h_n(\theta) \to 0$ for each $\theta \in \Theta$ as $n \to \infty$ and so that

$$\int \sup_n ||\nabla h_n(\theta)||^2 g(\theta)d\theta < \infty. \tag{5.3}$$

This flexibility to choose $\{h_n\}$ other than as in the proof of Theorem 3.1 will only very rarely be useful if $\Theta = \mathbb{R}^p$, however it is usually essential when $\Theta \neq \mathbb{R}^p$.

One common class of examples has $\Theta = \mathop{X}\limits_{i=1}^{p} (-\infty,0)$. A natural choice of $\{h_n\}$ is then

$$h_n(\theta) = \begin{cases} 1 & \Lambda \leq 1 \\ 1 - \dfrac{\ell n\, \Lambda}{\ell n\, n} & 1 \leq \Lambda \leq n \\ 0 & \Lambda \geq n \qquad n = 2,3,4... \end{cases} \tag{5.4}$$

with $\Lambda^2 = \Lambda^2(\theta) = \sum_{i=1}^{p} \ell n^2 |\theta_i|$.

The growth condition (5.3), enabling the proof that $A_n \to 0$, is then

$$\int_{\Theta-S'} \frac{g(\theta)}{\theta_i^2 \Lambda(\theta) \ell n^2 (\Lambda(\theta) \vee 2)} d\theta < \infty \tag{5.5}$$

with $S' = \{\theta: \Lambda(\theta) < 1\}$.

Weighted quadratic loss functions: The methods of Section 3 can readily be extended to quadratic type losses more general than (2.1). Thus (2.1) will now be replaced by a loss of the form

$$L(\theta,a) = \sum_{i=1}^{p} v_i(\theta)(a_i - \beta_i \nabla_i \psi(\theta))^2 \tag{5.6}$$

$$= \sum_{i=1}^{p} v_i(\theta)(a_i - \beta_i E_\theta(X_i))^2$$

with $\beta_i > 0$ being fixed constants, and

$$\nabla_i \psi(\theta) = (\nabla\psi(\theta))_i = \frac{\partial}{\partial\theta_i} \psi(\theta).$$

It seems clear to us that the following considerations could be further readily extended to a loss of the form

$$L(\theta,a) = (a-B(\theta)\nabla\psi(\theta))'V(\theta)(a-B(\theta)\nabla\psi(\theta))$$

with $V(\theta)$ positive definite and $B(\theta)$ non-singular. To preserve algebraic and conceptual simplicity in the statement of Theorem 5.1, below, we have not pursued this possibility.

Other (nearly conjugate) priors: Note that the prior density $g(\theta) = c$ is a conjugate prior for the exponential family. If g satisfies the flatness condition (3.2), then the prior $g(\theta)$ can be thought of as nearly equal to this conjugate prior, since (3.2) forces g to behave asymptotically much like a constant. (More precisely, $\nabla \ln g \sim \nabla \ln c = 0$.) Other conjugate priors are of interest, as well as priors affiliated with them in the above sense. Such priors do not satisfy the flatness condition (3.2). Fortunately the theory can be easily modified to accommodate them.

Fix $\eta > -1$ and $\alpha \in \mathbb{R}^p$ and consider a prior density of the form

(5.7) $$g(\theta)e^{-\eta\psi(\theta)+\alpha\cdot\theta}$$

Let

$$I_x^*h = \int_\Theta h(\theta)e^{\theta\cdot(x+\alpha)-(\eta+1)\psi(\theta)}d\theta.$$

Replace the assumption (2.2) with

(5.8) $$I_x^*(|\nabla_i(v_i g)|) < \infty \quad \forall i,\ \forall\ x \in \mathcal{X}.$$

Let $\delta(x) = \delta_g^*(x)$ have coordinates

(5.9) $$\delta_i(x) = \frac{x_i+\alpha_i}{\eta+1} + \frac{I_x^*(\nabla_i(v_i g))}{(\eta+1)I_x^*(v_i g)}.$$

Note that under (5.8) and some further minor assumptions $\delta(x)$ is the generalized Bayes estimator corresponding to the density (5.7).

Growth condition: With the loss as in (5.6) and the prior density as in (5.7) the relevant growth condition now takes one of the following forms. If $\Theta = \mathbb{R}^p$:

(5.10) $$\sum_{i=1}^{p} \int_{\Theta-S} \frac{v_i(\theta)g(\theta)e^{-\eta\psi(\theta)+\alpha\cdot\theta}}{||\theta||^2 \ell n^2(||\theta||\vee 2)} d\theta < \infty.$$

(Compare this to (3.1).)

If $\Theta = \mathop{X}\limits_{i=1}^{p} (-\infty,0)$:

(5.11) $$\sum_{i=1}^{p} \int_{\Theta-S'} \frac{v_i(\theta)g(\theta)e^{-\eta\psi(\theta)+\alpha\cdot\theta}}{\theta_i^2\Lambda^2(\theta)\ell n^2(\Lambda(\theta)\vee 2)} d\theta < \infty.$$

(Compare this to (5.5).)

More generally: there exists $\{h_n\}$ satisfying (5.1) and (5.0) such that

$$(5.12) \qquad \sum_{i=1}^{p} \int (\nabla_i h_n(\theta))^2 v_i(\theta) g(\theta) e^{-\eta\psi(\theta)+\alpha\cdot\theta} d\theta \to 0.$$

(Compare this to (5.2). Note also that there is a natural extension of (5.3).)

Asymptotic flatness condition: This condition is now

$$(5.13) \qquad \sum_{i=1}^{p} \int I_x^*\{v_i g(\frac{\nabla_i(v_i g)}{v_i g} - \frac{I_x^*(\nabla_i(v_i g))}{I_x^*(v_i g)})^2\}\nu(dx) < \infty.$$

As in Lemma 3.1 this condition is implied by

$$(5.14) \qquad \sum_{i=1}^{p} \int_{\Theta} \frac{(\nabla_i[v_i(\theta)g(\theta)])^2}{v_i(\theta)g(\theta)} e^{-\eta\psi(\theta)+\alpha\cdot\theta} d\theta < \infty.$$

Here is a formal statement of the theorem.

THEOREM 5.1. *Let the loss be given by* (5.6). *Fix* $\eta > -1$ *and* g *satisfying* (5.8). *Assume that the growth condition* ((5.10) *or* (5.11) *or* (5.12)) *is satisfied and that the asymptotic flatness condition* ((5.14) *or* (5.13)) *is satisfied. Let* δ *be defined by* (5.9) *and assume the mild boundedness condition,* (3.4), *is satisfied. Then* δ *is admissible.*

Proof. The proof follows exactly the proof of Theorem 3.1. It is only necessary to substitute I_x^* for I_x and make some consequent changes in the relevant algebraic expressions, and to use the form of $\{h_n\}$ appropriate to the assumed growth condition. (Use (3.6) when $\Theta = \mathbb{R}^p$ and (5.4) when $\Theta = \times_{i=1}^{p} (-\infty,0)$.)

Karlin's theorem is a corollary of Theorem 5.1. This is given below.

COROLLARY 5.1. *Suppose* $L(\theta,a) = (a-\psi'(\theta))^2$, $p = 1$ *and* $\Theta = (a,b)$ *with* $-\infty \leq a < b \leq \infty$. *Suppose*

$$\int_a e^{\eta\psi(\theta)-\alpha\theta} d\theta = \infty$$

and

$$\int^{b} e^{\eta\psi(\theta)-\alpha\theta}\, d\theta = \infty .$$

Then the estimator $\delta(x) = (x+\alpha)/(\eta+1)$ *is admissible.*

Proof. Choose η, α as in this corollary, and $g \equiv 1$. Then δ^*_g is as given in the corollary. The flatness condition, (5.14), is trivially satisfied since $\nabla g \equiv 0$. The growth condition (5.12) is

$$\int (h_n'(\theta))^2 e^{-\eta\psi(\theta)+\theta}\, d\theta \to 0. \tag{5.15}$$

This condition is satisfied by the choice

$$h_n(\theta) = \begin{cases} \int_{\theta}^{b_n} e^{\eta\psi(t)-\alpha t}dt \Big/ \int_{(a+b)/2}^{b_n} e^{\eta\psi(t)-\alpha t}dt & \text{if } \frac{a+b}{2} \leqq \theta < b_n \\ \int_{a_n}^{\theta} e^{\eta\psi(t)-\alpha t}dt \Big/ \int_{a_n}^{(a+b)/2} e^{\eta\psi(t)-\alpha t}dt & \text{if } a_n \le \theta \le \frac{a+b}{2} \\ 0 & \text{otherwise} \end{cases}$$

where $a_n \searrow a$ and $b_n \nearrow b$. (This choice of h_n minimizes the left side of (5.15) subject to the constraints $h_n(a_n) = h_n(b_n) = 0$, $h_n((a+b)/2) = 1$).

Remarks. Example 6.3 involves a minor generalization of Theorem 5.1. Probably this type of generalization would be relevant to other problems involving discrete sample spaces. (It did not, however, seem to be of use in Example 6.2.).

It is of interest to inequire whether there is a valid converse to Theorem 5.1. That is, suppose the flatness condition (5.13) is satisfied but the general growth condition (5.12) is not, and the revised growth condition, outlined in Example 6.3 is also not satisfied. Does this imply that δ_g is inadmissible? Certain heuristic considerations indicate such a converse may be valid. In particular, in the normal setting of Example 4.1, this converse is valid (with a slightly modified flatness condition which may however, be implied by (5.13). Consult Brown [7].) A special case of this conjecture would be to determine whether the converse of Karlin's theorem is valid. This converse has been verified in special cases by Joshi [18] and by Johnstone [16], but completely general results have not yet been obtained.

VI. APPLICATIONS OF THEOREM 5.1

Example 6.1; *Gamma distributions.* Let X_i be independent gamma variables, $i = 1,\ldots,p$ with scale σ_i (unknown) and expectation $k\sigma_i$ (k is a known parameter). This forms an exponential family with natural parameter θ having coordinates $\theta_i = -\sigma_i^{-1}$ and with $\Theta = \mathop{X}_{i=1}^{p} (-\infty,0)$ and $\psi(\theta) = \sum_{i=1}^{p} -k\ \ell n|\theta_i|$. Note that $E_\theta(X_i) = \nabla_i\psi = k/|\theta_i|$. Consider a loss function of the form

$$L(\theta,a) = \Sigma|\theta_i|^{m+2}(a_i - k/|\theta_i|)^2 = \Sigma|\theta_i|^m(a_i|\theta_i| - k)^2.$$

The case $m = 0$ corresponds to the standard invariant quadratic loss.

The best invariant estimator is $\delta(x) = kx/(1+k)$, corresponding to the prior $\Pi|\theta_i|^{-m-1} = (\Pi|\theta_i|^{-2-m})e^{-\eta\psi(\theta)}$ with $\eta = 1/k$. Theorem 2 yields:

This estimator is admissible if $p = 1$, *or* $p = 2$ *and* $m = 0$ ($\Rightarrow$ standard invariant loss).

In other cases Theorem 5.1 fails for good reason, since δ is inadmissible by Berger [2].

For an admissible estimator use $\eta = 1$ and

$$g(\theta) = \frac{e(\theta)}{\Pi|\theta_j|^{m+2}(\Sigma|\theta_j|^{-m})^r} \quad \text{with} \quad r = p-1.$$

and with $e(\theta) = f(\Lambda(\theta))$ where f is an asymptotically flat function satisfying a suitable order condition, below. Condition (5.8) is satisfied if $m < k$. If $f(\lambda) = O((1+\lambda)^{2-p})$ then (5.11) is satisfied since substitution and some direct bounds yield (for $p \geqq 2$)

$$\sum \frac{v_i(\theta)g(\theta)e^{-\eta\psi(\theta)}}{\theta_i^2} = O\left(\frac{e(\theta)}{\prod_j |\theta_j|}\right)$$

for the given choice of $r = p-1$. If $f(\lambda) = O((1+\lambda)^{-p-\varepsilon})$, some $\varepsilon > 0$, then (5.14) is satisfied since substitution and some direct bounds yield

$$\sum (\nabla_i \ln v_i g)^2 v_i g\, e^{-\eta\psi(\theta)} = O\left(\frac{e(\theta)}{\prod |\theta_j|}\right).$$

(We expect that (5.13) will be satisfied under a somewhat less stringent growth condition on f. Whether or not it is satisfied under the more aesthetic condition $f = O((1+\lambda)^{2-p})$ we cannot foresee.)

We have found the form of the resultant generalized Bayes estimators hard to conveniently describe with precision. However, *when* $m = -1$ a very crude, heuristic approximation using (1) yields

$$\delta_i(x) = \frac{x_i}{1+\eta} + \frac{-rm\ q(x,m,k)}{(1+\eta)\Sigma(1/x_j)}$$

with $0 < \inf q < \sup q < \infty$. This compares well with Berger's [2] estimator

$$\delta_i(x) = \frac{x_i}{1+\eta} + \frac{-rm}{(1+\eta)^2\Sigma(1/x_j)}.$$

Presumably one can derive similar comparisons for other values of m. (Note also that for $m = +1$ we need $k > 1$, as does Berger.)

It is interesting to observe that only the value $r = p-1$ yields a prior satisfying the growth condition (5.11). One may reasonably presume that the other values of r lead to inadmissible estimators. This apparently corresponds to the fact that (for $m \leq 0$) Berger's estimator for his constant $c = p-1$ dominates his estimator for all other values of c. (See also Brown, L. [9], p. 10-12.)

Example 6.2; *Geometric distribution.* Let X_i be independent geometric (π_i) variables. Thus $P\{X_i = x\} = \pi_i^x(1-\pi_i)$, $x = 0,1,\ldots$ This forms an exponential family with natural parameter having coordinates $\theta_i = \ln \pi_i$ and with $\Theta = \mathop{X}\limits_{i=1}^{p} (-\infty,0)$ and $\psi(\theta) = -\sum_{i=1}^{p} \ln(1-e^{\theta_i})$. Note that $\nabla_i\psi(\theta) = e^{\theta_i}/(1-e^{\theta_i}) = \pi_i/(1-\pi_i)$ and $\partial^2/\partial\theta_i^2\ \psi(\theta) = \mathrm{Var}_\theta(X_i) = e^{\theta_i}/(1-e^{\theta_i})^2 = \pi_i/(1-\pi_i)^2$.

Consider the ordinary quadratic loss (2.1), and the estimator $\delta(x) = x/2$. This estimator is generalized Bayes for the conjugate prior $1\cdot e^{-\psi(\theta)}$. *When* $p = 1$ Theorem 5.1 (or Corollary 5.1) shows this estimator to be admissible. But *when* $p \geq 2$ the growth conditions (5.11) or (5.12) fails; and $\delta(x) = x/2$ is probably inadmissible.

Now, suppose

$$L(\theta,a) = \sum_{i=1}^{p} \frac{(1-\pi_i)^2}{\pi_i}\left(a_i - \frac{\pi_i}{1-\pi_i}\right)^2,$$

which is reasonable since $\mathrm{Var}\, X_i = \pi_i/(1-\pi_i)^2$. Then $\delta(x) = x/2$ is generalized Bayes for the prior $\left(\prod_{i=1}^{p} [e^{\theta_i}/(1-e^{\theta_i})^2]\right)e^{-\psi(\theta)}$.

When $p = 2$ condition (5.11) is now satisfied, so that $\delta(x) = x/2$ is admissible. The same result holds for

$$L(\theta,a) = \sum_{i=1}^{p} \frac{(1-\pi_i)^2}{\pi_i(1+\pi_i)}\cdot\left(a_i - \frac{\pi_i}{1-\pi_i}\right)^2$$

for which $\delta(x) = x/2$ is constant risk minimax.

It should be possible to use Theorem 5.1 to describe generalized priors which lead to admissible, and hopefully reasonable, estimators for the cases where $\delta(x) = x/2$ is inadmissible.

The above results generalize easily to situations where the X_i are negative binomial variables.

Example 6.3; *Poisson distributions.* Suppose X_i are independent Poisson variables with mean λ_i as in Example 4.2. Recall that $\theta_i = \ell n \ \lambda_i$. Now suppose

$$L(\theta,a) = \sum_{i=1}^{p} \lambda_i^{-1}(a_i-\lambda_i)^2.$$

This replaces the ordinary quadratic loss discussed in Example 4.2. Clevenson and Zidek [11] first studied this problem and recommended the estimator

$$\delta_{CZ}(X) = [1 - \frac{\beta+p-1}{\beta+p-1+\Sigma X_j}]X, \ p \geq 2, \ \beta \geq 0$$

which is generalized Bayes relative to the prior (in λ)

$$(6.1) \qquad f(\lambda) = (\Sigma \ \lambda_j)^{-(p-1)} \int_0^\infty u^{\beta+p-2}(u+\Sigma \ \lambda_j)^{-\beta}e^{-u}du.$$

This estimator satisfies $R(\theta,\delta_{Cz}) < p \equiv R(\theta,X)$. In terms of θ, the prior is of course $g(\theta) = \Pi e^{\theta_i} f(e^{\theta_1},\ldots,e^{\theta_p})$. We show this estimator is admissible if $\beta \geq 0$.

The proof requires a small but significant revision of Theorem 5.1. Note that if δ dominates δ_{Cz} then

$$(6.2) \qquad \delta_i(X) = 0 \text{ whenever } X_i = 0,$$

for otherwise $\lim_{\theta\to -\infty} R(\theta,\delta) = \infty$ whereas $R(\theta,\delta_{Cz}) \leq p$. Thus one may consider only the class of procedures satisfying (6.2) in the proof of Theorem 5.1. The revised growth condition (5.10) then becomes

(6.3) $$\sum \int_{R^p} (\nabla_i h_n(\theta))^2 v_i(\theta) g(\theta) j_i(\theta) d\theta < \infty$$

where $j_i(\theta) = P_\theta(X_i > 0) = 1-e^{-e^{\theta_i}}$. Similarly the asymptotic flatness conditions (5.13) and (5.14) should be modified as (6.4) and (6.5). In (6.4), $\mathcal{X}_i$ represents the set of all x for which x_i is a positive integer and x_j's are non-negative integers, and v is the discrete measure that put mass $(\Pi\, x_i!)^{-1}$ on $(x_1,\ldots,x_p)$.

(6.4) $$\sum_{i=1}^{p} \int_{\mathcal{X}_i} I_x\{v_i g(\frac{\nabla_i v_i g}{v_i g} - \frac{I_x \nabla_i v_i g}{I_x v_i g})^2\}\ v(dx) < \infty.$$

(6.5) $$\sum_{i=1}^{p} \int_{\Theta} \frac{[\nabla_i v_i(\theta) g(\theta)]^2}{v_i(\theta) g(\theta)} j_i(\theta) d\theta < \infty.$$

Let

$$\begin{aligned} h_n(\theta) &= 1 && \text{if } 0 \le \Lambda = \textstyle\sum \lambda_i < 1 \\ &= 1 - \frac{\ell n\ \Lambda}{\ell n\ n} && 1 < \Lambda < n \\ &= 0 && \text{otherwise.} \end{aligned}$$

We first prove that such h_n satisfies condition (5.0). Note $R(\theta, \delta_{CZ})$ is bounded by p and

(6.6) $$\int h_n^2(\theta) g(\theta) d\theta \le \int_{\Lambda \le n} f(\lambda) d\lambda.$$

Let $f_0(\sum \lambda_i)$ denote the integral term in the definition, (6.1), of $f(\lambda)$. Note that $f_0(t) = 0((1+t)^{-\beta})$, and in particular $f_0 \equiv$ constant for $\beta = 0$. Hence from (6.6)

(6.7) $$\int h_n^2(\theta) g(\theta) d\theta \le \int_{\Lambda \le n} \Lambda^{-p+1} 0((1+\Lambda)^{-\beta}) \Lambda^{p-1} d\Lambda\ dr_1,\ldots,dr_{p-1}$$

where $\lambda_1,\ldots,\lambda_p$ is transformed to Λ, $r_1,\ldots,r_{p-1}$ by the relation

$\Lambda = \sum \lambda_i$ and $\gamma_i = \lambda_i/\Lambda$. The upper bound in (6.7) is clearly finite. To check the growth condition (6.3), we note that

$$\nabla_i h_n(\theta) = -\lambda_i/[\Lambda \,\ell n\, n] \qquad 1 \leq \Lambda \leq n$$

$$= 0 \qquad \text{otherwise.}$$

Hence the ith term in (6.3) is bounded by

$$\frac{1}{\ell n^2 n} \int_{1 < \Lambda < n} (1-e^{-\lambda_i}) f(\lambda) \lambda_i/\Lambda^2 d\lambda.$$

Omitting $(1-e^{-\lambda i})$ and using the same transformation as in deriving (6.7), the last expression is smaller than

$$(6.8) \qquad \frac{1}{\ell n^2 n} \int_1^n f_0(\Lambda)/\Lambda \, d\Lambda$$

since $f_0(\Lambda) = 0((1+\Lambda)^{-\beta})$, so (6.8) approaches zero for $\beta \geq 0$.

The expression in (6.7) therefore goes to zero and the growth condition (6.3) is satisfied.

For the asymptotic flatness condition, we consider first (6.5). Note that

$$|\nabla_i v_i g/v_i g| \leq (p+\beta-1)\lambda_i/\Lambda.$$

Hence the ith term of (6.5) is bounded by

$$(6.9) \qquad \int (p+\beta-1)^2 (1-e^{-\lambda_i}) f(\lambda)/\lambda_i d\lambda.$$

Again the transformation used in obtaining (6.7) can be applied to (6.9) which gives

$$(6.10) \qquad \int (p+\beta-1)^2 (1-e^{-\Lambda r_i}) f_0(\Lambda)/[\Lambda \; r_i] d\Lambda \; dr_1 \ldots dr_{p-1}$$

$$\leq (p+\beta-1)^2 \int_0^\infty \int_0^\Lambda (1-e^{-u} 0((\Lambda+1)^{-\beta})/[u\Lambda] du d\Lambda.$$

Note that

$$\int_0^2 \int_0^\Lambda (1-e^{-u}) O((\Lambda+1)^{-\beta}) / [u\Lambda] du d\Lambda$$

is bounded by $kc \int_0^2 \int_0^\Lambda \Lambda^{-1} du\, d\Lambda = 2ck$ where c denotes

$\max_{0 \le u \le 2} (1-e^{-u})u^{-1} < \infty$, and $k = \max O[(\Lambda+1)^{-\beta}]$ for $0 < \Lambda < 2$.

Therefore the upper bound in (6.10) is, in turn, smaller than

$$(p+\beta-1)^2 (2ck + \int_2^\infty \int_0^\Lambda O((1+\Lambda)^{-\beta})(1-e^{-u}) / [u\Lambda] du d\Lambda.$$

Let Γ represent the double integral in the above expression. Again using the fact $(1-e^{-u})u^{-1} \le c$ for $0 \le u \le 1$, Γ is clearly less than

$$c \int_2^\infty \int_0^1 O((1+\Lambda)^{-\beta}) \Lambda^{-1} du d\Lambda$$

$$+ \int_2^\infty \int_1^\Lambda O((1+\Lambda)^{-\beta}) \Lambda^{-1} u^{-1} du d\Lambda.$$

Since $\int_2^\infty O((1+\Lambda)^{-\beta}) \Lambda^{-1} d\Lambda$ is finite, it is sufficient to show

$\int_2^\infty \int_1^\Lambda O((1+\Lambda)^{-\beta}) \Lambda^{-1} u^{-1} du d\Lambda < \infty$, to establish the asymptotic flatness condition. This is obvious for $\beta > 0$, since for sufficiently large Λ, $(1+\Lambda)^{-\beta} < (\ell n\ \Lambda)^{-3}$.

To verify the asymptotic flatness condition for $\beta = 0$, we consider (6.4), which clearly equals

$$(6.11) \qquad \sum_{i=1}^{p} \int_{\mathcal{X}_i} \{ I_x \frac{[\nabla_i v_i g]^2}{v_i g} - \frac{(I_x \nabla_i v_i g)^2}{I_x v_i g} \} \nu(dx).$$

Direct calculation gives the formula

$$(6.12)\qquad I_x \Lambda^{k_0} \prod_{i=1}^{p} \lambda_i^{k_i}$$

$$\overset{\text{defn.}}{=} \int \Lambda^{k_0} \prod_{i=1}^{p} \lambda_i^{k_i} e^{\theta x - \psi(\theta)} d\theta$$

$$= (z+k_0-1+\sum k_i)! \prod_{i=1}^{p} (k_i+x_i-1)!/[z-1+\sum k_i]$$

where $z = \sum x_i$ and k_0 and k_i's are arbitrary integers such that the factorials make sense. From (6.1), $g(\theta) = (p-2)!$ $(\Pi\lambda_i)(\sum\lambda_i)^{-p+1}$. By using (6.12), (6.11) can be shown to equal

$$(6.13)\qquad (p-1)^2(p-2)! \sum_{i=1}^{p} \int_{\mathcal{X}_i} \frac{(z-1)!}{(z+p-1)!}\left[\frac{x_i+1}{z+p} - \frac{x_i}{z+p-1}\right](\pi x_i!)\nu(dx)$$

$$= (p-1)^2(p-2)! \sum_{i=1}^{p} \sum_{x\varepsilon\mathcal{X}_i} \frac{(z-1)!}{(z+p-1)!}\left[\frac{x_i+1}{z+p} - \frac{x_i}{z+p-1}\right].$$

By adding all the terms corresponding to x such that $\sum x_i = z$, (6.13) equals the multiplication of $(p-1)^2(p-2)!$ and

$$(6.14)\qquad \sum_{z=1}^{\infty} \frac{(z-1)!}{(z+p-1)!}\left[1-\frac{z}{z+p-1}\right]\frac{(z+p-1)!}{z!(p-1)!},$$

since there are $(z+p-1)!/[z!(p-1)!]$ many points whose coordinates are non-negative integers summing up to z. The expression in (6.14) is now

$$\sum_{z=1}^{\infty} \frac{(p-1)}{(z+p-1)z(p-1)!}$$

which is clearly finite. The asymptotic flatness condition (6.4) is now satisfied for $\beta = 0$. Theorem 5.1 implies that δ_{CZ} is admissible if $\beta \geq 0$ and $p \geq 2$. This proves the conjecture of Brown (1979). For $\beta < 0$, δ_{CZ} is inadmissible as conjectured in Brown [8] and proved in Hwang [15]. The technique developed here therefore proves the best admissibility results that one can hope for δ_{CZ}.

After this paper was presented, Iain Johnstone [17] proved the admissibility of a wide class of specific estimators for this Poisson problem by using different methods. His results include our Example 6.3 as a special case.

REFERENCES

[1] Barndorff-Neilsen, O. (1977). *Information and Exponential Families in Statistical Theory*. John Wiley, New York.

[2] Berger, J. (1980). Improving on inadmissible estimators in continuous exponential families with applications to simultaneous estimation of Gamma scale parameters. *Ann. Statist.* *8*, 545-571.

[3] Berger, J. (1980). A robust generalized Bayes estimator and confidence region for a multivariate normal mean. *Ann. Statist.* *8*, 716-761.

[4] Berger, J. (1980). *Statistical Decision Theory: Foundations, Concepts, and Methods*. Springer-Verlag, New York.

[5] Berger, J. and Srinivasan, C. (1978). Generalized Bayes estimators in multivariate problems. *Ann. Statist.* *6*, 783-801.

[6] Blyth, C. R. (1951). On minimax statistical decision procedures and their admissibility. *Ann. Math. Statist.* *22*, 22-42.

[7] Brown, L. D. (1971). Admissible estimators, recurrent diffusions, and insoluble boundary value problems. *Ann. Math. Statist.* *42*, 855-904.

[8] Brown, L. D. (1979). A heuristic method for determining admissibility of estimators-with applications. *Ann. Statist.* 7, 961-994.

[9] Brown, L. D. (1981). The differential inequality of a statistical estimation problem. Preprint, Cornell University, Ithaca.

[10] Cheng, P. (1964). Minimax estimates of parameters of distributions belonging to the exponential family. *Chinese Math. - Acta 5*, 277-299.

[11] Clevenson, M. and Zidek, J. (1977). Simultaneous estimation of the mean of independent Poisson laws. *J. Amer. Statist. Assoc. 70*, 698-705.

[12] Ghosh, M. and Meeden, G. (1977). Admissibility of linear estimators in the one parameter exponential family. *Ann. Statist. 5*, 772-778.

[13] Hodges, J. L., Jr., and Lehmann, E. L. (1951). Some applications of the Cramer-Rao inequality. *Proc. Second Berkeley Symp. Math. Statist. Probab. 1*, Univ. of California Press, Berkeley.

[14] Hwang, J. T. (1979). Improving upon standard estimators in discrete exponential families with applications to Poisson and negative binomial cases. Submitted to Ann. Statist.

[15] Hwang, J. T. (1980). Semi Tail Upper Bounds on the class of a admissible estimators in discrete exponential families with applications to Poisson and Negative binomial families. Submitted to Ann. Statist.

[16] Johnstone, Iain (1981). Lecture in Purdue 3rd Symposium.

[17] Johnstone, Iain (1981). Admissible Estimators of Poisson Means, Birth-Death Processes and Discrete Dirichlet Problems. Ph.D. thesis, Cornell University, Ithaca.

[18] Joshi, V. M. (1969). On a theorem of Karlin regarding admissible estimates for exponential populations. *Ann. Math. Statist. 40*, 216-223.

[19] Karlin, S. (1958). Admissibility for estimation with quadratic loss. *Ann. Math. Statist. 29*, 411-415.

[20] Peng, J.C.M. (1975). Simultaneous estimation of the parameters of independent Poisson distributions. Technical Report 78, Dept. Statist., Stanford Univ.

[21] Portnoy, S. (1971). Formal Bayes estimation with application to a random effects model. *Ann. Math. Statist 42*, 1379-1402.

[22] Stein, C. (1955). A necessary and sufficient condition for admissibility. *Ann. Math. Statist. 26*, 518-522.

[23] Stein, C. (1956). Inadmissibility of the usual estimator for the mean of a multivariate normal distribution. *Proc. Third Berkeley Symp. Math. Statist. Probability 1*. University of California Press, Berkeley.

[24] Strawderman, W. (1971). Proper Bayes minimax estimators of the multivariate normal mean. *Ann. Math. Statist. 42*, 385-388.

[25] Zidek, James V. (1970). Sufficient conditions for admissibility under squared errors loss of formal Bayes estimators. *Ann. Math. Statist. 41*, 446-456.

SOME ASPECTS OF ESTIMATION IN HETEROSCEDASTIC LINEAR MODELS

Raymond J. Carroll[1]

Department of Statistics
The University of North Carolina
Chapel Hill, North Carolina, U.S.A.

David Ruppert[2]

Department of Statistics
The University of North Carolina
Chapel Hill, North Carolina, U.S.A.

Robert N. Holt, Jr.

School of Accounting
University of Georgia
Athens, Georgia, U.S.A.

I. INTRODUCTION

We shall consider a heteroscedastic linear model in which the variances are a function of the mean response, i.e.,

$$(1.1) \qquad Y_i = x_i' \beta + \sigma_i \varepsilon_i$$

$$= \tau_i + \sigma_i \varepsilon_i \qquad\qquad i = 1,\ldots,N.$$

Here $\{x_i\}$ are (px1) vectors, as is β, the unknown regression parameter. The errors $\{\varepsilon_i\}$ are i.i.d. and symmetrically distributed about zero. The possible heteroscedasticity is expressed

[1]Also at the National Heart, Lung and Blood Institute. Supported by the Air Force Office of Scientific Research under Grant AFOSR-80-0080.

[2]Supported by National Science Foundation Grant MCS78-01240.

ISBN 0-12-307501-7

through the terms $\{\sigma_i\}$ which depend on the mean response in the following way:

$$\sigma_i = \sigma\, H_*(\tau_i,\lambda) = H(\tau_i,\theta) \text{ with } \theta = (\sigma,\lambda). \tag{1.2}$$

In the model (1.1)-(1.2), $\theta = (\sigma,\lambda)$ is an unknown parameter, while H is a known function.

The model (1.1)-(1.2) often arises when a preliminary least squares fit shows that the dispersion of the residuals increases with the magnitude of the fitted values. Various special forms of (1.2) have been suggested including

$$\sigma_i = \sigma(1 + |\tau_i|)^\lambda; \quad \sigma_i = \sigma|\tau_i|^\lambda \quad \text{(Box and Hill [2]);}$$

$$\sigma_i = \sigma \exp(\lambda\tau_i) \quad \text{(Bickel [1]);} \tag{1.3}$$

$$\sigma_i = (1 + \lambda\tau_i^2)^{\frac{1}{2}} \quad \text{(Jobson and Fuller [12]).}$$

There is a large literature on estimating β in these heteroscedastic linear models; see Box and Hill [2], Carroll [3,4], Carroll and Ruppert [5,6,7], Dent and Hildreth [8], Fuller and Rao [9], Hildreth and Houck [10], Jobson and Fuller [12] and Sarkar [14]. If the $\{\sigma_i\}$ were known, a reasonable estimate based on the usual normal distribution theory is the weighted least squares estimate (WLSE) which solves

$$0 = \sum_{i=1}^{N} ((Y_i - x_i' \hat{\beta}_W)/\sigma_i)x_i/\sigma_i. \tag{1.4}$$

In general, of course, the $\{\sigma_i\}$ are unknown and must be estimated. These generalized least squares estimates (GLSE) usually take the following form. Suppose we have estimates $(\hat{\beta}_0,\hat{\theta})$ of (β,θ) (there are many ways to do this) which satisfy

$$N^{\frac{1}{2}}(\hat{\theta}-\theta) = \mathcal{O}_p(1), \; N^{\frac{1}{2}}(\hat{\beta}_0-\beta) = \mathcal{O}_p(1). \tag{1.5}$$

One then forms estimated $\hat{\sigma}_i$ by

(1.6) $\hat{\sigma}_i = H(t_i, \hat{\theta}), \quad t_i = x_i' \hat{\beta}_0.$

The estimate $\hat{\beta}_G$ is a weighted estimate based on $\hat{\sigma}_i$, i.e.,

$$0 = \sum_{i=1}^{N} ((Y_i - x_i' \hat{\beta}_G)/\hat{\sigma}_i) x_i/\hat{\sigma}_i. \tag{1.7}$$

If we denote the weighted cross-products matrix by

$$S = N^{-1} \sum_{i=1}^{N} x_i x_i'/\sigma_i^2, \tag{1.8}$$

it is well known that

$$N^{\frac{1}{2}}(\hat{\beta}_W - \beta) \overset{\mathcal{L}}{\Rightarrow} N(0, S^{-1})$$

$$N^{\frac{1}{2}}(\hat{\beta}_G - \beta) \overset{\mathcal{L}}{\Rightarrow} N(0, S^{-1}),$$

so that the WLSE and GLSE are asymptotically equivalent to first order.

The model (1.1) can be reduced to the usual homoscedastic linear model if the $\{\sigma_i\}$ are known. Define

$$Y_{i*} = Y_i/\sigma_i, \quad x_{i*} = x_i/\sigma_i, \qquad \varepsilon_{i*} = \varepsilon_i/\sigma_i.$$

Then, (1.1) becomes

$$Y_{i*} = x_{i*}' \beta + \varepsilon_{i*}. \tag{1.10}$$

One can exploit (1.10) to define robust and/or bounded influence regression estimates. For example, the generalization of Huber [11] M-estimates solves

$$0 = \sum_{i=1}^{N} \psi(Y_{i*} - x_{i*}' \hat{\beta}_{WR}) x_{i*} \tag{1.11}$$

$$= \sum_{i=1}^{N} \psi((Y_i - x_i' \hat{\beta}_{WR})/\sigma_i) x_i/\sigma_i.$$

Here ψ is an odd, monotone function. Note that if $\psi(x) = x$, then $\hat{\beta}_W = \hat{\beta}_{WR}$ so the WLSE is included in (1.11). If the $\{\sigma_i\}$ must be estimated as is the usual case in practice, then a robust GLSE $\hat{\beta}_{GR}$ would solve

$$(1.12) \qquad 0 = \sum_{i=1}^{N} \psi((Y_i - x_i' \hat{\beta}_{GR})/\hat{\sigma}_i) x_i/\hat{\sigma}_i .$$

Carroll and Ruppert [5] have proven that $\hat{\beta}_{WR}$ and $\hat{\beta}_{GR}$ have (in general) the same asymptotic limit distribution and that

$$(1.13) \qquad N^{\frac{1}{2}}(\hat{\beta}_{GR} - \beta) \overset{\mathcal{L}}{\Rightarrow} N(0, c_0 S^{-1}),$$

where

$$(1.14) \qquad c_0 = E\psi^2(\varepsilon_1)/\{E\psi'(\varepsilon_1)\}^2 .$$

In comparing different choices of ψ, note that (1.13) indicates that the asymptotic efficiency of a procedure depends on ψ only through c_0 of (1.14). Curiously, c_0 is a well-known constant; it is precisely the asymptotic efficiency of the sample mean relative to an M-estimate for the location problem of estimating the center of symmetry of a distribution (Huber [11]). At the normal model, this efficiency is slightly greater than one (because of the optimality of the sample mean), but at heavier-tailed models this efficiency becomes much smaller than one.

The model (1.1) is fairly special because it assumes that the errors differ in distribution only by scale factors. Even when this holds and we can make the simple substitution (1.10), we still must find estimates of $\{\sigma_i\}$; this point is discussed next.

II. ESTIMATING $\{\sigma_i\}$

Different models admit different methods for estimating $\{\sigma_i\}$. Most methods are based on the following idea. First fit least squares to the data (call it $\hat{\beta}_L$); form residuals

$$r_i = Y_i - x_i' \hat{\beta}_L$$

and then regress the squared residuals $\{r_i^2\}$ on the squares of (1.3). This is particularly simple in the third case for (1.3) in which

$$(2.1) \qquad \sigma_i^2 = \sigma^2(1 + \lambda\tau_i^2) = \alpha_1 + \alpha_2 \tau_i^2 .$$

The reparameterization (2.1) then allows us to compute the LSE for α_1 and α_2 by regressing r_i^2 on $(\alpha_1 + \alpha_2(x_i' \hat{\beta}_L)^2)$, see Jobson and Fuller [12]. For the other models we would have to perform nonlinear regression.

Doing (non)linear regression on squared residuals in order to estimate $\{\sigma_i\}$ is conceptually simple but not necessarily the best way to proceed. Our simulations (Carroll and Ruppert [6]) indicate that instead of performing (possibly nonlinear) least squares on squared residuals, one can often do better in small samples by performing robust regression on squared residuals, even at the normal model. The reason appears to be that squared residuals are very non-normal and heavy tailed, as well as being heteroscedastic. Even when the heteroscedasticity of the squared residuals is accounted for, we have found simple robust methods preferable. There is a major theoretical difficulty here in that in (2.1) for example, one cannot consistently and robustly estimate α_1 except at the normal model (see Carroll and Ruppert [7]).

For the first two cases in (1.3), one might try to take logarithms, e.g.,

$$\log r_i^2 \approx \log \sigma^2 + \lambda \log(1+|x_i' \hat{\beta}_L|).$$

Because a small squared residual will have a very large logarithm, one should use this approach only with caution (and one's favorite robust regression).

The normal theory maximum likelihood estimates for θ are generally difficult to compute. More importantly, they have a quadratic influence curve and can thus be expected to be particularly non-robust. This is unfortunate because at the normal model, the maximum likelihood estimate will likely be much better than the regression methods outline above. For a particularly nice example of this latter phenomenon, See Raab [13]. As we show below, it is possible to construct estimates of θ which have bounded influence and are at least based in part on likelihood ideas (for pseudo-models with heavier tails than the normal model).

In dealing with the first two cases of (1.3), we have had considerable success by using pseudo-likelihood ideas. Consider a convex function ρ with derivative ψ and consider the log pseudo-likelihood

$$\text{(2.2)} \qquad \mathrm{LPL} = -\sum \log \sigma_i - \sum \rho((Y_i - x_i' \beta)/\sigma_i)$$

when the data have a density proportional to

$$\text{(2.3)} \qquad \sigma_i^{-1} \exp(-\rho((Y_i - x_i' \beta)/\sigma_i)).$$

If for fixed σ_i one maximizes (2.2), the result is $\hat{\beta}_{WR}$ of (1.11). On the other hand, suppose β is known and suppose

$$\text{(2.4)} \qquad \sigma_i = H(\tau_i, \theta) \qquad (\tau_i = x_i'\beta)$$

$$= \sigma \exp(h(\tau_i)\lambda).$$

Then taking derivatives with respect to θ one is led to solving

$$(2.5) \qquad 0 = \sum_{i=1}^{N} [z_i(\theta)\psi(z_i(\theta))-1]\binom{1}{h(\tau_i)},$$

where

$$(2.6) \qquad z_i(\theta) = (Y_i - \tau_i)/\{\sigma \exp(h(\tau_i)\lambda)\}.$$

Because the term in square brackets in (2.5) is not bounded and hence would, in general, lead to an unbounded influence function for the estimated θ and an overall lack of robustness in our estimation procedure, we follow the common device used in the homoscedastic case by Huber [11] of replacing $x\psi(x) - 1$ by a function $\chi(\cdot)$, as well as replacing τ_i by $t_i = x_i\hat{\beta}_0$, thus leading to estimates obtained by solving

$$(2.7) \qquad 0 = \sum_{i=1}^{N} \chi\left(\left(\frac{Y_i-t_i}{\sigma}\right)e^{-h(t_i)\lambda}\right)\binom{1}{h(t_i)},$$

where $\hat{\beta}_0$ is a preliminary (robust) estimate of β. We make the assumptions that $\chi(\cdot)$ is an even function with $\chi(0) < 0$, $\chi(\infty) > 0$. In the model (1.2), σ is a free parameter defined so that

$$E\chi((Y_1 - \tau_1)/\sigma_1) = 0.$$

These estimates of $\theta = (\sigma,\lambda)$ are easily computed and we have proved that they satisfy (1.5). Monte-Carlo work shows that they have good properties for moderately sized samples; see Carroll [4]. They have bounded influence against outliers in the response.

It is clear that estimation of θ is a problem that has not been adequately treated. Most of our emphasis has been on obtaining reasonable estimates of θ so we can estimate β well. Estimation of a variance *function* (as in immunoassay, see Raab [13] is conceptually different.

We believe that our methods based on (2.7) could well prove useful in estimating a variance function up to a common scale factor if the model is one of the first two cases in (1.3).

III. AN EXAMPLE

In this section we present a simple data set and study who some of the previously discussed methods perform on it. It is not our intention to fully analyze this data; we are in fact confident that better analyses are possible, but we only want to provide some illustration of previously discussed techniques.

The data are listed in Table 1. These data were gathered from a U.S. company over a 24 month period. One common idea is

Table 1.
Finished good ending inventory in units and unit sales used in the example in the text.

INVENTORY	SALES
38599	16161
36315	16897
35847	21693
37315	17616
41892	19282
38689	20275
32839	16023
30106	14846
28087	15229
30357	17729
28779	15136
33753	12200
34430	14953
36414	13951
36969	18017
41239	13743
38401	17921
29299	15211
24099	12682
21729	13483
20258	15223
19749	14403
15716	14600

that in periods of high sales, one should have a larger inventory. The data represent the experience of the company, which wanted to see if its sales were predictive of ending inventory. One data point was removed because it was a very high leverage point, corresponding to sales of less than 1/2 that of any other month.

We fit the model

$Y_i = \beta_0 + \beta_1 X_i + \sigma_i \varepsilon_i$, where

Y_i = finished goods ending inventory in ith month

X_i = unit sales in ith month

$\tau_i = \beta_0 + \beta_i X_i$

$\sigma_i = \sigma(1 + |\tau_i|)^\lambda$.

In estimating β, we first used an unweighted estimate. The least squares estimates for (β_0, β_1) were $(.77, 1.51) \times 10^{-5}$. The Huber Proposal 2 estimate based on $\psi(x) = \max(-2, \min(x,2))$ Huber [11] was $(.78, 1.50) \times 10^{-5}$. Residual plots based on either unweighted estimate indicate a pattern of decreasing variances for increasing mean response, i.e., if one is fitting the Box-Hill variance model

$$\sigma_i = \sigma(1 + |\tau_i|)^\lambda,$$

we expect $\lambda < 0$. Our method was to start from an unweighted estimate, solve (2.7), then solve (1.12), and finally solve (2.7) and (1.2) in turn. With $\psi(x) = x$, the estimate of λ is $\hat{\lambda} = -3.57$, with essentially the same answer for $\psi(x) = \max(-2, \min(x,2))$. The weighted estimate of (β_0, β_1) was $(1.02, 1.36) \times 10^{-5}$ for both choices of ψ. The weighted and unweighted regression lines are very similar and indicate that for this company monthly sales do predict finished goods ending inventory. The large value of $|\hat{\lambda}|$ suggest that the Box-Hill model may not be appropriate and that we should perhaps have used Bickel's exponential model in (1.3). We also did some bootstrap analyses which also suggested the possible inappropriateness of the Box-Hill model.

Carroll [4] and Carroll and Ruppert [5] gives three examples for which the Box-Hill model does appear appropriate and for which the robust weighted estimates seem to give the best answers.

REFERENCES

[1] Bickel, P. J. (1978). Using residuals robustly I: tests for heteroscedasticity, nonlinearity. *Ann. Statist.* 6, 266-291.

[2] Box, G. E. P. and Hill, W. J. (1974). Correcting inhomogeneity of variance with power transformation weighting. *Technometrics* 16, 385-389.

[3] Carroll, R. J. (1982a). Adapting for heteroscedasticity in linear models. To appear in *Ann. Statist.*

[4] Carroll, R. J. (1982b). Robust estimation in certain heteroscedastic linear models when there are many parameters. Tentatively accepted by *Journal of Statistical Planning and Inference.*

[5] Carroll, R. J. and Ruppert, D. (1982a). Robust estimation in heteroscedastic linear models. To appear in *Ann. Statist.*

[6] Carroll, R. J. and Ruppert, D. (1982b). A comparison between maximum likelihood and generalized least squares in a heteroscedastic linear model. To appear in *J. Amer. Statist. Assoc.*

[7] Carroll, R. J. and Ruppert, D. (1982c). Robust estimation in random coefficient models; large sample theory and Monte-Carlo. Manuscript.

[8] Dent, W. T. and Hildreth, C. (1977). Maximum likelihood estimation in random coefficient models. *J. Amer. Statist. Assoc.* 72, 69-72.

[9] Fuller, W. A. and Rao, J. N. K. (1978). Estimation for a linear regression model with unknown diagonal covariance matrix. *Ann. Statist.* *6*, 1149-1158.

[10] Hildreth, C. and Houck, J. P. (1968). Some estimators for a linear model with random coefficients. *J. Amer. Statist. Assoc.* *63*, 584-595.

[11] Huber, P. J. (1981). *Robust Statistics*. John Wiley and Sons, New York.

[12] Jobson, J. D. and Fuller, W. A. (1980). Least squares estimation when the covariance matrix and parameter vector are functionally related. *J. Amer. Statist. Assoc.* *75*, 176-181.

[13] Raab, G. M. (1981). Estimation of a variance function, with application to immunoassay. *Applied Statistics* *30*, 32-40.

[14] Sarkar, N. (1981). Heteroscedasticity and transformation of variables in econometrics. Manuscript.

ESTIMATING THE MEAN OF THE SELECTED POPULATION

Arthur Cohen[1] and H. B. Sackrowitz

Department of Statistics
Rutgers University
New Brunswick, New Jersey, U.S.A.

I. INTRODUCTION AND SUMMARY

Estimating the mean of the selected population is a long standing and an important practical problem. The farmer not only wishes to select the type of fertilizer from a choice of k fertilizers, that produces the highest mean yield, but he wants an estimate of the mean for the fertilizer selected. The manufacturer not only wants the machine he selects from among k machines to be the most productive, he also wants an estimate of the mean output for the selected machine. Despite the problem's obvious importance in real world situations there is a very limited amount of statistical research devoted to this problem. Charles Stein [7] at a discussion session of an Institute of Mathematical Statistics Meeting in Amherst, Massachusetts discussed the problem. Specifically he considered the problem of k independent normal populations with unknown means and common known variance. Suppose one observation is taken from each population. Select the population corresponding to the largest observation and consider estimation of the mean of the selected population for a squared error loss function. Letting $X_{(1)}$ represent the maximum of the k observations, it is easily noted that $X_{(1)}$ is a generalized Bayes estimator when the generalized prior distribution is Lebesgue measure. For the case $k = 2$, Stein easily proves that

[1]Research supported by N.S.F. Grant No. MCS-78-24167.

ISBN 0-12-307501-7

$X_{(1)}$ is admissible and minimax. He proceeds to note that for $k = 2$ and especially for $k > 2$, the estimator $X_{(1)}$ is highly unsatisfactory. It is clearly heavily biased upward for the case where the means of the populations are equal or close. The bias is more severe as k increases and in fact the bias tends to infinity as $k \to \infty$. Thus, from a practical point of view, a consumer offered a choice of k different machines could easily be deceived if he selected the machine with the highest sample mean output, and estimated the mean output of the selected machine by the maximum of the k sample means. (He would be badly misled if all k machines were essentially the same, and he didn't know it.)

Dahiya [4] studied other estimators of the mean of the selected population for $k = 2$. He considered the normal case with common known variance. Guided by estimators and computations in Blumenthal and Cohen [1], Dahiya studied the bias and mean square error of four classes of estimators. For the case $k = 2$, bias and mean square error computations are feasible. Hsieh [6] conducted a study similar to that of Dahiya, except that he assumes the common variance is unknown.

In this paper, to start, we also consider the normal case with common known variance. We assume we have equal sample sizes for each of the k populations and thus the k sample means are a set of sufficient statistics. Our main contribution is for the cases where $k \geq 3$. We produce an estimator (a family of estimators) that has many desirable properties. The estimator is a convex weighted combination of the ordered sample means where the weights depend on the adjacent differences in the ordered means. The bias of the estimator is much less severe than the bias of $X_{(1)}$, where now $X_{(1)}$ represents the maximum of the sample means. The weights or coefficients multiplying the ordered sample means are ordered themselves in the following sense: If $X_{(1)} \geq X_{(2)} \geq \ldots \geq X_{(k)}$ represent the ordered sample means then coefficients $C_{(i),k}$, $i=1,2,\ldots,k$ are such that

$C_{(1),k} \geq C_{(2),k} \geq \ldots \geq C_{(k),k}$. If the estimator for the k population case is called d_k, and if $X_{(j)}$ is very much larger than $X_{(j+1)}$, then d_k reduces essentially to d_j in the sense that $X_{(j+1)}, \ldots, X_{(k)}$ get negligible weight, while the weights for $X_{(1)}, X_{(2)}, \ldots, X_{(j)}$, are essentially the weights in the estimator d_j. The estimator increases as $X_{(1)}$ increases while $X_{(2)}, \ldots, X_{(k)}$ remain fixed. The estimator is bounded below by $\bar{X} = \sum_{i=1}^{k} X_{(i)}/k$ and above by $X_{(1)}$. Furthermore one version of the estimator is such that if all the $X_{(i)}$'s are "close", we get exactly $\bar{X}$, whereas in *all* versions of the estimator, if $X_{(1)}$ is not "close" to $X_{(2)}$, then the estimator is essentially $X_{(1)}$. As is the case with the estimator $X_{(1)}$, d_k will have bounded risk. A Monte Carlo evaluation of the mean square error of the estimator will demonstrate its desirability, particularly when compared to the estimator $X_{(1)}$. A further Monte Carlo computation compares coverage probabilities of the confidence intervals $X_{(1)} \pm 1.96$ and $T_2 \pm 1.96$, where T_2 appears to be one of the more desirable estimators. The coverage probability computations strongly support the estimator T_2.

The rationale and derivation of the estimator is based on Bayesian and empirical Bayesian considerations. In fact the estimator, is in a sense, an empirical Bayes estimator. The first step in the derivation is to allow the vector of means to have a prior distribution which is multivariate normal with mean vector zero and whose covariance matrix is one of a set of k possibilities. Each possible covariance matrix is such that the means are correlated in a way so as to reflect the possibility that some of them or all of them are close together. By allowing the variance of each population mean to tend to infinity in such a way that the variances of the differences of means tend to finite constants, we allow for possibilities that the means are close or can be far apart. These latter statements should become clear in the derivation section. The data, or more specifically the ordering of the sample means, is used to choose from among the k possible covariance matrices and the data is used to estimate the parameters of the prior that appear in the expression for the a posteriori mean.

The estimators and their properties are given in Section 2. The Monte Carlo results are given in Section 3. We also show in Section 3 that the risk of $X_{(1)}$ is maximized when all the population means are equal. This is helpful as a baseline when examining and comparing mean square errors. The derivation is in Section 4. In Section 5 we study the case k = 2 and compare our estimators with some of Dahiya's [4]. We show that some of Dahiya's estimators are inadmissible for the squared error loss function. We conclude in Section 6 with some remarks about extensions. We indicate that the results of the paper are appropriate for other problems, including estimating a current mean, with applications in quality control.

II. ESTIMATORS AND PROPERTIES

Let X_{ij}, $i = 1,2,\ldots,k$; $j = 1,2,\ldots,n$ represent k independent random samples from k normal populations with means θ_i and common known variance σ^2. Let $X_1, X_2, \ldots, X_k$ represent the k sample means and $X_{(1)} > X_{(2)} \geq \ldots \geq X_{(k)}$ represent the ordered sample means. Without loss of generality we let the variance of X_i, $i=1,2,\ldots,k$ be 1. (In Section 6 we discuss the case where the variance is unknown.) The problem is to estimate the mean of the selected population, where the population selected corresponds to $X_{(1)}$. That is, if $(i_1, i_2, \ldots, i_k)$ is a permutation of $(1,2,\ldots,k)$ and $X_{i_1} > X_{i_2} \geq \ldots \geq X_{i_k}$, then the problem is to estimate θ_{i_1}. We evaluate estimators by their mean square error. Let the estimator $T_1 = X_{(1)}$. This estimator is admissible and minimax for k = 2 as was indicated by Stein [7]. However for $k \geq 2$ this estimator is biased upward and severely so as k gets larger. In fact if $\theta_1 = \theta_2 = \ldots = \theta_k$, the asymptotic bias is of order $(2 \log k)^{\frac{1}{2}}$ and so the bias tends to infinity with k. The heavy overall bias of T_1 makes it unsatisfactory. The family of estimators we propose is as follows: Let $\underset{\sim}{X} = (X_1, X_2, \ldots, X_k)$ and for the sake of a clearer presentation suppose $X_1 > X_2 \geq \ldots \geq X_k$. Let $\hat{r}_i$, i = 1,2,...,k-1 be non-negative functions of $X_{i+1} - X_i$. Then the estimator is

$$d_k(\underset{\sim}{X}) = \sum_{i=1}^{k} C_{i,k} X_i, \tag{2.1}$$

where

$$C_{i,k} = \begin{cases} (\beta_i - 1)/(\beta_1 \beta_2 \cdots \beta_i) & \text{for } i = 1,2,\ldots,k-1, \\ 1/(\beta_1 \beta_2 \cdots \beta_{k-1}) & \text{for } i = k, \end{cases} \tag{2.2}$$

and the β's are defined by

$$\beta_{k-1} = \hat{r}_{k-1} + 2 \tag{2.3}$$

and

$$\beta_i = \hat{r}_i + 2 - 1/\beta_{i+1} \qquad \text{for } i = 1,2,\ldots,k-2. \tag{2.4}$$

Various choices of $\hat{r}_i$ will be studied. From (2.1) to (2.4) we see that for k = 2, 3, and 4,

$$d_2(\underset{\sim}{X}) = [(\hat{r}_1+1)/(\hat{r}_1+2)]X_1 + [1/(\hat{r}_1+2)]X_2; \tag{2.5}$$

$$\begin{aligned} d_3(\underset{\sim}{X}) = {} & [(\hat{r}_1(\hat{r}_2+2)+\hat{r}_2+1)/((2+\hat{r}_1)(2+\hat{r}_2)-1)]X_1 \\ & + [(\hat{r}_2+1)/((2+\hat{r}_1)(2+\hat{r}_2)-1)]X_2 \\ & + [1/((2+\hat{r}_1)(2+\hat{r}_2)-1)]X_3; \end{aligned} \tag{2.6}$$

$$\begin{aligned} d_4(\underset{\sim}{X}) = {} & [(1+\hat{r}_3+\hat{r}_2(2+\hat{r}_3)+3\hat{r}_1+2\hat{r}_1\hat{r}_3+\hat{r}_1\hat{r}_2\hat{r}_3)/\hat{R}_4]X_1 \\ & + [(1+2\hat{r}_3+\hat{r}_2(2+\hat{r}_3))/\hat{R}_4]X_2+[(\hat{r}_3+1)/\hat{R}_4]X_3+[1/\hat{R}_4]X_4, \end{aligned} \tag{2.7}$$

where

$$\hat{R}_4 = [(2+\hat{r}_1)(2+\hat{r}_2)(2+\hat{r}_3)-(2+\hat{r}_3)(2+\hat{r}_1)].$$

We proceed to establish the properties of the estimators claimed in the introduction. To do so formally we prove two lemmas.

LEMMA 2.1. *The terms* β_i *defined in* (2.3) *and* (2.4) *are such that* $\beta_i > 1$, $i = 1,2,\ldots,k-1$.

Proof. Since $\hat{r}_{k-1} \geq 0$, it follows from (2.3) that $\beta_{k-1} = \hat{r}_{k-1} + 2 > 1$. Now use backward induction. Assume $\beta_{j+1} > 1$, then $\beta_j = \hat{r}_j + 2-1/\beta_{j+1} > 1$.

LEMMA 2.2. *The coefficients* C_{ik} *in* (2.1) *are such that*

$$C_{i,k}(\underset{\sim}{X})-C_{i+1,k}(\underset{\sim}{X}) = \hat{r}_j/\beta_1\beta_2\ldots\beta_i=\hat{r}_j\sum_{j=i+1}^{k} C_{j,k}(\underset{\sim}{X}),$$

$$j = 1,2,\ldots,k-1.$$

Proof. Use (2.2), (2.3), and (2.4).

Use Lemmas 2.1, 2.2, and the definition of $C_{i,k}$ to establish

THEOREM 2.3. *The family* $d_k(\underset{\sim}{X})$ *has the following properties:*

(a) $C_{i,k}(\underset{\sim}{X}) \geq 0$, $i = 1,2,\ldots,k$

(b) $\sum_{i=1}^{k} C_{i,k}(\underset{\sim}{X}) = 1$

(c) $C_{i,k}(\underset{\sim}{X}) \geq C_{i+1,k}(\underset{\sim}{X})$

(d) $\hat{r}_i = 0$ *implies* $C_{i,k}(\underset{\sim}{X}) = C_{i+1,k}(\underset{\sim}{X})$

(e) *if for some* m, $1 \leq m \leq k-1$, $\hat{r}_m \to \infty$, *then*

(i) $\beta_m \to \infty$

(ii) $C_{i,k}(\underset{\sim}{X}) \to 0 \quad i = m+1,\ldots,k$

(iii) $C_{i,k}(X_1,X_2,\ldots,X_k) \to C_{i,m}(X_1,X_2,\ldots,X_m)$,

$i = 1,2,\ldots,m.$

Properties (a) and (b) indicate that $d_k(\underset{\sim}{X})$ is a weighted combination of the order statistics where the weights are non-negative. Property (c) shows that the coefficients are monotone in the sense that a larger sample mean gets a larger weight. Property (d) will be used to insure that when $X_{(i)}$ and $X_{(i+1)}$ are very "close" then $X_{(i)}$ and $X_{(i+1)}$ will be treated the same way. Property (e) will be used to insure that when $X_{(m)}$ is much "larger" than $X_{(m+1)}$ then only $X_{(1)},X_{(2)},\ldots,X_{(m)}$ will be used in d_k, and then used as in d_m. Note that in Section 6, when we discuss the case where σ^2 is unknown, we show that the family of estimators will be equivariant under location and scale transformations. From properties (a), (b), and (c) it follows that

COROLLARY 2.4. *The estimator satisfies*

$$\bar{X} \le d_k(\underset{\sim}{X}) \le X_1,$$

where $\bar{X} = \sum_{i=1}^{k} X_i/k.$

THEOREM 2.5. *Fix* k. *Let* $\hat{r}_i$ *be such that* $|X_i - X_{i+1}| \le B\,\hat{r}_i + A$, *for some constants* $B > 0$ *and* A. *Then* $d_k(\underset{\sim}{X})$ *has bounded risk.*

Proof. It is easily seen that the risk of $X_{(1)}$ is bounded by k. (A sharper bound will be given in the next section.) Hence it suffices to show that if $X_1 \ge X_2 \ge X_3 \ldots \ge X_k$, $|X_1 - d_k(\underset{\sim}{X})| \le M$, for some constant $M < \infty$. Since $\sum_{i=1}^{k} C_{i,k}(\underset{\sim}{X}) = 1$,

$$|X_1 - d_k(\underset{\sim}{X})| = \sum_{i=2}^{k} C_{i,k}(\underset{\sim}{X})(X_1 - X_i)$$

$$= \sum_{i=2}^{k} C_{i,k}(\underset{\sim}{X}) \sum_{j=1}^{i-1} |X_j - X_{j+1}|$$

$$= \sum_{j=1}^{k-1} \sum_{i=j+1}^{k} C_{i,k}(\underset{\sim}{X}) |X_j - X_{j+1}|$$

$$\leq \sum_{j=1}^{k-1} (B\hat{r}_j + A) \sum_{i=j+1}^{k} C_{i,k}(\underset{\sim}{X})$$

$$= B \sum_{j=1}^{k-1} \hat{r}_j \sum_{i=j+1}^{k} C_{i,k}(\underset{\sim}{X}) + A \sum_{j=1}^{k-1} \sum_{i=j+1}^{k} C_{i,k}(\underset{\sim}{X})$$

$$= B \sum_{j=1}^{k-1} [C_{j,k}(\underset{\sim}{X}) - C_{j+1,k}(\underset{\sim}{X})] + A \sum_{i=2}^{k} \sum_{j=1}^{i-1} C_{i,k}(\underset{\sim}{X})$$

$$= B[C_{1,k}(\underset{\sim}{X}) - C_{k,k}(\underset{\sim}{X})] + A \sum_{i=2}^{k} (i-1) C_{i,k}(\underset{\sim}{X})$$

$$\leq B + (k-1)A,$$

where the third from last expression follows from Lemma 2.2.

At this point we indicate some of the choices of $\hat{r}_i$. The $\hat{r}_i$'s to be listed were primarily chosen by considerations used in the rationale and derivation to be given in Section 4. Nevertheless even under the constraints of the derivation some flexibility in the choice of $\hat{r}_i$'s is desirable. Basically the choices vary as to how much more or how much less one wants to hedge between $\bar{X}$ and $X_{(1)}$. Clearly if $\hat{r}_i^{(1)} < \hat{r}_i^{(2)}$, for any set of indices i, the corresponding estimators $d_k^{(1)}(\underset{\sim}{X}) < d_k^{(2)}(\underset{\sim}{X})$ and so $d_k^{(1)}$ will be closer to $\bar{X}$ but $d_k^{(2)}$ will be closer to $X_{(1)}$. In choosing from among the list of possible $\hat{r}_i$'s one should consult the Monte Carlo study of Section 3. The following then is a list of $\hat{r}_i$'s, all of which satisfy the condition of Theorem 2.5:

(2.8) $(X_i - X_{i+1})^2$

(2.9) $2(X_i - X_{i+1})2$

(2.10) $3(X_i - X_{i+1})^2$

(2.11) $$4(X_i - X_{i+1})^2$$

(2.12) $$(X_i - X_{i+1})^4$$

(2.13) $$\{[X_i - X_{i+1}]^2 - 2\}^+.$$

Remark 2.1. One might suggest the use of $\hat{r}_i = K|X_i - X_{i+1}|$. However in this case (2.1) would have an undesirable property. In fact, suppose X_1 were much larger than $X_2 = X_3 = \ldots = X_k$. This is a case where the estimator should be very close to $X_{(1)}$. One can show though, that as $\hat{r}_1 = K|X_1 - X_2| \to \infty$, while $\hat{r}_2 = \ldots = \hat{r}_{k-1} = 0$, (2.1) $\to X_{(1)} - (1/K)$. For example, when $k = 3$, we get from (2.6) that

(2.14) $$d_3(\underset{\sim}{X}) = X_{(1)} - [(\hat{r}_2+1)/D](X_{(1)} - X_{(2)}) - (1/D)(X_{(1)} - X_{(3)}).$$

where $D = (2+\hat{r}_1)(2+\hat{r}_2) - 1$. Use $\hat{r}_2 = 0$, $\hat{r}_1 = K(X_{(1)} - X_{(2)})$ and recognize that $d_3(\underset{\sim}{X}) \to X_{(1)} - 1/K$ as $\hat{r}_1 \to \infty$.

III. MONTE CARLO EVALUATION OF MEAN SQUARE ERRORS AND BIAS

In this section we report the results of a Monte Carlo study for the evaluation of mean square errors and bias. Bias computations are done for the case when all components of $\underset{\sim}{\theta}$ are equal. This situation is the most interesting for the study of bias. In this situation it is clear that the bias notion is meaningful and important. As a baseline or point of reference and as a check on the simulations we note that the mean square error for the estimator $X_{(1)}$ is maximized when all components of $\underset{\sim}{\theta}$ are equal. In particular then, the maximum risk is easily obtained by taking $\underset{\sim}{\theta} = \underset{\sim}{0}$. At the end of this section we prove that the risk of $X_{(1)}$ is maximized when all components of $\underset{\sim}{\theta}$ are equal, not only for the squared error loss function of this study, but for any symmetric bowl shaped loss function. We include one interesting

Monte Carlo run contrasting coverage probabilities for two fixed width confidence intervals based on our estimators.

The Monte Carlo study was done for the cases k = 3, 5, and 7. In all cases, 500 random numbers were generated and the mean square errors computed. For k = 3 the mean square errors were computed for $X_{(1)}$, T_1, T_2, T_3, T_4, T_5, and T_6. The estimators T_j, j = 1,...,6, correspond respectively to $\hat{r}_i$'s given by (2.8), (2.9), (2.10), (2.11), (2.12), (2.13). Each parameter value in $(\theta_1,\theta_2,\theta_3)$ was chosen to range from 0 to 5 in steps of .5. Since T_2 was the most satisfactory from several points of view in the case k = 3, we studied it and compared its mean square error with that of $X_{(1)}$ for k = 5 and k = 7. For k = 5, each parameter in $(\theta_1,\theta_2,\theta_3,\theta_4,\theta_5)$ assumed the values 0, 1, 3, 5, and 7. For k = 7, each parameter in $(\theta_1,\theta_2,\theta_3,\theta_4,\theta_5,\theta_6,\theta_7)$ assumed the values 0, 1, 2, 5, 8. Since the estimators are permutation invariant and location equivariant we need only report mean square errors for $\theta_1 \leq \theta_2 \leq \ldots \leq \theta_k$, and $\theta_1 = 0$, in the tables below.

We note that the exact mean square errors for $X_{(1)}$ at $\underset{\sim}{\theta} = \underset{\sim}{0}$ are obtainable from tables on expected values of normal order statistics. Hence for k = 3, the mean square error is 1.27566, for k = 5 it is 1.80000, for k = 7 it is 2.22751. We know from the theorem at the end of this section that these values represent the maximum of the risk for the estimator $X_{(1)}$. These values also serve as a check on the accuracy of the simulation.

Mean square errors are given in Tables 1, 2, and 3 for the cases k = 3, 5, and 7 respectively.

Among the seven estimators considered in Table 1 we prefer T_2. It shows considerable improvement on $X_{(1)}$ over wide portions of the parameter space studied. It is better than $X_{(1)}$ with only a few exceptions and its maximum risk is only 1.18. Whereas T_3 and T_4 have smaller maximum risks, they do not improve on $X_{(1)}$ as often, nor do they improve by as much as T_2. The estimator T_5 does not compare that favorably with $X_{(1)}$. T_6, as expected, is very good when the parameters in $\underset{\sim}{\theta}$ are close, but is not that

Table 1. Mean Square Errors, k = 3

θ_1	θ_2	θ_3	$X_{(1)}$	T_1	T_2	T_3	T_4	T_5	T_6
0.0	0.0	0.0	1.2744	0.7425	0.8920	0.9705	1.0199	0.8845	0.4628
0.0	0.0	0.50	1.2289	0.7581	0.8962	0.9672	1.0112	0.9135	0.5095
0.0	0.0	1.00	1.1525	0.7752	0.8834	0.9395	0.9744	0.9268	0.6771
0.0	0.0	1.50	1.0212	0.8110	0.8671	0.8985	0.9185	0.9381	1.0297
0.0	0.0	2.00	1.0045	0.9784	0.9746	0.9779	0.9809	1.0652	1.5331
0.0	0.0	2.50	1.0492	1.0600	1.0402	0.0373	1.0370	1.1268	1.6929
0.0	0.0	3.00	0.9340	1.0635	1.0023	0.9823	0.9721	1.0670	1.8861
0.0	0.0	3.50	1.0388	1.2302	1.1370	0.1057	1.0898	1.1626	2.1064
0.0	0.0	4.00	0.9451	1.1666	1.0576	1.0206	1.0019	1.0529	1.9890
0.0	0.0	4.50	0.9866	1.1478	1.0639	1.0375	1.0246	1.0503	1.6479
0.0	0.0	5.00	0.9217	1.0179	0.9632	0.9478	0.9407	0.9492	1.2703
0.0	0.50	0.50	1.2611	0.7484	0.8940	0.9700	1.0177	0.8949	0.4723
0.0	0.50	1.00	1.1102	0.7081	0.8192	0.8779	0.9150	0.8389	0.5864
0.0	0.50	1.50	1.1752	0.8648	0.9542	1.0010	1.0302	1.0104	0.9122
0.0	0.50	2.00	1.1581	1.0178	1.0528	1.0736	1.0870	1.1384	1.3242
0.0	0.50	2.50	1.0876	1.0470	1.0479	1.0540	1.0589	1.1310	1.6141
0.0	0.50	3.00	0.8956	0.9893	0.9401	0.9264	0.9201	1.0063	1.8014
0.0	0.50	3.50	1.0602	1.2516	1.1676	1.1376	1.1217	1.2281	2.1475
0.0	0.50	4.00	0.9529	1.1349	1.0494	1.0205	1.0056	1.0805	1.8490
0.0	0.50	4.50	0.9520	1.0819	1.0143	0.9934	0.9832	1.0253	1.6471
0.0	0.50	5.00	1.0539	1.2203	1.1366	1.1098	1.0965	1.1190	1.6968
0.0	1.00	1.00	1.2371	0.7785	0.9143	0.9840	1.0273	0.9448	0.6099
0.0	1.00	1.50	1.0706	0.7363	0.8305	0.8803	0.9115	0.8737	0.7146
0.0	1.00	2.00	0.9486	0.7197	0.7863	0.8216	0.8435	0.8712	0.9145
0.0	1.00	2.50	0.9945	0.8982	0.9188	0.9335	0.9434	1.0011	1.3336
0.0	1.00	3.00	1.0198	1.0385	1.0251	1.0235	1.0232	1.1207	1.7000
0.0	1.00	3.50	1.0203	1.1036	1.0613	1.0482	1.0416	1.1384	1.8259
0.0	1.00	4.00	1.0256	1.2226	1.1330	1.1016	1.0851	1.1800	2.0909
0.0	1.00	4.50	1.1068	1.2533	1.1829	1.1597	1.1479	1.2130	1.8595
0.0	1.00	5.00	0.9132	1.0454	0.9738	0.9524	0.9421	0.9645	1.5315
0.0	1.50	1.50	1.1300	0.7332	0.8528	0.9136	0.9511	0.8971	0.6272
0.0	1.50	2.00	1.1817	0.8048	0.9221	0.9808	1.0166	0.9811	0.7955
0.0	1.50	2.50	0.9877	0.8294	0.8737	0.8981	0.9133	0.9686	1.1417

Table 1 (continued). Mean Squares Errors, k = 3

θ_1	θ_2	θ_3	$X_{(1)}$	T_1	T_2	T_3	T_4	T_5	T_6
0.0	1.50	3.00	0.9791	0.9581	0.9559	0.9597	0.9627	1.0509	1.5087
0.0	1.50	3.50	1.1077	1.1786	1.1398	1.1289	1.1238	1.2146	1.9130
0.0	1.50	4.00	0.9241	1.0553	0.9912	0.9705	0.9601	1.0425	1.8454
0.0	1.50	4.50	1.0184	1.2280	1.1298	1.0958	1.0782	1.1613	2.0653
0.0	1.50	5.00	0.9745	1.1815	1.0797	1.0459	1.0289	1.0785	1.9061
0.0	2.00	2.00	1.0048	0.6867	0.7827	0.8321	0.8627	0.8423	0.7306
0.0	2.00	2.50	1.0725	0.7788	0.8668	0.9116	0.9391	0.9419	0.9237
0.0	2.00	3.00	0.9153	0.7838	0.8180	0.8390	0.8525	0.8936	1.1032
0.0	2.00	3.50	0.9760	0.9143	0.9238	0.9336	0.9405	1.0019	1.4288
0.0	2.00	4.00	1.0373	1.1005	1.0673	1.0584	1.0542	1.1484	1.8149
0.0	2.00	4.50	0.9818	1.0983	1.0303	1.0090	0.9984	1.0760	1.8758
0.0	2.00	5.00	0.9710	1.1302	1.0547	1.0296	1.0166	1.0910	1.8234
0.0	2.50	2.50	1.0638	0.7637	0.8579	0.9048	0.9331	0.9369	0.8597
0.0	2.50	3.00	0.9873	0.7252	0.8072	0.8485	0.8737	0.8792	0.8094
0.0	2.50	3.50	1.0080	0.8628	0.9015	0.9241	0.9385	0.9805	1.1896
0.0	2.50	4.00	1.0976	1.0746	1.0740	1.0786	1.0821	1.1591	1.6057
0.0	2.50	4.50	0.9950	1.0581	1.0202	1.0113	1.0077	1.0729	1.7898
0.0	2.50	5.00	0.9864	1.1323	1.0614	1.0390	1.0278	1.0977	1.8169
0.0	3.00	3.00	1.1020	0.7882	0.8809	0.9283	0.9575	0.9434	0.8838
0.0	3.00	3.50	1.0112	0.7604	0.8374	0.8770	0.9012	0.9055	0.8999
0.0	3.00	4.00	0.9695	0.8107	0.8526	0.8778	0.8939	0.9127	1.1210
0.0	3.00	4.50	1.0038	0.9729	0.9714	0.9767	0.9809	1.0427	1.4127
0.0	3.00	5.00	0.9865	1.0512	1.0117	1.0017	0.9973	1.0666	1.6828
0.0	3.50	3.50	0.9983	0.7560	0.8294	0.8670	0.8901	0.8966	0.8752
0.0	3.50	4.00	1.0684	0.8104	0.8895	0.9295	0.9539	0.9604	0.9412
0.0	3.50	4.50	0.9992	0.8081	0.8616	0.8917	0.9106	0.9245	1.0547
0.0	3.50	5.00	1.0815	1.0104	1.0257	1.0376	1.0454	1.1019	1.3267
0.0	4.00	4.00	0.9437	0.6718	0.7519	0.7934	0.8192	0.8037	0.6948
0.0	4.00	4.50	1.0755	0.8027	0.8866	0.9295	0.9557	0.9482	0.8361
0.0	4.00	5.00	1.0037	0.8170	0.8714	0.9005	0.9184	0.9391	1.0049
0.0	4.50	4.50	0.9134	0.6584	0.7321	0.7712	0.7956	0.7785	0.6799
0.0	4.50	5.00	1.0316	0.7688	0.8466	0.8873	0.9125	0.8993	0.8437
0.0	5.00	5.00	1.0586	0.7958	0.8736	0.9135	0.9382	0.9279	0.8015

Table 2. Mean Square Errors, k = 5

θ_1	θ_2	θ_3	θ_4	θ_5	$X_{(1)}$	T_2
0.0	0.0	0.0	0.0	0.0	1.7491	1.1052
0.0	0.0	0.0	0.0	1.0	1.5634	1.0351
0.0	0.0	0.0	0.0	3.0	0.9850	1.0862
0.0	0.0	0.0	0.0	5.0	0.9896	1.1030
0.0	0.0	0.0	0.0	7.0	0.9896	1.0413
0.0	0.0	0.0	1.0	1.0	1.5462	1.0254
0.0	0.0	0.0	1.0	3.0	0.9756	1.0132
0.0	0.0	0.0	1.0	5.0	0.9896	1.1226
0.0	0.0	0.0	1.0	7.0	0.9896	1.0482
0.0	0.0	0.0	3.0	3.0	0.9374	0.7708
0.0	0.0	0.0	3.0	5.0	0.9378	0.9937
0.0	0.0	0.0	3.0	7.0	0.9896	1.0924
0.0	0.0	0.0	5.0	5.0	0.9107	0.7450
0.0	0.0	0.0	5.0	7.0	0.9378	0.9718
0.0	0.0	0.0	7.0	7.0	0.9107	0.7425
0.0	0.0	1.0	1.0	1.0	1.5688	1.0199
0.0	0.0	1.0	1.0	3.0	1.0164	0.9708
0.0	0.0	1.0	1.0	5.0	0.9872	1.1320
0.0	0.0	1.0	1.0	7.0	0.9896	1.0543
0.0	0.0	1.0	3.0	3.0	0.9675	0.7704
0.0	0.0	1.0	3.0	5.0	0.9378	1.0035
0.0	0.0	1.0	3.0	7.0	0.9896	1.0956
0.0	0.0	1.0	5.0	5.0	0.9107	0.7471
0.0	0.0	1.0	5.0	7.0	0.9378	0.9753
0.0	0.0	1.0	7.0	7.0	0.9107	0.7427
0.0	0.0	3.0	3.0	3.0	1.1825	0.8130
0.0	0.0	3.0	3.0	5.0	0.9693	0.9432
0.0	0.0	3.0	3.0	7.0	0.9872	1.1178
0.0	0.0	3.0	5.0	5.0	0.9590	0.7634
0.0	0.0	3.0	5.0	7.0	0.9378	0.9946
0.0	0.0	3.0	7.0	7.0	0.9107	0.7458
0.0	0.0	5.0	5.0	5.0	1.1740	0.8142
0.0	0.0	5.0	5.0	7.0	0.9693	0.9349
0.0	0.0	5.0	7.0	7.0	0.9590	0.7616
0.0	0.0	7.0	7.0	7.0	1.1740	0.8161

Table 2 (continued). Mean Square Errors, k = 5

θ_1	θ_2	θ_3	θ_4	θ_5	$X_{(1)}$	T_2
0.0	1.0	1.0	1.0	1.0	1.6411	1.0508
0.0	1.0	1.0	1.0	3.0	1.0753	0.9593
0.0	1.0	1.0	1.0	5.0	0.9632	1.1017
0.0	1.0	1.0	1.0	7.0	0.9896	1.0604
0.0	1.0	1.0	3.0	3.0	1.0608	0.8271
0.0	1.0	1.0	3.0	5.0	0.9244	0.9846
0.0	1.0	1.0	3.0	7.0	0.9896	1.1009
0.0	1.0	1.0	5.0	5.0	0.9107	0.7492
0.0	1.0	1.0	5.0	7.0	0.9378	0.9787
0.0	1.0	1.0	7.0	7.0	0.9107	0.7429
0.0	1.0	3.0	3.0	3.0	1.2501	0.8578
0.0	1.0	3.0	3.0	5.0	0.9726	0.9422
0.0	1.0	3.0	3.0	7.0	0.9872	1.1220
0.0	1.0	3.0	5.0	5.0	0.9590	0.7641
0.0	1.0	3.0	5.0	7.0	0.9378	0.9972
0.0	1.0	3.0	7.0	7.0	0.9107	0.7461
0.0	1.0	5.0	5.0	5.0	1.1740	0.8129
0.0	1.0	5.0	7.0	7.0	0.9693	0.9364
0.0	1.0	5.0	7.0	7.0	0.9590	0.7619
0.0	1.0	7.0	7.0	7.0	1.1740	0.8156
0.0	3.0	3.0	3.0	3.0	1.4944	0.9764
0.0	3.0	3.0	3.0	5.0	1.0648	0.9519
0.0	3.0	3.0	3.0	7.0	0.9632	1.0986
0.0	3.0	3.0	5.0	5.0	1.0608	0.8260
0.0	3.0	3.0	5.0	7.0	0.9244	0.9826
0.0	3.0	3.0	7.0	7.0	0.9107	0.7485
0.0	3.0	5.0	5.0	5.0	1.2501	0.8585
0.0	3.0	5.0	5.0	7.0	0.9726	0.9404
0.0	3.0	5.0	7.0	7.0	0.9590	0.7636
0.0	3.0	7.0	7.0	7.0	1.1740	0.8129
0.0	5.0	5.0	5.0	5.0	1.4944	0.9802
0.0	5.0	5.0	5.0	7.0	1.0648	0.9507
0.0	5.0	5.0	7.0	7.0	1.0608	0.8255
0.0	5.0	7.0	7.0	7.0	1.2501	0.8591
0.0	7.0	7.0	7.0	7.0	1.4944	0.9820

Table 3. Mean Square Errors, k = 7

θ_1	θ_2	θ_3	θ_4	θ_5	θ_6	θ_7	$X_{(1)}$	T_2
0.0	0.0	0.0	0.0	0.0	0.0	0.0	2.1717	1.3273
0.0	0.0	0.0	0.0	0.0	0.0	1.0	1.9611	1.2564
0.0	0.0	0.0	0.0	0.0	0.0	2.0	1.4235	1.1311
0.0	0.0	0.0	0.0	0.0	1.0	1.0	1.8703	1.1944
0.0	0.0	0.0	0.0	0.0	1.0	2.0	1.4754	1.1209
0.0	0.0	0.0	0.0	0.0	2.0	2.0	1.3532	1.0191
0.0	0.0	0.0	0.0	1.0	1.0	1.0	1.8687	1.1909
0.0	0.0	0.0	0.0	1.0	1.0	2.0	1.5501	1.0944
0.0	0.0	0.0	0.0	1.0	2.0	2.0	1.4463	1.0130
0.0	0.0	0.0	0.0	2.0	2.0	2.0	1.4954	1.0213
0.0	0.0	0.0	1.0	1.0	1.0	1.0	1.9185	1.1999
0.0	0.0	0.0	1.0	1.0	2.0	2.0	1.6398	1.1117
0.0	0.0	0.0	1.0	1.0	2.0	2.0	1.5615	1.0597
0.0	0.0	0.0	1.0	2.0	2.0	2.0	1.6154	1.0860
0.0	0.0	0.0	2.0	2.0	2.0	2.0	1.6969	1.0923
0.0	0.0	1.0	1.0	1.0	1.0	1.0	1.9884	1.2291
0.0	0.0	1.0	1.0	1.0	1.0	2.0	1.7755	1.1638
0.0	0.0	1.0	1.0	1.0	2.0	2.0	1.7046	1.1266
0.0	0.0	1.0	1.0	2.0	2.0	2.0	1.7442	1.1476
0.0	0.0	1.0	2.0	2.0	2.0	2.0	1.8032	1.1511
0.0	0.0	2.0	2.0	2.0	2.0	2.0	1.8799	1.1757
0.0	1.0	1.0	1.0	1.0	1.0	1.0	2.1015	1.2942
0.0	1.0	1.0	1.0	1.0	1.0	2.0	1.9092	1.2381
0.0	1.0	1.0	1.0	1.0	2.0	2.0	1.8170	1.1830
0.0	1.0	1.0	1.0	2.0	2.0	2.0	1.8342	1.1909
0.0	1.0	1.0	2.0	2.0	2.0	2.0	1.8846	1.1956
0.0	1.0	2.0	2.0	2.0	2.0	2.0	1.9652	1.2257

Table 3 (continued). Mean Square Errors, k = 7

θ_1	θ_2	θ_3	θ_4	θ_5	θ_6	θ_7	$X_{(1)}$	T_2
0.0	2.0	2.0	2.0	2.0	2.0	2.0	2.0705	1.2837
0.0	2.0	2.0	2.0	2.0	2.0	5.0	1.1810	1.2315
0.0	2.0	2.0	2.0	2.0	2.0	8.0	1.0476	1.1261
0.0	2.0	2.0	2.0	2.0	5.0	5.0	1.1023	0.9050
0.0	2.0	2.0	2.0	2.0	5.0	8.0	1.0361	1.1213
0.0	2.0	2.0	2.0	2.0	8.0	8.0	1.0511	0.8730
0.0	2.0	2.0	2.0	5.0	5.0	5.0	1.3548	0.9493
0.0	2.0	2.0	2.0	5.0	5.0	8.0	1.0380	1.1208
0.0	2.0	2.0	2.0	5.0	8.0	8.0	1.0418	0.8613
0.0	2.0	2.0	2.0	8.0	8.0	8.0	1.3154	0.9323
0.0	2.0	2.0	5.0	5.0	5.0	5.0	1.5768	1.0271
0.0	2.0	2.0	5.0	5.0	5.0	8.0	1.0588	1.1450
0.0	2.0	2.0	5.0	5.0	8.0	8.0	1.0677	0.8771
0.0	2.0	2.0	5.0	8.0	8.0	8.0	1.3360	0.9399
0.0	2.0	2.0	8.0	8.0	8.0	8.0	1.5580	1.0213
0.0	2.0	5.0	5.0	5.0	5.0	5.0	1.8355	1.1525
0.0	2.0	5.0	5.0	5.0	5.0	8.0	1.1010	1.1858
0.0	2.0	5.0	5.0	5.0	8.0	8.0	1.0677	0.8788
0.0	2.0	5.0	5.0	8.0	8.0	8.0	1.3360	0.9375
0.0	2.0	5.0	8.0	8.0	8.0	8.0	1.5580	1.0159
0.0	2.0	8.0	8.0	8.0	8.0	8.0	1.8167	1.1443
0.0	5.0	5.0	5.0	5.0	5.0	5.0	2.0705	1.2911
0.0	5.0	5.0	5.0	5.0	5.0	8.0	1.1810	1.2290
0.0	5.0	5.0	5.0	5.0	8.0	8.0	1.1023	0.9044
0.0	5.0	5.0	5.0	8.0	8.0	8.0	1.3548	0.9497
0.0	5.0	5.0	8.0	8.0	8.0	8.0	1.5768	1.0274
0.0	5.0	8.0	8.0	8.0	8.0	8.0	1.9355	1.1531
0.0	8.0	8.0	8.0	8.0	8.0	8.0	2.0705	1.2928

good otherwise. We only study $X_{(1)}$ and T_2 in Table 2. The comparison here shows T_2 to be a substantial improvement on $X_{(1)}$. Its mean square error is mostly smaller than that of $X_{(1)}$, the differences are often large, and the maximum value of the mean square error is 1.11 compared to 1.75. (Recall the actual maximum, not based on simulation, is 1.80). In Table 3, for k = 7, again T_2 looks substantially better than $X_{(1)}$ for similar reasons. For k = 7, the mean square errors for $X_{(1)}$ are becoming sizeable and differences in risks are getting larger.

We remark that the statistician can hedge more or hedge less regarding alternatives to $X_{(1)}$. A greater hedge towards $\bar{X}$ is achieved with T_1 and T_6. Estimators closer to $X_{(1)}$ are T_3 and T_4.

Biases are given in Table 4 for the cases k = 3, 5, and 7 when all parameters are equal and without loss of generality equal to zero. The exact bias for $X_{(1)}$ is obtainable from tables on expected values of normal order statistics. For k = 3, 5, and 7 the biases are respectively .8624, 1.1163, and 1.35218. These values serve as a check on the accuracy of the simulation. An examination of Table 4 reveals the substantial reduction in bias when using the estimator T_2 as compared to X_1. The figures also verify that the simulations are quite accurate.

Table 4. Bias

	X_1	T_1	T_2	T_3	T_4	T_5	T_6
k = 3	.8516	.4752	.5850	.6398	.6737	.5298	.0970
k = 5	1.1382		.7986				
k = 7	1.3251		.9447				

Another Monte Carlo was run to contrast coverage probabilities for the fixed width confidence intervals $X_{(1)} \pm 1.96$ and $T_2 \pm 1.96$, for $k = 5$. Each parameter in $(\theta_1,\theta_2,\theta_3,\theta_4,\theta_5)$ assumed the values 0, 1, 2, 5, 8. The coverage probabilities given in Table 5 for the interval $T_2 \pm 1.96$, are much more satisfactory than those given for $X_{(1)} \pm 1.96$.

We conclude this section by proving that the risk of the estimator which is the maximum of $(X_1,X_2,\ldots,X_k)$ is maximized when all components of $\underset{\sim}{\theta}$ are equal for any symmetric bowl shaped loss function. Toward this end let $J(\underset{\sim}{X})$ be such that $X_{J(\underset{\sim}{X})} = \max(X_1,X_2,\ldots,X_k)$. Let $Z = X_{J(\underset{\sim}{X})} - \theta_{J(\underset{\sim}{X})}$. Then the density function of Z is

$$(3.1) \qquad f_{\underset{\sim}{\theta}}(z) = \varphi(z) \sum_{j=1}^{k} \prod_{i\neq j} \Phi(z+(\theta_i-\theta_j)),$$

where φ and Φ are respectively, the p.d.f. and c.d.f. of a standard normal distribution. Let $L(z)$ be any loss function such that $L(0) = 0$, $L(-z) = L(z)$ and $L(|z|)$ increases as $|z|$ increases. For example, for squared error loss $L(z) = z^2$. Let $R(X_{J(\underset{\sim}{X})},\underset{\sim}{\theta}) = E_{\underset{\sim}{\theta}} L(Z)$.

THEOREM 3.1. *The risk function* $R(X_{J(\underset{\sim}{X})},\underset{\sim}{\theta})$ *is maximized at* $\underset{\sim}{\theta} = \underset{\sim}{0}$.

Proof. Observe that the problem is symmetric (permutation invariant) in the indices of the observations and parameters. Hence without loss of generality we can confine ourselves to studying the risk over that portion of the parameter space where $\theta_1 = \theta_2 = \ldots = \theta_m \geq \theta_{m+1} \geq \theta_{m+2} \geq \ldots \geq \theta_k$ for some fixed m, $1 \leq m \leq k-1$. Use (3.1) in

Table 5. Coverage Probabilities, k = 5

θ_1	θ_2	θ_3	θ_4	θ_5	$X_{(1)}\pm1.96$	$T_2\pm1.96$
0.0	0.0	0.0	0.0	0.0	.9040	.9440
0.0	0.0	0.0	0.0	1.0	.9140	.9420
0.0	0.0	0.0	0.0	2.0	.9360	.9500
0.0	0.0	0.0	1.0	1.0	.9120	.9440
0.0	0.0	0.0	1.0	2.0	.9280	.9500
0.0	0.0	0.0	2.0	2.0	.9300	.9560
0.0	0.0	1.0	1.0	1.0	.9140	.9420
0.0	0.0	1.0	1.0	2.0	.9260	.9480
0.0	0.0	1.0	2.0	2.0	.9260	.9560
0.0	0.0	2.0	2.0	2.0	.9280	.9580
0.0	1.0	1.0	1.0	1.0	.9100	.9480
0.0	1.0	1.0	1.0	2.0	.9180	.9540
0.0	1.0	1.0	2.0	2.0	.9140	.9460
0.0	1.0	2.0	2.0	2.0	.9160	.9540
0.0	2.0	2.0	2.0	2.0	.9160	.9560
0.0	2.0	2.0	2.0	5.0	.9540	.9340
0.0	2.0	2.0	2.0	8.0	.9540	.9560
0.0	2.0	2.0	5.0	5.0	.9560	.9740
0.0	2.0	2.0	5.0	8.0	.9540	.9400
0.0	2.0	2.0	8.0	8.0	.9600	.9780
0.0	2.0	5.0	5.0	5.0	.9480	.9700
0.0	2.0	5.0	5.0	8.0	.9600	.9360
0.0	2.0	5.0	8.0	8.0	.9580	.9760
0.0	2.0	8.0	8.0	8.0	.9500	.9700
0.0	5.0	5.0	5.0	5.0	.9220	.9520
0.0	5.0	5.0	5.0	8.0	.9540	.9340
0.0	5.0	5.0	8.0	8.0	.9560	.9740
0.0	5.0	5.0	8.0	8.0	.9580	.9700
0.0	8.0	8.0	8.0	8.0	.9220	.9520

$$(3.2)\qquad E_{\tilde{\theta}}L(z) = \int_{-\infty}^{\infty} L(z)f_{\tilde{\theta}}(z)dz$$

$$= \int_{-\infty}^{\infty} L(z)\varphi(z)[m\Phi^{m-1}(z)\prod_{i=m+1}^{k}\Phi(z+(\theta_i-\theta_1))$$

$$+ \sum_{j=m+1}^{k}\Phi^{m}(z+\theta_1-\theta_j)\prod_{\substack{i=m+1\\ i\neq j}}^{k}\Phi(z+(\theta_i-\theta_j))]dz.$$

Use the fact $L(z) = L(-z)$, $\varphi(-z) = \varphi(z)$ and (3.2) to find

$$(3.3)\qquad \frac{E_{\tilde{\theta}}}{\partial\theta_1} = m\int_{-\infty}^{\infty} L(z)\phi(z)\Phi^{m-1}(z)\sum_{j=m+1}^{k} -\phi(z+(\theta_j-\theta_1))$$

$$\times \prod_{\substack{i=m+1\\ i\neq j}}^{k}\Phi(z+(\theta_i-\theta_1))dx$$

$$+ \int_{-\infty}^{\infty} L(z)\phi(z)\sum_{j=m+1}^{k} m\phi(z+(\theta_1-\theta_j))\Phi^{m-1}(z+(\theta_1-\theta_j))$$

$$\times \prod_{\substack{i=m+1\\ i\neq j}}^{k}\Phi(z+(\theta_i-\theta_j))dz$$

$$= -m\sum_{j=m+1}^{k}\int_{-\infty}^{\infty} L(z)\phi(z)\phi(z+(\theta_1-\theta_j))\Phi^{m-1}(-z)$$

$$\times \prod_{\substack{i=m+1\\ i\neq j}}^{k}\Phi(-z+(\theta_i-\theta_1))dz$$

$$+ m\sum_{j=m+1}^{k}\int_{-\infty}^{\infty} L(z)\phi(z)\phi(z+(\theta_1-\theta_j))\Phi^{m-1}(z+(\theta_1-\theta_j))$$

$$\times \prod_{\substack{i=m+1\\ i\neq j}}^{k}\Phi(z+(\theta_i-\theta_j))dz$$

$$= m \sum_{j=m+1}^{k} \int_{-\infty}^{\infty} L(z)\phi(z)\phi(z+(\theta_1-\theta_j))A_j(z;\underset{\sim}{\theta})dz,$$

where

$$A_j(z,\underset{\sim}{\theta}) = \Phi^{m-1}(z+(\theta_1-\theta_j)) \prod_{\substack{i=m+1\\ i\neq j}}^{k} \Phi(z+(\theta_i-\theta_j))-\Phi^{m-1}(-z)$$

$$\times \prod_{\substack{i=m+1\\ i\neq j}}^{k} \Phi(-z+(\theta_i-\theta_1)).$$

Note that

$$A_j(u-(\theta_1-\theta_j)/2;\underset{\sim}{\theta}) = -A_j(-u-(\theta_1-\theta_j)/2;\underset{\sim}{\theta}) \geq 0 \text{ for } u \geq 0.$$

Now

$$(3.4) \qquad \int_{-\infty}^{\infty} L(z)\phi(z)\phi(z+(\theta_1-\theta_j))A_j(z;\underset{\sim}{\theta})dz$$

$$=\phi((\theta_1-\theta_j)/\sqrt{2})\int_{-\infty}^{\infty} L(z)\phi(\sqrt{2}(z+(\theta_1-\theta_j)))A_j(z;\underset{\sim}{\theta})dz$$

$$= \phi((\theta_1-\theta_j)/\sqrt{2})\int_{-\infty}^{\infty} L(u-(\theta_1-\theta_j)/2)\phi(\sqrt{2}u)$$

$$\times A_j(u-(\theta_1-\theta_j)/2;\underset{\sim}{\theta})dz.$$

Partition the region of integration in (3.4) into $(-\infty,0)$ and $(0,\infty)$, make a change of variable, and (3.4) becomes

$$(3.5) \quad \phi((\theta_1-\theta_j)/\sqrt{2})\int_{0}^{\infty}[L(u-(\theta_1-\theta_j)/2)-L(-u-(\theta_1-\theta_j)/2]\phi(\sqrt{2}u)$$

$$\times A_j(u-(\theta_1-\theta_j)/2;\underset{\sim}{\theta})dz.$$

Since $L(u-\Delta) \leq L(-u-\Delta)$ for all $u \geq 0$, $\Delta \geq 0$, (3.5) ≤ 0. Thus $[E_{\underset{\sim}{\theta}} L(Z)]$ is maximized when $\theta_1 =\ldots= \theta_m$ are taken equal to θ_{m+1}. Since m was permitted to be any value such that $1 \leq m \leq k-1$, this completes the proof of the theorem.

IV. RATIONALE AND DERIVATION

The rationale is to find a Bayes or limit of Bayes estimator that would not have the unsatisfactory bias of $X_{(1)}$. Yet the estimator should estimate by $X_{(1)}$ if $X_{(1)}$ is "larger" than $X_{(2)}$. On the other hand if other observations are close to $X_{(1)}$ then they should be used, otherwise the undesirable bias will remain. Another consideration is to maintain bounded risk of the estimator. For the estimator to satisfy the above properties one requires a prior distribution on $\underset{\sim}{\theta}$ such that the componets of $\underset{\sim}{\theta}$ would be correlated. One is also led to the conjugate prior, namely the multivariate normal, with covariance matrix Σ, say. To accomplish a reduction of bias (relative to $X_{(1)}$) while maintaining bounded risk, a sequence of Σ's is chosen so that the variances tend to infinity at the same rate, the correlations tend to one at the same rate, but in such a way that the variances of the differences in the θ's tend to constants. To further "bridle" the components of θ, thus ensuring a reduction of undesirable bias the variance of $(\theta_i - \theta_{i+j})$ is assumed to be the sum of the variances of $(\theta_i - \theta_{i+1})$, $(\theta_{i+1} - \theta_{i+2}), \ldots, (\theta_{i+j-1} - \theta_{i+j})$.

A way to accomplish the above features is to let the θ's form a stochastic process with independent normal increments such that each increment has a possibly different variance. Furthermore the parameters are randomly assigned to populations.

The resulting estimator is empirical Bayes in the following two senses. First we "estimate" the assignment of parameters to populations by using the ordering of the sample means. Second, we use the data to estimate the prior covariance matrix. The resulting estimator is the usual posterior expected value of the selected mean.

We now, more formally, outline the derivation. The vector of sample means $\underset{\sim}{X}$ has been assumed to be multivariate normal with mean vector $\underset{\sim}{\theta}$ and covariance matrix I. We will select a prior distribution for θ from k! possible priors. Each such prior will be multivariate normal with mean vector $\underset{\sim}{0}$ and some covariance matrix. The covariance matrices of the priors are determined as follows: Let $(i_1, i_2, \ldots, i_k)$ be a random ordering of (1.2,...,k). Assume θ_{i_1} has a normal distribution with mean 0 and variance τ^2. Let $\theta_{i_2} = \theta_{i_1} + Z_1$, $\theta_{i_3} = \theta_{i_2} + Z_2, \ldots$, and $\theta_{i_k} = \theta_{i_{k-1}} + Z_{k-1}$, where the Z_i's are independent normal with means 0 and variances r_i, $i = 1,2,\ldots,k-1$. Hence $(\theta_{i_1}, \theta_{i_2}, \ldots, \theta_{i_k})$ has a multivariate normal distribution with mean vector $\underset{\sim}{0}$ and covariance matrix Γ, where

$$(4.1)\quad \Gamma = \begin{pmatrix} \tau^2 & \tau^2 & \tau^2 & \cdots & \tau^2 \\ \tau^2 & \tau^2+r_1 & \tau^2+r_1 & \cdots & \tau^2+r_1 \\ \tau^2 & \tau^2+r_1 & \tau^2+r_1+r_2 & \cdots & \tau^2+r_1+r_2 \\ \vdots & \vdots & \vdots & \ddots & \vdots \\ \tau^2 & \tau^2+r_1 & \tau^2+r_1+r_2 & \cdots & \tau^2+r_1+r_2+\ldots+r_{k-1} \end{pmatrix}.$$

Now we proceed as follows. We observe the ordering of the sample means. We then estimate the ordering $(i_1, i_2, \ldots, i_k)$ to be the coordinates corresponding to the ordered X's. That is, if $X_1 > X_2 \geq X_3 \geq \ldots \geq X_k$, then we choose $(\theta_1, \theta_2, \ldots, \theta_k)$ to have the covariance matrix Γ, and we estimate θ_1. If $X_2 > X_1 \geq X_3 \geq \ldots \geq X_k$, then $(\theta_2, \theta_1, \theta_3, \ldots, \theta_k)$ has the prior Γ and we estimate θ_2. Under these conditions the "Bayes", or perhaps more suitably the "empirical Bayes" estimator is the a posteriori expected value of the component corresponding to the largest sample mean.

If we take $X_1 \geq X_2 \geq \ldots \geq X_k$, let $\underset{\sim}{r} = (r_1, r_2, \ldots, r_{k-1})$ and $\underset{\sim}{e} = (1,1,\ldots,1)$, $\underset{\sim}{e}$ a 1xk vector, then

$$(4.2)\qquad d_k(\underset{\sim}{X};\, \tau^2, \underset{\sim}{r}) = E\{\theta_1 | \underset{\sim}{X}\} = \tau^2 \underset{\sim}{e}(I+\Gamma)^{-1}\underset{\sim}{X}',$$

since $\begin{pmatrix} \underset{\sim}{X}' \\ \theta_1 \end{pmatrix} \sim N\left(\begin{pmatrix} \underset{\sim}{0}' \\ 0 \end{pmatrix}, \begin{bmatrix} I+\Gamma & \tau^2 \underset{\sim}{e}' \\ \tau^2 \underset{\sim}{e} & \tau^2 \end{bmatrix}\right)$. We now indicate how the estimator may be put in the form of (2.1).

It is well known that for any non-singular kxk matrix $B = (b_{ij})$ with co-factors B_{ij} corresponding to the elements b_{ij}:

$$\sum_{j=1}^{k} b_{\nu j} B_{ij} = \begin{cases} |B| & \text{whenever } \nu = i \\ 0 & \text{otherwise} \end{cases} \tag{4.3}$$

$$B^{-1} = (B_{ij}/|B|). \tag{4.4}$$

Let B play the role of $(I+\Gamma)$ in (4.2), use the symmetry of $(I+\Gamma)$, and the fact that the first row (or column) of $(I+\Gamma)$ is nearly a multiple of the vector $\underset{\sim}{e}$. To wit,

$$C_{i,k} = \tau^2 \sum_{j=1}^{k} (B_{ij}/|B|) = |B|^{-1}\{(\tau^2+1)B_{i1}+\tau^2 \sum_{j=2}^{k} B_{ij}-B_{i1}\} \tag{4.5}$$

$$= \begin{cases} 1-B_{11}/|B| & \text{if } i = 1 \\ -B_{i1}/|B| & \text{if } i = 2,\dots,k. \end{cases}$$

To evaluate $|B|, B_{11},\dots,B_{k1}$, each corresponding matrix is handled in the following manner. From each row (*starting* with the last row and ending with the second row) subtract the previous row. Then do the same thing with the columns. The next set of manipulations are designed to make all the lower off diagonal elements equal to zero so that the value of the determinant will be the product of the diagonal elements. Start with the last column. Divide the last column by the last diagonal element and add it to the next to last column. Next take the (new) next to last column, divide it by the (new) next to last diagonal element and add it to the second from last column. Continue in this fashion until all lower off diagonal elements are zero. Obtain $|B|$ and the needed cofactors in this fasion to get $B_{i1}/|B|$. Then let $\tau^2 \to \infty$ and the result is (2.1).

Remark 4.1. We chose the covariance matrix from among k! covariance matrices. However it can be shown that if the $\ddagger$ in (4.1) is assigned to $(\theta_1,\theta_2,\ldots,\theta_k)$, then the same $\ddagger$ could be assigned to $(\theta_k,\theta_{k-1},\ldots,\theta_1)$ without changing the estimator. Hence the choice of priors is really from among k!/2.

V. TWO POPULATIONS

The case where k= 2 is the easiest to study in detail. Dahiya !41 considers four classes of estimators for this case and derives the bias and mean square error of these estimators. Two classes of estimators can be expressed in terms of the family of estimators we give in (2.5). That is, for proper choices of $\hat{r}_1$, we have Dahiya's estimators. We indicate that the two other classes of estimators studied by Dahiya are inadmissible. We are also able to make other choices of $\hat{r}_1$ that enable us to reduce the bias of Dahiya's estimators when $\theta_1 = \theta_2$.

Letting $Y = X_1-X_2$, Dahiya's estimators are as follows:

(5.1) $$T = X_2 + Y\,\Phi(Y),$$

where $\Phi(z)$ is the c.d.f. of the standard normal distribution.

(5.2) $$\begin{aligned} H_C &= (X_1 + X_2)/2 && \text{if } |Y| < C \\ &= X_{(1)} && \text{if } |Y| \geq C, \end{aligned}$$

where $C \leq 0$ is an arbitrary constant.

(5.3) $$\hat{M}_\lambda = X_{(1)} - \sqrt{2}\,\lambda\,\varphi(Y/\sqrt{2}),$$

where $\varphi(z)$ is the p.d.f. of the standard normal distribution.

(5.4) $$T_\lambda = T-\lambda[\varphi(Y/\sqrt{2})(1/\sqrt{2}) + Y\{\Phi(Y/\sqrt{2})-\Phi(Y)\}].$$

Write (5.1) as $X_1\Phi(Y) + X_2(1-\Phi(Y))$. Note that if $\hat{r}_1 = (2\Phi(Y)-1)/(1-\Phi(Y))$, (2.5) becomes (5.1). (We are tacitly assuming $Y > 0$ when we use (2.5). If $Y < 0$ $(\hat{r}_1+1)/(\hat{r}_1+2)$ would multiply X_2). Furthermore if $\hat{r}_1 = 0$ when $|Y| < C$ and $\hat{r}_1 = \infty$ when $|Y| \geq C$, (2.5) becomes (5.2). One of the estimators we recommend is (2.5) with $\hat{r}_1$ given in (2.9). That is $\hat{r}_1 = 2Y^2$. Such a choice of $\hat{r}_1$ yields an estimator which is further from $X_{(1)}$ than is Dahiya's estimator given in (5.1). To prove this we show that $h(Y) = \Phi(Y)-(2Y^2+1)/(2Y^2+2) \geq 0$, for $Y \geq 0$. In other words the multiplier of $X_{(1)}$ in the linear combination of $X_{(1)}$ and $X_{(2)}$ is larger for Dahiya's estimator. Note $h(0) = 0$, $h(\infty) = 0$, $h'(Y) = \varphi(Y)-Y/(Y^2+1)^2$, and $h'(0) > 0$. Next $h''(Y) = 4Y^2/(Y^2+1)^3-1/(Y^2+1)^2-Y\varphi(Y)$. If Y_0 denotes a solution to $h'(Y) = 0$, then $h''(Y_0) = -(1/(Y_0^2+1))[(Y_0^2-1)^2/(Y_0^2+1)^2] < 0$. Thus $h(Y) \geq 0$. The implication is that the estimator with $\hat{r}_1 = 2Y^2$ will be less biased when $\theta_1 = \theta_2$ than Dahiya's estimator (5.1) and furthermore we would expect the maximum risk to be less than the maximum risk of Dahiya's estimator. The Monte Carlo study in Section 3 supports this expectation.

We conclude this section by indicating that Dahiya's estimators (5.3) and (5.4) are inadmissible. Since the reasoning is the same for (5.3) and (5.4) we will show that (5.3) is inadmissible. To see this, reformulate the problem as follows: Let $Z = (X_1-X_2)/2$, $Z_0 = (X_1+X_2)/2$, $\omega = (\theta_1-\theta_2)/2$, $\eta = (\theta_1+\theta_2)/2$. Then (5.3) becomes

$$\text{(5.5)} \qquad \hat{M}_\lambda = Z_0 + |Z|-2\lambda\, \varphi(\sqrt{2}Z).$$

The problem is to estimate $\eta + \omega$ if $Z > 0$, or estimate $\eta - \omega$ if $Z < 0$. Restrict estimators to be of the form $Z_0 + \gamma(|Z|)$. Clearly if M_λ is inadmissible in this smaller class, it is inadmissible. The restriction reduces the problem to observing $|Z|$ and estimating ω if $Z > 0$, and $-\omega$ if $Z < 0$, with a squared error loss function. Using an argument similar to that used in Blumenthal and Cohen !21, Theorem 4.3, p. 515, a complete class of estimators, for this restricted problem, is the class of generalized Bayes estimators. Furthermore the restriction to $|Z|$

implies that the estimators must be symmetric. These facts imply that the generalized prior is symmetric, which in turn implies that the estimators in the complete class are such that $\gamma(0) = 0$. If we write $\hat{M}_\lambda = Z_0 + \gamma_M(|Z|)$, we see from (5.5) that $\gamma_M(0) = -2\lambda\,\varphi(0) \neq 0$. Hence $\hat{M}_\lambda$ is inadmissible.

VI. EXTENSIONS AND REMARKS

Remark 6.1. All the recommended estimators in Section 2, (See (2.1) to (2.4) and (2.8) through (2.12) are such that $\hat{r}_i$'s are functions of $(|X_i - X_{i+1}|)$. Estimators for the case where σ is known but not equal to 1 are obtained by replacing $|X_i - X_{i+1}|$ with $(|X_i - X_{i+1}|/\sigma)$ in all $\hat{r}_i$'s. If σ^2 is unknown but an estimate s^2 of σ^2, independent of $\underset{\sim}{X}$ is available, then the recommended estimator of the selected mean is obtained by replacing $|X_i - X_{i+1}|$ with $|X_i - X_{i+1}|/s$ in all $\hat{r}_i$'s.

Remark 6.2. The estimators suggested in Remark 6.1 are easily seen to be equivariant under location and scale transformations of the data.

Remark 6.3. The derivation given in Section 4 has some resemblance to the derivation of Bayes estimators of the current mean given by Chernoff and Zacks !31. We remark that our derivation and family of estimators, with minor modifications, could be appropriate for the problem of estimating the current mean. Our prior is more general than the one studied in Chernoff and Zacks and our estimation procedure, being empirical Bayes, is more flexible and more responsive to the data. As such, our procedure does yield interesting estimators, worthy of further study, for the problem of estimating the current mean.

Remark 6.4. Hoadley !51 studies a variation of the problem of estimating the current mean in a quality control context. His model is Poisson as opposed to normal and he seeks confidence interval estimates. Our method should be adaptable to the Poisson and other models and could possibly yield useful estimators for the quality control problem. An extension to confidence interval estimates will be studied in subsequent work.

ACKNOWLEDGMENT

The authors would like to thank Professor Saul Blumenthal for several suggestions and for his help in starting this study. We are also grateful to Marian Sackrowitz for writing the computer programs used in the Monte Carlo study.

REFERENCES

[1] Blumenthal, S. and Cohen, A. (1968). Estimation of the larger of two normal means. *J. Amer. Statist. Assoc. 63*, 861-876.

[2] Blumenthal, S. and Cohen, A. (1968). Estimation of the larger translation parameter. *Ann. Math. Statist. 39*, 502-516.

[3] Chernoff, H. and Zacks, S. (1964). Estimating the current mean of a normal distribution which is subjected to changes in time. *Ann. Math. Statist. 35*, 999-1018.

[4] Dahiya, R. C. (1974). Estimation of the mean of the selected population. *J. Amer. Statist. Assoc. 69*, 226-230.

[5] Hoadley, B. (1981). The quality measurement plan (QMP). *Bell System Tech. J.*, Feb. Issure.

[6] Hsieh, H. (1980). On estimating the mean of the selected population with unknown variance. Submitted to *J. Amer. Statist. Assoc.*

[7] Stein, C. (1964). Contribution to the discussion of Bayesian and non-Bayesian decision theory. Handout, Institute of Mathematical Statistics Meeting, Amherst, Mass.

A NEW LOOK AT BAYESIAN PREDICTION AND CALIBRATION[1]

William W. Davis

Lockheed Research Laboratories
Palo Alto, California, U.S.A.

Morris H. DeGroot

Carnegie-Mellon University
Pittsburgh, Pennsylvania, U.S.A.

I. INTRODUCTION

This paper is concerned with prediction, calibration, and model selection from the Bayesian perspective. In some applications of statistics, the knowledge of which particular model in a given set is correct can advance the forefront of science. In most problems, however, the true model, if there is one, does not belong to the given set and the selection process is (or should be) used basically as a tool in prediction. In the sampling theory approach to statistics, it is difficult to combine prediction functions obtained from different models into a single function. After the data have been collected, the sampling theorist typically simply selects one of the models and uses it for prediction. On the other hand, different models can be combined easily for prediction using the Bayesian methodology. In fact, the multi-model predictive density of a random variable based on all the models in a given finite set is simply a weighted average of the single model predictive densities.

The posterior probabilities of the models in the given set are important in both model selection and prediction. When a

[1]This research was partially supported under Grant SOC79-06386 from the National Science Foundation.

ISBN 0-12-307501-7

model must be selected, these probabilities will be considered together with the costs of various selections. In prediction, these probabilities provide the weights attached to the single model predictive densities. For simplicity, throughout this paper we will assume that there are only two models in the given set, but the extension to the general finite case is apparent.

Our main objective is to study the relationships among the predictive distributions that are appropriate for some dependent variable y under various sampling schemes for an independent variable x. It is assumed throughout the paper that the values of $u_i = (x_i, y_i)$ are potentially observable for $i = 1,\ldots,n+1$. As usual, we will let $u^{(n)} = (u_1,\ldots,u_n)$, with similar notation for $x^{(n)}$ and $y^{(n)}$. Both x_i and y_i may be vectors of arbitrary dimensions.

We will distinguish between problems in which the exact value of x_i is controlled by the experimenter for $i = 1,\ldots,n$, and problems in which x_i is stochastic and has a non-degenerate probability distribution because it is either passively observed or only partially controlled. We will assume that the design (i.e., whether x_i is controlled or stochastic) is the same for each component of $x^{(n)}$, but may be different for x_{n+1}. Thus, four designs are possible for $x^{(n+1)}$, which we denote M, M', M'', and M'''. These designs are defined in Table 1, where we also briefly indicate the statistical contexts in which they arise.

Table 1. Possible designs of $x^{(n+1)}$.

		x_{n+1}: Controlled	x_{n+1}: Stochastic
$x^{(n)}$	Controlled	M: Standard regression and control problems	M''': Designed calibration
	Stochastic	M'': Control of passively observed systems	M': Natural calibration

We will now discuss our assumptions for these designs more fully. Throughout this paper we will use the symbol p as a generic symbol to denote a density function, and we will follow the convention of labelling functions by their arguments. Densities or probabilities associated with the design M' will be denoted by a single prime, those associated with M'' by a double prime, etc.

The model M is called a *conditional model* because it is specified by the conditional densities $p(y_i|x_i, \theta)$, for $i = 1,\ldots,n+1$, where θ is a parameter vector. It is assumed that the components of $y^{(n+1)}$ are independent given θ. We also assume that these n+1 conditional distributions are identical, so it might be said that under this model we have exchangeable conditional distributions. If θ has prior density $p(\theta)$, then the joint density $p(\theta, y^{(n+1)}|x^{(n+1)})$ can be determined and used to calculate the predictive density $p(y_{n+1}|u^{(n)}, x_{n+1})$.

The model M' is called a *stochastic model* because all the components of $u^{(n+1)}$ are stochastic. It is assumed that the vectors $u_1,\ldots,u_{n+1}$ are i.i.d., given some parameter Δ, and that the density of each u_i can be factored as

$$(1)\quad p'(u_i|\Delta) = p(y_i|x_i, \theta)p'(x_i|\psi),$$

where the parameter vectors θ and ψ are functions of Δ. In general, θ and ψ need not be independent under the prior distribution of Δ. As indicated by (1), we assume that the conditional density of y_i given x_i is the same as the one given by the model M.

Suppose that it is of interest to predict y_{n+1}. We assume that the vector $u^{(n)}$ is observed but that x_{n+1} may or may not be observed. If Δ has prior density $p'(\Delta)$ then the relevant predictive density of y_{n+1} can be calculated from the joint density $p'(\Delta, u^{(n+1)})$. This density is $p'(y_{n+1}|x_{n+1}, u^{(n)})$ if x_{n+1} is observed and $p'(y_{n+1}|u^{(n)})$ otherwise. Both situations arise in practice. This model M' also occurs in natural calibration problems (see Aitchison and Dunsmore [1], p. 184).

The model M'' is appropriate when it is desired to control a system that has been passively observed for n time periods. We assume that $u_1,\dots,u_n$ are i.i.d. with a density that satisfies (1) and that the density of y_{n+1} is $p(y_{n+1}|x_{n+1}, \theta)$. The predictive density $p''(y_{n+1}|u^{(n)},x_{n+1})$ can then be determined from any given prior density $p''(\Delta)$.

The model M''' is useful for prediction in a system that was controlled for n time periods and then is passively observed. Although it has seldom been employed, this is the correct model for designed calibration. However, in this case, one is interested in the prediction of x_{n+1} rather than y_{n+1}, so that the relevant predictive density is $p'''(x_{n+1}|u^{(n)},y_{n+1})$.

In Section 2 we discuss the relationships among these predictive distributions. In Section 3, the results are then specialized to the case of the multivariate normal distribution.

In Section 4 we assume that there is uncertainty about which of two prediction models is correct. We consider three designs M, M', and M'' which are analogs of the ones just described. An analog of M''' is not considered since its applicability seems limited. The potential observables are $z_i = (w_i, x_i, y_i)$ for $i = 1,\dots,n+1$, where w_i, x_i, and y_i are vectors of arbitrary dimensions.

In each of these models, it is assumed that there is uncertainty about which of the variables w_i or x_i is useful in prediction or control. Either y_i and x_i are conditionally independent given w_i, or y_i and w_i are conditionally independent given x_i. For a discussion of this concept and many other examples of the use of conditional independence see Dawid [5]. Conditions are given which imply that the predictive density is the same under M, M', and M''. In Section 5, the results are again specialized to the case of the multivariate normal distribution. Finally, an application is mentioned in Section 6.

II. PREDICTIVE DISTRIBUTIONS

In this section we will begin by deriving the predictive distribution of y_{n+1} under the different models and comparing the results. We will then derive the distribution of x_{n+1} for use in calibration problems.

Under the model M, the posterior density of θ based on $u^{(n)}$ is

$$p(\theta|u^{(n)}) \propto p(\theta)p(y^{(n)}|x^{(n)}, \theta) = p(\theta)\prod_{1}^{n} p(y_i|x_i,\theta)$$

and the predictive density is

$$p(y_{n+1}|x_{n+1},u^{(n)}) = \int p(y_{n+1}|x_{n+1}, \theta)p(\theta|u^{(n)})d\theta. \tag{2}$$

Under the model M', the posterior density of (θ,ψ) is

$$p'(\theta,\psi|u^{(n)}) \propto p(y^{(n)}|x^{(n)}, \theta)\ p'(x^{(n)}|\psi)p'(\theta,\psi). \tag{3}$$

We will assume throughout this paper that the marginal density of θ is the same under models M and M', i.e., $p(\theta) = p'(\theta)$. If θ and ψ are independent in the prior distribution, then they are also independent in the posterior distribution and $p'(\theta|u^{(n)}) = p(\theta|u^{(n)})$. The predictive density of y_{n+1} depends on whether x_{n+1} is observed. If x_{n+1} is observed, the predictive density is

$$p'(y_{n+1}|x_{n+1}, u^{(n)}) \propto \int p'(u_{n+1}|\Delta)\ p'(\Delta|u^{(n)})d\Delta.$$

Under the assumption of prior independence of θ and ψ, it can be shown that

$$p'(y_{n+1}|x_{n+1}, u^{(n)}) = p(y_{n+1}|x_{n+1},u^{(n)}). \tag{4}$$

If x_{n+1} is not observed, the predictive density is

$$p'(y_{n+1}|u^{(n)}) = \int p'(y_{n+1}|\Delta)p'(\Delta|u^{(n)})d\Delta,$$

and under the assumption of prior independence this reduces to

$$p'(y_{n+1}|u^{(n)}) = \int p'(x_{n+1}|x^{(n)})p(y_{n+1}|x_{n+1},u^{(n)})dx_{n+1}.$$

This predictive density is an average of the densities given by (2) where the weight function is given by $p'(x_{n+1}|x^{(n)}) = \int p'(x_{n+1}|\psi)p'(\psi|x^{(n)})d\psi$.

Under the model M'', the predictive density is given by

$$(5) \qquad p''(y_{n+1}|x_{n+1},u^{(n)}) = \int p(y_{n+1}|x_{n+1},\theta)p'(\theta|u^{(n)})d\theta$$

where $p'(\theta|u^{(n)})$ is obtained from (3) as a marginal density. If θ and ψ are independent in the prior distribution, then (5) reduces to (2). A crucial assumption in the model M'' is that the conditional distributions of the controlled and uncontrolled systems coincide, although there is no guarantee that this must be the case in every real problem (see Box [4]). Without this assumption, the predictive distributions will not necessarily coincide.

Now we discuss the calibration problem and the relevance of the model M'''. In one common type of calibration problem, the values of the y_i's are obtained by using a quick, crude measurement method applied to n specimens and the values of the x_i's are obtained by using a slow, accurate method applied to the same specimens. The values of a future $(n+1)^{\underline{st}}$ specimen using these same methods are denoted by y_{n+1} and x_{n+1} respectively. The value of y_{n+1} is measured and used to predict x_{n+1}. For summaries of the previous literature on calibration, see Lindley [12] and Williford et al. [14].

Much of the work on the calibration problem has dealt with designed calibration and it is usually assumed that the entire vector $x^{(n+1)}$ is controlled but that x_{n+1} is not observed. This corresponds to the model M but with the additional feature that x_{n+1} plays the role of a parameter. Thus, the joint prior density $p(\theta,x_{n+1})$ must be specified. The density of x_{n+1} is then given by

$$p(x_{n+1}|u^{(n)},y_{n+1}) \propto \int p(\theta,x_{n+1})p(y^{(n+1)}|x^{(n+1)},\theta)d\theta.$$

If θ and x_{n+1} are independent in their joint prior density, this reduces to

$$p(x_{n+1}|u^{(n)},y_{n+1}) \propto p(x_{n+1})p(y_{n+1}|x_{n+1},u^{(n)}). \tag{6}$$

Since the value of x_{n+1} is unknown to the experimenter in this discussion, x_{n+1} must be regarded as stochastic (even though its value may have been "controlled" by someone else). Since, in addition, $x^{(n)}$ is controlled, the model M''' is more appropriate than M. Under the assumption that $p'''(u_{n+1}|\Delta) = p'(u_{n+1}|\Delta)$,

$$p'''(x_{n+1}|y_{n+1},u^{(n)}) \propto$$

$$\int p'''(\theta,\psi)p(y^{(n+1)}|x^{(n+1)},\theta)p'(x_{n+1}|\psi)d\Delta.$$

If one again assumes prior independence of θ and ψ, and consistency of their prior marginal densities in the sense that $p'''(\theta) = p(\theta)$ and $p'''(\psi) = p'(\psi)$, then

$$p'''(x_{n+1}|y_{n+1},u^{(n)}) \propto p'(x_{n+1})p(y_{n+1}|x_{n+1},u^{(n)}), \tag{7}$$

where $p'(x_{n+1}) = \int p'(x_{n+1}|\psi)p'(\psi)d\psi$. In general, the densities (6) and (7) will not coincide since $p(x_{n+1})$ will be assigned directly whereas $p'(x_{n+1})$ will be obtained from $p'(\psi)$.

Finally, we shall consider the calibration problem under the model M'. Although we could proceed along lines similar to the derivation of (7), the following alternate method is usually simpler: Since all components of $u^{(n+1)}$ are stochastic under M', the calibration problem is the same as the prediction problem with the roles of x and y reversed. To calculate the predictive density we assume that the density can be written in the form

$$p'(u_i|\Delta) = p'(x_i|y_i,\theta^*)p'(y_i|\psi^*) \text{ for } i = 1,\ldots,n+1 \tag{8}$$

where θ^* and ψ^* are parameters. If θ^* and ψ^* are independent under the prior distribution, then it follows from (2) and (4) that the appropriate density for calibration is

$$p'(x_{n+1}|y_{n+1},u^{(n)}) = \int p'(x_{n+1}|y_{n+1},\theta^*)p'(\theta^*|u^{(n)})d\theta^*, \tag{9}$$

where $p'(\theta^*|u^{(n)}) \propto p'(\theta^*)p'(x^{(n)}|y^{(n)},\theta^*)$. Since this is the predictive density for the conditional model with the roles of x and y reversed, the solution is known in many cases.

III. MULTIPLE REGRESSION

We now specialize the results just described to problems of prediction and calibration using regression equations. Under model M' we assume that the u_i's are i.i.d. and have a multivariate normal distribution. We assume that x_i and y_i are vectors of dimensions d_1 and d_2 respectively, and we partition the mean μ of u_i as $\mu' = (\mu_1', \mu_2')$ and the covariance matrix Σ as

$$\Sigma = \begin{pmatrix} \Sigma_{11} & \Sigma_{12} \\ \Sigma_{21} & \Sigma_{22} \end{pmatrix},$$

where μ_i is d_i-dimensional and Σ_{ij} is a matrix of dimension $d_i \times d_j$. We refer to the distribution of u_i as $N(\mu,\Sigma)$. In this case Δ is composed of the distinct components of (μ,Σ). It is easy to see that the density of u_i satisfies (1) with ψ containing the distinct components of (μ_1, Σ_{11}) and θ containing the distinct components of $(\beta,\Sigma_{22.1})$ where $\beta' = (a\ A)$ with $A = \Sigma_{21}\Sigma_{11}^{-1}$, $a = \mu_2 - A\mu_1$, and $\Sigma_{22.1} = \Sigma_{22} - \Sigma_{21}\Sigma_{11}^{-1}\Sigma_{12}$. This stochastic model implies that the conditional distribution of y_i given x_i and θ, denoted by $\mathcal{L}(y_i|x_i,\theta)$, is given by

$$\mathcal{L}(y_i|x_i,\theta) = N(\beta' x_i^*, \Sigma_{22.1}), \quad i = 1,\ldots,n+1, \tag{10}$$

where $x_i^{*\prime} = (1, x_i')$.

In this problem, a conjugate family of prior distributions for Δ is the family of normal/inverted Wishart distributions. Diaconis and Ylvisaker [7] have given a justification for choosing this particular family in terms of linear posterior expectations. We say that Σ has the inverted Wishart distribution with parameters (α, R), and we write $\Sigma \sim IW(\alpha,R)$, if the precision matrix Σ^{-1} has the Wishart distribution with parameters (α, R^{-1}). If $\mathcal{L}(\mu|\Sigma) = N(m, \nu^{-1}\Sigma)$ and $\Sigma \sim IW(\alpha,R)$, then we write $(\mu,\Sigma) \sim NIW(m,\nu,\alpha,R)$. In this case the prior distribution of (μ, Σ^{-1}) is in the normal/Wishart family (DeGroot [6], Section 9.10). With these assumptions, the hyperparameter α denotes the degrees of freedom of the distribution of Σ^{-1}, and $E(\Sigma^{-1}) = \alpha R^{-1}$.

In the next theorem we assume that (μ,Σ) has a normal/inverted Wishart distribution and we give the distribution of (θ,ψ). A noteworthy feature of this theorem is the result that θ and ψ are independent (see also Barndorff-Nielsen [3], Corollary 9.3). In stating the theorem it is useful to employ the notation $\otimes$ for the Kronecker product of two matrices and the "vec" notation. If Q is a matrix with r columns $(q_1,\ldots,q_r)$, then $\text{vec}(Q) = (q_1',\ldots,q_r')$. The proof of the theorem can be obtained by standard multivariate techniques and is omitted.

THEOREM 1. *Suppose that* $(\mu,\Sigma) \sim NIW(m,\nu,\alpha,R)$. *Then* θ *and* ψ *are independent and have the following distributions:*

(i) $\psi = (\mu_1,\Sigma_{11}) \sim NIW(m_1, \nu, \alpha-d_2, R_{11})$

(ii) $\mathcal{L}[\text{vec}(\beta)|\Sigma_{22.1}] = N[\text{vec}(\beta_0), \Sigma_{22.1} \otimes \Gamma]$ *and*

$\Sigma_{22.1} \sim IW(\alpha, R_{22.1})$, *where* $\beta_0' = (m_2 - R_{21}R_{11}^{-1}m_1 \quad R_{21}R_{11}^{-1})$,

$$\Gamma = \begin{pmatrix} \nu^{-1} + m_1'R_{11}^{-1}m_1 & -m_1'R_{11}^{-1} \\ -R_{11}^{-1}m_1 & R_{11}^{-1} \end{pmatrix},$$

m *is partitioned in the same fashion as* μ, *and* $R = (R_{ij})$ *is partitioned in the same fashion as* Σ.

This theorem, together with (4), shows that the predictive density for the stochastic model M' coincides with the predictive density for the conditional model M if one uses a prior distribution in the conjugate family. This predictive density can be found using the methodology of Ando and Kaufman [2].

Under the stochastic model, the conditional distributions (10) form the traditional multivariate regression model. The conjugate prior distribution for the parameters of this model is

$$\mathcal{L}[\text{vec}(\beta)|\Sigma_{22.1}] = N[\text{vec}(\beta_0), \Sigma_{22.1} \otimes \Gamma]$$

and

$$\Sigma_{22.1} \sim IW(\alpha, R).$$

Theorem 1 shows that this class of prior distributions is also obtained by considering the marginal distributions of θ that arise from the conjugate family of prior distributions for Δ in the stochastic model. The same property is true for ψ: The conjugate family for ψ is the normal/inverted Wishart family, and Theorem 1 shows that this is the family of marginal distributions of ψ that arise from the conjugate family for Δ.

By definition, a conjugate prior density for a parameter has the same form as the likelihood function of the parameter based on a set of observations. Therefore, it has been pointed out to us by John Pratt, that a proof of Theorem 1 can be developed based on a demonstration that the likelihood function of Δ can be factored as in (1).

It is interesting to note that although any prior distribution in the conjugate family for Δ leads to independent prior distributions for θ and ψ which are in their own conjugate families, the converse is not true. That is, if we assume independent members of the conjugate family for θ and ψ, the distribution of Δ will not necessarily be a normal/inverted Wishart distribution. Theorem 1 shows that the hyperparameters of the distributions of θ and ψ are related, and unless the hyperparameters of the distributions of θ and ψ have this structure, they will not lead to a normal/inverted Wishart prior distribution for Δ. It should be emphasized that (4) holds for any prior distribution such that θ and ψ are independent, and in particular, it holds when θ and ψ are independent with distributions in their conjugate families.

We now consider the calibration problem. The most common application of calibration is when there are two variables that are approximately linearly related. The assumption of bivariate normality implies that both regressions are linear. Bayesian solutions of the calibration problem have been given by Dunsmore [8] using a non-informative prior distribution on the parameters of the bivariate normal distribution, and by Hoadley [11] and Williford et al. [14] assuming fixed independent variables.

We assume a sample from the bivariate normal distribution and factor the density using (8). If Δ has a conjugate prior distribution, then Theorem 1 shows both that θ and ψ are independent and that θ^* and ψ^* are independent. It is well known that the density given by (9) is in the Student t family (Ando and Kaufman [2]).

IV. PREDICTIVE DISTRIBUTIONS WITH DIFFERENT POSSIBLE MODELS

Suppose now that there is uncertainty about which of the vectors of independent variables w or x is useful in the prediction of y. We shall let $z_i = (w_i, x_i, y_i)$ and $v_i = (w_i, x_i)$ for $i = 1,\ldots,n+1$.

Under model M, the components of $v^{(n+1)}$ are controlled and we assume that the components of $y^{(n+1)}$ are independent for given values of the parameters. We consider two possible versions M_1 and M_2 of this model. If M_1 is true, the density of y_i given v_i is of the form $p(y_i|w_i, \theta_1)$ and does not depend on x_i. If M_2 is true, the density of y_i given v_i is of the form $p(y_i|x_i, \theta_2)$ and does not depend on w_i.

Although no simple model will be correct in any particular problem, it is convenient for purposes of prediction to restrict attention to a small set of possibilities. Therefore, we assign prior probabilities $p(M_1)$ and $p(M_2)$ to M_1 and M_2, where $p(M_1) + p(M_2) = 1$, and assign prior density $p(\theta_i)$ to the parameters of M_i for $i = 1,2$. The predictive density is then

$$(11) \qquad p(y_{n+1}|z^{(n)},v_{n+1}) = \sum_{i=1}^{2} p(M_i|z^{(n)})p_i(y_{n+1}|z^{(n)},v_{n+1})$$

where $p(M_i|z^{(n)})$ is the posterior probability of M_i and $p_i(y_{n+1}|z^{(n)},v_{n+1})$ is the predictive density for y_{n+1} if M_i is true. The posterior probabilities can be obtained from the relation

$$(12) \qquad \frac{p(M_1|z^{(n)})}{p(M_2|z^{(n)})} = \frac{p(M_1)}{p(M_2)} B(M_1,M_2)$$

where the Bayes factor $B(M_1,M_2)$ is given by

$$B(M_1,M_2) = \frac{\int p(y^{(n)}|w^{(n)},\theta_1)p(\theta_1)d\theta_1}{\int p(y^{(n)}|x^{(n)},\theta_2)p(\theta_2)d\theta_2}.$$

The predictive density under M_i is

$$(13) \qquad p_i(y_{n+1}|z^{(n)},v_{n+1}) = \int p(y_{n+1}|\theta_i,v_{n+1})p(\theta_i|z^{(n)})d\theta_i,$$

where $p(\theta_i|z^{(n)})$ is the posterior density of θ_i.

Now we consider the stochastic model M' in which all the components of z_i are stochastic and the n+1 components of $z^{(n+1)}$ are i.i.d. for given values of the parameters. We introduce two possible versions M_1' and M_2' are we let $p'(z^{(n)}|\Delta_i)$ denote the density of $z^{(n)}$ if M_i' is true, where Δ_1 and Δ_2 are parameter vectors. We assume that the conditional density $p'(y_i|v_i,\Delta_1)$ reduces to $p(y_i|w_i,\theta_1)$ under M_1' and $p'(y_i|v_i,\Delta_2)$ reduces to $p(y_i|x_i,\theta_2)$ under M_2'. The predictive density $p'(y_{n+1}|z^{(n)},v_{n+1})$ can be determined once prior probabilities $p'(M_i')$ and prior densities $p'(\Delta_i)$ have been assigned. We will assume that the prior distributions of the stochastic and conditional models are consistent in the sense that $p'(M_i') = p(M_i)$ and the marginal density of θ_i under M_i' coincides with the prior density of θ_i under M_i. We now give a set of conditions which imply that the predictive density under model M' coincides with the predictive density under model M.

THEOREM 2. *Under the following conditions* (A) *and* (B), *the predictive density* $p'(y_{n+1}|z^{(n)},v_{n+1})$ *coincides with* $p(y_{n+1}|z^{(n)},v_{n+1})$ *given by* (11):

(A) *The densities* $p'(z^{(n)}|\Delta_1)$ *and* $p'(z^{(n)}|\Delta_2)$ *satisfy the relations*

$$p'(z^{(n)}|\Delta_1) = p(y^{(n)}|w^{(n)},\theta_1)p'(v^{(n)}|\psi),$$
(14)
$$p'(z^{(n)}|\Delta_2) = p(y^{(n)}|x^{(n)},\theta_2)p'(v^{(n)}|\psi).$$

(B) *The prior density for* Δ_i *implies that* θ_i *and* ψ *are independent, and that the marginal distribution of* ψ *is the same for* i = 1,2.

Proof. The predictive density under M' is

$$p'(y_{n+1}|z^{(n)},v_{n+1}) = \sum_{i=1}^{2} p'(M_i'|z^{(n)})p_i'(y_{n+1}|z^{(n)},v_{n+1}), \tag{15}$$

where the summands in (15) can be obtained from relations analogous to (12) and (13). If θ_i and ψ are independent under the prior distribution in model M_i', then they are also independent under the posterior distribution. In fact, the posterior density of (θ_i, ψ) under M_i' will be $p'(\theta_i, \psi | z^{(n)}) \propto p'(\theta_i | z^{(n)}) p'(\psi | v^{(n)})$, where $p'(\theta_1 | z^{(n)}) \propto p(\theta_1) p(y^{(n)} | w^{(n)}, \theta_1), p'(\theta_2 | z^{(n)}) \propto p(\theta_2) p(y^{(n)} | x^{(n)}, \theta_2)$ and $p'(\psi | v^{(n)}) \propto p'(\psi) p'(v^{(n)} | \psi)$. This shows that the posterior distribution of θ_i under M_i' coincides with its distribution under M_i. If the prior distribution of ψ is the same under both M_1' and M_2', then prior independence of the parameters guarantees that $p(M_i | z^{(n)}) = p'(M_i' | z^{(n)})$ for $i = 1,2$. The predictive density given M_1' is

$$p_1'(y_{n+1} | z^{(n)}, v_{n+1}) \propto \int p(y_{n+1} | w_{n+1}, \theta_1) p'(\theta_1 | z^{(n)}) d\theta_1,$$

which coincides with the predictive density for M_1. A similar relation holds between M_2' and M_2, which completes the proof.

Two crucial assumptions of (14) are:

(i) The marginal density of $v^{(n)}$ is the same under M_1' and M_2'.

(ii) Under M_1', $y^{(n)}$ and $x^{(n)}$ are conditionally independent given $w^{(n)}$, and under M_2', $y^{(n)}$ and $w^{(n)}$ are conditionally independent given $x^{(n)}$. Thus, unless $y^{(n)}$ and $v^{(n)}$ are independent or their joint distribution is degenerate, only one of the models M_1' and M_2' can be correct.

Under the same conditions one can establish the same result for M''.

IV. THE NORMAL DISTRIBUTION

Now we specialize the results of the previous section to multivariate normal distributions. Under model M' we assume that $z_1, \ldots, z_{n+1}$ are i.i.d and have the $N(\mu, \Sigma)$ distribution. We partition $\mu' = (\mu_1', \mu_2', \mu_3')$ and $\Sigma = (\Sigma_{rs})$ to conform with the dimensions d_1, d_2, and d_3 of w_i, x_i, and y_i. As usual, we shall let

$$\Sigma_{rs.t} = \Sigma_{rs} - \Sigma_{rt}\Sigma_{tt}^{-1}\Sigma_{ts} \quad \text{for } r,s,t = 1,2,3.$$

The distribution of y_i under model M is obtained from the conditional distribution of y_i given v_i and is given by

$$\mathcal{L}(y_i|v_i) = N[\mu_3+\Gamma_1(w_i-\mu_1) + \Gamma_2(x_i-\mu_2), \Sigma_{33.12}],$$

where $\Gamma_1 = \Sigma_{31.2}\Sigma_{11.2}^{-1}$, $\Gamma_2 = \Sigma_{32.1}\Sigma_{22.1}^{-1}$, and $\Sigma_{33.12} = \Sigma_{33}-\Gamma_1\Sigma_{13}-\Gamma_2\Sigma_{23}$. The variables y_i and x_i are conditionally independent given w_i if and only if $\Gamma_2 = 0$, and y_i and w_i are conditionally independent given x_i if and only if $\Gamma_1 = 0$.

We assume that the prior distributions are consistent in the sense that $p'(M_i') = p(M_i)$ for $i = 1,2$. We also assume that either $\Gamma_1 = 0$ or $\Gamma_2 = 0$, but not both, so that $p(M_1) + p(M_2) = 1$.

Under model M_1' a prior distribution is assigned to the distinct components of $\Delta_1 = (\mu,\Sigma)$ except Σ_{32}, which is determined from the condition that $\Gamma_2 = 0$ under M_1'. Other consequences of the condition $\Gamma_2 = 0$ are

(i) $\Gamma_1 = \Sigma_{31}\Sigma_{11}^{-1}$,

(ii) $\Sigma_{33.12} = \Sigma_{33.1}$,

(iii) $|\Sigma| = |\Sigma_{11}||\Sigma_{22.1}||\Sigma_{33.1}|$.

Thus, Σ is positive definite when each of the terms on the right hand side of (iii) is positive. This will be the case if (w_i,x_i) and (w_i,y_i) have non-degenerate normal distributions with dimensions d_1+d_2 and d_1+d_3 respectively. Similar remarks apply to model M_2'.

In order to use Theorem 2 we define θ_1 to contain the distinct components of $\tau_1' = (\mu_3-\Gamma_1\mu_1\ \Gamma_1)$ and $\Sigma_{33.1}$, θ_2 to contain the distinct components of $\tau_2' = (\mu_3-\Gamma_2\mu_2\ \Gamma_2)$ and $\Sigma_{33.2}$, and ψ to contain the distinct components of

$$\begin{pmatrix} \mu_1 \\ \mu_2 \end{pmatrix} \quad \text{and} \quad \begin{pmatrix} \Sigma_{11} & \Sigma_{12} \\ \Sigma_{21} & \Sigma_{22} \end{pmatrix}.$$

A crucial assumption in Theorem 2 is that θ_i and ψ are independent under the prior distribution in model M_i'. The next theorem categorizes the prior distributions in a certain family that satisfy this assumption. Since it should be easier in practice to assess the prior distribution of $\gamma_1' = (\mu_3 \quad \Sigma_{31})$ than the distribution of τ_1, the prior distributions are stated for γ_1. Without loss of generality, we state the theorem for model M_1'.

THEOREM 3. *Suppose that* ψ *and* $\Sigma_{33.1}$ *are independently distributed and that* $\mathcal{L}[\text{vec}(\gamma_1)|\psi, \Sigma_{33.1}] = N[\text{vec}(A_1), \Sigma_{33.1} \otimes B_1]$. *Then* θ_1 *and* ψ *are independent if and only if* $A_1 = U_1'Q_1$ *and* $B_1 = U_1'R_1U_1$ *where*

$$U_1 = \begin{pmatrix} 1 & 0' \\ \mu_1 & \Sigma_{11} \end{pmatrix},$$

Q_1 *is an arbitrary matrix of dimension* $(d_1+1) \times d_3$ *and* R_1 *is an arbitrary positive definite matrix of dimension* $(d_1+1) \times (d_1+1)$.

Proof. Since $\tau_1' = U_1'^{-1}\gamma_1$, it follows from a property of the multivariate normal distribution that

$$\mathcal{L}[\text{vec}(\tau_1')|\psi,\Sigma_{33.1}]=N[\text{vec}(U_1'^{-1}A_1),\Sigma_{33.1}\otimes U_1'^{-1}B_1U_1^{-1}]. \tag{16}$$

Since ψ and $\Sigma_{33.1}$ are assumed to be independent, θ_1 and ψ will be independent if and only if τ_1 and ψ are conditionally independent given $\Sigma_{33.1}$. Suppose first that $A_1 = U_1'Q_1$ and $B_1 = U_1'R_1U_1$. Then from (16),

$$\mathcal{L}[\text{vec}(\tau_1')|\psi,\Sigma_{33.1}] = N[\text{vec}(Q_1),\Sigma_{33.1} \otimes R_1].$$

Since this distribution does not depend on ψ, it follows that τ_1

and ψ are conditionally independent given $\Sigma_{33.1}$. Conversely, if τ_1 and ψ are conditionally independent given $\Sigma_{33.1}$, the quantities $U_1'^{-1}A_1$ and $U_1'B_1U_1'^{-1}$, which we denote by Q_1 and R_1 respectively, do not depend on ψ. This completes the proof.

With the assumption of multivariate normality and the hypothesis that either $\Gamma_1 = 0$ or $\Gamma_2 = 0$, equation (14) is satisfied. If the prior distribution for ψ is the same under M_1' and M_2', and a prior distribution of the form given in Theorem 3 is assumed under both M_1' and M_2', then the predictive distributions for y_{n+1} will be the same under M and M'.

VI. AN APPLICATION

We now specialize the discussion in Section 5 to the case in which $d_i = 1$ for 1,2,3. Under M' we assume that the z_i's are i.i.d. with a trivariate normal distribution. Under M_1', the variables $y^{(n)}$ and $x^{(n)}$ are conditionally independent given $w^{(n)}$, and under M_2', the variables $y^{(n)}$ and $w^{(n)}$ are conditionally independent given $x^{(n)}$.

The conditional models M_1 and M_2 can be stated in the form

$$M_1: \quad y_i = \alpha_1 + \beta_1 w_i + e_{1i},$$

$$M_2: \quad y_i = \alpha_2 + \beta_2 x_i + e_{2i},$$

where $v_i = (w_i, x_i)$ is considered fixed for $i = 1,\ldots,n+1$, the e_{1i}'s are i.i.d. with the $N(0,\sigma_1^2)$ distribution, and the e_{2i}'s are i.i.d. with the $N(0,\sigma_2^2)$ distribution.

As in Section 5, we assume consistency of the prior distributions for the parameters of M_i' and M_i, and we also assume that exactly one of the models M_1' and M_2' is true.

Friedman and Meiselman [9] and Friedman and Schwartz [10] studied a problem of this form involving yearly time series measurements where w_i denotes autonomous spending in a given year i, x_i denotes the money supply, and y_i denotes consumption. Both of these studies used transformed values of the variables z_i to make the independence of the errors reasonable, but for simplicity we will assume the assumptions are satisfied for the original measurements. If consumption and spending are conditionally independent given the money supply, the monetarist's position is supported. If consumption and the money supply are conditionally independent given spending, the Keynesian position is supported.

Zellner ([15], Section 10.4) used this example to motivate the problem of choosing between two regression models where the independent variables are considered fixed, and assumed conjugate prior distributions for the parameters of the conditional models. With this approach, however, there is no guarantee that only one of the models is correct. In fact, although the independent variables of this example are usually called exogeneous, they are influenced by many random factors and can be considered to be random. If z_i has a trivariate normal distribution, then without further conditions, both M_1 and M_2 will be true. However, it follows from Theorem 3 and the discussion in Section 5 that a family of prior distributions can be constructed such that exactly one of these models is true and the predictive distributions are the same for the stochastic and the conditional models.

ACKNOWLEDGMENTS

We are grateful to James M. Dickey and Joseph B. Kadane for their helpful comments.

REFERENCES

[1] Aitchison, J. and Dunsmore, I. R. (1975). *Statistical Prediction Analysis*. Cambridge University Press, Cambridge.

[2] Ando, A. and Kaufman, G. W. (1965). Bayesian analysis of the independent multinormal process-neither mean nor precision known. *J. Amer. Statist. Assoc.* *60*, 347-358.

[3] Barndorff-Nielsen, O. (1978). *Information and Exponential Families in Statistical Theory*. John Wiley, New York.

[4] Box, G.E.P. (1966). The use and abuse of regression. *Technometrics* *8*, 625-629.

[5] Dawid, A. P. (1979). Conditional independence in statistical theory. *J. Roy. Statist. Soc. Ser. B* *41*, 1-31.

[6] DeGroot, M. H. (1970). *Optimal Statistical Decisions*. McGraw-Hill, New York.

[7] Diaconis, P. and Ylvisaker, D. (1979). Conjugate priors for exponential families. *Ann. Statist.* *7*, 269-281.

[8] Dunsmore, I. R. (1968). A Bayesian approach to calibration. *J. Roy. Statist. Soc. Ser. B* *30*, 396-405.

[9] Friedman, M. and Meiselman, D. (1963). The relative stability of monetary velocity and the investment multiplier in the United States, 1897-1958. The Commission on Money and Credit Research Study, *Stabilization Policies*. Prentice-Hall, Englewood Cliffs, New Jersey.

[10] Friedman, M. and Schwartz, A. J. (1963). Money and business cycles. *Rev. Econ. Statist.* *45* (supp.) 32-78.

[11] Hoadley, B. (1970). A Bayesian look at inverse regression. *J. Amer. Statist. Assoc.* *65*, 356-369.

[12] Lindley, D. V. (1972). *Bayesian Statistics: A Review*. Society for Industrial and Applied Mathematics, Philadelphia.

[13] Raiffa, H. and Schlaifer, R. (1961). *Applied Statistical Decision Theory*. Harvard Business School, Boston.

[14] Williford, W. O., Carter, M. C., and Field, J. C. (1979). A further look at the Bayesian approach to calibration. *J. Statist. Comput. Simulation* 9,47-69.

[15] Zellner, A. (1971). *An Introduction to Bayesian Inference in Econometrics*. John Wiley, New York.

ASSESSING PROBABILITY ASSESSORS: CALIBRATION AND REFINEMENT[1]

Morris H. DeGroot

and

Stephen E. Fienberg

Department of Statistics
Carnegie-Mellon University
Pittsburgh, Pennsylvania, U.S.A.

I. INTRODUCTION

You have just been hired by the management of a local television station to assist them in evaluating the candidates for a soon-to-be-filled position as station weatherman. Each of the candidates has made a sequence of probability forecasts of the event "rain", announcing the probability p_j on the jth trial of the sequence. Before making the next forecast the candidate learns the value of y_j, which is 1 if "rain" occurs, and is 0 otherwise. The basic data available to you for each candidate is a set of pairs $\{(p_j, y_j): j = 1,2,\ldots,n\}$, and from this information you are to assess the candidates, and possibly determine which is the best probability assessor. The purpose of this paper is to provide a probabilistic framework into which to set this problem of assessing probability assessors.

In the weatherman problem, we have taken care to ensure that each forecast is made in light of full information of the outcome

[1]The preparation of this paper was partially supported by the National Science Foundation under grant SES-7906386 and by the Office of Naval Research Contract N0014-80-C-0637 at Carnegie-Mellon University. Reproduction in whole or in part is permitted for any purpose of the United States Government.

ISBN 0-12-307501-7

of previous forecasts, i.e., with feedback. From a subjective probability perspective the announced probability forecasts form a sequence of conditional probabilities in which each term expresses the candidate's degree of belief given all of the information available at the time of the forecast. The probability distribution of these conditional probabilities, found by letting the number of trials $n \to \infty$, is of central concern in this paper.

The notion of calibration concerns the relationship between the probability distribution of conditional probabilities and the long-run frequencies of rain given a particular probabilistic assessment value. Roughly speaking a probability assessor is said to be well-calibrated if, for those trials on which he forecasts the probability x, the long-run frequency of rain is x. Pratt [21] and Dawid [7] show that a probability assessor who is coherent in the sense of de Finetti [8] must be well-calibrated almost surely. In Section 2, we make more formal this notion of calibration, and, in Section 3, we show that some well-calibrated forecasters are clearly superior to others. We suggest a formal sense in which a given well-calibrated forecaster can be "more refined" and thus "better" than another. Then in Section 4, we demonstrate the link between the concept of refinement and that of sufficiency in the comparison of experiments. This link leads in Section 5 to a rather simple condition for determining whether one well-calibrated forecaster is more refined than another. In Section 6, this condition is exploited in order to determine a "least-refined" forecaster.

Calibration and refinement, as presented in this paper, refer only to the full probability distribution of the assessor's conditional forecasts. However, in the television station example which began this section, and elsewhere in statistical practice, we do not know either this distribution or the long-run frequencies of rain. All that we get to see is a finite set of forecasts and the associated indicators of whether or not rain occurred, i.e., $\{(p_j,y_j): j = 1,2,\ldots,n\}$. In Section 7, we briefly review some scoring rules suggested for such sample situations, and indicate how they relate to the probabilistic concepts of calibration and refinement.

For the forecasting problems considered in the first six sections of the paper there are only two possible outcomes, rain or no rain. We take care in these sections to preserve the orientation of outcomes and work *only* with the forecasters' assessments of the probability of rain. Kadane and Lichtenstein [15] show that the loss of orientation leads to the inability to recalibrate a forecaster's assessments. Finally, in Section 8 we discuss extensions of the calibration and refinement structure to forecasting problems with $s > 2$ outcomes. In these problems, we require the ordered vector of assessed probabilities for the s possible outcomes and the associated indicator vector which summarizes which outcome actually occurs.

II. WELL-CALIBRATED FORECASTERS

Consider a weather forecaster who day after day must specify his subjective probability x that there will be at least a certain amount of rain at some given location. For simplicity, we shall refer to the occurrence of this well-specified event as "rain." Thus, we may say simply that, at the beginning of each day, the forecaster must specify his probability of rain, and that at the end of each day it is observed whether or not rain actually did occur.

We shall refer to the probability x specified by the forecaster on any particular day as his *prediction*. Both for realism and simplicity, we assume that the prediction x is restricted to a finite set of values $0 = x_0 < x_1 < \ldots < x_k = 1$. (In many weather forecasts, $k = 10$ and $x_j = j/10$.) We assume that the forecaster's predictions can be observed over a large number of days, and we shall let $\nu(x)$ denote the probability function (or frequency function) of his predictions over those days. Thus, we can think of $\nu(x)$ either as the probability that the forecaster's prediction on a randomly chosen day will be x, or in the frequency sense as the proportion of days on which his prediction is x. We shall let $\mathcal{X}$ denote the set of possible predictions $\{x_0, x_1, \ldots, x_k\}$ and let $\mathcal{X}^+$ denote the subset of $\mathcal{X}$ containing only those points for which $\nu(x) > 0$.

To evaluate the forecaster, we must compare the actual occurrences of rain or no rain with his predictions, and for $x \in \mathcal{X}^+$ we shall let $\rho(x)$ denote the conditional probability of rain given that the prediction is x. The forecaster is said to be *well-calibrated* (see, e.g., Dawid [7]) if $\rho(x) = x$ for all values of $x \in \mathcal{X}^+$. In words, the forecaster is well-calibrated if among all those days for which the prediction is x, the proportion of rainy days is also x, and this is true for every value of x. In meterology, the criterion of calibration is referred to as validity (Miller [18]), or reliability (Murphy [19]), and the well-calibrated forecaster is said to be *perfectly reliable*.

For obvious reasons, being well-calibrated is usually regarded as a desirable characteristic of a forecaster. It has been pointed out elsewhere (DeGroot [12]), however, that it is typically easy for any forecaster to make himself well-calibrated by specifying predictions that do not represent his subjective probabilities and in which he does not believe. Furthermore, as Dawid ([7]) has stated, even if the forecaster's true probabilities make him well-calibrated, "this does not necessarily mean that they are 'accurate' in all respects; and even if they are accurate, they may not be of much *substantive* value if the forecaster is a poor meteorologist." Thus, a well-calibrated forecaster is not necessarily a good forecaster, and we shall now consider the problem of comparing well-calibrated forecasters.

III. REFINEMENT

In this section, we shall restrict attention to well-calibrated forecasters. Let μ denote the relative frequency of days on which it rains. In meteorology, μ is sometimes called the *climatological probability*. For any well-calibrated forecaster, it must be true that

$$(3.1) \qquad \sum_{x \in \mathcal{X}} x\nu(x) = \mu.$$

Throughout this paper we shall assume that $0 < \mu < 1$.

In order to emphasize the possible differences that can exist among such forecasters, we shall begin by considering two extreme types. Suppose that $\mu \in \mathcal{X}$. Then the forecaster A_0 whose prediction each day is μ will be well-calibrated, although his predictions are completely useless for any purpose whatsoever. The predictions of A_0 are characterized by the degenerate probability function

$$(3.2) \qquad \begin{aligned} \nu_{A_0}(\mu) &= 1, \\ \nu_{A_0}(x) &= 0 \quad \text{for} \quad x \neq \mu. \end{aligned}$$

When $\mu \in \mathcal{X}$, we shall refer to A_0 as the *least-refined* forecaster.

Next, consider a well-calibrated forecaster A^0 whose predictions are characterized by the following probability function:

$$(3.3) \qquad \begin{aligned} \nu_{A^0}(1) &= \mu, \\ \nu_{A^0}(0) &= 1-\mu, \\ \nu_{A^0}(x) &= 0 \quad \text{for} \quad x \neq 0,1. \end{aligned}$$

It can be seen from (3.3) that the only probabilities of rain that forecaster A^0 ever specifies are 0 and 1, and since A^0 is well-calibrated, his predictions are always correct. We shall refer to A^0 as the *most-refined* forecaster. In meteorology, A_0 is said to exhibit zero *sharpness*, and A^0 to exhibit perfect sharpness (Sanders [22]).

It is clear from A_0 and A^0 that quite different types of behavior are possible among well-calibrated forecasters, ranging from useless to perfect predictions. We shall now describe a concept that yields a partial ordering on the class of all well-calibrated forecasters and justifies our referring to A_0 and A^0 as the least and the most refined members of this class.

A *stochastic transformation* $h(x|y)$ is a function defined on $\mathcal{X}\times\mathcal{X}$ such that

$$\text{(3.4)} \qquad \begin{aligned} &h(x|y) \geq 0 \text{ for } x \in \mathcal{X} \text{ and } y \in \mathcal{X}, \\ &\sum_{x\in\mathcal{X}} h(x|y) = 1 \quad \text{for} \quad y \in \mathcal{X}. \end{aligned}$$

Now consider two arbitrary well-calibrated forecasters whose predictions are characterized by the probability functions $\nu_A(x)$ and $\nu_B(x)$. We say that A is *at least as refined as* B if there exists a stochastic transformation h such that the following relations are satisfied:

$$\text{(3.5)} \qquad \sum_{y\in\mathcal{X}} h(x|y)\nu_A(y) = \nu_B(x) \qquad \text{for } x \in \mathcal{X},$$

$$\text{(3.6)} \qquad \sum_{y\in\mathcal{X}} h(x|y)y\nu_A(y) = x\nu_B(x) \quad \text{for } x \in \mathcal{X}.$$

By subtracting (3.6) from (3.5) we get

$$\text{(3.7)} \qquad \sum_{y\in\mathcal{X}} h(x|y)(1-y)\nu_A(y) = (1-x)\nu_B(x) \qquad \text{for } x \in \mathcal{X},$$

which adds a touch of symmetry when (3.7) is paired with (3.6).

Together, the relations (3.5) and (3.6), or (3.6) and (3.7), state that if we know the predictions of forecaster A, then we can simulate the predictions of forecaster B by using an auxiliary randomization based on the stochastic transformation h as follows: If A makes the prediction y on a particular day, then we simulate a prediction x in accordance with the conditional probability distribution $h(x|y)$. The prediction x will then have exactly the same probabilistic properties as the predictions of forecaster B. The relation (3.5) guarantees that we will obtain each prediction x with the same frequency $\nu_B(x)$ that B does, and the relation (3.6) guarantees that our predictions will still be well-calibrated.

To see that any forecaster A is at least as refined as the least-refined forecaster A_0, let us define the stochastic transformation h, as follows:

$$(3.8)\qquad \begin{aligned} h(\mu|y) &= 1 \quad \text{for } y \in \mathcal{X}, \\ h(x|y) &= 0 \quad \text{for } x \neq \mu . \end{aligned}$$

Then it follows from (3.1) that (3.5) and (3.6) are satisfied when ν_B is replaced by ν_{A_0} as defined by (3.2).

Similarly, to see that the most refined forecaster A^0 is at least as refined as any other forecaster B, let us define the stochastic transformation h as follows:

$$(3.9)\qquad \begin{aligned} h(x|1) &= \frac{1}{\mu}\, x\nu_B(x) \quad \text{for } x \in \mathcal{X}, \\ h(x|0) &= \frac{1}{1-\mu}\,(1-x)\nu_B(x) \quad \text{for } x \in \mathcal{X}. \end{aligned}$$

Since B is well-calibrated, it follows from (3.1) that the function h defined in (3.9) has the properties required of a stochastic transformation. The definition of $h(x|y)$ for $y \neq 0,1$ is irrelevant since forecaster A^0 never makes a prediction other than 0 or 1. The relations (3.5) and (3.6) will now be satisfied when ν_A is replaced by ν_{A^0} as defined by (3.3).

Since the relationship among well-calibrated forecasters defined by the concept of one being at least as refined as another is both reflexive and transitive, this relationship induces a partial ordering among those forecasters. We do not obtain a total ordering, however, as the next examples shows.

Suppose that A and B are well-calibrated forecasters characterized by the following probability functions:

$$\nu_A(x) = \begin{cases} .1 & \text{for} \quad x = 0, \\ .8 & \text{for} \quad x = .5, \\ .1 & \text{for} \quad x = 1, \end{cases} \tag{3.10}$$

and

$$\nu_B(x) = \begin{cases} .5 & \text{for} \quad x = .1, \\ .5 & \text{for} \quad x = .9. \end{cases} \tag{3.11}$$

Here $\mu = .5$.

In this example, A is not at least as refined as B. To see this, suppose on the contrary that there were a stochastic transformation $h(x|y)$ that satisfied (3.5) and (3.6), and let

$$a = h(.1|0), \; b = h(.1|.5), \text{ and } c = h(.1|1). \tag{3.12}$$

Then for $x = .1$, the relations (3.5) and (3.6) become

$$\begin{aligned} (.1)a + (.8)b + (.1)c &= .5, \\ (.4)b + (.1)c &= .05. \end{aligned} \tag{3.13}$$

The two equations in (3.13) imply that $a-c = 4$, which is an impossibility since both $0 \leq a \leq 1$ and $0 \leq c \leq 1$.

On the other hand, neither is B at least as refined as A. To see this, we need only note that on 20 percent of the days, A makes predictions of rain or no rain that are certain to be correct (because A is well-calibrated) whereas B never makes correct predictions with certainty. Thus, in this example neither A nor B is at least as refined as the other.

IV. SUFFICIENCY

In Section 2 we characterized the predictive behavior of any forecaster, regardless of whether or not he was well-calibrated, by the functions $\nu(x)$ and $\rho(x)$. In effect, we represented the joint distribution of the prediction x and the indicator of rain in terms of the marginal distribution of x and the conditional probability $\rho(x)$ of rain given the prediction x. But it is also useful at times to use an alternative factorization of this joint distribution (see, e.g., Lindley, Tversky, and Brown [17] and Lindley [16]).

Let θ denote the indicator of rain, so $\theta = 1$ if rain occurs on a particular day and $\theta = 0$ otherwise, and for any given forecaster let $f(x|\theta)$ denote the conditional probability function of the forecaster's predictions given θ. In other words, for $\theta = 1$, $f(x|\theta)$ represents the frequency function of the forecaster's predictions on days when rain actually occurs. It follows that for $x \in \mathcal{X}$,

(4.1) $$\mu f(x|1) = \rho(x)\nu(x),$$

(4.2) $$(1-\mu)f(x|0) = [1-\rho(x)]\nu(x).$$

It follows from (4.1) that the probability functions $f(x|\theta)$ for $\theta = 0$ and $\theta = 1$ characterize the forecaster's predictive behavior.

Now consider two forecasters A and B characterized by the functions $f_A(x|\theta)$ and $f_B(x|\theta)$. Following the original work of Blackwell ([1], [2]) on the comparison of experiments, we say that forecaster A is *sufficient* for forecaster B if there exists a stochastic transformation $h(x|y)$ such that

(4.3) $$\sum_{y\in\mathcal{X}} h(x|y)f_A(y|\theta) = f_B(x|\theta) \text{ for } x\in\mathcal{X} \text{ and } \theta = 0,1$$

(see, e.g., DeGroot [11], Sec. 14.17). The interpretation of (4.3) is similar to that given in Section 3: forecaster A is sufficient for forecaster B if we can simulate the predictions of

B from the predictions of A by using an auxiliary randomization based on the stochastic transformation h.

As before, the relationship of sufficiency induces a partial ordering among all forecasters. Since we have applied this relationship to all forecasters, however, and not just to those who are well-calibrated, it is not necessarily true that if A is sufficient for B then A is at least as "good" a forecaster as B. For example, suppose that A never makes a prediction other than $x = 0$ or $x = 1$, but that he is always wrong about whether or not it is going to rain. Then A is sufficient for every other forecaster, even though he is the worst possible forecaster. Of course, if we knew that A was always wrong, his predictions would be just as useful to us as those of a forecaster who was always correct.

THEOREM 1. *Consider two forecasters* A *and* B *whose predictive behavior is characterized by the functions* $\nu_A(x)$, $\rho_A(x)$, $\nu_B(x)$, *and* $\rho_B(x)$. *Then forecaster* A *is sufficient for forecaster* B *if and only if there exists a stochastic transformation* h *such that the following relations are satisfied:*

$$(4.4) \qquad \sum_{y \in \mathcal{X}} h(x|y)\nu_A(y) = \nu_B(x) \quad \text{for } x \in \mathcal{X},$$

$$(4.5) \qquad \sum_{y \in \mathcal{X}} h(x|y)\rho_A(y)\nu_A(y) = \rho_B(x)\nu_B(x) \quad \text{for } x \in \mathcal{X}.$$

Proof. Consider any fixed value $x \in \mathcal{X}$. It follows from (4.1) that for $\theta = 1$, the relation (4.3) is the same as (4.5). Furthermore, it follows from (4.2) that for $\theta = 0$, the relation (4.3) is the same as the relation

$$(4.6) \qquad \sum_{y \in \mathcal{X}} h(x|y)[1-\rho_A(y)]\nu_A(y) = [1-\rho_B(x)]\nu_B(x),$$

which, in view of (4.5), is equivalent to (4.4).

Recall now that a forecaster is well-calibrated if $\rho_A(x) = x$ for all $x \in \mathcal{X}^+$. The following result follows immediately in the light of relations (3.5) and (3.6).

THEOREM 2. *Consider two well-calibrated forecasters* A *and* B. *Then forecaster* A *is at least as refined as forecaster* B *if and only if forecaster* A *is sufficient for forecaster* B.

V. CONDITIONS FOR SUFFICIENCY

In this section we shall again consider two well-calibrated forecasters A and B. In order to determine whether or not A is sufficient for B based on the discussion in the previous sections, it is necessary to determine whether or not there exists a stochastic transformation that satisfies either the relations (3.5) and (3.6) or the relations (4.3). Attempts to establish the existence or non-existence of such a stochastic transformation can be frustrating and fruitless. Fortunately, Blackwell and Girshick [3] and Bradt and Karlin [4] have provided some direct methods for determining whether or not A is sufficient for B that eliminate the necessity of having to consider stochastic transformations.

For any forecaster, A, let

(5.1) $$\alpha_A(x) = f_A(x|1) + f_A(x|0) \quad \text{for} \quad x \in \mathcal{X},$$

and for $0 \leq t \leq 1$, let $\mathcal{S}_A(t)$ denote the subset of points in $\mathcal{X}$ such that $f_A(x|1) < t\,\alpha_A(x)$. Furthermore, let

(5.2) $$F_A(t) = \sum_{x \in \mathcal{S}_A(t)} \alpha_A(x) \quad \text{for } 0 \leq t \leq 1$$

and

(5.3) $$C_A(t) = \int_0^t F_A(u)\,du \qquad \text{for} \quad 0 \leq t \leq 1.$$

Then, as demonstrated in Theorem 12.4.1 of Blackwell and Girshick [3], forecaster A is sufficient for forecaster B if and only if $C_A(t) \geq C_B(t)$ for all t in the interval $0 \leq t \leq 1$.

A brief heuristic interpretation of this result is as follows. Suppose that the parameter θ has prior probabilities given by $\Pr(\theta=1) = \Pr(\theta=0) = \frac{1}{2}$. Then $\frac{1}{2}\alpha_A(x)$ is the marginal distribution of x for forecaster A. Furthermore, if we let $\pi_A(x)$ denote the posterior probability $\Pr(\theta=1|x)$ for forecaster A, then $\mathcal{S}_A(t)$ denotes the set of values of x for which $\pi_A(x) < t$. It can now be seen from (5.2) that $\frac{1}{2}F_A(t)$ is the distribution function of the posterior probability $\pi_A(x)$ for forecaster A. For an informative forecaster, the values of $\pi_A(x)$ will tend to be concentrated near 0 and 1, and away from their mean value $E_A[\pi_A(x)] = \frac{1}{2}$. The condition that $C_A(t) \geq C_B(t)$ for all t in the interval $0 \leq t \leq 1$ is equivalent to the condition that $E_A\{\varphi[\pi_A(x)]\} \geq E_B\{\varphi[\pi_B(x)]\}$ for every continuous convex function φ. In this sense, the condition expresses the notion that the probability distribution of $\pi_A(x)$ is more spread out from $\frac{1}{2}$ than the probability distribution of $\pi_B(x)$.

We are now ready to establish the main result of this section. Recall that the set $\mathcal{X}$ comprises the points $x_0 < x_1 < \ldots < x_k$.

THEOREM 3. *Consider two well-calibrated forecasters* A *and* B. *Then forecaster* A *is sufficient for forecaster* B *if and only if the following inequalities are satisfied:*

$$\sum_{i=0}^{j-1} (x_j - x_i)[\nu_A(x_i) - \nu_B(x_i)] \geq 0 \text{ for } j = 1,\ldots,k-1. \tag{5.4}$$

Proof. Since both A and B are well-calibrated, it follows from (4.1) and (4.2) that

$$\frac{f_A(x|1)}{\alpha_A(x)} = \frac{f_B(x|1)}{\alpha_B(x)} = \frac{(x/\mu)}{(x/\mu)+[(1-x)/(1-\mu)]} \tag{5.5}$$

whenever $\alpha_A(x)$ and $\alpha_B(x)$ are non-zero. Even if either $\alpha_A(x)$ or $\alpha_B(x)$ is zero for some $x \varepsilon \mathcal{X}$, without loss of generality we still may define (5.5) to be satisfied. Next, for $0 \leq t \leq 1$ and $x \varepsilon \mathcal{X}$, define

$$(5.6) \qquad s(t,x) = t\left(\frac{1-x}{1-\mu}\right) - (1-t)\,\frac{x}{\mu}.$$

Then both the sets $\mathcal{S}_A(t)$ and $\mathcal{S}_B(t)$ contain precisely those points $x \varepsilon \mathcal{X}$ for which $s(t,x) > 0$. Since the sets $\mathcal{S}_A(t)$ and $\mathcal{S}_B(t)$ are identical, we shall denote this common set simply by $\mathcal{S}(t)$.

From (5.2) and (5.3) we can write

$$C_A(t) = \int_0^t \Big[\sum_{x \varepsilon \mathcal{S}(u)} \alpha_A(x) \Big] du.$$

For each $x \varepsilon \mathcal{X}$, $\alpha_A(x)$ contributes to the integral over a certain set of u-values of length $t - f(x|1)/\alpha_A(x)$. Thus we can re-express $C_A(t)$ as

$$(5.7) \qquad C_A(t) = \sum_{x \varepsilon \mathcal{S}(t)} [t\alpha_A(x) - f_A(x|1)].$$

Next, using (4.1) and (4.2) and the fact that A is well-calibrated, we can rewrite (5.7) as follows:

$$(5.8) \qquad C_A(t) = \sum_{x \varepsilon \mathcal{S}(t)} s(t,x)\nu_A(x).$$

Furthermore, if we rewrite $s(t,x)$, as given by (5.6), in the form

$$(5.9) \qquad s(t,x) = \frac{1}{\mu(1-\mu)} \{t\mu - [t\mu + (1-t)(1-\mu)]x\},$$

then it can be seen that $\mathcal{S}(t)$ contains precisely those points $x \varepsilon \mathcal{X}$ for which the quantity inside braces in (5.9) is positive. Thus, $C_A(t)$ can be expressed as follows:

$$(5.10) \qquad C_A(t) = \frac{1}{\mu(1-\mu)} \sum_{x \varepsilon \mathcal{X}} \{t\mu - [t\mu + (1-t)(1-\mu)]x\}^+ \nu_A(x),$$

where, as usual, the notation $(m)^+$ denotes the positive part of the quantity m.

For forecaster B, the function $C_B(t)$ is also given by (5.10) with $\nu_A(x)$ replaced by $\nu_B(x)$. Let

$$L_A(t) = \mu(1-\mu)C_A(t) \tag{5.11}$$

and let $L_B(t)$ be defined similarly. Then it follows from Theorem 12.4.1 of Blackwell and Girshick [3], as cited earlier, that forecaster A is sufficient for forecaster B if and only if $L_A(t) \geq L_B(t)$ for all t in the interval $0 \leq t \leq 1$.

Corresponding to the points $0 \leq x_0 < x_1 <\ldots< x_k \leq 1$ in $\mathcal{X}$, let the points $0 \leq t_0 < t_1 <\ldots< t_k \leq 1$ be defined by the relations

$$t_j\mu-[t_j\mu+(1-t_j)(1-\mu)]x_j = 0 \text{ for } j = 0,1,\ldots,k. \tag{5.12}$$

Then both $L_A(t)$ and $L_B(t)$ are continuous, piecewise linear functions over the interval $0 \leq t \leq 1$ with $L_A(0) = L_B(0) = 0$ and $L_A(1) = L_B(1) = 1$, and with vertices at the points $t_0, t_1,\ldots,t_k$. Furthermore, $L_A(t_0) = L_B(t_0) = 0$ and, for $j = 1,\ldots,k$,

$$\frac{L_A(t_j)}{t_j\mu+(1-t_j)(1-\mu)} = \sum_{i=0}^{j-1} (x_j-x_i)\nu_A(x_i), \tag{5.13}$$

with an analogous expression for forecaster B.

Finally, we note that when $j = k$, the right-hand side of (5.13) can be reduced as follows by using (3.1):

$$\begin{aligned}\sum_{i=0}^{k-1} (x_k-x_i)\nu_A(x_i) &= x_k[1-\nu_A(x_k)] - [\mu-x_k\nu_A(x_k)] \\ &= x_k - \mu.\end{aligned} \tag{5.14}$$

Thus, $L_A(t_k) = L_B(t_k)$. We have now established that forecaster A is sufficient for forecaster B if and only if $L_A(t_j) \geq L_B(t_j)$

for j = 1,...,k-1. It follows from (5.13) that these k-1 inequalities are equivalent to the k-1 inequalities (5.4).

We make use of this theorem in the next section.

VI. THE LEAST-REFINED, WELL-CALIBRATED FORECASTER

In Section 3, we required that $\mu \varepsilon \mathcal{X}$ in order to ensure that the least-refined forecaster who is well-calibrated will always announce μ as his forecast. Suppose now that $\mu \notin \mathcal{X}$, and let x_L and x_U be the pair of adjacent values in $\mathcal{X}$ just bracketing μ, i.e., $x_L < \mu < x_U$. Then let A_0' be a well-calibrated forecaster characterized by the probability function:

$$\nu_{A_0'}(x_U) = (\mu - x_L)/(x_U - x_L),$$

(6.1) $$\nu_{A_0'}(x_L) = (x_U - \mu)/(x_U - x_L),$$

$$\nu_{A_0'}(x) \quad = 0 \text{ for } x \neq x_U \text{ or } x_L.$$

It can be seen from (6.1) that A_0' concentrates his forecasts as closely as possible to μ given the permissible forecast values. Thus, there is an intuitive sense in which A_0' is not as refined as another forecaster who spreads out his probabilities over at least some of the other values of x. We make this notion precise in the following theorem.

THEOREM 4. *The well-calibrated forecaster* A_0', *whose probability function* $\nu_{A_0'}(x)$ *is given by* (6.1), *is least refined among all other well-calibrated forecasters.*

Proof. Consider any other well-calibrated forecaster A. Then, from Theorem 2, A is at least as refined as A_0' if and only if A is sufficient for A_0', and, from Theorem 3, this is true if and only if

$$(6.2) \qquad \sum_{i=0}^{j-1} (x_j - x_i)[\nu_A(x_i) - \nu_{A_0'}(x_i)] \geq 0 \quad \text{for} \quad j = 1,2,\ldots,k-1.$$

To verify (6.2), we note that for $j = 1,\ldots,L$,

$$(6.3) \qquad \sum_{i=0}^{j-1} (x_j - x_i)[\nu_A(x_i) - \nu_{A_0'}(x_i)] = \sum_{i=0}^{j-1} (x_j - x_i)\nu_A(x_i),$$

which clearly is nonnegative since $x_j > x_i$ and $\nu_A(x)$ is a probability function. For $j = U$, recalling that $U = L+1$, we have

$$\begin{aligned} &\sum_{i=0}^{L} (x_U - x_i)[\nu_A(x_i) - \nu_{A_0'}(x_i)] \\ (6.4) \qquad &= \sum_{i=0}^{L} (x_U - x_i)\nu_A(x_i) - (x_U - x_L)\nu_{A_0'}(x_L) \\ &= \sum_{i=0}^{L} (x_U - x_i)\nu_A(x_i) - (x_U - \mu), \end{aligned}$$

where the final expression follows from (6.1). Since A is well-calibrated, we can now use (3.1) to rewrite the expression following the final equality sign in (6.4) as follows:

$$\begin{aligned} &\sum_{i=0}^{L} (x_U - x_i)\nu_A(x_i) - \sum_{i=0}^{k} (x_U - x_i)\nu_A(x_i) \\ (6.5) \qquad &= \sum_{i=U}^{k} (x_i - x_U)\nu_A(x_i) \geq 0. \end{aligned}$$

Similarly, for $j = U+1,\ldots,k$, the left-hand side of expression (6.2) equals

$$\sum_{i=j}^{k} (x_i - x_j)\nu_A(x_i) \geq 0.$$

The use of Theorem 3 is critical to the preceding proof, for otherwise we would need to construct the actual stochastic transformation $h(x|y)$ going from ν_A to $\nu_{A_0'}$, simultaneously ensuring that the calibration condition holds. We have found this to be a nontrivial task.

VII. SCORING RULES FOR ASSESSMENT

In the television station example introduced in Section 1, we get to see a finite set of forecasts and the associated indicators of whether or not rain occurred, i.e., $\{(p_j, y_j): j = 1,2,\ldots,n\}$. Several authors have suggested scoring rules to be used to assess probability assessors in such situations. Here we relate some of these to the probabilistic concepts of calibration and refinement.

One of the earliest scoring rule proposals suggested in the context of meteorological forecasts is the "Brier Score",

$$(7.1) \qquad BS_n = \frac{1}{n} \sum_{j=1}^{n} (p_j - y_j)^2,$$

which the forecaster is to attempt to minimize (Brier [5]). In the case of binary outcomes (rain, no rain), Winkler [26] notes that the Brier Score is equivalent to the general quadratic scoring rule proposed by de Finetti [10], designed to oblige the forecaster "to express his true feelings" (de Finetti [9]).

Other general classes of "strictly proper" scoring rules include Good's [13] logarithmic scoring rule and the spherical scoring rule (see Staël von Holstein [24] and Savage [23]).

If we let n_i equal the number of days out of n on which the forecaster predicts rain with probability x_i, and r_i the number of these n_i days on which it actually does rain, we can rewrite the Brier Score of (7.1) as

$$(7.2) \qquad BS_n = \frac{1}{n} \sum_{i=0}^{k} n_i \left(x_i - \frac{r_i}{n_i}\right)^2 + \frac{1}{n} \sum_{i=0}^{k} n_i \frac{r_i}{n_i} \left(1 - \frac{r_i}{n_i}\right),$$

or as

$$(7.3) \qquad BS_n = \frac{1}{n}\sum_{i=0}^{k} n_i\left(x_i - \frac{r_i}{n_i}\right)^2 + \frac{r}{n}\left(1-\frac{r}{n}\right) - \frac{1}{n}\sum_{i=0}^{k} n_i\left(\frac{r_i}{n_i} - \frac{r}{n}\right)^2,$$

where $\sum_{i=0}^{k} r_i = r$. Tukey, Mosteller, and Fienberg [25] suggest a variant of (7.2) which essentially allows the two components on the right-hand side to be given different weights.

To understand how the components of the Brier Score relate to the concepts discussed here we let $n \to \infty$ in such a manner that $r_i/n_i \to \rho(x_i)$ and $n_i/n \to \nu(x_i)$. Then

$$(7.4) \qquad \lim_{n\to\infty} \frac{r_i}{n} = \rho(x_i)\nu(x_i)$$

and

$$(7.5) \qquad \lim_{n\to\infty} \frac{r_i^2}{n_i n} = \rho^2(x_i)\nu(x_i).$$

Any sampling scheme of trials with these limiting properties suffices for our purposes. Thus, from (7.2) we have

$$BS = \lim_{n\to\infty} BS_n$$

$$(7.6) \qquad = \sum_{i=0}^{k} \nu(x_i)[x_i-\rho(x_i)]^2 + \sum_{i=0}^{k} \nu(x_i)\rho(x_i)[1-\rho(x_i)].$$

The first term on the right-hand side of (7.6) is the weighted mean square difference between the forecasted probability x_i and the frequency of rain $\rho(x_i)$. As such it is a measure of calibration. If the forecaster is well-calibrated, this term equals zero.

The second term on the right-hand side of (7.6) measures the dispersion of the results of the forecaster's predictions. As such it rewards the forecaster for spreading his predictions as much as possible, and thus is a measure of the forecaster's refinement. The following theorem shows that there is a direct relationship between this term and the concepts of refinement and sufficiency presented in Sections 3 and 4.

THEOREM 5. *If forecaster* A *is sufficient for forecaster* B, *then*

$$\sum_{x\in\mathcal{X}} \nu_A(x)\rho_A(x)[1-\rho_A(x)] \leq \sum_{x\in\mathcal{X}} \nu_B(x)\rho_B(x)[1-\rho_B(x)]. \tag{7.7}$$

Proof. Since A is sufficient for B, from (4.5) we have

$$\begin{aligned} \sum_x \rho_B(x)\nu_B(x) &= \sum_x \sum_y h(x|y)\rho_A(y)\nu_A(y) \\ &= \sum_y [\sum_x h(x|y)]\rho_A(y)\nu_A(y) \\ &= \sum_y \rho_A(y)\nu_A(y). \end{aligned} \tag{7.8}$$

Next, by applying both (4.4) and (4.5) we have

$$\begin{aligned} \nu_B(x)\rho_B^2(x) &= \frac{[\sum_y h(x|y)\rho_A(y)\nu_A(y)]^2}{\sum_h h(x|y)\nu_A(y)} \\ &= [\sum_y h(x|y)\nu_A(y)][\sum_y \frac{h(x|y)\nu_A(y)}{\sum_{y'} h(x|y')\nu_A(y')}\rho_A(y)]^2 \\ &\leq [\sum_y h(x|y)\nu_A(y)][\sum_y \frac{h(x|y)\nu_A(y)}{\sum_{y'} h(x|y')\nu_A(y')}\rho_A^2(y)] \\ &= \sum_y h(x|y)\nu_A(y)\rho_A^2(y), \end{aligned} \tag{7.9}$$

where the inequality is a special case of Jensen's inequality. Summing (7.9) over x now yields

$$\sum_x \nu_B(x)\rho_B^2(x) \le \sum_x \sum_y h(x|y)\nu_A(y)\rho_A^2(y)$$

$$(7.10) \qquad = \sum_y [\sum_x h(x|y)]\nu_A(y)\rho_A^2(y)$$

$$= \sum_y \nu_A(y)\rho_A^2(y).$$

Finally, combining (7.8) and (7.10) yields the inequality (7.7).

We recall from Section 5 that forecaster A is sufficient for forecaster B if and only if $C_A(t) \geq C_B(t)$, where $C_A(t)$ is defined by (5.3), and that this condition is equivalent to

$$(7.11) \qquad E_A\{\varphi[\pi_A(x)]\} \geq E_B\{\varphi[\pi_B(x)]\}$$

for every continuous convex function φ. Theorem 5 is, in effect, a special case of this equivalence. From (7.11) we can construct a class of generalized limiting scoring rules that replace the second term of (7.6) by

$$(7.12) \qquad \sum_{x\in\mathcal{X}} \nu(x)\varphi[\rho(x)].$$

The actual assessment of probability assessors based on a finite set of forecasts requires a careful description of the stochastic mechanisms associated with the production of predictions for the forecasters being compared. We shall present such a description in a separate paper.

VIII. MULTIVARIATE FORECASTS

In the preceding sections we have considered events with $s = 2$ possible outcomes (e.g., rain, no rain). Yet climatological forecasting often involves $s > 2$ outcomes (e.g., rain, snow, and neither rain nor snow, or a set of temperature ranges). In such situations the probability assessor specifies a vector of probabilities $\underset{\sim}{x}$, restricted to a finite set of values lying in the (s-1)-dimensional simplex. If the conditional probabilities of the s outcomes given the prediction $\underset{\sim}{x}$ is represented in vector form by $\underset{\sim}{\rho}(\underset{\sim}{x})$, then the multivariate forecaster is well-calibrated if $\underset{\sim}{\rho}(\underset{\sim}{x}) = \underset{\sim}{x}$ for all $\underset{\sim}{x} \in \mathcal{X}$. Note that this well-calibrated multivariate forecaster is also well-calibrated, in the sense of Section 2, for each binary problem formed by combining the s outcomes into two groups; however, a forecaster who is "marginally" well-calibrated for predicting "rain" or "no rain" may no longer be well-calibrated when "no rain" is divided into two or more possible outcomes.

More formally, let $\underset{\sim}{x} = (x_1,\ldots,x_s)$ and $\underset{\sim}{\rho}(\underset{\sim}{x}) = [\rho_1(\underset{\sim}{x}),\ldots,\rho_s(\underset{\sim}{x})]$. Furthermore, let $\mathcal{I} = \{I_1,\ldots,I_k\}$ represent a partition of the set $\{1,\ldots,s\}$ into k nonempty, mutually exclusive, and exhaustive sets $I_1,\ldots,I_k$. Then a forecaster is said to be *marginally well-calibrated with respect to the partition* $\mathcal{I}$ if

$$\sum_{i \in I_j} \rho_i(\underset{\sim}{x}) = \sum_{i \in I_j} x_i \quad \text{for } j = 1,\ldots,k \text{ and } \underset{\sim}{x} \in \mathcal{X}. \tag{8.1}$$

Similarly, we can develop the notion of conditionally well-calibrated forecasters. Consider again the problem treated in Sections 2-7, in which $s = 2$ and the forecaster simply specifies his probability x of rain. The forecaster may be well-calibrated for some, but not all, values of x. In other words, it may be true that $\rho(x) = x$ when x belongs to some subset $\mathcal{X}_0$ of $\mathcal{X}$, but not for all values of $x \in \mathcal{X}$. In this case, we may say that the forecaster is conditionally well-calibrated, given that $x \in \mathcal{X}_0$.

Now consider the general multivariate forecasting problem introduced in this section. Let the partition $\mathcal{I}$ be as defined here, and let $\mathcal{X}_0$ denote a proper subset of $\mathcal{X}$. Then a forecaster is said to be *conditionally well-calibrated with respect to the partition* $\mathcal{I}$, given that $\underset{\sim}{x} \in \mathcal{X}_0$, if the relation (8.1) is satisfied for $j = 1,\ldots,k$ and all $\underset{\sim}{x} \in \mathcal{X}_0$.

For well-calibrated multivariate forecasters, we can define the concept of refinement by means of a multivariate stochastic transformation. Moreover, this notion of refinement can again be directly linked to sufficiency in the comparison of experiments with a finite number of outcomes. Finally, the concept of one forecaster being marginally or conditionally more refined than another can be developed.

Critical to the multivariate versions of calibration and refinement as proposed in this section is the orientation of the vector of forecasted probabilities $\underset{\sim}{x}$. Each component of $\underset{\sim}{x}$ refers to a specific outcome. This methodology should be contrasted with the multivariate approach, described for example by Lichtenstein, Fischhoff, and Phillips [15], in which the forecaster "selects the single most likely alternative and states the probability that it is correct." Kadane and Lichtenstein [14] show that such a loss of orientation leads to the inability to recalibrate a forecater's assessments. From the discussion here, it should be clear that a careful description of calibration and refinement in both the binary and multivariate settings requires a well-specified set of outcomes, and probability assessments specifically tied to those outcomes.

REFERENCES

[1] Blackwell, D. (1951). Comparison of experiments. *Proc. Second Berkeley Symp. Math. Statist. Probability*. University of California Press, Berkeley.

[2] Blackwell, D. (1953). Equivalent comparison of experiments. *Ann. Math. Statist.* 24, 265-272.

[3] Blackwell, D. and Girshick, M. A. (1954). *Theory of Games and Statistical Decisions*. John Wiley, New York.

[4] Bradt, R. N. and Karlin, S. (1956). On the design and comparison of certain dichotomous experiments. *Ann. Math. Statist.* 27, 390-409.

[5] Brier, G. W. (1950). Verification of forecasts expressed in terms of probability. *Monthly Weather Review* 78, 1-3.

[6] Dawid, A. P. (1980). Discussion of papers on "Improving judgements using feedback." *Bayesian Statistics, Proc. of the First Int. Meeting*. (J. M. Bernardo, et al., eds.) University Press, Valencia, Spain, 418-419.

[7] Dawid, A. P. (1981). The well-calibrated Bayesian. *J. Amer. Statist. Assoc.* To Appear.

[8] de Finetti, B. (1937). Foresight: Its logical laws, its subjective sources. *Studies in Subjective Probability* (1964). (H. E. Kyburg and H. E. Smokler, eds.) John Wiley, New York.

[9] de Finetti, B. (1962). Does it make sense to speak of 'Good Probability Appraisers'? *The Scientist Speculates--An Anthology of Partly-Baked Ideas*. (I. J. Good, gen. ed.) Basic Books, New York.

[10] de Finetti, B. (1965). Methods for discriminating levels of partial knowledge concerning a test item. *British J. Math. Statist. Psych.* *18*, 87-123.

[11] DeGroot, M. H. (1970). *Optimal Statistical Decisions*. McGraw-Hill, New York.

[12] DeGroot, M. H. (1979). Comments on Lindley, et al. *J. Roy. Statist. Soc.* (A) *142*, 172-173.

[13] Good, I. J. (1952). Rational decisions. *J. Roy. Statist. Soc.* (B) *14*, 107-114.

[14] Kadane, J. B., and Lichtenstein, S. (1981). Calibration in perspective. Unpublished manuscript.

[15] Lichtenstein, S., Fischhoff, B. and Phillips, L. D. (1977). Calibration of probabilities: the state of the art. *Decision Making and Change in Human Affairs*. (H. Jungermann and G. de Zeeuw, eds.) D. Reidel Publishing Comapny, Dordrecht, Holland, 275-324.

[16] Lindley, D. V. (1981). The improvement of probability judgements. Unpublished manuscript.

[17] Lindley, D. V., Tversky, A., and Brown, R. V. (1979). On the reconciliation of probability assessments. *J. Roy. Statist. Soc.* (A) *142*, 146-180.

[18] Miller, R. G. (1962). Statistical prediction by discriminant analysis. *Meteorological Monographs* *4*, No. 25.

[19] Murphy, A. H. (1973). A new vector partition of the probability score. *J. Applied Meteorology 12*, 595-600.

[20] Murphy, A. H. and Winkler, R. L. (1977). Reliability of subjective probability forecasts of precipitation and temperature. *Appl. Statist. 26*, 41-47.

[21] Pratt, J. W. (1962). Must subjective probabilities be realized as relative frequencies? Unpublished seminar paper. Harvard University Grad. School of Bus. Administration.

[22] Sanders, F. (1963). On subjective probability forecasting. *J. Applied Meteorology 2*, 191-201.

[23] Savage, L. J. (1971). Elicitation of personal probabilities and expectations. *J. Amer. Statist. Assoc. 66*, 783-801.

[24] Staël von Holstein, C.-A. S. (1970). *Assessment and Evaluation of Subjective Probability Distributions.* Economic Research Institute, Stockholm School of Economics, Stockholm.

[25] Tukey, J. W., Mosteller, F. and Fienberg, S. E. (1965). Scoring probability forecasts. Memorandum NS-37, Dept. of Statistics, Harvard University.

[26] Winkler, R. L. (1967). The quantification of judgment: some methodological suggestions. *J. Amer. Statist. Assoc. 62*, 1105-1120.

BAYES RULES FOR LOCATION PROBLEMS

Persi Diaconis[1]

Department of Statistics
Stanford University
Stanford, California, U.S.A.

David Freedman[2]
Department of Statistics
University of California
Berkeley, California, U.S.A.

I. INTRODUCTION

The problem treated here is estimation of a location parameter when the error distribution is not completely known. Previous work from a Bayesian point of view is reviewed in Section 2. Some new nonparametric results are described. For example: let $X_i = \theta + \varepsilon_i$, $1 \leq i \leq n$ be observed. Put prior distributions on θ and $\varepsilon : \theta \sim \mu(d\theta)$ and $\varepsilon \sim D_\alpha$, where D_α is the Dirichlet prior with parameter α. The posterior distribution is computed. The Bayes estimate of θ under squared error loss is

$$(1.1) \qquad \hat{\theta} = \frac{\int \theta \ \Pi^* \alpha'(X_i - \theta)\mu(d\theta)}{\int \Pi^* \ \alpha'(X_i - \theta)\mu(d\theta)},$$

the product being over distinct X_i only. Some frequentist properties of $\hat{\theta}$ are derived in Section 3. Roughly, if the parameter measure α is long-tailed like a Cauchy distribution, then $\hat{\theta}$ is inconsistent, in the sense that there are random variables X_i, symmetric about 0, such that $\hat{\theta}$ oscillates indefinitely between two wrong answers as n tends to infinity. It is also shown that $\hat{\theta}$ is robust, in the sense of having a bounded influence curve, for α

[1]Research partially supported by NSF Grant MCS-80-24649.

[2]Research partially supported by NSF Grant MCS-80-02535.

ISBN 0-12-307501-7

having tails exponential or longer. In Section 4 some extensions such as symmetrized Dirichlet priors are considered. The overall conclusions do not change: The estimate $\hat{\theta}$ given in (1.1) with α' log convex, having exponential tails, is the only Bayes estimate which is both robust and consistent.

II. BAYESIAN ESTIMATION OF A LOCATION PARAMETER

In the basic measurement error model, variables $X_i = \theta + \varepsilon_i$ are observed. In the simplest case, the distribution of the ε_i is assumed independent and identically distributed from the known density f. If a prior measure $\mu(d\theta)$ is put on θ, then the posterior distribution of θ is proportional to the likelihood $\Pi f(X_i-\theta)$. The mean of the posterior is often chosen as an estimator. This gives

$$(2.1) \qquad \hat{\theta} = \frac{\int \theta \, \Pi f(X_i-\theta)\mu(d\theta)}{\int \Pi f(X_i-\theta)\mu(d\theta)}.$$

The assumption that the distribution of the ε_i is known may not be realistic. Consider a finite collection of error densities f_j and put prior weight w_j on the jth model; the posterior distribution of θ is readily calculated. It leads to a posterior mean of the following form:

$$(2.2) \qquad \hat{\theta} = \sum_{j=1}^{k} w_j^* \hat{\theta}_i.$$

In (2.2), $\hat{\theta}_j$ is the Bayes rule given in (2.1), assuming that model j is correct. The weights w_j^* are proportional to w_j times the integrated likelihood factor $\int \Pi f_j(X_i-\theta)\mu(d\theta)$. The estimator in (2.2) does a natural thing: it weights the Bayes estimate assuming that the jth model is correct by the prior probability of the jth model times a likelihood ratio type goodness of fit statistic for correctness of the jth model.

It is easy to extend the analysis to infinite collections of models. For example, Box and Tiao [4] consider error densities proportional to $\exp\{|(x-\theta)/\sigma|^a\}$. They put priors on θ, σ, and a. Fraser [11] considers the family of t-distributions and puts flat priors on θ, a scale parameter, and the number of degrees of freedom. Dempster [5] considers some other families and gives an extensive review of the literature. Hogg [15], in reviewing the adaptive approach to robustness, notes that it is quite close in spirit to the Bayesian approaches considered above: one does some form of goodness of fit test to weight possible models after having seen the data.

The parametrized families described above are admittedly ad hoc. Another approach is to attempt to work with priors over all possible error distributions. We state the results of a simple set of assumptions; θ and ε are assumed independent. A prior $\mu(d\theta)$ is put on θ and a Dirichlet prior with parameter α is put on the space of all probability distributions on the real line. We will not review the properties of Dirichlet priors here. An excellent review is in Ferguson [10].

THEOREM 1. *Let α be a finite, absolutely continuous measure with density α'. Let μ be a probability measure on the real line. Put a prior on the product of the real line and all probability measures on the real line by taking the product measure $\mu\times D_\alpha$. The posterior distribution given a sample of size n is of the form:*

$$\nu\, D_\beta. \tag{2.3}$$

In (2.3), ν is absolutely continuous with respect to μ, and has density

$$c(\underset{\sim}{X})\ \Pi^*\ \alpha'(X_i-\theta) \tag{2.4}$$

with

(2.5) $$c(\underset{\sim}{X})^{-1} = \int \Pi^* \alpha'(X_i - \theta)\mu(d\theta).$$

and $\beta = \alpha + \Sigma\, \delta_{X_i - \theta}$. *The* * *on the products in* (2.4) *and* (2.5) *signifies that these products are over distinct values of* X_i *only. For fixed* θ, D_β *is a probability on the set of probabilities. A measure is put on the product space by integration with respect to* ν.

COROLLARY 1. *The posterior mean of* θ *is*

$$c(\underset{\sim}{X}) \int \theta\, \Pi^* \alpha'(X_i - \theta)\mu(d\theta)$$

with c *given by* (2.5).

Remarks. A detailed proof of Theorem 1 and the theorems involving symmetrized Dirichlet priors in Section 4 will appear elsewhere. The arguments use the following technique: the space $\mathbb{R}$ is discretized, the computation carried out for a Dirichlet prior on the integers, and then a limit is taken. The Bayes rule in Corollary 1 is somewhat surprising in appearance. Aside from the * on the product, it is the same as in the rule (2.1) assuming that the density f equals the prior mean α'. For continuous data, the * plays no role, and it appears as if the posterior distribution on the error space is not contributing. One way of understanding this is to relate it to the following phenomena discovered by Korwar and Hollander [16]. If a Dirichlet prior is put on the set of probabilities on the line, then the distribution of the distinct observations, conditioned on being distinct, is iid from the measure α normalized to be a probability.

We close this section with some remarks about identifiability and symmetry. In the problem discussed here, the parameter space is the product of the real line and all probabilities. Since the pair $(\theta, F(x))$, $(\theta+\theta_0, F(x+\theta_0))$ give rise to the same sampling distribution, the parameter point $(\theta, F(x))$ is not identifiable without further assumptions. Under the assumptions of Theorem 1, in the Bayesian framework, the parameter point *is* identifiable because the measures $D_{\alpha+\delta_\theta}$ are all mutually singular as θ varies.

One approach around the identifiability question is to use symmetry, restricting attention to symmetric error distributions. We next describe an appropriate version of de Finetti's theorem for symmetric location problems. In the subjectivist treatment of inference problems, parameters are often introduced through de Finetti's theorem. In the nonparametric framework, this says that an exchangeable real valued sequence of random variables is a mixture of iid variables and so describable by specifying a prior distribution over the parameter space of all probabilities on the real line. We wondered what in addition to exchangeability was needed to force the prior to be a mixture of symmetric location families. This problem is solved in Freedman and Diaconis [14]. We state the main result here. A sequence of random variables $\{X_i\}_{i=1}^{\infty}$ is called *location symmetric* if for every m, the distribution of $X_1 - \frac{1}{m}(X_2 + \ldots + X_{m+1})$ is symmetric about zero. The sequence is *conditionally location symmetric* if for every n, given $X_1, \ldots, X_n$, the process: $X_{n+1}, X_{n+2}, \ldots,$ is location symmetric. Informally, an exchangeable sequence is location symmetric if it is symmetric about the mean as a location estimate. It is conditionally location symmetric if the future is location symmetric, no matter what the past. The following theorem appears in Freedman and Diaconis [14].

THEOREM. *Let* $X = (X_1, X_2, \ldots)$ *be a sequence of random variables. Then* X *is exchangeable and conditionally location symmetric if and only if there is a probability* ν *on the product of the real line and the set* $\mathbb{S}$ *of symmetric probabilities on the real line such that for all* n, *and* $x_1, \ldots, x_n$,

$$P\{X_1 \leq x_1, \ldots, X_n \leq x_n\} = \int_{\mathbb{R}} \int_{\mathbb{S}} \prod_{i=1}^{n} F(x_i - \theta)\nu(d\theta, dF).$$

It would be of interest to characterize situations in which the prior measure ν splits into a product measure. It would be of interest to characterize location mixtures of Dirichlet priors, as used in Theorem 1.

III. CONSISTENCY AND ROBUSTNESS OF $\hat{\theta}$

Some frequentist properties of the Bayes estimate $\hat{\theta}$ are given.

Consistency. Let $\{P_\theta\}_{\theta\in\Theta}$ be a family of probabilities on a measurable space. Let P_θ^∞ denote the infinite product measure. Let μ be a prior probability measure on Θ, and let μ_n be the posterior distribution on Θ given $X_1,\ldots,X_n$. The pair (θ,μ) is *consistent* if for P_θ^∞ almost all sequences $X_1,X_2,\ldots$, the posterior μ_n converges to a point mass at θ in distribution. Consistency has been investigated by Freedman [12], LeCam [18], Schwartz [19] and others. The main results show that, under strong regularity assumptions on the family P_θ, (θ,μ) is consistent if and only if θ is in the support of μ. Often the assumptions include a Euclidean Θ, ruling out nonparametric Bayesian procedures. Indeed, Freedman [12] presented the following counterexample. Let Θ be the set of all probabilities on the integers $\{0, 1, 2,\ldots,\}$. Let G_p denote the geometric distribution with parameter p. There is a prior μ on Θ which puts positive probability on every neighborhood of $G_{\frac{1}{4}}$ such that for $G_{\frac{1}{4}}$ almost all sequences $X_1,X_2,\ldots$, the posterior of μ given $X_1,\ldots,X_n$ converges to a point mass at $G_{\frac{1}{2}}$. Freedman [13] shows that this type of inconsistency is generic: for almost all θ and μ (in the topological sense) the pair (θ,μ) is inconsistent.

To insure consistency, Freedman [12] introduced the class of Dirichlet and tail free priors on the space of all probabilities. He proved that if μ is such a prior, then (θ,μ) is consistent for every θ. This work was extended by Fabius [8] and Ferguson [9]. Ferguson [10] contains an extensive bibliography.

In view of the fact that the Dirichlet prior was introduced to get consistency, it is somewhat surprising that the Bayes estimate $\hat{\theta}$ of Corollary 1, is not consistent:

THEOREM 2. *Let $\hat{\theta}$ as in Corollary 1, be based on the prior $\mu \times D_\alpha$ with α standard Cauchy. There is a sequence of random variables X_i having common infinitely differentiable density symmetric about zero, supported by the interval $[-2,2]$, with the following asymptotics for $\hat{\theta}$.*

(3.1) *For almost all sample sequences, there are subsequences n_j^+ and n_j^- and a positive γ such that $\hat{\theta}_{n_j^+} \to \gamma$ and $\hat{\theta}_{n_j^-} \to -\gamma$. Thus the Bayes estimate $\hat{\theta}_n$ oscillates indefinitely between $-\gamma$ and γ and fails of almost sure consistency.*

(3.2) *For any $\varepsilon > 0$ and each large n, with probability arbitrarily close to 1, either $|\hat{\theta}_n - \gamma| < \varepsilon$ or $|\hat{\theta}_n + \gamma| < \varepsilon$. In the limit these two events each have probability $\frac{1}{2}$. Thus $\hat{\theta}_n$ is not even consistent in probability.*

Remarks. 1. We have proved similar results for the M-estimate based on the Cauchy density in Diaconis and Freedman [6]. The following heuristic computation may help explain the connection. The product $\Pi\, \alpha'(x_i - \theta)$ equals $\exp\{\Sigma\, M(x_i - \theta)\}$, with $M = \log \alpha'$. The maximum of the product is at the associated M-estimate: the θ which maximizes $\Sigma\, M(x_i - \theta)$. Because of the arguments for Laplace's method $\int \theta\, \Pi\, \alpha'(x_i - \theta)\mu(d\theta) / \int \Pi\, \alpha'(y_i - \theta)\mu(d\theta)$ is close to this maximizing value. This value was shown to oscillate in the M-estimate paper cited above.

2. The counterexample constructed in Theorem 2 is bimodal. The positive results in Section 4 of Diaconis and Freedman [6] suggest the following: if the X_i have a symmetric strongly unimodal density, then $\hat{\theta}$ is consistent for any α. Further, if the density α' is log convex, then $\hat{\theta}$ is consistent for any symmetric

X_i. Apparently, if α' is not log convex, a sequence X_i can be constructed so that $\hat{\theta}_n$ behaves as in Theorem 2.

3. The support of the prior $\mu \times D_\alpha$ is all of the parameter space. Thus Theorem 1 provides a natural example of an inconsistent Bayes rule. Note that by a result of Doob (see Schwartz [19]) $\hat{\theta}$ *is* consistent if the process generating $X_i = \theta + \varepsilon_i$ is as follows: pick θ from μ; pick F from D_α and then ε_i iid from F.

4. Theorem 2 is related to results of Berk [1], [2], [3] who discusses the asymptotic behavior of Bayes rules when the model is wrong. Berk applies this to almost surely finite sequential tests in problems with nuisance parameters.

Robustness. The motivation for studying the Bayes estimates described in Section 2 is the basic problem of robustness. One measure of the robustness of an estimate $\hat{\theta}$ is the influence curve

$$IC(x,\hat{\theta},F) = \lim_{\varepsilon \to 0} \frac{1}{\varepsilon} \{\hat{\theta}\{(1-\varepsilon)F + \varepsilon\delta_x\} - \hat{\theta}\{F\}\}.$$

This measures the effect of a point mass at x. If the influence curve is bounded for all x, then changing the value of one sample point arbitrarily will only change $\hat{\theta}$ by a bounded amount. An extensive review of these ideas is in Huber [17]. A heuristic computation, based on ideas in Huber [17], suggests that the influence curve of the M-estimate asymptotically equivalent to Bayes estimate $\hat{\theta}_n$ of Corollary 1 is proportional to

$$\frac{\alpha''(x)}{\alpha'(x)}.$$

This is bounded if α is any t distribution or an exponential; it is unbounded when the tails of α go to zero faster than exponential.

The conclusions of the frequentist analysis presented above can be briefly summarized: in the class of Bayes estimates based on a Dirichlet prior, the following conditions are (roughly) necessary and sufficient to guarantee that the estimate is both robust and consistent.

• α must have a log-convex-density with exponential tails. Such estimates are very similar to the Huber estimates with eventually constant ψ-functions proposed by Huber in 1964!

IV. SOME VARIATIONS

Several variations will be briefly described in this section. The first variation puts a prior on the set of symmetric error distributions. The other variations, due to Hani Doss, involve tail free priors, and another method of symmetrizing.

A probability P on $\mathbb{R}$ is *symmetric* if $P(A) = P(-A)$ for all Borel sets A. Let $\mathcal{S}$ denote the symmetric probabilities. Let π^+ denote the probabilities on $[0,\infty)$. Define a map from π^+ into $\mathcal{S}$, by $P \to \check{P}$ where

$$\check{P}(A) = P(A \cap \{0\}) + \frac{1}{2} P(A \cap (0,\infty)) + \frac{1}{2} P(-A \cap (0,\infty)).$$

It is easy to check that this map is 1-1 and onto. If λ is a probability on π^+, the image of λ under the map will be denoted by $\check{\lambda}$. Form an exchangeable sequence $X = (X_1,X_2,\ldots,)$ as follows: pick θ from μ and F from $\check{\lambda}$. Let $X_i = \theta + \varepsilon_i$ where ε_i are iid from F. For some choices of λ, it is possible to compute the posterior of θ and F, and thus the posterior mean of θ. The final result is reasonably simple to describe in the following case.

THEOREM 3. *Suppose that α is a bounded measure on $[0,\infty)$ and μ is a probability on $(-\infty,\infty)$. Suppose that α and μ are absolutely continuous. Put prior $\mu \times \check{D}_\alpha$ on $(-\infty,\infty) \times \mathcal{S}$. Let the values $X_1,\ldots,X_n$, and $(X_i+X_j)/2$ be distinct. Then the posterior mean of θ is*

$$\frac{\int_{-\infty}^{\infty} \theta\, w(\theta)d\theta + \sum_{i<j} \frac{X_i+X_j}{2} w_{ij}}{\int_{-\infty}^{\infty} w(\theta)d\theta + \sum_{i<j} w_{ij}}$$

with $w(\theta) = \mu'(\theta) \prod \alpha'(X_i-\theta)$,

$$w_{ij} = \alpha'\left(\frac{X_i-X_j}{2}\right) \mu'\left(\frac{X_i-X_j}{2}\right) \prod_{k\neq i,j} \alpha'\left(X_k - \frac{X_i+X_j}{2}\right).$$

Remarks. When the sample size n is large, the terms involving an integral are negligible and the posterior mean is essentially a weighted average of the averages $(X_i+X_j)/2$. If μ' and α' are strongly unimodal densities such as normal or Cauchy densities, the weights w_{ij} are relatively large only when X_i and X_j are close to each other and the estimate $(X_i+X_j)/2$ is close to the other data points X_k.

Preliminary computations, which we hope to report elsewhere, indicate that symmetrization does not change the findings reported in Section 3. The Bayes rule can be inconsistent unless $\log \alpha'$ is convex and the associated influence curve is bounded only if α' has tails like the exponential or longer.

Hani Doss has carried out similar computations with more general priors λ. These are reported in Doss [7]. The associated Bayes rules when λ is tail free or neutral to the right are too complex to report here. It is not clear as of this writing if the estimates are consistent or robust. Doss has suggested an interesting way to circumvent the problem of symmetry. His idea is to choose a random error distribution F which has median zero. In greater detail, let λ be a prior on π^+. Let F_1 and F_2 be chosen independently from λ. Let $F(t) = \frac{1}{2} F_1(t) + \frac{1}{2} F_2(-t)$. This F had median zero. When λ is D_α, the atoms to the left and right of zero are independent and the "atomic part" of the estimate in Theorem 3 goes away.

THEOREM 4 (Doss). *Let* α *be absolutely continuous on* $[0,\infty)$ *let* μ *be a probability on* $(-\infty,\infty)$. *Let* $F(t) = \frac{1}{2} F_1(t) + \frac{1}{2} F_2(-t)$ *with* F_i iid *from* D_α. *Then the posterior mean of* θ, *assuming that all the* X_i *are distinct, is*

$$\hat{\theta} = \frac{\int_{-\infty}^{\infty} \theta \prod_{i=1}^{n} \alpha'(X_i-\theta) M(\underset{\sim}{X},\theta)\mu(d\theta)}{\int \prod_{i=1}^{n} \alpha'(X_i-\theta) M(\underset{\sim}{X},\theta)\mu(d\theta)},$$

with

$$M(\underset{\sim}{X},\theta) = \left\{ \prod_{i=1}^{nF_n(\theta)} \frac{\alpha(\infty)}{\alpha(\infty)+i-1} \right\} \cdot \left\{ \prod_{i=1}^{n(1-F_n\theta)} \frac{\alpha(\infty)}{\alpha(\infty)+i-1} \right\},$$

where F_n *is the empirical distribution function of* $X_i,\ldots,X_n$.

Remarks. The approach in Theorem 4 gets around the problem of symmetry by asking for an estimate of the median of the observed X_i. Again, preliminary computations indicate that the factor $M(\underset{\sim}{X},\theta)$ does not change the qualitative behavior of the estimate, so the conclusions of Section 3 apply to this estimate as well.

ACKNOWLEDGMENT

We thank Hani Doss for allowing us to describe some of his unpublished research in Section 4.

REFERENCES

[1] Berk, R. (1966). Limiting behavior of posterior distributions when the model is incorrect. *Ann. Math. Statist.* 37, 51-58.

[2] Berk, R. (1970a). Consistency a posteriori. *Ann. Math. Statist.* 41, 894-906.

[3] Berk, R. (1970b). Stopping times of SPRTS - based on exchangeable models. *Ann. Math. Statist.* *41*, 979-990.

[4] Box, G. E. P., and Tiao, G. C. (1973). *Bayesian Inference in Statistical Analysis*. Addison-Wesley, Reading.

[5] Dempster, A. P. (1975). A subjective look at Robustness. Research Report S-33, Harvard University.

[6] Diaconis, P., and Freedman, D. (1981). On inconsistent M-estimates. Stanford University Technical Report No. 170, Stanford. To appear, *Ann. Statist.*

[7] Doss, H. (1981). Unpublished Ph.D. dissertation, Stanford University.

[8] Fabius, J. (1964). Asymptotic behavior of Bayes estimates. *Ann. Math. Statist.* *35*, 846-856.

[9] Ferguson, T. (1973). A Bayesian analysis of some nonparametric problems. *Ann. Statist.* *1*, 209-230.

[10] Ferguson, T. (1974). Prior distributions on spaces of probability measures. *Ann. Statist.* *2*, 615-629.

[11] Fraser, D. A. S. (1976). Necessary analysis and adaptive inference. *J. Amer. Statist. Assoc.* *71*, 99-113.

[12] Freedman, D. (1963). On the asymptotic behavior of Bayes estimates in the discrete case. *Ann. Math. Statist.* *34*, 1386-1403.

[13] Freedman, D. (1965). On the asymptotic behavior of Bayes estimates in the discrete case II. *Ann. Math. Statist.* 35, 454-456.

[14] Freedman, D., and Diaconis, P. (1981). De Finetti's theorem for symmetric location families. To appear, *Ann. Statist.*

[15] Hogg, R. V. (1974). Adaptive robust procedures. *J. Amer. Statist. Assoc.* *69*, 909-922.

[16] Huber, P. (1981). *Robust Statistics*. Wiley, New York.

[17] Korwar, R. M. and Hollander, M. (1973). Contributions to the theory of Dirichlet Processes. *Ann. Prob.* *1*, 705-711.

[18] LeCam, L. (1953). On same asymptotic properties of the maximum likelihood estimates and related Bayes estimates. *Univ. Calif. Pub. Statist. 1*, 277-330 (1955).

[19] Schwartz, L. (1965). On Bayes procedures. *Z. Wahrsch. Verw. Gebiete 4*, 10-26.

Note added in Proof. The paper: Dalal, S. R. (1979). Nonparametric and Robust Bayes estimation of location. *Optimizing Methods in Statistics* (ed. by J. S. Rustagi), 141-166, Academic Press, has some overlap with the present paper.

A METHOD FOR EVALUATING IMPROPER PRIOR DISTRIBUTIONS[1]

Morris L. Eaton

Department of Theoretical Statistics
University of Minnesota
Minneapolis, Minnesota, U.S.A.

I. INTRODUCTION

In this paper, we explore a formulation of a decision problem which, among other things, allows the evaluation of improper prior distributions via the posterior distributions they define. This formulation arose from an attempt to decide whether or not some of the classical fiducial distributions were in a decision theoretic sense "reasonable" (e.g., admissible, minimax) decision rules. For example, if X given θ is $N(\theta,1)$, then the pivotal $X-\theta$ leads to the fiducial distribution "θ given X is $N(X,1)$". Within the Bayesian framework, this posterior distribution for θ arises by assuming θ has the improper prior distribution $d\theta$ (Lebesgue measure) on R^1. In the traditional estimation problem (e.g., estimating θ with quadratic loss) it is ordinarily the case that the non-randomized estimators form an essentially complete class. Thus, the randomized decision rule "θ given X is $N(X,I)$" cannot be reasonable in a traditional formulation of the estimation problem where decision rules are compared via their risk functions. This situation led to a re-examination of the decision theoretic formulation of the estimation problem and resulted in the reformulation of such problems which we will now briefly describe.

Consider a sample space $(\mathcal{X},\mathcal{F})$ and a parameter space $(\Theta,\mathcal{B})$

[1]This work was supported in part by National Science Foundation Grant MCS77-25112.

ISBN 0-12-307501-7

where $\mathcal{B}$ is some natural σ-algebra of subsets of Θ. Let $M(\mathcal{B})$ be the set of all probability measures defined on $\mathcal{B}$. Consider an observable $X \in \mathcal{X}$ whose distribution, given θ, is one of a family $\mathcal{P} = \{P_\theta | \theta \in \Theta\}$. By an *inference* we mean a function δ mapping $\mathcal{X}$ into $M(\mathcal{B})$ - that is, for each x, $\delta(\cdot|x)$ is a probability distribution defined on $(\Theta,\mathcal{B})$. A similar point of view was also taken in Bernardo [2]. This is just the usual definition of a randomized decision rule (at this point all measurability issues will be ignored). In the language of decision theory, $M(\mathcal{B})$ is the action space. Suppose a loss function L defined on $M(\mathcal{B}) \times \Theta$ to $[0,\infty)$ is specified; $L(\nu,\theta)$ measures the loss for action $\nu \in M(\mathcal{B})$ when θ is the "state of nature". The *risk function of* δ is defined by

$$R(\delta,\theta) = \int_{\mathcal{X}} L(\delta(\cdot|x),\theta)P(dx|\theta)$$

for any inference δ. The domain of definition of the risk function is extended to $M(\mathcal{B})$ by

$$\bar{R}(\delta,\pi) = \int R(\delta,\theta)\pi(d\theta), \quad \pi \in M(\mathcal{B}).$$

Now, we ask "What properties should R have?". First suppose a Bayesian has a prior distribution π which represents beliefs about θ. The rules of probability dictate the Bayesian's inference about θ after seeing X - namely, the Bayesian's inference is just the posterior distribution calculated from the model $\mathcal{P} = \{P(\cdot|\theta)|\theta \in \Theta\}$ and the prior π. Let $Q_\pi(\cdot|x)$ be the calculated posterior distribution when X = x so that Q_π is an inference. In order that our formulation lead the Bayesian to the inference Q_π (via minimizing the average risk) the risk function must satisfy

$$\text{(1.1)} \qquad \bar{R}(\delta,\pi) \geq \bar{R}(Q_\pi,\pi)$$

for all inferences δ and $\pi \in M(\mathcal{B})$. To pinpoint the issues involved, let us summarize the arguments which led to (1.1).

(i) Given $X = x$, an inference about θ is a probability distribution on Θ (supposedly reflecting our knowledge about θ based on X and whatever else we know)

(ii) If a Bayesian's prior opinion is given by π, then the Bayesian's inference must be Q_π

(iii) In order that our formulation of the decision problem be consistent with the accepted methods of updating prior information, inequality (1.1) must hold.

The obvious question is whether or not such R's exist. First observe that the space X played a secondary role in the above argument. In particular, if X consists of only one point (no information about θ is contained in X) then (1.1) becomes

$$\int L(\nu,\theta)\pi(d\theta) \geq \int L(\pi,\theta)\pi(d\theta), \quad \pi,\nu \in M(\mathcal{B}). \tag{1.2}$$

(Here, we have replaced δ by ν in (1.1) and suppressed the dependence on x since there is only one x). Hence, if (1.1) is to hold for all experiments, then (1.2) must hold. Conversely, if (1.2) holds, then

$$\begin{aligned}\bar{R}(\delta,\pi) &= \int_\Theta \int_X L(\delta(\cdot|x),\theta)P(dx|\theta)\pi(d\theta) \\ &= \int_X \int_\Theta L(\delta(\cdot|x),\theta)Q_\pi(d\theta|x)m_\pi(dx)\end{aligned} \tag{1.3}$$

where m_π is the marginal distribution of X when the prior is π. Using (1.2) (with $\nu = \delta(\cdot|x)$ and π replaced by $Q_\pi(\cdot|x)$) on the right most member of (1.3) yields

$$\begin{aligned}\bar{R}(\delta,\pi) &\geq \int_X \int_\Theta L(Q_\pi(\cdot|x),\theta)Q_\pi(d\theta|x)m_\pi(dx) \\ &= \int_\Theta \int_X L(Q_\pi(\cdot|x),\theta)P_\theta(dx)\pi(d\theta) = \bar{R}(Q_\pi,\pi)\end{aligned} \tag{1.4}$$

which is just (1.1).

Loss functions which satisfy criteria (1.2) have arisen in a number of other contexts. For example, Brier [5] introduced such a criteria in scoring weathermen on their weather forecasts and

Good [10] independently introduced this criteria in a more general context. For a survey and an extensive bibliography dealing primarily with the case when Θ is a finite set, see Savage [15]. For Θ infinite when densities are assumed, see Hendrickson and Buehler [11]. In Section 2, we will describe a class of L's which satisfy (1.2) in the general context described above.

Since it was a Bayesian argument which led to (1.2), L's which satisfy (1.2) will be called fair Bayes loss functions (FBLF). Further, a decision problem with the property that a Bayesian's decision rule is just the Bayesian's posterior distribution will be called a fair Bayes decision problem (FBDP). For the remainder of this paper, all decision problems will be FBDP's.

Given a FBDP and a prior π, then the appropriate inference (decision rule) is the posterior Q_π. Under fairly mild regularity conditions, such decision rules will be admissible as they are Bayes rules. Traditional justifications for using certain improper priors to induce posterior distributions have included

(i) analytic tractability

(ii) invariance arguments

(iii) the fact that such procedures yield answers which agree with answers obtained from likelihood methods.

Classically, these posterior distributions are then used to define point estimates or testing procedures as if they were defined by proper priors. That some proposed improper priors yield rather questionable solutions to statistical problems is well documented. For example, Stein [17] provided an example where the resulting statistical procedure was uniformly inadmissible. The examples in Dawid, Stone and Zidek [7] demonstrate that the acritical use of improper priors can lead to rather disturbing marginalization problems. However, the recent work of Sudderth [19] has clarified the marginalization situation somewhat.

Within the context of FBDP's there is a fairly natural way of evaluating improper priors. Suppose γ is an improper prior on $(\Theta,\mathcal{B})$ and γ defines a posterior Q_γ (see Section 2 for a discussion). Since Q_γ is an inference, it can be compared to all other inferences via its risk function. For example, we can ask whether or not Q_γ is minimax or admissible. What we are proposing is that γ be evaluated on the basis of the risk function $R(Q_\gamma,\cdot)$. In particular, if Q_γ is inadmissible for a variety of FBDP's, this would suggest that the use of γ as a prior is inappropriate. On the other hand, if Q_γ could be shown to be minimax and admissible in a number of problems, perhaps γ could be used for other problems of a similar nature. Thus, we have a fairly well defined problem - namely, to discover conditions under which Q_γ is admissible or inadmissible. Although our remarks have been directed at Q_γ's which arise from improper priors via a manipulation resulting in a posterior distribution, the same remarks apply to any other argument (e.g., the pivotal argument) which leads to a conditional distribution on Θ (that is, an inference).

Here is a brief synopsis of the remainder of this paper. In the next section, we detail our technical assumptions and describe a large class of FBLF's. This leads to the formal definition of a FBDF. Section 3 contains a discussion of a class of FBLF's called quadratic loss functions. For such loss functions, we also discuss sufficient conditions for admissibility. In Section 4, we present a few results for translation problems. In particular it is shown that for the normal distribution the "Pitman posterior" in one-dimensional translation problems is admissible and minimax. There are a number of problems of interest which do not fit directly into the framework described in Section 2. A modification of this framework is proposed in Section 5 so that marginal estimation problems and prediction problems can be handled directly.

The recent Ph.D. thesis of Gatsonis [9] contains some results which bear a similarity to the work here although the description of his problem and that given here are quite different. The loss functions used by Gatsonis are related to those introduced in Hendrickson and Buehler [11].

II. FAIR BAYES DECISION PROBLEMS

Suppose X and Θ are separable metric spaces so their Borel σ-algebras, say F and B, are countably generated. Assume that

$$(2.1) \qquad P = \{P(\cdot|\theta)|\theta \in \Theta\}$$

is a family of probability measures defined on the sample space (X,F). Let $M(B)$ be the set of all probability measures defined on (Θ,B). When equipped with the weak*-topology, $M(B)$ is a separable metric space and B^* will denote the Borel σ-algebra generated by the weak*-topology (see Parthasarathy (1967), Sec. II.6). It is also known that B^* is the smallest σ-algebra for which all of the functions $\pi \to \int_\Theta f d\pi$ are measurable where

(i) f is an arbitrary bounded continuous function

or

(ii) f is the indicator of any element of a collection of sets which generates B.

For a discussion of this, see Dubins and Freedman [8], Parthasarathy [14] and Blackwell, Freedman and Orkin [4]. The measurable space $(M(B),B^*)$ will be the action space for the decision problem to be studied here. As usual, a *decision rule* δ is a measurable function defined on (X,F) taking values in $(M(B),B^*)$. For reasons discussed in Section 1, decision rules will sometimes be called *inferences*.

Remark 2.1: The usual definition of a (randomized) decision rule δ (with Θ as the action space) goes as follows: δ: $B \times X \to [0,1]$ is assumed to satisfy (i) $\delta(\cdot|x) \in M(B)$ for each

$x \in \mathcal{X}$ and (ii) $\delta(B|\cdot)$ is assumed to be $\mathcal{F}$ measurable for each $B \in \mathcal{B}$. That this definition coincides with our definition follows from the remarks above concerning $\mathcal{B}^*$ (see Dubins and Freedman [8]).

Let $\mathcal{D}$ be the class of all decision rules. For $\delta \in \mathcal{D}$, we will use the notation $\delta(\cdot|x)$ to denote the value of δ at $x \in \mathcal{X}$ so $\delta(\cdot|x) \in M(\mathcal{B})$. Recall that a loss function L is a jointly measurable non-negative function defined on $M(\Theta) \times \Theta$. The extension of L to $M(\Theta) \times M(\Theta)$, is

$$\bar{L}(\nu,\pi) \equiv \int_{\Theta} L(\nu,\theta)\pi(d\theta). \tag{2.2}$$

Let $\epsilon_\theta \in M(\mathcal{B})$ denote the probability measure concentrated at $\theta \in \Theta$. Using this notation, $\bar{L}(\nu,\epsilon_\theta) = L(\nu,\theta)$. With the discussion in Section 1 as motivation, we make the following

Definition 2.1. The loss function L is called a fair Bayes loss function (FBLF) if $\bar{L}(\nu,\pi) \geq \bar{L}(\pi,\pi)$ for all $\nu,\pi \in M(\Theta)$.

Here is an interesting class of FBLF's.

Example 2.1. Consider a jointly measurable function K on $\Theta \times \Theta$ to R^1 such that $K(\theta,\eta) = K(\eta,\theta)$ and

$$\iint K(\theta,\eta)\mu(d\theta)\mu(d\eta) \geq 0 \tag{2.3}$$

for all bounded signed measures μ. (For example, if $f_1,\ldots,f_k$ are bounded measurable functions, then $K(\theta,\eta) = \Sigma f_i(\theta)f_i(\eta) = K(\eta,\theta)$ and (2.3) obviously holds.) Given such a K, define $\langle\cdot,\cdot\rangle$ by

$$\langle\mu_1,\mu_2\rangle = \iint K(\theta,\eta)\mu_1(d\theta)\mu_2(d\eta)$$

for bounded signed measures μ_1 and μ_2.

PROPOSITION 2.1. *Given* $\langle\cdot,\cdot\rangle$, *define* L *by*

$$L(\nu,\theta) = \langle\nu-\epsilon_\theta, \nu-\epsilon_\theta\rangle.$$

Then L *is a* FBLF.

Proof. Using the bilinearity and symmetry of $<\cdot,\cdot>$ compute as follows:

$$\begin{aligned}\bar{L}(\nu,\pi) &= \int<\nu-\epsilon_\theta,\ \nu-\epsilon_\theta>\pi(d\theta) = \int<\nu-\pi+\pi-\epsilon_\theta,\nu-\pi+\pi-\epsilon_\theta>\pi(d\theta)\\ &= <\nu-\pi,\nu-\pi> + \int<\pi-\epsilon_\theta,\pi-\epsilon_\theta>\pi(d\theta)\\ &= <\nu-\pi,\nu-\pi> + \bar{L}(\pi,\pi) \geq \bar{L}(\pi,\pi).\end{aligned}$$

The third equality follows from the formula

$$\int<\nu,\epsilon_\theta>\pi(d\theta) = <\nu,\pi>,\quad \nu,\pi \in M(\mathcal{B}).$$

The above inequality follows from (2.3) so the proof is complete.

Loss functions of the type given in Proposition 2.1 will be called *quadratic loss functions* since $<\cdot,\cdot>$ is a positive semi-definite quadratic form.

Given any loss function L, the *risk function* R defined on $\mathcal{D} \times \Theta$ is

$$R(\delta,\theta) = \int_{\mathcal{X}} L(\delta(\cdot|x),\theta)P(dx|\theta).$$

For $\pi \in M(\mathcal{B})$, the *integrated risk* is

$$\bar{R}(\delta,\pi) = \int R(\delta,\theta)\pi(d\theta)$$

so $\bar{R}(\delta,\epsilon_\theta) = R(\delta,\theta)$. Of course, if $\bar{R}(\delta,\theta) \geq \bar{R}(\delta_0,\pi)$ for all δ, then δ_0 is a Bayes rule for π.

Given $\pi \in M(\mathcal{B})$, to define the posterior distribution, first construct the joint measure on product sets by

$$\lambda(F \times B) \equiv \int_B P(F|\theta)\pi(d\theta),\quad F \in \mathcal{F},\ B \in \mathcal{B}.$$

Then, extend λ in the obvious way to $\mathcal{F} \times \mathcal{B}$ and let

$$m_\pi(F) = \lambda(F \times \Theta)$$

be the *marginal distribution* on $(\mathcal{X},\mathcal{F})$. If $Q_\pi \in \mathcal{D}$ exists which satisfies

$$\lambda(F \times B) = \int_F Q_\pi(B|x)m_\pi(dx), \quad F \in \mathcal{F},\ B \in \mathcal{B},$$

then $Q_\pi(\cdot|x)$ is the *posterior distribution* on Θ given x. Sufficient conditions to guarantee the existence of Q_π are that X and Θ be complete separable metric spaces (see Parthasarathy [14], Chapter 5, Section 7). When Q_π exists, the equation

$$(2.4) \qquad \iint h(x,\theta)P(dx|\theta)\pi(d\theta) = \iint h(x,\theta)\lambda(dx,d\theta)$$
$$= \iint h(x,\theta)Q_\pi(d\theta|x)m_\theta(dx)$$

holds for all $\mathcal{F} \times \mathcal{B}$ measurable h which are λ-integrable.

Now, suppose that L is a FBLF, $\pi \in M(\mathcal{B})$ and the posterior Q_π exists.

PROPOSITION 2.2. *For* $\pi \in M(\mathcal{B})$, *the Bayes rule is* Q_π.

Proof. It must be verified that

$$(2.5) \qquad \bar{R}(\delta,\pi) \geq \bar{R}(Q_\pi,\pi) \text{ for } \delta \in \mathcal{D}.$$

Using (2.4) we have

$$\bar{R}(\delta,\pi) = \iint L(\delta(\cdot|x),\theta)P(dx|\theta)\pi(d\theta)$$
$$= \iint L(\delta(\cdot|x),\theta)Q_\pi(d\theta|x)m_\pi(dx)$$
$$\geq \iint L(Q_\pi(\cdot|x),\theta)Q_\pi(d\theta|x)m_\pi(dx)$$
$$= \iint L(Q_\pi(\cdot|x),\theta)P(dx|\theta)\pi(d\theta) = R(Q_\pi,\pi).$$

The inequality above follows from (2.2) and Definition (2.1). The proof is complete.

Definition 2.2. Any decision problem with action space $(M(\mathcal{B}),\mathcal{B}^*)$ for which (2.5) holds will be called a *fair Bayes decision problem* (FBDP).

We will now argue that FBDP's provide a structure within which methods of assigning probabilities to subsets of Θ (that is, making inferences) can be evaluated. The first point is that the rules of probability force a (proper) Bayesian to assign probabilities in a certain way - namely, via the posterior. It is appropriate to evaluate other methods of making inferences within a system which provides that Bayesians behave consistently. Any inference δ can be judged via its risk function, assuming, of course, we agree that risk functions are an appropriate measure of the behavior of δ. Given this, a method of making inferences can be judged via the decision rules it produces. In particular, the use of an improper prior distribution to define an inference can be judged by the inference it produces. Of course, two properties of an inference δ which can be assessed via its risk function are admissibility and minimaxity.

To be precise, assume that $\gamma \not\equiv 0$ is a σ-finite measure on $(\Theta,\mathcal{B})$ and $\mathcal{P} = \{P(\cdot|\theta)|\theta \in \Theta\}$ is a parametric model on $(\mathcal{X},\mathcal{F})$. Again define λ on $\mathcal{F} \times \mathcal{B}$ by

$$\lambda(F \times B) = \iint I_F(x) I_B(\theta) P(dx|\theta)\gamma(d\theta)$$

and extend in the obvious manner so λ is a σ-finite measure. Then, define the marginal measure on $(\mathcal{X},\mathcal{F})$ by

$$m_\gamma(F) = \lambda(F \times \Theta).$$

To proceed further, it is necessary to *assume* that m_γ is σ-finite. This condition must be checked for each particular example. Let $\mathcal{F} \times \Theta$ denote the sub-σ-algebra of $\mathcal{F} \times \mathcal{B}$ consisting of all sets of the form $F \times \Theta$ with $F \in \mathcal{F}$. Then, the restriction of λ to $\mathcal{F} \times \Theta$ (that is, m_γ) is σ-finite by assumption. Given a set $B \in \mathcal{B}$, the Radon-Nikodym theorem implies the existence of an $\mathcal{F} \times \Theta$ measurable function, say Q_B, such that

$$\int_{\mathcal{X}\times\Theta} I_F(x) Q_B(x,\theta)\lambda(d\theta,dx) = \lambda(F \times B)$$

for all $F \in \mathcal{F}$. Since Q_B is $\mathcal{F} \times \Theta$ measurable, it cannot depend on the argument θ so we will write $Q_B(x)$ for $Q_B(x,\theta)$. It is easy to show $0 \le Q_B \le 1$ a.e. λ. Now, under suitable regularity conditions (e.g., $\mathcal{X}$ and Θ both complete separable metric spaces), we can find a decision rule Q_γ such that for each $B \in \mathcal{B}$ $Q_\gamma(B|\cdot) = Q_B(\cdot)$ a.e. m_γ. (A proof of this parallels the proof of Theorem 8.1, Chapter 5 of Parthasarathy [14]). This implies that

$$\iint I_F(x) I_B(\theta) Q_\gamma(d\theta|x) m_\gamma(d\theta)$$

$$= \iint I_F(x) I_B(\theta) P(dx|\theta)\gamma(d\theta), \; F \in \mathcal{F}, \; B \in \mathcal{B}.$$

Any such decision rule which has this property will be called a formal posterior distribution. Such posterior distributions have been proposed as decision rules. It is our suggestion that these decision rules be evaluated via their risk functions in FBDP's. In the next two sections, we look at some special cases.

III. QUADRATIC LOSS PROBLEMS

In this section, we consider a decision problem with a quadratic loss function given by

$$L(\nu,\theta) = \langle \nu-\epsilon_\theta, \nu-\epsilon_\theta \rangle, \; \nu \in M(\mathcal{B})$$

where

$$\langle \mu_1,\mu_2 \rangle \equiv \iint K(\theta,\eta)\mu_1(d\theta)\mu_2(d\eta)$$

for any two bounded signed measures μ_1 and μ_2. Here, K is a symmetric positive semi-definite kernel so $\langle \mu,\mu \rangle \geq 0$ for all bounded signed measures μ on $(\Theta,\mathcal{B})$. According to the results of the previous section, such an L gives rise to a FBDP. We also make the following two simplifying assumptions:

(3.1) the kernel K is bounded - say $|K(\theta,\eta)| \leq C$ for all $\theta,\eta \in \Theta$.

(3.2) for each $\delta \in \mathcal{D}$, the risk function $R(\delta,\cdot)$ is continuous.

These assumptions will make our discussion of admissibility easier. They will be verified directly for the problem of the next section.

Remark 3.1. Without assumption (3.2), the notion of almost admissibility is more appropriate to what follows.

PROPOSITION 3.1. *In order that* δ_0 *be admissible, it is sufficient that for each non-empty open set* $\mathcal{O} \subseteq \Theta$,

$$\inf_{\pi \in \Pi(\mathcal{O})} \frac{1}{\pi(\mathcal{O})} \int [R(\delta_0,\theta) - R(Q_\pi,\theta)]\, \pi(d\theta) = 0 \tag{3.3}$$

where $\Pi(\mathcal{O})$ *is the set of* $\pi \in M(\mathcal{B})$ *such that* $\pi(\mathcal{O}) > 0$.

Proof. This result is a minor modification of Stein's conditions (see Stein [16]), but the proof is easy so it is included. Suppose δ_0 is not admissible. Then there exists a δ_1 such that $R(\delta_1,\theta) \leq R(\delta_0,\theta)$ for all $\theta \in \Theta$, with strict inequality for some $\theta \in \Theta$. The continuity assumption on $R(\delta,\cdot)$ implies there exists an $\epsilon > 0$ such that

$$\mathcal{O} = \{\theta | R(\delta_1,\theta) < R(\delta_0,\theta) - \epsilon\}$$

is open and non-empty. Then, for each $\pi \in \Pi(\mathcal{O})$, we have

$$\frac{1}{\pi(\mathcal{O})} \int [R(\delta_0,\theta) - R(Q_\pi,\theta)]\pi(d\theta)$$

$$= \frac{1}{\pi(\mathcal{O})} \int [R(\delta_0,\theta) - R(\delta_1,\theta)]\, \pi(d\theta) + \frac{1}{\pi(\mathcal{O})} \int [R(\delta_1,\theta) - R(Q_\pi,\theta)]\, \pi(d\theta)$$

$$\geq \frac{1}{\pi(\mathcal{O})} \int_{\mathcal{O}} [R(\delta_0,\theta) - R(\delta_1,\theta)]\, \pi(d\theta) > \epsilon$$

which contradicts (3.3). The proof is complete.

The following result provides a useful first step in trying to verify (3.3). If μ is any bounded signed measure, $||\mu||^2$ will mean $\langle\mu,\mu\rangle$ so $||\cdot||$ is a semi-norm.

PROPOSITION 3.2. *For any quadratic loss function,*

$$\int_{\Theta} [R(\delta,\theta) - R(Q_\pi,\theta)]\, \pi(d\theta) = \int_{\mathcal{X}} ||\delta(\cdot|x) - Q_\pi(\cdot|x)||^2 m_\pi(dx) \tag{3.4}$$

where m_π *is the marginal distribution on* $\mathcal{X}$.

Proof. The identity $\int < \mu, \epsilon_\theta > \pi(d\theta) = <\mu,\pi>$ is used below. The proof is a calculation similar to that given in the proof of Proposition 2.2. For $\pi \in M(\Theta)$, we have

$$(3.5) \qquad \Psi(\pi,\delta) = \int[R(\delta,\theta) - R(Q_\pi,\theta)]\pi(d\theta)$$

$$= \int\int[||\delta(\cdot|x)-\epsilon_\theta||^2 - ||Q_\pi(\cdot|x)-\epsilon_\theta||^2]P_\theta(dx)\pi(d\theta)$$

$$= \int\int[<\delta(\cdot|x),\delta(\cdot|x)> -2 < \delta(\cdot|x)-Q_\pi(\cdot|x), \epsilon_\theta>$$

$$- <Q_\pi(\cdot|x),Q_\pi(\cdot|x)>]Q_\pi(d\theta|x)m_\pi(dx)$$

$$= \int[<\delta(\cdot|x),\delta(\cdot|x)> -2 < \delta(\cdot|x)-Q_\pi(\cdot|x),Q_\pi(\cdot|x)>$$

$$- <Q_\pi(\cdot|x),Q_\pi(\cdot|x)>]m_\pi(dx)$$

$$= \int||\delta(\cdot|x)-Q_\pi(\cdot|x)||^2 m_\pi(dx).$$

This completes the proof.

To show δ_0 is admissible, it suffices to show that for each open set $\mathcal{O}$,

$$(3.6) \qquad \inf_{\pi\in\Pi(\mathcal{O})} \frac{\Psi(\pi,\delta_0)}{\pi(\mathcal{O})} = 0.$$

There are a couple of upper bounds on $\Psi(\pi,\delta_0)$ which may be of use in the verification of (3.6).

PROPOSITION 3.3. *Given δ and π, assume that for all $x \in X$, $\delta(\cdot|x)$ and $Q_\pi(\cdot|x)$ are both absolutely continuous with respect to a fixed probability measure ξ on Θ. Let $\alpha(\cdot|x)$ and $q_\pi(\cdot|x)$ be the densities of $\delta(\cdot|x)$ and $Q_\pi(\cdot|x)$ with respect to ξ. If $|K(\theta,\eta)| \le C$ for all $\theta,\eta \in \Theta$, then*

$$(3.7) \qquad \Psi(\pi,\delta) \le C\int_X[\int_\Theta|\alpha(\theta|x)-q_\pi(\theta|x)|\xi(d\theta)]^2 m_\pi(dx)$$

$$\le C\int_X\int_\Theta(\alpha(\theta|x)-q_\pi(\theta|x))^2\xi(d\theta)m_\pi(dx).$$

Proof. Using Proposition (3.2) and the definition of $||\cdot||$, we have

$$\Psi(\pi,\delta) = \int_{X} ||\delta(\cdot|x)-Q_\pi(\cdot|x)||^2 m_\pi(dx)$$

$$= \int[\int\int K(\theta,\eta)[\delta(d\theta|x)-Q_\pi(d\theta|x)][\delta(d\eta|x)-Q_\pi(d\eta|x)]]m_\pi(dx)$$

$$= \int[\int\int K(\theta,\eta)[\alpha(\theta|x)-q_\pi(\theta|x)][\alpha(\eta|x)$$

$$- q_\pi(\eta|x)]\xi(d\theta)\xi(d\eta)]m_\pi(dx)$$

$$\leq C\int[\int\int|\alpha(\theta|x)-q_\pi(\theta|x)||\alpha(\eta|x)$$

$$- q_\pi(\eta|x)|\xi(d\theta)\xi(d\eta)]m_\pi(dx)$$

$$= C\int[\int|\alpha(\theta|x) - q_\pi(\theta|x)|\xi(d\theta)]^2 m_\pi(dx)$$

which is the first inequality. Applying Cauchy-Schwarz yields the second inequality so the proof is complete.

Another upper bound for $\Psi(\pi,\delta)$ can be given in terms of the Hellinger distance (see Kakutani [12]). Given two probability measures π_1 and π_2, the squared Hellinger distance is given by

$$(3.8) \qquad H^2(\pi_1,\pi_2) = \int\left[\left(\frac{d\pi_1}{d\beta}\right)^{\frac{1}{2}} - \left(\frac{d\pi_2}{d\beta}\right)^{\frac{1}{2}}\right]^2 d\beta$$

where β is any measure which dominates both π_1 and π_2. Of course, the value of $H(\pi_1,\pi_2)$ does not depend on the choice of β. For $\pi_1,\pi_2 \in M(\Theta)$, let α_i be the density of π_i with respect to β. Then

$$(3.9) \qquad ||\pi_1-\pi_2||^2$$

$$= \int\int K(\theta,\eta)[\alpha_1(\theta)-\alpha_2(\theta)][\alpha_1(\eta)-\alpha_2(\eta)]\beta(d\theta)\beta(d\eta)$$

$$\leq C[\int|\alpha_1(\theta) -\alpha_2(\theta)|\beta(d\theta)]^2$$

$$= C[\int |\alpha_1^{\frac{1}{2}}(\theta)-\alpha_2^{\frac{1}{2}}(\theta)||\alpha_1^{\frac{1}{2}}(\theta) + \alpha_2^{\frac{1}{2}}(\theta)|\beta(d\theta)]^2$$

$$\leq CH^2(\pi_1,\pi_2)\int(\alpha_1^{\frac{1}{2}}(\theta) + \alpha_2^{\frac{1}{2}}(\theta))^2\beta(d\theta)$$

$$= 2CH^2(\pi_1,\pi_2)[1 + \int\alpha_1^{\frac{1}{2}}(\theta)\alpha_2^{\frac{1}{2}}(\theta)\beta(d\theta)]$$

$$\leq 4CH^2(\pi_1,\pi_2).$$

This leads to

PROPOSITION 3.4. *Given* δ *and* π,

$$\Psi(\pi,\delta) \leq 4C\int H^2(\delta(\cdot|x),Q_\pi(\cdot|x))m_\pi(dx). \tag{3.10}$$

Proof. Apply (3.9) with $\pi_1 = \delta(\cdot|x)$, $\pi_2 = Q_\pi(\cdot|x)$ and use Proposition 3.2.

An upper bound similar to (3.10) was given by Stein [18] in his study of admissibility in classical decision theory problems. This suggests that admissibility in the present context will be closely connected to admissibility in more classical problems - at least in problems where Stein's upper bound is valid.

IV. A SIMPLE EXAMPLE

Our discussion in this section will be centered around the estimation of a univariate normal mean. Unfortunately, space limitations prohibit the inclusion of some of the detailed calculations. Suppose X is N(θ,1). For this example $\mathcal{X} = \Theta = R^1$ (a sufficiency argument shows we need only consider the case of one observation). Consider the particular inference δ_0 which specifies that θ is N(x,1) when X = x - that is, $\delta(\cdot|x)$ is the N(x,1) distribution on R^1. To define a FBLF, consider the kernel

$$K_t(\theta,\eta) = \exp[it(\theta-\eta)]$$

for $t \in R^1$ and $\theta,\eta \in R^1$. Note that K_t is complex valued. It is easy to verify that the bilinear from $<\cdot,\cdot>$ defined on pairs of bounded signed measures by

$$<\mu_1,\mu_2>_t = \iint K_t(\theta,\eta)\mu_1(d\theta)\mu_2(d\eta)$$

is positive semi-definite. The calculation given in Example 2.1 shows that the loss function L_t defined by

$$L_t(\nu,\theta) = <\nu-\epsilon_\theta, <\nu-\epsilon_\theta>_t$$

is a FBLF for each t. Further, the continuity of the risk function $R_t(\delta,\cdot)$ for each decision rule is easily verified using the analytic properties of the $N(\theta,1)$ distribution.

Given $\sigma > 0$, let π_σ denote the $N(0,\sigma^2)$ distribution and let Q_σ denote the posterior distribution of θ when X is $N(\theta,1)$. Thus $Q_\sigma(\cdot|x)$ is a $N(cx,c)$ distribution where $c = \sigma^2/(1+\sigma^2)$. Also, the marginal distribution of X is $N(0,1+\sigma^2)$ which is denoted by m_σ. Let $||\cdot||_t$ denote the semi-norm defined by K_t.

LEMMA 4.1. *For each non-empty open set* $\mathcal{O} \subseteq R^1$,

$$\lim_{\sigma\to\infty} \sup_t (\pi_\sigma(\mathcal{O}))^{-1} \int ||\delta_0(\cdot|x)-Q_\sigma(\cdot|x)||_t^2 m_\sigma(dx) = 0. \tag{4.1}$$

Proof. Since each $\mathcal{O}$ contains an interval, it is sufficient to establish (4.1) where $\mathcal{O} = (a,b)$, $-\infty < a < b < \infty$. In this case, note that $\sigma\pi_\sigma(\mathcal{O}) \to (b-a)$ as $\sigma \to \infty$ so it suffices to verify (4.1) with $(\pi_\sigma(\mathcal{O}))^{-1}$ replaced by σ. From the special form of K_t, it is clear that $||\delta_0(\cdot|x) - Q_\sigma(\cdot|x)||_t^2$ is the modulus squared of the difference between the characteristic functions of $\delta_0(\cdot|x)$ and $Q_\sigma(\cdot|x)$ evaluated at t. Since the two distributions are normal, a calculation yields

$$(4.2)\qquad \Delta_\sigma(x,t) = ||\delta_0(\cdot|x) - Q_\sigma(\cdot|x)||_t^2$$

$$= |\exp(itx - \tfrac{1}{2}t^2) - \exp(ictx - \tfrac{1}{2}c^2t^2)|^2$$

where $c = \sigma^2/(1+\sigma^2)$. Integrating $\Delta_\sigma(x,t)$ with respect to $m_\sigma(dx)$ yields

$$(4.3)\qquad \sup_t \int \Delta_\sigma(x,t) m_\sigma(dx)$$

$$= \sup_t\{\exp[-t^2] + \exp[-c^2t^2] - 2\exp[-t^2(1+ \tfrac{c(c-1)}{2})]\}$$

$$\leq \sup_t\{|\exp[-t^2]-\exp[-c^2t^2]|$$

$$+ 2|\exp[-t^2(1+ \tfrac{c(c-1)}{2})]-\exp[-c^2t^2]|\}$$

$$\leq 3 \sup_t|\exp[-t^2]-\exp[-c^2t^2]|$$

$$+ 2 \sup_t|\exp[-t^2(1+ \tfrac{c(c-1)}{2})]-\exp[-t^2]|.$$

Now, it is a routine but tedious calculation to compute the two suprema in the final term of (4.3). Using this result, one then can show that

$$\lim_{\sigma\to\infty} \sigma \sup_t \int \Delta_\sigma(x,t) m_\sigma(dx) = 0$$

which completes the proof.

PROPOSITION 4.1. *Let* k *be a complex valued function defined on* R^1 *such that* $k(0) = 1$ *and the kernel* K *given by* $K(\theta,\eta) = k(\theta-\eta)$ *satisfies* $K(\theta,\eta) = \overline{K(\theta,\eta)}$ *where the bar denotes complex conjugate. Assume* K *is positive semi-definite and let* L *be the* FBLF *defined by* K. *Then* δ_0 *is admissible in the* FBDP *defined by* L.

Proof. The assumption that $k(0) = 1$ together with the assumption that K is positive semi-definite allows us to invoke Bochner's Theorem to conclude that

$$K(\theta,\eta) = \int_{-\infty}^{\infty} K_t(\theta,\eta)H(dt)$$

where H is a distribution function on R^1. To show δ_0 is admissible, we will verify (3.3) using (3.4) and Lemma 4.1. As in the proof of Lemma 4.1, it suffices to take $\mathcal{O} = (a,b)$ where $-\infty < a < b < \infty$ and it suffices to show that

$$\lim_{\sigma\to\infty} \sigma\int ||\delta_0(\cdot|x) - Q_\sigma(\cdot|x)||^2 m_\sigma(dx) = 0, \tag{4.4}$$

where $||\cdot||$ is the semi-norm defined by K. But, for any bounded signed measure μ,

$$||\mu||^2 = \langle\mu,\mu\rangle = \int\langle\mu,\mu\rangle_t H(dt) = \int||\mu||_t^2 H(dt).$$

Substituting this into (4.4) and using Lemma 4.1 yields

$$\lim_{\sigma\to\infty} \sigma\int\int ||\delta_0(\cdot|x) - Q_\sigma(\cdot|x)||_t^2 H(dt)m_\sigma(dx)$$

$$\leq \lim_{\sigma\to\infty} \sigma \sup_t \int ||\delta_0(\cdot|x) - Q_\sigma(\cdot|x)||_t^2 m_\sigma(dx) = 0.$$

This completes the proof.

We close this section with a few remarks.

Remark 4.1. For the problem above with a general bounded kernel K, it should be possible to show that δ_0 is admissible via (3.3) and (3.4) by using the upper bounds given in Proposition 3.3 or Proposition 3.4. I have been unable to carry out the calculations thus far.

Remark 4.2. For loss functions of the type assumed in Proposition 4.1, the resulting decision problem is invariant (in the traditional sense) under translations. Of course, the group G is

R^1 and G acts in the obvious way on $\mathcal{X}$ and Θ. The action of G on decision rules is defined by

$$(\hat{g}\delta)(B|x) = \delta(g^{-1}B|g^{-1}x), \; g \in G$$

where B is a Borel set of Θ and $x \in \mathcal{X}$. Then δ is called invariant if $\hat{g}\delta = \delta$. Since the group G acts transitively on Θ, any invariant decision rule will have constant risk. The best of all the invariant rules is δ_0 - this follows from its admissibility, but an appeal to a general result of Stein is more appropriate (see Zidek [20]) - namely, under conditions which hold for this problem, the best invariant rule is obtained by using the right Haar measure as a prior (improper) distribution and calculating the posterior distribution. Of course, Lebesgue measure is the right Haar measure on G and δ_0 is the formal posterior distribution for this improper prior. Since δ_0 is a best invariant decision rule, that it is minimax follows from a result due to Kiefer [13].

Remark 4.3. When X is $N_p(\theta, I_p)$ and $p \geq 3$, it is natural to ask if the obvious decision rule, δ_0, which specifies that θ given $X = x$ is $N(x, I_p)$ is admissible. One suspects not because of the existence of Stein-type estimators when $p \geq 3$. Here is what I know so far. For the kernel K given by

$$K(\theta,\eta) = \exp[-\tfrac{1}{2}\,||\theta-\eta||^2]$$

which defines a FBLF and a FBDP, δ_0 is minimax (Kiefer's Theorem [13]) but δ_0 is not admissible. Consider a decision rule of the form

$$\delta_1(\cdot|x) \text{ is } N(u(x), I_p)$$

where

$$u(x) = x - \left(\frac{a}{b+||x||^2}\right) x.$$

Then there exists an a (small and positive) and a b (large and positive) so that δ_1 dominates δ_0. Methods similar to those in Brown [6] are used to establish this claim. The proof is tedious and offers virtually no guidance in the important problem of finding a prior (proper or improper) so that the corresponding posterior dominates δ_0. A result similar to the above has recently been established by Gatsonis [9].

V. SOME EXTENSIONS

In this section we extend our formulation of the decision problem to include the marginal estimation of parameters problem and the prediction problem. To discuss the first problem, again assume $(\mathcal{X},\mathcal{F})$ is the sample space, $(\Theta,\mathcal{B})$ is the parameter space and a model $\{P(\cdot|\theta)|\theta \in \Theta\}$ is given. Rather than requiring an inference from $\mathcal{X}$ to $\mathcal{M}(\mathcal{B})$, we now consider a σ-algebra $\mathcal{B}_0 \subseteq \mathcal{B}$, and define an inference to be measurable map from $\mathcal{X}$ to $\mathcal{M}(\mathcal{B}_0)$ where $\mathcal{M}(\mathcal{B}_0)$ is the set of all probability measures on $(\Theta,\mathcal{B}_0)$. An example will illustrate how this situation arises.

Example 5.1. Suppose $X_1,\ldots,X_n$ is a random sample from a $N(\mu,\sigma^2)$ population with μ and σ^2 both unknown. Thus, $\mathcal{X} = R^n$ and $\Theta = \{\theta|\theta = (\mu,\sigma^2),\ \mu \in R^1,\ \sigma^2 > 0\}$, so $\mathcal{B}$ is the set of Borel sets of Θ. If we are only interested in inferences about μ, then we take $\mathcal{B}_0 \subseteq \mathcal{B}$ to be

$$\mathcal{B}_0 = \{C \times (0,\infty)\,|\,C \text{ is a Borel set of } R^1\}.$$

Given any probability measure $\pi \in \mathcal{M}(\mathcal{B})$, its projection to $\mathcal{M}(\mathcal{B}_0)$ is given by simply restricting π to $\mathcal{B}_0$. For this example, the projection corresponds to "integrating out σ" or "marginalizing". That is, we can define $\tilde{\pi}$ on R^1 by $\tilde{\pi}(C) = \pi(C \times (0,\infty))$ so $\tilde{\pi}$ is just the marginal of π and provides an inference for $\mu \in R^1$.

To continue with the general discussion, for $\pi \in M(\mathcal{B})$, let $\hat{\pi}$ denote the restriction of π to $\mathcal{B}_0$ so $\hat{\pi} \in M(\mathcal{B}_0)$. In what follows, we assume that all elements of $M(\mathcal{B}_0)$ are obtained by the restriction of elements of $M(\mathcal{B})$. A sufficient condition for this is that both $(X, \mathcal{B})$ be Polish and $\mathcal{B}_0$ be countably generated (see Ascherl and Lehn [1] for a discussion). Given a loss function L defined on $M(\mathcal{B}_0) \times \Theta$, define $\bar{L}$ on $M(\mathcal{B}_0) \times M(\mathcal{B})$ by

$$\bar{L}(\nu,\pi) = \int L(\nu,\theta)\pi(d\theta).$$

Then L is a <u>FBLF</u> if $\bar{L}(\nu,\pi) \geq \bar{L}(\hat{\pi},\pi)$ for all $\nu \in M(\mathcal{B}_0)$ and $\pi \in M(\mathcal{B})$. Any such FBLF will give rise to a risk function R and its extension $\bar{R}$. When L is a FBLF, it is easy to show that

$$\bar{R}(\delta,\pi) \geq \bar{R}(\hat{Q}_\pi,\pi).$$

The proof of this is the same as given in Proposition 2.2. In other words, given a FBLF and π, the Bayes solution to the decision problem is obtained by projecting the posterior distribution. Examples of L's which are FBLF's are easily constructed as in Example 2.1 by taking the kernal K to be $\mathcal{B}_0 \times \mathcal{B}_0$ measurable. The verification of this is essentially that given for Proposition 2.1. Given such a quadratic loss function, all of the results in Section 3 are valid with virtually no modifications.

We now briefly indicate how the prediction problem can be formulated within the present contrext. Suppose (X, F) is a sample space, (Z, G) is is a space of values for future observables and $(\P, C)$ is a parameter space. The observation $X \in X$ is assumed to have a distribution belonging to a family $P = \{P(\cdot|z,\eta)\ z \in Z, \eta \in \P\}$. The future observable Z is assumed to have a distribution in the family $S = \{S(\cdot|\eta)|\eta \in \P\}$. The decision problem is to make an inference about Z after observing X. Let $(\Theta,\mathcal{B}) = (Z \times \P, G \times C)$ be the "parameter space" for this problem. Rather than consider the set of all "prior" distributions on $(\Theta,\mathcal{B})$, our assumptions require us to look only at distributions on $(\Theta,\mathcal{B})$, say π, which have the form

$$\pi(dz,d\eta) = S(dz|\eta)\xi(d\eta) \tag{5.1}$$

where ξ is an arbitrary prior on $(\P,\mathcal{C})$ - that is, $\xi \in M(\mathcal{C})$. In other words, the model assumptions specify the conditional distribution of z given η which is exactly what (5.1) means. Let $M_0(\mathcal{G} \times \mathcal{C})$ be distributions of the form (5.1). Since the problem is to make an inference about z, a decision rule should be a function from $\mathcal{X}$ to $M(\mathcal{G})$. However, it is a bit more consistent to identify $M(\mathcal{G})$ with projections of measures in $M(\mathcal{B})$. To be more precise, let $\mathcal{B}_0$ be the sub-σ-algebra of $\mathcal{B}$ defined by

$$\mathcal{B}_0 = \{G \times \P | G \in \mathcal{G}\}.$$

Thus, the restriction of $\pi \in M(\mathcal{B})$ to $\mathcal{B}_0$ defines a distribution in $M(\mathcal{G})$ and conversely. Finally, an *inference*, δ, is a measurable function defined on $\mathcal{X}$ taking values in $M(\mathcal{B}_0)$.

With the above formulation of the prediction problem, we have a problem very similar to the marginalization problem discussed earlier in the section. The only difference is that the prior distributions are of a restricted form because of our prior assumptions concerning the model. It is now a routine matter to extend the earlier notions. A loss function $L(\delta,\theta)$ is a FBLF if for $\pi \in M_0(\mathcal{G} \times \mathcal{C})$,

$$\int L(\delta,\theta)\pi(d\theta) \geq \int L(\hat{\pi},\theta)\pi(d\theta)$$

where $\hat{\pi}$ is the restriction of π to $\mathcal{B}_0$ ($\hat{\pi}$ is the marginal of π on $(\mathcal{Z},\mathcal{G})$). Given such a FBLF, the risk function R will have the property that

$$\int R(\delta,\theta)\pi(d\theta) \geq \int R(\hat{Q}_\pi,\theta)\pi(d\theta) \tag{5.2}$$

for $\pi \in M_0(\mathcal{G} \times \mathcal{C})$. Here, $\hat{Q}_\pi$ is the projection of the posterior Q_π onto $\mathcal{B}_0$. In other words, given a π of the form (5.1) and $x \in \mathcal{X}$, we have a posterior distribution, say $Q_\pi(\cdot|x)$ defined on

$(\mathcal{Z} \times \P, \mathcal{G} \times \mathcal{C})$. Then, the projection of $Q_\pi(\cdot|x)$ is defined by

$$\hat{Q}_\pi(G \times \P|x) \equiv Q_\pi(G \times \P|x)$$

for each set $G \in \mathcal{G}$ - that is, $\hat{Q}_\pi(\cdot|x)$ is the marginal distribution of $Q_\pi(\cdot|x)$ on the space $(\mathcal{Z}, \mathcal{G})$. Of course, $\hat{Q}_\pi(\cdot|x)$ is ordinarily called the predictive distribution. The above argument shows that if L is a FBLF, then given $\pi \in M_0(\mathcal{G} \times \mathcal{C})$, the Bayes solution to the decision problem (the prediction problem) is just the predictive distribution. As with the marginalization problem described earlier, examples of FBLF's are provided by $\mathcal{B}_0 \times \mathcal{B}_0$ measurable kernels which are positive semi-definite (as argued in Example 2.1).

REFERENCES

[1] Ascherl, A. and Lehn, J. (1977). Two principles for extending probability measures. *Manuscripta Math.* 21, 43-50.

[2] Bernardo, J. M. (1979). Expected information as expected utility. *Ann. Statist.* 7, 686-690.

[3] Blackwell, D. (1956). On a class of probability spaces. *Proc. 3rd Berkeley Symp. Math. Statist. Prob.* II, 1-6.

[4] Blackwell, D., Freedman, D. and Orkin, M. (1974). The optimal reward operator in dynamic programming. *Ann. Probab.* 2, 926-941.

[5] Brier, G. W. (1950). Verification of forecasts expressed in terms of probability. *Monthly Weather Rev.* 78, 1-3.

[6] Brown, L. D. (1966). On the admissibility of invariant estimators of one or more location parameters. *Ann. Math. Statist.* 37, 1087-1131.

[7] Dawid, A. P., Stone M. and Zidek, J. V. (1973). Marginalization paradoxes in Bayesian and structural inference. *J. Roy. Statist. Soc. Ser. B* 35, 189-233.

[8] Dubins, L. and Freedman, D. (1964). Measurable sets of measures. *Pacific J. Math.* 14, 1211-1222.

[9] Gatsonis, C. A. (1981). Estimation of the posterior density of a location parameter. Ph.D. Thesis, Cornell University, Ithaca.

[10] Good, I. J. (1952). Rational decisions. *J. Roy. Statist. Soc. Ser. B 14*, 357-364.

[11] Hendrickson, A. D. and Buehler, R. J. (1971). Proper scores for probability forecasters. *Ann. Math. Statist. 42*, 1916-1921.

[12] Kakutani, S. (1948). On equivalence of infinite product measures. *Ann. Math. 49*, 214.

[13] Kiefer, J. C. (1957). Invariance, minimax sequential estimation and continuous time processes. *Ann. Math. Statist. 28*, 573-601.

[14] Parthasarathy, K. R. (1957). *Probability Measures on Metric Spaces*. Academic Press, New York.

[15] Savage, L. J. (1971). The elicitation of personal probabilities and expectations. *J. Amer. Statist. Assoc. 66*, 783-801.

[16] Stein, C. (1955). A necessary and sufficient condition for admissibility. *Ann. Math. Statist. 26*, 518-522.

[17] Stein, C. (1956). Some problems in multivariate analysis, Part I. Stanford University Technical Report No. 6, Stanford.

[18] Stein, C. (1965). Approximation of improper prior measures by prior probability measures. *Bernoulli, Bayes, Laplace Anniversary Volume*, J. Neyman and L. LeCam (eds.). Springer-Verlag, Berlin.

[19] Sudderth, W. (1981). Finitely additive priors, coherence and the marginalization paradox. *J. Roy. Statist. Soc. Ser. 42*, 339-341.

[20] Zidek, J. V. (1969). A representation of Bayes invariant procedures in terms of Haar measure. *Ann. Inst. Statist. Math. 22*, 291-308.

A MOMENT FREE CONSISTENCY PROOF FOR THE LSEs AND MODEL IDENTIFICATION IN MIXED AUTOREGRESSIONS

F. Eicker

Abteilung Statistik
Dortmund University
Dortmund, West Germany

I. INTRODUCTION AND MODEL IDENTIFICATION

1.1 *Introduction*

Let $y_1, y_2, \ldots$ be observed real random variables (r.v.'s). The model for the y_t considered in this paper is partly autoregressive, partly exogenous linear regressive one as follows

$$(1.1) \qquad y_t = y_{t-1}\alpha_1 + \ldots + y_{t-p}\alpha_p + z_{t1}\gamma_1 + \ldots + z_{tq}\gamma_q + \varepsilon_t \quad (t \in \mathbb{N}).$$

The α's and γ's are unknown real constants for which in this paper we consider only their ordinary least squares estimates $\binom{\alpha}{\gamma}_{LSE}$ (LSE; defined in (1.3) below). The z_{tj} are known real (exogenous) regression constants and the ε_t are unobservable real r.v.'s on a common p-space. No moment or specific distributional assumptions will be made on the ε_t now. The values of p and q are assumed known here. For simplicity we put $y_o = \ldots = y_{1-p} = 0$. The following notations are convenient:

$Z \equiv Z_n = (z_{tj};\ t = 1,\ldots,n;\ j = 1,\ldots,q)$, $n \in \mathbb{N}$, form the (non-stochastic) part of the regression matrices in (1.1). In the sequel the subscript n usually will be suppressed where this should cause no confusion. Furthermore let

$$L \equiv L_n = \begin{pmatrix} 0 & & & & \\ 1 & 0 & & \cdots & \\ & 1 & 0 & & \\ & & \cdots & & \\ & 0 & \cdots & 1 & 0 \end{pmatrix}_{n\times n}$$

$n \in \mathbb{N}$, be the shift or lag matrices, and let

ISBN 0-12-307501-7

$$\mathcal{L}_y := (L_y, \ldots, L^p y)_{n\times p}.$$

(This notation will also be used with other vectors than y or with matrices). This is the stochastic part of the combined total regression matrix $X: = (\mathcal{L}_y, Z)_{n\times(p+q)}$ of the linear stochastic model (1.1) (which incidentally has also been called a linear difference equation. It should also be pointed out that in the theory of stationary processes the term autoregression is used in a narrower sense than above). In matricial notation the model (1.1) with n observations becomes

$$(1.2) \qquad y = X\binom{\alpha}{\gamma} + e = (\mathcal{L}_y, Z)\binom{\alpha}{\gamma} + e$$

where

$y': = (y_1, \ldots, y_n)$, $e': = (\varepsilon_1, \ldots, \varepsilon_n)$,

$$(\alpha', \gamma'): = (\alpha_1, \ldots, \alpha_p; \gamma_1, \ldots, \gamma_q).$$

The normal equations with LSEs $\binom{\alpha}{\gamma}_{LSE}$ are:

$$(1.3) \qquad X'X \binom{\alpha}{\gamma}_{LSE} = X'y.$$

The aim of this paper is to present a new method of proving consistency results of the LSE's as $n \to \infty$ under rather general conditions. The main result is Proposition 2.1 of Section 2.2. Since it does not require the existence of any moments of the ε_t nor a specific dependence structure,it in this respect generalizes most existing approaches, in particular the best result on weak consistency obtained so far, namely a theorem by R. Willers [7] (Satz 4), which is stated as Example 3.1 below. The influence of the tails of the error d.f.'s is hence reduced. Loosely speaking the assumptions on the errors concern the speed of the convergence to zero of sample-covariance-type expressions. In another example Cauchy-distributed error sequences are admitted.

The proof given in Section 2 emphasizes the geometrical and algebraic structure of the problem and essentially separates it from the probabilistic aspect. It is quite straightforward and its principles are probably more interesting than the resulting conditions on the errors which are admittedly not of immediate practical usefulness. In order to obtain from them more conventionally looking conditions the appropriate theorems of probability theory (e.g. on martingale convergence, on mixing or stationary sequences, laws of large numbers) may be applied.

Another group of recent papers on the linear model (1.1) and the more general one with arbitrary stochastic regression matrices X assumes that the ε_t form a martingale difference sequence. Then strong consistency results can be obtained (comp. [1] and [2] and the literature cited there).

As a side result of Proposition 2.1 as it stands the consistent estimation by least squares of the parameters of the autoregressive part alone can be asserted under quite general conditions on the exogenous variables ((2.4) below) and on the error distributions ((2.2'), (2.3')), no matter whether the LSEs $\hat{\gamma}$ of the deterministic regression part are consistent or not. Thus regarding its autoregression part the model has higher flexibility. It is very surprising, however, how quite severely the model assumptions must be restricted just in order to enforce in addition also the consistency of the $\hat{\gamma}$'s. These additional assumptions are in fact so restrictive that the practical usefulness of the model or at least of ordinary least squares becomes doubtful and consequently the validity of the model in a particular application must be carefully scrutinized. The futility of certain applications of model (1.1) and of the LS-method to real data has here its cause.

However there seems to be a kind of balance between the restrictiveness of the assumptions on the regressors Z and those on the errors ε_t: two sets of additional assumptions implying the consistency of the $\hat{\gamma}$ are being given, the first one being quite restrictive regarding the error distributions ((2.2) and (2.3) below) and weak regarding the regressors Z (see (2.4)). Conversely in the second set the error distributions are much less restricted (see (2.2'), (2.3'), (2.1)) but strong assumptions on the Z as known from earlier research results have to be imposed ((2.3"), (2.3"')). The stronger set of assumptions on the errors implies a high degree of asymptotic near-independence of the ε_t; white noise is an example satisfying these assumptions. In contrast the weaker set admits stronger dependencies.

The reason for these unfortunate and surprising facts which have such strong bearing upon the whole philosophy behind the model and on its practicability seems to be closely related to identifiability properties of the parameters in the model (1.1). We shall discuss these only briefly subsequently but a simple and realistic example of non-identifiability of the exogenous regression part of the observed vectors y will now be given.

1.2 *Modelling and Model Identification*

According to (2.7a; see below) the model (1.2) may in an equivalent but for some purposes more meaningful may be written as

$$(1.4) \qquad y = C(Z\gamma + e) = CZ\gamma + \eta, \ \eta := Ce,$$

which shows the structure of the deterministic regression $CZ\gamma$ of y on Z more clearly than (1.1); here $C \equiv C_n(\alpha)$ is given by (2.6). (1.4) is merely a deterministic regression with the parameter vector α,γ and it is non-linear since C (in contrast to C^{-1}) depends nonlinearily on α. But the new error sequence $\eta := Ce$ now depends also on the same parameter α and hence so does its distribution. But in most regression problems the error d.f. is merely a nuisance quantity not to be estimated. One must ask oneself whether the model (1.1) or equivalently (1.4) really is appropriate for the phenomenon and the data to be modelled. Probably in most cases it is not. It must be kept in mind, however, that in the purely autoregressive situation ($Z \equiv 0$, $q = 0$, γ absent) which is a special case of our model, of course it is just the probabilistic structure, at least its aspect expressed by α, which is of interest and to be estimated. Probably since (1.1) is intended as a mixed regression it may be difficult to decide in a given situation which of the two aspects, the deterministic representation or the probabilistic structure is of primary interest. The answer may in addition be obscured by the cursory fact that simultaneous analysis is relatively simple because (1.1) is linear both in α and γ.

We shall first now construct an *example of non-identifiability* of the deterministic regression part in the model (1.4), i.e. there exist two different parameter vectors (α,γ), $(\bar{\alpha},\bar{\gamma})$ with $\alpha \neq \bar{\alpha}$, $\gamma \neq \bar{\gamma}$ and matrices $Z \neq 0$ such that in case $\xi_t := Ey_t$ exists and $E\,\varepsilon_t = 0$

(1.5) $$\xi_t = \xi_{t-1}\alpha_1 + \ldots + \xi_{t-p}\alpha_p + z_{t1}\gamma_1 + \ldots + z_{tq}\gamma_q \qquad \forall t$$

or in the general case

(1.6) $$CZ\gamma = \bar{C}Z\bar{\gamma} \text{ or equivalently } \bar{C}^{-1}Z\gamma = C^{-1}Z\bar{\gamma}$$

since C^{-1} and $\bar{C}^{-1}$ are commutative lower triangular Toeplitz matrices. The second notation of (1.6) has the great advantage (besides being linear in the γ's for α fixed) to also be linear in the α's (γ fixed) - but still bilinear in the parameters $\binom{\alpha}{\gamma}$ all together.

Many examples satisfying (1.6) can be found. One easily verifies that the following simple one is a non-pathological case: put $q = 2$, $p = 1$;

$$\alpha = 1/2,\ \gamma' = (2.2);\ \bar{\alpha} = 1/4,\ \bar{\gamma}' = (1,3);$$

$$Z' = \begin{pmatrix} 1 & 1 & \ldots\ldots & 1 \\ & & & \\ 1 & 2 & \ldots\ldots & n \end{pmatrix}.$$

In concluding the introduction it should be stressed that this paper does not pay attention to the important practical aspects of computability nor to measurement errors in the Z's.

II. MAIN RESULTS

PROPOSITION 2.1. *The* LSEs $\binom{\alpha}{\gamma}_{LSE}$ *defined by* (1.3) *for the parameters* α,γ *in the model* (1.1) *are weakly consistent under alternative sets of assumptions. In both sets we assume that the error sequence* (ε_t), $t \in \mathbb{N}$ *satisfies*

$$(2.1) \qquad \sum_1^n \varepsilon_t^2 \to \infty \text{ and } \varepsilon_n^2/\sum_1^n \varepsilon_t^2 \to 0 \quad \text{a.s.} \quad \text{as } n \to \infty$$

and that (2.4) *and* (2.5) *below hold. The consistency of* α_{LSE} *alone holds irrespective of consistency of* γ_{LSE} *under the additional assumptions* (2.2'), (2.3'):

$$(2.2') \qquad \Big(\sum_{t=1}^{n-j} \varepsilon_t \varepsilon_{t+j}\Big)/\sum_1^n \varepsilon_t^2 \to 0 \quad \text{i.p.} \quad \text{for } j = 1,2,\ldots$$

$$(2.3') \qquad \Big(\sum_{t=1}^{n} a_{nt}\varepsilon_t\Big)\Big(\sum_1^n a_t^2 \sum_1^n \varepsilon_t^2\Big)^{-1/2} \to 0 \quad \text{i.p.}$$

for every double sequence of constants $(a_{1n},\ldots,a_{nn}) \in R^n$, $n \in \mathbb{N}$.

In addition γ_{LSE} *is consistent if the stronger assumptions*

$$(2.2) \qquad \Big(\sum_1^n \varepsilon_t^2\Big)^{-1/2} \max_{j=1,\ldots,n} \Big|\sum_{t=1}^{n-j} \varepsilon_t \varepsilon_{t+j}\Big| = 0_p(1)$$

and

$$(2.3) \qquad \Big(\sum_{t=1}^{n} a_{nt}^2\Big)^{-1/2} \sum_{t=1}^{n} a_{nt}\, \varepsilon_t = 0_p(1)$$

for all $(a_{n1},\ldots,a_{nn})$ *hold. If only* (2.2')/(2.3') *hold then*

(2.3'') $\lambda_{max}(P)/\lambda_{min}(P) < c < \infty \qquad \forall n,\ P: = Z'Z$

(2.3''') $\sum_1^n \varepsilon_t^2/\lambda_{min}^2(P) = 0_p(1)$

suffice for the consistency of γ_{LSE} *(as well as of* α_{LSE}*). Further assumptions are throughout: the (non-stochastic) regressors satisfy*

(2.4) $\lambda_{min}(P) \to \infty;$

moreover, the true parameters $\alpha_1,\ldots,\alpha_p$ *of the autoregressive part satisfy the stability assumption,* i.e. *the roots* ζ *of*

(2.5) $\zeta^p - \alpha_1\zeta^{p-1} - \ldots - \alpha_p = 0$ *are in modulus strictly* < 1.

Several comments and examples to this proposition are given in Section 3.

Remark 1. In order to verify (2.3') for a particular error sequence (ε_t) it suffices under (2.1) to verify them only for the particular triangular arrays (a_{nt}) of constants with non-zero rows $a \equiv a_{(n)}$ and satisfying the uniform asymptotic negligibility (uan) condition

(2.3'') $\max_{t=1,\ldots,n} a_{nt}^2/\sum_{s=1}^n a_{ns}^2 \to 0 \qquad$ as $n \to \infty$.

Denote the set of all such arrays by A.

To see this let $\delta > o$ be arbitrarily given and let

$$T_n: = \{t \in \{1,\ldots,n\}: |a_{nt}| > \delta||a_{(n)}||\}.$$

Necessarily $|T_n| < \delta^{-2}$ for all n. Hence by (2.1) [which is equivalent with $\varepsilon_{k_n}^2/\sum_1^n \varepsilon_t^2 \to 0$ for any sequence (k_n) of naturals. Indirect proof.]

$$(*) \qquad \sum_{t\in T_n} a_{nt}\ \varepsilon_t/||a_{(n)}|| \to 0 \quad \text{a.s.}$$

Since $\delta > 0$ was arbitrary there exists a sequence $\delta_n \downarrow 0$ such that (*) still holds. But then the remaining set of constants $\{a_{nt},\ t \notin T_n,\ n \in \mathbb{N}\} \in A$ for which (2.3') was assumed to hold.

Remark 2. Note that (2.3) implies $\varepsilon_n = 0_p(1)$ so that, under (2.1a), (2.1b) would follow. Anyway, the consistent estimation of γ under the present setup is somewhat problematical.

Remark 3. It has been pointed out that often in practice the length of the various exogenous regressors (columns of Z) grow with comparable speeds as n grows. Hence the assumptions (2.4) may often be too general, and narrower conditions on the Z_n should be traded in against wider conditions on the ε_t. (2.3"), (2.3" ') are of this type, although these conditions may be too extreme in the opposite direction.

2.1 *Simple Properties of the Model*

for the discussion of the theorem and for its proof we need the following preliminary properties and notations. Put

$$(2.6) \qquad C_n^{-1} \equiv C^{-1} := I_n - \sum_{j=1}^{p} \alpha_j\ L_n^j, \text{ with } \alpha_j'\text{s satisfying (2.5).}$$

Then the inverse of $C = \sum_{j=0}^{n-1} c_j\ L^j$ and $|c_j| < \text{const}\ \rho^j\ \forall n,j$ for some constant $0 < \rho < 1$ (comp. 3.3 and [4], p. 462). The c_j can be determined algebraically from the α_i and they are independent of n. Moreover

$$(2.7) \qquad 0 < c' < \lambda_{min}(C'C) \leq \lambda_{max}(C'C) < c'' \leq \infty\ \forall n,$$

with constants c', c" independent of n.

The model equation (1.2) can now be resolved for y:

$$(2.7a) \qquad y = C(Z\ \gamma + e) = CZ\gamma + C\ e$$

with non linear deterministic exogenous regression part $CZ\gamma$ and a new error sequence $C\,e$. The original model (1,2) then can be rewritten in order to investigate its probabilistic properties in the form

$$y = L_{C(Z\gamma+e)}\alpha + Z\gamma + e = Z_L\binom{\alpha}{\gamma} + L_{Ce}\alpha + e$$

where

$$\text{(2.7b)} \qquad Z_L := (L_{CZ\gamma}, Z) = C(L_{Z\gamma}, C^{-1} Z)$$

is the deterministic part.

A crucial property of the model for fixed (though unknown) α,γ is the collinearity or near-collinearity of the matrix

$$\bar{Z} := (L_{Z\gamma}, C^{-1} Z).$$

which is a function of Z_L. In view of consistency only a suitable weaker concept of *asymptotic* (near-)collinearity is needed. We note that only $\bar{Z}$ depends on γ, the error $C\,e$ does not. It is important to remember the non-trivial and non-pathological example of a strictly collinear matrix $\bar{Z}$ for all n with Z satisfying (2.4) (comp. the Introduction). In such a case no consistent estimation of γ can be possible and the same is true for some sort of asymptotic near-collinearity usually. As was pointed out this is only a property of the regression matrices Z and the parameter constellation and is completely independent of the error sequence.

Next for any $n\times k$-matrix or n-vector A put, like in Section 1

$$L_A := (LA, \ldots, L^p A).$$

Note e.g., $L_{Ce} = CL_e$. For the $n\times q$ partial non-stochastic regression matrix $Z \equiv Z_n$ we put $Z^2 := Z'Z \equiv P$ and assume n so large that P is non-singular under assumption (2.4). Similarly, e.g., put $L^2_{Ce} := L'_{Ce} L_{Ce}$. Further let, now always for n large enough,

$$(2.8) \qquad Q: = I - Z\,P^{-1}Z' = Q^2$$

the $n\times n$ - projection matrix on span $Z^{\perp}$, the linear subspace $\subset R^n$ spanned by n-q linearly independent vectors orthogonal to the columns of Z_n, $I \equiv I_n: = \mathrm{diag}(1,\ldots,1)$, the n-th identity matrix. Define further the $p\times p$-matrix

$$(2.9) \qquad T: = L_{Ce}^2 + L'_{CZ\gamma}Q\,L_{CZ\gamma} = (CL_e)^2 + (QL_{CZ\gamma})^2$$

and

$$(2.10) \qquad M: = \begin{pmatrix} T^{1/2} & 0 \\ P^{-1/2}Z'L_{CZ\gamma} & P^{1/2} \end{pmatrix}_{(p+q)\times(p+q)} = \begin{pmatrix} T^{1/2} & 0 \\ 0 & P^{1/2} \end{pmatrix}\begin{pmatrix} I_p & 0 \\ P^{-1}Z'L_{CZ\gamma} & I_q \end{pmatrix}.$$

According to Lemma 2.2 below $|T| > 0$ on events Ω_n with $P\Omega_n \to 1$ under assumptions (2.1), (2.2) and (2.5). Thus on Ω_n there exists T^{-1} and one verifies or concludes from general matrix algebra

$$(2.11) \qquad M^{-1} = \begin{pmatrix} T^{-1/2} & 0 \\ -P^{-1}\,Z'L_{CZ\gamma}\quad T^{-1/2} & P^{-1/2} \end{pmatrix} = \begin{pmatrix} I_p & 0 \\ -P^{-1}\,Z'L_{CZ\gamma} & I_q \end{pmatrix}\begin{pmatrix} T^{-1/2} & 0 \\ 0 & P^{-1/2} \end{pmatrix}$$

[If one prefers this equality to hold on the entire sample space one may replace the inverse matrices of T and M on Ω_n^c by suitable generalized inverses. But if (weak or strong) consistency holds in the above theorem it is of no interest what happens on the Ω_n^c.] Further

$$
(2.12)\qquad
\begin{aligned}
M'M &= \left(\begin{array}{c|c} L_{Ce}^2 + L_{CZ\gamma}^2 & L'_{CZ\gamma}\ Z \\ \hline Z'\ L_{CZ\gamma} & P \end{array}\right) \\
&= Z_L^2 + (L_{Ce},0)^2 \qquad (Z_L: = (L_{CZ\gamma},Z)),
\end{aligned}
$$

$$
\begin{aligned}
(M'M)^{-1} &= M^{-1}M'^{-1} \\
&= \left(\begin{array}{c|c} T^{-1} & -T^{-1}L'_{CZ\gamma}ZP^{-1} \\ \hline -P^{-1}Z'L_{CZ\gamma}T^{-1} & P^{-1}Z'L_{CZ\gamma}T^{-1}L'_{CZ\gamma}ZP^{-1}+P^{-1} \end{array}\right)
\end{aligned}
$$

$$
(2.13)\qquad
\begin{aligned}
&= \left(\begin{array}{c|c} T^{-1/2} & 0 \\ \hline 0 & P^{-1/2} \end{array}\right) \times \\
&\left(\begin{array}{c|c} I_p & -T^{-1/2}L'_{CZ\gamma}ZP^{-1/2} \\ \hline -P^{-1/2}Z'L_{CZ\gamma}T^{-1/2} & I_q+P^{-1/2}Z'L_{CZ\gamma}T^{-1}L'_{CZ\gamma}ZP^{-1/2} \end{array}\right)\times \\
&\times \left(\begin{array}{c|c} T^{-1/2} & 0 \\ \hline 0 & P^{-1/2} \end{array}\right) .
\end{aligned}
$$

The regression matrix $X = (L_y,Z)$ in the model (1.2) can now be rewritten using $L_{CZ\gamma + Ce} = L_{CZ\gamma} + L_{Ce}$ in the form

$$
(2.14)\qquad X = (L_{CZ\gamma},Z) + (L_{Ce},0).
$$

We use the notation $X_n = O_P(1)$, in words (X_n) is stochastically bounded, if for any $\eta > 0$ there exist constants $K_\eta > 0$ independent of n and an $n_\eta \in \mathbb{N}$ such that

$$
(2.15)\qquad P(|X_n| > K_\eta) < \eta \qquad \forall n > n_\eta .
$$

2.2 *Proof of the Theorem*

The normal equations (1.3) are equivalent to

$$(2.16) \qquad X^2 \binom{\hat{\alpha}}{\hat{\gamma}} = X'e \text{ where } \binom{\hat{\alpha}}{\hat{\gamma}} := \binom{\alpha}{\gamma}_{LSE} - \binom{\alpha}{\gamma}.$$

It is to be shown $\binom{\hat{\alpha}}{\hat{\gamma}} \underset{P}{\rightarrow} 0$.

In the course of the proof it will be shown for a finite number of sequences of r.v.'s depending on the e_t's that they are simultaneously bounded i.p. or converge to zero stochastically under the assumptions of the theorem. The r.v.'s of these sequences will be inserted into certain expressions or inequalities and thus again finitely many new sequences of r.v.'s will be obtained. In this process the simultaneous boundedness or convergence properties or the original sequences will be exploited and can as well be stated simultaneously for the new set of sequences. The ultimate sequence thus obtained is that of the LSE's whose (simultaneous) stochastic convergence to the parameters then is exhibited.

We have with Z_L defined by (2.7b)

$$(2.17) \qquad X^2 = (Z_L + (L_{Ce},0))^2 = M'M + \binom{L'_{Ce}}{0} Z_L + Z'_L(L_{Ce},0)$$

and we will show first

$$(2.18) \qquad X^2 = M'(I + o_P(1))M.$$

Here o_P is a $(p+q)\times(p+q)$-matrix whose elements are $o_P(1)$. To a large extent the following proof rests upon the fact that under the assumptions (especially (2.3)) the lagged error vectors $L^j e$ and the columns of Z_L are in some sense nearly asymptotically orthogonal. Consequently certain mixed products in (2.17) can be neglected.

Moreover, the algebraic decomposition of the main term M'M of X'X in (2.17) - which accomplishes a partial diagonalization of

X^2 - is essentially equivalent to the orthogonal decomposition (projection) onto $M(Z)$, the linear space in R^n spanned by the (linearly independent) column vectors of Z, and on its orthocomplement in R^n, denoted by $pr_{\tilde{Z}}$ resp. $pr_{Z^\perp}$. It is provided by the n×n-projection matrices $\tilde{Z}\tilde{Z}'$ ($\tilde{Z} := ZP^{-1/2}$ having orthonormal columns) resp. $Q = I_n - \tilde{Z}\tilde{Z}'$ already defined under (2.8). In obvious notation the whole matrix of columns of $L_{CZ\gamma}$ projected on $M(Z)$ is denoted resp. given by

$$(2.19) \qquad pr_{\tilde{Z}} L_{CZ\gamma} = \tilde{Z}\tilde{Z}' L_{CZ\gamma} =: L_Z .$$

Similarly

$$(2.20) \qquad pr_{Z^\perp} L_{CZ\gamma} = QL_{CZ\gamma} =: L_\perp .$$

Then in

$$(2.21) \qquad X = (L_{Ce} + L_Z + L_\perp, Z) = (L_{Ce},0) + (L_\perp,0) + (L_Z,Z)$$

the last three matrices are mutually columnwise exactly resp. stochastically asymptotically near-orthogonal. Consequently (2.17) splits up further as follows

$$(2.22) \qquad X^2 = \begin{pmatrix} L_{Ce}^2 & 0 \\ 0 & 0 \end{pmatrix} + \begin{pmatrix} L_\perp^2 & 0 \\ 0 & 0 \end{pmatrix} + \begin{pmatrix} L_Z^2 & L_Z'Z \\ Z'L_Z & Z^2 \end{pmatrix} + A$$

with

$$(2.23) \qquad A := \begin{pmatrix} L_{Ce}' & Z_L \\ 0 & \end{pmatrix} + (Z_L' L_{Ce},0)$$

$$(Z_L := (L_{CZ\gamma},Z) = (L_\perp + L_Z,Z)).$$

Under our assumption the sum of the first three matrices on the r.h.s. of (2.22) will be shown to be the leading terms and to equal M'M. Noting (2.9) we have

$$(2.24)\qquad X^2 = \begin{pmatrix} T & 0 \\ 0 & 0 \end{pmatrix} + M_2^2 + A = M'M + A, \qquad \left[\begin{pmatrix} T & 0 \\ 0 & 0 \end{pmatrix} = M_1^2\right]$$

if we split up

$$(2.25)\qquad M = \begin{pmatrix} M_1' \\ \hline M_2' \end{pmatrix}, \quad M_1' := (T^{1/2}, 0), \quad M_2' := (\tilde{Z}' L_{CZ\gamma}, P^{1/2})$$

so that

$$(2.26)\qquad M'M = M_1 M_1' + M_2 M_2'.$$

Note here

$$(2.27)\qquad L_Z^2 = L'_{CZ\gamma} \tilde{Z}\, \tilde{Z}' L_{CZ\gamma}, \quad L_Z' Z = L'_{CZ\gamma} \tilde{Z}\, \tilde{Z}' Z = L'_{CZ\gamma} \tilde{Z}\, P^{-1/2+1}$$

$$= L'_{CZ\gamma} \tilde{Z}\, P^{1/2}.$$

The notation (2.26) shows the parallelism of the algebraic decomposition of X^2 (i.e. essentially (2.26)), and the above geometric decomposition. We note incidentally that in a purely algebraic treatment the following identity may be used: consider the matrices $A(n\times n)$ non-singular, $B(n\times m)$, $C(m\times n)$, $D(m\times m)$, $E: = D-CA^{-1}B$ (Schur complement). Then

$$\left(\begin{array}{c|c} A & B \\ \hline C & D \end{array}\right) = \left(\begin{array}{c|c} A & 0 \\ \hline C & I_m \end{array}\right) \left(\begin{array}{c|c} I_n & A^{-1}B \\ \hline 0 & E \end{array}\right).$$

Regarding geometric decompositions, many similar projections onto two ore more (upto p+q) mutually orthogonal linear subspaces of the R^n could be explicitly executed. They are equivalent to partial diagonalizations algebraically. In particular, pr $CZ\gamma$ for $\gamma \neq 0$ might be rewarding. Another example is the p+q-fold orthogonal decomposition on p+q orthogonal subspaces accomplished by the operator $pr_{a_1} + \ldots + pr_{a_{p+q}}$ where a_j are the orthonormal columns of $Z_L\, Z_L^{-1/2}$. It would lead to a complete diagonalization of Z_L^2 and thus (nearly) of

$$X^2 - \begin{pmatrix} L_{Ce}^2 & 0 \\ 0 & 0 \end{pmatrix}.$$

However, it appears that none of these various procedures would yield any substantial advantages in the proof (or even weaker assumptions of the theorem). Hence we shall stick to the approach begun with (2.17) and investigate first the matrix T now.

Let $\lambda_{min}A$, $\lambda_{max}A$ denote the largest and smallest eigenvalue of any p×p symmetric positive definite matrix A. We first strengthen Lemma 2.2. Let c, c', c_1, c_1' be positive finite constants independent of n. Then on events Ω_n with $P\,\Omega_n \to 1$ under the assumptions (2.5) and under (2.2'): $e'\,L^j e = o_p(||e||^2)$ for $j = 1,2,\ldots,p$ we have for any fixed γ [using the notation $a \vee b := \max\{a,b\}$ for reals a,b]

$$(2.28)\quad a)\quad c_1(||e||^2 \vee \lambda_{min}(QL_{CZ\gamma})^2) < \lambda_{min}T < c(||e||^2 \vee \lambda_{min}(QL_{CZ\gamma})^2)$$

$$(2.29)\quad b)\quad c_1'(||e||^2 \vee \lambda_{max}(QL_{CZ\gamma})^2) < \lambda_{max}T < c'(||e||^2 \vee \lambda_{max}(QL_{CZ\gamma})^2).$$

With the earlier notation $QL_{CZ\gamma} = L_\perp$ we obtain from the definition $T = L_{Ce}^2 + L_\perp^2$ hence the assertions follow immediately from (2.7) and Lemma 2.2 below.

We now show that in the representation (2.22) of X^2 the matrix A can be neglected compared with M'M, more precisely (comp. (2.18))

$$(2.29)\qquad X^2 = M'(I_{p+q} + o_p(1))M.$$

The matrix A contains

$$(2.30)\qquad \left(\begin{array}{cc} L'_{Ce} & Z_L \\ \hline & 0 \end{array}\right) = \left(\begin{array}{cc|c} L'_{Ce} & L_\perp & 0 \\ \hline & 0 & 0 \end{array}\right) + \left(\begin{array}{c} L'_{Ce} \\ 0 \end{array}\right) (L_Z, Z) =: A_1 + A_2$$

plus the transpose of this. Hence it suffices to consider first

$$(2.31)\qquad M'^{-1} A_1 M^{-1} = \left(\begin{array}{c|c} T^{-1/2} L'_e (C' L_\perp T^{-1/2}) & 0 \\ \hline 0 & 0 \end{array}\right).$$

Let N be the modal matrix of $L_\perp^2$, i.e. $L_\perp N$ has orthogonal columns and $N' L_\perp^2 N =: \Delta^2$, a diagonal matrix. Then using $T \overset{d}{=} L_{Ce}^2 + L_\perp^2$ we have $N'TN =: \Delta(I_p + S)\Delta$ where S is a positive definite matrix. Consequently

$$(2.32)\qquad L_\perp T^{-1} L'_\perp = L_\perp N (N'TN)^{-1} N' L'_\perp = L_\perp N \Delta^{-1} (I_p + S)^{-1} \Delta^{-1} N' L'_\perp .$$

If a column of $L_\perp N$ has length zero the corresponding element of Δ^{-1} may be replaced by one. Then the columns of $L_\perp N \Delta^{-1}$ are orthogonal and of uniformly bounded length resp. zero. The elements of $(I_p + S)^{-1}$ are uniformly bounded by a positive constant. Now the elements of $L'_e (C' L_\perp T^{-1/2})$ are of the shape $(1 + o_p(1)) e' L^{j'} a = o_p(||e||)$, the latter by assumption (2.3'), with vectors a bounded in norm uniformly in n. Since $\lambda_{\min} T^{-1} > c||e||^2$ on Ω_n by (2.28b) we finally have

$$(2.33)\qquad M'^{-1} A_1 M^{-1} = o_p(1).$$

Next in (2.30) it is to be considered $M'^{-1} A_2 M^{-1}$ which gives rise to

$$(2.34)\qquad (L_Z, Z) M^{-1} = (L_Z, Z) \left(\begin{array}{c|c} I_p & 0 \\ \hline -P^{-1} Z' L_{CZ\gamma} & I_q \end{array}\right) \left(\begin{array}{c|c} T^{-1/2} & 0 \\ \hline & P^{-1/2} \end{array}\right)$$

$$= (0, ZP^{-1/2}) =: (0, \tilde{Z})$$

with orthonormal columns in $\tilde{Z}$. Consequently

$$(2.35) \qquad M'^{-1}A_2M^{-1} = M'^{-1}\begin{pmatrix} L'_e \\ 0 \end{pmatrix} C'(0,\tilde{Z}) = M'^{-1}\left(\begin{array}{c|c} 0 & o_p(||e||) \\ \hline 0 & 0 \end{array}\right)$$

$$= \left(\begin{array}{c|c} 0 & T^{-1/2}\ o_p(||e||) \\ \hline 0 & 0 \end{array}\right) = o_p(1)$$

where $o_p(\cdot)$ denote matrices with $o(\cdot)$-elements due to (2.3') and (2.28). This proves (2.18).

Next the right-hand side of the normal equations (2.16) premultiplied by $(M')^{-1}$ will be shown to satisfy

$$M'^{-1}X'e$$

$$(2.36a) \qquad = \left(\begin{array}{c|c} T^{-1/2} & 0 \\ \hline 0 & P^{-1/2} \end{array}\right)\left(\begin{array}{c|c} I_p & -L'_{CZ\gamma}\tilde{Z}P^{-1/2} \\ \hline 0 & I_q \end{array}\right) \times$$

$$\times \left\{\begin{pmatrix} L'_{Ce}+L'_{\perp} \\ \hline 0 \end{pmatrix} + \begin{pmatrix} L'_Z \\ \hline Z' \end{pmatrix}\right\} e$$

$$(2.36b) \qquad = \begin{pmatrix} T^{-1/2}(L'_{Ce}+L'_{\perp}) \\ \hline \tilde{Z}' \end{pmatrix} e = ||e|| \cdot o_p(1)$$

under (2.2'), (2.3') with a (p+q)-vector $o_p(1)$ as is seen as follows. For the last q components of (2.36b) the assertion is obvious from (2.3'). In

$$L'_{Ce}\ e = \left(\sum_{j=0}^{n-1} c_j\ e'\ L^{j+1}\ e, \ldots, \sum_{j=0}^{n-1} c_j\ e'\ L^{j+p} e\right)$$

each of the sequences $||e||^{-2}e'\ L^j e =: X_{jn} \to 0$ i.p. by (2.2') for any $j > 0$. Then there exists a sequence $j_n \uparrow \infty$ such that $\max_{j=1,\ldots,j_n} |X_{jn}| \to 0$ i.p. because if $\Omega_{jn} := (|X_{jn}| < \varepsilon)$ then

$P\Omega_{jn} \underset{n\to\infty}{\to} 1 \ \forall j$ and hence there exists $j_n \uparrow \infty$ such that

$P(\bigcap_{j=1}^{j_n} \Omega_{jn}) \to 1$. Using this and the fact that by the Cauchy-Schwarz inequality surely $\sup_{j,n}|X_{jn}| \le 1$ we have for $k = 1,\ldots,p$

$$(2.37) \qquad ||e||^{-2}\left|\sum_{j=o}^{n-1} c_j \ e'L^{j+k} \ e\right|$$

$$\le \max_{j=o,\ldots,j_n-k} |X_{jn}| c' \sum_{j=o}^{j_n} \rho^j + c'\rho^{j_n}(1-\rho)^{-1}$$

$$\to 0 \text{ i.p.}$$

where $|c_j| < c' \ \rho^j$, $0 < p < 1$.

Next in (2.36b) put $B: = (L_\perp' \ L_\perp)^{1/2}$ and use a generalized inverse B^{-1} if necessary. Obviously

$$\lambda_p(B^{-1} \ TB^{-1}) = \lambda_p(I_p + B^{-1} \ L_{Ce}^2 \ B^{-1}) \ge 1.$$

Now

$$(2.38) \qquad ||T^{-1/2}L_\perp' \ e||^2 \le \lambda_1(B \ T^{-1} \ B)||B^{-1}L_\perp' \ e||^2 = o_p(||e||^2)$$

by (2.3'). Hence (2.36b) is completely proved.

Now the normal equations (NEs) are equivalent to

$$(2.39) \qquad M\binom{\hat{\alpha}}{\gamma} = ||e||o_p(1).$$

With (2.12) is follows that

$$(2.40) \qquad ||M\binom{\hat{\alpha}}{\gamma}||^2 = ||Z_L\binom{\hat{\alpha}}{\gamma}||^2 + ||CL_e\hat{\alpha}||^2 = ||e||^2 \ o_p(1).$$

By (2.7) and since $||e||^{-2}L_e^2 = I_p + o_p(1)$ under (2.2') it follows in particular $o_p(1) \geq ||\hat{\alpha}||^2$, i.e. $\hat{\alpha} \to 0$ i.p.. Next then (2.40) reduces to

$$(2.41) \qquad ||Z_L \begin{pmatrix} o_p(1) \\ \hat{\gamma} \end{pmatrix} ||^2 = ||e||^2 \, o_p(1).$$

Now since for every admitted α and γ-vector, $\gamma \neq 0$, any $p > 0$, $q > 1$, we can easily construct Z-matrices such that $\text{rk } Z_L < p + q$ for all n, consistency of $\hat{\gamma}$ cannot be inferred from (2.41). Therefore now and only now the stronger assumptions (2.2), (2.3) are invoked. We will show that they imply for the NE's instead of (2.39)

$$(2.42) \qquad M\binom{\hat{\alpha}}{\hat{\gamma}} = O_p(1).$$

If then we can also show $\lambda_{min} M^2 \to \infty$ i.p. both relations together again imply the weak consistency of $\binom{\hat{\alpha}}{\hat{\gamma}}$.

To show that the right hand side (r.h.s.) (2.36a) of the NEs is now $O_p(1)$ consider first the term $T^{-1/2} L'_{Ce} e$ arising in (2.36a). It satisfies, involving (2.28),

$$(2.43) \qquad ||T^{-1/2} L'_{Ce} e||^2 \leq \lambda_{max}(T^{-1}) ||L'_{Ce} e||^2$$

$$\leq (c' + o_p(1)) ||e||^{-2} \sum_{j=1}^{p} (e'CL^j e)^2, \; c' > 0 \text{ constant.}$$

Now

$$|e'CL^j e| = |\sum_{k=o}^{n-1} c_k e'L^{j+1} e| \leq c'' \sup_{k>o} k^{-M} |e'L^k e| \sum_{j=o}^{\infty} \rho^j j^M$$

with constants $c'' > 0$ and $\rho \in (0,1)$ and $M > 0$ arbitrarily large. With the assumption (2.2) one then obtains for (2.43)

$$(2.44) \qquad ||T^{-1/2} L'_{Ce} e||^2 = O_p(1).$$

Similarly, since by definition of T the rows of $T^{-1/2} L'_I$ have length $\leq$ 1, (2.3) immediately implies for the second term in (2.36a) $T^{-1/2} L_{\perp}' e = O_p(1)$. Now in the third term of (2.36a) we use $(I_p, - L'_{CZ\gamma} \tilde{Z} P^{-1/2}) \begin{pmatrix} L'Z \\ --- \\ Z \end{pmatrix} = 0$. Hence only $\tilde{Z}'e = O_p(1)$ remains.

Now consistency of $\hat{\alpha},\hat{\gamma}$ follows if we have shown

$$(2.45) \qquad \lambda_{min} (M'M) \to \infty;$$

this is true solely under (2.1), (2.2'), (2.4) and (2.5). Now by (2.12) we have

$$M'M = (L_{CZ\gamma}, Z)^2 + (CL_e, 0)^2$$

and each of the two matrix sequences $A_n := (L_{C_n Z_n \gamma}, Z_n)^2$ and $B_n := (C_n L_{e_{(n)}}, 0)^2$ are increasing in the sense that, e.g., $A_{n+1} - A_n = a_{n+1} a'_{n+1} \geq 0$ where a_n' is the n-th row of A_n. Now Lemma 2.1 is applicable since for any fixed non-zero vector $c = \binom{b}{d}$, $b \in R^p$, $d \in R^q$ we have $||Mc||^2 \to \infty$ because if $b \neq 0$ then already $b'B_n b \to \infty$ as fast as $const||e_{(n)}||^2$ due to assumption (2.1) and if $b = 0$ then necessarily $d \neq 0$ implying $||Mc|| = ||Zd|| \to \infty$ like $const\ \lambda_{min}(P)$ due to assumption (2.4).

Finally it remains to prove that (2.2'), (2.3') and (2.3") besides the other assumptions imply consistency of γ_{LSE}. This may be seen from the last q of the set of NE's (2.16):

$$Z'L_Z \hat{\alpha} + P \hat{\gamma} = Z'e$$

or equivalently, with $\tilde{Z} := Z P^{-1/2}$,

$$(2.46) \qquad P^{-1/2} \tilde{Z}' L_Z \hat{\alpha} + \hat{\gamma} = ||e|| P^{-1/2} o_p(1) = o_p(1)$$

where the two last equalities follow from assumptions (2.3') and (2.3' "). The first term in (2.46) tends to zero due to Schwarz inequality and due to (2.3") and because $\hat{\alpha} \to 0$ i.p.. This completes the proof of Theorem 2.1.

The lemma used repeatedly in the above proof has been applied and proved e.g. by Drygas [3] (see also [6], p.38). It states:

LEMMA 2.1. *Let* A_n *be a sequence of real symmetric* $k \times k$ *matrices satisfying* $A_{n+1} - A_n \geq 0 \ \forall n \in \mathbb{N}$. *Then* $\lambda_{min} A_n \to \infty$ iff

$$c'A_n c \to \infty \text{ for every fixed non zero vector } c \in R^k. \tag{2.47}$$

LEMMA 2.2. *The matrices* T, C, L_e *defined above satisfy under the assumptions (the first one follows from* (22))

$$e'L^j e = o_p(||e||^2) \ \forall\ j = 1,\dots,p \text{ and } ||e|| \to \infty, \tag{2.48}$$

and under (2.1) *and* (2.5) *the relation*

$$\lambda_{min} T \geq \lambda_{min} L^2_{Ce} \geq c\ \lambda_{min} L^2_e \doteq c||e||^2(1+o_p(1)) \to \infty \tag{2.49}$$

with $\lambda_{min} C^2 \geq c > 0$, c *independent of* n. *Here* $o_p(1)$ *can be replaced by an* a.s. *convergent null sequence* o(1) *if* (2.47) *holds* a.s..

Proof. The last inequality in (2.49) follows from Lemma 2.1, because $L^2_{e_{n+1}} - L^2_{e_n}$ is positive semi-definite $\forall n$ on the entire sample space; moreover for any constant $a \in R^p$, $a \neq 0$,

$$a'L^2_e a = ||L_e a||^2 = ||(\sum_{j=1}^{p} a_j L^j)e||^2 = \sum_1^p a_j^2||L^j e||^2 +$$

$$+ 2\sum_{i \neq j} a_i a_j\ e'L'^i L^j e \to \infty$$

since $||e|| \to \infty$ a.s. by the assumptions of the lemma and since then for $i \neq j$ from $\{1,\dots,p\}$ we have
$e'L'^i L^j e = o_p(||e||^2)$ resp. a.s..

III. EXAMPLES AND COMMENTS

First it will be shown in Example 1 that Willers' result [7] (Satz 4) follows easily from Theorem 2.1.

Example 3.1 [7]. Let the sequence $\varepsilon_1, \varepsilon_2, \ldots$ satisfy

$$(3.1) \qquad E\varepsilon_t = 0,\ E\varepsilon_t^2 > \underline{\sigma}^2 > 0,\ E\varepsilon_t^4 < \mu < \infty \quad \forall t,$$

and let it be quasiindependent of order four, i.e. the mixed moments of the ε_t upto order 4 behave as if the ε_t were independent. Then conditions (2.1) - (2.3) of Proposition 2.1 concerning e are satisfied. If also (2.4) and (2.5) hold the theorem is true and consistency holds.

In order to prove this we will show first (3.2) rather than the stronger (2.2). (3.2) is needed in (2.43) and is defined by

$$(3.2) \qquad ||e||^{-1}\, e'CL^j e = 0_p(1) \qquad (j = 1,\ldots,p)$$

i.e. we have to show that

$$(3.3) \qquad P(||e||^{-1}|e'CL^j e| > \delta)$$

is as small > 0 as we like for any δ and large n. We first show that the first of the properties (2.1) holds: for any constant $c \in (0,\underline{\sigma}^2)$ we have

$$(3.4) \qquad 1\text{-}PA = PA^c \underset{n\to\infty}{\to} 0, \quad A: = (||e||^2 \geq cn)$$

since

$$\begin{aligned}(3.5) \quad PA^c &\leq P((||e||^2 - E||e||^2 < (c-\underline{\sigma}^2)n) \leq \\ &\leq P((||e||^2 - E||e||^2)^2 > (c-\underline{\sigma}^2)^2 n^2) \\ &\leq (c-\underline{\sigma}^2)^{-2} n^{-2}\ E(||e||^2 - E||e||^2)^2 \\ &\leq n^{-1}\ \mu(c-\underline{\sigma}^2)^{-2} \to 0;\end{aligned}$$

here $E(\sum_t(\varepsilon_t^2 - E\varepsilon_t^2)^2)^2 < \mu n$ has been used.

Now in (3.3) with $\kappa := \delta\sqrt{c}$ and a suitable constant $\rho \in (0,1)$

(3.6) $$P(||e||^{-1}|e'CL^{j}e| > \delta) \leq o(1) + P(|e'CL^{j}e| > \kappa\sqrt{n})$$

$$\leq o(1) + P(\sum_{k=o}^{n-1} \rho^{k}|e' L^{j+k}e| > \kappa\sqrt{n})$$

$$\leq o(1) + \kappa^{-1}n^{-1/2}\sum_{k} \rho^{k} E|e' L^{j+k}e| = o(1)+\text{const}/\kappa;$$

here we use

(3.7) $$E|e' L^{m}e| \leq (E(e'L^{m}e)^{2})^{1/2} \leq \mu^{1/2}n^{1/2} \text{ for } m > 0.$$

Next, condition (2.3) is also satisfied since $E(e'a)^{2} \leq ||a||^{2}\mu^{1/2}$ and thus by Markov's inequality for any $\delta > 0$

(3.8) $$P(|e'a|/||a|| > \delta) \leq \delta^{-2}||a||^{-2}E(e'a)^{2} = \delta^{-2}\mu^{1/2} \quad \forall n.$$

Condition (2.1) is trivially satisfied.

One can also show that (2.2) is satisfied (although this isn't needed anymore since (3.2) holds). Using (3.4), the Markov inequality and (3.7) we have

(3.9) $$P(AA_{mn}) \leq P(|e' L^{m}e| > Km^{M}(cn)^{1/2})$$

$$\leq K^{-1}m^{-M}c^{-1/2}\mu^{1/2}.$$

Hence, if we let w.l.o.g. $M > 2$ so that $\sum_{m} m^{-M} = O(1)$, then

(3.10) $$P(\bigcup_{m} A_{mn}) = P(A^{c} \cup A_{mn}) + P(A \cup A_{mn})$$

$$\leq o(1) + K^{-1}c^{-1/2}\mu^{1/2}O(1) < \varepsilon$$

for almost all n if K is chosen large enough.

Example 3.2. The conditions (2.1), (2.2'), (2.3') of Proposition 2.1 are satisfied for ε_{t} i.i.d. standard Cauchy (and then also for numerous other sequences with heavy-tailed d.f.s.). In a technical note the author has shown

$$(3.2.1) \qquad P(o(n^2) < ||e_{(n)}||^2 < n^2/o(1)) \to 1.$$

Hence (2.1) holds. In Section 3 of that note (2.2') is shown to be satisfied. (2.3') holds since firstly $\sum_{t=1}^{n} a_{nt}\,\varepsilon_t =: S_n$ has a Cauchy d.f. centered at 0 and with scale parameter $\sum_{t=1}^{n} |a_{nt}| =: \lambda_n$ (Johnson-Kotz [6], p. 156). Next, denoting

$$\alpha_n := \max_{t=1,\ldots,n} |a_{nt}|/||a_{(n)}||$$

($\to 0$ by assumption) and

$$\Omega_n := (||e_{(n)}|| > n.\alpha_n^{1/2})$$

(so that $P\Omega_n \to 1$ by (3.2.1)) we have

$$q_n := (||e_{(n)}||\ ||a_{(n)}|)^{-1}|\sum_{t=1}^{n} a_{nt}\,\varepsilon_t|$$

$$\leqq \frac{|S_n|}{\lambda_n}\, n\,\alpha_n (n\,\alpha_n^{1/2})^{-1}\, 1_{\Omega_n} + q_n 1_{\Omega_n^c}$$

$$= O_p(\alpha_n^{1/2}) + o_p(1) \to 0 \text{ i.p..}$$

Hence $\alpha_{LSE} \to \alpha$ i.p.. But (2.3) in general does not hold and thus $\gamma_{LSE} \to \gamma$ i.p. cannot be asserted.

Remark 3.3. *On Strong Consistency.* In principle the proof of Theorem 2.1 should go through if the weak assumptions on null convergence and on boundedness are replaced by their strong counterparts. However, the basic problem of parameter identifiability is not touched by these probabilistic postulates at all and represents a separate aspect of the proof as it were. Instead of (2.2) we now postulate for example the existence of an a.s. finite r.v. X such that

$$(3.11) \qquad ||e||^{-2}|e'\, L^j e| < X \quad \text{a.s.} \quad \forall n,\ \forall\, j = 1,\dots,p$$

and

$$||a||^{-1}|e'a| < X \quad \text{a.s.} \quad \forall n$$

and for all a of some subspaces $\subset R^n$ of fixed and finite dimension. However, it looks like that the strong version of (2.2) is empty, i.e. there may be no error sequence (ε_t) satisfying

$$(3.12) \qquad ||e||^{-1} \max_{j=1,\dots,n-1} |e'\, L^j e| < X \quad \text{a.s.} \quad \forall n.$$

Not even condition (2.43) may be satisfied as the example of white noise, $\varepsilon_t \sim N(0,1)$ i.i.d., suggests. Here $n^{-1}||e_{(n)}||^2 \to 1$ a.s. and there exists e.g. $\lim_n \mathcal{D}(n^{-1/2}\, e'L^j e)$ (see [5]).

If strong consistency is to be recovered much stronger assumptions on the Z-sequence than (2.4), namely e.g. (2.3''), (2.3'') seem necessary. Under conditions of this type strong consistency is proved e.g. in [2] Section 3. They also occur in the analysis of stationary time series (comp. e.g. [5]).

Remark 3.4. *On the Stability Assumption.* In autoregression analysis the following representation of the lag-matrix C and of the stability condition is useful. In (2.5) of Theorem 2.1 the characteristic polynomial

$$(2.5) \qquad f(\xi) := \xi^p - \alpha_1\, \xi^{p-1} - \dots - \alpha_p = 0$$

occurs. Let it have the roots $z_1,\dots,z_p$ (complex in general). Then the α_j are the symmetric functions of the roots:

$$\alpha_1 = \sum_{j=1}^{p} z_j, \quad \alpha_2 = - \sum_{i \neq j} z_i z_j \quad \text{etc.}$$

and f factorizes into $f(\xi) = \sum_{j=1}^{p} (\xi - z_j)$. To this there corresponds the matrix factorization

$$(3.13) \qquad C^{-1} := I - \sum_{i}^{p} \alpha_j L^j = \prod_{j=1}^{p} (I - z_j L)$$

as is easily verified. The (Toeplitz) matrix factors $I - z_j L$ commute and are easily verified to have simple inverses (also commuting)

$$(3.14) \qquad (I - zL)^{-1} = \sum_{m=o}^{n-1} z^m L^m, \text{ any complex } z,\ n \in \mathbb{N}.$$

Hence

$$(3.15) \qquad C = \prod_{j=1}^{p} \left(\sum_{m=0}^{n-1} z_j^m L^m \right)$$

from which a proof of the remark following (2.6) could be derived.

The stability assumption about (2.5) is equivalent to requiring of the p new complex and in general mutually mathematically independent parameters z_j

$$(3.16) \qquad |z_j| < 1, \qquad j = 1, \ldots, p.$$

This concerns only p real parameters iff all α_j are real which is of course assumed. Then also all non-real z_j occur in conjugate pairs.

Remark 3.5. *An Alternate Model.* As an alternative model to (1.1) which may avoid some of the shortcomings of (1.1) one may consider the following compromise if it makes sense phenomenologically

$$(3.17) \qquad y = -L_{Z\gamma}\alpha + Z\gamma + u = C_{\alpha}^{-1} Z\gamma + u$$

which is bilinear in the parameters α and γ. Minimizing

$$||y - Z\gamma + L_{Z\gamma}\alpha||^2$$

leads to the 'normal equations'

$$L'_{Z\gamma}(Z\gamma - y) = L^2_{Z\gamma}\ \alpha \text{ and } Z'C'^{-1}y = (Z'C'^{-1}C^{-1}Z)\gamma.$$

Model (3.17) of course is much less complicated then $y = CZ\gamma + v$ which latter involves all the possible lags of $Z\gamma$.

Remark 3.6. *Regression Consistency.* In most regression problems the main goal is the maximum possible expansion (i.e. representation) of the observed (known) vector $y \in R^n$ for fixed or a set of sizes n in terms of observed regression quantities Z (here assumed to be deterministic). The estimation and identification of regression parameters is a separate question of a principally different nature and is often of secondary or auxiliary importance. In case of more than one regressors here the question of linear and/or of other functional interrelations among them is of fundamental importance and with it the question of selection of suitable regressors - obviously a different subject area than close fitting. In addition, of course, in this procedure the causality structure must be clear beyond doubt. If there were no casual dependence of the y's on the regression quantities then regression analysis would have to try to explore to the 'maximum possible' extent the interdependence between both by mutual representation, e.g. by orthogonal regression. Since in this paper t represents time and we think of autoregressive schemes we implicitly assume clear causal dependence of y_t on the regressors comprised in the matrix Z. In the ordinary (i.e. un-weighted) least squares approach 'maximum explanation', equivalently 'close representation' or 'approximation' is defined via minimizing the sum of squares. There may or may not exist a unique minimizing approximant defined by the infimum of the sum of squares. If for increasing n the regression vector combinations approximating y converge componentwise to y we may speak of *consistent regression*. This is obviously a more general and weaker concept than consistency of parameters, which makes sense in the particular case that the competing set of approximants has a parametric representation like in our case (1.1) or (3.17). Here the question arises whether or not in case of existence of a unique approximant it has a unique parametric representation at least in the asymptotic case $n \to \infty$. In applications as well as in theory it is often of primary and of more fundamental interest whether or not a unique approximant exists at all and what it is. Uniqueness of its parametric representation (the second question above) is conceptually and practically a question of a different nature. It often depends only on peripherical circumstances (e.g. the particular choice or collinearity of regression vectors) and is closely related to the problems of parameter identifiability. On the other hand of course the values of the parameters in a linear regression may characterize the size of influence of a regressor. Some further clarification is still needed. In the above mentioned 'representation of y in terms of Z' we think of some functional representation of each y_t in terms of the matrix $(z_{sj})_{s \leq t;\ j = 1,\ldots,q} \equiv Z_t$, i.e.

$$(3.18) \qquad y_t = f_t(Z_t) + \text{error} \quad (t = 1,\ldots,n).$$

We seek functions f_t such that the unexplained remainders remain as small as possible. In any such regression situation a class of admissible functions f_t must be specified and each f_t depends on a fixed finite number of free parameters, in our case (α,γ), which we want to choose to obtain 'best fit'. (So at present certain problems of regression analysis may have to be excluded.) The simplest case not considered here explicitly is linear regression: $y_t = \sum_{j=1}^{q} \gamma_j z_{tj}$, $t = 1,\ldots,n$. In the case of (1.1) as suggested by the probabilistic scheme generating the y i.e. $y = C(Z\gamma+e)$ we may look for a data-analyting description of y in the nonlinear form

$$(3.19) \qquad y = C_\alpha Z\gamma + \text{unexplained remainder}$$

where $C_\alpha := (I - \sum_{k=1}^{p} \alpha_k L^k)^{-1}$ depends in a highly implicit form on α. The p parameter components of α and the q components of γ should be chosen so as to keep the present errors as small as possible, i.e. to yield the maximum possible deterministic representation of y. The probabilistic structure of the error sequence should allow for such a representation. Then a LS-fit defined by

$$(3.20) \qquad \inf_{\alpha,\gamma} ||y - C_\alpha Z\gamma||^2 = \inf_{\alpha,\gamma} ||C_\alpha(C_\alpha^{-1}y - Z\gamma)||^2$$

should make sense. Achieving this fit analytically may be difficult or impossible. In particular, in general the set of competing regression vectors does not form a linear subspace $M \subset R^n$ so that the LS-fit is not given by the orthogonal projection $pr_M\, y$ of y onto M. However, an approximate fitting with the help of a computer is quite possible. Anyway, the second expression of (3.20) shows that certainly its minimum is *not* obtained by minimizing

$$(3.21) \qquad \inf_{\alpha,\gamma} ||C_\alpha^{-1}y - Z\gamma||^2 = \inf_{\alpha,\gamma} ||y - \sum_{k=1}^{p} \alpha_k L^k y - Z\gamma||^2$$

which would lead to the simple least squares fit having the well-known explicit solution being considered in this paper. For an alternative procedure compare Section 3.4. Otherwise the questions raised here are not pursued further in this paper.

Remark 3.7. *Asymptotic Model Identification.* This concept occurs already in the simplest case of one linear (non-zero non-stochastic) regressor z_t $(t \in \mathbb{N})$ in the linear model

$$(3.22) \qquad y_t = \gamma z_t + \varepsilon_t \qquad (t = 1,\ldots,n).$$

The concept appears to be especially suitable for consistency investigations of the LSE of the parameter γ. It is easy to visualize situations where the parameters of model (3.22) are identifiable for some n+1 but not for n, with $\mathcal{D}(\varepsilon_1,\ldots,\varepsilon_n) \equiv \mathcal{D}(e_n)$, defined by the marginal of $\mathcal{D}(\varepsilon_1,\ldots,\varepsilon_{n+1})$. A sufficient condition on $\mathcal{D}(e_n)$, $n \in \mathbb{N}$, and on $(z_t)_{t\in\mathbb{N}}$ for asymptotic identifiability of γ as well as of the $\mathcal{D}(e_n)$ $(n \in \mathbb{N})$ appears to be

$$(3.23) \qquad z'\,e = o_p(||z||^2)$$

where $z \equiv z_{(n)} := (z_1,\ldots,z_n)'$; $e \equiv e_{(n)} := (\varepsilon_1,\ldots,\varepsilon_n)$. For non identifiability of γ would mean that there exists a $\gamma' \neq \gamma$ such that y_t had also the representation $y_t = \gamma' z_t + \varepsilon_t'$ (all t) besides (3.22) which would imply $\varepsilon_t' = (\gamma-\gamma')z_t+\varepsilon_t$ (all t). But then

$$\sum_{t=1}^{n} z_t\,\varepsilon_t' = (\gamma-\gamma)'||z||^2 + o_p(||z||^2) \neq o_p(||z||)^2).$$

In the case of multiple (k-dimensional) non-stochastic regression with regression matrices $Z \equiv Z_n$, (3.23) is to be replaced by

$$(3.24) \qquad Z'e = o_p(\lambda_{min}(Z'Z))$$

with $o_p(\cdot)$ a k-dimensional vector in order to ensure asymptotic identifiability of $\gamma \in R^k$ and of $\mathcal{D}(e_n)$.

REFERENCES

[1] Anderson, T. W. and Taylor, J. B. (1979). Conditions for strong consistency of least squares estimates in linear models. *Ann. Statist.* 7, 484-489.

[2] Christopeit, N. and Helmes, K. (1979). Strong consistency of generalized least squares estimators. *Ann. Statist.* 7, 795-800.

[3] Drygas, H. (1971). Consistency of the least squares and Gauss-Markov estimators in regression models. *Z. Wahrsch. Verw. Gebiete* 17, 309-326.

[4] Eicker, F. (1963). Über die Konsistenz von Parameterschätzfunktionen für ein gemischtes Zeitreihen-Regressionsmodell. *Z. Wahrsch. Verw. Gebiete* 1, 456-477.

[5] Grenander, U. and Rosenblatt, M. (1957). *Statistical Analysis of Stationary Time Series.* Wiley, New York.

[6] Johnson, N. I. and Kotz, S. (1970). *Continuous Univariate Distributions.* Houghton-Mifflin, New York.

[7] Willers, R. (1978). Schwache Konsistenz von Kleinst-Quadrate-Schätzern für Regressions- und Streuungsparameter in Linearen Modellen. Dissertation, Dortmund University.

SEQUENTIAL ESTIMATION WITH DIRICHLET PROCESS PRIORS

Thomas S. Ferguson[1]

Department of Mathematics
University of California at Los Angeles
Los Angeles, California, U.S.A.

I. INTRODUCTION AND SUMMARY

The purpose of this article is to investigate two simple sequential nonparametric problems from a Bayesian viewpoint using a Dirichlet process prior, the estimation of a distribution function on the real line, and the estimation of the mean of a distribution on the real line.

Let F denote a distribution function on the real line, $\mathbb{R}$, and let $X_1, X_2, \ldots$ represent a sample from F. In the problem of estimating F, the statistician is to choose a distribution function $\hat{F}$ with loss measured by the function

$$L(F, \hat{F}) = \int (F(x) - \hat{F}(x))^2 dW(x) \tag{1.1}$$

where W is some finite measure (weight function) on $\mathbb{R}$. In the problem of estimating the mean of F, the statistician chooses a point $\hat{\mu} \in \mathbb{R}$ and loses the amount

$$L(F, \hat{\mu}) = (\mu - \hat{\mu})^2 \tag{1.2}$$

where $\mu = \int x dF(x)$ is assumed to exist for this problem. There is a positive cost $c > 0$ each time the statistician looks at a new observation. After each observation, the statistician must decide whether to take another observation or to stop sampling and choose an estimate.

[1]This research was supported by the National Science Foundation under Grant No. MCS 80-02732.

ISBN 0-12-307501-7

We attempt to find Bayes solutions to these problems when the prior distribution of F is the Dirichlet process, $\mathcal{D}(\alpha)$, where α is a given finite non-null measure on $\mathbb{R}$. See [3] for the elementary facts about this prior that are used below. In problem (1.1), it is assumed that α and W have no common atoms. It is useful to use the distribution function form of the measure α, in which α has the representation $\alpha = MF_0$, where $M = \alpha(\mathbb{R})$ is a positive number, and that F_0 is a distribution function. Thus, let $F \in \mathcal{D}(MF_0)$. Then $\mathcal{E}F = F_0$. Moreover, if $X_1, X_2, \ldots, X_n$ is a sample from F, then the posterior distribution of F given $X_1, \ldots, X_n$ is $\mathcal{D}((M+n)F_n)$ where

$$(1.3) \qquad F_n = \frac{M}{M+n} F_0 + \frac{n}{M+n} \hat{F}_n,$$

where $\hat{F}_n$ is the sample distribution function,

$$(1.4) \qquad \hat{F}_n(x) = \frac{1}{n} \sum_1^n I_{[X_i,\infty)}(x)$$

and $I_S(x)$ represents the indicator function of the set S.

We recommend the use of the 1- or 2-stage look-ahead rules for these problems. The theorems of this paper give a partial justification for this recommendation. In Theorems 1 and 3, it is seen that the k-stage look-ahead modified rules are easily computed for k as large as $[(M+n+2)/2]$, and the resulting rule is seen to be comparable to the 1-stage look-ahead rule. In Theorems 2 and 4, conditions are given under which the 1-stage look-ahead rule is optimal.

II. ESTIMATING A DISTRIBUTION FUNCTION

Let $F \in \mathcal{D}(MF_0)$ and let $X_1, \ldots, X_n$ be a sample of fixed size n from F. In estimating F with loss (1.1), the Bayes estimate is $\mathcal{E}(F|X_1, \ldots, X_n) = F_n$ of (1.3) and the minimum Bayes risk is

$$(2.1) \qquad \int \mathrm{Var}\ (F(x)|X_1,\ldots,X_n)dW(x)$$

$$= \frac{1}{M+n+1} \int F_n(x)(1-F_n(x))dW(x).$$

In the extension of this problem to the sequential case, it is well-known (see, for example [2] Theorem 7.1) that once we decide to stop, the Bayes terminal estimate is the same as for the fixed sample size problem, so that if we stop after observing $X_1,\ldots,X_n$, the Bayes terminal estimate is F_n. Thus we are only concerned with finding the Bayes stopping rule.

It is only in very exceptional parametric cases that an optimal stopping rule can be found explicitly. Usually, an approximation to the optimal rule is sought, for example the rule optimal among those limited to a fixed bounded number N of observations. However, it is still only in special parametric cases -- when there exists a small dimensional sufficient statistic whatever the sample size -- that such a rule can be computed for moderate N in a reasonable length of time. In the problems considered here, sufficiency does not reduce the dimensionality of the observations, and the backward induction method necessary to compute such rules involves the approximation of functions of N variables.

As a practical matter, there are some very good suboptimal rules. These are the k-stage look-ahead rules.

The k-*stage look-ahead rule* (k-*sla*) *is the rule that at each stage stops or continues according to whether the rule optimal among those taking at most* k *more observations stops or continues.* Usually, and it is so for our problems, the 1-sla is trivial to compute. The 2-sla involves a 1-dimensional numerical integration to be performed at each stage, while the 3-sla (about as complex as one would like to consider) involves a 2-dimensional numerical integration at each stage.

The 1-sla is not only easy to compute; it is reasonably good for estimation problems, and the 2-sla or 3-sla is generally quite good. In fact, Bickel and Yahav [1] have shown that for sufficiently regular estimation problems with quadratic loss, the 1-sla is asymptotically pointwise optimal as $c \to 0$.

A simplification may be made in these rules. This is due to the fact that in our problems, if the k-stage look-ahead rule tells you to continue, it is optimal to continue, for there is at least one rule that continues (but stops in at most k stages) and gives a smaller expected cost plus loss than stopping at once. This property suggests a simplification of the 2-sla: use the 1-sla until it tells you to stop and then use the 2-sla. Similarly, the 3-sla is equivalent to: use the 1-sla until it tells you to stop, (then the 2-sla until it tells you to stop), and then use the 3-sla.

Let us evaluate the 1-stage look-ahead rule, sometimes called the "myopic" rule. First, we discover what it requires us to do at the very first stage before looking at any observations. If we stop and make a terminal decision without sampling, we lose (2.1) with $n = 0$, namely

$$\frac{1}{M+1} \int F_0(1-F_0)dW. \tag{2.2}$$

If we take one observation X_1 and then stop, we lose, conditional on X_1, the amount $c+(M+2)^{-1} \int F_1(1-F_1)dW$. On the average, we expect to lose

$$c+(M+2)^{-1}\mathcal{E}\int F_1(1-F_1)dW = c + \frac{M}{(M+1)^2} \int F_0(1-F_0)dW. \tag{2.3}$$

This computation is easily made using (1.3), (1.4) and $\mathcal{E}\hat{F}_1 = F_0$, which holds since the marginal distribution of X_1 is F_0. Therefore, the 1-stage look-ahead rule calls for stopping without taking any observations if (2.2) $\leq$ (2.3), or equivalently, if

$$\int F_0(1-F_0)dW \leq c(M+1)^2. \tag{2.4}$$

After observing $X_1,\ldots,X_n$, the 1-stage look-ahead rule calls for stopping if the updated posterior distribution satisfies an updated version of (2.4). That is, *the* 1-*stage look-ahead rule calls for stopping after the first* n *for which*

$$\int F_n(1-F_n)dW \leq c(M+n+1)^2. \tag{2.5}$$

Since the left side is bounded above by $W(\mathbb{R})/4$, and the right side increases to infinity as n tends to infinity, the 1-stage look-ahead rule eventually calls for stopping, and bounds on the maximum sample size can be found.

When the 1-sla finally tells us to stop, how can we tell if it is optimal to stop? Two partial answers to this question are given in Theorems 1 and 2 below. The first theorem involves the notion of the k-stage modified sequential decision problem, due originally to Magwire [4]. The only difference between this problem and the ordinary sequential decision problem is that if stage k is reached the terminal loss is set equal to zero, in which case it is certainly optimal to stop.

The k-*stage look-ahead modified rule* (k-*slam*) *is the rule that at each stage stops or continues according to whether the rule optimal* for the modified problem in which the terminal loss is set to zero if you take k more observations stops or continues.

In contrast to the k-sla which never takes too many observations, the k-slam never takes too few. *If the* k-*slam calls for stopping, it is optimal to stop,* for any rule that continues costs at least as much as the best rule for the modified problem which is the cost of stopping without taking any further observations. The optimal Bayes rule therefore lies somewhere between the k-sla and the k-slam. Bickel and Yahav [1] have shown that the 1-slam is asymptotically pointwise optimal as $c \to 0$ for sufficiently regular hypothesis testing problems.

If the 1-sla is myopic, the 1-slam is very myopic. It compares the expected terminal loss of taking no further observations with the cost of one more observation. It does not depend on the distribution of that observation. In our problem, the 1-slam calls for stopping without taking any observations if

$$\frac{1}{M+1} \int F_0(1-F_0)dW \le c. \tag{2.6}$$

The general 1-*slam therefore calls for stopping after the first* n *for which*

$$\int F_n(1-F_n)dW \le c(M+n+1). \tag{2.7}$$

This differs from the 1-sla only in the term (M+n+1) replacing $(M+n+1)^2$, but this is a very big difference if M or n is large. Since we expect the 1-sla to be reasonably good, this means we expect the 1-slam to be poor. However, the following theorem shows that we can completely describe the k-slam for $k \le M/2 + 1$. This leads to a modified rule that is comparable to the 1-sla.

This theorem is based on two simple lemmas.

LEMMA 1.

$$\int F_n(1-F_n)dW = \frac{M}{M+n} \int F_0(1-F_0)dW + \frac{n}{M+n} \int \hat{F}_n(1-\hat{F}_n)dW + \frac{Mn}{(M+n)^2} \int (F_0-\hat{F}_n)^2 dW. \tag{2.8}$$

This identity is easily checked by straightforward calculation using (1.3).

LEMMA 2. *If* j *and* k *are non-negative integers and if* $M \ge 2(k-1)$ *then*

$$(k-j)(M+j)(M+j+1) \le kM(M+1). \tag{2.9}$$

Proof. The result is obvious with equality if j = 0. So assume j > 0. From $(k-j)(M+j)(M+j+1)-kM(M+1) = kj(2M+1)+kj^2 - j(M+j)(M+j+1)$, we see that (2.9) holds if and only if

$$k(2M+j+1) \le (M+j)(M+j+1). \tag{2.10}$$

Using the assumption $M \ge 2(k-1)$ or $k \le M/2+1$, we will be finished if we show $(M/2+1)(2M+j+1) \leq (M+j)(M+j+1)$ or $(M+2)(M+(j+1)/2) \leq (M+j)(M+j+1)$. This is true with equality if $j = 1$, while for $j \geq 2$, $(M+2) \leq (M+j)$ and $M+(j+1)/2 \leq M+j+1$, completing the **proof**.

THEOREM 1. *If* $M \geq 2(k-1)$, *then the* k-*slam calls for stopping at stage* 0 *if and only if* $\int F_0(1-F_0)dW \leq k(M+1)c$.

Proof. The k-slam calls for stopping if and only if $\frac{1}{M+1}\int F_0(1-F_0)dW \leq c + \phi_1$ where, inductively, $\phi_k = 0$ and for $j = k-1,\ldots,1$.

$$\phi_j = \mathcal{E}[\min(\frac{1}{M+j+1}\int F_j(1-F_j)dW,\ c + \phi_{j+1})|X_1,\ldots,X_{j-1}].$$

Suppose that $\int F_0(1-F_0)dW = k(M+1)c$; we will show $\phi_j = (k-j)c$ for $j = 1,\ldots,k-1$. An application of (2.8) shows

$$\int F_j(1-F_j)dW \geq \frac{M}{M+j}\int F_0(1-F_0)dW \quad \text{a.s.}$$
$$= \frac{M(M+1)kc}{M+j}.$$

Inductively, using Lemma 2,

$$\frac{1}{M+k}\int F_{k-1}(1-F_{k-1})dW \geq \frac{M(M+1)kc}{(M+k)(M+k-1)} \geq c \quad \text{so} \quad \phi_{k-1} = c$$
$$\vdots$$
$$\frac{1}{M+2}\int F_1(1-F_1)dW \geq \frac{M(M+1)kc}{(M+2)(M+1)} \geq (k-1)c \quad \text{so } \phi_1 = (k-1)c.$$

Thus, if $\int F_0(1-F_0)dW = k(M+1)c$, the k-slam is indifferent. For larger values of c it is uniquely optimal to stop, and for smaller values of c, it is uniquely optimal to continue, completing the proof.

Since it is easy to use, we prefer the k-slam to the 1-slam where $k = \lfloor M/2+1 \rfloor$ ($\lfloor x \rfloor$ is the greatest integer less than or equal to x.) In fact, since M increases with n, we may let k depend on n and use the $\lfloor (M+n+2)/2 \rfloor$-slam: *stop after the first* n *for which*

$$\int F_n(1-F_n)dW \le c(M+n+1)\lfloor (M+n+2)/2 \rfloor . \tag{2.11}$$

This is much closer to the 1-sla (2.5).

This theorem is of use in the evaluation of the (k+1)-slam where $k \le (M+1)/2$ with the numerical computation of only one integral since after one observation M increases by 1 and the k-slam is then immediately computable.

We now consider the possible optimality of the 1-stage look-ahead rule. We have noted that if the 1-sla calls for continuing at a certain n, it is optimal to continue at that n. When the loss function is bounded as is the case here, there is a simple sufficient condition for the converse. *If the 1-stage look-ahead rule calls for stopping at a certain* n, *and if for almost all futures starting from that time the 1-stage look-ahead rule calls for stopping, then it is optimal to stop at that* n. This condition is well-known (see for example, [2] Theorems 7.5 and 7.6), but it is rather strong, and useful only in special cases. In our case, if (2.5) holds almost surely for $n = 0,1,2,\ldots$, then it is optimal to stop without taking any observations. The following theorem shows that this can occasionally occur.

THEOREM 2. *Conditions* (2.5) *hold almost surely for* $n = 0,1,2,\ldots$, *provided*

(i) $\int F_0(1-F_0)dW \le c(M+1)^2$

(ii) $M \max(\int F_0 dW, \int(1-F_0)dW) \le 4c(M+1)^3$, *and*

(iii) $M \ge (\sqrt{5} - 1)/2 = .618\ldots$.

Proof. Condition (2.4) is exactly condition (i). To evaluate the other inequalities (2.5) we need

$$\int F_n(1-F_n)dW = (M+n)^{-2} \int (MF_0+n\hat{F}_n)(M(1-F_0)+n(1-\hat{F}_n))dW \tag{2.12}$$

$$= (M+n)^{-2}\{M^2 \int F_0(1-F_0)dW + M\sum_{i=1}^{m} [\int_{-\infty}^{X_i} F_0dW + \int_{X_i}^{\infty} (1-F_0)dW]$$

$$+ n^2 \int \hat{F}_n(1-\hat{F}_n)dW\}.$$

It is easy to see that for all x,

$$\int_{-\infty}^{x} F_0dW + \int_{x}^{\infty}(1-F_0)dW \le \max(\int F_0dW, \int(1-F_0)dW) \tag{2.13}$$

so that using (i) and (ii),

$$\int F_1(1-F_1)dW \le (M+1)^{-2}\{M^2 \int F_0(1-F_0)dW$$

$$+ M \max(\int F_0dW, \int(1-F_0)dW)\}$$

$$\le (M+1)^{-2}\{M^2c(M+1)^2 + 4c(M+1)^3\} = c(M+2)^{-2} \quad \text{a.s.}$$

It remains to be shown that (2.5) holds a.s. for n = 2,3,... . The summation in the last term on the right side of (2.12) may be bounded as follows.

$$n^2 \int\hat{F}_n(1-\hat{F}_n)dW \le \frac{n^2}{4} \int dW \le \frac{n^2}{2} \max(\int F_0dW, \int(1-F_0)dW).$$

Therefore, from (i), (ii), and (2.12),

$$\int F_n(1-F_n)dW \le \frac{c(M+1)^2}{(M+n)^2} \{M^2 + 4n(M+1) + 2n^2 \frac{M+1}{M}\} \quad \text{a.s.}$$

Thus (2.5) holds a.s. if

$$(M+1)^2\{M^2+4n(M+1) + 2n^2 \frac{M+1}{M}\} \le (M+n+1)^2(M+n)^2.$$

This reduces to the inequality

$$0 \le n^3+2n^2(2M+1) + n[4M^2-5-2M^{-1}]-2(M+1)(3M+2). \tag{2.14}$$

As a function of n, the right side of (2.14) has positive slope for $n \geq 2$ when (iii) is satisfied. Therefore, (2.5) holds a.s. for all $n \geq 2$ if (2.14) holds a.s. for $n = 2$; that is, if

$$0 \leq 2M^2 + 6M + 2 - 4M^{-1} = 2(M+2)(M^2 + M - 1)M^{-1}.$$

This is satisfied if $M^2 + M - 1 \geq 0$ which is exactly condition (iii), completing the proof.

This theorem gives conditions for the 1-stage look-ahead rule to be optimal at the initial stage. If (i) is satisfied, so that the 1-stage look-ahead rule calls for stopping, then it is optimal to stop without taking any observations provided (ii) and (iii) are satisfied. At subsequent stages, F_0 and M are updated to F_n and M+n so that condition (iii) becomes automatically satisfied.

COROLLARY. *If, after* $n \geq 1$ *observations have been taken, the 1-stage look-ahead rule calls for stopping, it is optimal to stop provided*

$$(2.15) \qquad (M+n)\max\{\int F_n dW, \int (1-F_n)dW\} \leq 4c(M+n+1)^3.$$

How likely is it, when (2.5) becomes satisfied for the first time, that (2.15) will be satisfied also? In a practical case where we expect to take many observations before stopping, we expect approximate equality in (2.5) when we do stop. In such a case, (2.15) becomes approximately

$$(2.16) \qquad \max\{\int F_n dW, \int (1-F_n)dW\} \leq 4 \int F_n(1-F_n)dW$$

(assuming M is small compared to n). Since F_n converges almost surely to the true F, this gives us an indication of how likely it will be that the 1-sla will stop only when it is optimal to stop.

As an example, let $F_0(x) = x$ on [0,1], the uniform distribution, and suppose $dW = dx$ on [0,1]. Then

$\int F_0(1-F_0)dW = \int_0^1 x(1-x)dx = 1/6$, and $\int F_0 dW = \int (1-F_0)dW = 1/2$. The 1-sla calls for stopping without taking any observations if $1/6 \leq c(M+1)^2$. This condition implies condition (ii) of Theorem 1, since $4c(M+1)^3 \geq 4(M+1)/6 \geq M/2$. Therefore, the 1-sla is optimal at the initial stage if $M \geq .618\ldots$. If the 1-sla calls for at least one observation, and if M is large, it is likely that condition (2.15) will be satisfied a.s. when we stop. This is because (2.16) is satisfied for $n = 0$ (i.e. $1/2 \leq 2/3$), and, if M is large, it is likely that F will be close to the uniform. It is possible, though, that the 1-sla will call for stopping after the first observation and that it will not be optimal to stop. In cases when (2.15) is not satisfied when you stop, it is best to check the 2-sla.

We mention that the results of this section carry over to estimating a distribution function in d-dimensions. The statements of Theorems 1 and 2 are the same except that condition (ii) of Theorem 2 must be replaced by the more general statement

(ii') $$M \max_z \{\int [F_0(x)(1-I_{[z,\infty)}(x)) + (1-F_0(x))I_{[z,\infty)}(x)]dW(x)\}$$
$$\leq 4c(M+1)^3.$$

Here, $[z,\infty)$ represents the set of points $x \in \mathbb{R}^d$ such that the inequality $z \leq x$ holds for each coordinate. In general for $d \geq 2$, (ii') does not reduce to (ii). The proofs were written to apply to this generalization unchanged.

Let us look briefly at the difficulties involved in computing the 2-sla and 3-sla. If we stop without sampling, we lose (2.2). If we take one observation X_1, and use the best 1-stage look-ahead procedure from there, we pay c plus the minimum of (2.2) and (2.3) updated by one observation, namely,

$$(2.17)\qquad c+\min\left(\frac{1}{M+2}\int F_1(1-F_1)dW, c + \frac{M+1}{(M+2)^2}\int F_1(1-F_1)dW\right)$$

$$= c+ \frac{1}{M+2}\int F_1(1-F_1)dW + \min\left(0, c- \frac{1}{(M+2)^2}\int F_1(1-F_1)dW\right).$$

Thus, for the 2-sla, we stop without taking observations if (2.2) is smaller than the expectations of (2.17), that is if

$$(2.18)\qquad \frac{1}{(M+1)^2}\int F_0(1-F_0)dW \le c - \mathcal{E}\ \max\left(0, \frac{1}{(M+2)^2}\int F_1(1-F_1)dW-c\right).$$

This differs from the 1-sla of (2.4) by the subtraction of the nonnegative term on the right. The expectation in this term can be computed using numerical approximations without too much difficulty.

Similarly, for the 3-sla, if we take one observation and use the best 2-stage procedure from there, we pay c plus the minimum of (2.2) and the expectation of (2.17) updated by one observation. The rule corresponding to (2.18) is more completed and can be evaluated in general only by iterated numerical integration.

III. ESTIMATING THE MEAN OF A DISTRIBUTION

Let $F \in \mathcal{D}(\alpha)$ where $\alpha = MF_0$ as before, and consider estimating the mean μ of F with loss (1.2) based on a sample of fixed size n, $X_1,\ldots,X_n$ from F. It is assumed that the second moment of F_0 is finite. The Bayes estimate of μ is

$$(3.1)\qquad \mu_n = \frac{M}{M+n}\mu_0 + \frac{n}{M+n}\bar{X}_n$$

where $\mu_0 = \int x dF_0$ is the prior estimate of the mean and $\bar{X}_n = n^{-1}\Sigma_1^n X_i$. The minimum conditional Bayes risk is

$$(3.2)\qquad \mathrm{Var}(\mu|X_1,\ldots,X_n) = \sigma_n^2/(M+n+1)$$

where σ_n^2 is the variance of the distribution F_n. It may be computed in a formula analogous to (2.8)

$$\sigma_n^2 = \int (x-\mu_n)^2 dF_n(x) = (M\sigma_0^2 + ns_n^2 + \frac{Mn}{M+n}(\bar{X}_n-\mu_0)^2)/(M+n) \tag{3.3}$$

where σ_0^2 is the variance of the distribution F_0 and $s_n^2 = n^{-1}\Sigma_1^n(X_i - \bar{X}_n)^2$.

Let us evaluate the 1-sla for the sequential problem. If we stop without sampling, our expected loss is $\sigma_0^2/(M+1)$. If we take one observation and stop, our conditional expected loss plus cost given X_1 is $c + \sigma_1^2(M+2)^{-1}$, so on the average we expect to lose

$$c + \frac{1}{M+2}\mathcal{E}\,\sigma_1^2 = c + \frac{1}{(M+1)(M+2)}(M\sigma_0^2 + \frac{M}{M+1}\sigma_0^2)$$

$$= c + \frac{M}{(M+1)^2}\sigma_0^2.$$

At the first stage, the 1-sla calls for stopping if

$$\sigma_0^2 \leq c(M+1)^2. \tag{3.4}$$

Hence, the 1-stage look ahead rule is: *stop after the first* n *for which*

$$\sigma_n^2 \leq c(M+n+1)^2. \tag{3.5}$$

On the other hand, the 1-slam calls for stopping without taking any observations if $\sigma_0^2 \leq c(M+1)$, so that the general 1-slam is: *stop after the first* n *for which*

$$\sigma_n^2 \leq c(M+n+1). \tag{3.6}$$

The difference between the stopping rules (3.5) and (3.6) is great if M or n is large. However, we can narrow the gap by considering the k-slam as in the following analogue of Theorem 1.

THEOREM 3. *If* $M \geq 2(k-1)$, *then the* k-*slam calls for stopping if and only if* $\sigma_0^2 \leq k(M+1)c$.

The proof of this theorem is exactly the same as Theorem 1 with $\int F_n(1-F_n)dW$ replaced by σ_n^2 and the use of Lemma 1 replaced by (3.3).

As before, we may use the k-slam and allow k to depend on n: *the* $\lfloor \frac{M+n+2}{2} \rfloor$-*slam calls for stopping after the first* n *for which*

$$\sigma_n^2 \leq (M+n+1)\left\lfloor \frac{M+n+2}{2} \right\rfloor c. \tag{3.7}$$

The difference between the stopping rules (3.5) and (3.7) is not great, and the optimal stopping rule lies between them.

As before, if the 1-sla calls for continuing at a certain n, it is optimal to continue at that n. If the 1-sla calls for stopping at a certain n, and if for almost all futures proceeding from that n the 1-stage look-ahead calls for stopping, it is optimal to stop at that n. A glance at (3.5) shows that if F_n were the distribution function of an unbounded distribution, (3.5) could not hold almost surely, since s_n^2 and $\bar{X}_n$ may take unboundedly large values. To obtain a result similar to Theorem 1, we must therefore assume that the distribution of X_1 is bounded. In the following theorem, we take the distribution of $|X_1|$ to be bounded by 1.

THEOREM 4. *Assume that* α *gives all of its mass to the interval* $[-1,1]$. *Then, conditions* (3.5) *are satisfied a.s. for* $n = 0,1,2,\ldots$, *provided*

(i) $\sigma_0^2 \leq c(M+1)^2$

(ii) $M(1+|\mu_0|)^2 \leq c(3M+4)(M+1)^2$, *and*

(iii) *if* $M|\mu_0| < 1$, *then* $1 + \frac{M}{2}\,{}^2_0 \leq c(3M^2 + 10M + 9)$.

Proof. Condition (3.5) with n = 0 is exactly condition (i). With n = 1, (3.5) is satisfied since

$$\sigma_1^2 = \frac{M}{M+1}\sigma_0^2 + \frac{M}{(M+1)^2}(X_1-\mu_0)^2$$

$$\le \frac{M}{M+1}\sigma_0^2 + \frac{M}{(M+1)^2}(1+|\mu_0|)^2 \quad \text{a.s.}$$

$$\le Mc(M+1) + c(3M+4) = c(M+2)^2$$

using only (i) and (ii). To show (3.5) for $n \ge 2$, it is sufficient to show

$$s_n^2 + \frac{M}{M+n}(\bar{X}_n-\mu_0)^2 \le c\,\frac{M+n}{n}(M+n+1)^2 - c\,\frac{M(M+1)^2}{n} \quad \text{a.s.}$$

$$= c[n^2 + n(3M+2)+(M+1)(3M+1)]$$

using (i). Since all $|X_i| \le 1$ a.s., we have

$$s_n^2 = \frac{1}{n}\sum_1^n X_i^2 - \bar{X}_n^2 \le 1 - \bar{X}_n^2 \quad \text{a.s.}$$

so that it is sufficient to show

$$1-\bar{X}_n^2 + \frac{M}{M+n}(\bar{X}_n-\mu_0)^2 \le c[n^2+n(3M+2)+(M+1)(3M+1)] \quad \text{a.s.} \tag{3.8}$$

We seek the maximum of the left side of this inequality over variation of $\bar{X}_n$ in [-1,1]. The function $1-x^2 + M(x-\mu_0)^2/(M+n)$ is quadratic in x with maximum at $x = -M\mu_0/n$.

Case 1. $M|\mu_0| < 1$. In this case, the maximum occurs at a point inside the interval [-1,1] for all n. Thus it is sufficient to show (3.8) with $\bar{X}_n$ replaced by $-M\mu_0/n$, namely

$$1 + \frac{M}{n}\mu_0^2 \le c[n^2 + n(3M+2)+(M+1)(3M+1)]$$

for all $n \ge 2$. But the left side is decreasing in n and the right side is increasing in n, so it is sufficient to show this inequality for $n = 2$. For $n = 2$, this reduces to (iii).

Case 2. $M|\mu_0| \geq 1$. For $n \geq M|\mu_0|$, the left side of (3.8) is bounded above by $1 + \frac{M}{n}\mu_0^2$ as in Case 1. For $1 \leq n \leq M|\mu_0|$, the maximum of (3.8) as $\bar{X}_n$ varies in $[-1,1]$ occurs at ± 1, and the maximum value is $M(1+|\mu_0|)^2/(M+n)$. These bounds for the left side of (3.8) are decreasing in n, and the right side is increasing in n, so it is sufficient to show this inequality for $n = 1$. But this is exactly (3.5) which we have already shown to be satisfied. This completes the proof.

The conditions of Theorem 4 are sufficient for the optimality of the decision to stop without taking any observations. Unfortunately, conditions (ii) and (iii) are somewhat stronger than their counterparts of Theorem 2 although (iii) could be weakened slightly. This makes it less likely that the theorem will be of use, partly because, no doubt, the 1-stage look-ahead rule is less likely to be optimal.

The uniform distribution on $[-1,1]$ is a critical case. Let F_0 be the distribution function of $\mathcal{U}(-1,1)$, so that $\mu_0 = 0$ and $\sigma_0^2 = 1/3$. The 1-stage look-ahead rule calls for stopping without taking any observations if

$$(3.9) \qquad \frac{1}{3} \leq c(M+1)^2.$$

Condition (ii), that $M \leq c(3M+4)(M+1)^2$, and condition (iii), that $1 \leq c(3M^2 + 10M + 9)$, are then automatically satisfied. Thus, it is optimal to stop without taking observations if M and c are such that (3.9) is satisfied.

Thus, for the uniform distribution (ii) and (iii) are satisfied when (i) is, but barely. If the variance σ_0^2 were any smaller than 1/3, (ii) would not follow from (i) except for special values of M. Also, if the mean μ_0 were not exactly zero, (ii) would not follow in general from (i). The same goes for condition (iii).

If c is such that the sample size will be at least moderate before the 1-stage look-ahead calls for stopping, then we expect approximate equality in (i) with σ_0^2 and M updated. With M large, in order that (i) imply (ii) and (iii), it is necessary that $\sigma_0^2 \geq 1/3$ and μ_0 be close to zero. All in all, it is likely that the 1-stage look-ahead rule is optimal when stopping occurs only if the true distribution is U-shaped. More recourse to the 2-stage or 3-stage look-ahead rule will probably be required for this problem than for the problem of estimation of a distribution function.

The 2-stage look-ahead rule may be computed as in the earlier problem, and is found to have a similar form: stop without taking any observations if

$$\frac{\sigma_0^2}{(M+1)^2} \leq c - \mathcal{E} \max(0, \frac{\sigma_1^2}{(M+2)^2} - c).$$

REFERENCES

[1] Bickel, P. J., and Yahav, J. A. (1965). Asymptotically pointwise optimal procedures in sequential analysis. *Proc. Fifth Berkeley Symp. Math. Statist. Prob. I*, 401-413.

[2] Ferguson, T. S. (1967). *Mathematical Statistics: A decision theoretic approach.* Academic Press, New York and London.

[3] Ferguson, T. S. (1973). A Bayesian analysis of some nonparametric problems. *Ann. Statist. 1*, 209-230.

[4] Magwire, C. A. (1953). Sequential decisions involving the choice of experiments. Ph.D. thesis, Stanford University.

EXPANSIONS FOR POSTERIOR PROBABILITY AND INTEGRATED BAYES RISK

J. K. Ghosh

Indian Statistical Institute
Calcutta, India

B. K. Sinha

Department of Mathematics and Statistics
University of Pittsburgh
Pittsburgh, Pennsylvania, U.S.A.

S. N. Joshi
Indian Statistical Institute
Calcutta, India

I. INTRODUCTION

Asymptotic expansion of the posterior distribution has been investigated by Johnson ([8], [7]). Considering a one parameter family of distribution in the independent and identically distributed (i.i.d.) set up, he proves under certain regularity conditions, that with probability one under a fixed value of the parameter, the suitably centered and scaled posterior distribution possesses an asymptotic expansion in powers of $n^{-1/2}$, with the standard normal as the leading term. (Johnson expands only the posterior distribution function but his expansion is valid for the posterior probability of any Borel set.) The proof involves, among other things, repeated use of a version of the uniform strong law. Employing yet another version of the uniform strong law (for a precise statement see Lemma 4.1) and proceeding analogously as in Johnson [8], the following uniform variant of the main result on asymptotic expansion of the posterior can be obtained.

Statistical Decision Theory and Related Topics III, Vol. 1

ISBN 0-12-307501-7

Let the parameter space Θ be a possibly unbounded interval. Consider a bounded open subinterval Θ_1 whose closure $\bar{\Theta}_1$ is properly contained in Θ. *Fix a prior* ρ *such that* $\rho(\theta) > 0$ *on* $\bar{\Theta}_1$. Choose a constant $r > 0$. Then under certain regularity conditions which are stronger than Johnson's and depend on r, $\exists\ n_o$ and $M(0 < M < \infty)$ such that $\forall n > n_o$

$$(1.1) \qquad P_{\theta_o}\Big[\Big|F_n(\xi) - \Phi(\xi) - \sum_{j=1}^{K} \gamma_j(\xi, \underline{x}_n) n^{-j/2}\Big| \le M \cdot n^{-(K+1)/2} \text{ uniformly in } \xi\Big] = 1 - 0(n^{-r}), \text{ uniformly in } \theta_o \in \Theta_1,$$

where $\underline{x}_n = (x_1, \ldots, x_n)$, $F_n(\xi) = P[\sqrt{n}(\theta - \hat{\theta}_n)b \le \xi / \underline{x}_n]$,

$\Phi(\xi) = \frac{1}{\sqrt{2\pi}} \int_{-\infty}^{\xi} \exp(-x^2/2)dx$, $\hat{\theta}_n$ is the maximum likelihood estimate (m.l.e.), $(-b^2)$ is the second derivative of the loglikelihood at $\hat{\theta}_n$ and other quantities are as defined in Johnson [8]. (This is essentially our Corollary 2.1). Here K is such that $\rho(\theta)$ is (K+1) times continuously differentiable. It may be noted that if $r > 1$, by the Borel Cantelli Lemma, (1.1) implies Johnson's result. Conversely, Johnson's result implies (1.1) if $N_{\underline{x}}$ (as defined in Johnson [8]) has finite r^{th} order moment. In the special case of exponential families (1.1) holds for all $r > 0$ provided $\bar{\Theta}_1$ is contained in the interior of the natural parameter space. This result or rather a slight variant of it has been observed by Alvo [2]; see in this connection his Corollaries 1 and 2.

While results of Johnson or the one given above in (1.1) are important, a Bayesian would be more interested in versions which hold with a large probability under P_ρ, rather than merely P_{θ_o} (where P_ρ denotes the marginal probability measure of X under the prior ρ). Arguments needed for (1.1) also lead to

$$(1.2) \qquad P_\rho[|F_n(\xi) - \Phi(\xi) - \sum_{j=1}^{K} \gamma_j(\xi,\underline{x}_n)\cdot n^{-j/2}| \le M\cdot n^{-(K+1)/2}\cdot|C_n|^{-1} \text{ uniformly in } \xi] = 1 - 0(n^{-r})$$

provided certain regularity conditions hold and ρ is positive on a bounded interval (a_o,b_o), $\rho = 0$ on $(a_o,b_o)^c$ and ρ is $(K+1)$ times continuously differentiable on $[a_o,b_o]$. (All priors in this paper will satisfy such conditions unless stated otherwise and (a_o,b_o) will have the meaning assigned here) (vide Theorem 2.1). Since $|C_n|^{-1}$ is an unbounded random quantity, (1.2) ceases to be true if the error term in the expansion is replaced by constant $n^{-(K+1)/2}$. (See in this connection Example 1 of Section 6).

If ρ behaves like a polynomial of degree K at both end points of the support we shall say ρ is of type D_K; in this case we can estimate (vide Proposition 2.1) the P_ρ-probability that $\hat{\theta}_n$ lies in neighbourhoods of the two end points whose lengths tend to zero at a certain rate. This enables us to prove (vide Theorem 2.2) that with a large P_ρ-probability the error $M\, n^{-(K+1)/2}\cdot|C_n|^{-1}$ as well as the terms $\gamma_j\, n^{-j/2}$ tend to zero as $n \to \infty$. For a subclass D_∞ of infinitely differentiable priors the same end is achieved in Theorem 2.3 via Proposition 2.2. To get a flavour of these results and see the significant role played by the rate of decay near the end-point of the support, consider the following immediate consequence of Theorems 2.2 and 2.3. Let the common density $f(x,\theta)$ be $C(\theta)\exp(\theta.T(x) + \phi(x))$ and let $[a_o,b_o]$ be a subset of the interior of the natural parameter space. Then for any $K \ge 0$, $\varepsilon > 0$ and $r > 0$

$$P_\rho[|F_n(\xi) - \Phi(\xi) - \sum_{j=1}^{K} \gamma_j(\xi,\underset{\sim}{x}_n)\, n^{-j/2}|$$

$$\leq M\cdot n^{-([K+1]/2-\varepsilon)}]$$

$$= 1-o(n^{-r}) \text{ if } \rho \text{ is of type } D_\infty$$

$$= 1 - 0(n^{-\frac{(S+1)}{S}(\frac{S-K-2}{2}+\varepsilon)}) - 0(n^{-\frac{(S+1)}{K+1}\cdot\varepsilon})$$

if ρ is of type D_S, $S > K+2$.

Our regularity assumptions on the density are collected in Section 3 (Note that assumption AV is taken from Pfanzagl [10].) The preliminary lemmas needed for Section 2 are presented in Section 4.

One of the main applications of these techniques is in expanding the integrated Bayes risk. This is done in Section 5. For estimation with squared error loss the integrated Bayes risk R_ρ can be expanded (vide Theorem 5.1) in the form

$$R_\rho = a_1\cdot n^{-1} + a_2\cdot n^{-2} + o(n^{-2})$$

where $a_1 = \int(I(\theta))^{-1}\rho(\theta)d\theta$, $I(\theta)$ is Fisher information and a_2 is defined in Theorem 5.1. Similar results for coverage probability of posterior confidence sets may not be difficult to get along similar lines provided Edgeworth expansions are available for derivatives of the log likelihood function.

The examples in Section 6 show in various ways that the unboundedness of $|C_n|^{-1}$ can't be ignored with impunity In particular we show that Corollary 2 of Alvo [2] is false; it is also shown that even for a normal with unknown mean, there is no expansion for the integrated Bayes risk up to $o(n^{-2})$ for the uniform prior on [0,1].

Even though Alvo's Corollary 2 and hence the proof of his main result (viz. Theorem 4) is invalid, the result turns out to be correct, at least if one restricts the prior as in our Theorems 2.2 and 2.3; the proof of this is contained in Section 8.

Section 7 is about second order efficiency. Roughly speaking we use the expansions for the integrated Bayes risk to justify certain heuristic arguments of Ghosh and Subramanyam [5]. The proof of second order efficiency of the m.l.e. obtained in this way is different from that in Ghosh, Sinha and Wieand [4]; the results obtained and assumptions are also somewhat different. (see also in this connection Pfanzagl and Wefelmeyer [12] and Akahira and Takeuchi [1].)

After most of this paper was written the authors were informed by Professor A. Novikov of a similar investigation by Burnašev [3]. Burnašev has announced without proof an expansion of the integrated Bayes risk for a location parameter family under rather general conditions on the prior. (Burnašev seems to have missed one term in his expansion.) In the last section we assume conditions on the prior similar to Burnašev's and show how our main results (namely Theorems 2.2, 2.3 and 5.1) can be obtained by minor modifications in the arguments given in Sections 2 and 5.

II. MAIN RESULTS

THEOREM 2.1. *Let the assumptions* AI *to* AV *hold for some* $r_1 \geq 3$ *and* $r_2 \geq 2$. *Let* ρ *be* K+1 *times continuously differentiable on* $[a_o, b_o]$. *Then* $\exists$ $M(0 < M < \infty)$ *such that*

$$(2.1) \qquad P_\rho[|F_n(\xi)-\Phi(\xi) - \sum_{j=1}^{K} \gamma_j(\xi, \underline{x}_n)\cdot n^{-j/2}| \leq M\cdot n^{-(K+1)/2}\cdot|C_n|^{-1} \text{ uniformly in } \xi] = 1 - O(n^{-r_1/2}) - o(n^{-r_2/2}),$$

where $C_n = \sum_{j=0}^{K} \beta_j(\underline{x}_n)\cdot n^{-j/2}$ *and* β_j's *and* γ_j's *are as in Johnson* [8]. *(See Remark* 2.1 *for comments on* β_j's *and* γ_j's; *also note that* (2.4) *and* (2.7a) *imply that with* P_ρ*-probability tending to one* C_n^{-1} *is bounded).*

Hence forward M will be used as a generic constant independent of ξ.

Proof. Note that if $|A-a| \leq R_1$, $|B-b| \leq R_2$ and $|\frac{A}{B}| \leq C$ then

$$(2.2) \qquad |\frac{A}{B} - \frac{a}{b}| \leq |b|^{-1}(R_1 + C\, R_2).$$

The posterior is a ratio whose numerator, say A, and denominator, say B, are approximated in (4.3) and (4.4); also R_n occurring in (4.3) and (4.4) is bounded by $M\, n^{-(K+1)/2}$, vide Remark 4.1. Hence using (2.2) with C = 1 and $b = C_n$, (4.3) and (4.4) we have uniformly in $\theta \in [a_o, b_o]$

$$(2.3) \qquad P_\theta[|F_n(\xi)-\Phi(\xi) - \sum_{j=1}^{K} \gamma_j(\xi, \underline{x}_n)\cdot n^{-j/2}|$$

$$\leq M\cdot n^{-(K+1)/2}\cdot|C_n|^{-1} \text{ uniformly in } \xi]$$

$$= 1 - O(n^{-r_1/2}) - o(n^{-r_2/2})$$

which gives us (2.1). Q.E.D.

In view of Lemmas 4.2, 4.5 and 4.6, under appropriate assumptions we have uniformly in $\theta \in [a_o, b_o]$

$$(2.4) \qquad P_\theta(A_n) = 1 - O(n^{-r_1/2}) - o(n^{-r_2/2}),$$

where

$$A_n = \{-M < a_{k,n}(\hat{\theta}_n) < M,\ k = 1,\ldots,K+2,\ 0 < \delta_1 < b^{-1} < M\},$$

$a_{k,n}$'s are as defined in Lemma 4.5.

REMARK 2.1. Note that $\beta_o(\underline{x}_n) = \sqrt{2\pi}\,\rho(\hat{\theta}_n)$,

$$\beta_j(\underline{x}_n) = \sum_{i=1}^{j} a_{n,j,i}\rho^{(i)}(\hat{\theta}_n),\ j \geq 1 \text{ and} \tag{2.5}$$

$$\gamma_j(\xi,\underline{x}_n) = \sum_{\underline{i}\in I_j} k_{n,j,\underline{i}} \prod_{k\in\underline{i}} \rho^{(k)}(\hat{\theta}_n)\rho^{-1}(\hat{\theta}_n) \tag{2.6}$$

$$I_j = (\underline{i} = \{i_1,\ldots,i_\alpha\}: \sum_{r=1}^{\alpha} i_r \leq j,\ \alpha = 1,\ldots,j),$$

where $a_{n,j,i}$ $(1 \leq i \leq j,\ 1 \leq j \leq K)$ and $k_{n,j,\underline{i}}$ $(\underline{i} \in I_j, 1 \leq j \leq K)$ are bounded (uniformly in ξ, in the later case) on A_n. By (2.5) we get

$$C_n = \rho(\hat{\theta}_n)(\sqrt{2\pi} + n^{-1/2}C_{n,0} + \sum_{j=1}^{K} C_{n,j}\rho^{(j)}(\hat{\theta}_n)\rho^{-1}(\hat{\theta}_n)\cdot n^{-j/2}), \tag{2.7}$$

where $C_{n,j}(0 \leq j \leq K)$ are bounded on A_n.

The quantities C_n^{-1} and γ_j $(1 \leq j \leq K)$ are unbounded; but it is clear that they are bounded on $A_n \cap (\rho(\hat{\theta}_n) > \epsilon)$ for any $\epsilon > 0$. Now if $\theta \in \Theta_1$, $\bar{\Theta}_1 \subset (a_o,b_o)$, then by Lemma 4.2, uniformly in $\theta \in \Theta_1$

$$P_\theta(\rho(\hat{\theta}_n) > \epsilon) = 1-o(n^{-r_2/2}) \text{ for some } \epsilon > 0. \tag{2.7a}$$

This along with (2.4) and (2.3) gives the following result.

COROLLARY 2.1. *Let the assumptions* AI *to* AV *hold for some* $r_1 \geq 3$ *and* $r_2 \geq 2$. *Let* ρ *be* K+1 *times continuously differentiable on* $[a_o,b_o]$. *Let* Θ_1 *be such that* $\bar{\Theta}_1 \subset (a_o,b_o)$. *Then uniformly in* $\theta \in \Theta_1$,

$$P_\theta[|F_n(\xi)-\Phi(\xi)-\sum_{j=1}^{K}\gamma_j(\xi,\underline{x}_n)n^{-j/2}|$$

$$\leq M\cdot n^{-(K+1)/2} \textit{ uniformly in } \xi]$$

$$= 1 - O(n^{-r_1/2})-o(n^{-r_2/2}).$$

As explained in the introduction we now study the behaviour of the error $n^{-(K+1)/2}\cdot|C_n|^{-1}$ and terms in the expansion under P_ρ. We begin with a few definitions.

DEFINITION 1. The prior ρ is said to be of type D_K, $2 \leq K < \infty$, if

(i) $\rho(\theta) > 0$ on a bounded interval (a_o,b_o) and $\rho(\theta) = 0$ on $(a_o,b_o)^c$,

(ii) it has (K-1) continuous derivatives on $[a_o,b_o]$,

(iii) $\exists\ c_i > 0$ and $c_i' > 0 (0 \leq i \leq K-2)$ such that for $0 \leq i \leq K-2$,

$$\rho^{(i)}(\theta) = (\theta-a_o)^{K-i}(c_i+o(1)) \text{ for } \theta \text{ near } a_o$$

$$= (b_o-\theta)^{K-i}(c_i'+o(1)) \text{ for } \theta \text{ near } b_o,$$

where $\rho^{(i)}(\theta) = \frac{d^i}{d\theta^i}\rho(\theta)$ and $\rho^{(o)}(\theta) = \rho(\theta)$.

If the degrees of the polynomials at the two end points do not coincide, only minor modifications are needed in Proposition 2.1 and hence in the Theorem 2.2.

Definition 2. The prior ρ is said to be of type D_∞ if

(i) same as (i) of Definition 1,

(ii) it is infinitely differentiable on $[a_o,b_o]$,

(iii) $\rho^{v-1}(\theta)\cdot\rho^{(i)}(\theta) \to 0$ as $\theta \to a_o$ or b_o for all $v > 0$ and $i = 1,2,\ldots$.

(iv) ρ is monotone near a_o and b_o.

An example of this kind of prior is

$$\rho(\theta) = \text{constant}\cdot\exp\{\frac{-1}{\theta(1-\theta)}\}, 0 < \theta < 1$$
$$= 0 \qquad \text{elsewhere.}$$

PROPOSITION 2.1. *Let the assumptions* AI *to* AIII *and* AV *hold for some* $r_2 \geq 2$. *Let* ρ *be of type* D_S. *Then for any* $C, \acute{C} (0 < C, \acute{C} < \infty)$ *and* $0 < 2m \leq S$

$$(2.8) \qquad P_\rho[\hat{\theta}_n - a_o < C\cdot n^{-\frac{m}{S}}] = 0(n^{-\frac{(S+1)}{S}\cdot m}) + o(n^{-r_2/2})$$

$$= P_\rho[b_o - \hat{\theta}_n > C\cdot n^{-\frac{m}{S}}]$$

and

$$(2.9) \qquad P_\rho[\rho(\hat{\theta}_n) > \acute{C}\cdot n^{-m}] = 1 - 0(n^{-\frac{(S+1)}{S}\cdot m}) - o(n^{-r_2/2}).$$

Proof. For simplicity let $a_o = 0$ and $b_o = 1$. Note that for any $\acute{C}$, $\exists$ C $(0 < \acute{C}, C < \infty)$ such that

$$(2.10) \qquad (\hat{\theta}_n > C\cdot n^{-\frac{m}{S}}) \cap (\hat{\theta}_n < 1 - C\cdot n^{-\frac{m}{S}}) \Rightarrow (\rho(\hat{\theta}_n) > \acute{C}\cdot n^{-m}).$$

Hence it suffices to prove (2.8).

$$P_\rho[\hat{\theta}_n < C\cdot n^{-m/S}] = E_\rho P_\theta[\sqrt{n}(\hat{\theta}_n - \theta)\beta(\theta) < \sqrt{n}(C\cdot n^{-m/S} - \theta)\cdot\beta(\theta)]$$

(see Lemma 4.3 for the definition of $\beta(\theta)$)

$$= E_\rho P_\theta[\sqrt{n}(\hat{\theta}_n - \theta)\beta(\theta) < - u\cdot\beta(\theta)], \quad u = \sqrt{n}(\theta - C\, n^{-m/S})$$

$$\leq \int_{u<0} \rho(\theta)d\theta + \int_{0 < u < \alpha\cdot\sqrt{\log n}} P_\theta[\sqrt{n}(\hat{\theta}_n - \theta)\beta(\theta) < - u\beta(\theta)]\rho(\theta)d\theta$$
$$+ \int_{u > \alpha\cdot\sqrt{\log n}} P_\theta[\sqrt{n}(\hat{\theta}_n - \theta)\beta(\theta) < - u\beta(\theta)]\rho(\theta)d\theta = I_1 + I_2 + I_3.$$

Note that I_1 is $O(n^{-\frac{(S+1)}{S}\cdot m})$ as ρ is of type D_S and I_3 is $o(n^{-r_2/2})$ in view of Lemma 4.3. In view of Lemma 4.4,

$$I_2 = \int_{0 < u < \alpha\cdot\sqrt{\log n}} [(1-\Phi(u\beta(\theta))) + \frac{v(u,\theta)}{\sqrt{n}}]\cdot(\frac{u}{\sqrt{n}} + \frac{C}{n^{m/S}})^S \frac{du}{\sqrt{n}}$$

for sufficiently large n;
where $|v(u,\theta)| < K_1\ \forall u,\ \forall\ \theta \in [0,1]$, for some K_1 and for sufficiently large n. Hence

$$\begin{aligned} I_2 &= \int_{0 < u < \alpha\cdot\sqrt{\log n}} [1-\Phi(u\beta(\theta))](\frac{u}{\sqrt{n}} + \frac{C}{n^{m/S}})^S \frac{du}{\sqrt{n}} + o(n^{-m-\frac{1}{2}}) \\ &= n^{-m-\frac{1}{2}} \int [1-\Phi(u\beta(\frac{u}{\sqrt{n}} + \frac{C}{n^{m/S}}))] \\ &\quad \times I_{(0,\alpha\cdot\sqrt{\log n})} (C + \frac{u}{n^{(1/2-m/S)}})^S du + o(n^{-m-\frac{1}{2}}). \end{aligned}$$

Let $\beta' = \inf_{\theta\in[0,1]} \beta(\theta)$; then $0 < \beta' < \infty$. Now if $2m < S$, then for sufficiently large n the integrand is dominated by $C_1^S\cdot[1-\Phi(u\beta')]I_{(0,\infty)}$ (for some $0 < C_1 < \infty$) which is integrable, showing $I_2 = O(n^{-m-1/2})$ by the dominated convergence thoerem. Similar arguments hold for $2m = S$. The other part of (2.8) can be proved analogously. Q.E.D.

PROPOSITION 2.2. *Let the assumptions* AI *to* AIII *and* AV *hold for some* $r_2 \geq 2$. *Let* ρ *be of type* D_∞. *Then for any* C $(0 < C < \infty)$ *we have*

$$P_\rho[\rho(\hat{\theta}_n) > C\cdot n^{-m}] = 1 - O(n^{-m}) - o(n^{-r_2/2}). \tag{2.11}$$

Proof. For simplicity let $a_o = 0$ and $b_o = 1$. Note that the inverse function ρ^{-1} can be defined in a neighbourhood of 0 and 1. Let ρ_1^{-1} and ρ_2^{-1} be the inverse of ρ near 0 and 1 respectively.

$$P_\rho[\rho(\hat{\theta}_n) < C\cdot n^{-m}] = E_\rho P_\theta[\rho(\hat{\theta}_n) < C\cdot n^{-m}]$$

$$= E_\rho P_\theta[\rho_1^{-1}(C\cdot n^{-m}) > \hat{\theta}_n]$$

$$+ E_\rho P_\theta[\rho_2^{-1}(C\cdot n^{-m}) < \hat{\theta}_n].$$

As in the Proposition 2.1 and using the same notations as there we need to prove

$$I_2 = \int_{0 < u < \alpha\cdot\sqrt{\log n}} [1-\Phi(u\beta(\theta))]\rho(\frac{u}{\sqrt{n}} + \rho_1^{-1}(C\cdot n^{-m}))\frac{du}{\sqrt{n}} = 0(n^{-m}). \tag{2.12}$$

Now,

$$\rho(\frac{u}{\sqrt{n}} + \rho_1^{-1}(C\cdot n^{-m})) = C\cdot n^{-m} + \frac{u}{\sqrt{n}}\rho^{(1)}(\rho_1^{-1}(C\cdot n^{-m})) + \dots$$

$$\dots + (\frac{u}{\sqrt{n}})^{[2m]+1}\cdot \frac{1}{([2m]+1)!}\rho^{([2m]+1)}(\theta_n^*),$$

where $[x]$ denotes the integral part of x and θ_n^* is between $\frac{u}{\sqrt{n}} + \rho_1^{-1}(C\cdot n^{-m})$ and $\rho_1^{-1}(C\cdot n^{-m})$. Let $\rho_1^{-1}(C\cdot n^{-m}) = \theta_n$, i.e. $\rho(\theta_n) = C\cdot n^{-m}$ (which implies that θ_n is near zero). Since ρ is is of type D_∞,

$$n^{(m-r/2)}\rho^{(r)}(\rho_1^{-1}(C\cdot n^{-m})) = \rho^{(r/2m-1)}(\theta_n)\rho^{(r)}(\theta_n)\cdot C^{(1-r/2m)}\to 0.$$

Thus $n^{-m}\cdot\rho(\frac{u}{\sqrt{n}} + \rho_1^{-1}(C\cdot n^{-m}))$ can be expressed as a polynomial of degree $([2m]+1)$ in u with bounded coefficients for sufficiently large n. Now using similar arguments as in the proof of (2.9) proof of (2.12) is completed.

THEOREM 2.2. *Let assumptions* AI *to* AV *hold for some* $r_1 \geq 3$ *and* $r_2 \geq 2$. *Let* ρ *be of type* D_{K+2}; *then for* $0 < \ell < \frac{K+1}{2}$, $\exists$ $\epsilon > 0$ *such that*

$$(2.13) \qquad P_\rho[|F_n(\xi)-\Phi(\xi)-\sum_{j=1}^{K}\gamma_j(\xi,\underline{x}_n)\cdot n^{-j/2}| \leq M\cdot n^{-\ell},$$

$$|\gamma_j(\xi,\underline{x}_n)\cdot n^{-j/2}| \leq M\cdot n^{-\epsilon\cdot j}, 1 \leq j \leq K \textit{ uniformly in } \xi]$$

$$= 1 - 0(n^{-\frac{K+3}{K+2}(\frac{K+1}{2}-\ell)}) - 0(n^{-r_1/2}) - o(n^{-r_2/2}).$$

Proof. For simplicity let $a_o = 0$ and $b_o = 1$. Let

$$B_n = [\hat{\theta}_n > C\cdot n^{-\frac{(K+1)}{2(K+2)}+\frac{\ell}{K+2}}] \cap [1-\hat{\theta}_n > C\cdot n^{-\frac{(K+1)}{2(K+2)}+\frac{\ell}{K+2}}].$$

Hence using (2.8) for some $\acute{C}$,

$$(2.14) \qquad B_n \Rightarrow \rho(\hat{\theta}_n) > \acute{C}\cdot n^{-(K+1)/2+\ell}.$$

Now note that on B_n

$$\text{Max}(\hat{\theta}_n^{-1}\cdot n^{-1/2}, (1-\hat{\theta}_n)^{-1}\cdot n^{-1/2}) < C\cdot n^{-\epsilon}$$

for

$$0 < \epsilon \leq [\frac{1}{2} - \frac{1}{K+2}(\frac{K+1}{2}-\ell)].$$

Hence on B_n

$$|\frac{\rho^{(i)}(\hat{\theta}_n)}{\rho(\hat{\theta}_n)}| \leq M\cdot(\hat{\theta}_n)^{-i} \leq M\cdot n^{(\frac{1}{2}-\epsilon)\cdot i}.$$

So in view of (2.14) and Remark 2.1

$$B_n \cap A_n \Rightarrow (|C_n|^{-1} \le M \cdot n^{-\ell + \frac{K+1}{2}})$$

$$\cap [|\gamma_j(\xi, \underset{-}{x}_n) \cdot n^{-j/2}| \le M \cdot n^{-\epsilon \cdot j} \quad 1 \le j \le K \text{ uniformly in } \xi]$$

for some $\epsilon > 0$. This along with (2.4), (2.9) and Theorem 2.1 gives us the result. Q.E.D.

Remark 2.2. Suppose AI to AV hold with K replaced by $K'(K' > K)$ for some $r_1 \ge 3$ and $r_2 \ge 2$ and ρ is of type $D_{K'+2}$. Then one would expect better probability bounds in (2.12). This indeed is the case. This can be achieved by first getting a $(K' + 1)$ term expansion for $F_n(\xi)$ with $M \cdot n^{-\ell} (0 < \ell < \frac{K+1}{2})$ as the error term and then bounding $\sum_{j=K+1}^{K'} |\gamma_j(\xi, \underset{-}{x}_n) \cdot n^{-j/2}|$ by $M \cdot n^{-\ell}$. The probability bound for the statement of (2.12) now turns out to be

$$1 - O(n^{-\frac{(K'+3)}{K'+2}(\frac{K'}{2} - \ell)}) - O(n^{-(K'+3)(\frac{1}{2} - \frac{\ell}{K+1})})$$

$$- O(n^{-r_1/2}) - o(n^{-r_2/2}),$$

which clearly becomes better with larger K.

Below we investigate the case when ρ is of type D_∞.

THEOREM 2.3. *Let the assumptions* AI *to* AV *hold for some* $r_1 \ge 3$ *and* $r_2 \ge 2$ *and* ρ *be of type* D_∞; *then for any* $0 < \ell < \frac{j+1}{2} \le \frac{K+1}{2}$ *and* $\epsilon > 0$

$$P_\rho[|F_n(\xi) - \Phi(\xi) - \sum_{i=1}^{j} \gamma_i(\xi, \underset{-}{x}_n) n^{-i/2}| \le M \cdot n^{-\ell},$$

$$|\gamma_i(\xi, \underset{-}{x}_n) \cdot n^{-i/2}| \le M \cdot n^{-\frac{i}{2} + \epsilon} \quad 1 \le i \le j \text{ uniformly in } \xi]$$

$$= 1 - O(n^{-\frac{(K+1)}{2}+\ell}) - O(n^{-r_1/2}) - o(n^{-r_2/2}).$$

Proof. By (iii) of Definition 2 we have for any $v > 0$

$$|\rho^{(i)}(\hat{\theta}_n)\rho^{-1}(\hat{\theta}_n)| = |\rho^{(i)}(\hat{\theta}_n)\cdot\rho^{v-1}(\hat{\theta}_n)\cdot\rho^{-v}(\hat{\theta}_n)| \leq M\cdot\rho^{-v}(\hat{\theta}_n).$$

Hence using (2.4) and Remark 2.1 for any $\epsilon > 0$ and $m > 0$

$$(\rho(\hat{\theta}_n) > n^{-m}) \cap A_n$$

$$\Rightarrow (|C_n|^{-1} \leq M\cdot n^{-m}, \sum_{i=j+1}^{K} |\gamma_i(\xi,\underline{x}_n)\cdot n^{-i/2}| \leq M\cdot n^{-\ell},$$

$$|\gamma_i(\xi,\underline{x}_n)\cdot n^{-i/2}| \leq M\cdot n^{-\frac{i}{2}+\epsilon} \quad 1 \leq i \leq j).$$

This along with (2.4), (2.11) (with $m = \frac{K+1}{2} - \ell$) and (2.1) gives the result. Q.E.D.

III. ASSUMPTIONS

Let $X_1, X_2, \ldots$ be a sequence of i.i.d. random variables having common distribution function $F(x,\theta)$, parametrized by $\theta \in \Theta$, Θ being an open interval of R. Let $f(x,\theta)$ be the density of $F(x,\theta)$ w.r.t. a σ-finite measure μ. Let the parameter θ have a prior distribution which has density $\rho(\cdot)$ w.r.t. Lebesgue measure. Let $[a_o,b_o] \subset \Theta$ be such that $\rho(\theta) > 0$ on (a_o,b_o) and $\rho(\theta) = 0$ on $(a_o,b_o)^c$. Let $c < a_o$ and $d > b_o$ be such that $[c,d] \subset \Theta$. We need to make the following assumptions.

AI: $f(x,\theta)$ is measurable in x for each $\theta \in [c,d]$.

AII: $\int |f(x,\theta)-f(x,\theta')|d\mu(x) > 0 \ \forall\, \theta,\theta' \in [c,d], \theta \neq \theta'$.

AIII: For each x, $f(x,\theta)$ admits partial derivatives w.r.t. θ of order up to two which are continuous in $[c,d]$.

AIV: 1) For each x, $f(x,\theta)$ admits partial derivatives of order upto $K+3$ $(K \geq 0)$ which are continuous in $[c,d]$.

2) For every $\theta \in [a_o,b_o]$ there exists a neighbourhood (nhbd) U_θ such that

$$\sup_{\theta' \in U_\theta} E_{\theta'} \left|\frac{d^i}{d\theta^i} \log f(X,\theta')\right|^{r_1} < \infty, \quad 1 \leq i \leq K+2.$$

3) For every $\theta \in [a_o,b_o]$, $\exists$ a nhbd U_θ and measurable functions $H_\theta(x)$ and $A_\theta(x)$ such that

a) $$\left|\frac{d^{K+3}}{d\theta^{K+3}} \log f(x,\theta')\right| \leq H_\theta(x), \ \forall\ \theta' \in U_\theta \text{ and } \forall x,$$

b) $$\left|\frac{d^{K+3}}{d\theta^{K+3}} \log f(x,\theta') - \frac{d^{K+3}}{d\theta^{K+3}} \log f(x,\theta'')\right|$$

$$\leq |\theta'-\theta''| A_\theta(x), \quad \forall \theta',\theta'' \in U_\theta \text{ and } \forall x.$$

c) $$\operatorname*{Sup}_{\theta' \in U_\theta} E_{\theta'}(H_{\theta'}(X)^{r_1}) < \infty.$$

d) $$\operatorname*{Sup}_{\theta' \in U_\theta} E_{\theta'}(A_{\theta'}(X)) < \infty.$$

AV: 1) For every $\theta \in (c,d)$ $\exists$ a nhbd U_θ such that

$$\operatorname*{Sup}_{\theta' \in U_\theta} E_{\theta'}(|\log f(X,\theta)|^{r_2+1}) < \infty.$$

2) $E_\theta(\frac{d}{d\theta} \log f(X,\theta)) = 0, \ \forall\ \theta \in (c,d).$

3) For every $\theta \in [c,d]$, $\theta' \in (c,d)$, $\exists$ nhbds V_θ and $W_{\theta'}$ such that for all nhbds $V \subset V_\theta$ of θ,

$$\operatorname*{Sup}_{\alpha \in W_{\theta'}} E_\alpha(|\operatorname*{Sup}_{\sigma \in V} \log f(X,\sigma)|^{r_2+1}) < \infty.$$

4) For every $\theta \in (c,d)$

a) $I(\theta) = E_\theta(-\frac{d^2}{d\theta^2} \log f(X,\theta) > 0.$

b) $I_1(\theta) = E_\theta(-\frac{d}{d\theta} \log f(X,\theta))^2 > 0.$

5) $I(\theta)$ and $I_1(\theta)$ are continuous on (c,d).

6) For every $\theta \in (c,d)$, $\exists$ a nhbd U_θ and a measurable function $m(x,\theta)$ such that

a) $\left|\frac{d^2}{d\theta^2} \log f(x,\theta') - \frac{d^2}{d\theta^2} \log f(x,\theta'')\right| \leq |\theta'-\theta''| m(x,\theta),$

$\forall \theta',\theta'' \in U_\theta \quad \forall x.$

b) $\sup_{\theta' \in U_\theta} E_{\theta'}(m(X,\theta)^{r_2+1}) < \infty.$

c) $\sup_{\theta' \in U_\theta} E_{\theta'}(|\frac{d^2}{d\theta^2} \log f(X,\theta')|^{r_2+1}) < \infty.$

7) For every $\theta \in (c,d)$ $\exists$ a nhbd U_θ such that

$\sup_{\theta' \in U_\theta} E_{\theta'}(|\frac{d}{d\theta} \log f(X,\theta')|^{r_2+2}) < \infty.$

Note that if AIV holds, then on $[a_o,b_o]$ $I(\theta)$ equals $I_1(\theta)$ and is continuous.

IV. SOME LEMMAS

In this section we collect all the Lemmas needed for the proofs of the results in the Sections 2 and 5. Following is a version of the Lemma 1 of Ghosh, Sinha and Wieand [4].

LEMMA 4.1. *Let* C *be a compact interval and let* $U(x,t)$ *be a real valued function measurable in* x *for each* $t \in C$ *and continuous in* t *for each* x. *Let* $X_1, X_2, \ldots$ *be a sequence of* i.i.d. r.v.s *having a common* d.f.F_θ, $\theta \in \Theta$, *and let* $H(x)$ *and* $A(x)$ *be measurable functions such that*

a) $|U(x,t)| \leq H(x), \forall\ t \in C, \forall x,$

b) $|U(x,t) - U(x,t')| \leq |t-t'|A(x), \forall t,t' \in C, \forall x,$

c) $\sup_{\theta\in\Theta} E_\theta(H(X)^r) < \infty,\ r \geq 3,$

d) $\sup_{\theta\in\Theta} E_\theta(A(X)) < \infty.$

Then for given $\epsilon > 0, \exists\ K(\epsilon)(0 < K(\epsilon) < \infty)$ *and* n_o *such that*

$$P_{F_\theta}[\sup_{t\in C}|n^{-1}\sum_{i=1}^{n} U(x_i,t) - E_{F_\theta}(U(X,t))| < \epsilon]$$

$$\geq 1-K(\epsilon)\cdot n^{-r/2}, \forall\theta \in \Theta, \forall n \geq n_o.$$

LEMMA 4.2. *Let assumptions* AI *to* AIII *and* AV *hold for some* $r_2 \geq 2$. *Then for* $\epsilon > 0$ *and* $\delta > 0$, *uniformly on compact subsets of* (c,d), *we have*

$$(4.1)\qquad P_\theta[|\hat\theta_n - \theta| \leq \varepsilon, \sum_{i=1}^{n} \frac{d}{d\theta} \log f(x_i,\hat\theta_n) = 0 \text{ and}$$

$$\frac{1}{n}\sum_{i=1}^{n}(\log f(x_i,\hat\theta_n+\emptyset) - \log f(x_i,\hat\theta_n) < -\epsilon, \forall |\emptyset| > \delta]$$

$$= 1 - o(n^{-r_2/2}),$$

where the m.l.e. $\hat\theta_n$ *is such that*

$$\sup_{\theta\in[c,d]} \prod_{i=1}^{n} f(x_i,\theta) = \prod_{i=1}^{n} f(x_i,\hat\theta_n).$$

Proof. (4.1) with r_2 replaced by 2 can be obtained from Lemma 4 of Michel and Pfanzagl [9]. Now (4.1) can be obtained as suggested in proof of Lemma 3 of Pfanzagl [10]. Q.E.D.

Following is Lemma 3 of Pfanzagl [10].

LEMMA 4.3. *Let assumptions* AI *to* AIII *and* AV *hold for some* $r_2 \geq 2$. *Then* $\exists$ *constant* $c_1 (0 < c_1 < \infty)$ *such that uniformly on compact subsets of* (c,d)

$$P_\theta\left[\frac{|\hat{\theta}_n - \theta|}{\beta(\theta)} \leq c_1 \cdot n^{-1/2}(\log n)^{1/2}\right] = 1 - o(n^{-r_2/2}),$$

where $\beta(\theta) = I^{1/2}(\theta) I_1^{-1}(\theta)$.

Following is the Theorem of Pfanzagl [11].

LEMMA 4.4. *Let assumptions* AI *to* AIII *and* AV *hold for some* $r_2 \geq 2$. *Then uniformly in* $\theta \in [a,b]$ *and uniformly over all measurable convex sets* E,

$$|P_\theta[n^{1/2}\beta^{-1}(\theta)(\hat{\theta}_n - \theta) \in E] - \Phi(E)| = 0(n^{-1/2}),$$

where Φ *denotes probability measure corresponding to a standard normal variable as well as its* d.f.

LEMMA 4.5. *Let assumptions* AI *to* AV *hold for some* $r_1 \geq 3$ *and* $r_2 \geq 2$. *Then* $\exists$ M $(0 < M < \infty)$ *such that uniformly in* $\theta \in [a_o, b_o]$

$$P_\theta[-M < a_{k,n}(\hat{\theta}_n) < M] = 1 - o(n^{r_2/2}) - 0(n^{-r_1/2}) \text{ for}$$

$k = 1,\ldots,K+3$ *where* $a_{k,n}(\theta) = \frac{1}{k!n} \sum_{i=1}^{n} \frac{d^k}{d\theta^k} \log f(x_i, \theta)$.

Proof. Applying Lemma 4.1 to $a_{k,n}$ $(k = 1,\ldots,K+3)$, for every $\delta > 0$ we get M $(0 < M < \infty)$ such that uniformly in $\theta \in [a_o, b_o]$ we have

$$P_\theta[-M < a_{kn}(\theta') < M \text{ for } \forall |\theta' - \theta| < \delta \text{ and } k = 1,\ldots,K+3]$$

$$= 1 - 0(n^{-r_1/2}).$$

Combining this with Lemma 4.2 we get the result. Q.E.D.

LEMMA 4.6. *Let assumptions* AI *to* AIV *hold with* $r_1 \geq 3$. *Then for* $\epsilon > 0$ $\exists$ $\delta > 0$ *such that uniformly in* $\theta \in [a_o, b_o]$

$$P_\theta[E_\theta(-2a_{2,n}(\theta)) - \epsilon \leq -2a_{2,n}(\theta') \leq E_\theta(-2a_{2,n}(\theta)) + \epsilon,$$

$$\forall |\theta-\theta'| < \delta] = 1 - 0(n^{-r_1/2}).$$

Proof. Applying Lemma 4.1 to $-2a_{2,n}(\theta)$ we get $\delta_1 > 0$ such that uniformly in $\theta \in [a_o, b_o]$ we have

$$P_\theta[E_\theta(-2a_{2,n}(\theta')) - \frac{\epsilon}{2} \leq -2a_{2,n}(\theta') \leq E_\theta(-2a_{2,n}(\theta') + \frac{\epsilon}{2},$$

$$\forall |\theta-\theta'| < \delta_1] = 1 - 0(n^{-r_1/2}).$$

Now

$$E_\theta(-2a_{2,n}(\theta')) = E_\theta(-2a_{2,n}(\theta)) + (\theta'-\theta)E_\theta(-a_{3n}(\theta)) \frac{3!}{2} + \ldots$$

$$+ \ldots + \frac{(K+2)!}{(K-1)!} (\theta'-\theta)^{K-1} E_\theta(-a_{K+2,n}(\theta)) + \frac{(K+3)!}{K!}$$

$$(\theta'-\theta)^K E_\theta(-a_{K+3,n}(\theta_1)),$$

where θ_1 lies between θ and θ'. Hence in view of AIV, $\exists$ $\delta_2 > 0$ such that

$$|E_\theta(-2a_{2,n}(\theta')) - E_\theta(-2a_{2,n}(\theta))| < \frac{\epsilon}{2} \; \forall |\theta-\theta'| < \delta_2,$$

$$\forall \; \theta \in [a_o, b_o]. \qquad \text{Q.E.D.}$$

The proof of the following Lemma is similar to that of Lemma 2.2 of Johnson [8]. Instead of his (2.5), in our case, we use Lemma 4.6 along with Lemma 4.2.

LEMMA 4.7. *Let assumptions* AI *to* AV *hold for some* $r_1 \geq 3$ *and* $r_2 \geq 2$. *Then* $\exists$ $\delta_2 > 0$ *such that uniformly in* $\theta \in [a_o, b_o]$

$$P_\theta[n^{-1}\sum_{i=1}^{n}(\log f(x_i,\hat{\theta}_n+\emptyset b^{-1})-\log f(x_i,\hat{\theta}_n)) \le -\frac{\emptyset^2}{6}, \forall|\emptyset| \le \delta_2]$$

$$= 1 - o(n^{-r_2/2}) - 0(n^{-r_1/2}).$$

Here $b^2(\theta) = (-2a_{2,n}(\theta))$ *and* $b^2 = b^2(\hat{\theta}_n)$.

Remark 4.1. Note that (4.2), (4.3) and (4.4) below are similar to the (2.11), (2.21) and (2.22) of Johnson [8] respectively with slightly different remainder R_n. We need the remainder in this form mainly to display clearly the contribution of ρ to the remainder. In what follows

$$R_n = \sum_{r=1}^{r_o} n^{-(K+r)/2}|\rho^{(K+r)}(\hat{\theta}_n)| + n^{-(K+1)/2}\sum_{r=0}^{K}|\rho^{(r)}(\hat{\theta}_n)|$$

$$+ n^{-(K+r_o+1)/2} \quad \text{with } \rho^{(0)}(\theta) = \rho(\theta)$$

and $\rho^{(k)}(\theta) = \dfrac{d^k}{d\theta^k}\rho(\theta)$.

LEMMA 4.8. *Let assumptions* AI *to* AV *hold with some* $r_1 \ge 3$ *and* $r_2 \ge 2$. *Let* ρ *be* $K+r_o+1$ *times continuously differentiable on* $[a_o,b_o]$ *for some* $r_o \ge 0$. *Then* $\exists$ M $(0 < M < \infty)$ *such that for sufficiently small* $\delta > 0$ *and uniformly in* $\theta \in [a_o,b_o]$ *we have*

$$P_\theta[\int_{-\delta}^{\delta}|\exp[n\sum_{K=2}^{K+3} a_{k,n}(\hat{\theta}_n)(\emptyset b^{-1})^k]\rho_K(\hat{\theta}_n+\emptyset b^{-1})$$

$$- \prod_{i=1}^{n}[f(x_i,\hat{\theta}_n+\emptyset b^{-1})/f(x_i,\hat{\theta}_n)]\rho(\hat{\theta}_n+\emptyset b^{-1})|d\emptyset$$

$$\le M\cdot R_n\cdot n^{-1/2}]$$

$$= 1 - o(n^{-r_2/2}) - 0(n^{-r_1/2}).$$

Here $\rho_K(\theta) = \rho(\hat{\theta}_n) + \sum_{r=1}^{K} \frac{(\theta-\hat{\theta}_n)^r}{r!} \rho^{(r)}(\hat{\theta}_n)$.

Proof. Proof of this lemma is similar to that of Lemma 2.4 of Johnson [8]. Here we use the Lemmas 4.5, 4.6 and 4.7 instead of his corresponding results and expand $\rho(\cdot)$ up to $K+r_o+1$ terms instead of K+1 terms. Hence there exists constant M_2 such that for sufficiently small $\delta > 0$ and uniformly in $\theta \in [a_o,b_o]$ we have

$$P_\theta\{\int_{-\delta}^{\delta} |\exp[n \sum_{k=1}^{K+3} a_{k,n}(\hat{\theta}_n)(\emptyset b^{-1})^k]\rho_K(\hat{\theta}_n+\emptyset b^{-1})$$

$$- \prod_{i=1}^{n} [f(x_i,\hat{\theta}_n+\emptyset b^{-1})/f(x_i,\hat{\theta}_n)]\rho(\hat{\theta}_n+\emptyset b^{-1})|d\emptyset$$

$$\leq \int_{-\delta}^{\delta} e^{-\frac{n\emptyset^2}{2}} [\sum_{r=1}^{r_o} \frac{|\emptyset b^{-1}|^{K+r}}{(K+r)!} |\rho^{(K+r)}(\hat{\theta}_n)|$$

$$+ M_2 \frac{|\emptyset b^{-1}|^{K+r_o+1}}{(K+r_o+1)!} |\rho^{(K+r_o+1)}(\theta_n^*)|]d\emptyset\}$$

$$= 1 - O(n^{-r_1/2}) - o(n^{-r_2/2}),$$

where θ_n^* is between $\hat{\theta}_n$ and $\hat{\theta}_n+\emptyset b^{-1}$. Now using similar arguments as in the proof of Lemma 2.4 of Johnson [8] we get the result.

Q.E.D.

Now as we don't want to confound terms involving ρ and its derivatives with the remainder we expand $\exp[\omega\psi_{K_n}(z)]$ (see 2.14 of Johnson [8] for notations and other details) instead of $\rho_K(\hat{\theta}_n+zb^{-1})\exp[\omega\psi_{K_n}(z)]$. Thus in our case bounding $c_{\ell,m}(\underset{\sim}{x}_n)$ with the help of Lemmas 4.5 and 4.6, instead of his (2.18) we get constants M_r $(1 \leq r \leq K)$ such that uniformly in $\theta \in [a_o,b_o]$

$$P_\theta\{|P_K(\phi, n\phi^3, \underline{x}_n) - \sum_{\ell+m\leq K} c_{\ell,m}(\underline{x}_n)\phi^\ell(n\phi^3)^m|$$

$$\leq \sum_{r=0}^{K} M_r|\rho^{(r)}(\hat{\theta}_n)|[|\phi|^{K+1}+|n\phi^3|^{K+1}+ \sum_{K-r+1\leq i+j\leq K}|\phi|^i|n\phi^3|^j]|\phi|^r$$

for $|\phi| < n^{-1/3}\} = 1 - O(n^{-r_1/2}) - o(n^{-r_2/2})$.

Hence, using our versions of his results and using similar arguments, as in the proof of (2.21) and (2.22) of Johnson [8], we get (4.3) and (4.4). Q.E.D.

LEMMA 4.9. *Let assumptions* AI *to* AV *hold with* $r_1 \geq 3$ *and* $r_2 \geq 2$ *and let* ρ *be* $K+r_o+1$ *times continuously differentiable on* $[a_o, b_o]$ *for some* $r_o \geq 0$. *Then* $\exists$ M $(0 < M < \infty)$ *such that uniformly in* $\theta \in [a_o, b_o]$ *we have*

$$(4.3)\qquad P_\theta\{|\int_{-\infty}^{\infty} \rho(\hat{\theta}_n+\phi b^{-1}) \prod_{i=1}^{n} [f(x_i, \hat{\theta}_n+\phi b^{-1})/f(x_i, \hat{\theta}_n)]d\phi$$

$$- \sum_{j=0}^{K} \beta_j(\underline{x}_n)n^{-\frac{1}{2}(j+1)}| \leq M\cdot n^{-\frac{1}{2}}\cdot R_n\}$$

$$= 1 - O(n^{-r_1/2}) - o(n^{-r_2/2})$$

and

$$(4.4)\qquad P_\theta\{|\int_{-\infty}^{\xi\cdot n^{-1/2}} \rho(\hat{\theta}_n+\phi b^{-1}) \prod_{i=1}^{n} [f(x_i, \hat{\theta}_n+\phi b^{-1})/f(x_i, \hat{\theta}_n)]$$

$$- \sum_{j=0}^{K} \alpha_j(\xi, \underline{x}_n)n^{-\frac{1}{2}(j+1)}| \leq M\cdot n^{-1/2}\cdot R_n \text{ uniformly in } \xi\}$$

$$= 1 - O(n^{-r_1/2}) - o(n^{-r_2/2}),$$

where the α_j *and* β_j *are as defined in Johnson* [8].

V. EXPANSIONS FOR POSTERIOR AND INTEGRATED BAYES RISK

Let $A_n = \{-M < a_{3,n}(\hat{\theta}_n) < M,\ 0 < \delta < b^{-1}(\hat{\theta}_n) < M\}$. Then $\exists$ $\delta > 0$ and M such that under appropriate assumptions (vide Lemmas 4.2, 4.4 and 4.6)

$$(5.1) \qquad P_\rho(A_n) = 1 - o(n^{-2}).$$

LEMMA 5.1. *Let assumptions* AI *to* AV *hold with some* $K \geq 2$, $r_1 > 4$ *and* $r_2 \geq 4$. *Let* ρ *be of type* D_{5+r_o} *for some* r_o, $6 < r_o < \infty$. *Then* $\exists$ $\in > 0$ *and* $\delta > 0$ *such that*

$$(5.2) \qquad P_\rho[|E(\theta/\underset{\sim}{x}_n) - \hat{\theta}_n - \lambda_{1,2,n}(\underset{\sim}{x}_n)\cdot n^{-1}| \leq M\cdot n^{-(\frac{3}{2}+\in)},$$

$$|n^{-1}\cdot \frac{\rho^{(1)}(\hat{\theta}_n)}{\rho(\hat{\theta}_n)}| \leq M\cdot n^{-\delta}]$$

$$= 1 - o(n^{-2}),$$

where

$$\lambda_{1,2,n}(\underset{\sim}{x}_n) = b^{-1}(6a_{3,n}(\hat{\theta}_n)\, b^{-3} + \frac{\rho^{(1)}(\hat{\theta}_n)}{\rho(\hat{\theta}_n)}\cdot b^{-1}).$$

Expression for $\lambda_{1,2,n}$ as given by Johnson [8] is not correct. It should be as given above. In this lemma we get an expansion for the Bayes estimate as in Theorem 3.1 of Johnson [8]. In this connection note that Johnson expands to less terms than are allowed by the assumptions for his Theorem 3.1; in the following we are in effect expanding the Bayes estimate up to $n^{-3/2}$ and using the fact that the coefficient of this term is zero.

Proof. Following the proof of (4.3) (vide Theorem 3.1 of Johnson [8]) with $\rho(\hat{\theta}_n + \emptyset b^{-1})$ replaced by $\emptyset\rho(\hat{\theta}_n + \emptyset b^{-1})$ we get

$$(5.3a)\qquad P_\rho\{|\int_{-\infty}^{\infty} \phi\rho(\hat\theta_n+\phi b^{-1}) \prod_{i=1}^{n} [f(x_i,\hat\theta_n+\phi b^{-1})/f(x_i,\hat\theta_n)]d\phi$$

$$- (b^{-1}\cdot\rho^{(1)}(\hat\theta_n) + b^{-3}a_{3,n}(\hat\theta_n)\cdot\rho(\hat\theta_n))\cdot n^{-1}\cdot\sqrt{2\pi}|$$

$$\leq M\cdot n^{-1/2}\cdot R_{1n}\}$$

$$= 1-o(n^{-2}),$$

$$R_{1n} = n^{-(4+r_o)/2} + n^{-2}\sum_{r=0}^{2}|\rho^{(r)}(\hat\theta_n)|$$

$$+ \sum_{r=1}^{r_o} n^{-(3+r)/2}|\rho^{(2+r)}(\hat\theta_n)|$$

(vide Remark 4.1). Using (4.3), (2.2) and (5.3a) we have

$$P_\rho\{|E(\theta-\hat\theta_n/\underset{\sim}{x}_n)| \leq M\cdot(n^{-1}\cdot|\lambda_{1,2,n}(\underset{\sim}{x}_n)|+|C_n|^{-1}\cdot n^{1/2}\cdot R_{1n})$$

$$= n^{-1/2}\cdot M\cdot\delta_n \quad \text{(say)}\}$$

$$= 1 - o(n^{-2}). \quad \text{(vide Remark 2.1 for } C_n).$$

Now again using (4.3), (5.3a) and (2.2) but this time (2.2) with $C = n^{-1/2}\cdot\delta_n\cdot M\cdot b$, we get

$$(5.3)\qquad P_\rho\{|E(\theta/\underset{\sim}{x}_n)-\hat\theta_n-\lambda_{1,2,n}(\underset{\sim}{x}_n)\cdot n^{-1}| \leq M\cdot|C_n|^{-1}\cdot R_n\}$$

$$= 1 - o(n^{-2}),$$

where $R_n = R_{1n}(1 + \delta_n)$.

For simplicity let $a_o = 0$ and $b_o = 1$. Consider the case $r_o < \infty$. By Remark 2.1, (2.10) and using the forms of R_n and $\lambda_{1,2,n}(\underset{\sim}{x}_n)$ for every $\epsilon_1 > 0$, $\exists$ $\epsilon > 0$ and $\delta > 0$ such that on A_n

$$(5.4)\qquad (\hat{\theta}_n \geq M\cdot n^{-(1/6-\epsilon_1)}, \hat{\theta}_n \leq 1-M\cdot n^{-(1/6-\epsilon_1)})$$

$$\Rightarrow \{|C_n|^{-1}\cdot R_n \leq M\cdot n^{-(\frac{3}{2}+\epsilon)}, |n^{-1}\cdot\frac{\rho^{(1)}(\hat{\theta}_n)}{\rho(\hat{\theta}_n)}| \leq M\cdot n^{-\delta}\}.$$

For the case $r_o < \infty$, the proof of (5.2) is completed by using (5.3), (5.4) and (5.1). The case $r_o = \infty$ follows easily. Q.E.D.

Let

$$(5.5)\qquad \Delta_n = [|E(\theta/\underline{x}_n)-B_n| \leq M\cdot n^{-(\frac{3}{2}+\epsilon)},$$

$$|\lambda_{1,2,n}(\underline{x}_n)\cdot n^{-1}| \leq M\cdot n^{-\delta}] \cap A_n,$$

where $B_n = \hat{\theta}_n + \lambda_{1,2,n}(\underline{x}_n)\cdot n^{-1}$ and ϵ and δ as in Lemma 5.1. Note that B_n is bounded on Δ_n and $P_\rho(\Delta_n) = 1 - o(n^{-2})$.

PROPOSITION 5.1. *Let assumptions* AI *to* AV *hold with some* $K \geq 2$, $r_1 > 4$ *and* $r_2 \geq 4$. *Let* ρ *be of type* D_S, $11 < S \leq \infty$. *Then*

$$(5.6)\qquad E_\rho[(B_n-\theta)^2\cdot I_{\Delta_n}] = a_1\cdot n^{-1}+a_2\cdot n^{-2}+o(n^{-2}),$$

where $a_1 = \int I^{-1}(\theta)\rho(\theta)d\theta$,

$$a_2 = \int\{H_{2,2}(\theta)-\frac{1}{4}I^{-4}(\theta)\ell_3^2(\theta)-4I^{-3}(\theta)\cdot\frac{d}{d\theta}\log\rho(\theta)\cdot\frac{d}{d\theta}I(\theta)$$

$$-I^{-2}(\theta)(\frac{d}{d\theta}\log\rho(\theta))^2 + I^{-3}(\theta)\cdot\frac{d}{d\theta}\ell_3(\theta)$$

$$-3I^{-4}(\theta)\ell_3(\theta)\frac{d}{d\theta}(I(\theta))\}\rho(\theta)d\theta,$$

$$\ell_i(\theta) = E_\theta(\frac{d^i}{d\theta^i}\log f(X,\theta)),$$

$$\ell_{i,j}(\theta) = E_\theta\{\frac{d^i}{d\theta^i} \log f(X,\theta)\cdot\frac{d^j}{d\theta^j} \log f(X,\theta)\},\ 1 \le i,j \le 4,$$

$\ell_{i,o}(\theta) = \ell_i(\theta)$ *and*

$$H_{2,2}(\theta) = E_\theta\{(\frac{d}{d\theta} \log f(X,\theta))^3\cdot(\frac{d^3}{d\theta^3} \log f(X,\theta))\}\cdot I^{-4}(\theta)$$

$$+ \frac{15}{4}\ell_3^2(\theta)\cdot I^{-4}(\theta)+12(\ell_{1,2}(\theta)+\ell_3(\theta))I^{-4}(\theta)$$

$$+ 6\ell_{1,2}^2(\theta)\cdot I^{-4}(\theta)$$

$$+ 2E_\theta\{(\frac{d}{d\theta} \log f(X,\theta))^2\cdot(\frac{d^2}{d\theta^2} \log f(X,\theta))\}\cdot I^{-3}(\theta)$$

$$+ \ell_4(\theta)\cdot I^{-3}(\theta)+3\ell_{1,3}(\theta)\cdot I^{-3}(\theta)$$

$$+ E_\theta(\frac{d^2}{d\theta^2} \log f(X,\theta))^2\cdot I^{-3}(\theta)$$

(*vide* (3.3) *of Gusev* [6]). *We also use following notations*

$\ell_{i,n}(\theta) = (i!)a_{i,n}(\theta)$ *and* $I_n(\theta) = -2a_{2,n}(\theta)$ *for* $n > 4$.

Proof. Note that under the assumptions of the Proposition, by Gusev [6] we have uniformly in $\theta \in [a_o,b_o]$

$$(5.7) \qquad E_\theta(\hat\theta_n-\theta) = \frac{\ell_3(\theta)+2\ell_{1,2}(\theta)}{2I^2(\theta)}\cdot n^{-1} + 0(n^{-2})$$

$$E_\theta(\hat\theta_n-\theta)^2 = I^{-1}(\theta)\cdot n^{-1} + H_{2,2}(\theta)\cdot n^{-2} + o(n^{-2})$$

$$E_\theta(\hat\theta_n-\theta)^i = 0(n^{-2}),\quad i = 3,4,$$

and

$$(5.7a) \qquad \ell_{1,3}(\theta) + \ell_4(\theta) = \frac{d}{d\theta}\ell_3(\theta),\ \ell_{1,2}(\theta)+\ell_3(\theta)= \frac{d}{d\theta}(-I(\theta)).$$

Let

$$I_{n,\theta} = \{|\hat{\theta}_n-\theta| \le c_n, \sum_{i=1}^{n} \frac{d}{d\theta} \log f(x_i,\hat{\theta}_n) = 0,$$

$$|\ell_{2,n}(\hat{\theta}_n)-\ell_2(\hat{\theta}_n)| \le c_n,$$

$$|\ell_{3,n}(\hat{\theta}_n)-\ell_3(\hat{\theta}_n)| \le c_n, 0 < \delta < I_n(\theta_n^*) < M \text{ and}$$

$$M < \ell_{i,n}(\theta_n^*) < M,$$

for i = 3,4,5 and θ_n^* between $\hat{\theta}_n$ and $\theta\}$, where $c_n = c_1 \cdot n^{-1/2} (\log n)^{1/2}$, c_1 as in Lemma 4.3. Note that by applying Lemma 1 of Pfanzagl [10] to $\ell_{2,n}(\theta)$ and $\ell_{3,n}(\theta)$ and our Lemma 4.1 to $\ell_{i,n}$ (i = 3,4,5) in view of our Lemma 4.3 we have uniformly in $\theta \in [a_o,b_o]$

(5.8) $$P_\theta(I_{n,\theta}) = 1 - o(n^{-2}).$$

Now,

(5.9) $$E_\theta[(B_n-\theta)^2 \cdot I_{\Delta_n}] = E_\theta[(B_n-\theta)^2(I_{\Delta_n \cap I_{n,\theta}} + I_{\Delta_n \cap I^c_{n,\theta}})].$$

For simplicity, let $a_o = 0$ and $b_o = 1$. First we consider the case $16 < S < \infty$. Let $a_n = 2c_n$ and $b_n = 1-2c_n$. Note that

(5.10) $$\int_o^{a_n} E_\theta[(B_n-\theta)^2 \cdot I_{\Delta_n}]\rho(\theta)d\theta = o(n^{-2})$$

$$= \int_{b_n}^{1} E_\theta[(B_n-\theta)^2 \cdot I_{\Delta_n}]\rho(\theta)d\theta$$

and $\int_o^1 E_\theta[(B_n-\theta)^2 \cdot I_{\Delta_n \cap I^c_{n,\theta}}]\rho(\theta)d\theta = o(n^{-2})$.

Using (5.9) and (5.10) we get

(5.11) $$E_\rho[(B_n-\theta)^2 \cdot I_{\Delta_n}] = \int_{a_n}^{b_n} E_\theta[(B_n-\theta)^2 \cdot I_{\Delta_n \cap I_{n,\theta}}]\rho(\theta)d\theta + o(n^{-2}).$$

Expanding $\lambda_{1,2,n}(\hat{\theta}_n)$ around θ and denoting the first and second derivatives of $\lambda_{1,2,n}$ by $\lambda^{(1)}_{1,2,n}$ and $\lambda^{(2)}_{1,2,n}$ respectively we have

$$(B_n-\theta) = (\hat{\theta}_n-\theta)+\lambda_{1,2,n}(\theta)\cdot n^{-1}+(\hat{\theta}_n-\theta)\cdot n^{-1}\cdot\lambda^{(1)}_{1,2,n}(\theta)$$

$$+n^{-1}\cdot\frac{(\hat{\theta}_n-\theta)^2}{2}\lambda^{(2)}_{1,2,n}(\xi)$$

$$= (\hat{\theta}_n-\theta)+n^{-1}\cdot I_n^{-1}(\theta)\left[\frac{\ell_{3,n}(\theta)\cdot I_n^{-1}(\theta)}{2}+\frac{d}{d\theta}\log\rho(\theta)\right]$$

$$+ (\hat{\theta}_n-\theta)\cdot n^{-1}\cdot\{I_n^{-3}(\theta)\ell^2_{3,n}(\theta)+\frac{1}{2}\cdot I_n^{-2}(\theta)\ell_{4,n}(\theta)$$

$$+ I_n^{-1}(\theta)\frac{d^2}{d\theta^2}\log\rho(\theta)+I_n^{-2}(\theta)\cdot\ell_{3,n}(\theta)\frac{d}{d\theta}\log\rho(\theta)\}$$

$$+ n^{-1}\cdot\frac{(\hat{\theta}_n-\theta)^2}{2}\lambda^{(2)}_{1,2,n}(\xi),$$

where ξ is between $\hat{\theta}_n$ and θ. Now we use

$$(I_n(\theta))^{-r} = (I(\theta))^{-r}-r(I_n(\theta)-I(\theta))(I(\theta))^{-(r+1)}$$

$$+ r\cdot(r+1)\frac{1}{2}\cdot(I_n(\theta)-I(\theta))^2\cdot(I_n^*)^{-(r+2)},$$

where I_n^* is between $I_n(\theta)$ and $I(\theta)$ and

$$(\hat{\theta}_n-\theta) = I^{-1}(\theta)\ell_{1,n}(\theta)-(\hat{\theta}_n-\theta)\cdot I^{-1}(\theta)\cdot(I_n(\theta)-I(\theta))$$

$$+\frac{(\hat{\theta}_n-\theta)^2}{2}\ell_{3,n}(\theta_n^*)\cdot I^{-1}(\theta)$$

where θ_n^* is between $\hat{\theta}_n$ and θ. Write $(B_n-\theta)^2 = E_{1,n}+E_{2,n}$ where

$$E_{1,n} = (\hat{\theta}_n-\theta)^2+n^{-2}\cdot I^{-2}(\theta)\cdot[\frac{d}{d\theta}\log\rho(\theta)+\frac{1}{2}I^{-1}(\theta)\ell_3(\theta)]^2$$

$$+ n^{-1}.I^{-2}(\theta)(I^{-1}(\theta)\ell_{1,n}(\theta)[\ell_{3,n}(\theta)-\ell_3(\theta)]+(\hat{\theta}_n-\theta)^2\ell_4(\theta))$$

$$+ 2\cdot n^{-1}I^{-3}(\theta)\ell_3(\theta)(-I^{-1}(\theta)\ell_{1,n}(\theta)[I_n(\theta)-I(\theta)] + (\hat{\theta}_n-\theta)^2\ell_3(\theta))$$

$$+ 2\cdot n^{-1}I^{-1}(\theta)(\hat{\theta}_n-\theta)^2\frac{d^2}{d\theta^2}\log\rho(\theta)$$

$$+ 2\cdot n^{-1}I^{-2}(\theta)\frac{d}{d\theta}\log\rho(\theta)(-I^{-1}(\theta)\ell_{1,n}(\theta)[I_n(\theta)-I(\theta)] + (\hat{\theta}_n-\theta)^2\ell_3(\theta))$$

$$+ 2\cdot n^{-1}I^{-1}(\theta)(\hat{\theta}_n-\theta)(\frac{1}{2}I^{-1}(\theta)\ell_3(\theta) + \frac{d}{d\theta}\log\rho(\theta)).$$

We now prove that

$$\int_{a_n}^{b_n} E_\theta[E_{2n}\, I_{\Delta_n\cap I_{n,\theta}}]\rho(\theta)d\theta = o(n^{-2}). \tag{5.12}$$

Choose a term of $E_{2,n}$, say,

$$2n^{-1}\cdot\frac{\rho^{(1)}(\theta)}{\rho(\theta)}(I(\theta))^{-1/2}\cdot n^{-1}\cdot\frac{(\hat{\theta}_n-\theta)^2}{2}\cdot\lambda^{(2)}_{1,2,n}(\xi).$$

We prove that

$$n^{-2}\cdot\int_{a_n}^{b_n}\frac{\rho^{(1)}(\theta)}{\rho(\theta)}\cdot I^{-1}(\theta)\cdot E_\theta[(\hat{\theta}_n-\theta)^2\cdot\lambda^{(2)}_{1,2,n}(\xi)\cdot I_{\Delta_n\cap I_{n,\theta}}]\rho(\theta)d\theta = o(n^{-2}). \tag{5.13}$$

Note that for sufficiently small $\epsilon > 0$

(5.14)
$$n^{-2}\cdot\int_{a_n}^{\epsilon} E_\theta[(\hat\theta_n-\theta)^2\cdot \frac{\rho^{(1)}(\theta)}{\rho(\theta)}\cdot\frac{\rho^{(1)}(\xi)^3}{\rho(\xi)}\cdot I_{\Delta_n\cap I_{n,\theta}}]\rho(\theta)d\theta$$

$$\le M\cdot n^{-3}\cdot\log n\cdot\int_{2c_n}^{\epsilon}\theta^{-1}\cdot(\theta-c_n)^{-3}\cdot\theta^S d\theta$$

$$= M\cdot n^{-3}\cdot\log n\int_{c_n}^{\epsilon-c_n}(\theta+c_n)^{S-1}\cdot\theta^{-3}d\theta$$

$$= o(n^{-2}) \text{ as } S > 16.$$

Now it is not difficult to see that (5.14) and similar observations give us (5.13). Similarly handling other terms of $E_{2,n}$ one gets (5.12). Using (5.11) and (5.12) we get

(5.15)
$$E_\rho[(B_n-\theta)^2\cdot I_{\Delta_n}]$$

$$= \int_{a_n}^{b_n} E_\theta[E_{1,n}\cdot I_{\Delta_n\cap I_{n,\theta}}]\rho(\theta)d\theta + o(n^{-2}).$$

We have

(5.16)
$$\int_{a_n}^{b_n} E_\theta[E_{1,n}\, I_{(\Delta_n\cap I_{n,\theta})^c}]\rho(\theta)d\theta$$

$$\le \int_{a_n}^{b_n}[E_\theta(E_{1,n}^2)\rho(\theta)]^{\frac{1}{2}}\cdot[P_\theta(\Delta_n^c\cup I_{n,\theta}^c)\rho(\theta)]^{\frac{1}{2}}d\theta$$

$$\le \{\int_{a_n}^{b_n}E_\theta(E_{1,n}^2)\rho(\theta)d\theta\}^{\frac{1}{2}}\cdot\{\int_{a_n}^{b_n}P_\theta(\Delta_n^c\cup I_{n,\theta}^c)\rho(\theta)d\theta\}^{\frac{1}{2}}$$

$$= o(n^{-2}),$$

using (5.5), (5.8), (5.7) and (iii) of Definition 1. Moreover, integrating term by term and utilizing the polynomial decay of $\rho^{(1)}(\theta), \rho^{(2)}(\theta)$ and $\frac{(\rho^{(1)}(\theta))^2}{\rho(\theta)}$ near the two end points, in view of (5.7) we have

$$\int_0^{a_n} E_\theta(E_{1,n})\rho(\theta)d\theta = o(n^{-2}) = \int_{b_n}^1 E_\theta(E_{1,n})\rho(\theta)d\theta. \tag{5.17}$$

Combining (5.15), (5.16) and (5.17) we get

$$E_\rho[(\hat{\theta}_n-\theta)^2 \cdot I_{\Delta_n}] = \int_0^1 E_\theta(E_{1,n})\rho(\theta)d\theta + o(n^{-2}).$$

This in view of (5.17) proves the Proposition for $11 < S < \infty$.

When ρ is of type D_∞, let $a_n = \rho_1^{-1}(n^{-3})$ and $b_n = \rho_2^{-1}(n^{-3})$ (see Proposition 2.2 for the definitions of ρ_1^{-1} and ρ_2^{-1}). Now to get (5.6), similar arguments as above can be given, the only difference being the demonstration of the conclusion of (5.17). Note that for sufficiently small $\epsilon > 0$ and for sufficiently large n

$$n^{-2}\int_{a_n}^{\epsilon} E_\theta\{(\hat{\theta}_n-\theta)^2 \cdot \frac{\rho^{(1)}(\theta)}{\rho(\theta)} \cdot \frac{\rho^{(1)}(\xi)^3}{\rho(\xi)} \cdot I_{\Delta_n \cap I_{n,\theta}}\}\rho(\theta)d\theta$$

$$\leq M \cdot n^{-3}\int_{a_n}^{\epsilon} \rho^{-v_1}(\theta) \cdot \rho^{-v_2}(\theta-c_n)\rho(\theta)d\theta,$$

where $v_1 > 0$ and $v_2 > 0$ can be made arbitrarily small by choosing $\epsilon > 0$. Now

$$\rho^{-v_2}(\theta-c_n) = [\rho(\theta)+\sum_{i=1}^{6}\frac{(-c_n)^i}{i!}\rho^{(i)}(\theta)+\frac{(-c_n)^7}{7!}\rho^{(7)}(\theta_n)]^{-v_2}$$

(where θ_n is between θ and $\theta-c_n$)

$$= \rho^{-v_2}(\theta)[1+\sum_{i=1}^{6}\frac{(-c_n)^i\rho^{(i)}(\theta)}{i!} + \frac{(-c_n)^7}{7!}\frac{\rho^{(7)}(\theta_n)}{\rho(\theta)}]^{-v_2}$$

$$\leq M\cdot\rho^{-v_2}(\theta) \text{ for } \theta = \theta_n.$$

The conclusion of (5.17) is now proved in view of monotone nature of ρ near the end points along with other observations. Q.E.D.

Let

$$B_n' = \hat{\theta}_n + I^{-1}(\hat{\theta}_n)(\frac{1}{2} I^{-1}(\hat{\theta}_n)\ell_3(\hat{\theta}_n) + \frac{d}{d\theta}\log\rho(\hat{\theta}_n))\cdot n^{-1}.$$

PROPOSITION 5.2. *Under the assumptions of Proposition* 5.1

$$E_\rho[(B_n'-\theta)^2\cdot I_{\Delta_n}] = a_1\cdot n^{-1} + a_2\cdot n^{-2} + o(n^{-2}).$$

Proof. Let

$$C(\theta) = I^{-1}(\theta)(\frac{1}{2} I^{-1}(\theta)\ell_3(\theta) + \frac{d}{d\theta}\log\rho(\theta)).$$

$$(B_n'-\theta) = (\hat{\theta}_n-\theta) + n^{-1}\cdot C(\theta) + n^{-1}\cdot(\hat{\theta}_n-\theta)\cdot C^{(1)}(\theta)$$

$$+ n^{-1}\cdot\frac{(\hat{\theta}_n-\theta)^2}{2}\cdot C^{(2)}(\theta_n^*),$$

where $C^{(i)}(\theta) = \frac{d^i}{d\theta^i}C(\theta)$ and θ_n^* is between $\hat{\theta}_n$ and θ. As in the case of B_n, we write

$$(B_n'-\theta)^2 = E_{1,n}' + E_{2,n}'$$

where

$$E_{1,n}' = (\hat{\theta}_n-\theta)^2 + n^{-2}\cdot I^{-2}(\theta)[\frac{1}{2} I^{-1}(\theta)\ell_3(\theta) + \frac{d}{d\theta}\log\rho(\theta)]^2$$

$$+ n^{-1}\cdot I^{-2}(\theta)[I^{-1}(\theta)\ell_{1,n}(\theta)(\ell_{3,n}(\theta)-\ell_3(\theta)) + (\hat{\theta}_n-\theta)^2\ell_4(\theta)]$$

$$+ 2n^{-1}\cdot I^{-3}(\theta)\ell_3(\theta)(\hat{\theta}_n-\theta)^2 \frac{d}{d\theta}(-I(\theta))$$

$$+ 2n^{-1}\cdot I^{-1}(\theta)(\hat{\theta}_n-\theta)[\frac{1}{2} I^{-1}(\theta)\ell_3(\theta)+ \frac{d}{d\theta}\log \rho(\theta)]$$

$$+ 2n^{-1}\cdot I^{-1}(\theta)(\hat{\theta}_n-\theta)^2 \frac{d^2}{d\theta^2}\log \rho(\theta)$$

$$+ 2n^{-1}\cdot I^{-2}(\theta)(\hat{\theta}_n-\theta)^2 \frac{d}{d\theta}\log \rho(\theta) \frac{d}{d\theta}(-I(\theta)).$$

Now proceeding as in the case of Proposition 5.1 the proof is completed.

Definition 5.1. An estimate T_n is called an approximate Bayes estimate of order β w.r.t. the loss function L and prior ρ if

$$|E_\rho[L(T_n,\theta)] - \text{Inf } E_\rho[L(T'_n,\theta)]| = o(n^{-\beta}),$$

the above infimum being taken over all estimates depending only on $\underset{\sim}{x}_n$.

Let

$$B^*_n = B_n \text{ if } B_n \in (a_o,b_o)$$

$$= a_o \text{ if } B_n \leq a_o$$

$$= b_o \text{ if } B_n \geq b_o$$

and

$$B''_n = B'_n \text{ if } B'_n \in (a_o,b_o)$$

$$= a_o \text{ if } B'_n \leq a_o$$

$$= b_o \text{ if } B'_n \geq b_o.$$

THEOREM 5.1. *Under the assumptions of Proposition* 5.1, *the Bayes risk*, R_ρ, w.r.t. *the squared error loss function has the following expansion*

$$R_\rho = a_1 \cdot n^{-1} + a_2 \cdot n^{-2} + o(n^{-2}).$$

COROLLARY 5.1. *Under the assumptions of Proposition* 5.1, B_n^* *and* B_n'' *are approximate Bayes estimates of order* 2, w.r.t. *the squared error loss function.*

Proof. As B_n^* is the natural truncation of B_n

$$E_\rho[(B_n-\theta)^2 \cdot I_{\Delta_n}] \geq E_\rho[(B^*_n-\theta)^2 \cdot I_{\Delta_n}] \tag{5.18}$$

$$= E_\rho[(B_n^*-\theta)^2]+o(n^{-2}).$$

The last equality is due to (5.5) and the fact that B_n^* is bounded (on Δ_n^c). Now

$$E_\rho[E(\theta/\underline{x}_n)-\theta)^2] \geq E_\rho[(E(\theta/\underline{x}_n)-B_n+B_n-\theta)^2 \cdot I_{\Delta_n}] \tag{5.18a}$$

$$= E_\rho[(B_n-\theta)^2 \cdot I_{\Delta_n}]+E_\rho[(E(\theta/\underline{x}_n)-B_n)^2 \cdot I_{\Delta_n}]$$

$$+ 2E_\rho[(E(\theta/\underline{x}_n)-B_n)(B_n-\theta) \cdot I_{\Delta_n}]$$

$$= I_1 + I_2 + I_3, \text{ say.}$$

Note that
$I_2 = o(n^{-2})$ (vide Lemma 5.1),

$$I_3 \leq 2\, E_\rho^{\frac{1}{2}}[(B_n-\theta)^2 \cdot I_{\Delta_n}]\; E_\rho^{\frac{1}{2}}[(E(\theta/\underline{x}_n)-B_n)^2 \cdot I_{\Delta_n}]$$

$= o(n^{-2})$ (vide Lemma 5.1 and Proposition 5.1).

Hence in view of (5.18)

$$E_\rho[(B_n^*-\theta)^2] \leq a_1 \cdot n^{-1}+a_2 \cdot n^{-2}+o(n^{-2}) \leq E_\rho[(E(\theta/\underline{x}_n)-\theta)^2]+o(n^{-2}).$$

Remark 5.1. If the assumptions AI to AV hold with some $K \geq 4$, $r_1 > 4$, $r_2 \geq 4$ and ρ is of type D_S $(20 < S \leq \infty)$ then as in the case of Lemma 5.1, $\exists$ $\epsilon > 0$ and $\delta > 0$ such that

$$P_\rho\{|E[(\theta-\hat{\theta}_n)^2 \cdot b^2/\underline{x}_n]-n^{-1}\cdot\lambda_{2,2}(\underline{x}_n)-n^{-2}\cdot\lambda_{2,4}(\underline{x}_n)|$$

$$\leq M\cdot n^{-(2+\epsilon)}, |n^{-i}\cdot\lambda_{2,2i}(\underline{x}_n)| \leq M\cdot n^{-\delta}, 1= 1,2\}$$

$$= 1 - o(n^{-2}),$$

where $\lambda_{2,2}$ and $\lambda_{2,4}$ are as in Theorem 3.1 of Johnson [8]. This along with Lemma 5.1 gives us the expansion for the posterior risk, i.e., $\exists$ $P_1(\underline{x}_n)$, $P_2(\underline{x}_n)$, $\epsilon > 0$ and $\delta > 0$ such that

$$P_\rho\{|E[(\theta-E(\theta/\underline{x}_n))^2/\underline{x}_n]-n^{-1}\cdot P_1(\underline{x}_n)-n^{-2}\cdot P_2(\underline{x}_n)|$$

$$\leq M\cdot n^{-(2+\epsilon)}, |n^{-i}\cdot P_i(\underline{x}_n)| \leq M\cdot n^{-\delta}, i = 1,2\}$$

$$= 1 - o(n^{-2}).$$

Remark 5.2. If the assumptions AI to AV hold with some $K \geq 2$, $r_1 > 3$, $r_2 > 2$ and ρ is of type D_S $(5 \leq S \leq \infty)$ then it is easy to see that $\hat{\theta}_n$ is approximate Bayes of order 1 w.r.t. the squared error loss function and using similar arguments as in the Proposition 5.1 and Theorem 5.1 one can get

$$R_\rho = a_1\cdot n^{-1} + o(n^{-1}).$$

VI. SOME COUNTEREXAMPLES

We begin with an example to show that

$$P_\rho[|F_n(\xi)-\Phi(\xi)| \leq M\cdot n^{-1/2} \text{ uniformly in } \xi]$$

cannot be made of order $1-o(n^{-r})$ for all $r > 0$ even in the case where $X_1, X_2, \ldots, X_n$ are i.i.d. $N(\theta,1)$. (An example on similar lines can be constructed to show that (1.2)' does not hold for all $r > 0$ in general, where (1.2)' denotes (1.2) with error term $M \cdot n^{-(K+1)/2} \cdot |C_n|^{-1}$ replaced by $M \cdot n^{-(K+1)/2}$).

Example 1. Consider $X_1, X_2, \ldots, X_n$ i.i.d. $N(\theta,1)$ variables, $-\infty < \theta < \infty$ and a prior

$$\begin{aligned} \rho(\theta) &= K \cdot \theta^5 (1-\theta)^5 \quad \text{for } 0 \leq \theta \leq 1 \\ &= 0 \qquad\qquad \text{elsewhere.} \end{aligned}$$

Now,

$$0 = P[\theta < 0/\underline{x}_n] = P[\sqrt{n}(\theta - \bar{x}_n) < -\sqrt{n} \cdot \bar{x}_n/\underline{x}_n],$$

where $\hat{\theta}_n = n^{-1} \sum_{i=1}^{n} x_i = \bar{x}_n$. Hence $F_n(\xi) = 0$ for $\xi = -\sqrt{n}\,\bar{x}_n$ and to get a counter-example it is enough to show that for some $0 < \epsilon < \frac{1}{2}$

$$\text{(6.1)} \qquad P_\rho[\Phi(\xi) > n^{-\frac{1}{2}+\epsilon}] \text{ cannot be made of order } n^{-r} \text{ for all } r > 0.$$

Note that if $c < (2-4\epsilon)^{1/2}$ and n is sufficiently large then

$$\begin{aligned} P_\rho[\Phi(\xi) > n^{-\frac{1}{2}+\epsilon}] &\geq P_\rho[-\sqrt{n}\,\bar{x}_n > -c \cdot \sqrt{\log n}] \\ &= \int P_\theta[\sqrt{n}(\bar{x}_n - \theta) < c \cdot \sqrt{\log n} - \sqrt{n} \cdot \theta]\rho(\theta)d\theta \\ &\geq \frac{1}{2} \int_{0 < \theta < d \cdot n^{-1/2} \cdot \sqrt{\log n}} \rho(\theta)d\theta \quad \text{if } (c-d) > 0 \\ &= K \cdot (\log n)^3 \cdot n^{-3}, \end{aligned}$$

which proves (6.1).

The above example also suggests that Corollary 2 of Alvo [2] is not true. To get a counter-example to the corollary it is enough to show that for some $0 < \epsilon_1 < 1$

$$(6.2) \qquad P_\rho[|E(\theta/\underline{x}_n)-\hat{\theta}_n| < M\cdot n^{-1+\epsilon_1}] \text{ cannot be made of order } n^{-1},$$

implying that even the first moment of Alvo's $N_{\underline{x}}$ is infinity. Now as in the case of our Lemma 5.1 we have

$$(6.3) \qquad P_\rho[|E(\theta/\underline{x}_n)-\hat{\theta}_n-\lambda_{1,2,n}(\underline{x}_n)\cdot n^{-1}| \leq M\cdot n^{-(1+\epsilon)}]$$

$$\geq 1-0(n^{-(1-\epsilon)\cdot\frac{6}{5}}) \text{ for } 0 < \epsilon < 1.$$

Here $\lambda_{1,2,n}(\underline{x}_n) = \rho^{(1)}(\hat{\theta}_n)/\rho(\hat{\theta}_n)$. Also by modifying the proof of Proposition 2.1 it is not difficult to get that for any $0 < \epsilon_1 < \frac{1}{2}$

$$P_\rho[|\lambda_{1,2,n}(\underline{x}_n)\cdot n^{-1}| > M\cdot n^{-1+\epsilon_1}] \geq 0(n^{-6\cdot\epsilon_1}).$$

This along with (6.3) gives

$$P_\rho[|E(\theta/\underline{x}_n)-\hat{\theta}_n| > M\cdot n^{-1+\epsilon_1}]$$

$$\geq 0(n^{-6\cdot\epsilon_1}) - 0(n^{-(1-\epsilon)\cdot\frac{6}{5}}).$$

Now choosing ϵ_1 sufficiently small we get (6.2).

Now we give an example which demonstrates (A) the Bayes risk need not have an expansion of the form $a_1\cdot n^{-1}+a_2\cdot n^{-2}+o(n^{-2})$ where a_1 and a_2 are constants and (B) a Bayes estimate, in general, cannot be improved by an estimate of the form $\hat{\theta}_n + \frac{d(\hat{\theta}_n)}{n}$, where $d(\theta)$ is a smooth (i.e. twice continuously differentiable) function of θ, in the sense

$$(6.4) \qquad E_\theta(E(\theta/\underline{x}_n)-\theta)^2 \geq E_\theta(\hat{\theta}_n+\frac{d(\hat{\theta}_n)}{n}-\theta)^2 + o(n^{-2})$$

uniformly in θ belonging to an interval say (0,1).

Example 2. Let $X_1, X_2, \ldots, X_n$ be i.i.d. $N(\theta,1)$ and the prior $\rho(\theta)$ be uniform over (0,1). It is easy to see that for any $K > 0$, if we take $r_K = \{(\frac{K}{2}+1)^2-1\}/2$ and $d_K(\theta) = -\frac{(K+2)}{2}\theta^{r_K}$, then $\exists\ n_o(K)$ such that the Bayes risk of $\hat{\theta}_n + \frac{d_K(\hat{\theta}_n)}{n}$ is

$$(6.5) \qquad R(\hat{\theta}_n + \frac{d_K(\hat{\theta}_n)}{n}) = \frac{1}{n} - \frac{K}{n^2} + R_n,$$

where $|R_n| < n^{-2}\ \forall n \geq n_o(K)$. We shall prove that

$$(6.6) \qquad R(E(\theta/\underline{x}_n)) = n^{-1} + o(n^{-1}).$$

Since K in (6.5) is arbitrary, (6.5) and (6.6) imply that $R(E(\theta/\underline{x}_n)) = n^{-1}-a_n$ where $a_n > 0$ and $a_n \cdot n^2 \to \infty$. This demonstrates (A). Also (B) is demonstrated for if there exists a twice continuously differentiable function $d(\theta)$ such that (6.4) holds then $n^{-1} + d_1 \cdot n^{-2} + o(n^{-2}) \leq n^{-1}-a_n$, where

$$R(\hat{\theta}_n + \frac{d(\hat{\theta}_n)}{n}) = n^{-1}+d_1 \cdot n^{-2}+o(n^{-2})$$

and d_1 is a constant. To prove (6.6), note that for $\theta \in (n^{-1/2}\log n,\ 1-n^{-1/2}\log n) = S_n$,

$$P_\theta(\bar{x}_n \in (0,1)) = 1-o(n^{-3}),$$

i.e. $P_\theta(\rho(\bar{x}_n) = 1) = 1-o(n^{-3})$, and hence we can get

$$P_\theta[|E(\theta/\underline{x}_n)-\bar{x}_n| \leq n^{-3}] = 1 - o(n^{-3}).$$

Thus we have for $\theta \in S_n$

$$E_\theta(E(\theta/\underline{x}_n)-\theta)^2 = E_\theta(\bar{x}_n-\theta)^2 + o(n^{-2}).$$

Now it is easy to see that (6.6) follows if we prove

$$E_\theta[h^2(\underline{x}_n)\cdot I_{[|\sqrt{n}\,\bar{x}_n-\theta|< c\cdot(\log n)^{1/2}]}] < M,\ \forall\ \theta \in S_n^c, \tag{6.7}$$

where $E(\theta/\underline{x}_n) = \bar{x}_n + h(\bar{x}_n)/\sqrt{n}$ and c is chosen suitably. First assume $\theta \in (0,n^{-1/2}\log n)$ and note that

$$h(\underline{x}_n) = [\int_{-\sqrt{n}\,\bar{x}_n}^{-\sqrt{n}\,\bar{x}_n+\sqrt{n}} z\, e^{-z^2/2}dz]\cdot[\int_{-\sqrt{n}\,\bar{x}_n}^{-\sqrt{n}\,\bar{x}_n+\sqrt{n}} e^{-z^2/2}dz]^{-1}$$

$$< e^{-n\bar{x}_n^2/2}[\Phi(-\sqrt{n}\,\bar{x}_n + \sqrt{n})-\Phi(-\sqrt{n}\,\bar{x}_n)]^{-1}$$

$$\le M\cdot(-\sqrt{n}\,\bar{x}_n) \quad \text{if} \quad 0 < c' < -\sqrt{n}\,\bar{x}_n.$$

Since $\theta \in (0,n^{-1/2}\log n)$, $\exists\ t_o > 0$ such that

$$|h(\bar{x}_n)|\cdot I_{[|\sqrt{n}\,\bar{x}_n-\theta|< c\cdot(\log n)^{1/2}]}$$

$$< \sqrt{t_o} \text{ on } (\sqrt{n}\,\bar{x}_n > 0) \cup (0 < -\sqrt{n}\,\bar{x}_n < c').$$

Note that

$$h(\bar{x}_n)\cdot I_{[|\sqrt{n}\,\bar{x}_n-\theta|< c\cdot(\log n)^{1/2}]} \ge 0$$

for sufficiently large n. Hence

$$E_\theta h^2(\bar{x}_n)\cdot I_{[|\sqrt{n}\,\bar{x}_n-\theta|< c\cdot(\log n)^{1/2}]}$$

$$< t_o + \int_{t_o}^{\infty} P_\theta[|\sqrt{n}(\bar{x}_n-\theta)|<-\frac{t^{1/2}}{M} - \sqrt{n}\,\theta]dt$$

$$\le M \quad \text{for} \quad \theta \in (0,n^{-1/2}\cdot\log n),$$

and similarly (6.7) can be proved for $\theta \in (1-n^{-1/2}\cdot\log n, 1)$.

VII. SECOND ORDER EFFICIENCY (S.O.E.)

In this section we investigate the S.O.E. of m.l.e. as indicated in Section 4 of Ghosh and Subramanyam [5] and give rigorous proofs based on ideas developed there. The basic idea is to get approximate Bayes estimates for a sequence of priors which converge to a degenerate distribution at a point, say θ_o, of the parameter space Θ, at a certain rate and then to utilize (4.18) of Ghosh and Subramanyam [5].

Let the assumptions AI to AV hold with some $K \geq 3$, $r_1 > 4$ and $r_2 > 4$. Define the m.l.e. $\hat{\theta}_n$ as in Lemma 4.2. Roughly speaking we show how, given an efficient estimate T_n, we can get an estimate $\hat{\theta}^*_n$ depending only on $\hat{\theta}_n$ such that $\hat{\theta}^*_n$ is better upto $o(n^{-2})$ than T_n at any $\theta_o \in [a_o, b_o]$.

We also assume that on $[c,d]$, $b_o(\theta)$ is twice continuously differentiable and $H_{2,2}(\theta)$ (vide (5.7)) is continuously differentiable on $[a_o, b_o]$ where $b_o(\theta) = (\ell_3(\theta)+2\ell_{1,2}(\theta))(2I^2(\theta))^{-1}$. Let the sequence of priors $\rho_n(\theta)$ be defined as

$$\rho_n(\theta) = K_n\cdot\exp[-(\theta-\theta_o+(\log n)^{-1/4})^{-1}\cdot(\theta_o-\theta+(\log n)^{-1/4})^{-1}]$$

$$\text{for } \theta \in (\theta_o-(\log n)^{-1/4}, \theta_o+(\log n)^{-1/4}) = V_n$$

$$= 0 \quad \text{elsewhere.}$$

Note that

$$1 \geq \int_{\theta_o-(\log n)^{-1/2}}^{\theta_o+(\log n)^{-1/2}} \rho_n(\theta)d\theta \geq K_n\cdot 2\cdot(\log n)^{-1/2} e^{-c\cdot(\log n)^{1/2}},$$

where $c > 0$, which provides an upper bound for K_n. One now checks easily that (in what follows ε denotes an arbitrary positive number)

$$(7.1)\qquad |\rho_n^{(i)}(\theta)| \leq n^{\epsilon},\ \forall\ \theta,\ \forall\ n \geq n_o(\varepsilon,i),\ i = 0,1,2,\ldots,$$

$\rho_n(\theta)$ is of type D_∞ for each $n \geq 1$, and

$$(7.2)\qquad |\rho_n^{(i)}(\theta)|\cdot\rho_n^{v-1}(\theta) \leq K_n^v\cdot M(k,v),\ \forall\ \theta \in V_n,\ \forall\ n \geq 1,$$

and $i = 1,\ldots,k$ where $0 < M(k,v) < \infty$ depends only on v and k. Now it is easy to see that Proposition 2.2 holds, i.e.

$$(7.3)\qquad P_{\rho_n}(\rho_n(\hat{\theta}_n) > n^{-m}) = 1-0(n^{-m})-o(n^{-(r_2-\epsilon)/2}),$$

and that Lemmas 4.8 and 4.9 hold with R_n (vide Remark 4.1) having term $n^{-(K+r_o+1-\epsilon)/2}$ instead of $n^{-(K+r_o+1)/2}$ (vide (7.1)). Also note that (7.1), (7.2) and (7.3) suffice to bound $|C_n|^{-1}$ of Theorem 2.1 with a suitable bound. Thus Proposition 5.2 holds with all the expressions appropriately defined (i.e. by replacing ρ by ρ_n) so we have

$$(7.4)\qquad E_{\rho_n}[(B_n''-\theta)^2\cdot I_{\Delta_n}] = a_{1,n}\cdot n^{-1}+a_{2,n}\cdot n^{-2}+o(n^{-2}),$$

where

$$B_n'' = \hat{\theta}_n+d_n(\hat{\theta}_n)\cdot n^{-1},d_n(\theta) = (\ell_3(\theta)+\frac{\rho_n^{(1)}(\theta)}{\rho_n(\theta)})\cdot(I(\theta))^{1/2}.$$

Now let $c_{1,n} < \theta_0$ and $c_{2,n} > \theta_o$ be such that

$$\rho_n(c_{1,n}) = n^{-3} = \rho_n(c_{2,n}).$$

Then it is not difficult to see that

$$(7.5)\qquad \text{on } (|\hat{\theta}_n-\theta| < c_n),\rho(\hat{\theta}_n) = 0(n^{-3}) \text{ for } \theta\ \varepsilon\ (c_{1n},c_{2n}),$$

(7.6) $\quad P_\theta(\Delta_n) = 1-o(n^{-(2+\varepsilon)})$ for $\theta \varepsilon (c_{1n}, c_{2n})$.

For an estimate T_n of θ we need the following conditions.

(t_1) $\quad E_\theta(T_n-\theta)^2 = n^{-1}\cdot I^{-1}(\theta)+n^{-2}\cdot g(\theta)+o(n^{-2})$ uniformly in $\theta \in [a_o,b_o]$, where $g(\theta)$ is a twice continuously differentiable function for $\theta \varepsilon [a_o,b_o]$;

(t_2) $\quad E_\theta(T_n-\theta) = n^{-1}\cdot b(\theta)+o(n^{-(1+\epsilon)})$, the error being uniform in $\theta \in [a_o,b_o]$ and $b(\theta)$ a twice continuously differentiable function of $\theta \varepsilon [c,d]$;

(t_3) $\quad \sup_{\theta\varepsilon[a_o,b_o]} E_\theta(T_n-\theta)^4 < M < \infty$.

THEOREM 7.1. *Let* T_n *be an estimate satisfying* (t_1) *to* (t_3). *Then*

$$E_{\theta_o}(T_n-\theta)^2 \geq E_{\theta_o}(\hat{\theta}^*_n-\theta)^2 + o(n^{-2}) \text{ for } \theta_o \in [a_o,b_o],$$

where $\hat{\theta}^*_n = \hat{\theta}_n - \frac{1}{n}(b_o(\hat{\theta}_n)-b(\hat{\theta}_n))$.

Proof. Let $J_{n\theta} = \{|\hat{\theta}_n-\theta| < c_n\}$ (vide Proposition 5.1 for definition of c_n). Note that

(7.7) $\quad P_\theta(J_{n\theta}) = 1-o(n^{-(2+\varepsilon)})$ uniformly in $\theta \varepsilon [a_o,b_o]$.

Now on $\Delta_n \cap J_{n\theta}$ in view of (7.2) and (7.5), for $\theta \varepsilon (c_{1n}, c_{2n})$, we have, with $g_n(\theta) = (b_o(\theta)-b(\theta)+d_n(\theta))$, $f(\theta) = (b_o(\theta)-b(\theta))$ and primes denoting derivatives for g_n, f, b_o and b

$$(B''_n-\theta)^2 = (\hat{\theta}^*_n-\theta)^2 + \frac{1}{n^2} g_n^2(\theta) + \frac{2}{n}(\hat{\theta}_n-\theta)g_n(\theta) - \frac{2}{n^2} g_n(\theta)f(\theta)$$

$$+ \frac{2}{n}(\hat{\theta}_n-\theta)^2 g'_n(\theta) + o(n^{-(2+\varepsilon)}),$$

$$(T_n-\theta)^2 = (T_n'-\theta)^2 - \frac{1}{n^2} g_n^2(\theta) - \frac{2}{n} g_n(\theta)(T_n-\theta)$$

$$- \frac{2}{n} g_n'(\theta)(T_n-\theta)(\hat{\theta}_n-\theta)$$

$$- \frac{1}{n} (\hat{\theta}_n-\theta)^2 (T_n-\theta) g_n''(\theta_{1n}) + o(n^{-(2+\varepsilon)}),$$

where $T_n' = T_n + \frac{1}{n} g_n(\hat{\theta}_n)$ and θ_{1n} is between $\hat{\theta}_n$ and θ. Hence using (t_1) to (t_3), (7.2), (7.6), (7.7) and (5.7) along with the fact that $\hat{\theta}_n \varepsilon [c,d]$ we get for uniformly in $\theta \varepsilon (c_{1n}, c_{2n})$

(7.8) $$E_\theta(\hat{\theta}_n^*-\theta)^2 - E_\theta(B_n''-\theta)^2 I_{\Delta_n \cap J_{n\theta}}$$

$$= - \frac{1}{n^2} g_n^2(\theta) - \frac{2}{n} g_n(\theta) b_o(\theta) + \frac{2}{n^2} g_n(\theta) f(\theta)$$

$$- \frac{2}{n^2} g_n'(\theta) \cdot I^{-1}(\theta) + o(n^{-(2+\varepsilon)}), \text{ and}$$

(7.9) $$E_\theta(T_n-\theta)^2 I_{\Delta_n \cap J_{n\theta}} - E_\theta(T_n'-\theta) I_{\Delta_n \cap J_{n\theta}}$$

$$= - \frac{1}{n^2} g_n^2(\theta) - \frac{2}{n} g_n(\theta) b(\theta) - \frac{2}{n^2} g_n(\theta) I^{-1}(\theta)$$

$$+ \frac{2}{n} E_\theta(T_n-\hat{\theta}_n)^2 g_n'(\theta) + o(n^{-(2+\varepsilon)}).$$

Let $B_n''^*$ and $T_n'^*$ denote natural truncations on Δ_n of B_n'' and T_n' respectively. Then the Bayes property of $B_n''^*$ (vide Theorem 5.1) along with (7.8) and (7.9) implies

(7.10) $$0 \leq \int E_\theta(T_n-\theta)^2 \rho_n(\theta) d\theta - \int E_\theta(\hat{\theta}_n^*-\theta)^2 \rho_n(\theta) d\theta$$

$$+ \delta_n + \varepsilon_o + o(n^{-(2+\varepsilon)}),$$

where ε_o is a positive quantity and

$$|\delta_n| \leq \frac{2}{n} \int E_\theta (T_n - \hat{\theta}_n)^2 |g_n'(\theta)| \rho_n(\theta) d\theta$$

$$\leq \frac{2}{n} n^\varepsilon E_{\rho_n} (T_n - \hat{\theta}_n)^2$$

$$\leq 2\, n^{-1+\varepsilon} (E_{\rho_n}^{1/2} (T_n - E(\theta/\underline{x}_n))^2 + E_{\rho_n}^{1/2} (\hat{\theta}_n - E(\theta/\underline{x}_n))^2)^2$$

$$\leq 2\, n^{-2-\varepsilon}$$

as

$$E_{\rho_n} (T_n - E(\theta/\underline{x}_n))^2 = E_{\rho_n} (T_n - \theta)^2 - E_{\rho_n} (E(\theta/\underline{x}_n) - \theta)^2$$

$$= O(n^{-2}) = E_{\rho_n} (\hat{\theta}_n - E(\theta/\underline{x}_n))^2.$$

Hence using (t_2) and (5.7),

$$0 \leq \int [\frac{g(\theta)}{n^2} - \frac{g_1(\theta)}{n^2}] \rho_n(\theta) d\theta + \varepsilon_o + o(n^{-(2+\varepsilon)})$$

(where

$$g_1(\theta) = g_o(\theta) + f^2(\theta) - 2f(\theta) b_o(\theta) - 2f'(\theta) b_o(\theta)$$

is the coefficient of n^{-2} in the expansion of $E_\theta(\hat{\theta}_n^* - \theta)^2$), i.e.

$$0 \leq n^{-2} \int (g(\theta_o) - g_1(\theta_o) + (\theta - \theta_o)(g'(\theta_1) - g_1'(\theta_1))) \rho_n(\theta) d\theta$$

$$+ \varepsilon_o + o(n^{-(2+\varepsilon)}),\ \theta_1 \text{ between } \theta \text{ and } \theta_o.$$

Hence $E_{\theta_o} (\hat{\theta}_n^* - \theta)^2 \leq E_{\theta_o} (T_n - \theta)^2 + o(n^{-2})$. Q.E.D.

VIII. APPLICATION TO BAYESIAN SEQUENTIAL ESTIMATION

As pointed out in Section 6, Alvo's Corollary 2 is not true and hence his proof of Theorem 4 (Alvo [2]) is not correct. The conclusion of Theorem 4 happens to be essentially true if the prior is of type D_∞ or D_S $(S \geq 30)$. For D_∞ a proof is given below; it is a modification of Alvo's based on the results of Section 5. The proof for priors of type D_S is similar. We now assume Alvo's [2] setup with a D_∞ prior and *adopt his notations*.

We have to prove

$$(8.1) \qquad \rho(\psi,N) = 2c^{1/2}E(\sigma(\theta))+c\cdot E(\ell(\theta))+o(c)$$

where, as in Alvo,

$$N = \text{least integer } n \geq 1 \text{ such that } n \geq c^{-1/2}\cdot\bar{\sigma}_n.$$

As in the case of our Lemma 5.1 we can get a set A_n such that for some K and $\beta > 3$, $P_\psi(A_n) \geq 1-K\cdot n^{-\beta}$, $\forall\, n \geq 1$, and such that on A_n we have

(a) $|E(\theta/\underline{x}_n)-\hat{\theta}_n-\lambda_{1,2}\cdot n^{-1}-\lambda_{1,4}\cdot n^{-2}| < R_n\cdot n^{-3}$,

(b) $|E(\theta/\underline{x}_n)-\hat{\theta}_{n-1}| < R_n\cdot n^{-1}$,

(c) $|\bar{\ell}_n-\hat{\ell}_n| < R_n\cdot n^{-1}$,

(d) $|(\bar{\sigma}_n)^2-(\hat{\sigma}_n)^2| < R_n\cdot n^{-1}$,

(e) $|E[(\theta-\hat{\theta}_n)^2/\underline{x}_n]-(\hat{\sigma}_n)^2\cdot(n^{-1}+\lambda_{2,4}\cdot n^{-2})| < R_n\cdot n^{-3}$,

(f) $|\hat{\ell}_n| < R_n$,

(g) $|\bar{x}_{n-1}| < R_n$ and $|x_n| < R_n$,

where R_n is the generic notation for a random term with the property that $R_n\cdot n^{-\delta} < M$ for some M and $0 < \delta < \frac{1}{2}$, $\forall\, n \geq 1$. Also, M will be used as a generic constant. (Note that one can obtain (c) and (d) by replacing $\emptyset^r\rho$ by $\ell(\theta)\rho(\theta)$ and $\sigma^2(\theta)\rho(\theta)$ respectively in Theorem 3.1 of Johnson [8] and then proceeding as in the case of our Lemma 5.1).

We now estimate $E(\rho_o(\psi_N)\cdot I_{A_N})$. Following Alvo and using (a), (c), (d) and (e) on A_n the posterior risk is given by

$$(8.2)\qquad \rho_o(\psi_n) = 2c^{1/2}\cdot\bar{\sigma}_n + \bar{\ell}_n\cdot c + n^{-1}(\bar{\sigma}_n - n\cdot c^{1/2})^2$$
$$+ \bar{\ell}_n\cdot[(\bar{\sigma}_n)^2 - n^2\cdot c]\cdot n^{-2} + R_n\cdot n^{-3}.$$

Now on $(N = n)\cap A_n$,

$$0 \geq (\bar{\sigma}_n)^2 - n^2\cdot c > (\bar{\sigma}_n)^2 - (\bar{\sigma}_{n-1})^2 + (2n-1)\cdot c$$
$$= \sigma^2(\hat{\theta}_n) - \sigma^2(\hat{\theta}_{n-1}) + (2n-1)\cdot c + R_n\cdot n^{-1},$$

(by using (b) and (d))

$$= \frac{1}{n}(x_n - \bar{x}_{n-1})D'(\bar{x}_n^*)\cdot 2\sigma(\theta_n^*)\sigma'(\theta_n^*) + (2n-1)\cdot c + R_n\cdot n^{-1},$$

where $\bar{x}_n^*$ is between $\bar{x}_n$ and $\bar{x}_{n-1}$, θ_n^* is between $\hat{\theta}_n$ and $\hat{\theta}_{n-1}$ and D is the map which takes $\bar{x}_n$ to $\hat{\theta}_n$. Also on $(N = n)$

$$\delta\cdot c^{-1/2} \leq n \leq [Kc^{-1/2}] + 1, \text{ where } 0 < \delta \leq \bar{\sigma}_n \leq K < \infty$$

and [g] denotes the integral part of g (existence of such δ and K is ensured by the compact support of ψ). Hence on $(N = n)\cap A_n$, in view of (c), (f) and (g),

$$|\bar{\ell}_n[(\bar{\sigma}_n)^2 - n^2\cdot c]\cdot n^{-2}| < M\cdot c^{1+\epsilon} \text{ for some } \epsilon > 0.$$

Using similar arguments, on $(N = n)\cap A_n$ we have

$$n^{-1}\cdot(\bar{\sigma}_n - n\cdot c^{1/2})^2 < M\cdot c^{1+\epsilon} \quad \text{for some } \epsilon > 0.$$

Thus

(8.3) $$\left| \sum_{n\geq 1} E[\{n^{-1}\cdot[\bar{\sigma}_n - n\cdot c^{1/2}]^2 + \bar{\ell}_n\cdot[(\bar{\sigma}_n)^2 - n^2\cdot c]\cdot n^{-2} + R_n\cdot n^{-3}\}\cdot I_{(N=n)\cap A_n}]\right|$$

$$\leq M\cdot c^{1+\epsilon} \sum_{n\geq 1} P(N=n)$$

$$= M\cdot c^{1+\epsilon} \quad \text{for some } \epsilon > 0.$$

Now

$$E[\bar{\sigma}_n\cdot I_{(N=n)}\cdot I_{(N=n)\cap A_n^c}]$$

$$\leq E^{1/2}[(\bar{\sigma}_n)^2\cdot I_{(N=n)}]\cdot P^{1/2}((N=n)\cap A_n^c)$$

$$\leq \{1+E[(\bar{\sigma}_n)^2\cdot I_{(N=n)}]\}P^{1/2}((N=n)\cap A_n^c).$$

Hence

$$\sum_{n\geq 1} E[2\bar{\sigma}_n\cdot c^{1/2}\cdot I_{(N=n)\cap A_n^c}]$$

$$\leq 2\cdot c^{1/2}\{M\cdot c^{\beta/2}\cdot E\sigma^2 + M\cdot c^{\beta/2}([K\cdot c^{1/2}]+1)\}$$

since

$$E^2(\sigma/\underset{-}{x}_n) = (\bar{\sigma}_n)^2 \leq E(\sigma^2/\underset{-}{x}_n) = (\overline{\sigma^2})_n,$$

which is a martingale,

(8.4) $$\leq M\cdot c^{1+\epsilon} \quad \text{for some } \epsilon > 0.$$

Using similar arguments

(8.5) $$\sum_{n\geq 1} E\{\bar{\ell}_n\cdot c\cdot I_{(N=n)\cap A_n^c}\}$$

$$\leq M\cdot c^{1+\epsilon} \text{ for some } \epsilon > 0.$$

Since $\bar{\sigma}_n$ and $\bar{\ell}_n$ are martingales and N is finite, $E(\bar{\sigma}_N) = E(\sigma(\theta))$ and $E(\bar{\ell}_N) = E(\bar{\ell}(\theta))$. Hence by (8.4) and (8.5)

$$E[\{c^{1/2}\cdot\bar{\sigma}_N + c\cdot\bar{\ell}_N\}\cdot I_{A_N}] = c^{1/2}E(\sigma(\theta))+cE(\ell(\theta))+o(c),$$

and so by (8.2) and (8.3)

$$E(\rho_o(\psi_N)\cdot I_{A_N}) = 2c^{1/2}E(\sigma(\theta))+cE(\ell(\theta))+o(c).$$

The proof of (8.1) is completed by noticing that

$$\begin{aligned}\rho(\psi,N) &= E(\rho_o(\psi_N))\\ &= \sum_{n\geq 1} E\{\rho_o(\psi_n)\cdot I_{(N=n)\cap A_n}\} + o(c).\end{aligned}$$

IX. RELATION WITH THE WORK OF BURNAŠEV

Let the prior $\rho \in C^3(R)$ be such that $\rho(\theta) > 0$ on (a_o,b_o) and $\rho(\theta) = 0$ on $(a_o,b_o)^c$. Suppose for some $\delta > 0$, $\exists\ \delta_1 > 0$ such that

i) $\int\left|\frac{d}{d\theta}\log\rho(\theta)\right|^{2+\delta_1}\rho(\theta)d\theta < \infty$,

ii) $\int\left|\frac{d^2}{d\theta^2}\log\rho(\theta)\right|^{1+\delta_1}\rho(\theta)d\theta < \infty$,

iii) $\int_{D(\varepsilon)}\rho(\theta)d\theta = O(\varepsilon^{2+\delta_1})$ as $\varepsilon \to 0$,

where

$$D(\varepsilon) = \{\theta:\ \sup_{|z|<\varepsilon}\frac{|\rho^{(3)}(\theta+z)|}{\rho(\theta)} > \varepsilon^{-(3-\delta)}\}.$$

(Burnasev [3] has conditions (i) and (ii), and (iii) with

$$D(\varepsilon) = \{\theta: \sup_{|z|<\varepsilon} \left|\frac{d^3}{d\theta^3} \log \rho(\theta+z)\right| > \varepsilon^{(3-\delta)}\}$$

along with the condition

$$\int_{D^c(\varepsilon)} \rho(\theta) \sup_{|z|<\varepsilon} \left|\frac{d^3}{d\theta^3} \log \rho(\theta+z)\right| d\theta = O(\varepsilon^{-(1-\delta)})).$$

Below we sketch a proof of Theorem 5.1 when ρ satisfies (i) to (iii) above and $r_2 > 6$. Note that if $|A-a| \le n^{-1/2}R_{1n}$, $|B-b_1| \le R_{1n}$ and $|\frac{A}{B}| \le C$ then using (2.2) repeatedly it is easy to get

$$(9.1) \qquad \left|\frac{A}{B} - \frac{a}{b_1}\right| \le (C+n^{-1/2})(|b_1|^{-1}R_{1n})^K$$

$$+ \left(\left|\frac{a}{b_1}\right| + n^{-1/2}\right) \sum_{r=1}^{K-1} (|b_1|^{-1}R_{1n})^r$$

$$= R_{nK} \quad \text{(say)} \quad \text{for } K = 1,2,\ldots .$$

Let

$$A_{n\theta} = \{\underset{\sim}{x}_n: |E(\theta/\underset{\sim}{x}_n) - \hat{\theta}_n - n^{-1}\cdot\lambda_{1,2,n}(\underset{\sim}{x}_n)| < M\cdot R'_{nK}\} \cap I_{n\theta},$$

where R'_{nK} is R_{nK} of (9.1) with

$$A = \int \emptyset\rho(\hat{\theta}_n+\emptyset b^{-1}) \prod_{i=1}^{n} [f(x_i,\hat{\theta}_n + \emptyset b^{-1})/f(x_i,\hat{\theta}_n)]d\emptyset,$$

$$B = \int \rho(\hat{\theta}_n+\emptyset b^{-1}) \prod_{i=1}^{n} [f(x_i,\hat{\theta}_n+\emptyset b^{-1})/f(x_i,\hat{\theta}_n)]d\emptyset,$$

$$b_1 = n^{-1/2}\cdot C_n, \ \frac{a}{b} = n^{-1}\cdot b\cdot\lambda_{1,2,n}(\underset{\sim}{x}_n), \text{ and}$$

$$R_{1n} = M\cdot c_n^4\{\sum_{i=o}^{2} |\rho^{(i)}(\hat{\theta}_n)| + \sup_{|z|<c_n} |\rho^{(3)}(\hat{\theta}_n+z)|\}.$$

Hence using (5.8) and arguments similar to the proofs of (5.3a) and (4.3) we get

(9.2) $$P_\theta(A_{n\theta}) = 1-o(n^{-2}) \text{ uniformly in } \theta \in [a_o,b_o].$$

In view of (i) to (iii), $\exists\ \delta_o > 0$ and $\delta_2 > 0$ such that

(9.3) $$P_\rho(D_n) = o(n^{-1-\delta_2}), \text{ where}$$

$$D_n = \{\theta: \frac{|\rho^{(1)}(\theta)|}{\rho(\theta)} > n^{1/2-\delta_o} \text{ or } \frac{|\rho^{(2)}(\theta)|}{\rho(\theta)} > n^{1-\delta_o} \text{ or}$$

$$y_{n\theta} = \operatorname*{Sup}_{|z|<2c_n} \frac{|\rho^{(3)}(\theta+z)|}{\rho(\theta)} > (2c_n)^{-3+\delta_o}\}.$$

Note that in view of (i), (ii) and the fact $\int y_{n\theta}\rho(\theta)d\theta < M$ we have

(9.4) $$E(R'^2_{nK} \cdot I_{A_{n\theta}} \cdot I_{D_n^c}) = o(n^{-2})$$

for sufficiently large K depending on δ_o.

CLAIM 1: (5.6) *holds with* I_{Δ_n} *replaced by* $I_{A_{n\theta}} \cdot I_{D_n^c}$.

Proof. Note that the statements

(9.5) $$E_\rho[(B_n-\theta)^2 \cdot I_{A_{n\theta}} \cdot I_{D_n^c}] = E_\rho[E_{1n} \cdot I_{A_{n\theta}} \cdot I_{D_n^c}] + o(n^{-2})$$

and

$$E_\rho[E_{1n} \cdot I_{A^c_{n\theta}} \cdot I_{D_n^c}] = o(n^{-2})$$

are analogous to (5.15) and (5.16) respectively and can be proved similarly if we bound quantities like $\rho^{-i}(\theta)\rho^{(i)}(\theta)$ and $y_{n\theta}$ on D_n^c by using the definition of D_n^c, and use the integrability conditions (i) and (ii) and the fact $\int y_{n\theta}\rho(\theta)d\theta < M$. Also in view of (i), (ii) and (9.3) it is easy to see that

$$E(E_{1n}\cdot I_{D_n}\cdot I_{A_{n\theta}}) = o(n^{-2}). \qquad \text{Q.E.D.}$$

CLAIM 2. $\int_{D_n} E_\theta(E(\theta/\underset{\sim}{x}_n)-\theta)^2\,\rho(\theta)d\theta = o(n^{-2})$.

Proof. Let

$$\begin{aligned}\tilde{\theta}_n &= E(\theta/\underset{\sim}{x}_n) \quad \text{if} \quad |\hat{\theta}_n - E(\theta/\underset{\sim}{x}_n)| < 3c_n \\ &= \hat{\theta}_n \qquad \text{otherwise.}\end{aligned}$$

Let

$$B_n = \{\underset{\sim}{x}_n : |\hat{\theta}_n - E(\theta/\underset{\sim}{x}_n)| > 3c_n\},$$

$$G_{n\theta} = \{(\theta,\underset{\sim}{x}_n): |\hat{\theta}_n - \theta| < c_n\},$$

and let B_n also denote $(a_o,b_o)\times B_n$. Clearly $P_\rho(G^c_{n\theta}) = o(n^{-2}\cdot c_n^2)$. On $G_{n\theta}\cap B_n$, $c_n^2 < (E(\theta/\underset{\sim}{x}_n)-\theta)^2-(\hat{\theta}_n-\theta)^2$; hence

$$0 \geq R(\rho,E(\theta/\underset{\sim}{x}_n))-R(\rho,\tilde{\theta}_n) \geq c_n^2 P_\rho(G_{n\theta}\cap B_n)-K\cdot P_\rho(G^c_{n\theta}),$$

and so we have $P_\rho(G_{n\theta}\cap B_n) = o(n^{-2})$. Now

$$E_\rho(E(\theta/\underset{\sim}{x}_n)-\theta)^2\cdot I_{D_n} = J_1 + J_2 + J_3 + J_4,$$

where (vide (9.3))

$$J_1 = E_\rho(E(\theta/\underset{\sim}{x}_n)-\theta)^2\cdot I_{D_n\cap B^c_n\cap G_{n\theta}} \leq c_n^2 P_\rho(D_n) = o(n^{-2}),$$

$$J_2 = E_\rho(E(\theta/\underset{\sim}{x}_n)-\theta)^2\cdot I_{D_n\cap B^c_n\cap G^c_{n\theta}} \leq K\ P_\rho(G^c_{n\theta}) = o(n^{-2}),$$

$$J_3 = E_\rho(E(\theta/\underline{x}_n)-\theta)^2 \cdot I_{D_n \cap B_n \cap G_{n\theta}} \leq K\, P_\rho(G_{n\theta} \cap B_n) = o(n^{-2}),$$

$$J_4 = E_\rho(E(\theta/\underline{x}_n)-\theta)^2 \cdot I_{D_n \cap B_n \cap G^c_{n\theta}} \leq K\, P_\rho(G^c_{n\theta}) = o(n^{-2}). \quad \text{Q.E.D.}$$

Now using Claim 2 and (9.2) we have

$$E_\rho[\sqrt{n}(E(\theta/\underline{x}_n)-\theta)]^2 = I_1 + I_2 + I_3 + o(n^{-1}),$$

where I_i's are defined as in (5.18a) with I_{Δ_n} replaced by $n \cdot I_{A_{n\theta}} \cdot I_{D^c_n}$. Using (9.4) we get $I_2 = o(n^{-1})$. Also it is easy to see that $I_3 = o(n^{-1})$, hence

$$E_\rho[\sqrt{n}(E(\theta/\underline{x}_n)-\theta)]^2 = I_1 + o(n^{-1}) = a_1 + a_2 \cdot n^{-1} + o(n^{-1}).$$

Remark 9.1. If ρ is continuously differentiable with $\rho(\theta) > 0$ on (a_o, b_o) and $\rho(\theta) = 0$ on $(a_o, b_o)^c$ and if for some $\delta > 0$

$$\int_{D^c_1(\varepsilon)} \sup_{|z|<\varepsilon} \frac{|\rho^{(1)}(\theta+z)|^2}{\rho(\theta)}\, d\theta = O(\varepsilon^{-(1-\delta)}), \text{ where}$$

$$D_1(\varepsilon) = \{\theta: \sup_{|z|<\varepsilon} \frac{|\rho^{(1)}(\theta+z)|}{\rho(\theta)} > \varepsilon^{-(1-\delta)}\},$$

then we have $R_\rho = a_1 \cdot n^{-1} + o(n^{-1})$. Also it is clear that when ρ is uniform over (a_o, b_o) the above expansion for R_ρ holds. Also note that if $X_1, X_2, \ldots, X_n$ are iid $N(\theta, 1)$ and ρ is uniform over $(-h/\sqrt{n}, h/\sqrt{n})$ then the Bayes estimate is given by

$$\frac{z}{\sqrt{n}} + \frac{1}{\sqrt{n}} \int_{-h-z}^{h-z} t\, e^{-\frac{t^2}{2}}\, dt \Big/ \int_{-h-z}^{h-z} e^{-\frac{t^2}{2}}\, dt,$$

where z is $N(\sqrt{n} \cdot \theta, 1)$, and so the coefficient of the n^{-1} term in the Bayes risk is not one. This is due to the fact that some of the error terms neglected earlier now assume magnitude of order n^{-1}. This would be true for certain other smooth priors also if they are supported on $(-h/\sqrt{n},\ h/\sqrt{n})$.

Remark 9.2. Instead of (i) to (iii) let ρ satisfy

$$\int_{D(\varepsilon)} [(\sup_{|z|<\varepsilon} |\rho^{(3)}(\theta+z)|+|\rho^{(1)}(\theta)| + |\rho^{(2)}(\theta)|)\rho^{-1}(\theta)]^{K_1}\rho(\theta)d\theta < \infty, \text{ for some } K_1 \geq 1. \tag{9.6}$$

Note that (vide (2.3))

$$P_\theta[|F_n(\xi)-\Phi(\xi)-\sum_{j=1}^{2}\gamma_j(\xi,\underline{x}_n)\cdot n^{-j/2}|$$

$$\leq M\cdot n\cdot^{1/2}\cdot R_{1n}\cdot|C_n|^{-1} \text{ uniformly in } \xi]$$

$$= 1-0(n^{-r_1/2})-o(n^{-r_2/2}) \text{ uniformly in } \theta \in [a_o,b_o].$$

Hence using (9.6) we get

$$P_\rho[|F_n(\xi)-\Phi(\xi)-\sum_{j=1}^{2}\gamma_j(\xi,\underline{x}_n)\cdot n^{-j/2}|$$

$$< M\cdot n^{-(3/2-\delta)} \text{ uniformly in } \xi]$$

$$= 1-0(n^{-r_1/2})-o(n^{r_2/2})-0(n^{-\delta K})-\int_{D_n}\rho(\theta)d\theta.$$

Remark 9.3. Note that priors of type D_S $(S \geq 4)$ or D_∞ satisfy both Burnašev's as well as our conditions (i) to (iii).

REFERENCES

[1] Akahira, M. and Takeuchi, K. (1976). On the second order asymptotic efficiencies of estimators. *Proceedings of the Third Japan-USSR Symposium on Probability Theory*, G. Maruyama and J. V. Prokhorov (eds.). Lecture Notes in Mathematics 550, Springer-Verlag, Berlin.

[2] Alvo, M. (1977). Bayesian sequential estimation. *Ann. Statist.* *5*, 955-968.

[3] Burnašev, M. V. (1979). Asymptotic expansions of the integral risk of statistical estimators of location parameter in a scheme of independent observations. *Soviet Math. Dokl.* *20*, 788-791.

[4] Ghosh, J. K., Sinha, B. K. and Wieand, H. S. (1981). Second order efficiency of the M.L.E. w.r.t. any bounded bowl-shaped loss function. *Ann. Statist.* *8*, 506-521.

[5] Ghosh, J. K. and Subramanyam, K. (1974). Second order efficiency of maximum likelihood estimators. *Sankhyā Ser.* A, *36*, 325-358.

[6] Guesev, S. I. (1976). Asymptotic expansions associated with some statistical estimators in the smooth case II. Expansions of moments and distributions. *Theory Probab. Appl.* *21*, 14-32.

[7] Johnson, R. A. (1967). An asymptotic expansion for posterior distributions. *Ann. Math. Statist.* *38*, 1899-1906.

[8] Johnson, R. A. (1970). Asymptotic expansions associated with posterior distributions. *Ann. Math. Statist.* *41*, 851-864.

[9] Michel, R. and Pfanzagl, J. (1971). The accuracy of the normal approximation for minimum contrast estimates. *Z. Wahrsch. Verw. Gebiete* *18*, 73-84.

[10] Pfanzagl, J. (1973a). Asymptotic expansions related to minimum contrast estimators. *Ann. Statist.* *1*, 993-1026.

[11] Pfanzagl, J. (1973b). The accuracy of the normal approximation for estimates of vector parameters. *Z. Wahrsch. Verw. Gebiete* *25*, 171-198.

[12] Pfanzagl, J. and Wefelmeyer, W. (1978). A third order optimum property of the maximum likelihood estimator. *J. Multivariate Anal.* *8*, 1-29.

SELECTION PROCEDURES FOR A PROBLEM IN ANALYSIS OF VARIANCE[1]

Shanti S. Gupta

Department of Statistics
Purdue University
West Lafayette, Indiana, U.S.A.

Deng-Yuan Huang
Institute of Mathematics
Academia Sinica
Taipei, Taiwan

I. INTRODUCTION

For a randomized complete block design with one observation per cell, we express the observable random variables $X_{i\alpha}$ $(i = 1,\ldots,k;\ \alpha = 1,\ldots,n)$ as

$$(1.1)\qquad X_{i\alpha} = \mu + \beta_\alpha + \tau_i + \epsilon_{i\alpha},\quad \sum_{i=1}^{k} \tau_i = 0,$$

where μ is the mean-effect, $\beta_1,\ldots,\beta_n$ are the block effects (nuisance parameters for the fixed effects model), $\tau_1,\ldots,\tau_k$ are the treatment effects, and $\epsilon_{i\alpha}$ are the error components. We assume that the errors within each block are jointly normally distributed.

We assume that the quality of a treatment is judged by the largeness of the τ_i's. A 'population' π_i is called the best if τ_i is the largest. In general, it may be complicated to derive suitable tests for appropriate hypotheses, in which the

[1]This research was supported by the Office of Naval Research contract N00014-75-C-0455 at Purdue University. Reproduction in whole or in part is permitted for any purpose of the United States Government.

ISBN 0-12-307501-7

experimenter may really be interested. We apply the subset selection approach (using certain basic hypotheses) and thus obtain more appropriate information regarding the treatments. A subset selection procedure is designed to select a subset so as to include the best population. Selection of any suhset that contains the best is called a correct selection (CS). Roughly speaking, any two populations that are in the same selected subset, will not be considered as "significantly different" (based on the given set of observations). If all populations are selected, we claim that all treatments are not significantly different. In general, for achieving the objective of the experimenter, one should establish a suitable set of basic hypotheses. Depending on the objective one should proceed to consider different ways of formulating the basic hypotheses. In this paper, we discuss a method based on subset selection rules to test the hypothesis that all τ_i, $i \in I$, are not significantly different and greater than $\tau_j + \Delta$ for all $j \in J$, if the hypothesis is not rejected, we wish to make a claim of the type: $\tau_i = \tau^* > \tau_j + \Delta$ for all $i \in I$ and $j \in J$, where I and J form a partition of $\{1,2,\ldots,k\}$. The process of making such a claim will be called *hypothesis identification*. This is achieved by setting up certain basic hypotheses regarding the τ_i's and using a subset selection procedure to test these basic hypotheses. It should be pointed out that in identifying an appropriate hypothesis, we assume that the constant Δ in the claim is specified by the experimenter, say, based on past experience. Associated with the tests of the basic hypotheses using a selection rule, there are error probabilities and the infimum of the probability of a correct selection for the rule employed. These are related to the power function of these tests. The sum of the average (over the basic hypotheses tested) of the error probabilities and one minus the infimum of the probability of a correct selection is called the *identification risk*. The main theorem of the paper discusses the derivation of an optimal selection rule in the sense of minimizing the identification risk. For a more general theory of multiple decisions from ranking and selection approach, one can refer to a recent monograph by Gupta and Huang [1]. A general survey of the entire field is provided in Gupta and Panchapakesan [2].

Let $\underline{Y}$ be a random observable vector with probability distribution depending upon a parameter $\underline{\tau}' = (\tau_1,\ldots,\tau_k) \in \Omega$. Consider a family of hypotheses testing problems as follows:

$$(1.2) \qquad H_0\colon\ \underline{\tau} \in \Omega_0 \quad \text{vs} \quad H_i\colon\ \underline{\tau} \in \Omega_i,\ 1 \le i \le k,$$

where $\Omega_0 = \{\underline{\tau}|\tau_1 = \ldots = \tau_k\}$ and $\Omega_i = \{\underline{\tau}|\tau_i > \max_{j\neq i} \tau_j\}$, i=1,2,...,k. A test of the hypotheses (1.2) will be defined to be a vector $(\delta_1(\underline{y}),\ldots,\delta_k(\underline{y}))$, where the elements of the vector are ordinary test functions; when $\underline{y}$ is observed we reject H_0 in favor of H_i with probability $\delta_i(\underline{y})$, $1 \le i \le k$. The power function of a test $(\delta_1,\ldots,\delta_k)$ is defined to be the vector $(\beta_1(\underline{\tau}),\ldots,\beta_k(\underline{\tau}))$, where $\beta_i(\underline{\tau}) = E_{\underline{\tau}}\delta_i(\underline{Y})$, $1 \le i \le k$. For $\underline{\tau} \in \Omega_i$, $\beta_i(\underline{\tau})$ is the probability of a correct selection P(CS) and $\delta_i(\underline{y})$ is the individual selection probability of selecting the best population π_i. Let S_γ be the set of all the tests $(\delta_1,\ldots,\delta_k)$ such that

$$(1.3) \qquad E_{\underline{\tau}}\delta_i(\underline{Y}) \le \gamma,\ \underline{\tau} \in \Omega_0,\quad 1 \le i \le k,$$

where γ is the upper bound on the error probabilities associated with the treatment effects.

For each i, $(1 \le i \le k)$, we would like to have $\beta_i(\underline{\tau})$ large when $\underline{\tau} \in \Omega_i$ subject to (1.3). For $\underline{\tau} \in \Omega_i$, if we make $\beta_i(\underline{\tau})$ large, then $\beta_j(\underline{\tau})$ should be small for $j \neq i$.

It should be pointed out that in the formulation and proof of the optimal selection procedure, results from Neyman-Pearson theory are used.

II. FORMULATION OF AN OPTIMAL SELECTION PROCEDURE

Assume that

$$\underline{X}'_{\alpha} = (X_{1\alpha},\ldots,X_{k\alpha}),$$

$\alpha = 1,\ldots,n$, are independently and identically distributed random vectors with the following distribution:

$$(2.1) \qquad (2\pi\sigma^2)^{-\frac{1}{2}kn}|\Lambda|^{-\frac{1}{2}}\exp[-\frac{1}{2\sigma^2}(\underline{x}-\underline{\theta})'\Lambda^{-1}(\underline{x}-\underline{\theta})],$$

where $\underline{x}' = (x_{11},\ldots,x_{k1};\ldots;x_{1n},\ldots,x_{kn})$ and $\underline{\theta}' = (\theta_{11},\ldots,\theta_{k1};\ldots;\theta_{1n},\ldots,\theta_{kn})$, $\theta_{i\alpha} = \mu + \beta_{\alpha} + \tau_i$, $i = 1,\ldots,k$; $\alpha = 1,2,\ldots,n$ and Λ is a known positive definite kn x kn correlation matrix defined as follows:

$$\Lambda = (\lambda_{ij})_{kn\times kn} = \begin{bmatrix} \Lambda_1 & 0 & \cdots & 0 \\ 0 & \Lambda_1 & \cdots & 0 \\ \vdots & \vdots & & \vdots \\ 0 & 0 & \cdots & \Lambda_1 \end{bmatrix},$$

where

$$\Lambda_1 = \begin{bmatrix} 1 & & \lambda \\ & \ddots & \\ \lambda & & 1 \end{bmatrix}_{k\times k}.$$

We rewrite the original model as the general linear model as follows:

$$\underline{X} = \underline{\theta} + \underline{\epsilon}, \qquad \underline{\epsilon} \sim N(\underline{0}, \sigma^2\Lambda).$$

Since our interest lies only in differences between pairs of τ_i's, we can make the following transformation thereby eliminating the nuisance parameters β_i. For any i, let

$$\underline{Y}_i = C\,\underline{\tau}_i + \underline{\eta}, \qquad \underline{\eta} \sim N(\underline{0}, \sigma^2\Sigma_i),$$

where $\underset{-}{\tau}_i' = (\tau_{i1},\ldots,\tau_{ik})$, $\tau_{ij} = \tau_i - \tau_j$, $j \neq i$,

$$\underset{-}{Y}_i' = (Y_{i11},\ldots,Y_{ik1};\ldots;\, Y_{i1n},\ldots,Y_{ikn})_{1x(k-1)n},$$

$$Y_{ij\ell} = X_{i\ell} - X_{j\ell},\ i \neq j;\ i,j = 1,\ldots,k;\ \ell = 1,\ldots,n,$$

$$\underset{-}{Y}_i = A_i \underset{-}{X}, \qquad \underset{-}{\eta} = A_i \underset{-}{\epsilon},$$

$$A_i = \begin{bmatrix} A_{i1} & & & \\ & A_{i1} & & 0 \\ & 0 & \ddots & \\ & & & A_{i1} \end{bmatrix}_{(k-1)nxkn},$$

$$\Sigma_i = A_i\ \Lambda\ A_i' = \begin{bmatrix} A_{i1}\Lambda_1 A_{i1}' & & 0 \\ & \ddots & \\ 0 & & A_{i1}\Lambda_1 A_{i1}' \end{bmatrix}_{(k-1)nx(k-1)n},$$

$$A_{i1} = \begin{array}{c} \\ \\ \\ \\ \\ \\ \\ \end{array}\begin{matrix} & & & i & \\ -1 & 0\ldots\ldots\ldots 0 & & 1 & 0\ldots\ldots\ldots\ldots\ldots 0 \end{matrix}$$

$$A_{i1} = \begin{bmatrix} -1 & 0\ldots\ldots\ldots 0 & 1 & 0\ldots\ldots\ldots\ldots\ldots 0 \\ 0 & -1 \quad 0\ldots\ldots 0 & 1 & 0\ldots\ldots\ldots\ldots\ldots 0 \\ \ldots & \ldots\ldots\ldots\ldots\ldots & \ldots & \ldots\ldots\ldots\ldots\ldots\ldots \\ 0\ldots\ldots\ldots 0 & -1 & 1 & 0\ldots\ldots\ldots\ldots\ldots 0 \\ 0\ldots\ldots\ldots\ldots\ldots 0 & & 1 & -1 \quad 0\ldots\ldots\ldots 0 \\ \ldots & \ldots\ldots\ldots\ldots\ldots & \ldots & \ldots\ldots\ldots\ldots\ldots\ldots \\ 0\ldots\ldots\ldots\ldots\ldots & & 1 & 0\ldots\ldots\ldots 0 \quad -1 \end{bmatrix}\begin{matrix} \\ \\ \\ i-1 \\ i+1 \\ \\ (k-1)xk, \end{matrix}$$

$$C' = [I,\ldots,I]_{(k-1)x(k-1)n},$$

where each of the identity matrices in C' is (k-1)x(k-1). The maximum likelihood estimator of $\underset{-}{\tau}_i$ is as follows:

$$\hat{\underset{-}{\tau}}_i = (C'\Sigma_i^{-1}C)^{-1}C'\Sigma_i^{-1}\underset{-}{Y}_i.$$

Since

$$A_{i1}\ \Lambda_1\ A_{i1}' = (1-\lambda)\begin{bmatrix} 2 & & 1 \\ & \ddots & \\ 1 & & 2 \end{bmatrix}_{(k-1)x(k-1)},$$

it is clear that

$$(A_{i1}\ \Lambda_1\ A_{i1}')^{-1} = (1-\lambda)^{-1}\frac{1}{k}\begin{bmatrix} k-1 & & -1 \\ & \ddots & \\ -1 & & k-1 \end{bmatrix} = V_i,$$

$$C'\Sigma_i^{-1}C = n(A_{i1}\ \Lambda_1\ A_{i1}')^{-1} = \frac{n}{k(1-\lambda)}\begin{bmatrix} k-1 & & -1 \\ & \ddots & \\ -1 & & k-1 \end{bmatrix},$$

$$(C'\Sigma_i^{-1}C)^{-1} = \frac{1-\lambda}{n}\begin{bmatrix} 2 & & 1 \\ & \ddots & \\ 1 & & 2 \end{bmatrix}_{(k-1)x(k-1)},$$

$$C'\Sigma_i^{-1} = [I\ldots I]\begin{bmatrix} V_i & & 0 \\ & \ddots & \\ 0 & & V_i \end{bmatrix}$$

$$= [V_i,\ldots,V_i],$$

and

$$(C'\Sigma_i^{-1}C)^{-1}C'\Sigma_i^{-1} = \frac{1-\lambda}{n}\begin{bmatrix} 2 & & 1 \\ & \ddots & \\ 1 & & 2 \end{bmatrix}[V_i,\ldots,V_i]$$

$$= \frac{1}{n}[I,\ldots,I].$$

Hence,

$$\hat{\underset{-}{\tau}}_i = (C'\Sigma_i^{-1}C)^{-1}C'\Sigma_i^{-1}\underset{-}{Y}_i$$

$$= \frac{1}{n}\begin{bmatrix} \sum_{\ell=1}^{n} Y_{i1\ell} \\ \vdots \\ \sum_{\ell=1}^{n} Y_{ik\ell} \end{bmatrix} = \begin{bmatrix} Y_{i1} \\ \vdots \\ Y_{ik} \end{bmatrix} = \begin{bmatrix} \bar{X}_i - \bar{X}_1 \\ \vdots \\ \bar{X}_i - \bar{X}_k \end{bmatrix},$$

where $\bar{X}_i = \frac{1}{n}\sum_{j=1}^{n} X_{ij}$, $1 \le i \le k$.

The joint density of $Y_{i11},\ldots,Y_{ik1};\ldots;Y_{i1n},\ldots,Y_{ikn}$ is the following:

$$p_{\underline{\tau}_i}(\underline{y}_i) = (2\pi\sigma^2)^{-\frac{1}{2}(k-1)n}|\Sigma_i|^{-\frac{1}{2}} \exp[-\frac{1}{2\sigma^2}(\underline{y}_i - C\underline{\tau}_i)'\Sigma_i^{-1}(\underline{y}_i - C\underline{\tau}_i)]$$

where

$$\Sigma_i = A_i \Lambda A_i' = (1-\lambda)\begin{bmatrix} J & & 0 \\ & \ddots & \\ 0 & & J \end{bmatrix}_{(k-1)n\mathrm{x}(k-1)n},$$

$$J = \begin{bmatrix} 2 & & 1 \\ & \ddots & \\ 1 & & 2 \end{bmatrix}_{(k-1)\mathrm{x}(k-1)},$$

and

$$\Sigma_i^{-1} = \begin{bmatrix} V_i & & 0 \\ & \ddots & \\ 0 & & V_i \end{bmatrix}.$$

Now, we specify the Ω_i's as follows: (Note that this is a different specification from that given earlier.)

$$\Omega_i = \{\underline{\tau} | \tau_i \geq \max_{j\neq i} \tau_j + \Delta\sigma\}, \quad 1 \leq i \leq k,$$

and

$$\bar{\Omega} = \bigcup_{i=1}^{k} \Omega_i.$$

Assume that σ is known. Let

$$\underline{\Delta}_i' = (\Delta\sigma,\ldots,\Delta\sigma)_{1\mathrm{x}(k-1)}, \quad i = 1,\ldots,k, \quad \Delta > 0.$$

Thus

$$\frac{p_{\underline{\Delta}_i}(\underline{y}_i)}{p_{\underline{0}}(\underline{y}_i)} = \exp \frac{1}{2\sigma^2}\{-(\underline{y}_i - C\underline{\Delta}_i)'\Sigma_i^{-1}(\underline{y}_i - C\underline{\Delta}_i) + \underline{y}_i'\Sigma_i^{-1}\underline{y}_i$$

$$= \exp\{\frac{1}{\sigma^2}\underline{\Delta}_i'C'\Sigma_i^{-1}\underline{y}_i - \frac{1}{2\sigma^2}\underline{\Delta}_i'C'\Sigma_i^{-1}C\,\underline{\Delta}_i\}$$

$$= \exp\{\frac{n\Delta}{(1-\lambda)k\sigma}(y_{i1} + \ldots + y_{ik}) - \frac{1}{2\sigma^2}\underline{\Delta}_i'C'\Sigma_i^{-1}C\underline{\Delta}_i\}.$$

Hence, we can rewrite

$$\frac{p_{\underline{\Delta}_i}(\underline{y}_i)}{p_{\underline{0}}(\underline{y}_i)} \geq d'$$

as $y_{i1} + \ldots + y_{ik} \geq d''\sigma$.

Let a selection rule $\delta^0 = (\delta_1^0, \ldots, \delta_k^0)$ be defined by

$$\delta_i^0(\underline{y}_i) = \begin{cases} 1 & \text{if } p_{\underline{\Delta}_i}(\underline{y}_i) \geq d'p_{\underline{0}}(\underline{y}_i), \\ 0 & \text{otherwise} \end{cases}$$

such that

(2.2) $$E_{\underline{\tau}}\delta^0(\underline{Y}_i) = \gamma, \ \underline{\tau} \in \Omega_0.$$

Then δ^0 maximizes

(2.3) $$\inf_{\bar{\Omega}} P(CS|\delta)$$

among all selection rules $\delta \in S(\gamma)$.

Note that $\delta_i^0(\underline{y}_i)$ is also based on the maximum likelihood estimators $\hat{\underline{\tau}}_i$ of $\underline{\tau}_i$. Since for any $\delta \in S(\gamma)$,

$$\underline{\tau} \in \bar{\Omega} = \bigcup_{i=1}^{k} \Omega_i \text{ implies } \underline{\tau} \in \Omega_i \text{ for some } i,$$

it is clear that

$$P(CS|\delta) = \int \delta_i(\underline{y}_i)p_{\underline{\tau}}(\underline{y}_i)d\nu(\underline{y}_i)$$

$$\geq \min_{1\leq i\leq k} \inf_{\underline{\tau}\in\Omega_i} \int \delta_i(\underline{y}_i)p_{\underline{\tau}}(\underline{y}_i)d\nu(\underline{y}_i).$$

We have

$$\inf_{\underline{\tau}\in\bar{\Omega}} P(CS|\delta) = \min_{1\leq i\leq k} \inf_{\underline{\tau}\in\Omega_i} \int \delta_i(\underline{y}_i)p_{\underline{\tau}}(\underline{y}_i)d\nu(\underline{y}_i).$$

For any $\delta \in S(\gamma)$, it follows that

$$\int (\delta_i-\delta_i^0)(p_{\underline{\Delta}_i} - d'p_{\underline{0}}) \leq 0$$

which implies

$$\int\delta_i^0\, p_{\underline{\Delta}_i} \geq \int\delta_i p_{\underline{\Delta}_i}.$$

Since $\delta_i^0(\underline{y}_i)$ is nondecreasing in $\underline{y}_i$, we have

$$\inf_{\underline{\tau}\in\bar{\Omega}} P(CS|\delta^0) = \min_{1\leq i\leq k} \int \delta_i^0(\underline{y}_i)p_{\underline{\Delta}_i}(\underline{y}_i)d\nu(\underline{y}_i)$$

$$\geq \min_{1\leq i\leq k} \int\delta_i(\underline{y}_i)p_{\underline{\Delta}_i}(\underline{y}_i)d\nu(\underline{y}_i)$$

$$\geq \min_{1\leq i\leq k} \inf_{\underline{\tau}\in\Omega_i} \int \delta_i(\underline{y}_i)p_{\underline{\tau}}(\underline{y}_i)d\nu(\underline{y}_i)$$

$$= \inf_{\underline{\theta}\in\bar{\Omega}} P(CS|\delta).$$

We rewrite δ^0 as follows:

$$\delta_i^0(\underline{y}_i) = \begin{cases} 1 & \text{if} \quad y_{i1} +\dots+ y_{ik} \geq d''\sigma, \\ 0 & \text{otherwise.} \end{cases}$$

Thus, the optimal subset selection rule is as follows:

$$\delta_i^0(\underline{x}) = \begin{cases} 1 & \text{if } \bar{x}_i \geq \frac{1}{k-1} \sum_{j\neq i} \bar{x}_j + d\sigma, \\ 0 & \text{otherwise.} \end{cases}$$

where $d = \frac{d''}{k-1}$.

Now, we wish to determine d and n. We make the following transformation:

$$z_{ik} = [1\ldots1]_{1\times(k-1)} \begin{bmatrix} y_{i1} \\ \vdots \\ y_{ik} \end{bmatrix}, \quad \text{and}$$

$$\tau = \tau_{i1} +\ldots+ \tau_{ik} = (k-1)\tau_i - \sum_{j\neq i} \tau_j.$$

Since the distribution of

$$\hat{\underline{\tau}}_i = \begin{bmatrix} Y_{i1} \\ \vdots \\ Y_{ik} \end{bmatrix} = (C'\Sigma_i^{-1}C)^{-1}C'\Sigma_i^{-1}\underline{Y}_i$$

is $(2\pi\sigma^2)^{-\frac{1}{2}k}|\Sigma_{1i}|^{-\frac{1}{2}}\exp[-\frac{1}{2\sigma^2}(\hat{\underline{\tau}}_i - \underline{\tau}_i)'\Sigma_{1i}^{-1}(\hat{\underline{\tau}}_i-\underline{\tau}_i)]$, where

$\Sigma_{1i} = \frac{1-\lambda}{n} J$, the distribution of Z_{ik} is

$$[2\pi\sigma^2(1-\lambda)k(k-1)\frac{1}{n}]^{-\frac{1}{2}}\exp[-\frac{n}{2\sigma^2(1-\lambda)k(k-1)}(z_{ik}-\tau)^2].$$

Hence

$$\text{(2.4)} \qquad E_{\underline{0}}\delta_i^0(\underline{Y}_i) = P(Z_{ik} \geq d''\sigma)$$

$$= \Phi[-\frac{d''\sqrt{n}}{\sqrt{(1-\lambda)k(k-1)}}] = \gamma,$$

and

$$(2.5)\qquad \inf_{\underline{\tau}\in\bar{\Omega}} P_{\underline{\tau}}(CS\,|\,\delta^0)$$

$$= \min_{\underline{1<i<k}} \int \delta_i^0(\underline{y}_i)p_{\underline{\Delta}_i}(\underline{y}_i)d\nu(\underline{y}_i)$$

$$= \min_{\underline{1<i<k}} P_{\underline{\Delta}_i}(Z_{ik} \geq d''\sigma)$$

$$= \min_{\underline{1<i<k}} P_{\underline{\Delta}_i}\left(\frac{(Z_{ik}-(k-1)\Delta)\sqrt{n}}{\sqrt{(1-\lambda)k(k-1)}} \geq \frac{(d''-(k-1)\Delta)\sqrt{n}}{\sqrt{(1-\lambda)k(k-1)}}\right)$$

$$= \Phi\left[-\frac{(d''-(k-1)\Delta)\sqrt{n}}{(1-\lambda)k(k-1)}\right] = P^*.$$

For given γ, P^*, k, λ, and Δ, we can find d'' and the smallest number of blocks, n, to satisfy equations (2.4) and (2.5). Note that this n is also the minimum sample size for the case of one observation per cell in the completely randomized block design.

We rewrite (2.4) and (2.5) as

$$\Phi\left[-\frac{d\sqrt{n(k-1)}}{\sqrt{(1-\lambda)k}}\right] = \gamma$$

and

$$\Phi\left[-\frac{(d-\Delta)\sqrt{n(k-1)}}{\sqrt{(1-\lambda)k}}\right] = P^*.$$

Let z_{P^*} and z_γ represent the upper percentage points corresponding to P^* and γ, respectively of the standard normal distribution. Then we have

$$d = -\frac{z_\gamma \Delta}{z_{p^*} - z_\gamma},$$

and

$$n = \left\langle \frac{(1-\lambda)k(z_{P^*} - z_\gamma)^2}{(k-1)\Delta^2} \right\rangle,$$

where $\langle a \rangle$ is the smallest integer greater than or equal to a.

Summarizing the previous results, we obtain the following theorem.

THEOREM. *Under model* (1.1) *with the stated assumptions on* $\underline{\epsilon}_\alpha$, *an optimal procedure for selecting a subset of the "best" or "worthwhile" treatments based on the observed data* $\underline{x}$ *and satisfying the conditions* (2.2) *and* (2.3) *is: Select the population* π_i *with probability* $\delta_i^0(\underline{x})$ *given by*

$$\delta_i^0(\underline{x}) = \begin{cases} 1 & \text{if} \quad \bar{x}_i \geq \frac{1}{k-1} \sum_{j \neq i} \bar{x}_j + d\sigma, \\ 0 & \text{otherwise,} \end{cases}$$

where the smallest values of d *and* n *are given by*

$$d = -\frac{z_\gamma \Delta}{z_{P*} - z_\gamma},$$

and

$$n = \left\langle \frac{(1-\lambda)k(z_{P*} - z_\gamma)^2}{(k-1)\Delta^2} \right\rangle.$$

Furthermore, we have established the following connection between the selection procedure and the hypothesis identification problem as follows: If $\pi_{i_1}, \pi_{i_2}, \ldots, \pi_{i_j}$ $(j < k)$ *are selected, we say that these populations are not significantly different and make the hypothesis identification*

$$H_i^!: \quad \tau_{i_1} = \ldots = \tau_{i_j} \geq \max_{\substack{1 \leq \ell \leq k \\ \ell \notin \{i_1, \ldots, i_j\}}} \tau_\ell + \Delta\sigma.$$

Note that the overall identification risk connected with this problem is $\leq \gamma + (1-P^*)$.

Remark: It should be pointed out that for some pairs (γ, P^*), δ^0 may not select any population. This is to be interpreted as not identifying any one of the appropriate hypotheses.

We consider some special cases to provide an idea as to the appropriate identification of one of the hypotheses. For $\gamma = 0.05$, $\lambda = 0.5$ and $P^* = 0.95, 0.90, 0.80$; then

(i) $k = 2$,

$$H_0: \tau_1 = \tau_2,\ H_1': \tau_1 \geq \tau_2 + \Delta\sigma,\ H_2': \tau_2 \geq \tau_1 + \Delta\sigma.$$

In this case, for specified Δ-values, the smallest d and n needed for the optimal selection rule are given in the following table.

Table 1. d and n for various Δ, $k = 2$, and $P^* = 0.95, 0.90, 0.80$.

Δ	0.1	0.5	1.0	2.0
d	0.05,0.06,0.07	0.25,0.32,0.33	0.50,0.64,0.66	1.00,1.29,1.33
n	1089,858,620	44,35,25	11,9,7	3,3,2

(ii) $k = 3$,

$H_0: \tau_1 = \tau_2 = \tau_3$, $H_1': \tau_1 \geq \max(\tau_2, \tau_3) + \Delta\sigma$,

$H_2': \tau_2 \geq \max(\tau_1, \tau_3) + \Delta\sigma$, $H_3': \tau_3 \geq \max(\tau_1, \tau_2) + \Delta\sigma$,

$H_4': \tau_1 = \tau_2 \geq \tau_3 + \Delta\sigma$, $H_5': \tau_1 = \tau_3 \geq \tau_2 + \Delta\sigma$,

$H_6': \tau_2 = \tau_3 \geq \tau_1 + \Delta\sigma$.

For the optimal selection rule, the minimum value of d and n are computed (for specified values of Δ) and given in the following table.

Table 2. d and n for various Δ, $k = 3$, and $P^* = 0.95, 0.90, 0.80$.

Δ	0.1	0.5	1.0	2.0
d	0.05,0.06,0.07	0.25,0.32,0.33	0.50,0.64,0.66	1.00,1.29,1.33
n	817,644,465	33,26,19	9,7,5	3,2,2

(iii) $k = 4$,

H_0: $\tau_1 = \tau_2 = \tau_3 = \tau_4$, H'_1: $\tau_1 \geq \max(\tau_2,\tau_3,\tau_4) + \Delta\sigma$,

H'_2: $\tau_2 \geq \max(\tau_1,\tau_3,\tau_4) + \Delta\sigma$, H'_3: $\tau_3 \geq \max(\tau_1,\tau_2,\tau_4) + \Delta\sigma$,

H'_4: $\tau_4 \geq \max(\tau_1,\tau_2,\tau_3) + \Delta\sigma$, H'_5: $\tau_1 = \tau_2 \geq \max(\tau_3,\tau_4) + \Delta\sigma$,

H'_6: $\tau_1 = \tau_3 \geq \max(\tau_2,\tau_4) + \Delta\sigma$, H'_7: $\tau_1 = \tau_4 \geq \max(\tau_2,\tau_3) + \Delta\sigma$,

H'_8: $\tau_2 = \tau_3 \geq \max(\tau_1,\tau_4) + \Delta\sigma$, H'_9: $\tau_2 = \tau_4 \geq \max(\tau_1,\tau_3) + \Delta\sigma$,

H'_{10}: $\tau_3 = \tau_4 \geq \max(\tau_1,\tau_2) + \Delta\sigma$, H'_{11}: $\tau_1 = \tau_2 = \tau_3 \geq \tau_4 + \Delta\sigma$,

H'_{12}: $\tau_1 = \tau_2 = \tau_4 \geq \tau_3 + \Delta\sigma$, H'_{13}: $\tau_1 = \tau_3 = \tau_4 \geq \tau_1 + \Delta\sigma$,

H'_{14}: $\tau_2 = \tau_3 = \tau_4 \geq \tau_1 + \Delta\sigma$.

For the optimal selection rule, the minimum value of d and n are computed (for specified values of Δ) and given in the following table.

Table 3. d and n for various Δ, k=4, and P* = 0.95,0.90,0.80.

Δ	0.1	0.5	1.0	2.0
d	0.05,0.06,0.07	0.25,0.32,0.33	0.50,0.64,0.66	1.00,1.29,1.33
n	726,572,413	30,23,17	8,6,5	2,2,2

Note that P* is the probability of correct selection for the associated subset selection rule, while the error probability γ is controlled at 5 percent level. The identification risk is 0.05 + (1-P*). We can explain the cases described above as follows: for k = 2, if the selected subset contains π_i only, we identify H'_i, i = 1,2; if it contains π_1 and π_2, we identify H_0. For k = 3, if the selected subset contains π_i only, we identify H'_i, i = 1,2,3; if it contains π_1 and π_2, π_1 and π_3, or π_2 and π_3 only, we identify H'_4, H'_5 or H'_6, respectively. Similar discussion applies to the case k = 4.

Now, we discuss the case where σ^2 is unknown. For any i, the maximum likelihood estimators of $\underline{\tau}_i$ and σ^2 are:

$$\hat{\underline{\tau}}_i = (C'\Sigma_i^{-1}C)^{-1}C^{-1}\Sigma_i^{-1}\underline{Y}_i = \begin{bmatrix} Y_{i1} \\ \vdots \\ Y_{ik} \end{bmatrix}$$

and

$$\hat{\sigma}^2 = \frac{1}{(k-1)(n-1)} \underline{Y}_i'[\Sigma_i^{-1} - \Sigma_i^{-1}C(C'\Sigma_i^{-1}C)^{-1}C'\Sigma_i^{-1}]\underline{Y}_i.$$

We know that $\hat{\sigma}^2$ and $\hat{\underline{\tau}}_i$ are independent and the distribution f(s) of $s = \frac{\hat{\sigma}}{\sigma}$ is $\sqrt{\chi_p^2(s)}$ with $p = (k-1)(n-1)$.

As before, we define the selection rule as follows:

$$\varphi_i^0(\hat{\underline{\tau}}_i,\hat{\sigma}) = \begin{cases} 1 & \text{if } y_{i1} + \ldots + y_{ik} \geq d_1\hat{\sigma}, \\ 0 & \text{otherwise,} \end{cases}$$

or

$$\varphi_i^0(\underline{x},\hat{\sigma}) = \begin{cases} 1 & \text{if } \bar{x}_i \geq \frac{1}{k-1}\sum_{j\neq i}\bar{x}_j + \frac{d_1}{k-1}\hat{\sigma} \\ 0 & \text{otherwise.} \end{cases}$$

Conditionally, for an observed value of $\hat{\sigma}$, we can discuss the optimality as before. However, the constant d and n can be determined without any difficulty by (2.8) and (2.9). Since

$$E_{\underline{\tau}}\varphi_i^0(\hat{\underline{\tau}}_i,\hat{\sigma}) = \gamma, \qquad \underline{\tau} \in \Omega_0$$

we get

$$(2.6) \qquad \int \Phi[-\frac{d_1 s\sqrt{n}}{\sqrt{(1-\lambda)k(k-1)}}] f(s)ds = \gamma,$$

and

$$\inf_{\bar{\Omega}} P(CS|\varphi^0)$$

$$(2.7)\qquad = \int \Phi\left[-\frac{(d_1 s-(k-1)\Delta)\sqrt{n}}{\sqrt{(1-\lambda)k(k-1)}}\right]f(s)ds = P^*.$$

This gives

$$(2.8)\qquad t\left[-\frac{d_1\sqrt{n(n-1)}}{\sqrt{(1-\lambda)k}};\ (k-1)(n-1),0\right] = \gamma,$$

and

$$(2.9)\qquad t\left[-\frac{d_1\sqrt{n(n-1)}}{\sqrt{(1-\lambda)k}};\ (k-1)(n-1),\ \frac{\Delta\sqrt{n(k-1)}}{\sqrt{(1-\lambda)k}}\right] = P^*,$$

where $t(a;\ b,\ c)$ is the percentage point of the noncentral t with b degrees of freedom and the noncentrality parameter c.

ACKNOWLEDGMENT

The authors with to thank Professor S. Panchapakesan for a critical reading of this paper and for suggestions to improve the presentation of this paper.

REFERENCES

[1] Gupta, S. S. and Huang, D. Y. (1981). *Multiple Statistical Decision Theory*. Lecture Notes in Statistics (6), Springer-Verlag, New York.

[2] Gupta, S. S. and Panchapakesan, S. (1979). *Multiple Decision Procedures*. John Wiley and Sons, New York.

ON THE PROBLEM OF FINDING A BEST POPULATION WITH RESPECT TO A CONTROL IN TWO STAGES[1]

Shanti S. Gupta

Department of Statistics
Purdue University
West Lafayette, Indiana, U.S.A.

Klaus-J. Miescke

Department of Mathematics
Mainz University
Mainz, West Germany

I. INTRODUCTION

Let $\pi_1,\ldots,\pi_k$ be k populations associated with unknown parameters $\theta_1,\ldots,\theta_k \in \Omega \subseteq \mathbb{R}$. Let $\theta_0 \in \Omega$ be a given control value such that every π_i with $\theta_i > \theta_0$ is assumed to be "good", and "bad" otherwise, $i = 1,\ldots,k$. We consider the problem: how to find the best population (i.e. that one associated with the largest parameter) among the good ones (if there is any) in two stages by screening out non-best (or bad) populations in the first stage.

Assume that samples $\{X_{ij}\}_{j=1,\ldots,n}$ and $\{Y_{ij}\}_{j=1,\ldots,m}$ can be drawn from π_i at the first and the second stage, respectively, $i = 1,\ldots,k$, which are mutually independent. Let U_i and V_i be real-valued sufficient statistics for θ_i with respect to these samples which have densities f_{θ_i} and g_{θ_i}, respectively, with respect to the Lebesgue measure on $\mathbb{R}$, $i = 1,\ldots,k$. The families $\{f_\theta\}_{\theta\in\Omega}$ and $\{g_\theta\}_{\theta\in\Omega}$ are assumed to be known and to have monotone

[1]This research was supported by the Office of Naval Research Contract N00014-75-C-0455 at Purdue University. Reproduction in whole or in part is permitted for any purpose of the United States Government.

ISBN 0-12-307501-7

non-decreasing likelihood ratios (MLR). Finally, let $W_i = T(U_i, V_i)$ be a real-valued sufficient statistic for θ_i with respect to (U_i, V_i), which has a density h_{θ_i} with respect to the Lebesgue measure on $\mathbb{R}$, where the family $\{h_\theta\}_{\theta \in \Omega}$ also has MLR. For notational convenience, let $\underline{U} = (U_1, \ldots, U_k)$, and let $\underline{V}$, $\underline{W}$ etc. have analogous meaning.

In this paper we will study a certain class of 2-stage procedures (S,d), defined as follows. Let S denote any subset selection procedure based on $\underline{U}$, i.e. S: $\mathbb{R}^k \to \{s | s \subseteq \{1,\ldots,k\}\}$ measurable with respect to Borel sets in $\mathbb{R}^k$, where an empty subset is admitted. S *acts as a screening procedure in the first stage*. Let $d = \{d_s\}_{s \subseteq \{1,\ldots,k\}}$ with $d_\emptyset = 0$ and $d_{\{i\}} = i$, $i = 1,\ldots,k$. Moreover, for every $s \subseteq \{1,\ldots,k\}$ with size $|s| \geq 2$, let d_s: $\mathbb{R}^k \times \mathbb{R}^k \to s$, where $d_s(\underline{u}, \underline{v})$ depends only on variables u_i and v_i with $i \in s$, and where d_s is measurable with respect to the Borel sets in their joint space $\mathbb{R}^{2|s|}$. d *represents the set of final decisions* at the first stage and the second stage, respectively. The introduction of the (at the first sight) somewhat complicated looking structure d will prove to be very convenient in the sequel. Now we are ready to define our 2-stage procedures in a concise way.

Definition 1. *2-stage procedure* (S,d).

Stage 1. Take observations (i.e. the X-samples) from $\pi_1, \ldots, \pi_k$. Select all populations π_i with $i \in s = S(\underline{U})$. If $s = \emptyset$, stop, and decide $d_\emptyset = 0$ (i.e. "no population is good"). If $s = \{i\}$ for some $i \in \{1,\ldots,k\}$, stop, and decide $d_{\{i\}} = i$ (i.e. "π_i is good and the best one"). If $|s| \geq 2$, proceed to Stage 2.

Stage 2. Take additional observations (i.e. the Y-samples) from all populations π_i with $i \in s$ and make the final decision $d_s(\underline{U}, \underline{V})$ (i.e. "π_{i_0} is good and the best one", if $d_s(\underline{U}, \underline{V}) = i_0$, say, for some $i_0 \in s$.).

Throughout this paper we will restrict consideration to procedures (S,d) which are completely (i.e. with respect to both, S and d) invariant under permutations of the k populations $\pi_1,\ldots,\pi_k$.

In Section 2 it will be shown that under any reasonable loss structure the optimal final decisions are always the natural ones, i.e. are associated with the largest sufficient statistic among those coming from the populations which still are eligible. This result can be derived from Lehmann's [10] version of the "Bahadur-Goodman-Theorem". In Section 3 a natural type 2-stage procedure will be studied which screens out in the first stage by means of a UMP-test ("$\theta \leq \theta_0$" versus "$\theta > \theta_0$") at a fixed level, which is applied separately to $U_1,\ldots,U_k$, respectively. Finally, in Section 4 it will be shown that under a fairly general loss structure (cost for sampling plus loss for final decision) and for every i.i.d. prior there exists a Bayes 2-stage procedure which is completely monotone (i.e. where also the subset selections are made in terms of the largest observations), provided that a certain condition (Assumption (A) or (B)) is satisfied. This result will be derived by a two-fold application of Eaton's [3] more general version of the "Bahadur-Goodman-Theorem". Throughout the following we shall repeatedly study, as an example, the case of k normal populations with unknown means $\theta_1,\ldots,\theta_k$ and a common known variance $\sigma^2 > 0$.

II. OPTIMALITY OF THE NATURAL FINAL DECISIONS

In this section we assume that a loss structure is given which we will specify only with respect to final decisions, and without reference to the control θ_0. This allows us to state the results in a more general setting including also the non-control ("finding the best population") problems such as those studied by Tamhane and Bechhofer [14].

Definition 2. *Loss structure* L.

Let us assume that for every procedure (S,d) subsequent decisions S = s and $d_s = i$, $i \in s$, result in a real-valued loss $L(s,i,\underline{\theta})$ at $\underline{\theta} = (\theta_1,\ldots,\theta_k) \in \Omega^k$, which is integrable and has the following two properties:

(a) L is permutation invariant (i.e. $L(\pi s,\pi i,\pi\underline{\theta}) = L(s,i,\underline{\theta})$ in the sense of Eaton [3] for all permutations π), and:

(b) For every $\underline{\theta} \in \Omega^k$ and $i,j \in \{1,\ldots,k\}$ with $\theta_i < \theta_j$, $L(\{i\},i,\underline{\theta}) \geq L(\{j\},j,\underline{\theta})$; and $s \subseteq \{1,\ldots,k\}$ with $i,j \in s$ implies $L(s,i,\underline{\theta}) \geq L(s,j,\underline{\theta})$.

The risk of a procedure (S,d) at $\underline{\theta} \in \Omega^k$ is given by

$$
\begin{aligned}
(1)\quad r_{\underline{\theta}}(S,d) &= E_{\underline{\theta}}(L(S(\underline{U}),\ d_{S(\underline{U})}(\underline{U},\underline{V}),\ \underline{\theta})) \\
&= L(\emptyset,0,\underline{\theta})P_{\underline{\theta}}\{S(\underline{U}) = \emptyset\} \\
&+ \sum_{i=1}^{k} L(\{i\},i,\underline{\theta})P_{\underline{\theta}}\{S(\underline{U})=\{i\}\,|\,|S(\underline{U})|=1\}P_{\underline{\theta}}\{|S(\underline{U})|=1\} \\
&+ \sum_{s,|s|\geq 2} \Big(\sum_{i\in s} L(s,i,\underline{\theta})P_{\underline{\theta}}\{d_s(\underline{U},\underline{V})=i\,|\,S(\underline{U})=s\}\Big)P_{\underline{\theta}}\{S(\underline{U})=s\}.
\end{aligned}
$$

Our first result is with respect to final decisions at Stage 1.

LEMMA 1. *Let* (S,d) *be a 2-stage procedure and let* $\tilde{S}$ *be the same procedure as* S *with the only modification that for all* $\underline{u} \in \mathbb{R}^k$ *with* $|S(\underline{u})| = 1$, $\tilde{S}(\underline{u}) = \{i\}$ *implies* $u_i = \max_{j=1,\ldots,k} u_j$, $i \in \{1,\ldots,k\}$. *Then* $r_{\underline{\theta}}(\tilde{S},d) \leq r_{\underline{\theta}}(S,d)$ *for all* $\underline{\theta} \in \Omega^k$.

Proof. For a fixed (S,d), let $A = \{\underline{u} \in \mathbb{R}^k \mid |S(\underline{u})| = 1\}$. Let $\underline{\theta} \in \Omega^k$ with $P_{\underline{\theta}}\{\underline{U} \in A\} > 0$. The conditional distribution of $\underline{U}$, given $\underline{U} \in A$, has the following density w.r.t. the Lebesgue measure

$$(2)\qquad P_{\underline{\theta}}\{\underline{U} \in A\}^{-1} \prod_{i=1}^{k} f_{\theta_i}(u_i)\ I_A(\underline{u}),\quad \underline{u} \in \mathbb{R}^k.$$

Since by the invariance of S, A is permutation symmetric and moreover, $P_{\underline{\theta}}\{U \in A\}$ is a permutation symmetric function of $\underline{\theta} \in \Omega^k$, (2) is of the form assumed in Lehmann [10]. Also, $L(\{i\}, i, \underline{\theta})$ satisfies the monotonicity property (5) of Lehmann [10]. Thus by his main result the first sum in (1) is for $(\tilde{S}, d)$ smaller or equal to that one for (S,d). Since all other terms in (1) are the same for both procedures the proof is completed.

The proof w.r.t. final decisions at Stage 2 is similar but a bit more complicated. For simplicity, let us assume from now on that the mapping $(u,v) \to (u,T(u,v))$ for (u,v) in the interior of $\mathcal{D} = \bigcup_{\theta \in \Omega} (\text{support}(f_\theta) \times \text{support}(g_\theta))$ is one-to-one and continuously differentiable. Thus we have a function $\tilde{T}$ with $(u,v) = (u, \tilde{T}(u, T(u,v)))$, $(u,v) \in \mathcal{D}$ with analogous properties.

LEMMA 2. *For every* $\underline{\theta} \in \Omega^k$, $s = \{i_1, \ldots, i_t\}$ *and Borel set* $A \subseteq \mathbb{R}^k$ *with* $P_{\underline{\theta}}\{\underline{U} \in A\} > 0$ *which is* s-*permutation symmetric (i.e.* $I_A(\underline{u})$, $\underline{u} \in \mathbb{R}^k$, *is symmetric in* $(u_{i_1}, \ldots, u_{i_t})$ *as well as in the* k-t *remaining variables), the conditional distribution of* $\underline{W}$, *given* $\underline{U} \in A$, *has a density w.r.t. Lebesgue measure of the type*

$$(3) \qquad c(\underline{\theta}) \prod_{i=1}^{k} \tilde{h}_{\theta_i}(w_i)\, p(\underline{w}), \quad \underline{w} \in \mathbb{R}^k,$$

where $c\colon \Omega^k \to \mathbb{R}_+ = \{\xi \mid \xi \geq 0\}$ *is* s-*permutation symmetric,* $\tilde{h}_\theta\colon \mathbb{R} \to \mathbb{R}_+$ *is measurable,* $p\colon \mathbb{R}^k \to \mathbb{R}_+$ *is measurable* s-*permutation symmetric, and* $\{\tilde{h}_\theta\}_{\theta \in \Omega}$ *has* MLR.

Proof. Let $\underline{\theta} \in \Omega^k$ and $A \subseteq \mathbb{R}^k$ be given as stated above. Then the conditional distribution of $(\underline{U}, \underline{V})$, given $\underline{U} \in A$, has the following density w.r.t. Lebesgue measure.

$$(4) \qquad P_{\underline{\theta}}\{\underline{U} \in A\}^{-1} \prod_{i=1}^{k} f_{\theta_i}(u_i) g_{\theta_i}(v_i) I_A(\underline{u}), \quad \underline{u}, \underline{v} \in \mathbb{R}^k.$$

Since $W_i = T(U_i,V_i)$ is sufficient for θ_i, $i = 1,\ldots,k$, by the factorization theorem there exist non-negative measurable functions $\tilde{h}_\theta$ and G with $f_\theta(u)g_\theta(v) = \tilde{h}_\theta(T(u,v))G(u,v)$, $u,v \in \mathbb{R}, \theta \in \Omega$. After inserting this into (4) and after a standard change of variables, we see that the conditional distribution of $(\underline{U},\underline{W})$ with $W_i = T(U_i,V_i)$, $i = 1,\ldots,k$, given $\underline{U} \in A$, has the density

$$(5) \qquad P_{\underline{\theta}}\{\underline{U} \in A\}^{-1} \prod_{i=1}^{k} \tilde{h}_{\theta_i}(w_i)G(u_i,\tilde{T}(u_i,w_i)) \left|\frac{\partial\tilde{T}(u_i,w_i)}{\partial w_i}\right| I_A(\underline{u}), \quad \underline{u},\underline{w} \in \mathbb{R}^k.$$

Thus by integrating out the variables $\underline{u} \in \mathbb{R}^k$ we see that the conditional distribution of $\underline{W}$, given $\underline{U} \in A$, has a density of the form (3) w.r.t. the Lebesgue measure. Here $c(\underline{\theta}) = P_{\underline{\theta}}\{\underline{U} \in A\}^{-1}$ which, apparently, is s-permutation symmetric. Moreover,

$$(6) \qquad p(\underline{w}) = \int_A \prod_{i=1}^{k} G(u_i,\tilde{T}(u_i,w_i)) \left|\frac{\partial\tilde{T}(u_i,w_i)}{\partial w_i}\right| d\underline{u}, \quad \underline{w} \in \mathbb{R}^k,$$

which also is s-permutation symmetric. Finally, since by assumption the family of densities for $W_i = T(U_i,V_i)$, $i = 1,\ldots,k$, $\{h_\theta\}_{\theta\in\Omega}$, has MLR, $\{\tilde{h}_\theta\}_{\theta\in\Omega}$ has also MLR. This completes the proof of Lemma 2.

COROLLARY 1. *For every* $\underline{\theta} \in \Omega^k$, $s = \{i_1,\ldots,i_t\}$ *and Borel set* $A \subseteq \mathbb{R}^k$ *with* $P_{\underline{\theta}}\{\underline{U} \in A\} > 0$ *which is* s*-permutation symmetric, the conditional distribution of* $(W_{i_1},\ldots,W_{i_t})$, *given* $\underline{U} \in A$, *has a density w.r.t. the Lebesgue measure of the type*

$$(7) \qquad c(\underline{\theta}) \prod_{j=1}^{t} \tilde{h}_{\theta_{i_j}}(\xi_j)p_{\underline{\theta}'}(\underline{\xi}), \quad \underline{\xi} \in \mathbb{R}^t,$$

where c *and* $\{\tilde{h}_\theta\}_{\theta\in\Omega}$ *are the same as in* (3), $\underline{\theta}' = (\theta_{j_1},\ldots,\theta_{j_{k-t}})$ *with* $\{i_1,\ldots,i_t\} \cup \{j_1,\ldots,j_{k-t}\} = \{1,\ldots,k\}$, *and* $p_{\underline{\theta}'}(\underline{\xi})$ *is permutation symmetric in* $\underline{\theta}'$ *as well as in* $\underline{\xi} \in \mathbb{R}^t$.

Proof. This follows from Lemma 2 by integrating out in (3) the variables $w_{j_1},\ldots,w_{j_{k-t}}$. Especially thereby we get for $(w_{i_1},\ldots,w_{i_t}) \in \mathbb{R}^t$

$$p_{\underline{\theta}'}(w_{i_1},\ldots,w_{i_t}) = \int_{\mathbb{R}^{k-t}} \prod_{r=1}^{k-t} \tilde{h}_{\theta_{j_r}}(w_{j_r})p(w_1,\ldots,w_k) \, d(w_{j_1},\ldots,w_{j_{k-t}}), \tag{8}$$

which now can be seen to have the symmetry properties stated above. Thus the proof is completed.

Now we are ready to prove the main result of this section.

THEOREM 1. *Let* (S,d) *be a 2-stage procedure and let* $\tilde{S}$ *be the modification of* S *(given in Lemma* 1*) which uses the optimal final decision at Stage* 1. *Let* $d^* = \{d_s^*\}_{s \subseteq \{1,\ldots,k\}}$ *be the set of natural final decisions, i.e. where for every* $s \subseteq \{1,\ldots,k\}$ *with* $|s| \geq 2$, $i \in s$, $\underline{u}, \underline{v} \in \mathbb{R}^k$ *and* $d_s^*(\underline{u},\underline{v}) = i$ *implies* $T(u_i,v_i) = \max_{j\in s} T(u_j,v_j)$. *Then* $r_{\underline{\theta}}(\tilde{S},d^*) \leq r_{\underline{\theta}}(S,d)$ *for all* $\underline{\theta} \in \Omega^k$.

Proof. Let $\underline{\theta} \in \Omega^k$ be fixed. In view of Lemma 1 we only have to show that $r_{\underline{\theta}}(S,d^*) \leq r_{\underline{\theta}}(S,d)$. Thus by (1) it suffices to prove that for every $s \subseteq \{1,\ldots,k\}$ with $|s| \geq 2$ and $P_{\underline{\theta}}\{S(\underline{U}) = s\} > 0$,

$$\sum_{i\in s} L(s,i,\underline{\theta})P_{\underline{\theta}}\{d_s^*(\underline{U},\underline{V}) = i|S(\underline{U}) = s\} \tag{9}$$

$$\leq \sum_{i\in s} L(s,i,\underline{\theta})P_{\underline{\theta}}\{d_s(\underline{U},\underline{V}) = i|S(\underline{U}) = s\}.$$

Let $s \subseteq \{1,\ldots,k\}$ with $|s| \geq 2$ be fixed. Let $A = \{\underline{u} \in \mathbb{R}^k | S(\underline{u}) = s\}$. By the invariance property of S, A is s-permutation symmetric. In the conditional situation, given $S(\underline{U}) = s$ or, equivalently, given $\underline{U} \in A$, $\underline{W}$ is sufficient for

$\underline{\theta} \in \Omega^k$. This can be seen from (4) and the sentence following (4). Thus, similar as one concludes in the theory of selection procedures, if $s = \{i_1,\ldots,i_t\}$ with $1 \le i_1 <\ldots< i_t \le k$, say, then we can assume that $d_s(\underline{u},\underline{v})$ is a function of $(T(u_{i_1},v_{i_1}),\ldots,T(u_{i_t},v_{i_t}))$. By Corollary 1 the conditional distribution of $(W_{i_1},\ldots,W_{i_t})$, given $\underline{U} \in A$, has a density w.r.t. the Lebesgue measure of the form (7) or, respectively,

$$(10) \qquad c_{\underline{\theta}'}(\theta_{i_1},\ldots,\theta_{i_t}) \prod_{j=1}^{t} \tilde{h}_{\theta_{i_j}}(\xi_j) p_{\underline{\theta}'}(\underline{\xi}), \quad \underline{\xi} \in \mathbb{R}^t,$$

where $c_{\underline{\theta}'}: \Omega^t \to \mathbb{R}_+$ and $p_{\underline{\theta}'}: \mathbb{R}^t \to \mathbb{R}_+$ are permutation symmetric functions, $p_{\underline{\theta}'}$ is measurable and $\{\tilde{h}_\theta\}_{\theta\in\Omega}$ has MLR. Therefore this distribution satisfies all conditions assumed by Lehmann [10]. Since moreover, $L(s,i,\underline{\theta})$, $i \in s$, satisfies the condition (5) in his paper, it follows from his version of the "Bahadur-Goodman Theorem" that inequality (9) holds. This completes the proof of the theorem.

Remark 1. Let (S,d) be any 2-stage procedure. Then, after having made a decision $S = s$, say, the final decision $d = i$, say, can be viewed as being a partition $(s\setminus\{i\}, \{i\})$ of s into two subsets of sizes $|s|-1$ and 1, respectively. If, more generally, partitions into q subsets of s of fixed sizes $r_1,\ldots,r_q$ are to be made, where q, $r_1,\ldots,r_q$ depend on $|s|$, then the more general version of the "Bahadur-Goodman-Theorem" by Eaton [3] can be applied. Thus, if the loss structure in this setting is compatible with the one assumed by Eaton [3], then the set of natural partitions in terms of the ordered W_i's is optimal.

By Theorem 1 we know now especially, that after having made a decision $S(\underline{U}) = s$, say, it is always better to make a final decision in terms of the largest W_{i_0} among the W_i with $i \in s$, than to make it in terms of the largest V_{i_0} among the V_i with $i \in s$. This fact appears to be interesting enough to be formulated in a slightly more general form in the following Corollary 2.

COROLLARY 2. *For every* $\underline{\theta} \in \Omega^k$, $s \subseteq \{1,\ldots,k\}$ *and* s-*permutation symmetric Borel set* $A \subseteq \mathbb{R}^k$ *with* $P_{\underline{\theta}}\{\underline{U} \in A\} > 0$ *the following holds true. Let* $e_i = P_{\underline{\theta}}\{W_i = \max_{j\in s} W_j | \underline{U} \in A\}$ *and* $f_i = P_{\underline{\theta}}\{V_i = \max_{j\in s} V_j\}$, $i \in s$. *Then the* e_i's *and* f_i's *are ordered in the same order as the* θ_i's *with* $i \in s$ *and, moreover, the vector of* e_i's *majorizes the vector of* f_i's.

Proof. Without loss of generality, let $s = \{1,\ldots,t\}$ with $t \geq 2$ and $\underline{\theta} \in \Omega^k$ with $\theta_1 \leq \ldots \leq \theta_t$. If $A \subseteq \mathbb{R}^k$ has the properties stated above, take any permutation invariant S with $S(\underline{u}) = s$ if $\underline{u} \in A$ and with $|S(\underline{u})| \leq 1$ otherwise. Let $r \in \{1,\ldots,t-1\}$ be fixed and take any loss structure L with $L(s,i,\underline{\theta}) = 1(0)$ if $i \leq (>) r$, $i \in s$. Let $d_s(\underline{u},\underline{v}) = i$ if $v_i = \max_{j\in s} v_j$, $i \in s$, where ties are broken at random. Then by Theorem 1 we get $r_{\underline{\theta}}(S,d^*) \leq r_{\underline{\theta}}(S,d)$ or, more specifically, by inequality (9) we get $f_{r+1} + \ldots + f_t \leq e_{r+1} + \ldots + e_t$, since, obviously, we have $f_1 + \ldots + f_t = e_1 + \ldots + e_t = 1$. Moreover, that $f_1 \leq \ldots \leq f_t$ holds is well known. Finally, $e_1 \leq \ldots \leq e_t$ follows from Corollary 1 and Lemma 4.1 of Eaton. Thus the proof is completed.

Example (Normal Case). Let us look at the special case where $\pi_1,\ldots,\pi_k$ are normal populations $N(\theta_1,\sigma^2),\ldots,N(\theta_k,\sigma^2)$ with unknown means $\theta_1,\ldots,\theta_k \in \mathbb{R}$ and a common known variance $\sigma^2 > 0$. Let U_i and V_i be the arithmetic means of the observations in samples $\{X_{ij}\}_{j=1,\ldots,n}$ and $\{Y_{ij}\}_{j=1,\ldots,m}$, respectively, $i = 1,\ldots,k$. In several parts of this paper we shall return to this special case which henceforth will be denoted as the *normal case*.

Thus we have $U_i \sim N(\theta_i,p)$ and $V_i \sim N(\theta_i,q)$, $i = 1,\ldots,k$, which are mutually independent, where $p = \sigma^2/n$ and $q = \sigma^2/m$. Let W_i be the overall arithmetic mean for π_i, $i = 1,\ldots,k$. Then

$W_i = T(U_i,V_i) = (qU_i + pV_i)/(q+p) \sim N(\theta_i,(q^{-1} + p^{-1})^{-1})$, and

$V_i = \tilde{T}(U_i,W_i) = W_i + p^{-1}q(W_i-U_i)$, $i = 1,\ldots,k$.

Since all our assumptions concerning the underlying distributions are satisfied, all results derived so far are valid in this case. And from Corollary 2, one can derive interesting inequalities.

Remark 2. Without going into details it should be pointed out that analogous results to the ones derived in this section can be obtained in more general sequential settings, provided that the stopping rule is permutation invariant.

III. A NATURAL TYPE 2-STAGE PROCEDURE

In this section we will study 2-stage procedures (S,d) from a non-decision theoretic point of view. Let a correct decision (CD) at $\underline{\theta} \in \Omega^k$ be $d = 0$ (i.e. $S = \emptyset$) if $\theta_1,\ldots,\theta_k \leq \theta_0$, and be $d = i$ if

$$\theta_i = \max_{j=1,\ldots,k} \theta_j > \theta_0,$$ otherwise. Let us assume that the experimenter wishes to have a procedure (S,d) which at Stage 1 has a small expected number of selected bad populations, denoted by $E_{\underline{\theta}}(N_b)$ (a small expected overall sampling amount or a small similar measure of economical performance), and a large probability of a correct selection $P_{\underline{\theta}}(CD)$ at points $\underline{\theta} \in \Omega^k$ where

$\max_{j=1,\ldots,k} \theta_j > \theta_0$, subject to the *basic* P_*-*condition*

$\inf\{P_{\underline{\theta}}(CD) \mid \underline{\theta} \in \Omega^k, \theta_1,\ldots,\theta_k \leq \theta_0\} \geq P_*$, where P_* is a prespecified constant with $0 < P_* < 1$.

The following procedure may, sometimes, be applied in practice. The experimenter takes the UMP test for H: $\theta \leq \theta_0$ versus K: $\theta > \theta_0$ at level $\alpha = 1-P_*^{1/k}$ and selects all populations π_i which are shown to be significantly good by statistics U_i, $i = 1,\dots,k$. His final decision may be the natural one based on the V_i's associated with the populations which are selected at Stage 1. From Corollary 2 it follows that this procedure can be improved with respect to $P_{\underline{\theta}}(CD)$ without any changes in the expected number of selected good populations $E_{\underline{\theta}}(N_g)$, $E_{\underline{\theta}}(N_b)$ and $P_{\underline{\theta}}\{S(\underline{U}) = \emptyset\}$. This procedure $\mathcal{P}$ will be studied now in more detail. For convenience, let us define it without using the terminology of hypothesis testing.

Definition 3. *Procedure* $\mathcal{P}$. Let $\mathcal{P}$ be the 2-stage procedure (S,d^*) with $S(\underline{u}) = \{i | u_i > a, i = 1,\dots,k\}$, where $a \in \mathbb{R}$ is determined by $P_{\theta_0}\{U_1 \leq a\}^k = P_*$.

That $\mathcal{P}$ satisfies the basic P_*-condition follows from the fact that U_i is stochastically non-decreasing in $\theta_i \in \Omega$, $i = 1,\dots,k$, which in turn is a well-known consequence of the MLR property of $\{f_\theta\}_{\theta\in\Omega}$.

In the next two steps we establish formulas for the distribution of final decisions under $\mathcal{P}$ and derive a basic monotonicity property.

THEOREM 2. *For every* $\underline{\theta} \in \Omega^k$

$$
(11) \qquad P_{\underline{\theta}}\{d^*_{S(\underline{U})}(\underline{U},\underline{V}) = i\} = \begin{cases} \prod_{j=1}^{k} P_{\theta_j}\{U_j \leq a\} = \prod_{j=1}^{k} F_{\theta_j}(-\infty), i = 0, \\ \int_{\mathbb{R}} \prod_{\substack{j=1 \\ j\neq i}}^{k} F_{\theta_j}(\lambda)\,dF_{\theta_i}(\lambda), \ i = 1,\dots,k, \end{cases}
$$

where for $\theta_r \in \Omega$, $\lambda \in \mathbb{R} \cup \{-\infty\}$, $r = 1,\dots,k$,

(12) $$F_{\theta_r}(\lambda) = E_{\theta_r}[I_{(-\infty,a]}(U_r) + (1-I_{(-\infty,a]}(U_r))I_{(-\infty,\lambda]}(W_r)].$$

Proof. For $r \in \{1,\ldots,k\}$ take the improper random variable defined by $Z_r = -\infty$ (W_r) if $U_r \leq (>)a$, which obviously has the distribution function $F_{\theta_r}(\lambda)$, $\lambda \in \mathbb{R} \cup \{-\infty\}$. Now, for $i = 1,\ldots,k$ we have

(13) $$\{Z_i = \max_{j=1,\ldots,k} Z_j, \text{ and } Z_i > -\infty\}$$

$$= \{W_i = \max\{W_j | U_j > a, \ j = 1,\ldots,k\}, \text{ and } U_i > a\}$$

$$= \{d^*_{S(\underline{U})}(\underline{U},\underline{V}) = i\}.$$

Therefore, in view of the independence of $Z_1,\ldots,Z_k$, (11) follows for $i = 1,\ldots,k$. The proof of (11) for $i = 0$ is straightforward.

THEOREM 3. *$\{F_\theta\}_{\theta\in\Omega}$, as given in* (12), *is a stochastically non-decreasing family of distribution functions on* $\mathbb{R} \cup \{-\infty\}$.

Proof. Let $\lambda \in \mathbb{R} \cup \{-\infty\}$ be fixed and let $H_{a,\lambda}$ be an auxiliary function defined by

(14) $$H_{a,\lambda}(u,v) = (1-I_{(-\infty,a]}(u))(1-I_{(-\infty,\lambda]}(T(u,v))), (u,v) \in \mathcal{D}.$$

By the assumptions made in Section 1 we can assume that $T(u,v)$ is a non-decreasing function in u as well as in v, $(u,v) \in \mathcal{D}$. Thus $H_{a,\lambda}$ has the same monotonicity properties. Now by $W_1 = T(U_1,V_1)$ and (12) we have

(15) $$F_{\theta_1}(\lambda) = 1-E_{\theta_1}[(1-I_{(-\infty,a]}(U_1))(1-I_{(-\infty,\lambda]}(W_1))]$$

$$= 1-E_{\theta_1}[H_{a,\lambda}(U_1,V_1)], \quad \theta_1 \in \Omega.$$

Since U_1 and V_1 are stochastically non-decreasing in $\theta_1 \in \Omega$ and independent, $E_{\theta_1}[H_{a,\lambda}(U_1,V_1)]$ is non-decreasing in $\theta_1 \in \Omega$. This follows from Lehmann [8]. Thus the proof is completed.

From Theorems 2 and 3 several desirable properties of procedure $\mathcal{P}$ can be derived. Properties 1-4 can be proved with standard techniques (especially integration by parts) from single stage selection theory. The masses in $\{-\infty\}$ have to be taken into consideration, but they cause no serious problems. Thus, we omit the proofs for brevity.

PROPERTY 1. *For every* $i \in \{1,\ldots,k\}$, $P_{\underline{\theta}}\{d^*_{S(\underline{U})}(\underline{U},\underline{V}) = i\}$ *is non-decreasing in* θ_i *and non-increasing in* θ_j, $j \neq i$, $\underline{\theta} \in \Omega^k$.

PROPERTY 2. *For every* $\underline{\theta} \in \Omega^k$ *with* $\theta_1 \leq \cdots \leq \theta_k$, $P_{\underline{\theta}}\{d^*_{S(\underline{U})}(\underline{U},\underline{V}) = i\}$ *is non-decreasing in* $i \in \{1,\ldots,k\}$.

PROPERTY 3. *For every non-empty set* $M \subseteq \{1,\ldots,k\}$, $P_{\underline{\theta}}\{d^*_{S(\underline{U})}(\underline{U},\underline{V}) \in M\}$ *is non-decreasing (non-increasing) in* θ_i *with* $i \in M (i \notin M)$, $\underline{\theta} \in \Omega^k$.

PROPERTY 4. $E_{\underline{\theta}}(N_g)$ $(E_{\underline{\theta}}(N_b))$ *is non-decreasing in* θ_i *with* $\theta_i > \theta_0$ $(\theta_i \leq \theta_0)$, $i = 1,\ldots,k$, $\underline{\theta} \in \Omega^k$.

PROPERTY 5. *For every* $\underline{\theta} \in \Omega^k$ *with* $\theta_1,\ldots,\theta_k < \theta_0$, $P_{\underline{\theta}}\{S(\underline{U}) = \emptyset\}$ *tends to* 1 *for large* n. *For every* $\underline{\theta} \in \Omega^k$ *with* $\theta_1,\ldots,\theta_{k-t} < \theta_0 < \theta_{k-t+1},\ldots,\theta_{k-1} < \theta_k$, $t \in \{1,\ldots,k\}$, $P_{\underline{\theta}}\{S(\underline{U}) = \{k-t+1,\ldots,k\}$, $d^*_{S(\underline{U})}(\underline{U},\underline{V}) = k\}$ *tends to* 1 *for large* n *and* m.

Proof. The first assertion follows from the well known consistency properties of the UMP-test mentioned at the beginning of this section. For $\underline{\theta} \in \Omega^k$ with $\theta_1,\ldots,\theta_{k-t} < \theta_0 < \theta_{k-t+1},\ldots,\theta_{k-1} < \theta_k$, $t \in \{1,\ldots,k\}$, by the same reasons, $P_{\underline{\theta}}\{S(\underline{U}) = \{k-t+1,\ldots,k\}\}$ tends to 1 for large n. Since, moreover, $P_{\underline{\theta}}\{W_k = \max_{j=1,\ldots,k} W_j\}$ tends to 1 for large n+m (see Miescke [11]), the proof is completed.

Next we like to show along the lines of Tamhane and Bechhofer, in an informal way of proof, that procedure $\mathcal{P}$ is preferable to the corresponding 1-stage procedure $\mathcal{P}_0$, say, from an economical point of view. Let $\tilde{U}_1,\ldots,\tilde{U}_k$ be of the same type as $U_1,\ldots,U_k$, but based on samples of size n_0 from $\pi_1,\ldots,\pi_k$. Then $\mathcal{P}_0$ decides as follows:

$$(16) \qquad S_0(\underline{\tilde{U}}) = \begin{cases} \emptyset & \text{if } \tilde{U}_1,\ldots,\tilde{U}_k \le a_0 \\ \{i\} & \text{if } \tilde{U}_i = \max\limits_{j=1,\ldots,k} \tilde{U}_j \text{ and } \tilde{U}_i > a_0, \end{cases}$$

$$i = 1,\ldots,k,$$

where a_0 is determined by $P_{\underline{\theta}_0}\{\tilde{U}_1 \le a_0\}^k = P_*$. The version of $\mathcal{P}_0$ in the *normal case* was studied by Bechhofer and Turnbull [1]. Now, if an optimal allocation of observations is derived subject to a criterion which can be met by the use of monotonicity properties of $P_{\underline{\theta}}$\{final decision is "i"\} in $\theta_1,\ldots,\theta_k$, $i = 1,\ldots,k$, then the allocation problem has to be solved for both, $\mathcal{P}$ and $\mathcal{P}_0$, at the same points $\underline{\theta} \in \Omega^k$. Since then $\mathcal{P}_0$ can be viewed to be a special version of $\mathcal{P}$ with $n = n_0$ and $m = 0$, we conclude as follows:

PROPERTY 6. *In every allocation problem subject to a criterion which can be met by the use of monotonicity properties of* $P_{\underline{\theta}}$*{final decision is "i"} in* $\theta_1,\ldots,\theta_k$, $\underline{\theta} \in \Omega^k$, $i = 1,\ldots,k$, $\mathcal{P}$ *is at least as economical as* $\mathcal{P}_0$.

Finally, let us consider the class C of procedures which are of the same type as $\mathcal{P}$ but use another level α test at Stage 1. Then by the properties of the UMP level α test we get

PROPERTY 7. *For every fixed* n, m *and* α *(or* P_*, *respectively),* $\mathcal{P}$ *maximizes (minimizes)* $E_{\underline{\theta}}(N_g)$ $(E_{\underline{\theta}}(N_b))$ *within the class* C, *uniformly in* $\underline{\theta} \in \Omega^k$.

To summarize the results so far derived, and especially in view of Properties 4, 5 and 7, $\mathcal{P}$ appears to be a reasonable procedure if the experimenter wishes to screen out the bad populations at Stage 1, to keep the good ones (if there are any) at the same time, and finally to select the best population (if it is good).

On the other hand, let us look at the case where the experimenter is looking for the best population (if it is good) but wishes to keep the expected overall sampling amount small. Then at points $\underline{\theta} \in \Omega^k$ where more than one population is good, $\mathcal{P}$ might possibly not very effectively screen out. Here an additional screening mechanism seems to be appropriate, i.e. a subset selection procedure for the first stage, which has to be combined with a procedure of the type S considered so far.

In the *normal case*, analogous to what Tamhane and Bechhofer [14] proposed in the non-control setting, a natural choice for the additional screening mechanism could be Gupta's [5] maximum means procedure. This leads to a 2-stage procedure $\mathcal{P}_\Delta = (S_\Delta, d^*)$ with

$$S_\Delta(\underline{u}) = \{i \mid u_i > a_\Delta \text{ and } u_i \geq \max_{j=1,\ldots,k} u_j - p^{1/2}\Delta,\quad i = 1,\ldots,k\}, \tag{17}$$

where $\Delta \geq 0$ is fixed and a_Δ has to be determined such that S_Δ meets the basic P_*-condition. Note that for $\Delta = 0$ (∞), $\mathcal{P}_\Delta$ is of the type $\mathcal{P}_0(\mathcal{P})$.

Since we again have enlarged the class of 2-stage procedures, we are led to a more economical type of procedure in the sense of Property 6. Moreover, for $\Delta > 0$ and $\underline{\theta} \in \Omega^k$ with $\theta_0 < \max_{j=1,\ldots,k} \theta_j$, the probability of making a correct final decision at Stage 1 already, tends to 1 for large n. But, on the other hand, $\mathcal{P}_\Delta$ for $0 < \Delta < \infty$ is much more difficult to implement in practice. The problems arising here are of the same type as discussed in Tamhane and Bechhofer [14], Gupta and Miescke [6] and Miescke and Sehr [13].

IV. BAYESIAN 2-STAGE PROCEDURES

From now on let us assume that the parameters $\underline{\theta} = (\theta_1,\ldots,\theta_k)$ vary randomly according to a permutation invariant product prior τ on the Borel sets of Ω^k. We will study the form of Bayesian 2-stage procedures under a loss structure L given by

$$(18)\qquad L(s,i,\underline{\theta}) = \begin{cases} 0 & \text{if } s = \emptyset \\ \ell(\theta_0-\theta_i) & \text{if } s = \{i\} \\ c|s|+\ell(\theta_0-\theta_i) & \text{if } |s| \geq 2 \end{cases}$$

$i = 1,\ldots,k$, $\underline{\theta} \in \Omega^k$, where $c \geq 0$ is a constant and $\ell\colon \mathbb{R} \to \mathbb{R}$ is non-decreasing, integrable, with $\ell(0) = 0$. The overall Bayes risk is given by

$$(19)\qquad \int_{\Omega^k} \Big[\sum_{i=1}^{k} \ell(\theta_0-\theta_i)P_{\underline{\theta}}\{S(\underline{U}) = \{i\}\} + \sum_{s,|s|\geq 2} (c|s| + \sum_{i\in s} \ell(\theta_0-\theta_i)P_{\underline{\theta}}\{d_s(\underline{U},\underline{V})=i|S(\underline{U})=s\})P_{\underline{\theta}}\{S(\underline{U})=s\}\Big]d\tau(\underline{\theta}).$$

By Theorem 1 we can restrict our consideration to Bayes procedures (S^B,d^B) with $d^B = d^*$ and the property that $\underline{u} \in \mathbb{R}^k$ and $S^B(\underline{u}) = \{i\}$ implies $u_i = \max_{j=1,\ldots,k} u_j$, $i = 1,\ldots,k$. Therefore at every point $\underline{u} \in \mathbb{R}^k$ an optimal subset selection procedure S^B decides in favor of a subset $s \subseteq \{1,\ldots,k\}$ which is associated with the smallest of the values given in the following scheme.

s	Posterior risk at $\underset{\sim}{u} \in \mathcal{S}^k$, $\mathcal{S} = \bigcup_{\theta\in\Omega}$ support (f_θ)
$\emptyset$	0
$\{i\}$	$E\{\ell(\theta_0-\Theta_i)\mid \underset{\sim}{U} = \underset{\sim}{u}\}$, $u_i = \max_{j=1,\ldots,k} u_j$
$\{i_1,\ldots,i_t\}$	$tc + E\{\min_{j=1,\ldots,t} E\{\ell(\theta_0-\Theta_{i_j})\mid \underset{\sim}{U} = \underset{\sim}{u}, \underset{\sim}{V}\}\mid \underset{\sim}{U} = \underset{\sim}{u}\}$,
	$1 \leq i_1 < \ldots < i_t \leq k$, $t \geq 2$.

Note that in the last expression the inner conditional expectation is viewed as being a function of $\underset{\sim}{V}$, and that the outer one is the expectation with respect to the conditional distribution of $\underset{\sim}{V}$, given $\underset{\sim}{U} = \underset{\sim}{u}$.

Definition 4. A 2-stage procedure (S,d) is called *monotone* if $(S,d) = (\tilde{S},d^*)$ in the sense of Theorem 1 and, moreover, if for every $\underset{\sim}{u} \in \mathbb{R}^k$, $i,j \in \{1,\ldots,k\}$ with $u_i < u_j$, $i \in S(\underset{\sim}{u})$ implies $j \in S(\underset{\sim}{u})$.

Next we wish to find sufficient conditions under which there exist Bayes 2-stage procedures which are monotone. For this purpose let $\underset{\sim}{u} \in \mathcal{S}^k$ with $u_1 \leq \ldots \leq u_k$ and $t \in \{2,\ldots,k-1\}$ be fixed. In Goel and Rubin [4] an optimal s with $|s| = t$ could be derived directly from Eaton's result. In our situation this is not possible since now the conditional expected loss, given $\underset{\sim}{U} = \underset{\sim}{u}$, does not simply depend on $S(\underset{\sim}{u})$, but also on $\underset{\sim}{u}$. Let us now try to find sufficient conditions under which the posterior risk at $\underset{\sim}{u}$ is minimal for the set $\{k-t+1,\ldots,k\}$ among all sets $s \subseteq \{1,\ldots,k\}$ with $|s| = t$. An optimal s with $|s| = t$ minimizes

(20) $$E\{\min_{j\in s} E\{\ell(\theta_0 - \Theta_j)\mid \underset{\sim}{U} = \underset{\sim}{u}, \underset{\sim}{V}\}\mid \underset{\sim}{U} = \underset{\sim}{u}\}$$

$$= \int_{\mathbb{R}^k} \min_{j\in s} \int_{\Omega^k} \ell(\theta_0 - \theta_j) \prod_{i=1}^{k} f_{\theta_i}(u_i) g_{\theta_i}(v_i) d\tau(\underset{\sim}{\theta}) d\underset{\sim}{v}\ \beta(\underset{\sim}{u}),$$

where $\beta(\underline{u}) = (\int_{\Omega^k} \prod_{i=1}^{k} f_{\theta_i}(u_i)d\tau(\underline{\theta}))^{-1}$ is of no relevance for our problem and thus can be ignored in the sequel. From the remark following (4) we see that the integral on the r.h.s. of (20) can be rewritten as

$$(21) \qquad \int_{\mathbb{R}^k} \min_{j\in s} \int_{\Omega^k} \ell(\theta_0-\theta_j) \prod_{i=1}^{k} \tilde{h}_{\theta_i}(T(u_i,v_i))d\tau(\underline{\theta}) \prod_{r=1}^{k} G(u_r,v_r)d\underline{v}.$$

A change of variables $w_i = T(u_i,v_i)$ (or $v_i = \tilde{T}(u_i,w_i)$, respectively) modifies (21) to

$$(22) \qquad \int_{\mathbb{R}^k} \min_{j\in s} \int_{\Omega^k} \ell(\theta_0-\theta_j) \prod_{i=1}^{k} \tilde{h}_{\theta_i}(w_i)d\tau(\underline{\theta}) \prod_{r=1}^{k} G(u_r,\tilde{T}(u_r,w_r)) \left|\frac{\partial\tilde{T}(u_r,w_r)}{\partial w_r}\right| d\underline{w}.$$

Now we are in a position to apply Eaton's main result iteratively, first to the inner integral (i.e. the 2nd stage scenario), and then to the outer one (i.e. the 1st stage scenario). Let L_s: $\mathbb{R}^k \to \mathbb{R}$ be defined by

$$(23) \qquad L_s(\underline{w}) = \min_{j\in s} \int_{\Omega^k} \ell(\theta_0-\theta_j) \prod_{i=1}^{k} \tilde{h}_{\theta_i}(w_i)d\tau(\underline{\theta}), \quad \underline{w} \in \mathbb{R}^k.$$

LEMMA 3. *For every* $\underline{w} \in \mathbb{R}^k$, $s \subseteq \{1,\ldots,k\}$ *with* $|s| = t$, $i \in s$, $j \in \{1,\ldots,k\} \setminus s$, $\tilde{s} = (s\setminus\{i\}) \cup \{j\}$ *and* $w_i \le w_j$ *implies* $L_{\tilde{s}}(\underline{w}) \le L_s(\underline{w})$.

Proof. Let $r \in \{1,\ldots,k\}$ and $\underline{w} \in \mathbb{R}^k$ be fixed. Then except for a normalizing factor depending on $\underline{w}$,

$R_r = \int_{\Omega^k} \ell(\theta_0-\theta_r) \prod_{i=1}^{k} \tilde{h}_{\theta_i}(w_i)d\tau(\underline{\theta})$ can be viewed as being the posterior risk ($\underline{w}$ are the given "observations" and $\underline{\theta}$ are the "parameters") for decision $\{r\}$ in a fixed size 1 subset selection problem of the type treated in Eaton [3]. The loss function hereby is $\tilde{L}_{\{i\}}(\underline{\theta}) = \ell(\theta_0-\theta_i)$, $\underline{\theta} \in \Omega^k$, $i = 1,\ldots,k$, which clearly satisfies the monotonicity and invariance properties (3.4) and (3.5) of Eaton [3]. Thus by his Lemma 4.1 we know that $R_1,\ldots,R_k$ are ordered in the reverse order to $w_1,\ldots,w_k$. This completes the proof.

In view of Lemma 3 we know now that an optimal s with $|s| = t$ minimizes

$$(24) \qquad \int_{\mathbb{R}^k} L_s(\underline{w}) \prod_{i=1}^{k} G(u_i,\tilde{T}(u_i,w_i)) \left| \frac{\partial \tilde{T}(u_i,w_i)}{\partial w_i} \right| d\underline{w},$$

which can be viewed to be (except for a normalizing factor depending on $\underline{u}$) the posterior risk ($\underline{u}$ are the "observations" and $\underline{w}$ the "parameters") for decision s in a fixed size t subset selection problem of the type treated in Eaton [3]. The loss function $L_s(\underline{w})$ hereby satisfies (by Lemma 3) the monotonicity property (3.4) and, obviously, also the invariance property (3.5) of Eaton [3]. Thus by his Lemma 4.1 we see that the following Assumption (A) is sufficient for the existence of a monotone optimal s with $|s| = t$.

Assumption (A). The distributions are as stated in Section 1, and the function $G(u,\tilde{T}(u,w)) \left.\frac{\partial \tilde{T}(\xi,\eta)}{\partial \eta}\right|_{(\xi,\eta) = (u,w)}$, $(u,w) \in \{(u,T(u,v)) \mid (u,v) \in \mathcal{D}\}$, has MLR.

THEOREM 4. *Under Assumption* (A), *for every loss structure* L *of type* (18) *and every permutation invariant product prior* τ, *there exists a 2-stage Bayes procedure* (S^B,d^B) *which is monotone.*

It is now of interest to find simple sufficient conditions for Assumption (A) to hold true. For exponential families we get the following.

Assumption (B). The underlying distributions for all observations from $\pi_1, \ldots, \pi_k$ belong to an exponential family with densities $a(\theta)b(x)\exp\{\theta x\}$, $x \in \mathbb{R}$, $\theta \in \Omega$, w.r.t. the Lebesgue measure on $\mathbb{R}$, where the function $b(x)$, $x \in \mathbb{R}$, is log-concave (i.e. the densities are strongly unimodal.)

THEOREM 5. *Assumption* (B) *implies Assumption* (A).

Proof. Let $U_i = \sum_{j=1}^{n} X_{ij}$, $V_i = \sum_{j=1}^{m} Y_{ij}$ and $W_i = U_i + V_i$, $i = 1,\ldots,k$. Thus we have $T(u,v) = u+v$ and $\tilde{T}(u,w) = w-u$, $u, v, w \in \mathbb{R}$. The density of U_i is $a(\theta_i)^n b^{*n}(u)\exp\{\theta_i u\}$, $u \in \mathbb{R}$, and the density of V_i is $a(\theta_i)^m b^{*m}(v) \exp\{\theta_i v\}$, $v \in \mathbb{R}$, $i = 1,\ldots,k$, where $b^{*n}(b^{*m})$ denotes the n-fold (m-fold) convolution of b with respect to the Lebesgue measure on $\mathbb{R}$. It follows that

$$(25) \qquad G(u,\tilde{T}(u,w)) \left.\frac{\partial \tilde{T}(\xi,\eta)}{\partial \eta}\right|_{(\xi,\eta) = (u,w)} = b^{*n}(u)b^{*m}(w-u), \quad u,w \in \mathbb{R}.$$

Let the function $b(x)$, $x \in \mathbb{R}$, be log-concave. Then by Ibragimov [7], the function $b^{*m}(x)$, $x \in \mathbb{R}$, has the same property. But this is equivalent for $b^{*m}(w-u)$ to have MLR in $w \in \mathbb{R}$ w.r.t. $u \in \mathbb{R}$ (cf. Lehmann [9], p. 330), and therefore it is also equivalent for Assumption (A) to hold true.

Remark 3. It is not difficult to see that in the general case the following conditions are sufficient for Assumption (A) to hold true: $T(u,v) = \varepsilon_1 u + \varepsilon_2 v$, $u,v \in \mathbb{R}$, $\varepsilon_1,\varepsilon_2 > 0$, and $\{g_\theta\}_{\theta\in\Omega}$ is a family of log-concave (i.e. strongly unimodal) densities. This follows directly from the factorization identity $f_\theta(u)g_\theta(v) = \tilde{h}_\theta(T(u,v))G(u,v)$, $u,v \in \mathbb{R}$, $\theta \in \Omega$.

For the remainder of this section let us consider the *normal case* in more detail. Here, Assumption (B) is satisfied with $b(x) = \exp\{-x^2/2\sigma^2\}$, $x \in \mathbb{R}$, and thus Theorem 4 is valid in this case. Let us assume that apriori $\Theta_1,\ldots,\Theta_k$ are independently identically distributed random normals with mean θ_0 and variance $r > 0$. Then at $\underline{u} \in \mathbb{R}^k$ with $u_1 \leq \ldots \leq u_k$ the optimal procedure selects at Stage 1 in favor of the smallest value in the following scheme.

s	Posterior risk at $\underline{u} \in \mathbb{R}^k$ with $u_1 \leq \ldots \leq u_k$
$\emptyset$	0
$\{k\}$	$E^0[\ell(\alpha_2(\theta_0-u_k) + \alpha_1 Q_0)]$
$\{k-t+1,\ldots,k\}$	$tc + E[\min_{j\geq k-t+1} E^0(\ell(\alpha_2(\theta_0-u_j)+\alpha_3 Q_j+\alpha_4 Q_0))]$, $t \geq 2$,

where $Q_0,Q_1,\ldots,Q_k$ are auxiliary random variables which are independent standard normals, E^0 denotes expectation w.r.t. Q_0, and

$\alpha_1 = (rp(p+r)^{-1})^{1/2}$, $\alpha_2 = r(p+r)^{-1}$, $\alpha_3 = pr[(p+r)(pq+pr+qr)]^{-1/2}$,

$\alpha_4 = [rpq/(pq+pr+qr)]^{1/2}$.

Similar to what was done by Goel and Rubin [4], let us show next that the Bayes solution at $\underline{u} \in \mathbb{R}^k$ with $u_1 \leq \ldots \leq u_k$ can be determined in the following short way. Let r_t denote the posterior risk for decision $s = \{k-t+1,\ldots,k\}$, $t = 0,1,\ldots,k$. At first one computes r_0, r_1. Then $r_2,r_3,\ldots$ are computed successively until $r_{i_0} \leq r_{i_0+1}$ occurs for the first time. If now $r_0(r_1) = \min\{r_0,r_1,r_{i_0}\}$ then $s = \emptyset$ ($\{k\}$) and otherwise, $s = \{k-i_0+1,\ldots,k\}$ is the final decision. This method is justified by the following result.

LEMMA 4. *Let* $\underline{u} \in \mathbb{R}^k$ *with* $u_1 \leq \ldots \leq u_k$ *be fixed and let* r_0, $r_1,\ldots,r_k$ *be defined as stated above. Then* $r_2 - r_3 \geq r_3 - r_4 \geq \ldots \geq r_{k-1} - r_k$.

Proof. Let $Z_1,\dots,Z_k$ be random variables defined by $Z_j = -E^0(\ell(\alpha_2(\theta_0-u_j) + \alpha_3 Q_j + \alpha_4 Q_0))$, $i = 1,\dots,k$. Then by $u_1 \le \dots \le u_k$ and the fact that ℓ is non-decreasing we have $Z_1 \underset{st}{\le} Z_2 \underset{st}{\le} \dots \underset{st}{\le} Z_k$ (where "$\underset{st}{\le}$" denotes stochastic ordering). Moreover, $r_t = tc - E(\max_{j \ge k-t+1} (Z_j))$, $t = 2,\dots,k$. Thus, for $t \ge 2$, by Chernoff and Yahav [2] we get

$$r_t - r_{t+1} = E(\max_{j \ge k-t} Z_j) - E(\max_{j \ge k-t+1} Z_j) - c$$

$$= \int_{\mathbb{R}} \prod_{j \ge k-t+1} P\{Z_j \le \lambda\} P\{Z_{k-t} > \lambda\} d\lambda - c,$$

which clearly is non-increasing in t, $t = 2,\dots,k-1$.

Let us finally take a brief look at the special case of a linear loss function $\ell(\xi) = a\xi$, $\xi \in \mathbb{R}$, $a > 0$, where we can choose $a = 1$ (since other values of a can be compensated in the cost c). Then the decision at Stage 1 is based on the following scheme.

s	Posterior risk at $\underline{u} \in \mathbb{R}^k$ with $u_1 \le \dots \le u_k$
$\emptyset$	0
$\{k\}$	$\alpha_2(\theta_0-u_k)$
$\{k-t+1,\dots,k\}$	$\alpha_2(\theta_0-u_k)+tc-\alpha_2 E(\max_{j \ge k-t+1} (u_j-u_k+\alpha_3\alpha_2^{-1}Q_j))$, $t \ge 2$.

Lower and upper bounds for the expectations in this scheme can be found in Miescke [12] to approximate the Bayes procedure. Note that if for a $t \in \{2,\dots,k\}$ $tc \ge \alpha_3 E(\max_{j=1,\dots,t} Q_j)$, then at most t-1 populations are selected at the first stage. Thus in the case of $2c \ge \alpha_3 \pi^{-1/2}$ the Bayes-procedure is of the type $\mathcal{P}_0$ (cf. (16)). And for the case of k = 2 populations the Bayes-procedure is of the type $\mathcal{P}_\Delta$ (cf. (17)), except for an area in the neighborhood of (θ_0, θ_0) where the Bayes-procedure selects both populations.

ACKNOWLEDGMENTS

The authors are grateful to Professors H. Rubin and A. Rukhin for several helpful comments.

REFERENCES

[1] Bechhofer, R. E. and Turnbull, B. W. (1978). Two (k+1)-decision selection procedures for comparing k normal means with a specified standard. *J. Amer. Statist. Assoc. 73*, 385-392.

[2] Chernoff, H. and Yahav, J. A. (1977). A subset selection problem employing a new criterion. *Statistical Decision Theory and Related Topics II* (S. S. Gupta and D. S. Moore eds.). Academic Press, New York, 93-119.

[3] Eaton, M. L. (1967). Some optimum properties of ranking procedures. *Ann. Math. Statist. 38*, 124-137.

[4] Goel, P. K. and Rubin, H. (1977). On selecting a subset containing the best population - a Bayesian approach. *Ann. Statist.* 5, 969-983.

[5] Gupta, S. S. (1956). On a decision rule for a problem in ranking means. Mimeo. Ser. No. 150, Inst. of Statist., Univ. of North Carolina, Chapel Hill.

[6] Gupta, S. S. and Miescke, K. J. (1981). On the least favorable configurations in certain two-stage selection procedures. To appear in *Essays in Statistics and Probability* (P. R. Krishnaiah, ed.). North-Holland, Amsterdam.

[7] Ibragimov, I. A. (1956). On the composition of unimodal distributions. *Theor. Probability Appl. 1*, 255-260.

[8] Lehmann, E. L. (1955). Ordered families of distributions. *Ann. Math. Statist. 26*, 399-419.

[9] Lehmann, E. L. (1959). *Testing Statistical Hypotheses.* John Wiley, New York.

[10] Lehmann, E. L. (1966). On a theorem of Bahadur and Goodman. *Ann. Math. Statist.* 37, 1-6.

[11] Miescke, K. J. (1979). Identification and selection procedures based on tests. *Ann. Statist.* 7, 207-219.

[12] Miescke, K. J. (1979). Bayesian subset selection for additive and linear loss functions. *Comm. Statist. A-Theory Methods* 8, 1205-1226.

[13] Miescke, K. J. and Sehr, J. (1980). On a conjecture concerning the least favorable configuration of certain two-stage selection procedures. *Comm. Statist. A-Theory Methods* 9, 1609-1617.

[14] Tamhane, A. C. and Bechhofer, R. E. (1979). A two-stage minimax procedure with screening for selecting the largest normal mean (II): an improved PCS lower bound and associated tables. *Comm. Statist. A-Theory Methods* 8, 337-358.

THE BERRY-ESSEEN BOUND FOR U - STATISTICS

R. Helmers

Mathematisch Centrum
Amsterdam, The Netherlands

W. R. Van Zwet

Department of Mathematics
University of Leiden
Leiden, The Netherlands

I. INTRODUCTION

A more or less satisfactory and reasonably complete theory of Berry-Esseen bounds and Edgeworth expansions is available only for sums of independent random variables and vectors. In recent years, however, Berry-Esseen bounds and Edgeworth expansions were also obtained for several statistics of a different structure, which occur in estimation and hypothesis testing problems. To obtain such results for statistics T_N in cases where no explicit representation for the characteristic function of T_N is known, one may proceed by first obtaining a so-called stochastic expansion for T_N. This means that one approximates T_N sufficiently accurately by a statistic T'_N of a simpler structure and then proves the desired results for T'_N instead of T_N. In many of the cases that were considered, T'_N is a smooth function of a sum of independent random vectors and the problem can be solved by appealing to the classical theory for such sums and translating the result into one for T'_N. Thus the classical theory can be extended beyond its original domain of application.

There are other cases, however, where the natural stochastic expansion T'_N is of a different type. In particular, it appears to be quite common that T'_N is a U - statistic, i.e.

Statistical Decision Theory and Related Topics III, Vol. 1

ISBN 0-12-307501-7

$$(1.1) \qquad T'_N = \sum_{1 \le i_1 < \ldots < i_k \le N} \sum h(X_{i_1}, \ldots, X_{i_k}),$$

where $X_1, \ldots, X_N$ are independent and identically distributed (i.i.d.) random variables. Examples of statistics T_N for which this is the case are one-sample linear rank statistics and linear combinations of order statistics. For a more detailed account of what has been said so far and for references to relevant literature, the reader is referred to Van Zwet [13].

In view of this, it would be of considerable interest to have a theory of Berry-Esseen bounds and Edgeworth expansions for U - statistics, similar to the one for sums of independent random variables and vectors. Such a theory would not only be a meaningful generalization of the classical case from a purely probabilistic point of view, but it could also be extended to statistics possessing stochastic expansions of the type (1.1).

As yet, Edgeworth expansions for U - statistics have only been established under very restrictive assumptions (cf. Janssen [10] and Callaert, Janssen and Veraverbeke [4]) and much work remains to be done on this problem. However, results of Berry-Esseen type showing that the distribution function of a standardized U-statistic tends to its normal limit at the rate of $N^{-\frac{1}{2}}$, have been obtained in increasing generality by Bickel [1], Chan and Wierman [6] and Callaert and Janssen [3]. These authors discuss U - statistics of order 2, viz.

$$(1.2) \qquad U_N = \sum_{1 \le i < j \le N} \sum h(X_i, X_j),$$

but Chan and Wierman as well as Callaert and Janssen point out that all results carry over to U - statistics of any fixed order and also to the multi-sample case (cf. also Janssen [10]). The best of these results is that of Callaert and Janssen who assume that $E|h(X_1, X_2)|^3 < \infty$. In the present paper we relax this moment condition even further. The results are applied to Von Mises functionals and an example is given to indicate the improvement over previous work. For simplicity we too restrict attention to U - statistics of order 2.

II. THE BERRY-ESSEEN THEOREM

Let $X_1, X_2, \ldots$ be i.i.d. random variables with common distribution function F. Define the U - statistic U_N by (1.2), where h is a symmetric function of two variables with

$$(2.1) \qquad E\, h(X_1,X_2) = 0, \quad E|h(X_1,X_2)|^p < \infty,$$

for some $p > 5/3$. Let g be given by

$$(2.2) \qquad g(x) = E(h(X_1,X_2)\,|\,X_1=x) = \int h(x,y)\,d\,F(y)$$

and suppose that

$$(2.3) \qquad E\, g^2(X_1) > 0, \quad E|g(X_1)|^3 < \infty.$$

If we take

$$\psi(x,y) = h(x,y) - g(x) - g(y),$$

then the random variable $\psi(X_1,X_2)$ has the property that

$$(2.4) \qquad E(\psi(X_1,X_2)\,|\,X_1) = E(\psi(X_1,X_2)\,|\,X_2) = 0$$

almost surely (a.s.) and

$$(2.5) \qquad U_N = (N-1)\sum_{i=1}^{N} g(X_i) + \sum_{1\le i<j\le N} \psi(X_i,X_j).$$

Let

$$(2.6) \qquad \tau_N^2 = (N-1)^2 N\, E\, g^2(X_1)$$

denote the variance of the first term on the right in (2.5) and let Φ be the standard normal distribution function.

THEOREM 2.1. *Suppose that* (2.1) *and* (2.3) *are satisfied for some* $p > 5/3$. *Then there exists a positive number* C_p *depending on* h *and* F *only through* p *and such that for every* $N \geq 2$,

$$\sup_x |P(\tau_N^{-1} U_N \leq x) - \Phi(x)| \leq C_p N^{-\frac{1}{2}} \left[\frac{E|g(X_1)|^3}{\{Eg^2(X_1)\}^{3/2}} + \frac{E|h(X_1,X_2)|^p}{\{Eg^2(X_1)\}^{\frac{1}{2}p}} \right]. \tag{2.7}$$

In the special case where (2.1) holds for $p = 2$, U_N possesses a finite variance σ_N^2 which is given by

$$\sigma_N^2 = \tau_N^2 + \frac{N(N-1)}{2} E\, \psi^2(X_1, X_2). \tag{2.8}$$

Obviously

$$1 \leq \frac{\sigma_N}{\tau_N} \leq 1 + \frac{Eh^2(X_1,X_2)}{2N\, Eg^2(X_1)}$$

and hence σ_N may replace τ_N in (2.7) to yield

COROLLARY 2.1. *There exists a universal constant* C *such that for every* $N \geq 2$,

$$\sup_x |P(\sigma_N^{-1} U_N \leq x) - \Phi(x)| \leq C N^{-\frac{1}{2}} \left[\frac{E|g(X_1)|^3}{\{Eg^2(X_1)\}^{3/2}} + \frac{Eh^2(X_1,X_2)}{Eg^2(X_1)} \right], \tag{2.9}$$

provided (2.1) *and* (2.3) *are satisfied for* $p = 2$.

We note that the result of this corollary was announced without proof in Helmers [9], p. 56, and quoted and applied subsequently by Callaert and Veraverbeke [5] and Müller-Funk and Witting [11]. It also occurs in Borovskikh [2] but the proof given there is incomplete and ignores a crucial part of the argument.

III. PROOF OF THEOREM 2.1

Assume that (2.1) and (2.3) are satisfied for some $p > 5/3$ so that the quantities

$$a = \frac{E|g(X_1)|^3}{\{Eg^2(X_1)\}^{3/2}}, \quad b_p = \frac{E|h(X_1,X_2)|^p}{\{Eg^2(X_1)\}^{\frac{1}{2}p}}$$

are both finite. If $p \geq 2$, (2.2) ensures that $b_2 \geq 1$ and this implies that for $p > 2$, $b_p \geq b_2^{\frac{1}{2}p} \geq b_2$. It is therefore sufficient to prove the theorem for $5/3 < p \leq 2$ and we shall restrict attention to this case. Define, for $m = 1,\ldots,(N-1)$,

$$(3.1) \qquad \Delta_N(m) = \sum_{i=1}^{m} \sum_{j=i+1}^{N} \psi(X_i,X_j).$$

We shall need the following bounds for moments.

LEMMA 3.1. *If* (2.1) *and* (2.3) *hold for some* $5/3 < p \leq 2$, *then*

$$(3.2) \qquad \frac{E|\psi(X_1,X_2)|}{\{Eg^2(X_1)\}^{\frac{1}{2}}} \leq 2(2a+b_p),$$

$$(3.3) \qquad \frac{E|\psi(X_1,X_2)g(X_1)g(X_2)|}{\{Eg^2(X_1)\}^{3/2}} \leq 5a + 2b_p,$$

$$(3.4) \qquad E\left|\frac{\Delta_N(m)}{\tau_N}\right|^p \leq 4(2a+b_p)m\, N^{-(3/2)p+1}$$

for $m = 1,\ldots,N-1$ *and* $N = 2,3,\ldots$.

Proof. By the c_r - inequality and Lemma 1 of Chatterji [7]

$$E|\psi(X_1,X_2)|^p \leq 2^{p-1} E|h(X_1,X_2)|^p + 4\, E|g(X_1)|^p$$

$$\leq 2^{p-1}E|h(X_1,X_2)|^p + 4\, \{Eg^2(X_1)\}^{\frac{1}{2}p},$$

and since $a \geq 1$,

$$\frac{E|\psi(X_1,X_2)|^p}{\{Eg^2(X_1)\}^{\frac{1}{2}p}} \leq 4a + 2^{p-1}b_p \leq 2(2a+b_p). \tag{3.5}$$

As $p \geq 1$, this implies that the left-hand side in (3.2) is bounded by $\{2(2a+b_p)\}^{1/p} \leq 2(2a+b_p)$ which proves (3.2). To prove (3.3) we take $q^{-1} = 1-p^{-1}$, so that $2 \leq q < 5/2$. Because $xy \leq x^p + y^q$ for nonnegative x and y,

$$\frac{E|\psi(X_1,X_2)g(X_1)g(X_2)|}{\{Eg^2(X_1)\}^{3/2}} \leq \frac{E|\psi(X_1,X_2)|^p}{\{Eg^2(X_1)\}^{\frac{1}{2}p}} + \frac{\{E|g(X_1)|^q\}^2}{\{Eg^2(X_1)\}^q}$$

$$\leq \frac{E|\psi(X_1,X_2)|^p}{\{Eg^2(X_1)\}^{\frac{1}{2}p}} + \frac{\{E|g(X_1)|^{5/2}\}^2}{\{Eg^2(X_1)\}^{5/2}} \leq 5a + 2b_p$$

by (3.5) and Schwarz's inequality.

For $i = 1,\dots,m$, define

$$Z_i = \sum_{j=i+1}^{N} \psi(X_i,X_j).$$

Obviously, $EZ_m = 0$ and in view of (2.4) $E(Z_i|Z_{i+1},\dots,Z_m) = 0$ a.s. for $i = 1,\dots,m-1$, so that $Z_m, Z_{m-1},\dots,Z_1$ is a martingale difference sequence. Since $p \in [1,2]$, it follows from Lemma 1 of Chatterji [7] that

$$E|\Delta_N(m)|^p = E|\sum_{i=1}^{m} Z_i|^p \leq 2^{2-p} \sum_{i=1}^{m} E|Z_i|^p.$$

But $\psi(X_i,X_{i+1}),\ldots,\psi(X_i,X_N)$ is another martingale difference sequence and hence

$$E|\Delta_N(m)|^p \le 2^{4-2p} \sum_{i=1}^{m} \sum_{j=i+1}^{N} E|\psi(X_i,X_j)|^p$$

$$\le 2^{4-2p}\ m(N-1)E|\psi(X_1,X_2)|^p$$

and (3.4) follows from (2.6) and the first part of (3.5) because $N \ge 2$. □

Now fix $p \in (5/3,2]$ and assume that (2.1) and (2.3) are satisfied. As $|e^{ix}-1-ix| \le 2|x|^p$ for all real x, we have for every $m = 1,\ldots,N-1$ and $N = 2,3,\ldots$,

$$\phi_N(t) = E\ \exp\{it\ \tau_N^{-1}\ U_N\}$$

$$= E[\exp\{it\ \tau_N^{-1}(U_N-\Delta_N(m))\}(1+it\ \tau_N^{-1}\Delta_N(m))] + R_N,$$

$$|R_N| \le 2|t|^p\ \tau_N^{-p}\ E|\Delta_N(m)|^p \le 8(2a+b_p)mN^{-(3/2)p+1}|t|^p.$$

Let χ denote the characteristic function of $g(X_1)$, thus

$$\chi(t) = E\ \exp\{it\ g(X_1)\}.$$

Taking $m = (N-1)$ first and using (2.4) as well as the independence of $X_1,X_2,\ldots,$ we see that

$$|E\ \tau_N^{-1}\Delta_N(N-1)\exp\{it\ \tau_N^{-1}(U_N-\Delta_N(N-1))\}|$$

$$= |\tau_N^{-1} \sum_{1\le r<s\le N} E\psi(X_r,X_s)\exp\{it\ \tau_N^{-1}(N-1)\sum_{k=1}^{N} g(X_k)\}|$$

$$\le \frac{N(N-1)}{2\tau_N}|E\psi\ (X_1,X_2)\exp\{it\ \tau_N^{-1}(N-1)(g(X_1)+g(X_2))\}|$$

$$\times|\chi(\tau_N^{-1}(N-1)t)|^{N-2}$$

$$= \frac{N(N-1)}{2\tau_N} \left| E\psi(X_1,X_2) \prod_{k=1}^{2} [\exp\{it\ \tau_N^{-1}(N-1)g(X_k)\}-1] \right|$$

$$\times \left|\chi(\tau_N^{-1}(N-1)t)\right|^{N-2}$$

$$\leq \frac{N(N-1)^3 t^2}{2\tau_N^3} \left|\chi(\tau_N^{-1}(N-1)t)\right|^{N-2} E|\psi(X_1,X_2)g(X_1)g(X_2)|$$

$$\leq \frac{1}{2}(5a+2b_p)N^{-\frac{1}{2}}t^2\left|\chi(\tau_N^{-1}(N-1)t)\right|^{N-2},$$

because of (2.6) and (3.3). Similarly, we find that for $m \leq N-2$,

$$\left|E\ \tau_N^{-1}\Delta_N(m)\exp\{it\ \tau_N^{-1}(U_N-\Delta_N(m))\}\right|$$

$$= \Big|\tau_N^{-1} \sum_{r=1}^{m} \sum_{s=r+1}^{N} E\ \psi(X_r,X_s)\exp\{it\ \tau_N^{-1}[(N-1)\sum_{k=1}^{N} g(X_k)$$

$$+ \sum_{m<k<\ell\leq N} \psi(X_k,X_\ell)]\}\Big| \leq \frac{m(N-1)}{\tau_N} E|\psi(X_1,X_2)|\left|\chi(\tau_N^{-1}(N-1)t)\right|^{m-2}$$

$$\leq 2(2a+b_p)m\ N^{-\frac{1}{2}}\left|\chi(\tau_N^{-1}(N-1)t)\right|^{m-2}$$

because of (2.6) and (3.2). Finally we note that for $|t| \leq T_N = a^{-1}N^{\frac{1}{2}}$,

$$\left|\chi(\tau_N^{-1}(N-1)t)-1+\frac{t^2}{2N}\right| \leq \frac{(N-1)^3|t|^3}{6\tau_N^3} E|g(X_1)|^3$$

$$\leq \frac{1}{6}a|t|^3 N^{-3/2} \leq \frac{t^2}{6N}$$

and hence

$$\left|\chi(\tau_N^{-1}(N-1)t)\right| \leq 1-\frac{t^2}{3N} \leq \exp\{-\frac{t^2}{3N}\}.$$

Combining these computations for $m = (N-1)$ and $m \leq (N-2)$ respectively we find that for $|t| \leq T_N = a^{-1}N^{\frac{1}{2}}$,

$$(3.6)\qquad \phi_N(t) = [\chi(\tau_N^{-1}(N-1)t)]^N + R_N',$$

$$|R_N'| \le 8(2a+b_p)N^{-(3/2)p+2}|t|^p +$$

$$+ \frac{1}{2}(5a+2b_p)N^{-\frac{1}{2}}|t|^3\exp\{-\frac{(N-2)t^2}{3N}\}$$

and

$$(3.7)\qquad |\phi_N(t)| \le 8(2a+b_p)m\, N^{-(3/2)p+1}|t|^p + \exp\{-\frac{mt^2}{3N}\} +$$

$$+ 2(2a+b_p)m\, N^{-\frac{1}{2}}|t|\exp\{-\frac{(m-2)t^2}{3N}\}$$

for $m = 1,\dots,N-2$.

From the proof of the classical Berry-Esseen theorem for sums of i.i.d. random variables we borrow the fact that

$$(3.8)\qquad \int_{-T_N}^{T_N} |t|^{-1}|(\chi(\tau_N^{-1}(N-1)t))^N - e^{-\frac{1}{2}t^2}|dt \le c_1\, a\, N^{-\frac{1}{2}},$$

where we shall write $c_1, c_2, \dots$ to denote universal constants.

Take $\varepsilon = (3p-5)/(2p)$ so that $0 < \varepsilon \le \frac{1}{4}$, and define $T_N' = \min(N^{\varepsilon}, T_N)$. It follows from (3.6) and (3.8) that

$$(3.9)\qquad \int_{-T_N'}^{T_N'} |t|^{-1}|\phi_N(t) - e^{-\frac{1}{2}t^2}|dt \le c_2(a+b_p)N^{-\frac{1}{2}}.$$

For $T_N' \le |t| \le T_N$ we use (3.7) with $m = [3N\log N/t^2]$. Clearly there exists a natural number N_p depending only on p, such that for $N \ge N_p$ and $T_N' \le |t| \le T_N$ we do indeed have $1 \le m \le N-2$ for this choice of m and such that (3.7) yields

$$(3.10)\qquad \int_{T_N' \le |t| \le T_N} |t|^{-1}|\phi_N(t) - e^{-\frac{1}{2}t^2}|dt \le c_3(a+b_p)N^{-\frac{1}{2}}$$

for every $N \geq N_p$. It follows that (3.10) will hold for all $N \geq 2$ if we allow c_3 to depend on p and together with (3.9) this implies

$$(3.11) \qquad \int_{|t| \leq T_N} |t|^{-1} |\phi_N(t) - e^{-\frac{1}{2}t^2}| dt \leq C'_p (a+b_p) N^{-\frac{1}{2}}$$

where C'_p depends only on p. Application of Esseen's smoothing lemma (cf. Feller [8] p. 538) completes the proof of the theorem.

IV. EXTENSION AND APPLICATIONS

The gist of Theorem 2.1 is that the U - statistic structure (2.4) - (2.5) permits us to ignore the second order term $\tau_N^{-1} \sum\sum \psi(X_i, X_j)$, even though it only possesses moments of a much lower order than the leading term $\tau_N^{-1} (N-1) \sum g(X_i)$. Many variations on this theme are possible and we shall briefly discuss one here. We shall show that if the functions g and ψ contain terms of lower order, then the contributions of such terms can be neglected under even weaker moment conditions than those imposed on g and ψ in Theorem 2.1.

Let α, β, r and s be real numbers satisfying

$$(4.1) \qquad \alpha \geq \frac{1}{2}, \; \beta \geq 0, \; r > \frac{3}{1+2\alpha}, \quad s > \frac{5}{3+2\beta}.$$

Take h, g, ψ, U_N and τ_N as in Section 2 and define (cf. (2.5))

$$(4.2) \qquad V_N = U_N + (N-1)N^{-\alpha} \sum_{i=1}^{N} \tilde{g}(X_i) + N^{-\beta} \sum_{1 \leq i < j \leq N} \sum \tilde{\psi}(X_i, X_j),$$

where $\tilde{\psi}$ is a symmetric function of its two variables. We assume that

$$(4.3) \qquad E|\tilde{g}(X_1)|^r < \infty \text{ and if } r \geq 1, \; E\,\tilde{g}(X_1) = 0,$$

(4.4) $E|\tilde{\psi}(X_1,X_2)|^s < \infty$ and if $s \geq 1$, $E(\tilde{\psi}(X_1,X_2)|X_1)=0$ a.s..

Thus V_N is another U - statistic which is obtained from U_N by replacing g and ψ by $g + N^{-\alpha}\tilde{g}$ and $\psi + N^{-\beta}\tilde{\psi}$ respectively. The assumptions $\alpha \geq \frac{1}{2}$ and $\beta \geq 0$ suggest that $\tau_N^{-1}(V_N-U_N)$ is stochastically of order $N^{-\frac{1}{2}}$, so that one may hope to obtain a Berry-Esseen theorem for $\tau_N^{-1}V_N$ under appropriate moment conditions. These conditions are spelled out in (4.3), (4.4) and the second part of (4.1) and we see that terms of small order do indeed require only mild moment assumptions.

THEOREM 4.1. *Suppose that* (4.1), (4.3), (4.4) *as well as the assumptions of Theorem* 2.1 *are satisfied. Then there exists a positive number* C *depending only on* α, β, r, s *and* p *and such that for every* $N \geq 2$,

$$\sup_x |P(\tau_N^{-1}V_N \leq x) - \Phi(x)| \leq C\, N^{-\frac{1}{2}}\left[\frac{E|g(X_1)|^3}{\{Eg^2(X_1)\}^{3/2}} + \right.$$

(4.5)

$$\left. + \frac{E|\psi(X_1,X_2)|^p}{\{Eg^2(X_1)\}^{\frac{1}{2}p}} + \frac{E|\tilde{g}(X_1)|^r}{\{Eg^2(X_1)\}^{\frac{1}{2}r}} + \frac{E|\tilde{\psi}(X_1,X_2)|^s}{\{Eg^2(X_1)\}^{\frac{1}{2}s}}\right].$$

The proof of this theorem is very similar to that of Theorem 2.1, though slightly more laborious. The random variable

$$\Delta_N^*(m) = \Delta_N(m) + (N-1)N^{-\alpha}\sum_{i=1}^{m+1} \tilde{g}(X_i)+N^{-\beta}\sum_{i=1}^{m}\sum_{j=i+1}^{N} \tilde{\psi}(X_i,X_j)$$

plays the part of $\Delta_N(m)$ in the earlier proof. When expanding the characteristic function we now use the inequality

$$|\exp\{i(x+y+z)\} - 1 - i(x+y+z)| \leq 4\ (|x|^p+|y|^r+|z|^s)$$

if p, r, s $\in [1,2]$; if r and/or s are in (0,1), then the corresponding linear terms iy and/or iz should be omitted from the expansion of the exponential. Moments of sums of order smaller than 1 are bounded simply by using $|\sum a_i|^s \leq \sum |a_i|^s$ for $0 < s < 1$. Apart from these rather obvious changes the proof contains no new elements and will therefore be omitted.

We conclude this section with two applications. The first of these concerns the Von Mises functional

$$M_N = \sum_{i=1}^{N} \sum_{j=1}^{N} h(X_i,X_j) = 2 \sum_{1\leq i<j\leq N} h(X_i,X_j) + \sum_{i=1}^{N} h(X_i,X_i)$$

(4.6)

$$= (N-1) \sum_{i=1}^{N} \{2g(X_i) + (N-1)^{-1} h(X_i,X_i)\} + 2 \sum_{1\leq i<j\leq N} \psi(X_i,X_j),$$

with h, g and ψ as in Section 2. The statistic $\frac{1}{2} M_N$ is of the form (4.2) with $\alpha = 1$, $\tilde{g}(x) = \frac{1}{2} N(N-1)^{-1} h(x,x)$ and $\tilde{\psi} = 0$. It follows that if for some $p > 5/3$ and $r > 1$, (2.1) and (2.3) hold and

$$E|h(X_1,X_1)|^r < \infty, \tag{4.7}$$

then we have the Berry-Esseen bound

$$\sup_x |P(\tfrac{1}{2} \tau_N^{-1} M_N \leq x) - \Phi(x)| = \mathcal{O}(N^{-\frac{1}{2}}), \tag{4.8}$$

where τ_N^2 is given by (2.6). Note that we have omitted the assumption $E\, h(X_1,X_1) = 0$ even though $r > 1$ (cf. (4.3)), because $\tau_N^{-1} N\, E\, h(X_1,X_1) = \mathcal{O}(N^{-\frac{1}{2}})$ in any case and a non-random contribution of this order leaves (4.8) unaffected. The bound (4.8) was obtained earlier by Boos and Serfling who assume finite moments of orders $p = 3$ and $r = 3/2$ for $|h(X_1,X_2)|$ and $|h(X_1,X_1)|$ respectively (cf. Serfling [12], p. 230).

Berry-Esseen bounds for U - statistics have been used by a number of authors to obtain similar bounds for various Studentized statistics (e.g. Helmers [9] for Studentized linear combinations of order statistics and Callaert and Veraverbeke [5] for Studentized U - statistics).

Since the main argument is the same in each case, we may as well apply our results to the simplest of these statistics, which is of course Student's t. Let $X_1, X_2, \ldots$ be i.i.d. random variables with

$$(4.9) \qquad E\,X_1 = 0,\ E\,X_1^2 = 1,\ E|X_1|^r < \infty$$

for some $r > 4$. Define $\bar{X} = N^{-1} \sum_{i=1}^{N} X_i$ and

$$(4.10) \qquad T_N = \left(\frac{N-1}{N}\right)^{\frac{1}{2}} \frac{\sum_{i=1}^{N} X_i}{\left\{\sum_{i=1}^{N} (X_i - \bar{X})^2\right\}^{\frac{1}{2}}} .$$

Then

$$(4.11) \qquad \sup_x |P(T_N \le x) - \Phi(x)| = \mathcal{O}(N^{-\frac{1}{2}}).$$

A proof of this result starts by noting that $\{T_N \le x\} = \{S_N \le x_N\}$, where

$$S_N = \frac{\sum_{i=1}^{N} X_i}{\left\{\sum_{i=1}^{N} X_i^2\right\}^{\frac{1}{2}}}, \quad x_N = \left(\frac{N}{N-1+x^2}\right)^{\frac{1}{2}} x.$$

It follows that it suffices to prove (4.11) with T_N replaced by S_N.

By Markov's inequality and that of Marcinkiewicz, Zygmund and Chung,

$$P\left(\frac{|\sum (X_i^2 - 1)|}{N} \ge \frac{N^{-\frac{1}{4}}}{\log N}\right) \le \left(\frac{\log N}{N^{3/4}}\right)^{r/2} E|\sum (X_i^2 - 1)|^{r/2}$$

$$= \mathcal{O}((N^{-\frac{1}{4}} \log N)^{r/2}) = \mathcal{O}(N^{-\frac{1}{2}})$$

and hence

$$(4.12)\qquad \left(\frac{N}{\sum X_i^2}\right)^{\frac{1}{2}} = \left(1 + \frac{\sum(X_i^2-1)}{N}\right)^{-\frac{1}{2}} = 1 - \frac{1}{2N}\sum(X_i^2-1) + \mathcal{O}\left(\frac{N^{-\frac{1}{2}}}{(\log N)^2}\right)$$

uniformly on a set of probability $1 - \mathcal{O}(N^{-\frac{1}{2}})$. In view of the Berry-Esseen theorem for $N^{-\frac{1}{2}}\sum X_i$ we have

$$P(|N^{-\frac{1}{2}}\sum X_i| \geq \log N) = \mathcal{O}(N^{-\frac{1}{2}})$$

and as a result

$$S_N = N^{-\frac{1}{2}}\sum X_i(1 - \frac{1}{2N}\sum(X_i^2-1)) + \mathcal{O}(N^{-\frac{1}{2}})$$

uniformly on a set of probability $1 - \mathcal{O}(N^{-\frac{1}{2}})$. It is therefore sufficient to prove (4.11) with T_N replaced by

$$N^{-\frac{1}{2}}\sum X_i(1 - \frac{1}{2N}\sum(X_i^2-1)) + \frac{1}{2}N^{-\frac{1}{2}}E\,X_1^3$$

$$= N^{-\frac{1}{2}}\sum\{X_i - \frac{1}{2N}(X_i^3-X_i-EX_1^3)\} - \frac{1}{2}N^{-3/2}\sum_{i\neq j}\sum X_i(X_j^2-1).$$

But this is of the form $\tau_N^{-1}V_N$ studied in Theorem 4.1 with $g(x) = x$, $\psi(x,y) = -\frac{1}{2}(N-1)N^{-1}\{x(y^2-1) + y(x^2-1)\}$, $\alpha = 1$, $\tilde{g}(x) = -\frac{1}{2}(x^3-x-EX_1^3)$ and $\tilde{\psi} = 0$. The conditions of Theorem 4.1 reduce to (4.9) for some $r > 10/3$. As we have $r > 4$ the theorem may be applied and the proof is complete.

This Berry-Esseen theorem for Student's t provides us with a convenient yardstick to measure the strength of our results. If one recalls that (4.9) for $r = 3$ is needed to establish the classical Berry-Esseen bound for $N^{-\frac{1}{2}}\sum X_i$, then one must admit that the present condition (4.9) for some $r > 4$ is still considerably worse. It is small consolation that the full force of this condition is needed only to bound the remainder term in

(4.12); elsewhere any $r > 10/3$ would have been sufficient. However, if one compares with what could previously be obtained, one sees that some progress has certainly been made. A similar analysis based on the best previous result of Callaert and Janssen [3] would require (4.9) for $r = 6$. If one would use only Theorem 2.1 or Corollary 2.1 of the present paper, one would need (4.9) for $r = 9/2$ (cf. Helmers [9] and Callaert and Veraverbeke [5]).

REFERENCES

[1] Bickel, P. J. (1974). Edgeworth expansions in nonparametric statistics. *Ann. Statist. 2*, 1-20.

[2] Borovskikh, Yu.V. (1979). Approximation of U - statistics distribution (in Ukrainian). *Proc. Ukrainian Acad. Sci. A. 9*, 695-698.

[3] Callaert, H. and Janssen, P. (1978). The Berry-Esseen theorem for U - statistics. *Ann. Statist. 6*, 417-421.

[4] Callaert, H., Janssen, P. and Veraverbeke, N. (1980). An Edgeworth expansion for U - statistics. *Ann. Statist. 8*, 299-312.

[5] Callaert, H. and Veraverbeke, N. (1981). The order of the normal approximation for a studentized U - statistic. *Ann. Statist. 9*, 194-200.

[6] Chan, Y. K. and Wierman, J. (1977). On the Berry-Esseen theorem for U - statistics. *Ann. Probability 5*, 136-139.

[7] Chatterji, S. D. (1969). An L^p - convergence theorem. *Ann. Math. Statist. 40*, 1068-1070.

[8] Feller, W. (1971). *An Introduction to Probability Theory and Its Applications*, Vol. 2, 2nd Edition, Wiley, New York.

[9] Helmers, R. (1978). Edgeworth expansions for linear combinations of order statistics. Ph.D. Thesis, University of Leiden; also *Mathematical Centre Tract 105* (1981), Mathematisch Centrum, Amsterdam.

[10] Janssen, P. (1978). De Berry-Esseen stelling en een asymptotische ontwikkeling voor U - statistieken. Ph.D. Thesis, University of Leuven.

[11] Müller-Funk, U. and Witting, H. (1981). On the rate of convergence in the CLT for signed linear rank statistics. To appear in *Proc. Colloquium on Nonparametric Statistical Inference*, I. Vincze (ed.), Budapest.

[12] Serfling, R. J. (1980). *Approximation Theorems of Mathematical Statistics*, Wiley, New York.

[13] Van Zwet, W. R. (1977). Asymptotic expansions for the distribution functions of linear combinations of order statistics. *Statistical Decision Theory and Related Topics, II*, S. S. Gupta and D. S. Moore (eds.), 421-437, Academic Press, New York.

Γ-MINIMAX PROCEDURES FOR SELECTING GOOD LOCATION PARAMETERS IN SOME MULTIVARIATE DISTRIBUTIONS

Ping Hsiao

Department of Mathematics
Wayne State University
Detroit, Michigan, U.S.A.

I. INTRODUCTION

In many of the experimental situations, the experimenter is confronted with the problem of making decisions regarding k populations and frequently the goal is to partition these k populations into two groups: the "good" populations and the "bad" populations. Following the initial investigations by Paulson [14], many different formulation of this problem have been studied and contributions have been made by Dunnett [4], Lehmann [12], Tong [19], Randles and Hollander [15], Gupta and Kim [8] and Gupta and Hsiao [5]. A more detailed reference can be found in Chapter 20 of Gupta and Panchapakesan [8].

When making statistical inference, unless we can specify the prior distribution of the unknown parameters exactly, a complete Bayes analysis cannot be performed. When lack of full prior information, Robbins [16] suggested that attention be paid to the case in which the prior distribution is a member of some given family Γ of distributions. Blum and Rosenblatt [2] used this idea and formed the Γ-minimax principle. Under this principle, one is required to choose a decision rule that minimizes the maxmum expected risk over Γ. Γ-minimax principal has been applied to various statistical decision problems by Jackson, O'Donovan, Zimmer and Deely [10], Solomon [17] [18], DeRouen and Mitchell [3], Gupta and Huang [6] [7], Berger [1] Miescke [13], Gupta and Kim [8] and Gupta and Hsiao [5].

Statistical Decision Theory and Related Topics III, Vol. 1

ISBN 0-12-307501-7

The problem considered in this paper can be best illustrated by the following example. Suppose that there are k investment plans and each plan consists of p many investments. The profit of the jth investment in plan i can be measured by a random variable X_{ij} which we assume to follow a distribution with an unknown location parameter θ_{ij}. We say that plan i is good if certain linear combination of θ_{ij} $(1 \leq j \leq p)$ is greater than a given amount $c_i + \varepsilon_i$ and is bad if it is less than c_i. If it is known from outside sources or past experiences that plan i is good with probability between λ_{iL} and λ_{iu}; and bad with probability between λ'_{iL} and λ'_{iu}, then Γ-minimax principle can be approximately applied. Our goal in this paper is to search for Γ-minimax rules for selecting the good populations.

In Section 2, notations and definitions are introduced, and a formulation of the problem is given. In Section 3, a Γ-minimax rule is derived and it is shown that the result of Randles and Hollander [15] is a special case of this paper. In Section 4, we reduce the problem to the case that populations are normally distributed with known covariance matrix. Minimax rules are derived as a byproduct of the Γ-minimax rules and some more optimal properties of the Γ-minimax rules are found.

II. NOTATIONS AND FORMULATION OF THE PROBLEM

Let $\pi_1, \pi_2, \ldots, \pi_k$ be k independent populations. Suppose that the probability density function of π_i is $f_i(\underset{\sim}{x} - \underset{\sim}{\theta}_i)$ with $\underset{\sim}{\theta}_i = (\theta_{i1}, \ldots, \theta_{ip})'$ as a location parameter for $1 \leq i \leq k$. We define π_i to be a good population if $\underset{\sim}{\beta}'_i \underset{\sim}{\theta}_i \geq c_i + \varepsilon_i$ and a bad population if $\underset{\sim}{\beta}'_i \underset{\sim}{\theta}_i \leq c_i$ where $\underset{\sim}{\beta}'_i = (\beta_{i1}, \ldots, \beta_{ip})$ is a specified p-dimensional vector and c_i, ε_i are specified constants. Let $\Theta = \{\underset{\approx}{\theta} | \underset{\approx}{\theta} = (\underset{\sim}{\theta}_1, \ldots, \underset{\sim}{\theta}_k), \underset{\sim}{\theta}_i \in \mathbb{R}^p \text{ for } 1 \leq i \leq k\}$ be the parameter space and $\Theta/\Theta_i = \{(\underset{\sim}{\theta}_1, \ldots, \hat{\underset{\sim}{\theta}}_i, \ldots, \underset{\sim}{\theta}_p) | \underset{\sim}{\theta}_j \in \mathbb{R}^p \text{ for all } j \neq i\}$ where $(\underset{\sim}{\theta}_1, \ldots, \hat{\underset{\sim}{\theta}}_i, \ldots, \underset{\sim}{\theta}_p)$ means that $\underset{\sim}{\theta}_i$ is deleted from $\underset{\approx}{\theta}$. A decision rule $\underset{\approx}{\delta}$ contains k components and is defined by

$\delta(\underset{\approx}{x}) = (\delta_1(\underset{\approx}{x}),\ldots,\delta_k(\underset{\approx}{x}))$ where δ_i's are measurable functions from $\mathbb{R}^{kp}$ to $[0,1]$, where $\underset{\approx}{x} = (\underset{\sim}{x}_1,\ldots,\underset{\sim}{x}_k)$, $\underset{\sim}{x}_i = (x_{i1},\ldots,x_{ip})$ for $1 \leq i \leq k$, and $\delta_i(\underset{\approx}{x})$ denotes the probability of selecting π_i as a good population given $\underset{\approx}{X} = \underset{\approx}{x}$. The objective is to select all the good populations while rejecting the bad ones. Let L_1 be the loss incurred when we fail to select a good population and L_2 the loss for each bad population selected. Let $G_i = \{\underset{\approx}{\theta}|\underset{\sim}{\beta}'_i\underset{\sim}{\theta}_i \geq c_i+\varepsilon_i\}$ and $B_i = \{\underset{\approx}{\theta}|\underset{\sim}{\beta}'_i\underset{\sim}{\theta}_i \leq c_i\}$ for $1 \leq i \leq k$, then the loss function can be expressed by

$$L(\underset{\approx}{\theta},\underset{\sim}{\delta}) = \sum_{i=1}^{k} L^{(i)}(\underset{\approx}{\theta}, \delta_i) \text{ where}$$

(2.1) $$L^{(i)}(\underset{\approx}{\theta}, \delta_i) = L_1(1-\delta_i)I_{G_i}(\underset{\approx}{\theta}) + L_2\,\delta_i\,I_{B_i}(\underset{\approx}{\theta})$$

and I_A denotes the indicator function of A.

The risk function is $R(\underset{\sim}{\theta}, \underset{\sim}{\delta}) = \sum_{i=1}^{k} R^{(i)}(\underset{\approx}{\theta}, \delta_i)$ where $R^{(i)}(\underset{\approx}{\theta}, \delta_i) = E[L^{(i)}(\underset{\approx}{\theta}, \delta_i(\underset{\approx}{X}))]$. The Bayes risk of $\underset{\sim}{\delta}$ wrt a prior distribution τ is $r(\tau, \underset{\sim}{\delta}) = \sum_{i=1}^{k} r^{(i)}(\tau, \delta_i)$ where $r^{(i)}(\tau, \delta_i) = E[R^{(i)}(\underset{\approx}{\theta}, \delta_i)]$.

Now, assume that partial information is available to the decision maker such that the prior distribution is a member of

$$\Gamma = \{\tau|\lambda_{iL} \leq P_\tau(G_i) \leq \lambda_{iu}, \lambda'_{iL} \leq P_\tau(B_i) \leq \lambda'_{iu} \text{ for all } 1 \leq i \leq k\}$$

where λ_{iL}, λ_{iu}, λ'_{iL} and λ'_{iu} are given constants satisfying $\lambda_{iL} \geq 0$, $\lambda'_{iL} \geq 0$, $\lambda_{iu} + \lambda'_{iu} \leq 1$ for $1 \leq i \leq k$ and $P_\tau(B) = \int_B d\tau(\underset{\approx}{\theta})$ for all $B \subset \Theta$. In this framework, a rule $\underset{\sim}{\delta}^*$ is called a Γ-minimax rule if $\sup_{\tau\in\Gamma} r(\tau, \underset{\sim}{\delta}^*) = \inf_{\delta\in D} \sup_{\tau\in\Gamma} r(\tau, \underset{\sim}{\delta})$ where $D = \{\underset{\sim}{\delta}|\underset{\sim}{\delta}$ is a decision rule$\}$. A component decision rule δ_i^* is said to be a Bayes rule for the ith component problem wrt a prior τ if $r^{(i)}(\tau, \delta_i^*) = \inf_{\underset{\sim}{\delta}\in D} r^{(i)}(\tau, \delta_i)$. In the next section, the component Bayes rules of a certain prior distribution are found, from which a Γ-minimax rule is derived.

III. DERIVING A Γ-MINIMAX RULE

Let $\underset{\sim}{x} = (x_1,\ldots,x_p)$, $\underset{\sim}{x}' = (x_1',\ldots,x_p')$. We define that $\underset{\sim}{x} \leq \underset{\sim}{x}'$ if $x_i \leq x_i'$ for all $1 \leq i \leq p$. Lehmann [11] proved that if $\underset{\sim}{X}$ has a cdf $F(\underset{\sim}{x} - \underset{\sim}{\theta})$ and $\delta(\underset{\sim}{x})$ is a real-valued function such that $\delta(\underset{\sim}{x}) \leq \delta(\underset{\sim}{x}')$ for $\underset{\sim}{x} \leq \underset{\sim}{x}'$, then $E_{\underset{\sim}{\theta}}[\delta(\underset{\sim}{X})] \leq E_{\underset{\sim}{\theta}}'[\delta(\underset{\sim}{X})]$ for $\underset{\sim}{\theta} \leq \underset{\sim}{\theta}'$. The following lemma generalizes this result.

LEMMA 3.1. *Let* $\{F(\underset{\sim}{x} - \underset{\sim}{\theta}\}$, *be a class of distributions and* $\underset{\sim}{\beta}$ *be an arbitrary vector. If* δ *is a real-valued function such that* $\delta(\underset{\sim}{x} + t\underset{\sim}{\beta}) \geq \delta(\underset{\sim}{x} + s\underset{\sim}{\beta})$ *for all* $\underset{\sim}{x}$ *for* $t \geq s$, *then* $E_{\underset{\sim}{\theta}+t\underset{\sim}{\beta}}[\delta(\underset{\sim}{X})] \geq E_{\underset{\sim}{\theta}+s\underset{\sim}{\beta}}[\delta(\underset{\sim}{X})]$ *for any* $\underset{\sim}{\theta}$, *where* $E_{\underset{\sim}{\theta}}[\delta(\underset{\sim}{X})] = \int\delta(\underset{\sim}{x})dF(\underset{\sim}{x}-\underset{\sim}{\theta})$ *is assumed to exist for all* $\underset{\sim}{\theta}$.

Proof. Let A be a non-singular matrix with $\underset{\sim}{\beta}$ as its first column. Let $\underset{\sim}{Y} = A^{-1}\underset{\sim}{X}$ and $\hat{\delta}(\underset{\sim}{x}) = \delta(A\underset{\sim}{x})$. Then when $\underset{\sim}{X} \sim f(\underset{\sim}{x} - \underset{\sim}{\theta})$, we have $\underset{\sim}{Y} \sim c\hat{f}(\underset{\sim}{y} - \underset{\sim}{\eta})$ where $c = |\det A|$, $\hat{f}(\underset{\sim}{x}) = f(A\underset{\sim}{x})$ and $\underset{\sim}{\eta} = A^{-1}\underset{\sim}{\theta}$. Let $g(\underset{\sim}{\theta}) = E_{\underset{\sim}{\theta}}[\delta(\underset{\sim}{X})]$ and $\hat{g}(\underset{\sim}{\eta}) = E_{\underset{\sim}{\eta}}[\hat{\delta}(\underset{\sim}{Y})]$. Now,

$$\hat{\delta}(\underset{\sim}{y} + t\underset{\sim}{e}_1) = \delta(A\underset{\sim}{y} + tA\underset{\sim}{e}_1) = \delta(A\underset{\sim}{y} + t\underset{\sim}{\beta}) \geq \delta(A\underset{\sim}{y}+s\underset{\sim}{\beta}) = \hat{\delta}(\underset{\sim}{y}+s\underset{\sim}{e}_1)$$

for $t \geq s$, hence $\hat{\delta}$ is increasing in its first component. Since $\underset{\sim}{\eta}$ is a location parameter of $\underset{\sim}{Y}$, we get $\hat{g}(\underset{\sim}{\eta} + t\underset{\sim}{e}_1) \geq \hat{g}(\underset{\sim}{\eta} + A\underset{\sim}{e}_1)$ for all $\underset{\sim}{\eta}$. But

$$g(\underset{\sim}{\theta}) = \int \delta(\underset{\sim}{x})f(\underset{\sim}{x}-\underset{\sim}{\theta})d\underset{\sim}{x} = \int \delta(A\underset{\sim}{y})f(A\underset{\sim}{y}-AA^{-1}\underset{\sim}{\theta})|\det A|d\underset{\sim}{y}$$

$$= \int \hat{\delta}(\underset{\sim}{y})\hat{f}(\underset{\sim}{y}-A^{-1}\underset{\sim}{\theta})d\underset{\sim}{y} = \hat{g}(A^{-1}\underset{\sim}{\theta}).$$

Thus,

$$g(\underset{\sim}{\theta} + t\underset{\sim}{\beta}) = \hat{g}(A^{-1}\underset{\sim}{\theta} + tA^{-1}\underset{\sim}{\beta}) = \hat{g}(A^{-1}\underset{\sim}{\theta} + t\underset{\sim}{e}_1)$$

$$\geq \hat{g}(A^{-1}\underset{\sim}{\theta} + s\underset{\sim}{e}_1) = g(\underset{\sim}{\theta} + s\underset{\sim}{\beta}).$$

This finishes the proof.

The next lemmas has been widely used to solve for Γ-minimax rules. It is stated here for completeness.

LEMMA 3.2 (Randles and Hollander [15]).

If there exists a prior distribution $\tau^* \in \Gamma$ *such that* δ_i^* *is a Bayes rule for the* i^{th} *component problem* wrt τ^* *and* δ_i^* *satisfies* $\sup_{\tau\in\Gamma} r^{(i)}(\tau, \delta_i^*) = r^{(i)}(\tau^*,\delta_i^*)$ *for all* $i = 1,2,\ldots,k$, *then* $\underset{\sim}{\delta}^* = (\delta_1^*,\ldots,\delta_k^*)$ *is a Γ-minimax rule.*

Now, for any $\tau \in \Gamma$,

$$r^{(i)}(\tau,\delta_i) = \int_{G_i}\int_{\mathcal{X}} L_1(1-\delta_i(\underset{\approx}{x}))\prod_{\ell=1}^{k} f_\ell(\underset{\sim}{x}_\ell-\underset{\sim}{\theta}_\ell)d\underset{\sim}{x}_\ell d\tau(\underset{\approx}{\theta}) \tag{3.1}$$

$$+ \int_{B_i}\int_{\mathcal{X}} L_2\delta_i(\underset{\approx}{x})\prod_{\ell=1}^{k} f_\ell(\underset{\sim}{x}_\ell-\underset{\sim}{\theta}_\ell)d\underset{\sim}{x}_\ell d\tau(\underset{\approx}{\theta}).$$

The τ^* appeared in Lemma 3.2 is called the least favorable prior distribution. This suggests that in our problem we may define τ^* to be the prior distribution in Γ such that $\underset{\sim}{\theta}_1,\ldots,\underset{\sim}{\theta}_k$ are independent under τ^* and $P_{\tau^*}[\underset{\sim}{\theta}_i = \underset{\sim}{\varphi}_i] = \lambda_{iu}$, $P_{\tau^*}[\underset{\sim}{\theta}_i = \underset{\sim}{\psi}_i] = \lambda'_{iu}$ and $P_{\tau^*}[\underset{\sim}{\theta}_i = \frac{1}{2}(\underset{\sim}{\varphi}_i + \underset{\sim}{\psi}_i)] = 1 - \lambda_{iu} - \lambda'_{iu}$, where $\underset{\sim}{\varphi}_i = (c_i+\varepsilon_i)\underset{\sim}{\beta}_i/||\underset{\sim}{\beta}_i||^2$ and $\psi_i = c_i\underset{\sim}{\beta}_i/||\underset{\sim}{\beta}_i||^2$ for $1 \leq i \leq k$. By substituting τ^* into (3.1) and use Fubini Theorem, we get

$$r^{(i)}(\tau^*,\delta_i) = \int_{\mathcal{X}_i} L_1(1-\delta_i(\underset{\approx}{x}))f_i(\underset{\sim}{x}_i-\underset{\sim}{\varphi}_i)\{\int_{\mathcal{X}/\mathcal{X}_i}\int_{\{\underset{\approx}{\theta}|\underset{\sim}{\theta}_i = \underset{\sim}{\varphi}_i\}}$$

$$\prod_{j\neq i} f_j(\underset{\sim}{x}_j-\underset{\sim}{\theta}_j)d\tau^*(\underset{\approx}{\theta})d\underset{\sim}{x}_j\}_1 d\underset{\sim}{x}_i + \int_{\mathcal{X}_i} L_2\delta_i(\underset{\approx}{x})f_i(\underset{\sim}{x}_i-\underset{\sim}{\psi}_i)$$

$$\{\int_{\mathcal{X}/\mathcal{X}_i}\int_{\{\underset{\approx}{\theta}|\underset{\sim}{\theta}_i = \underset{\sim}{\psi}_i\}} \prod_{j\neq i} f_j(\underset{\sim}{x}_j - \underset{\sim}{\theta}_j)d\tau^*(\underset{\approx}{\theta})d\underset{\sim}{x}_j\}_2\, d\underset{\sim}{x}_i,$$

where

$$\mathcal{X} = \{\underset{\approx}{x}|\underset{\approx}{x} = (\underset{\sim}{x}_1,\ldots,\underset{\sim}{x}_k),\ \underset{\sim}{x}_i \in \mathbb{R}^p \text{ for } 1 \leq i \leq k\}$$

$$\mathcal{X}/\mathcal{X}_i = \{(\underset{\sim}{x}_1,\ldots,\hat{\underset{\sim}{x}}_i,\ldots,\underset{\sim}{x}_k)|\underset{\sim}{x}_j \in \mathbb{R}^p \text{ for } j \neq i\} \text{ and}$$

$$\mathcal{X}_i = \{\underset{\sim}{x}_i|\underset{\sim}{x}_i \in \mathbb{R}^p\}.$$

Now,

$$\{\quad\}_1 = \int_{\{\underset{\approx}{\theta}|\underset{\sim}{\theta}_i = \underset{\sim}{\varphi}_i\}}\int_{\mathcal{X}/\mathcal{X}_i}\prod_{j\neq i} f_j(\underset{\sim}{x}_j - \underset{\sim}{\theta}_j)d\underset{\sim}{x}_j\ d\tau^*(\underset{\approx}{\theta})$$

$$= \int_{\{\underset{\approx}{\theta}|\underset{\sim}{\theta}_i = \underset{\sim}{\varphi}_i\}} d\tau^*(\underset{\approx}{\theta}) = P_{\tau^*}[\underset{\sim}{\theta}_i = \underset{\sim}{\psi}_i] = \lambda_{iu}.$$

Similarly, $\{\quad\}_2 = \lambda'_{iu}$. Then,

$$r^{(i)}(\tau^*,\delta_i) = \int_{\mathcal{X}_i} [L_2\lambda'_{iu}f_i(\underset{\sim}{x}_i-\underset{\sim}{\psi}_i) - L_1\lambda_{iu}f_i(\underset{\sim}{x}_i - \underset{\sim}{\varphi}_i)]\delta_i(\underset{\approx}{x})d\underset{\sim}{x}_i + L_1\lambda_{iu}, \tag{3.2}$$

hence the Bayes rule for the ith component problem wrt τ^* is

$$\delta_i^*(\underset{\sim}{x}_i) = \begin{cases} 1 & \text{if } L_1\lambda_{iu}\, f_i(\underset{\sim}{x}_i - \underset{\sim}{\varphi}_i) \geq L_2\lambda'_{iu}f_i(\underset{\sim}{x}_i-\underset{\sim}{\psi}_i) \\ 0 & \text{if } \qquad\qquad\qquad\qquad < \end{cases} \tag{3.3}$$

THEOREM 3.1. *Given* $\xi_i > 0$, *let*

(3.4) $$h_i(\underset{\sim}{y}) = f_i(\underset{\sim}{y} - \xi_i \underset{\sim}{\beta}_i)/f_i(\underset{\sim}{y}).$$

If (i) $h_i(\underset{\sim}{y} + \underset{\sim}{v}_i) = h_i(\underset{\sim}{y})$ *for all* $\underset{\sim}{v}_i$ *such that* $\underset{\sim}{v}_i' \underset{\sim}{\beta}_i = 0$ *and* (ii) $h_i(\underset{\sim}{y} + t\underset{\sim}{\beta}_i) \geq h_i(\underset{\sim}{y} + s\underset{\sim}{\beta}_i)$ *for all* $\underset{\sim}{y}$, *where* $t \geq s$, *then* $\underset{\sim}{\delta}^* = (\delta_1^*, \ldots, \delta_k^*)$ *is a* Γ-*minimax rule with* δ_i^**'s defined by* (3.3).

Proof.

(3.5) $$\delta_i^*(\underset{\sim}{x}_i) = I_{[f_i(\underset{\sim}{x}_i - \underset{\sim}{\varphi}_i)/f_i(\underset{\sim}{x}_i - \underset{\sim}{\psi}_i) \geq (L_2\lambda_{iu}')/(L_1\lambda_{iu})]}(\underset{\sim}{x}_i)$$

$$\doteq I_{[f_i(\underset{\sim}{y}_i - \xi_i\underset{\sim}{\beta}_i)/f_i(\underset{\sim}{y}_i) \geq b_i]}(\underset{\sim}{x}_i)$$

$$= I_{[h_i(\underset{\sim}{y}_i) \geq b_i]}(\underset{\sim}{x}_i)$$

where $\underset{\sim}{y}_i = \underset{\sim}{x}_i - \underset{\sim}{\psi}_i$, $\xi_i = \varepsilon_i/||\beta_i||^2$ and $b_i = \dfrac{L_2\lambda_{iu}'}{L_1\lambda_{iu}}$. Then,

$$\delta_i^*(\underset{\sim}{x}_i + s\underset{\sim}{\beta}_i) = I_{[h_i(\underset{\sim}{y}_i + s\underset{\sim}{\beta}_i) \geq b_i]}(\underset{\sim}{x}_i) \leq I_{[h_i(\underset{\sim}{y}_i + t\underset{\sim}{\beta}_i) \geq b_i]}(\underset{\sim}{x}_i)$$

$$= \delta_i^*(\underset{\sim}{x}_i + t\underset{\sim}{\beta}_i) \quad \text{for } s \leq t \text{ by (ii).}$$

So, by Lemma 3.1 we have

(3.6) $$E_{\underset{\sim}{\theta}_i + t\underset{\sim}{\beta}_i}[\delta_i^*(\underset{\sim}{X}_i)] \geq E_{\underset{\sim}{\theta}_i + s\underset{\sim}{\beta}_i}[\delta_i^*(\underset{\sim}{X}_i)]$$

for all $\underset{\sim}{\theta}_i$ and $t \geq s$. Now, let $\underset{\approx}{\theta} \in G_i$, then there exists $\underset{\sim}{\gamma}_i$ such that $\underset{\sim}{\gamma}_i'\underset{\sim}{\beta}_i = 0$ and $\underset{\sim}{\theta}_i = a_i\underset{\sim}{\beta}_i + b_i\underset{\sim}{\gamma}_i$ for some a_i and b_i. Since $\underset{\sim}{\beta}_i' \underset{\sim}{\theta}_i \geq c_i + \varepsilon_i$ so $a_i \geq (c_i + \varepsilon_i)/||\beta_i||^2$. Hence

$$E_{\underset{\sim}{\theta}_i}[\delta_i^*(\underset{\sim}{X}_i)] \geq E_{\underset{\sim}{\varphi}_i + b_i\underset{\sim}{\gamma}_i}[\delta_i^*(\underset{\sim}{X}_i)] \text{ by (3.6)}$$

$$= E_{\underset{\sim}{0}}[\delta_i^*(\underset{\sim}{X}_i - \underset{\sim}{\varphi}_i - b_i\underset{\sim}{\gamma}_i)]$$

$$= E_{\underset{\sim}{0}}[\delta_i^*(\underset{\sim}{X}_i - \underset{\sim}{\varphi}_i)] \text{ by (i)}$$

$$= E_{\underset{\sim}{\varphi}_i}[\delta_i^*(\underset{\sim}{X}_i)].$$

Thus, we have shown that $\inf_{\underset{\approx}{\theta} \in G_i} E_{\underset{\sim}{\theta}_i}[\delta_i^*(\underset{\sim}{X}_i)] = E_{\underset{\sim}{\varphi}_i}[\delta_i^*(\underset{\sim}{X}_i)]$. Similarly, $\sup_{\underset{\approx}{\theta} \in B_i} E_{\underset{\sim}{\theta}_i}[\delta_i^*(\underset{\sim}{X}_i)] = E_{\underset{\sim}{\psi}_i}[\delta_i^*(\underset{\sim}{X}_i)]$, for all $1 \le i \le k$. It follows that for all $\tau \in \Gamma$,

$$\gamma^{(i)}(\tau, \delta_i^*) = \int_{G_i} L_1(1-E_{\underset{\approx}{\theta}}[\delta_i^*(\underset{\sim}{X}_i)]d\tau(\underset{\approx}{\theta})$$

$$+ \int_{B_i} L_2 E_{\underset{\approx}{\theta}}[\delta_i^*(\underset{\sim}{X}_i)]d\tau(\underset{\approx}{\theta}) \text{ by (3.1)}$$

$$\le L_1(1-E_{\underset{\sim}{\varphi}_i}[\delta_i^*(\underset{\sim}{X}_i)]) \int_{G_i} d\tau(\underset{\approx}{\theta}) + L_2 E_{\underset{\sim}{\psi}_i}[\delta_i^*(\underset{\sim}{X}_i)] \int_{B_i} d\tau(\underset{\approx}{\theta})$$

$$\le L_1 \lambda_{iu}(1-E_{\varphi_i}[\delta_i^*(\underset{\sim}{X}_i)]) + L_2 \lambda'_{iu} E_{\underset{\sim}{\psi}_i}[\delta_i^*(\underset{\sim}{X}_i)]$$

$$= \gamma^{(i)}(\tau^*, \delta_i^*),$$

hence Lemma 3.2 implies that $\underset{\sim}{\delta}^*$ is a Γ-minimax rule.

Remarks: 1. In deriving the Γ-minimax rule, we did not use the fact that $\underset{\sim}{X}_1, \underset{\sim}{X}_2, \ldots, \underset{\sim}{X}_k$ have the same dimension. δ_i^* defined by (3.3) still defines a Γ-minimax rule if $\underset{\sim}{X}_i$ is p_i dimensional and P_i's are not necessarily equal for $i = 1,2,\ldots,k$.

2. If the loss function is generalized, i.e., let $L^{(i)}(\underset{\approx}{\theta}, \delta_i) = L_{i1}(1-\delta_i) I_{G_i}(\underset{\approx}{\theta}) + L_{i2}\delta_i I_{B_i}(\underset{\approx}{\theta})$ in (2.1), then by changing L_1 and L_2 to L_{i1} and L_{i2}, respectively, in (3.3), we still get a Γ-minimax rule.

3. The problem considered by Randles and Hollander [15] is a special case of the problem considered here. It is the case when all the populations are one dimensional and $c_i = \theta_o$, $\varepsilon_i = \Delta$, $\beta_i = 1$, $\lambda_{iL} = \lambda_{iu} = \pi_i$, $\lambda'_{iL} = \lambda'_{iu} = \pi'_i$ for all $1 \le i \le k$. It is easy to verify that conditions (i) and (ii) in Theorem 3.1 are

satisfied if f_i is a PF_2 function. Hence Theorem 3.1 of Randles and Hollander [15] can be treated as a corollary of our Theorem 3.1.

4. The rule $\underset{\sim}{\delta}^*$ depends on Γ only through the ratio of λ_{iu} and λ'_{iu} and is completely independent of the lower bounds λ_{iL} and $\lambda_{iL'}$. Thus (3.3) defines a Γ'-minimax rule for any Γ' such that

$$\tau^* \in \Gamma' \subset \{\tau | P_\tau(G_i) \le \lambda_{iu},\ P_\tau(B_i) \le \lambda'_{iu},\ \text{for } 1 \le i \le k\}.$$

5. The Γ-minimum rule defined by (3.3) is admissible because it is the unique Bayes rule (up to equivalence) wrt τ^*.

IV. REDUCE TO THE CASE OF MULTIVARIATE NORMAL DISTRIBUTION

In this section, we assume that $f_i(\underset{\sim}{x}-\underset{\sim}{\theta}) \propto \exp\{-(\underset{\sim}{x}-\underset{\sim}{\theta}_i)' \Sigma_i^{-1}(\underset{\sim}{x}-\underset{\sim}{\theta}_i)\}$ where Σ_i is a known p.d. covariance matrix for $1 \le i \le k$. Let

$$(4.1) \qquad \underset{\sim}{Y}_i = \Sigma_i^{-\frac{1}{2}}\underset{\sim}{X}_i,\ \underset{\sim}{\eta}_i = \Sigma_i^{-\frac{1}{2}}\underset{\sim}{\theta}_i \text{ and } \underset{\sim}{\alpha}_i = \Sigma_i^{\frac{1}{2}}\underset{\sim}{\beta}_i.$$

Then $\underset{\sim}{\eta}_i$ is a location parameter of $\underset{\sim}{Y}_i$ and the pdf of $\underset{\sim}{Y}_i$ is $g_i(\underset{\sim}{y}-\underset{\sim}{\eta}_i) \propto \exp\{-\frac{1}{2}(\underset{\sim}{y}-\underset{\sim}{\eta}_i)'(\underset{\sim}{y}-\underset{\sim}{\eta}_i)\}$. Now, under (4.1), π_i is good if $\underset{\sim}{\alpha}'_i\underset{\sim}{\eta}_i \ge c_i+\varepsilon_i$ and is bad if $\underset{\sim}{\alpha}'_i\underset{\sim}{\eta}_i \le c_i$. Also, (4.1) is a one-to-one transformation, so $\underset{\sim}{Y}_i$'s are sufficient statistics for X_i's, hence the problem about $(\underset{\sim}{X}_i, f_i, \underset{\sim}{\theta}_i, \underset{\sim}{\beta}_i)$'s is equivalent to that about $(\underset{\sim}{Y}_i, g_i, \underset{\sim}{\eta}_i, \underset{\sim}{\alpha}_i)$'s. In the new problem, (3.4) becomes

$$(4.2) \qquad h_i(\underset{\sim}{y}) = g_i(\underset{\sim}{y} - \xi_i\underset{\sim}{\alpha}_i)/g_i(\underset{\sim}{y}) = \exp\{\xi_i\underset{\sim}{\alpha}'_i\underset{\sim}{y} - \frac{1}{2}\xi_i^2\underset{\sim}{\alpha}'_i\underset{\sim}{\alpha}_i\}.$$

It is easy to see that $h_i(\underset{\sim}{y} + v_i) = h_i(\underset{\sim}{y})$ for all v_i such that $\underset{\sim}{v}'_i\underset{\sim}{\alpha}_i = 0$ and $h_i(\underset{\sim}{y} + t\underset{\sim}{\alpha}_i) \ge h_i(\underset{\sim}{y} + s\underset{\sim}{\alpha}_i)$ for $t \ge s$. Hence, by Theorem 3.1 $(\delta_1^*(\underset{\sim}{x}_1),\ldots,\delta_k^*(\underset{\sim}{x}_k))$ is a Γ-minimax rule, where

$$\delta_i^*(\underset{\sim}{x}_i) = \begin{cases} 1 & \text{if } h_i(\underset{\sim}{y}_i - c_i\underset{\sim}{\alpha}_i/||\underset{\sim}{\alpha}_i||]) \geq b_i \\ 0 & \qquad\qquad < \end{cases}$$

with h_i defined by (4.2), $\xi_i = \dfrac{\varepsilon_i}{||\underset{\sim}{\alpha}_i||^2}$ and b_i defined by (3.5).

After some lengthy computation,

$$(4.3)\quad \delta_i^*(x_i) = \begin{cases} 1 & \text{if } \underset{\sim}{\beta}_i' \underset{\sim}{x}_i \geq c_i + \varepsilon_i/2 + k_i \\ 0 & \qquad < \end{cases}$$

where $k_i = (\underset{\sim}{\beta}_i' \Sigma_i \underset{\sim}{\beta}_i) \log b_i/\varepsilon_i$, $1 \leq i \leq k$. If a random sample of size n_i is taken from π_i, $1 \leq i \leq k$, then by the principle of sufficiency, we can reduce consideration to $\bar{\underset{\sim}{X}}_1, \ldots, \bar{\underset{\sim}{X}}_k$ which has the effect of changing Σ_i to Σ_i/n_i and keep all the other configuration the same. The ith component of the Γ-minimax rule becomes

$$(4.4)\qquad \delta_i^*(\bar{\underset{\sim}{x}}_i) = I_{[\underset{\sim}{\beta}_i' \bar{\underset{\sim}{x}}_i \geq c_i + \varepsilon_i/2 + k_i/n_i]}(\bar{\underset{\sim}{x}}_i).$$

THEOREM 4.1. $\lim_{n\to\infty} \sup_{\tau\in\Gamma} r(\tau, \underset{\sim}{\delta}^*) = 0$ *where* $n = n_1 \wedge \ldots \wedge n_k$, $\underset{\sim}{\delta}^* = (\delta_1^*, \ldots, \delta_k^*)$, *and* δ_i^* *is defined by* (4.4) *for* $1 \leq i \leq k$.

Proof.

$$(4.5)\qquad \sup_{\tau\in\Gamma} r^{(i)}(\tau, \delta_i^*) = \gamma^{(i)}(\tau^*, \delta_i^*)$$

$$= L_1\lambda_{iu}(1 - E_{\underset{\sim}{\varphi}_i}[\delta_i^*(\bar{\underset{\sim}{X}}_i)]) + L_2\lambda_{iu}' E_{\underset{\sim}{\psi}_i}[\delta_i^*(\bar{\underset{\sim}{X}}_i)].$$

Now,

$$E_{\underset{\sim}{\varphi}_i}[\delta_i^*(\underset{\sim}{\bar{X}}_i)] = P_{\underset{\sim}{\varphi}_i}[\underset{\sim}{\beta}_i' \underset{\sim}{\bar{X}}_i \geq c_i + \varepsilon_i/2 + k_i/n_i]$$

$$= P[Z \geq (c_i + \varepsilon_i/2 + k_i/n_i - \underset{\sim}{\beta}_i' \underset{\sim}{\varphi}_i)/(\sigma_i^2/n_i)^{\frac{1}{2}}]$$

where $\sigma_i^2 = \underset{\sim}{\beta}_i' \Sigma_i \underset{\sim}{\beta}_i$

$$= 1 - \Phi((\sigma_i^2/n_i)^{\frac{1}{2}}(\ell_n b_i/\varepsilon_i) - (\varepsilon_i/2)(n_i/\sigma_i^2)^{\frac{1}{2}})$$

$$\to 1 \text{ as } n_i \to \infty.$$

Similarly $E_{\psi_i}[\delta_i^*(\underset{\sim}{\bar{X}}_i)] \to 0$ as $n_i \to \infty$. Hence,

$$0 \leq \lim_{n\to\infty} \sup_{\tau\in\Gamma} r(\tau, \underset{\sim}{\delta}^*) \leq \sum_{i=1}^{k} \lim_{n\to\infty} r^{(i)}(\tau, \delta_i^*) = 0.$$

This finishes the proof.

It is well known that if Γ consists of all the priors on Θ, then a Γ-minimax rule becomes a minimax rule. This suggests that in order to find minimax rule through Γ-minimax rule we should let Γ be as large as possible. Consider $\Gamma(\underset{\sim}{p}) = \{\tau | P_\tau(G_i) = p_i,\ P_\tau(B_i) = 1-p_i \text{ for all } 1 \leq i \leq k\}$ where $\underset{\sim}{p} = (p_1,\ldots,p_k)'$. Let $q_i = \log \dfrac{L_2(1-p_i)}{L_1 p_i}$, we can prove that

THEOREM 4.2. *If* q_i*'s (hence* p_i*'s) are chosen to satisfy*

$$(4.6) \qquad L_1\Phi\left(\frac{\sigma_i}{\varepsilon_i} q_i - \frac{\varepsilon_i}{2\sigma_i}\right) = L_2\left[1-\Phi\left(\frac{\sigma_i}{\varepsilon_i} q_i + \frac{\varepsilon_i}{2\sigma_i}\right)\right]$$

where $\sigma_i^2 = \underset{\sim}{\beta}_i' \Sigma_i \underset{\sim}{\beta}_i$ *for* $1 \leq i \leq k$. *Then the* $\Gamma(\underset{\sim}{p})$ *- minimax rule is actually a minimax rule.*

Proof. From (4.3) if $(\delta_1^*,\ldots,\delta_k^*)$ is the $\Gamma(\underset{\sim}{p})$-minimax rule then

$$\delta_i^*(\underset{\sim}{x}_i) = I_{[\underset{\sim}{\beta}_i' \underset{\sim}{x}_i \geq c_i + \varepsilon_i/2 + \sigma_i^2 q_i/\varepsilon_i]}(\underset{\sim}{x}_i).$$

For $\underset{\approx}{\theta} \in G_i$,

$$R^{(i)}(\underset{\approx}{\theta}, \delta_i^*) = L_1 P_{\underset{\sim}{\theta}_i}[\underset{\sim}{\beta}_i' \underset{\sim}{X}_i < c_i + \varepsilon_i/2 + \sigma_i^2 q_i/\varepsilon_i]$$

$$= L_1 \Phi([c_i + \varepsilon_i/2 + \sigma_i^2 q_i/\varepsilon_i - \underset{\sim}{\beta}_i' \underset{\sim}{\theta}_i]/\sigma_i).$$

Since $\underset{\sim}{\beta}_i' \underset{\sim}{\theta}_i \geq c_i + \varepsilon_i$ for all $\underset{\approx}{\theta} \in G_i$, so $\sup_{\underset{\approx}{\theta} \in G_i} R^{(i)}(\underset{\approx}{\theta}, \delta_i^*) = u_i$ where u_i is either side of (4.6).

Similarly, for $\underset{\approx}{\theta} \in B_i$,

$$R^{(i)}(\underset{\approx}{\theta}, \delta_i^*) = L_2 P_{\underset{\sim}{\theta}_i}[\underset{\sim}{\beta}_i' \underset{\sim}{X}_i \geq c_i + \varepsilon_i/2 + \sigma_i^2 q_i/\varepsilon_i]$$

$$= L_2[1 - \Phi([c_i + \varepsilon_i/2 + \sigma_i^2 q_i/\varepsilon_i - \underset{\sim}{\beta}_i' \underset{\sim}{\theta}_i]/\sigma_i)],$$

so $\inf_{\underset{\approx}{\theta} \in B_i} R^{(i)}(\underset{\approx}{\theta}, \delta_i^*) = L_2[1 - \Phi(\frac{\sigma_i}{\varepsilon_i} q_i + \frac{\varepsilon_i}{2\sigma_i})] = u_i$ by (4.6). Also $R^{(i)}(\underset{\approx}{\theta}, \delta_i^*) = 0$ for $\underset{\approx}{\theta} \notin G_i \cup B_i$. Hence $\sup R^{(i)}(\underset{\approx}{\theta}, \delta_i^*) = u_i$ for $1 \leq i \leq k$. Now, by (4.5)

$$r^{(i)}(\tau^*, \delta_i^*) = L_1 a \Phi(\frac{\sigma_i}{\varepsilon_i} q_i - \frac{\varepsilon_i}{2\sigma_i}) + L_2(1-a)[1 - \Phi(\frac{\sigma_i}{\varepsilon_i} q_i + \frac{\varepsilon_i}{2\sigma_i})]$$

$$= u_i.$$

Thus

$$r(\tau^*, \underset{\sim}{\delta}^*) = \sum_{i=1}^{k} r^{(i)}(\tau^*, \delta_i^*) = \sum_{i=1}^{k} u_i = \sum_{i=1}^{k} \sup_{\underset{\approx}{\theta}} R^{(i)}(\underset{\approx}{\theta}, \delta_i^*)$$

$$\geq \sup_{\underset{\approx}{\theta}} \sum_{i=1}^{k} R^{(i)}(\underset{\approx}{\theta}, \delta_i^*) = \sup_{\underset{\approx}{\theta}} R(\underset{\approx}{\theta}, \underset{\sim}{\delta}^*).$$

Note that $\underset{\sim}{\delta}^*$ is the Bayes rules wrt τ^*, so $\underset{\sim}{\delta}^*$ is a minimax rule.

Finally, in our problem if we let $c_i = \underset{\sim}{\beta}_o' \underset{\sim}{\theta}_o$ for all $1 \leq i \leq k$, where $\underset{\sim}{\beta}_o$ is given and $\underset{\sim}{\theta}_o$ is an unknown location parameter of a control population π_o, then we are faced with a slightly different problem. Γ-minimax rules can be found with the technique of this paper and that developed in Gupta and Hsiao [5].

REFERENCES

[1] Berger, R. L. (1977). Minimax, admissible, and Γ-minimax multiple decision rules. Ph.D. Thesis (Mimeo. Ser. No. 498), Dept. of Statist., Purdue Univ.

[2] Blum, J. R. and Rosenblatt, J. (1967). On partial a prior information in statistical inference. *Ann. Math. Statist.* *28*, 1671-1678.

[3] DeRouen, T. A. and Mitchell, T. J. (1974). A G_1-minimax estimator for a linear combination of binomial probabilities. *J. Amer. Statist. Assoc.* *69*, 231-233.

[4] Dunnett, C. W. (1955). A multiple comparison procedure for comparing several treatments with a control. *J. Amer. Statist. Assoc.* *50*, 1096-1121.

[5] Gupta, S. S. and Hsiao, P. (1981). On Γ-minimax, minimax, and Bayes procedures for selecting populations close to a control. To appear in *Sankhyā Ser. B*.

[6] Gupta, S. S. and Huang, D. Y. (L975). On Γ-minimax classification procedures. *Proceedings of the 40th Session on the International Statistical Institute 46*, Book 3, 330-335.

[7] Gupta, S. S. and Huang, D. Y. (1977). On some Γ-minimax subset selection and multiple comparison procedures. *Statistical Decision Theory and Related Topics II*, S. S. Gupta and D. S. Moore (eds.). Academic Press, New York.

[8] Gupta, S. S. and Kim, W. C. (1980). Γ-minimax and minimax rules for comparison of treatments with a control. To appear in the *Proceedings of International Conference in Statistics*, K. Matusita (ed.). North Holland Pub. Co., Amsterdam, The Netherlands.

[9] Gupta, S. S. and Panchapakesan, S. (1979). *Multiple Decision Procedures: Theory and Methodology of Selection and Ranking of Populations.* John Wiley, New York.

[10] Jackson, D. A., O'Donovan, T. M., Zimmer, W. J. and Deely, J. J. (1970). G_2-minimax estimation in the exponential family. *Biometrika 57*, 439-443.

[11] Lehmann, E. L. (1955). Ordered families of distributions. *Ann. Math. Statist. 26*, 399-419.

[12] Lehmann, E. L. (1961). Some Model I problems of selection. *Ann. Math. Statist. 32*, 990-1012.

[13] Miescke, K. J. (1979). Γ-minimax selection procedures in simultaneous testing problems. Mimeo. Ser. No. 79-1, Dept. of Statist., Purdue Univ.

[14] Paulson, E. (1952). On the comparison of several experimental categories with a control. *Ann. Math. Statist. 23*, 239-246.

[15] Randles, R. H. and Hollander, M. (1971). Γ-minimax selection procedures in treatment versus control problems. *Ann. Math. Statist. 42*, 330-341.

[16] Robbins, H. (1951). Asymptotically subminimax solutions of compound statistical decision problems. *Proc. Second Berkeley Symp. Math. Statist. Prob. 1*, 131-148. Univ. of California Press, Berkeley.

[17] Solomon, D. L. (1972). Λ-minimax estimation of a multivariate location parameter. *J. Amer. Statist. Assoc. 67*, 641-646.

[18] Solomon, D. L. (1972). Λ-minimax estimation of a scale parameter. *J. Amer. Statist. Assoc. 67*, 647-649.

[19] Tong, Y. L. (1969). On partitioning a set of normal populations by their locations with respect to a control. *Ann. Math. Statist. 40*, 1300-1324.